SIXTH EDITION

LEARNING DISABILITIES

Characteristics, Identification, and Teaching Strategies

WILLIAM N. BENDER

University of Georgia

PEARSON

Boston ▪ New York ▪ San Francisco
Mexico City ▪ Montreal ▪ Toronto ▪ London ▪ Madrid ▪ Munich ▪ Paris
Hong Kong ▪ Singapore ▪ Tokyo ▪ Cape Town ▪ Sydney

Executive Editor: *Virginia Lanigan*
Editorial Assistant: *Matthew Buchholz*
Senior Marketing Manager: *Kris Ellis-Levy*
Production Editor: *Gregory Erb*
Editorial Production Service: *Trinity Publishers Services*
Composition Buyer: *Linda Cox*
Manufacturing Buyer: *Linda Morris*
Electronic Composition: *Omegatype Typography, Inc.*
Photo Researcher: *PoYee Oster*
Cover Designer: *Kristina Mose-Libon*

For related titles and support materials, visit our online catalog at www.ablongman.com.

Between the time Website information is gathered and then published, it is not unusual for some sites to have closed. Also, the transcription of URLs can result in typographical errors. The publisher would appreciate notification where these errors occur so that they may be corrected in subsequent editions.

ISBN 10: 0-205-51553-3
ISBN 13: 978-0-205-51553-0

Library of Congress Cataloging-in-Publication Data
Bender, William N.
 Learning disabilities : characteristics, identification, and teaching strategies / William N.
Bender.—6th ed.
  p. cm.
Includes bibliographical references and indexes.
ISBN 0-205-51553-3 (casebound)
1. Learning disabled children—Education—United States. 2. Learning disabilities—United
 States—Case studies. I. Title.
LC4705.B46 2008
371.92'6—dc21
                        2007000632

Printed in the United States of America

10 9 8 7 6 5 4 3 2 1   RRD-VA   11 10 09 08 07

Photo Credits: Page 3: © Royalty Free/CORBIS; pp. 46, 72, 107: © T. Lindfors Photography; p. 138: © Frank Siteman; p. 179: © T. Lindfors Photography; pp. 217, 242: © Will Hart; pp. 271, 301, 324, 343, 368: © T. Lindfors Photography; p. 396: © Comstock Royalty Free.

CONTENTS

CHAPTER FOUR

Personality and Social Characteristics of Students with Learning Disabilities   107

CHAPTER FIVE

Assessment of Learning Disabilities   138

**SECTION II   CHARACTERISTICS OF STUDENTS WITH
LEARNING DISABILITIES   177**

CHAPTER SIX

Learning Characteristics in Reading and Language Arts   179

PREFACE

This text is a practical guide for the beginning teacher in the field of learning disabilities. Unlike many introductory texts in the field, this book is founded in the need to provide educationally relevant information as well as theoretical background. The author of this text has 29 years of experience working with children and adolescents who have learning disabilities. Several of those years involve direct teaching experience in a junior high school resource room for the learning disabled. Texts written by educational psychologists are generally accurate in content dealing with characteristics associated with learning disabilities, but this text also provides insight into educational concerns from a teacher's perspective, as well as the relevant scholarship.

For example, this book uses actual assessment and referral reports in order to present the characteristics of students with disabilities (see Chapter 5 and the Appendix). As a teacher, you need some experience in reading these reports as a part of your introduction to children with learning disabilities.

In all of the chapters, numerous instructional examples are given whenever a particular characteristic of the learning disabled is discussed. These instructional suggestions should assist in your later methods courses. Further, when scholarship in the field is unclear on a particular educational issue—differentiating learning disabilities from other disabilities such as mental retardation and behavioral disorders, for example—this book presents the most defensible options used today in the public schools and at the same time underscores the complex issues involved.

Finally, the field is replete with professional debates. Issues that have yet to be decided include changing theoretical perspectives on learning disabilities, multiple definitions of this population, and appropriate service delivery models for these students. Each of these issues is presented in a manner that allows and encourages the beginning teacher to make a tentative professional decision.

This book is prepared for upper-level undergraduates and beginning graduate students studying learning disabilities. The student should have completed several courses in general educational psychology and child development. However, because of the instructional strategies included within each chapter, even students with no exposure to education courses should be able to use this text successfully. Furthermore, given the educational approach of this text, the book should also be useful for parents. The section on selection of appropriate programs for college-bound students with learning disabilities (Chapter 13), for example, provides a practical guide for identification of the particular components that these students and their parents should look for in selection of a college program.

CHAPTER ORGANIZATION

The book is written in an educational format that facilitates learning in college students. A number of learning activities are included in each chapter format, as discussed below.

Chapter Objectives.   The beginning of each chapter includes objectives that indicate the types of activities the chapter will teach.

Keywords Lists.   At the beginning of each chapter, a vocabulary list of keywords is presented. These terms may be found in boldface type in the chapters and should be mastered prior to moving to succeeding chapters.

Interest Boxes and Figures.   The interest boxes and the figures present information that facilitates understanding of the points in the chapter. In some cases, this information is directly discussed in text; at other times, it is an adjunct to the text. Each interest box should be read as you read the relevant chapter section.

Questions and Activities.   At the end of each chapter, two types of activities are included in the questions and activities section. Answers to some of the questions are revealed directly in the chapter; other activities will further clarify the issues discussed in the chapter.

Use of the Learning Activities.   In order to gain the most from the use of this text, the student should take advantage of each of these learning activities. First, read the objectives presented at the front of each chapter because these provide a framework for later study. Next, read the introductory and summary sections of each chapter. These sections will highlight the content of the chapter and encourage you to attend to the major points. Glance at the keywords so that you can note them in the chapter. After these introductory activities, return to the beginning of the chapter and read the text and interest boxes as you come to them. After completion of the reading, complete the questions and activities at the end of the chapter.

THE CHALLENGE

By taking the course in which this text is used, you have embarked on a challenging series of studies. Although earlier courses in your instructional program were important, you may now be involved in your first course in the field of learning disabilities, and this course will require a measure of personal commitment from you. You should make a personal and professional commitment to master the concepts and ideas presented here because of the intense need for well-prepared teachers of students with learning disabilities. An earnest effort has been made to present the best educational ideas, the latest scholarship, and the issues that are still open to debate. It is up to you to gain insight into these complex issues.

In a broader sense, the field of learning disabilities is dynamic, challenging, and demanding. You, as a professional in the field in years to come, will help to decide many of the professional questions presented here. Also, other issues will crop up from time to time that will demand your best professional judgment. The discussion of inclusion in Chapter 9 was a hotly debated issue ten years ago. More recently the response to intervention eligibility procedure (Chapter 5) has drastically impacted the field. In order to get a handle on these dynamic changes, Chapter 14 presents a series of suggestions concerning how you, as a beginning teacher, may participate fully in these decisions. Such decision-making responsibility requires a commitment from each professional in the field.

Implicit to your understanding of and commitment to the field is familiarity with its vocabulary. Given the dynamic nature of the learning disabilities field, vocabulary is constantly evolving. Thus, new terms are frequently introduced, and others are used to mean different things by different people. To assist you in mastering the vocabulary, every effort has been made in this book to use terms consistently and definitively. You should be aware of variances in usage, however. For instance, *response to intervention (RTI)* is a relatively new term and there are many variations of meaning for it. Also, the terms *mainstreaming, general education,* and *full inclusion* are considered synonymous by some individuals but have slightly different meanings to others.

Finally, the challenge to become professionally involved requires a personal commitment from you for the sake of the students with learning disabilities whom you will teach. This challenge, in the final analysis, must be stated in personal, moral terms. These students historically have been ignored by our educational institutions and our society. Many have suffered emotionally because of the uninformed ridicule by other students and, in some rare cases, teachers. Yet most of the students with whom you will have contact will be individuals who have not given up the struggle to gain something through their educational endeavors and their personal/social lives.

Almost every professional in the field is constantly amazed at the triumph of spirit that is apparent in these students. In the face of consistent failure, many students with learning disabilities continue to attempt every reading assignment, every math assignment, and every language arts task. They constantly seek to achieve social acceptance from their peers, even at the cost of some unintentional ridicule and social embarrassment. These struggling students will amaze you, and you will quickly find that you wish to assist them in every way you can. You will learn a deep, abiding respect for these individuals. You will seek ways to assist them in their schoolwork and in their relationships with peers, teachers, and family members. You will do everything within your power to assure that these individuals are given something resembling an even chance in their education and in their lives. In the majority of cases, an even chance is all these students need to become very productive citizens in our society. The moral imperative then becomes clear: You must become the best teacher you can be. These remarkable students deserve nothing less.

INTRODUCTION TO LEARNING DISABILITIES

Since the early years of learning disabilities in the 1960s, when the term *learning disabilities* was first used, there has never been a period of greater upheaval and transition. This transition has arisen for several reasons, which are presented in the first few chapters. With the first federal legislation now over 25 years behind us, President George W. Bush created a commission to evaluate special education services nationwide. The report of the President's Commission on Excellence in Education resulted in dramatic change in how students with learning disabilities are identified. In December of 2004, the president enacted a number of recommendations from that report, including an emphasis on "response to intervention" as the defining characteristic of learning disabilities. Chapter 1 presents the history of the concept of learning disabilities, including the recent dynamic changes in the field. Chapter 2 presents the medical basis for learning disabilities, as well as some of the recent research in neurosciences. Chapters 3 and 4 provide information on characteristics of students with learning disabilities. Finally, Chapter 5 presents current diagnostic practice, as well as a step-by-step guideline for the newly emerging procedures concerning response to intervention.

CHAPTER ONE

CHANGING DEFINITIONS OF LEARNING DISABILITIES

CHAPTER OUTLINE

WHEN YOU COMPLETE THIS CHAPTER, YOU SHOULD BE ABLE TO:

1. Discuss the phases in the history of the field of learning disabilities and state the reasons for the transitions between each of these phases.

2. Identify and describe the four characteristics common to most definitions of learning disabilities.

3. Discuss the development of the discrepancy formula and recent responses to it among professional groups.

4. Identify the major perspectives in the field.

5. Describe the characteristics of a theoretical perspective.

6. Identify the major contributors to each perspective.

7. Identify the relative importance of each perspective during the last three decades.

KEYWORDS

visual-perceptual/motor theorists
William Cruickshank
Marianne Frostig
language theorists
language deficit
Samuel Orton

Grace Fernald
neurological perspective
Samuel Kirk
Task Force I
cognitive-processing perspectives
metacognition

learning-strategies approach
Howard Gardner
multiple intelligences
differentiated instruction
response to intervention

INTRODUCTION

Case Study 1

Timeko has had trouble in reading since he was in kindergarten. He experienced difficulty in mastering his letters, and his teacher noticed that Timeko had difficulty detecting the beginning and final consonant sounds for many common words. In grade 2 he did not learn as many vocabulary terms as many others in his class. In the late autumn of his second-grade year, the teacher began to chart Timeko's progress in mastering sight words as well as decoding unknown words. The teacher used a reading curriculum approved by the state curriculum board as scientifically validated, and her principal indicated that she utilized the activities in that curriculum appropriately. Thus, Timeko should have been making reading progress. However, the charts of his mastery of decoding skills indicates he is not improving, and the teacher has begun to suspect a learning disability.

Case Study 2

Adam has failed several subjects in the fourth grade, and his mother believes that this is related to his low reading skill. Although he has passed reading, he usually passes it with a "D" and sometimes a "C" grade. His mom has become concerned and has spoken to the fourth-grade teacher. The teacher indicated that Adam is in the lowest-level reading group but still seems to be performing poorly. Also, she mentioned several other problems, including spelling difficulty and poor handwriting skills. When a paragraph is assigned in class, he has difficulty writing it. In spite of these problems, Adam seems to have no difficulty in math, and he usually earns a "B" in that subject. His mom doesn't understand this because she sees that Adam studies very hard each night for at least an hour and a half.

Case Study 3

Heather succeeded during the first year of school with below-average grades, but when she got to the second grade, she began to have problems with some of her work. She cannot recognize words and does not understand the stories that she reads during reading time. She also has trouble when another student or the teacher reads the story. Although Heather can name the various characters in a story, she cannot seem to remember the plot very well; and if she has to tell the story to someone else, she tends to get the facts confused and is unable to recall the sequence of events. In spite of these problems, Heather is doing low-average work in math and is able to complete simple math operations as well as any other student.

Case Study 4

Thomas never read very well and, from the first grade on, always had problems with his handwriting. When he got to the fifth grade, the teacher decided that he needed some help in both of these areas, and she began to work with him during class. When she started, she was sure that the extra work would help because Thomas seemed to be motivated to improve his reading. As she worked with him, she noted that he would often say one word when he meant another. Also, he sometimes seemed to get his thoughts confused and was unable to communicate as clearly as the typical fifth-grade child. After some time, it became apparent that the extra work did not help, so in desperation, the teacher consulted with the special education teacher in the school to find out about having Thomas tested.

Each of the children described in the case studies is demonstrating a learning disability. A child or adolescent with a learning disability has difficulty in some facet of academic or behavioral functioning that is not related to any other disability. Often, these students perform very well, or acceptably well, in certain academic areas, while in other areas their performance is very low, as in case studies 2 and 3 above. At other times, some students seem to fail to respond to appropriate interventions as in case study 1, and that may be evidence of a learning disability (NJCLD, 2005). This type of problem is very frustrating for the students, particularly at the middle school grades and upper grades as the peer group assumes more importance in the child's life (Bender, 2002). For example, students with a learning disability may be embarrassed when reading aloud in class; almost all students with learning disabilities experience reading problems (Commission on Excellence in Special Education, 2001; National Reading Panel, 2000). Teachers often feel frustrated also because the student will perform well in one area and not in another. Finally, parents of these students often feel as if more should be done to provide an adequate education for their children. One can easily understand all of these frustrations when one considers the emotional and academic burden that many of these students carry. However, this brief set of case studies does not express the personal sense of frustration, loneliness, and failure that many students with learning disabilities experience. No understanding of the phenomenon of learning disabilities is complete unless one has a sense of what these feelings involve, and we must turn to the writings of individuals who are learning disabled for this insight (Reid & Button, 1995). The writings of Joshua Weistein (1994) can assist in this regard.

> I can still remember when I was first tested for dyslexia [i.e., a form of learning disabilities]. I was a klutzy little 8-year-old, curious and dumbfounded by the foreign world that I was slowly learning to understand. I recall sitting in a small office in Toronto, Canada, the beckoning sun shining through an array of windows, while a friend of my mother's administered a barrage of intelligence and reading tests to me. It wasn't the first time my parents had noticed a problem with my rote learning. For years I have been shunned by teachers, considered too unintelligent to participate in daily classroom activities. Alone and rejected, I stood in the corner of my first- and second-grade classes, unsure and perplexed as to why I couldn't take part in the learning process that my peers thought of as commonplace. I couldn't learn to read. I couldn't memorize my multiplication tables regardless of the incessant hours I spend transfixed by this foreign language and all the while, I had a confusing name stapled to my back: dyslexia.

This student shares with us the most profound sense of failure that is common in students with learning disabilities. There is so much failure at such an early age for many students with learning disabilities that one wonders why they don't merely give up. Nevertheless, through courageous efforts, often with the help of effective, concerned teachers, students with learning disabilities do manage to compensate for the disabilities and learn to succeed. Listen to this same student's resolution:

> By making me a very focused learner, dyslexia has given me a zest for solving problems that is applicable in all areas where I've wished to focus my attention. This has not always been easy, but I believe that because of my learning disability, I have learned substantially more. The high school I attend is renowned for its hard academic curriculum, and in the early years, I spent 2 or 3 nights a week at a tutor's home. I have compensated for difficulties with rote learning by identifying problems early, by learning conceptually, and by determining when I need help and seeking this help in the form of tutoring. (Weistein, 1994)

Clearly, Joshua received a great deal of special assistance and has learned to compensate for the learning disability. Joshua Weistein subsequently enrolled at Vassar College in Poughkeepsie, New York, pursuing a liberal arts degree in theater. Such is the power of determination, courage, and effective special education services for students with learning disabilities.

The Challenge

You are now entering the field of study involving learning disabilities, a relatively new and very lively area of great challenge and possibilities. This field has existed for slightly over four decades, and in that time, professionals, parents, and individuals who themselves experience learning disabilities have tried desperately to develop new approaches to deal with the set of problems described in the case studies. The challenge for you as a future professional in the field or a professional currently serving there is to improve the overall educational performance of students with learning disabilities while serving as an advocate for them in an attempt to alleviate some of their difficulties.

Your task will not be an easy one. Nevertheless, the opportunity is yours, and the rewards for helping these students are great, in terms of both your personal satisfaction and the success of the students you will teach. You must reach out to students just like Timeko, Joshua, Adam, Heather, and Thomas and assist them in dealing with their disabilities. This will be your overriding goal.

THE COMPLEX HISTORY OF LEARNING DISABILITIES

In understanding the history of the field of learning disabilities, students must focus on two things: the six distinct historical phases and a variety of different theoretical perspectives in each phase. The six historical phases include the clinical phase, the classroom transition phase, the consolidation phase, the expansion phase, the retrenchment phase, and the revitalization phase. Our task herein is to present these historical phases and the events that characterized each phase.

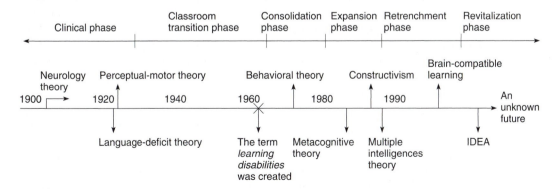

FIGURE 1.1   Time Line for Learning Disabilities

However, in addition to understanding these historical phases, it is important to know the theoretical perspectives in each phase, since the theories on learning disabilities helped define the history in each phase. Of course, no theory is static, and as research is conducted in the field, the theoretical perspectives change over time. In some cases, entirely different theories evolved into new perspectives in the field of learning disabilities. Adding to this complexity, the terms and definitions of the term *learning disabilities* changed from one historical period to the next. Figure 1.1 presents a historical time line, coupled with the dates associated with the various theoretical perspectives. In reading the next sections of this chapter, you should refer back to Figure 1.1, as this will greatly assist you in understanding the history of this complex field.

THE CLINICAL PHASE: EARLY EVOLUTION OF THE FIELD

The clinical phase began in the 1920s with the first tentative recognition of a group of children who were "different" from children with mental retardation. Until this time, the children who would today be considered learning disabled had been labeled mentally retarded because learning deficits were noted among these children and because no alternative disability or classification existed. The clinical phase ended around 1940, when this group of children with poorly understood learning characteristics was shown to be different from children with lower than normal levels of intelligence. At that point, an emphasis emerged that resulted in attempts to identify educational recommendations for these children who seemed to learn differently. This and subsequent historical phases, and the primary emphasis of each phase, are presented in Figure 1.2.

Research during the clinical phase took place in non–public school settings because that is where children with learning differences were then receiving their schooling. Further, many different clinical settings were associated with various early theories in the field. For example, numerous theorists who were later associated with the "visual-perceptual perspective on learning disabilities" either studied or were influenced by those who studied at the Wayne County Training School in Michigan, an institution for people who were retarded that tended to emphasize perception as the basis of learning problems. Alternatively, theorists who studied language development and language-related learning problems tended to be associated with university speech clinics. Several points should be made here. First, some early theories on learning disabilities—specifically, the visual-perceptual deficit theory and the language-deficit theory—evolved in part as a result of where the students were receiving services. Next, early research on learning disabilities was based on children who may have been more severely impaired than those classified by the public schools today as having learning disabilities because, at that time, only children with the most severe impairments were placed in clinical settings.

The difference between the types of children studied then and now results in a problematic transition to public school settings. For example, clinical settings tend to be dominated by medical models of thought, and clinicians use medical terms to designate problems. Whereas an educator may find that low levels of on-task time or attention in class may cause learning disability, a researcher in a clinical setting is likely to identify these problems as distractibility or as an attention-deficit disorder.

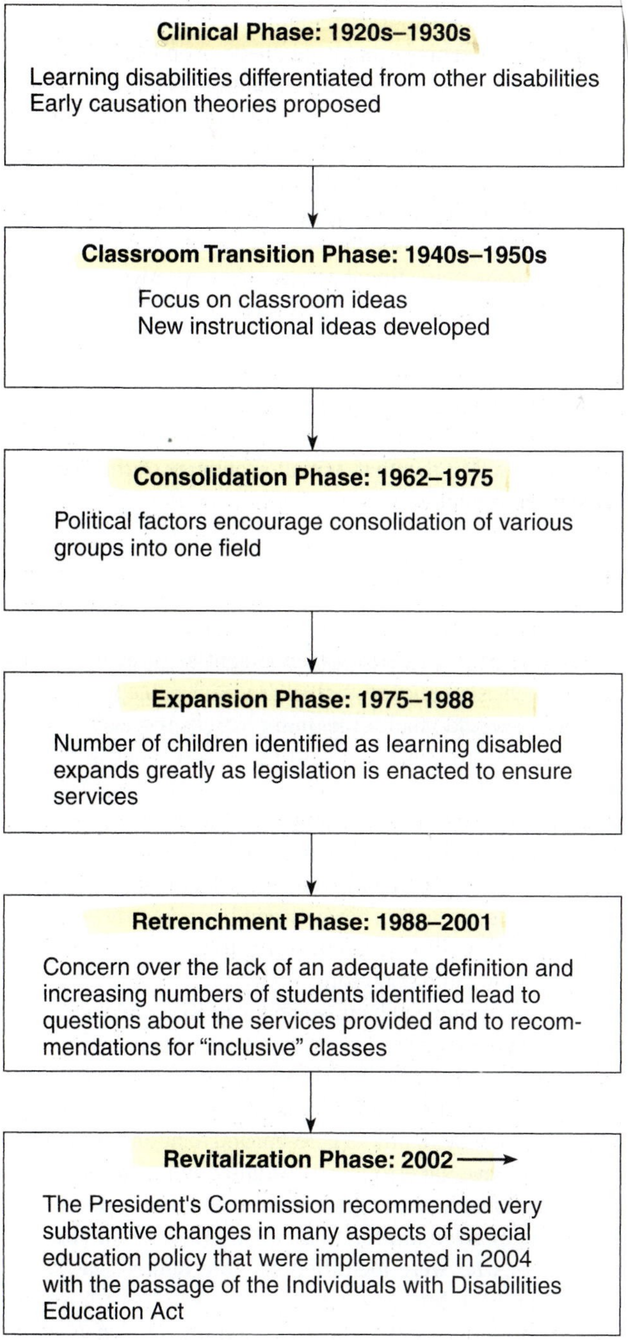

Clinical Phase: 1920s–1930s

Learning disabilities differentiated from other disabilities
Early causation theories proposed

Classroom Transition Phase: 1940s–1950s

Focus on classroom ideas
New instructional ideas developed

Consolidation Phase: 1962–1975

Political factors encourage consolidation of various
groups into one field

Expansion Phase: 1975–1988

Number of children identified as learning disabled
expands greatly as legislation is enacted to ensure
services

Retrenchment Phase: 1988–2001

Concern over the lack of an adequate definition and
increasing numbers of students identified lead to
questions about the services provided and to recommendations for "inclusive" classes

---

Revitalization Phase: 2002 ⟶

The President's Commission recommended very
substantive changes in many aspects of special
education policy that were implemented in 2004
with the passage of the Individuals with Disabilities
Education Act

FIGURE 1.2   Phases in the History of Learning Disabilities

As a student of the field, you should remember that many of the early terms in our field had their origins in clinical settings that used medically based terms rather than educational terms. Although sophisticated-sounding terminology may have temporarily improved the status of the profession historically (in 1978, Coles indicated that medical terms may carry more clout than educational terms), today's professional has little to gain and much to lose by using terms that are overly sophisticated and inconsistent with local and state department of education terminology. Like other complex professions (e.g., law, medicine, engineering), education has developed a terminology of its own, and these terms are much more useful and relevant to educational settings than borrowed medical terminology. Consequently, use of medically based terms in this section is provided merely as historical information.

Scholars in the field of learning disabilities disagree concerning the number of constituent groups in the history of the field (Commission, 2001; NJCLD, 2005), and there is increasing disagreement about the varied theoretical perspectives today. Several different groups of theorists are discussed in this text, but all groupings of this nature are rather arbitrary, and each includes subgroups.

Visual-Perceptual/Motor Theorists

As the name implies, the **visual-perceptual/motor theorists** were concerned with impaired visual perception and delayed motor development as possible causes of learning problems. This group of theorists believed that such visual-perceptual problems coupled with poor fine motor control would result in learning deficits that were independent of intelligence. Within this group, an emphasis on brain-based perceptual and motor disabilities was the major concern because problems with the brain and the central nervous system were considered the primary cause of learning problems (Moats & Lyon, 1993). The recognition that some children labeled retarded were in fact fairly capable of certain things while being completely incapable of some perceptual motor tasks resulted in the proliferation of labels attempting to represent the relationship between brain-based learning and difficulty in school subjects. Labels such as *brain injured, central nervous system dysfunction,* and *minimal brain dysfunction* were quite common.

The development of this group can be traced back to Kirk Goldstein. In studying veterans after World War I, Goldstein identified certain visual-perceptual problems in soldiers who had suffered brain injuries during battle. The clinical/medically based thought here is obvious. Goldstein was a student of Gestalt psychology and was interested in perception. He found that his subjects could not identify figure-ground relationships and, in some cases, lost the ability to read. Letter-reversal errors and design-copying problems were very common. The subjects were also observed to be hyperactive and easily distracted. Goldstein's work led to the use of the term *brain injured* to identify children with these types of problems. This group of children who were identified as brain injured was later incorporated into the category of learning disabilities.

In retrospect, the error in this logic is apparent; in short, similarity of symptoms does not necessarily imply similarity of cause. Thus, one should not assume that all learning disabilities are caused by brain injury simply because their symptoms seem to overlap with the symptoms of the brain-injured soldiers studied by Goldstein. However, for several decades (the 1930s to the 1960s), the assumption that all learning disabilities were related to brain injury of some unspecified type that resulted in a visual and/or perceptual-motor problem was central to the history of learning disability.

Goldstein's research influenced Alfred Strauss, who was working with children who were mentally retarded. Strauss and Heinz Werner, at the Wayne County Training School, studied in a clinical setting children whose retardation resulted from nongenetic factors. This nongenetic retardation was labeled *exogenous*. Also, these children were shown to exhibit hyperactivity and delays in responding to certain stimuli. Strauss and his co-workers identified seven criteria for identification of these children: perceptual disorders, perseveration (continuous repetition), thinking disorders, behavior disorders, slight neurological signs, history of neurological impairment, and no history of mental retardation. Aspects of these criteria are still found in later definitions of learning disability.

As the number of theorists associated with this theory grew, these visual-motor theorists developed numerous hypotheses that suggested a learning disability was the result of a deficit in visual or visual-motor ability. Because of the historical evidence indicating that certain injuries to the brain could cause visual-perceptual problems, a group of theorists, including **William Cruickshank** and **Marianne Frostig,** asserted that learning disabilities were a result of perceptual problems based on dysfunctions in the brain and central nervous system. If a child could not copy geometric designs with a certain degree of skill, this was assumed to indicate a problem of intrasensory integration, the integration of information between the child's sensory nervous system (the optic nerve that gathered the information) and the motor nervous system (that controlled the child's written response). Other indicators of this problem included an inability to copy from the blackboard, locate "hidden pictures" where the stimulus picture is partially covered, and perceive differences between letters that are mirror reversals of each other (e.g., b and d). In each example, the child must take in information visually, integrate it with known or relevant facts, and then produce the correct motor-nerve response.

Strauss and Werner were among the first to suggest that learning problems can be caused by something other than retardation, and it is difficult to overstate the importance of these perceptual-motor theorists. This was the first group of theorists who actively studied students with learning disabilities. Also, because of these perceptual characteristics, a different type of educational program was recommended for these students, including reduced exposure to potentially distracting stimuli. These leaders separated the brain-injured from the retarded populations and recommended different teaching strategies based on the characteristics of the individual learner. Of course, this last idea is now mandated in special education law and policy. Finally, as noted, many early leaders in the field of learning disabilities studied with Strauss and Werner, and thus their influence was multiplied.

One problem with this theoretical perspective is the inability of researchers to measure an ability in the brain (Hammill, 1993). Although behavioral responses such as copying were observable, the abilities upon which these responses were assumed to be based were hidden in the brain and central nervous system (CNS) and not directly measurable. Consequently, theorists such as Hammill (1993) and Vaughn and Linan-Thompson (2003) indicated that these abilities were only assumed to exist. In other words, low scores on visual-perceptual exercises may be a result of poor handwriting or lack of attention to detail in copying the designs, rather than a brain-based malfunction in the learning process.

Much of the controversy concerning assessment of students with learning disabilities is associated with the instruments developed to assess visual-perceptual deficits, and the weaknesses in many measurement instruments were noted early on (Moats & Lyon, 1993). Many of the assessments then in use had questionable reliability and validity. In general, a reliability figure of 0.90 or higher is recommended for any test that is used for placement of an individual child in a special program or curriculum, and even today few commercially available instruments that assess visual-motor skills are acceptable by this standard (Moats & Lyon, 1993). This ongoing concern for accurate assessment continues in the field today (Commission, 2001; NJCLD, 2005).

However, the problems with the measurement instruments did not prevent implementation of instruction for these presumed visual deficits. From the late 1950s through the 1970s, many public school classes for children with learning disabilities included various remediation exercises that were intended to correct these visual-perceptual problems. For example, a music liner was used on the blackboard, and children would be expected to draw lines between each of the stimulus lines without touching them. Such exercises were assumed to improve visual perception and, therefore, reading.

The assumption behind these training exercises suggested that if a teacher could remediate the visual-perceptual abilities, the improvement in design copying would result in improved reading scores for the child with learning disabilities. Of course, this assumption was highly questionable and has been largely discredited (Hammill, 1993; Moats & Lyon, 1993). Further, evidence accumulated to indicate the futility of many of these early training programs (Hammill, 1993; Moats & Lyon, 1993; Vaughn & Linan-Thompson, 2003). In spite of these early failures, there is some recent evidence that reading disabilities (i.e., one form of a learning disability) are associated with visual problems for some children (Eden, Stein, Wood, & Wood, 1995). Consequently, there are still many practitioners in the field who support the concept of some visual deficit as one potential cause of learning disabilities.

Language Theorists

During the clinical phase, another early perspective emerged from researchers studying languages. The **language theorists** were less unified than the visual-perceptual theorists in the early history of the field. The group was concerned with language development in young children, and later this was expanded to an emphasis on both spoken and written language across the age span. Language represents the use and interpretation of information in symbolic form, and spoken and written language have this interpretative basis in common. This group of theorists tended to view academic achievement in terms of the use of language because it was dominated by theorists who worked initially with children with speech delays and/or children who were deaf, and these problems were presumed to have a ripple effect that could cause academic delay in a number of school subjects. From this perspective, children would be described as learning disabled based on incomplete speech development, incorrect usage of various rules of grammar, inappropriate understanding of pronoun referents, and other speech and language problems. These were believed to be the basis of other difficulties in written language, reading, and communication skills.

Much of the early research of this group of theorists demonstrated relationships between language measures and academic skills. The emphasis on language arts and reading skills within the present instructional approaches to learning disabilities can be traced directly to this group. Like the visual-motor theorists, these researchers concentrating on language suggested a neurological basis for language-based learning disabilities. Some dysfunction in the sensory and motor nervous systems was assumed to be the culprit. The most notable of these theorists was Samuel Kirk.

In one sense, the major difference between this and the visual-deficit perspective was the mode of input for the stimulus information. For this group of theorists, the majority of information was taken in by hearing the stimulus rather than seeing it. With children who were late in learning language or who demonstrated problems in various types of language arts and reading, a **language deficit** was assumed to exist in the perceptual systems that involved either auditory input or some linguistic area in the brain. Indicators of this deficit included an inability to integrate several syllables into one word, recall a series of digits presented orally, or use the correct grammatical rules for simple plural formations.

The early language theorists started working with children with learning disabilities in the 1920s and 1930s. For example, as early as 1926, Head published a series of studies of adults who had lost the ability to read as a result of brain injuries acquired during World War I (Kirk, 1988). This series of studies was, at the time, viewed as independent of Goldstein's research on perception of soldiers with brain injury. However, in later years, this research strengthened the hypothesized connection between brain injury and learning problems in children.

Perhaps the major name associated with language research in the early period was **Samuel Orton.** Orton postulated that the normal dominance of one brain hemisphere in language (which develops in the left hemisphere of the brain in most children by about the age of 7 years) was lacking in children with language and reading problems. The lack of dominance and the language-related problems that were thought to result from it were labeled *strephosymbolia*—literally, "twisted symbols." Also, many of the children in his clinical setting—the Iowa State Psychopathic Hospital—were observed to have mixed or confused dominance of hand, eye, or foot. Such deficits led Orton to advocate an education approach that included phonic and kinesthetic aids (teaching aids designed for touch and/or movement). These concepts are still in use today in some classes for those with learning disabilities.

Charles Osgood, working in the area of language during this period, postulated a model of communication that attempted to demonstrate the information processing that transpired between presentation of a stimulus and the response. This model was to become the basis for further work designed to identify specific types of learning disabilities.

Grace Fernald, working at a clinical school at the University of California in 1921, developed a teaching approach for reading and writing. The approach focused on providing stimuli on a multisensory basis, using visual, auditory, kinesthetic, and tactile means. The student would see, hear, and form the movements involved in writing and touch an outlined shape of a letter or word when first exposed to it. Many special education programs today still incorporate these ideas in language arts instruction.

With these leading researchers working on language deficits, a great deal of research was done to demonstrate that children with learning disabilities were deficient in various language abilities such as use of proper syntax, semantics, and general use of language for communication. Overall, these early language-deficit theories, much like the visual-deficit perspective, have not continued to exert a major influence on the field. The measurement instruments and the recommended treatment strategies have received the same criticism as those based on the visual-deficit perspective.

Neurological Theorists

The medical profession has been very active in the field from the earliest historical periods—as discussed in Chapter 2. Studies of neurology have a certain appeal in the area of learning disabilities in that many students with learning disabilities demonstrate problems with various types of learning tasks, including attention, memory, and paired-associate learning. Thus, a large body of work in the field is based in this concern for the neurology of learning problems. Neurologically oriented theorists have provided hypotheses in the field of learning disabilities in three general areas: etiology, assessment, and treatment. However, only in the last area has medical science proven to be a major contributor to the field.

Some neurologically based problems have been tentatively identified as causes of learning disabilities. As mentioned previously, Orton (1937) was the first to suggest that children who experience learning disabilities seem to develop hemispheric specialization for language at a later stage of development. This developmental lag in hemispheric specialization was believed to cause delayed language and concomitant reading problems as well as confused laterality (an inability to identify left and right). While the idea of hemispheric specialization as a potential cause for learning disabilities has declined in recent years, some practitioners still advocate this formulation of learning problems based on hemispheric-specialization problems.

In the area of neurological assessment, great progress has been made in identification of neural structures associated with different types of learning tasks (Leonard, 2001; Sousa, 2001). Still, these assessment procedures are clinically oriented and thus are rarely used in schools today for identification of students with learning disabilities. However, research on how the human brain functions has grown dramatically within the last 15 years, as described in Chapter 2, and the application of some of these newly developed assessment procedures may increase over the next decade.

To date, the **neurological perspective** has not resulted in effective treatments for most students with disabilities (Hammill, 1993; Sousa, 2001), with the obvious exception of certain medication treatments for hyperactivity. Although some students with learning disabilities do demonstrate unusual brain activity during educational tasks, many children with learning disabilities do not. Also, many children who are not disabled demonstrate unusual brain activity patterns. Finally, even when unusual patterns of activity are present, very few relevant suggestions concerning appropriate remedial strategies for educational treatment have been forthcoming.

Early research in the other areas of neurology did not result in major contributions either. For example, suggestions that children who have learning disabilities demonstrate different brain hemispheric preferences for language have not been supported (Bender, 1987). Although neurological studies have been a major emphasis in the field, there has to date been no single breakthrough that this perspective can point to as an important contribution to either identification or educational treatments for students with learning disabilities. However, a great deal of research is ongoing; advances in medical diagnosis techniques, such as the positron emission tomography (PET) scan and the functional magnetic resonance imaging (fMRI), have documented numerous differences between the brains of individuals with and without learning disabilities (Hynd, Marshall, & Gonzalez, 1991; Leonard, 2001; Shaywitz & Shaywitz, 2006; Sousa, 2001). This perspective has thus received a resurgence of interest of late, and recent advances in this area are described in more detail in Chapter 2.

THE CLASSROOM TRANSITION PHASE: MOVING INTO THE SCHOOL SETTING

The early work on recognition of the existence of learning disabilities as a condition different from retardation was done in hospitals and institutions, particularly those previously mentioned. However, educational ideas based on this new condition were being translated into classroom terms by the 1940s and 1950s. For example, numerous students of the previously mentioned researchers had become interested in classroom application of the learning principles developed by their mentors. By 1940, much of the early groundwork for the field had been completed, and the shift to classroom applications had begun.

During this phase, from 1940 until the early 1960s, education for students with learning disabilities was not legally mandated. Consequently, even though the movement toward services in public school settings began at this time, most of the children who would today be considered learning disabled were still not receiving educational services in public schools. Rather, they were receiving services in clinics, where medical terminology and medical perspectives dominated, or were merely excluded from schooling altogether.

This medical domination of the early historical periods presented a problem for the field. Although medically based terms have been very useful in certain respects (e.g., *diagnosis* of learning problems and individualized educational *treatment* are themselves medical concepts), use of these terms does result in certain difficulties. Much of the current confusion about definitional issues and treatment approaches stems from the blurred transition between medically based settings, such as institutions for people who are retarded or speech/language clinics, and public school classrooms. As a new practitioner in this field, you are well advised to be cautious in your use of medical terminology in educational settings. However, to acquaint you with this information in the field of learning disabilities, more information on the medical basis of learning disabilities is provided in Chapter 2.

Visual-Motor Theorists

The visual-motor theorists, many of whom were students of Strauss and Werner, exerted a dominant influence over the field during the 1950s and 1960s. For example, Newell Kephart worked with Strauss on an early teaching methods textbook for children with brain injuries (Strauss & Kephart, 1955). Also, Kephart postulated that all learning was based on perceptual-motor development and thus expanded the concerns of this group of theorists to include various aspects of motor learning.

William Cruickshank also studied with Strauss and Werner and then applied their findings to youth with minimal brain dysfunction—the terminology of the day. He focused on distractibility and hyperactivity and recommended educational strategies for children with these problems. This was a critical conceptual link to later formulations of definitions for learning disability because, combined with the Strauss/Werner separation of various types of retardation, this concept provided the rationale for identification of this disorder as an entirely separate disability. Cruickshank's book, *A Teaching Method for Brain-Injured and Hyperactive Children* (Cruickshank, Bentzen, Ratzeburg, & Tannhauser, 1961), was one of the most influential methods books at the time concerning the education of individuals with learning disabilities. Interest Box 1.1 presents some of the recommendations made for the education of children with brain injuries.

skip this part

Language Theorists

The language theorists were also very busy establishing classroom-based educational interventions and assessment devices. For example, **Samuel Kirk,** who had studied with a colleague of Orton and worked at the Wayne County Training School, initiated long-term study of language usage in children without retardation. Kirk's major accomplishment was publication of the *Illinois Test of Psycholinguistic Abilities* (Kirk, McCarthy, & Kirk, 1968), which was designed to identify visual- and auditory-based language deficits that affected achievement in various academic subjects. The assumption was that educational recommendations could then be made for classroom instructional strategies. Also, Kirk served in

- - - - - ▬▬▬▬▬▬▬▬▬▬▬▬▬▬▬▬▬▬▬▬▬▬▬▬▬▬▬▬▬▬▬▬▬▬▬

INTEREST BOX 1.1

EARLY EDUCATIONAL RECOMMENDATIONS

These are the educational recommendations that were made originally by Werner and Strauss and later refined by Cruickshank. It is interesting to note the similarities to many of the strategies used today. Cruickshank recommended a reduced-stimuli environment, which included the following elements:

1. Reductions in external noise, light, and distracting stimuli in the classroom
2. Carpeted floors to reduce noise, bookshelves that close, and study cubicles that prevent the child from seeing other stimuli
3. Highlighted learning tasks—accomplished by using colors, large print, and unique lettering

The background for learning tasks was intended to be unstimulating, while the specific educational task was to include heightened stimuli such as bright colors. Such an environment was intended to heighten awareness of the specific educational stimuli. The teaching material was intended to include bright colors, with perhaps only one or two words of reading text per page. This was expected to encourage the child to attend to the learning task with less distraction.

The reduced-stimuli environment in combination with highlighted teaching materials was assumed to promote better attention and achievement. However, research did not show such innovations to be effective in increasing achievement.

several governmental capacities during the formative years of federal policy in the 1950s and 1960s, thus becoming a major force in the development of the field. He was the first person to use the term *learning disabilities*, which he coined in 1962.

During this period, Helmer Myklebust began working with children who were deaf, focusing on disorders of spoken language. However, this interest quickly expanded to include written language and reading. Myklebust advocated instruction through auditory or visual stimuli, based on the strength of the student in each area. During the 1970s and 1980s, research demonstrated that modality training was not as effective as had been hoped (Hammill, 1993; Moats & Lyon, 1993; Vaughn & Linan-Thompson, 2003), but the concept is still occasionally utilized in the field.

THE CONSOLIDATION PHASE: THE FIELD BECOMES UNIFIED

Although identification of discrete historical phases is rarely precise, this phase can be dated as beginning in 1962. In that year, the diverse advocacy groups concerned with children who had problems but who were not retarded agreed to join forces as educators concerned with learning disabilities. In order to understand the field of learning disabilities today, some understanding of the political events of that time period is necessary.

John F. Kennedy was president from 1960 until 1963, and in that office, he became one of the first national figures to publicly acknowledge mental retardation as a family reality—his sister Rosemary Kennedy was retarded. Kennedy created a national office, the Division for Handicapped Children, in the U.S. Office of Health, Education, and Welfare, to oversee funds for research on individuals with disabilities. This tentatively opened the door for public funding of services for research into the problems of students with a variety of disabilities (Kirk, 1988). However, children with identified perceptual problems or language delays were initially not included because the theorists had been unable to agree on a term and definition common to these conditions. For a brief period, there was some possibility that children with those problems would be excluded from research and program funds, and their parents were very concerned that children with this variety of learning problems were being ignored.

The First Definition of Learning Disability

However, Samuel Kirk, as the director of the new division, was aware of these parental concerns and interpreted his instructions to include the children who were being called brain injured, minimal brain dysfunctional, language delayed, and so on. This decision provided a political and financial reason for establishing a strong group identity among parents and professionals concerned with children who had these problems. By the early 1960s, many professionals had begun to recognize that the common element among these perceptual and language problems seemed to be an inability to learn that was not caused by low intelligence or environmental factors. The cause seemed to be dysfunction in the brain or central nervous system that affected the way a child processed information. Consequently, a meeting was held in Chicago, and Kirk, as the keynote speaker, recommended the term *learning disability* to include all children with perceptual and/or language problems. He defined this term as

> a retardation, disorder, or delayed development in one or more of the processes of speech, language, reading, spelling, writing, or arithmetic resulting from a possible cerebral dysfunction and/or emotional or behavioral disturbance and not from mental retardation, sensory deprivation, or cultural or instructional factors. (Kirk, 1988)

Note that this definition, similar to the criteria developed by Strauss, maintained the exclusion of retardation as a potential cause for learning disabilities. Also, the cause of the problem was assumed to be a brain dysfunction. Many of the later definitions of the term use these same concepts.

Based on this brief political history, one can see that the factors that led to the consolidation of the field of learning disabilities basically came from three areas: human factors, research factors, and funding factors. These factors are depicted in Figure 1.3.

The human factors included a growing awareness on the part of U.S. society of the needs of various disadvantaged groups. It is not accidental that the first national concern for children with disabilities came during the same decade as the national concern for the civil rights of minorities—the 1960s. A second human factor involved the formation of strong parental advocacy groups that sought funding for research on children's problems.

Research factors stemmed from research in earlier periods. First, during the 1960s, researchers in the field accepted the difference between a learning disability and mental retardation, and that widespread acceptance established learning disabilities as a separate disability that warranted research attention. Second, researchers identified a common denominator that unified the diverse groups—an unexplained inability to learn that was presumably based in some incapacity of the brain or central nervous system.

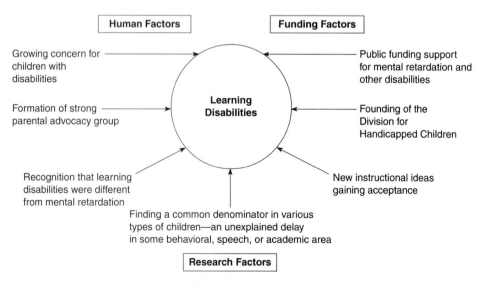

FIGURE 1.3   Factors in the Consolidation Phase

Funding constituted the third group of factors. The diverse groups concerned with language delay and visual-perceptual problems realized that, in order to secure funding from the government, they should form one unified group. The Division for Handicapped Children provided a funding mechanism for services to children who came to be recognized as having learning disabilities.

This consolidation of the various factions concerned with learning disabilities represents a milepost for several reasons. First, the initial two historical phases can be roughly dated by the activities of various researchers, but this third phase is dated by political events. The consolidation phase began at the meeting in 1962 that resulted from the political and financial reasons noted previously. This phase also ended with a political event, the passage of the Education for All Handicapped Children Act in 1975, that mandated education for all children with disabilities. Theorists have repeatedly indicated the political nature of the learning disabilities concept (Commission, 2001; Hammill, 1993; Moats & Lyon, 1993), and beginning with this phase of the history, this political connection is apparent. Also, with this consolidation of the diverse groups, the professionals and parents concerned with learning disabilities were united into a political force that could assist in the national recognition and funding for education for all children with learning disabilities.

Second, during this phase, researchers became so numerous that it is difficult to report all of the strides made. Furthermore, the dualism between language theorists and perceptual-motor theorists dissipated to some degree. The emphasis of theorists shifted to providing an adequate definition of *learning disability* and identifying the characteristics of the population. Finally, the 1963 meeting resulted in the creation of the Association for Children with Learning Disabilities. This group, now called the Learning Disabilities Association (LDA), became one of the most influential organizations concerned with the education of these children. With this politically active group in place, recognition of this newly established disability became the major focus.

Task Force I.   During the consolidation phase, the necessity to establish a national identity for individuals with learning disabilities was paramount. It was imperative to establish an adequate and widely accepted definition and to identify criteria based on that definition in order to secure funding for the education of these children. Consequently, the search intensified for a definition acceptable to all parties that adequately identified the group of children who should receive additional help. The National Society for Crippled Children and Adults, along with the National Institute of Neurological Diseases, sponsored a task force known as **Task Force I** with the intention of providing an adequate definition. In 1966, S. D. Clements, as the director of a task force, proposed a definition based on the earlier examples of Strauss and Kirk. This group chose to use the term *minimal brain dysfunction (MBD)* and defined the dysfunction as follows:

> Children of near average, average, or above average general intelligence with certain learning or behavioral disabilities ranging from mild to severe, which are associated with deviations of function of the central nervous system. These deviations may manifest themselves by various combinations of impairment in perception, conceptualization, language, memory, and control of attention, impulse, or motor function. (Clements, 1966)

As is apparent, several aspects of the early definitions are included in this definition. These include emphases on the association between the learning problems and problems in the brain or CNS, on average or above-average general intelligence, and on perception, language, thinking, and behavioral abnormalities.

The Early Federal Definition.   The U.S. Office of Education was given the responsibility of funding special education programs, and this resulted in the formation of the National Advisory Committee on Handicapped Children in 1968. A definition was formulated that would include all of the children who needed services but exclude other low-achieving children whose poor school performance was not related to disabilities. Under Kirk's leadership, the following definition of learning disabilities was proposed by this committee:

> Children with special learning disabilities exhibited a disorder in one or more of the basic psychological processes involved in understanding or in using spoken or written languages. These may be manifested in disorders of listening, thinking, talking, reading, writing, spelling, or arithmetic. They include conditions which have been referred to as perceptual handicaps, brain injury, minimal brain dysfunction, dyslexia, developmental aphasia, etc. They do not include learning problems which are due primarily to visual, hearing, or motor handicaps, to mental retardation, emotional disturbance, or environmental disadvantage. (Kirk, 1988)

This definition shows certain similarities to previous definitions. These include an emphasis on language-based difficulties as well as perceptual difficulties, an emphasis on cognitive processes (i.e., referred to as the "basic psychological processes" of thought), and a clause to exclude children with other disabilities. Also, use of phrases such as "may be manifested" and "one or more" resulted in later confusion concerning the true meaning of the definition. This definition is very important because of the timing of federal legislation. It was incorporated into federal law in the Learning Disabilities Act of 1969. Furthermore, the definition became the model from which most states subsequently wrote their state definitions of learning disabilities from 1973 to 1976. This is the period when Public Law (PL) 94-142, the Education for All Handicapped Children Act, was passed, and that legislation required states to serve children with all disabilities, including learning disabilities. Obviously, every state needed to define learning disabilities to determine which students needed services, and most looked to the 1968 federal definition as a model for these early state definitions of *learning disability*.

read this

Declining Influence of the Early Theories

Toward the end of the consolidation phase, in the 1970s, the influence of the early theories in learning disabilities began to decline. When viewed in retrospect, the early perspectives on learning disabilities—the visual-motor perspective, the language-deficit perspective, and the neurological perspective—were quite similar. Each was based on a presumed cognitive-processing deficit, that is, a central nervous system dysfunction. These cognitive-processing deficits, visual, perceptual-motor, attention, memory, or language deficits, were, in turn, believed to lead to academic failure and were assumed to be the basis of a learning disability. Thus, these cognitive-processing perspectives were all "medically based" in that the learning was presumed to reside within the child rather than in the interaction between the child and the learning environment. These theorists believed that a deficit in the cognitive or psychological process based on some type of malfunction in the brain was the causal factor in learning disabilities. The cognitive processes were believed to take place within the CNS and include such things as language, memory, attention, and perception (Hammill, 1993; Moats & Lyon, 1993).

Figure 1.4 illustrates the basic conceptualization of the cognitive-processing perspectives. Stimuli impact the brain and central nervous system, the basic psychological processes take place in the brain, and the student performs some type of behavioral response.

As you begin your studies in this field, you should remember that the early scholars representing the diverse historical roots of the field were proponents of different cognitive or mental processing concepts. For example, the language theorists believed that language delays were the cause of disabilities, whereas the visual-motor theorists believed problems in perception were the cause. The neurologists considered all learning problems to be based within the brain. Only in hindsight can these views be grouped. Further, during the 1940s and 1950s, these theorists were well aware of the differences between these various perspectives, and no truly different perspectives had emerged (Hammill, 1993). Although many more recent theories exist today, the popular press—and thus many parents and nonprofessionals—still perceive learning disabilities in ways consistent with the early processing perspectives.

Of course, there do seem to be several types of neurological involvement in some children with learning disabilities (Leonard, 2001; Sousa, 2001), but none of these early perspectives received singular validation as the major one in the field of learning disabilities. It is possible that students who are presently classified by schools as learning disabled have these medically based conditions, though no rigorous methods for measuring them are available today in the schools. Also, some of the training techniques that these perspectives

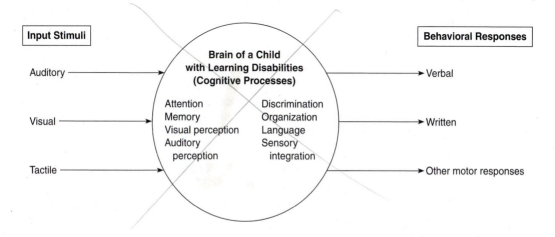

FIGURE 1.4   Early Perspectives

suggest may be valuable for particular children, though research has not supported these for the average child with learning disabilities (Hammill, 1993).

In the 1970s, most theorists and professionals in the field began to face the fact that these perspectives were largely invalidated and therefore highly questionable. For the majority of children with learning disabilities who are in special classes today, the emphasis on these cognitive-deficit assumptions is unwarranted. Because of the failure to validate any of the cognitive-processing perspectives, other theoretical perspectives have been forthcoming (Hammill, 1993). Still, as a professional in the field, you must realize that in spite of the decreasing influence of these perspectives, many theorists in the field have maintained their belief in these assumptions. Consequently, the belief that some children have a measurable brain-based dysfunction that causes learning disabilities is still a theoretical perspective encountered in the field. Also, many theorists and teachers believe that remediation activities need to be based on the strategies suggested by these processing perspectives.

Further, with the continuing definitional concerns in the field of learning disabilities, the emphasis on cognitive or psychological processing may reemerge (Hammill, 1993). Increasing sophistication in the study of brain-based learning processes (described more clearly in Chapter 2) may also lead to the reemergence of this emphasis (Leonard, 2001; Sousa, 2001; Shaywitz & Shaywitz, 2006).

Emergence of a New View: The Behavioral Perspective

With the decreasing influence of the language theorists and the visual-motor theorists during the latter part of this period, the predominance of the behavioral theorists began to emerge in the field of learning disabilities. Behavioral thought contributed very little to early phases in the development of the field. Only during the consolidation phase did behavioral theorists begin to influence education and special education in any significant manner.

However, the influence of behavioral thought during the latter part of the consolidation phase was both extensive and profound. It can be identified in several ways. First, the behavioral influence, with the concentration on specific measurable behaviors rather than cognitive processes, led to the declining sway of the visual-motor and language-deficit theories from the earlier periods. Second, the language of behavioral theory (e.g., objectives and individualized educational programs) began to dominate special education to such a degree that subsequent federal and state legislation was written in behavioral terms. That is, an individual educational plan must be written to stipulate goals and behavioral objectives based on stated, measurable criteria. All of these concepts and requirements stem from behavioral thought. Finally, the emphasis on teaching specific skills rather than training in visual and auditory-perceptual exercises increased during this period. Consequently, the earlier classroom-based treatments for students with learning disabilities were changed fairly significantly during the last few years of the consolidation phase. By the end of this phase, the behavioral perspective held the most power in the field, and special education law was written using the terms of behavioral psychology.

Behavioral psychologists tended to view the earlier perspectives on learning disabilities with some degree of skepticism and argued that instruction in special education classes should concentrate on specific skills that students with special needs would utilize in their everyday world (Hammill, 1993). Unlike the early cognitive-processing perspectives, the behavioral perspective is a unitary conceptualization of learning disabilities. Basically, it suggests that specific academic skills that form the basis of the school curriculum should be the basis for assessment and remediation for all students, including those with learning disabilities. Whereas the visual-perceptual proponents remediated reversal errors between b and d by providing various geometric designs for copying practice, the behavioral theorists provided direct-practice exercises using these specific letters, such as matching tasks or letter-find puzzles, in order to highlight discrimination between the letters. The emphasis was on the specific skill that the student needed to master, rather than some underlying basic perceptual process.

In fact, the growing influence of this behavioral perspective was a direct result of the failure of the earlier cognitive-processing perspectives to provide meaningful and successful remediation techniques to increase academic competence. This perspective also emphasized exact measurement of academic skills, as well as appropriate analysis of the educational task expected of the child.

For example, criterion-referenced testing is one technique associated with the behavioral perspective. Theorists using it argue that diagnosis and remediation of learning disabilities should be based on the skills to be mastered. Therefore, assessment based on the curriculum that the child with learning disabilities should master is required, and nebulous concepts such as intelligence assessment and patterns of cognitive ability are considered irrelevant for instructional purposes. Numerous terms are used to indicate this need to concentrate on skills, including *curriculum-based assessment, precision teaching, direct and daily measurement, direct instruction,* and *skill assessment.* Several of these behavioral interventions are described in more detail in Chapter 10.

The teaching techniques recommended by the behavioral perspective are not specialized techniques designed only for children with learning disabilities. Basically, they were borrowed from other, more traditional areas of education such as research in reading and math education for the elementary school child. Also, research concerning the remedial strategies used with children who are low achieving but not learning disabled has been used. Consequently, during the 1970s and 1980s, classes for children with learning disabilities that were based on this perspective were very similar to the reading and language arts classes for low-level readers, and a few theorists began to question the real need for specialized education for students with learning disabilities.

Research support for many of these instructional techniques is quite compelling. As early as the 1970s, the techniques used by the behavioral theorists and teachers were supported by the research in the field (Hammill, 1993; White, 1986), and that support has continued to the present day. Also, the strength of the research in this area accounts for the fact that this is one of the most influential perspectives in the field today. Research on both precision teaching and direct instruction has been particularly supportive (Hammill, 1993; White, 1986).

In spite of the success of the teaching methods associated with the behavioral perspective, this view of learning disabilities has been criticized. By stressing remediation of specific academic skills, this perspective may miss the accurate portrayal of the whole of learning disabilities. Concerns such as problem-solving skills, academic problems, inefficient methods of problem solution, emotional distress as a result of continued academic failure, and the interaction of these several factors in the overall development of a child may not receive the necessary attention from researchers who are proponents of this perspective. In effect, this perspective essentially places the learning disabilities specialist in the same role as a remedial skills teacher (Carlson, 1985; Vaughn & Linan-Thompson, 2003). Thus, the training of these teachers has been redefined to include remedial math and reading methods rather than any specialized techniques. The teachers of students with learning disabilities who apply this perspective tend to stress only basic skills, such as reading, language arts, and math, to the exclusion of other subject areas. Conversely, in many secondary classrooms for students with learning disabilities, tutoring in subject areas is the mainstay of the class. This raises certain ethical questions about the appropriate use of the special education teacher, who may merely function as a tutor (Carlson, 1985).

THE EXPANSION PHASE: SERVICES WIDEN

With the passage of PL 94-142, in 1975, a major growth of services for children identified with learning disabilities was initiated. During this phase, special education classes were established nationwide for students with learning disabilities, and the professionals and parents who had fought so hard to gain recognition, funding, and research attention for this group of students were euphoric. Services were now provided free of charge for students with disabilities by virtue of federal legislation and subsequent state mandates.

Definition and Identification Problems Arise

However, even in this great expansion of services, problems with the definition of learning disability continued to plague the field. When PL 94-142 passed, scholars had estimated that perhaps 2% of the school-aged population had learning disabilities, and this figure was included in the early draft, but not the final version, of PL 94-142 (Chalfant, 1985). However, because of the vague phrases in the federal definition of learning disabilities, the number of children so identified skyrocketed. For example, by 1983, the population of children in public schools identified as having learning disabilities had reached 3.8% (Chalfant, 1985)—a percentage much higher than had originally been forecast. By the 1990s, this figure had reached 5% (Hallahan, 1992). Also, in 1978, only 29% of all children identified as disabled were identified as learning disabled; but today that figure is much higher.

In 2001, 50% of students with disabilities were identified as learning disabled (Commission, 2001). This higher percentage necessitated increased federal and state funds to provide services for these pupils. As a result, growing percentages were of great concern to federal and state personnel who managed the budgets for education services. Clearly, the state definitions of learning disabilities in use were too ambiguous to allow for accurate identification, and funding agencies were very nervous because of the increased need for funds to provide specialized education for this growing population (Hallahan, 1992; NJ-CLD, 2005).

Consequently, at the same time that educational services for the learning disabled were being established in the 1975–1980 period, scholars and government administrators became concerned that almost any child who did poorly on his or her report card could be identified as learning disabled. States rapidly increased services at the same time that research-ers and practitioners—those who had to identify children with learning disabilities—were becoming more and more concerned with the growing numbers of students so identified. Thus, in the middle of the expansion phase, the roots of the next historical phase—re-trenchment—began. Clearly, the state and federal funds allocated to aid the education of this group of children could not be utilized to support programs for *all* children who had difficulty in school. A tighter definition was needed that would be specific enough to allow for adequate identification of children with learning disabilities without including every child who was low achieving.

There were several responses to this problem of overidentification. These are pre-sented in chronological order. First, the 1968 definition was revised slightly in the 1977 *Federal Register.* This revised definition read as follows:

> "Specific learning disability" means a disorder in one or more of the basic psychological processes involved in understanding or in using language, spoken or written, which may manifest itself in an imperfect ability to listen, think, speak, read, write, spell or to do math-ematical calculations. The term includes such conditions as perceptual handicaps, brain injury, minimal brain dysfunction, dyslexia, and development aphasia. The term does not in-clude children who have learning problems which are primarily the result of visual, hearing, or motor handicaps, of mental retardation, or emotional disturbance, or of environmental, cultural, or economic disadvantage. (U.S. Office of Education, 1977)

Reschly and Hosp (2004) reported that, as late as 2003, 41 states still based their state definition of learning disabilities on this 1977 federal definition, thus indicating the impor-tance of this definition. Further, most of the major components of the definition remained from the earlier definitions. However, the government failed to identify criteria that would clarify the phrase "basic psychological processes." Therefore, the only measurable identifi-cation criterion is the "disorder" list. Most states have operationalized this as a discrepancy between ability, as measured by intelligence tests, and school achievement in one subject or another. According to that definition, if the discrepancy between ability and achievement is great enough, it is considered evidence that a child is not reaching his or her academic potential, and a learning disability is presumed to be present.

Several organizations have since argued against this discrepancy model as a func-tional definition mechanism (Commission, 2001; Council for Learning Disabilities, 1987) because such discrepancies often include children who are low achieving and who have behavior problems or merely refuse to do the required homework. Clearly, children who are not even attempting their work should not be automatically considered learning disabled because specialized education is probably not needed or warranted in those cases. Again, this problem still haunts the field today (Commission, 2001; NJCLD, 2005).

As a second response to the overidentification problem, the National Joint Council on Learning Disabilities was formed in the late 1980s. It consisted of members of various pro-fessional organizations, including the American Speech-Language-Hearing Association, the Council for Learning Disabilities, the International Reading Association, the Associa-tion for Children with Learning Disabilities, the Division for Children with Communication Disorders, and the Orton Dyslexia Society. It proposed a definition that differed from the earlier ones in several major aspects:

Learning disabilities is a general term that refers to a heterogeneous group of disorders manifested by significant difficulties in the acquisition and use of listening, speaking, reading, writing, reasoning, or mathematical abilities. These disorders are intrinsic to the individual, presumed to be due to central nervous system dysfunction, and may occur across the life span. Problems in self-regulatory behaviors, social perception, and social interaction may exist with learning disabilities but do not by themselves constitute a learning disability. Although learning disabilities may occur concomitantly with other handicapping conditions (for example, sensory impairment, mental retardation, serious emotional disturbance) or with extrinsic influences (such as cultural differences, insufficient or inappropriate instruction) they are not the result of those conditions or influences. (Hammill, 1990)

Note that this definition specifies a population that exists across the age span, whereas earlier definitions focused only on school-aged persons. Also, this definition does not specifically exclude students who have a lower-than-average intelligence quotient (IQ), but merely states that the learning disability may not be the result of the lower IQ. This definition has been cited as one of the innovative definitions of the 1990s (Hammill, 1990), but it has not resulted in wide revision of state definitions of learning disability.

Although presenting so many definitions of learning disabilities may seem cumbersome, it helps underline the importance and difficulty of defining this term. Ideally, the core characteristics that make up a learning disability must be embedded within the definition of this term; subsequently, from the definition stem the actual diagnostic procedures. However, the field has historically fallen far short of this ideal (Commission, 2001; Stanovich, 1999; Tomasi & Weinberg, 1999).

For example, Siegel (1999) discusses a court case in which several students at Boston University presented evidence to document their learning disabilities and requested accommodations, including course substitutions for the foreign language requirement. When Boston University denied these accommodations, the students went to court and won the case, based in part on the fact that the definition of a learning disability was not clear. Siegel (1999) reports that Boston University itself had used varying procedures for identifying students with learning disabilities, with little consensus on what characteristics should be measured. This ambiguity of definition and diagnostic procedures for college-aged students with learning disabilities has been labeled "chaotic," suggesting a need for a more precise definition. At present, as a beginning practitioner in this field, you must become accustomed to the relatively fluid definitions of the term and apply the terminology and assessment procedures that are used in your state or school district until more precise terms and procedures evolve. Further, because of the recent enactment of the Individuals with Disabilities Education Act, the definition and assessment procedures for identifying students with learning disabilities are changing once again (Fuchs, Fuchs, & Compton, 2004; Mellard, Deshler, & Barth, 2004; Mellard, Byrd, Johnson, Tollefson, & Boesche, 2004; NJCLD, 2005).

A New Theory Emerges: Metacognition

During the expansion phase, as a result of dissatisfaction with the behavioral perspective, a number of researchers developed an alternative perspective on learning disabilities—a perspective today known as the metacognitive perspective. Joseph Torgesen (1975, 1977) is credited with the early development of the metacognitive perspective, though other schol-ars had formulated similar assumptions at about the same time (Kavale & Forness, 1986). Basically, this perspective suggests that children with learning disabilities do not or can-not develop the type of task-planning and task-execution strategies that some schoolwork requires, for a variety of cognitive and emotional reasons. The perspective is centered on a research conceptualization called **metacognition,** which suggests that children need to think about and plan out their thinking and their activities in order to complete a complex educational task.

For example, as one completes a task, one generally makes various statements to oneself concerning it. Torgesen (1977, 1980) reviewed research to suggest that children with learning disabilities do not give themselves such self-instruction with the same fre-quency or degree of accuracy as other children. He demonstrated that students with learn-ing disabilities were often unengaged or inactive in their learning efforts, and he used the term *inactive learner* as one early conceptualization of this idea (Torgesen, 1977). He also included emotional and personality factors in the perspective by suggesting that children with learning disabilities were more likely to have a lower self-concept, which in turn led to fewer attempts to plan the education task successfully. Finally, children with learning disabilities were viewed as having high external control (i.e., they perceived control over their grades and success in school as external to themselves—based perhaps on chance or the whim of the teacher). In short, if a student with learning disabilities generally thinks that he or she cannot complete the task and believes that completion will not necessarily be recognized and rewarded, then the student sees no reason to try.

Because of Torgesen's suggestion of dual causality—that learning disabilities result from both cognitive and emotional/personality causes—a wide array of research in the field of learning disabilities may be seen as a direct result of this metacognitive perspective. Many cognitive psychologists renewed their study of memory and attention in populations of individuals with learning disabilities in view of this concept in an effort to portray ac-curately the types of individual self-instruction students with learning disabilities provide for themselves when engaged in a learning task (Hallahan & Sapona, 1983; Torgesen, 1980; Torgesen & Licht, 1983). Also, a number of theorists studied self-concept, locus of control, and attributions for success in these populations (Bender, 1985; Bender, Rosenkrans, & Crane, 1999; Torgesen & Licht, 1983).

Research on the learning characteristics of children with learning disabilities was generally supportive of the metacognitive perspective, the theory that students with learn-ing disabilities were not cognitively and/or motivationally involved with the learning task (Torgesen, 1980). For example, researchers soon demonstrated that such children are much more likely to be off-task than children who do not have learning disabilities (Bender, 1985). Also, children with learning disabilities demonstrate a lack of memory and attention skills that facilitate learning (Bender, 2002; Liddell & Rasmussen, 2005).

Because of the important research in this area, numerous instructional techniques based on this perspective have been developed for use with children who have learning disabilities (Bender, 2002; Hallahan & Sapona, 1983). Donald Deshler and his associ-ates (Deshler, Schumaker, Lenz, & Ellis, 1984) developed an array of learning strategies for use with secondary school students with learning disabilities. These include acronyms that are easily remembered and that indicate a specific plan for students to follow in a particular type of learning situation. These learning strategies are discussed in more detail in Chapter 11.

Daniel Hallahan and his associates (Hallahan & Sapona, 1983) developed a system by which children with learning disabilities may be taught to monitor their own attention behavior. The system provides a metacognitive statement that children are trained to ask themselves repeatedly: "Am I paying attention?" The use of this procedure can drastically increase the attention behavior of children with learning disabilities (Bender, 2002). Self-monitoring is presented in more detail in Chapter 11, along with other metacognitive strategies.

The metacognitive perspective has dominated the field of learning disabilities for several reasons. First, the strategies developed have been supported by research and are very effective. Second, the perspective offers the advantage of specializing programs for the children with disabilities. Finally, this emphasis on a **learning-strategies approach** parallels a similar trend emphasizing metacognitive skills for all students.

In spite of the increasing support for the metacognitive perspective, several major criticisms are appropriate. First, it does not offer any method whereby a child with learning disabilities may be identified. For example, a great deal of research on the memory, attention, self-concept, and locus of control of children who are low achieving as well as those who are mentally disabled parallels the research results for children with learning disabilities. This suggests that differentiation of these groups might be difficult. Clearly, if the metacognitive perspective does not provide a mechanism for discrimination of children with learning disabilities from other children with or without disabilities, the perspective will begin to lose influence in the field, as did the earlier cognitive-processing perspectives and the behavioral perspective.

Second, Hammill (1993) pointed out that this metacognitive perspective suffers from many of the same problems as the earlier cognitive-processing views. Specifically, it seems to be as difficult—Hammill would say impossible—to measure a "metacognitive" process as it was to measure the cognitive processes of yesteryear. However, one important difference may be noted. Unlike some theorists from the 1970s, the metacognitive theorists have repeatedly operationalized their variables with rigor and are committed to validation studies to demonstrate the efficacy of the recommended treatments (Hammill, 1993).

read this

THE RETRENCHMENT PHASE

Beginning around 1988, the field of learning disabilities, and the entire field of special education, began a period of retrenchment. This period can be dated from 1988 because, by that year, the initial euphoria associated with the expansion phase had diminished, and several factors suggested to leaders in the field of learning disabilities that some degree of turf protection would become necessary if the field were to survive. In fact, numerous authors have indicated that the very existence of the field is occasionally called into question (Commission, 2001; Mather & Roberts, 1994).

At least two identifiable factors led to the retrenchment phase. First, the definition problems and the overidentification problems had not been solved by the late 1980s, and indeed are not solved today; the field has been wrestling with these issues for over 30 years

(Commission, 2001; Hammill, 1993; NJCLD, 2005; Stanovich, 1999; Tomasi & Weinberg, 1999). This is highly problematic because without an adequate definition, there is no method whereby students can effectively be placed in services or eliminated from services based on ineligibility. The field has continually been criticized for this lack of an adequate definition (Commission, 2001).

The second factor may be even more problematic; this is the movement toward inclusive classes (Zigmond, 2003). During the latter part of the expansion phase, concern with the increasing numbers of students identified as learning disabled continued to grow, and administrators began to search for methods to serve the ever-expanding number of students with learning disabilities. Madeline Will (1986, 1988), who served as the assistant secretary of the Office of Special Education and Rehabilitation Services in the Department of Education in Washington, DC, suggested that students with mild disabilities should be served without taking them from the mainstream (the regular education) classroom. This began the movement for "inclusion" of all students with special needs in mainstream classes for 100% of the school day.

Perhaps a brief explanation of services for students with learning disabilities is in order. During the expansion phase, the tendency had been to identify a child with a learning disability and pull that child out of the general education class for one or two periods each day in order to provide services in a special education class. The child would then continue in the general education class for the remainder of the day. However, with the ever-increasing numbers of students identified as learning disabled, the number of special education classes required was growing, as was the associated expense. Consequently, one part of the justification for "inclusion" was a concern for meeting these children's needs without increasing the number of pull-out special education classes, and the concept of the inclusive class was born.

In an inclusive classroom, the general education teacher and the special education teacher are present in the room together for some portion of the school day (Magiera & Zigmond, 2005). Thus, students with learning disabilities would receive the services from a trained special education teacher but would not be extracted from the general education class. Presumably, the teacher with expertise in learning disabilities could then serve in two or three general education classes, and the overall expense of special education could be limited.

Many researchers in the field have expressed concern with inclusive classes, based on the belief that the needs of students with learning disabilities would not be adequately met (Mather & Roberts, 1994). Further, numerous organizations that advocate for students with learning disabilities have expressed concern over the concept of inclusion (Commission, 2001; Mather & Roberts, 1994). Thus, the inclusive educational plan has met some resistance and became a primary factor in the retrenchment phase.

However, this is not to suggest that inclusion should necessarily be viewed as detrimental to students with learning disabilities. There are a number of reasons to believe that students' needs may be better served in inclusive classes than in pull-out special education programs. First, the negative stigma associated with going to the special education class can be minimized in inclusive classrooms, particularly if each teacher works with large numbers of kids with and without special needs. Also, in effective inclusive classes, teachers tend to serve as a sounding board and resource for each other, and the terrible isolation teachers often feel in traditional classes is minimized. Teachers in inclusive classes have a support person—another adult—to turn to if a problem arises, whereas teachers facing a behavioral outburst in a traditional class either have to handle it by themselves or hand the problem over to the principal. Still, the existence of these programs leaves many in the field concerned for the future of classes for students with learning disabilities and contributes to the retrenchment mentality.

Emerging Theoretical Views

During the expansion phase, several additional theoretical perspectives on learning disabilities began to emerge: constructivism, multiple intelligences theory, and brain-compatible instruction (Bender, 2002; Hearne & Stone, 1995; Mather & Roberts, 1994; Moats & Lyon, 1993; Sousa, 2001). Similar to the behavioral perspective in earlier years, each of these recently emerging perspectives was founded in the broader field of psychology and educational psychology, rather than exclusively in the area of learning disabilities. Thus, these are not merely theories in learning disabilities, but rather broader theories in education and learning, which have subsequently been applied to the study of learning disabilities. Given the recency of these developments, it seems premature to try to determine their overall impact at present (Moats & Lyon, 1993). However, the student in the field should have some background understanding of these concepts because these theoretical views are being discussed in the community of researchers and teachers associated with the field of learning disabilities.

Skip this passage **Constructivism.**   Constructivist thought suggests that learners construct knowledge based on background information and connections that can be made between ideas, facts, and concepts (Poplin, 1988). In many ways, this constructivist perspective represents a reaction to—and perhaps a rejection of—the concepts of behavioral thought, and topics such as task analysis and highly specific behavioral objectives are not included within this lexicon. In fact, one concept that has emerged from this perspective is "holistic" thought, which emphasizes that true understanding must stem from some conceptualization of the whole, rather than minute understanding of specific task-analyzed components.

According to Poplin (1988), one proponent of this view, learning is based on empowering the student to discover new meanings and the substantive interrelationship between events, rather than the meanings imposed by others. This emphasis on interrelationships and the meanings discovered by students suggests that assessment should be based in real-world activities and include components that document the student's interests and motivation. Constructivist theorists as a group are interested in how students solve problems. However, problem resolution through cognitive-strategy training or learning-strategies approaches is viewed as much too mechanical; therefore, the constructivists do not consider themselves proponents of metacognitive training as previously described.

The instructional implications of constructivism include an emphasis on real problems based on students' interest, motivation, and self-initiated solutions. New concepts must be constructed based on previously learned concepts, and students must concentrate not only on learning the new material, but also on how that learning takes place. Good teaching is viewed as effective interactional guiding of the student's search for meanings, rather than merely presentation of preselected curriculum materials.

The constructivist view has gained some adherents (Moats & Lyon, 1993), though it is much too early to tell if this perspective will become a major influence within the field of learning disabilities. Also, the implications of this view in both assessment and instruction for the field of learning disabilities are not yet clear.

Multiple Intelligences.   Since the early 1900s, there have been several competing views of intelligence. As you may recall from your early educational psychology courses, the predominant view in Western society regards intelligence as a relatively unified construct; that is, general intelligence is viewed as a single continuum of ability that can be measured by an assessment of the intelligence quotient. Thus, the concept of the IQ score as the single important determinant of adaptive ability arose, and this impacted the field of learning disabilities as well as every other area of educational psychology and special education. For example, today one aspect of the assessment and identification process for students with learning disabilities is the determination of their "general intelligence."

However, in contrast with this view, some theorists have always argued that intelligence really is multifaceted, that various abilities in different areas exist within each individual, and that these various abilities really have relatively little to do with each other. This raises the possibility that a single individual may have vastly differing abilities in different areas—written language versus math versus musical skills

Further, numerous theorists have argued over the last 100 years that intelligence as measured on standardized IQ tests has very little to do with creativity (Hearne & Stone, 1995; Stanford, 2003). These authors suggested that intelligence is not a single unitary construct, but that many different types of abilities should be measured to get a true picture of a child's overall capability in dealing with his or her environment. The most recent work based on this view is that of **Howard Gardner** (1983, 1993) on multiple intelligences. Gardner (1983) initially identified seven different types of intelligence (linguistic, logico-mathematical, musical-rhythmic, visual-spatial, bodily-kinesthetic, interpersonal, and intrapersonal). More recently, Gardner added an eighth intelligence—naturalistic. Each is viewed as relatively independent, and presumably a particular individual may be very capable in one or two areas and much less capable in others.

In applying this growing theoretical perspective of **multiple intelligences** to the field of learning disabilities, Hearne and Stone (1995) found numerous pieces of evidence suggesting that the multiple intelligences perspective may be a more appropriate view of learning disabilities than the more static view based on a unitary construct of general intelligence. For example, school assessments in almost every subject are heavily dependent upon linguistic and/or logico-mathematical understanding, and if a particular student is highly gifted in musical ability, indeed, if the student plays music better than anyone else at the school, but cannot read the tests given in that subject, the student can still fail in music (Hearne & Stone, 1995). What Gardner and others (Campbell, 1994) argue is that all demonstrations of the various multiple intelligences should be valued and used as the basis for instruction and for assessment of students in schools. Further, educators should seek to identify the child's strengths in all the different forms of intelligence and plan a school program building on the child's strengths. Of course, this concept could—and many researchers suggest that it will—revolutionize all education (Bender, 2002; Hearne & Stone, 1995).

Various researchers have discussed the application of multiple intelligences theory in the field of learning disabilities (Bender, 2002; Elias, 2004; Stanford, 2003). However, research on this concept is not highly developed, and consequently the multiple intelligences perspective has not yet been widely accepted as valid within the field of learning disabilities. Nevertheless, proponents of this view suggest that this perspective may be particularly useful in the field of learning disabilities, given the considerable variability of students with learning disabilities across the various academic areas, as well as the need to vary instructional tactics in the general education classroom in order to accommodate these learners (Bender, 2002; Hearne & Stone, 1995; Stanford, 2003). Further, the multiple intelligences perspective is currently exerting a considerable degree of influence in general education and is resulting in teachers utilizing a more diverse set of academic instructional tactics in general education. Many see this as a benefit for students with learning disabilities who are "included" in those classes (Bender, 2002; Elias, 2004; Tomlinson, 1999).

The most recent application of multiple intelligences theory is represented by the work of Carol Tomlinson. In her book *The Differentiated Classroom* (1999), Tomlinson suggested that teachers should vary their instructional techniques to address the various multiple intelligences in today's classrooms. This concept of **differentiated instruction** has received wide national and international attention and offers the opportunity for general and special education teachers to revitalize their instruction by incorporating a wider variety of teaching techniques into the class. Although there seems to be increasing emphasis on multiple intelligences and differentiated instruction in education generally (Bender, 2002), it is still too early to tell if these approaches will play a major role in the development of the construct of learning disabilities.

Brain-Compatible Learning.   During the late 1990s, an emerging perspective on learning disabilities developed: the brain-compatible learning perspective (Bender, 2002; Sousa, 1995, 2001; Shaywitz & Shaywitz, 2006; Sylwester, 1995). In some ways, this may be considered a reemergence of the neurological perspective on learning. Several medical technologies, such as PET scans and fMRI techniques (which are discussed in more detail in Chapter 2), have dramatically increased our understanding of how learning takes place in the human brain and the central nervous system. For this reason, some have dubbed the 1990s the "decade of the brain" (Sousa, 1995, 2001). Specifically, these technologies made it possible just before the millennium to actually observe learning processes in the living brain, as reflected by the consumption of sugars in the neurons. This emerging body of research, now referred to as brain-compatible learning research, has begun to impact education and has been interpreted by a number of theorists into recommended classroom practice for elementary and secondary education classes (Jensen, 1995; Sousa, 1995, 2001; Sylwester, 1995).

The brain-compatible learning research of today is much more solidly founded than the neurological perspective concepts of the 1960s, because current researchers have applied more rigorous scientific standards in their research. In fact, several notions concerning human memory have been superseded by other theories based on newly available data from this body of research. Specifically, although theorists have long suspected that there is a distinction between short-term memory and longer-term memory (Swanson, 1999), the emerging brain-compatible instruction research suggests several additional phases of memory (Sousa, 1995, 2001; Swanson, 1999). Further, the concept of short-term memory has been refined, and theorists currently prefer the concept of working memory. That is, in order for a fact to be successfully stored for recall (i.e., moved from short-term into long-term memory), the individual must work with the fact by assigning sense and meaning to it (Sousa, 1995; Swanson, 1999). In this way, working memory allows for long-term memory storage and subsequent retrieval of facts. Lee Swanson in particular has done a great deal of work in the area of working memory in students with learning disabilities (see Swanson, 1999, for a review).

Various other leaders in this field, such as David Sousa (1995, 2001), Robert Sylwester (1995), and Eric Jensen (1995), have made numerous suggestions for how the emerging information on the thinking process should impact the way teachers present information in the elementary and secondary classroom. For example, teachers should concentrate on providing verbal practice for students who are learning facts and concepts by having them discuss the facts or concepts with their classmates (Sousa, 1995). Further, teachers should offer some quiet time or "wait time" after asking a question prior to calling on a student for an answer. This 10- to 15-second wait time allows all students to process the question—to think about it and consider several answers—before the question is answered by a classmate. These are practical suggestions for instruction that are currently emerging from the growing knowledge of the brain and the learning process.

The new data on how the human brain works while processing information will impact how teachers construct the learning environment in their classrooms. From the late 1990s through today, teachers across the nation have flocked to workshops on "Brain-Compatible Learning," "The Learning Brain," and similar topics. Further, Sousa (2001) and Bender (2002) have now applied the emerging instructional suggestions specifically to students with learning disabilities. Thus, the brain-compatible learning perspective, which impacted elementary and secondary education rather dramatically from 1995 on, now seems positioned to impact learning disabilities in a similar fashion. Clearly, every practitioner in education will be seeing more on the concept of brain-compatible learning over the next decade.

THE REVITALIZATION PHASE: THE FUTURE OF LEARNING DISABILITIES

Given the concerns with ever-increasing numbers of students identified as needing special education, with some 50% of these students identified as having a learning disability, President George W. Bush appointed a Commission on Excellence in Special Education in 2001 to address the growing concerns noted in the retrenchment phase as described previously. This body was working not only immediately after the turn of the century, but also 25 years after Public Law 94-142—the first federal legislation mandating education for students with disabilities—was passed. Based on the issues raised in the retrenchment phase as well as the critically important timing already noted, the commission made an effort to structure its deliberations as an opportunity for revitalization in special education (Commission, 2001). This effort may be seen as the initiation of the beginning of the most recent phase in the history of special education for students with learning disabilities (Council for Exceptional Children, 2002). The primary findings of the commission are presented in Interest Box 1.2.

Based on these findings, the commission recommended many broad and sweeping changes in special education procedures, and many of these changes were enacted in the reauthorization of the Individuals with Disabilities Education Act (IDEA), which President Bush signed into law in December of 2004. This law is sometimes referred to as the Individuals with Disabilities Education Improvement Act or IDEIA of 2004, but for our purposes we will use IDEA to refer to this revised legislation. Among the various changes embodied in this legislation, the most important changes for practitioners in learning disabilities are modifications of the definition of a *learning disability* and in the related assessment procedures used to determine whether a particular student has a learning disability.

The definition of *learning disability* was modified to enable school districts to use a different assessment procedure to document a child's learning disability, and a bit of explanation is in order on this point. In the recent past, school districts have used a discrepancy between a child's intelligence and his or her academic scores to determine when a learning disability existed. This "discrepancy procedure" has not been satisfactory for a variety of reasons that will be discussed in more detail in Chapter 5. However, with the enactment of IDEA in 2004, the federal government now encourages use of a **response to intervention** (sometimes referred to as RTI) procedure in order to document a student's learning disability (Batsche et al., 2004; Fuchs, Fuchs, & Compton, 2004; Mellard, Deshler, & Barth, 2004; Mellard, Byrd, Johnson, Tollefson, & Boesche, 2004; NJCLD, 2005). The specific two sections of that modification follow:

> An LEA [i.e., a local education agency–school or school district] shall not be required to take into consideration whether a child has a severe discrepancy between achievement and intellectual ability in oral expression, listening comprehension, written expression, basic reading skill, reading comprehension, mathematical calculation, or mathematical reasoning.
>
> An LEA may use a process that determines if the child responds to scientific, research-based intervention as a part of the evaluation procedures.

Therefore, a school district is not now required to use a discrepancy procedure and instead may now use evidence of how the child responds to an instructional intervention to determine if the child has a learning disability. In short, if the child is provided effective instruction using a scientifically validated instructional curriculum and still does not positively respond to that intervention by demonstrating increased mastery of the content (i.e., if he or she does not demonstrate increased academic scores), then that child will be considered as potentially having a learning disability (Batsche et al., 2004; Fuchs, Fuchs, & Compton, 2004; NJCLD, 2005; McMaster, Fuchs, Fuchs, & Compton, 2005). There is much discussion and much uncertainty today concerning the exact implementation of this new RTI eligibility procedure, and more information will be presented in Chapter 5 on the RTI procedure itself. However, at this point, we should note three things:

INTEREST BOX 1.2

**FINDINGS OF THE COMMISSION ON EXCELLENCE
IN SPECIAL EDUCATION**

Finding 1. IDEA (Individuals with Disabilities Education Act) is generally providing basic legal safeguards and access for children with disabilities. However, the current system often places process above results and bureaucratic compliance above student achievement, excellence, and outcomes. The system is driven by complex regulations, excessive paperwork, and ever-increasing administrative demands at all levels—for the child, the parent, the local education agency, and the state education agency. Too often, simply qualifying for special education becomes an end point, not a gateway to more effective instruction and strong intervention.

Finding 2. The current system uses an antiquated model that waits for a child to fail, instead of a model based on prevention and intervention. Too little emphasis is put on prevention, early and accurate identification of learning and behavior problems, and aggressive intervention using research-based approaches. This means students with disabilities don't get help early when that help can be most effective. Special education should be for those who do not respond to strong and appropriate instruction and methods provided in general education.

Finding 3. Children placed in special education are general education children first. Despite this basic fact, educators and policymakers think about the two systems as separate and tally *the cost* of special education as a separate program, not as additional services with resultant add-on expenses. In such a system, children with disabilities are often treated not as children who are members of the general education community whose special instructional needs can be met with scientifically based approaches, but as separate, with unique costs. This creates incentives for misidentification and academic isolation, preventing the pooling of all available resources to aid learning. General education and special education share responsibilities for children with disabilities. They are not separable at any level—cost, instruction, or even identification.

Finding 4. When a child fails to make progress in special education, parents don't have adequate options and have little recourse. Parents have their child's best interests in mind, but they often do not feel they are empowered when the system fails them.

Finding 5. The culture of compliance has often developed from the pressures of litigation, diverting much energy from the public schools' first mission: educating every child.

Finding 6. Many of the current methods of identifying children with disabilities lack validity. As a result, thousands of children are misidentified every year, while many others are not identified early enough or at all.

Finding 7. Children with disabilities require highly qualified teachers. Teachers, parents, and education officials desire better preparation, support, and professional development related to the needs of serving these children. Many educators wish they had better preparation before entering the classroom as well as better tools for identifying needs early and accurately.

Finding 8. Research on special education needs enhanced rigor and the long-term coordination necessary to support the needs of children, educators, and parents. In addition, the current system does not always embrace or implement evidence-based practices once established.

Finding 9. The focus on compliance and bureaucratic imperatives in the current system, instead of academic achievement and social outcomes, fails too many children with disabilities. Too few successfully graduate from high school or transition to full employment and postsecondary opportunities, despite provisions in IDEA providing for transition services. Parents want an education system that is results oriented and focused on the child's needs—in school and beyond.

1. The revitalization phase has received a new emphasis from the commission report and the passage of IDEA of 2004.
2. The definition and eligibility assessment procedures for documenting a learning disability are changing currently based on these modifications embedded within IDEA of 2004.
3. Implementation of these RTI procedures will continue to be discussed in the field.

One other piece of federal legislation was passed during this retrenchment phase, which, together with IDEA of 2004, significantly impacts education for students with learning disabilities—the No Child Left Behind Education Act. This law was signed by President Bush in 2001 and mandates that all students in public schools—including students with special needs—be held accountable for their learning and meet state-identified educational standards by the 2013–2014 school year (Simpson, LaCava, & Graner, 2004). To meet those goals, states and school districts have identified benchmarks by which to measure progress toward those goals and have identified other interim benchmarks that specify "adequate yearly progress" toward those goals; this is sometimes shortened to "meet AYP." Needless to say, meeting AYP has become a hot-button issue in virtually every school in the United States and continues to be a challenge for many students with learning disabilities (Yell, Katsiyannas, & Shiner, 2006). This law also mandated implementation of scientifically validated curriculum, and this is the first time the federal government has publicly required teachers and/or school districts to use validated curriculum. For teachers in the field of learning disabilities, this impacts what reading and/or math curriculum may be used for instruction, and it demands that teachers be aware and fluent in discussions of the scientific evidence for the curricula they utilize.

All of these factors create an unknown future for the field of learning disabilities. As a practitioner who is entering the field, you will repeatedly hear discussions of meeting AYP among your colleagues and administrators. Further, you should remain abreast of the definition issues in this new legislation, as well as any RTI assessment procedures implemented by your school district over the next few years (Fuchs, Fuchs, & Compton, 2004; Mellard, Deshler, & Barth, 2004; Mellard, Byrd, Johnson, Tollefson, & Boesche, 2004; NJCLD, 2005).

A THEORETICAL BASIS FOR LEARNING DISABILITIES

Functions of a Theoretical Perspective

As discussed, many theoretical perspectives have emerged in the history of learning disabilities, and any practitioner can easily wonder which is the correct one. To answer this question, we would be well advised to consider the overall functions of any theoretical perspective. In fact, any understanding of the diverse theoretical perspectives on learning disabilities must include reference to the overall functions of a theoretical perspective. In short, a theory or theoretical perspective must serve several functions to be a meaningful contributor to a field of thought, and various perspectives in a particular field may be evaluated by how well they serve these functions.

First, a perspective must define the population it addresses. Such a definition may seem an easy task to the uninitiated. However, given the 50 different definitions provided by state governments for the same group of children and adolescents and the changing perspectives in the field, it is safe to assume that the definition of a learning disability offered by a particular perspective will be a crucial factor in evaluating that perspective.

Along with a definition, a perspective must identify group membership. Although many of the cognitive-deficit or basic psychological-processing perspectives provided definitions, these were not helpful in separating children with learning disabilities from groups with other types of disabilities. This function is crucial because of competition for funds for research and for teaching various groups of children. A theory must allow professionals to determine reliably whether a child has or does not have learning disabilities.

Next, a theory must guide research questions in the field. Because of the difficulty of proving any scientific hypothesis, a perspective must at least generate research questions that are amenable to disproof. For example, if a theory suggests that learning takes place because of some phenomenon that is unobservable or unmeasurable, the perspective must be removed from practical consideration because it cannot be disproved. Therefore, perspectives must generate suggestions that are subject to disproof through research. Further, as these suggestions are tested in research studies, if these ideas are not disproved, the suggestions are assumed to be accurate.

Finally, any perspective on learning disabilities must suggest meaningful educational treatments. These should be differentially effective in order to justify the distinctive cost of specialized programs. In other words, if a suggested treatment is effective for all students, the most appropriate method of teaching the students would be a combined program rather than a special class or specialized instruction for students with learning disabilities. Also, research must be presented to demonstrate that the suggested treatments are effective. Professional educators, like professional physicians, must know that the education treatment prescribed has demonstrated effectiveness.

Evaluation of Current Theories

Each of the major theoretical perspectives is represented in Interest Box 1.3 and cross-indexed with the four functions of a theoretical perspective noted previously. The general strengths and weaknesses of each of the major perspectives are shown. The emerging theories (constructivism, multiple intelligences, and brain-compatible instruction) are not presented because it is too early to determine their impact in the field of learning disabilities.

The early visual, language, and neurological processing perspectives are similar in that they each hypothesize a brain or CNS dysfunction that causes learning difficulty. The early definitions of learning disability were a result of these perspectives. The similarity between these perspectives breaks down, however, when theorists in the various areas attempt to apply the definition to identify students with learning disabilities. The measurement instruments and identification techniques suggested by each of these groups of theorists failed to meet acceptable standards in differentiating these children from those without learning disabilities (Hammill, 1993; Moats & Lyon, 1993). Thus, although these perspectives did offer early definitions of learning disabilities, they were ineffective in delineating accurate

■ ■ ■ ■ ■

INTEREST BOX 1.3
FUNCTIONS OF A THEORETICAL PERSPECTIVE

Perspective	Definition Provided	Group Membership	Research Guidance*		Educational Treatments
Visual-motor	Yes	No	Yes	No	No
Auditory language	Yes	No	Yes	Yes	No
Neurological	Yes	No	Yes	Yes	No
Behavioral	No	No	No	Yes	Yes
Metacognitive	Yes	No	No	Yes	Yes

*The first column concerns research for the early period (1950s to 1980s). The second column indicates whether the perspective is presently a major influence on research in the field.

assessments that would identify a student with a learning disability (see the "group membership" column in Interest Box 1.3).

The visual-perceptual, the language, and the neurological perspectives influenced the early research in the field, but not all of them influence research today. Current research is still heavily influenced by the auditory/language-deficit perspective as a result of the partial success in this area. However, less research is ongoing with school-identified populations of children with learning disabilities on the visual-perceptual perspective. Some recent advances in medical technology have resulted in an increase in research from the neurological perspective, though few children who experience learning disabilities are currently subjected to these assessment procedures. More information on the brain-compatible neurological research is presented in Chapter 2.

Finally, aside from drug-based interventions, based on the neurological perspective, none of the early perspectives has shown great promise in suggesting major treatment techniques for students with learning disabilities. Perhaps more than any other factor, this failure on the part of these perspectives led to their decreasing influence during the 1980s and 1990s.

The behavioral perspective became the most influential view in the 1970s because it allowed for documentation of academic progress in students with learning disabilities. The theorists who supported it demonstrated that the recommended techniques were effective, and teachers widely accepted the view that the appropriate role of a learning disabilities specialist was basic skill instruction and/or tutoring in subject content areas. The behavioral perspective also generated a great deal of research concerning the effectiveness of various teaching strategies, ranging from token economies to precision teaching. The effectiveness of the assessment techniques associated with this perspective is quite evident when compared with the dismal failure of assessment techniques generated by the earlier perspectives.

However, the overall failure of the behavioral perspective is apparent when the definition of populations of students with learning disabilities and group membership are considered. Theorists in this area have largely rejected any attempt to develop procedures to define such populations based on this perspective. In many cases, the techniques that work for students with learning disabilities were recommended for all students who were low achieving, thus sidestepping the need to identify children who experience learning disabilities.

The recent success of the metacognitive perspective is apparent when one reviews the research on the numerous learning strategies and self-monitoring techniques developed as a result of this perspective. Research has consistently confirmed the effectiveness of the techniques developed, and this perspective has been the most influential in research on students with learning disabilities for the last decade (Bender, 2002; Commission, 2001). Also, the strategies developed are finding increasing acceptance in classes for students with learning disabilities, as well as inclusive classes.

Despite these successes, the metacognitive perspective has not yet adequately addressed the issues of identification or remediation of students with learning disabilities. For example, perhaps all children who are low achieving and all children with mild mental disabilities should receive instruction using the learning strategies that were initially developed for students with learning disabilities. If this perspective is to continue to exert the influence over the field that it has enjoyed since the 1980s, these issues will have to be addressed.

COMPONENTS OF THE CURRENT DEFINITIONS OF LEARNING DISABILITIES

As this review of the history of learning disabilities demonstrates, various definitions of learning disabilities have been offered, modified, and/or rejected throughout the last five decades. As the definition modifications discussed previously show, the recently passed IDEA of 2004 did not offer a totally new definition of learning disabilities, but it nevertheless redefined the identification procedures for documenting a learning disability in a fundamental sense. Still, there are several components that have been constant in the traditional definitions of learning disabilities (Reschly & Hosp, 2004), and these remain in the current definition. Thus, understanding these components will provide every practitioner in the field a more thorough understanding of learning disabilities. These components are reviewed below.

The Psychological Process Criteria

The early assumption inherent in the definition of a learning disability was that some type of disability of perception, language, or cognition prevented an individual from learning. Discussion of these cognitive, mental, or psychological processes included terms such as *perception, attention,* and *sensory integration* (i.e., the ability to combine information obtained from several senses, notably hearing and vision). No exhaustive list of these processes has been compiled, and in the 1977 definition, the federal government refused to identify criteria for measuring these processes. In 2004, Reschly and Hosp indicated that 49 states *allowed* measurement of these basic psychological processes in the state definition of learning disabilities, and 13 states still *required* some measurement of these processes in the eligibility process.

Measurement of these basic psychological processes remains highly problematic because the theorists disagree on what the processes are and which should be measured (Hammill, 1993; Shaw et al., 1995). Also, the measurement devices used as indicators of various types of perceptual problems are not adequate for identification purposes (Shaw et al., 1995). For these reasons, the Commission on Excellence in Special Education (2001) omitted any emphasis on this component of the definition, though the recent IDEA 2004 did not address this measurement issue.

Exclusionary Criteria

The last part of the federal definition attempts to tell what a learning disability is not rather than what it is. This is like trying to define the color red by pointing to things that are not red. Such attempts at definition inevitably suggest a real problem in definition. However, this exclusionary clause has been common to the many definitions of learning disabilities. As early as the 1920s and 1930s, when Strauss identified his criteria for these students, conceptualizations of the disability have included some type of exclusionary clause.

More recently, the clause has been expanded to include numerous children who are culturally deprived or who have behavioral disorders, as two examples. This entails additional problems because it is often difficult to distinguish between various disabilities (Commission, 2001). For example, a child with learning disabilities and one with behavioral disorders often behave similarly, and no set criteria are provided that make the distinction between these disabilities clear (Commission, 2001).

Finally, the exclusionary criteria tie the definition of learning disability to the definitions of numerous other conditions. Therefore, if definitions of these other disabilities change, so does the definition of learning disability. One early 1970s change in the definition of mental retardation provides a good example. The traditional definitions of mental retardation stipulated that a child must have an IQ at least one standard deviation lower than normal in order to be considered mentally retarded. This results in an IQ of 85 or below on many of the widely used tests. This was the conceptualization of retardation in place when the term *learning disabilities* was coined, and the exclusionary clause in the definition of learning disabilities at that time ruled out any child with an IQ below 85.

However, since 1973, the definition of retardation has stated that it begins at two standard deviations below normal, in the IQ range of 70 and below. This change affected the types of children identified as learning disabled because now children with IQs between 70 and 85 were eligible for placement in classes for students with learning disabilities in many states. However, other states adapted their definitions of learning disabilities by stipulating that students with learning disabilities must have an IQ of 85 or higher to be identified. Clearly, this can get quite confusing, and as long as the exclusionary clause is in place in the definition of learning disabilities, there is nothing to rule out such changes again.

Further, many children whose IQs fall between 70 and 85 need either remedial or special education, and some of them may fall "between the cracks." They are clearly not retarded, but they may not be eligible for services as "learning disabled" either. These students generally end up being labeled as learning disabled in order to provide some type of educational placement where their education deficiencies can be addressed. Of course, these children tend to use the schools' resources that were intended for children with "real" learning disabilities. Taken together, these "backdoor" definitional variations indicate a continued weakness in the ability to identify children and adolescents who have learning disabilities, and the failure to differentiate students with learning disabilities from other students with different types of learning problems continues to threaten the field (Commission, 2001; Mather & Roberts, 1994; NJCLD, 2005).

Discrepancy Criteria

The assumption that students with learning disabilities are not performing as well academically as they should has led to a number of mathematical formulas that are used for identification of the learning disability. These are referred to as discrepancies. Basically, these discrepancies are used to indicate a substantial difference between intelligence, as measured on standardized IQ assessments, and achievement in a number of academic subject areas. Specific information on the various procedures for calculating discrepancies is presented in Chapter 5.

In 1976, the U.S. Department of Education indicated that some form of discrepancy that was unexplained by other factors was the only useful indicator of a learning disability. Also, Chalfant's (1985) report indicated that certain discrepancy procedures may be considered indicators of learning disability. However, in 1987, the Council for Learning Disabilities recommended that the use of discrepancy formulas be phased out, but the report did not recommend any type of alternative procedure.

In 2004, 48 states required a calculation of a discrepancy between intelligence and achievement as one component of the documentation of a learning disability (Reschly & Hosp, 2004). Also, we should note that, while the discrepancy between intelligence and achievement is not now required by the federal legislation, legislation does not specifically prohibit the use of such a discrepancy calculation. Thus, this discrepancy procedure may be utilized in some states in the future.

However, even before the recent change in legislation, there was some question as to how frequently discrepancies have actually been used, even in states that require such calculations. For example, MacMillan, Gresham, and Bocian (1998) report that schools often do not document a discrepancy between intelligence and achievement. Studying 150 children in five different districts in Southern California, these researchers demonstrated that even with a discrepancy clause in place in California's definition of learning disabilities, many students were identified as learning disabled who did not meet the criteria. Of the 61 students who were classified as learning disabled in this study, less than half (i.e., 29 students) met the discrepancy criteria. This suggests that over 50% of children receiving services in that research population were not learning disabled. These researchers suggest that the definition of learning disability was used by public schools as a nonspecific category to cover many types of children with many types of educational needs and to provide some services for them, a problem also noted by the Commission on Excellence in Special Education (2001).

Although the desire of educators to provide needed services may be admirable, it does not benefit students with learning disabilities to include other groups, because doing so effectively dilutes the available resources and services. As a new practitioner in the field, you will sit on various placement committees when this issue is discussed in relation to a particular child, and you will have to make decisions on what is appropriate for that child

INTEREST BOX 1.4

FACT SHEET OF COMMON CHARACTERISTICS OF STUDENTS WITH LEARNING DISABILITIES

1. Boys demonstrate learning disabilities much more frequently than girls, and in most classes for students with disabilities, boys outnumber girls three or four to one.
2. Most students diagnosed with learning disabilities are identified during the third- and fourth-grade years, and most of those students continue throughout their school years to receive services for learning disabilities.
3. A discrepancy between one's intellectual ability and reading achievement has been the defining characteristic of 90% of students (Commission, 2001).
4. Many students with learning disabilities will perform poorly on reading, writing, or language tasks but will perform acceptably in math. Although some students have a specific learning disability in math rather than reading and language arts, this type of disability is the exception rather than the rule.
5. Learning disabilities are often manifested in attention problems and/or high levels of distractibility in public school classes.
6. Some students with learning disabilities have difficulty organizing material when completing school assignments or in personal organization matters such as bringing the correct books to class or arriving at classes on time.
7. Some younger students experiencing learning disabilities demonstrate hyperactivity, or a tendency to fidget or move around the room much too frequently. This problem may be addressed through medical interventions involving prescribed drugs.
8. Difficulty in copying material from blackboards or performing other design-copying tasks is frequently a symptom of learning disabilities.

and others. Further, with the modifications of the learning disabilities definition from the IDEA of 2004 incorporated into law, one may anticipate that many schools and school districts will decrease the use of discrepancy as an eligibility consideration.

WHO ARE THESE KIDS?

When one reflects on the changes in definition within the field of learning disabilities and the numerous professional groups that have participated in the growth of this field, one should not be surprised that children with learning disabilities form a very heterogeneous group. For this reason, any discussion of general characteristics of children and youth with learning disabilities should be viewed as quite tentative. Although some children and youth with learning disabilities will demonstrate many of the general characteristics listed in Interest Box 1.4, others will not. However, certain characteristics of students with learning disabilities seem to be generally accepted among teachers and other professionals (Kavale & Reese, 1992; McLeskey, 1992).

QUESTIONS AND ACTIVITIES

1. Review older texts in the field and compare the sections on history with this chapter. What differences do you note?

2. Review the definitions presented in this chapter and note the discrepancies. What reasons can you give for these differences?

3. What historical phases do other scholars in the field propose? How do these compare to the present analysis of historical phases?

4. Prepare a role-play activity in which a visual/perceptual-motor theorist and a language theorist debate the nature of learning disabilities. What positions should be reflected in each position?

5. Which case study in this chapter represents the language theorists' view of a learning disability? Which represents the visual-motor theorists' view?

6. Obtain a copy of the definition of learning disabilities used in your state from the state Department of Education and compare that definition to the ones presented in this chapter. What components are present in the definition, and what implications does the state definition hold for identification of students with learning disabilities?

7. What is the relationship between the early theories, upon which the field was founded, and the more recent perspectives?

8. How do school psychologists perceive the learning disabilities perspective debate just described? How do parents perceive it?

9. Interview, with discretion, any secondary school pupils with learning disabilities whom you may know concerning their learning problems and relationships with their teachers and peers at school. What perspective do they demonstrate when discussing their own disabilities?

10. Review information on brain-compatible learning research and describe differences between current research and earlier neurological theories.

REFERENCES

Batsche, G., Elliott, J., Graden, J. L., Grimes, J., Kovaleski, J. F., Prasse, D., Reschly, D. J., Schrag, J., & Tilly, W. D. (2004). *Response to intervention: Policy considerations and implementation.* Alexandria, VA: National Association of State Directors of Special Education.

Bender, W. N. (2002). *Differentiating instruction for students with learning disabilities: Best teaching practices for general and special educators.* Thousand Oaks, CA: Corwin Press.

Bender, W. N. (1987). Inferred brain hemispheric preference and behavior of learning disabled students. *Perceptual and Motor Skills, 64,* 521–522.

Bender, W. N. (1985). Differential diagnosis based on the task related behavior of learning disabled and low achieving adolescents. *Learning Disability Quarterly, 8*(4), 261–266.

Bender, W. N., Rosenkrans, C. B., & Crane, M. K. (1999). Stress, depression, and suicide among students with learning disabilities: Assessing the risk. *Learning Disability Quarterly, 22*(2), 143–156.

Campbell, B. (1994). *The multiple intelligences handbook: Lesson plans and more.* Stanwood, WA: Campbell & Associates.

Carlson, S. A. (1985). The ethical appropriateness of subject-matter tutoring for learning disabled adolescents. *Learning Disability Quarterly, 8,* 310–314.

Chalfant, J. C. (1985). Identifying learning disabled students: A summary of the national task force report. *Learning Disabilities Focus, 1*(1), 9–20.

Commission on Excellence in Special Education (2001). *Revitalizing special education for children and their families.* Available from www.ed.gov/inits/commissionsboards/whspecialeducation.

Council for Exceptional Children (2002). Commission report calls for special education reform. *Today, 9*(3), 1–6.

Council for Learning Disabilities (1987). The CLD position statements. *Journal of Learning Disabilities, 20,* 349–350.

Cruickshank, W. M., Bentzen, F. A., Ratzeburg, R. H., & Tannhauser, M. T. (1961). *A teaching method for brain-injured and hyperactive children.* Syracuse, NY: Syracuse University Press.

Deshler, D. D., Schumaker, J. B., Lenz, B. K., & Ellis, E. S. (1984). Academic and cognitive interventions for LD adolescents: Part II. *Journal of Learning Disabilities, 17,* 170–187.

Eden, G. F., Stein, J. F., Wood, M. H., & Wood, F. B. (1995). Verbal and visual problems in reading disability. *Journal of Learning Disabilities, 28,* 272–290.

Elias, M. J. (2004). The connection between social-emotional learning and learning disabilities: Implications for practice. *Learning Disability Quarterly, 27*(1), 53–62.

Fuchs, D., Fuchs, L. S., & Compton, D. L. (2004). Identifying reading disabilities by responsiveness-to-instruction: Specifying measures and criteria. *Learning Disability Quarterly, 27*(4), 216–229.

Gardner, H. (1983). *Frames of mind: The theory of multiple intelligences.* New York: Basic Books.

Gardner, H. (1993). *Multiple intelligences: The theory in practice.* New York: Basic Books.

Hallahan, D. P. (1992). Some thoughts on why the prevalence of learning disabilities has increased. *Journal of Learning Disabilities, 25,* 523–528.

Hallahan, D. P., & Sapona, R. (1983). Self-monitoring of attention with learning disabled children: Past research and current issues. *Journal of Learning Disabilities, 16,* 616–620.

Hammill, D. D. (1990). On defining learning disabilities: An emerging consensus. *Journal of Learning Disabilities, 23,* 74–84.

Hammill, D. D. (1993). A brief look at the learning disabilities movement in the United States. *Journal of Learning Disabilities, 26,* 295–310.

Hearne, D., & Stone, S. (1995). Multiple intelligences and underachievement: Lessons from individuals with learning disabilities. *Journal of Learning Disabilities, 28,* 439–448.

Hynd, G. W., Marshall, R., & Gonzalez, J. C. (1991). Learning disabilities and presumed central nervous system dysfunction. *Learning Disability Quarterly, 14,* 283–296.

Jensen, E. (1995). *The learning brain.* Del Mar, CA: Turning Point.

Kavale, K. A., & Forness, S. R. (1986). School learning, time and learning disabilities: The disassociated learner. *Journal of Learning Disabilities, 19,* 130–138.

Kavale, K. A., & Reese, J. H. (1992). The character of learning disabilities: An Iowa profile. *Learning Disability Quarterly, 15,* 74–94.

Kirk, S. A. (1988). *Historical aspects of learning disabilities.* Unpublished paper of keynote speech, delivered at Rutgers University.

Kirk, S. A., McCarthy, J. J., & Kirk, W. D. (1968). *The Illinois test of psycholinguistic abilities.* Urbana, IL: University of Illinois Press.

Leonard, C. M. (2001). Imaging brain structure in children: Differentiating language disability and reading disability. *Learning Disability Quarterly, 24,* 141–157.

Liddell, G. A., & Rasmussen, C. (2005). Memory profile of children with nonverbal learning disability. *Learning Disabilities Research, 20*(3), 137–141.

MacMillan, D. L., Gresham, R. M., & Bocian, K. M. (1998). Discrepancy between definitions of learning disabilities and school practices: An empirical investigation. *Journal of Learning Disabilities, 31,* 314–326.

Magiera, K., & Zigmond, N. (2005). Co-teaching in middle school classrooms under routine conditions: Does the instructional experience differ for students with disabilities in co-taught and solo-taught classes? *Learning Disabilities Research, 20*(2), 79–85.

Mather, N., & Roberts, R. (1994). Learning disabilities: A field in danger of extinction? *Learning Disabilities Research and Practice, 9*(1), 49–58.

McLeskey, J. (1992). Students with learning disabilities at primary, intermediate, and secondary grade levels: Identification and characteristics. *Learning Disability Quarterly, 15,* 13–19.

McMaster, K. L., Fuchs, D., Fuchs, L. S., & Compton, D. L. (2005). Responding to nonresponders: An experimental field trial of identification and intervention methods. *Exceptional Children, 71*(4), 445–463.

Mellard, D. F., Byrd, S. E., Johnson, E., Tollefson, J. M., & Boesche, L. (2004). Foundations and research on identifying model responsiveness-to-intervention sites. *Learning Disability Quarterly, 27*(4), 243–256.

Mellard, D. F., Deshler, D. D., & Barth, A. (2004). LD identification: It's not simply a matter of building a better mousetrap. *Learning Disability Quarterly, 27*(4), 229–242.

Moats, L. C., & Lyon, G. R. (1993). Learning disabilities in the United States: Advocacy, science, and the future of the field. *Journal of Learning Disabilities, 26,* 282–294.

National Joint Committee on Learning Disabilities (NJCLD) (2005). Responsiveness to intervention and learning disabilities: A report prepared by the National Joint Committee on Learning Disabilities. *Learning Disability Quarterly, 28*(4), 249–260.

National Reading Panel (2000). *Teaching children to read: A report from the National Reading Panel.* Washington, DC: U.S. Government Printing Office.

Orton, S. (1937). *Reading, writing, and speech problems in children.* New York: Norton.

Poplin, M. S. (1988). Holistic/constructivist principles of the teaching/learning process: Implications for the field of learning disabilities. *Journal of Learning Disabilities, 21,* 401–416.

Reid, D. K., & Button, L. J. (1995). Anna's story: Narratives of personal experience about being labeled learning disabled. *Journal of Learning Disabilities, 28,* 602–614.

Reschly, D. J., & Hosp, J. L. (2004). State SLD identification policies and practices. *Learning Disability Quarterly, 27*(4), 197–213.

Shaw, S. F., Cullen, J. P., McGuire, J. M., & Brinckerhoff, L. C. (1995). Operationalizing a definition of learning disabilities. *Journal of Learning Disabilities, 28,* 586–597.

Shaywitz, S. E., & Shaywitz, B. A. (2006). Reading disability and the brain. *Educating Exceptional Children: 2005/2006.* Dubuque, IA: McGraw-Hill.

Siegel, L. S. (1999). Issues in the definition and diagnosis of learning disabilities: A perspective on *Guckenberger v. Boston University. Journal of Learning Disabilities, 32,* 304–319.

Simpson, R. L., LaCava, P. G., & Graner, P. S. (2004). The No Child Left Behind Act: Challenges and implications for educators. *Intervention in School and Clinic, 40*(2), 67–75.

Sousa, D. A. (1995). *How the brain learns: A classroom teacher's guide.* Reston, VA: National Association of Secondary School Principals.

Sousa, D. A. (2001). *How the special needs brain learns.* Thousand Oaks, CA: Corwin Press.

Stanford, P. (2003). Multiple intelligence for every classroom. *Intervention in School and Clinic, 39*(2), 81–86.

Stanovich, K. E. (1999). The sociopsychometrics of learning disabilities. *Journal of Learning Disabilities, 32,* 350–361.

Strauss, A. A., & Kephart, N. C. (1955). *Psychopathology and education of the brain-injured child: Vol. 2. Progress in theory and clinic.* New York: Grune & Stratton.

Swanson, H. L. (1999). Cognition and learning disabilities. In W. N. Bender (Ed.), *Professional issues in learning disabilities* (pp. 415–460). Austin, TX: ProEd.

Sylwester, R. (1995). *A celebration of neurons: An educator's guide to the human brain.* Alexandria, VA: Association for Supervision and Curriculum Development.

Tomasi, S. F., & Weinberg, S. L. (1999). Classifying children as LD: An analysis of current practice in an urban setting. *Learning Disability Quarterly, 22,* 31–42.

Tomlinson, C. (1999). *The differentiated classroom: Responding to the needs of all learners.* Alexandria, VA: Association for Supervision and Curriculum Development.

Torgesen, J. K. (1975). Problems and prospects in the study of learning disabilities. In E. M. Hetherington & O. Hagen (Eds.), *Review of child development research, Vol. 5.* Chicago: University of Chicago Press.

Torgesen, J. K. (1977). The role of non-specific factors in the task performance of learning disabled children: A theoretical assessment. *Journal of Learning Disabilities, 10,* 27–35.

Torgesen, J. K. (1980). The use of efficient task strategies by learning disabled children: Conceptual and educational implications. *Journal of Learning Disabilities, 13,* 364–371.

Torgesen, J. K., & Licht, B. G. (1983). The learning disabled child as an inactive learner: Retrospect and prospects. In J. D. McKinney & L. Feagans (Eds.), *Current topics in learning disabilities, Vol. 1.* Norwood, NJ: Ablex.

U.S. Office of Education (1977). Assistance to states for education of handicapped children: Procedures for evaluating specific learning disabilities. *Federal Register, 42,* 65082–65085.

Vaughn, S., & Linan-Thompson, S. (2003). What is special about special education for students with learning disabilities? *Journal of Special Education, 37*(3), 140–147.

Weistein, J. A. (1994). Growing up learning disabled. *Journal of Learning Disabilities, 27,* 142–143.

White, O. R. (1986). Precision teaching—Precision learning. *Exceptional Children, 52,* 522–534.

Will, M. (1986). *Educating students with learning problems: A shared responsibility.* Washington, DC: U.S. Department of Education.

Will, M. (1988). Educating students with learning problems and the changing role of the school psychologists. *School Psychology Review, 17,* 476–478.

Yell, M. L., Katsiyannas, A., & Shiner, J. G. (2006). The No Child Left Behind Act, adequate yearly progress, and students with disabilities. *Teaching Exceptional Children, 38*(4), 32–39.

Zigmond, N. (2003). Where should students with disabilities receive special education services? Is one place better than another? *Journal of Special Education, 37*(3), 193–199.

MEDICAL ASPECTS
OF LEARNING DISABILITIES

CHAPTER OUTLINE

WHEN YOU COMPLETE THIS CHAPTER, YOU SHOULD BE ABLE TO:

1. Identify the several different medically related issues in the field of learning disabilities.

2. Compare and contrast the medical and the educational models.

3. Describe the attempts to identify medically based causes of learning disabilities.

4. Discuss the genetic and biochemical causes for learning disabilities.

5. Describe several promising new medical technologies for assessment.

6. List the drug-based treatment approaches to control of behavior.

7. Describe the basic structure of the central nervous system.

8. Describe attention-deficit hyperactivity disorder.

KEYWORDS

CNS	temporal lobe	ADHD
neuron	frontal lobe	DSM-V
dendrites	parietal lobe	comorbidity
axon	occipital lobe	cranial nerves
neurotransmitters	NLD	CAT scan
cerebellum	BPPD	PET scan
cerebrum	teratogenic insult	magnetic resonance imaging
localization	fetal alcohol syndrome (FAS)	(MRI)
hemispheric specialization	DSM-IV	functional MRI (fMRI)

INTRODUCTION

The roots of the study of learning disabilities are in the medical field, and the relationships between the disciplines of medicine and learning disabilities are varied. First, much of the influence in the entire field of special education comes from medicine. For example, the legislation that facilitated special education service nationally requires that medical information be a part of each child's individual education program. Also, the terms that are used—*individual diagnosis of education problems* and *treatment approaches*—are medical in origin.

Second, medical information may play an important role in the identification of learning disabilities in some children. As the definitions in Chapter 1 indicated, medical causes such as vision deficits and auditory problems must be ruled out in order to classify a child as learning disabled. Information from a neurologist is also often used in identifying a child with learning disabilities. Clearly, teachers in the field of learning disabilities must have some understanding of medical contributions to the field in order to deal with the varied types of medical information that he or she will confront.

Finally, numerous medical treatments for learning disabilities have been proposed. Although some of these are quite controversial and at present unsupported, other treatments are strongly supported by the research and used quite frequently—drug interventions to combat hyperactivity are one example.

This chapter is intended to provide information on the medical background of learning disabilities. First, a comparison of the methods of the medical approach and the educational approach to learning disabilities is provided as a background for understanding the remainder of the chapter. Next, a discussion of the brain and central nervous system is presented. Then three different areas in which medical science research has affected the field of learning disabilities are discussed—etiological concerns, assessment, and treatment.

MEDICAL AND EDUCATIONAL MODELS

Medical = finding out what is wrong

educational = knowing what wrong and How to deal With it.

Practitioners in the medical field approach the study of children with learning disabilities in a different manner from educators. Whereas the educator is concerned with identification of the types of learning environments that may lead the child toward mastery of certain material, the medical model of thought places the burden of the disability squarely on the shoulders of the child. Whereas a medical orientation may lead a practitioner to search for abnormalities in the central nervous system of a child, an educator is more likely to search for a problem in the way the child interacts with his or her educational environment. Because of this emphasis on the manner in which the educator seeks environmental remedies, another term used for the educational model is the *ecological model*. This term demonstrates the concern educators feel for the relationship between the child and the learning environment—a concern that parallels the ecologist's concern for interactions between the organism and the environment. You may also hear the term *contextualist perspective* used as a synonym, suggesting an emphasis on the context in which learning takes place. When a problem arises, the educator may seek, as one example, a different instructional approach to which the child may respond more successfully, whereas the medical practitioner is likely to seek a drug treatment to alleviate the learning deficiency.

Although this is, in some sense, a gross oversimplification, the differences in the models of thought used in these two different professions cause some concern in communication between the practitioners in the two fields, as will be apparent later in this chapter. Interest Box 2.1 presents a brief comparison of the major differences between the medical and the educational models. You may wish to review these now and return to these points later in the chapter.

During the Bush administration, an effort has been undertaken to revitalize special education (Commission on Excellence in Special Education, 2001; NJCLD, 2005), and this effort has led to a report that will move the educational model of thought forward. For example, the recommendations of the commission suggest increased concentration on educational results and developing a model of prevention of school difficulties, rather than waiting for a child to fail in reading or math prior to diagnosis of a learning disability (more information on the new procedures on response to intervention is presented in Chapter 5). In fact, given the IDEA of 2004 legislation, it is quite likely that the educational perspective will be revitalized, and we may see considerable changes in how students with learning disabilities and other disabilities are identified. At a minimum, the focus on school-related learning problems and how teachers may help students remedy them will be enhanced as a result of this report, and the field will move further away from the early dominance of the medical model.

■ ■ ■ ■ ■

INTEREST BOX 2.1
MEDICAL AND EDUCATIONAL MODELS

A comparison of the medical and educational models of thought demonstrates the types of differences in assumptions and educational strategies that these two models entail. Such comparison is obviously somewhat oversimplified, but this contrast does suggest the types of differences between the two approaches.

Issue	Medical Model	Educational Model
Etiology	Cause resides in the child's biological and central nervous system makeup; awareness of this can suggest educational treatments	Cause resides in the interaction between the learner and the environment
Terminology	Tend to use terms that have basis in clinical practices	Use terms with more educational relevance
Assessment	Assess to label the child's disorder	Assess in order to help teach the child
Treatment	Tendency to use drug treatments to combat hyperactivity and attention problems	Tendency to use behavioral reinforcement programs

LEARNING AND THE NERVOUS SYSTEM

Learning is a function of the nerves within the body that make up the **CNS** (central nervous system)—the brain and the spinal column. This system is, in reality, a communication system in which various electrochemical impulses carry information. Some rudimentary understanding of this system will assist in your understanding of the medically based treatments of learning disabilities (Leonard, 2001; Shaywitz & Shaywitz, 2006).

Neurons

The basic unit of the system is the single **neuron,** or nerve cell. Figure 2.1 presents a diagram of several neurons. The neuron is a chemical and electrical system that responds in a complex fashion to an electric impulse from another neuron. Initially, the **dendrites,** or the sensory detectors of the neurons, detect a chemical transmission from another neuron and activate the cell. An electrical impulse is formed and travels throughout the cell, eventually traveling down the **axon,** or the long stem of the cell, to activate surrounding nerve cells (Sousa, 1995).

The dendrites are numerous and connect the neuron to hundreds of other neurons through a complex chemical system in which the production of the chemicals is controlled by the electrical impulse. Notice that the dendrites of one cell and the axons of other cells do not quite touch each other. The space in between is called the *synaptic gap.* As the electrical

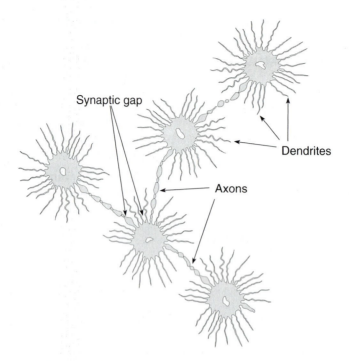

Synaptic gap

Dendrites

Axons

FIGURE 2.1   Five Neurons in the Brain

impulse reaches the synaptic gap, a set of chemicals—called **neurotransmitters**—is released. Dopamine, norepinephrine, and acetylcholine are several of the neurotransmitters
that are frequently mentioned in the national press, though over 50 have been identified.
These neurotransmitters in turn excite the axons of other neurons. However, not all messages pass the synaptic gap because also released at that gap is an entirely different class of
chemicals that may inhibit the electric impulse. These are referred to as *neuroinhibitors.*

   Learning is dependent on the connections made between neurons. There is considerable evidence from the brain-compatible learning literature that suggests that the neurons in
a child's brain make many more connections than those in an adult's (Sousa, 1995). Also,
the richer the environment experienced by children at an early age, the more numerous the
connections between neurons. Over time, neural connections that the brain finds useful are
strengthened and become permanent, whereas connections that are not frequently used are
eliminated (Sousa, 1999, 1995, 2001). This process is lifelong but appears to be greatest between 2 and 11 years of age. This pattern of brain development provides a strong argument for
early intervention educational and environmental enrichment programs. Unfortunately, most
students with learning disabilities are not diagnosed until the school-age years, and many are
not diagnosed until the third or fourth grade, when they are at the high end of this age range.
Nevertheless, this newly emerging information on the learning potential of younger children
has provided much of the research rationale for early intervention programs.

   The chemical/electrical signal system between neurons is quite complex, and you
need not understand these interactions completely. However, as an educator, you will want
to understand this rather elementary description of neuron interaction because a number

of the medical treatments that are often prescribed for children with learning disabilities apparently affect this transfer of information at the synaptic gap. For example, the use of various stimulants may affect the production of neurotransmitters and neuroinhibitors and thus lead to changes in such classroom behavior problems as hyperactivity. (For further explanation of these dynamics of brain cell interaction, see Booth & Burman, 2001; Richards, 2001; Sousa, 2001.)

Also, some researchers have indicated that biochemical abnormalities that affect these neurotransmitters may potentially cause learning disabilities (Shaywitz & Shaywitz, 2006). Parents who have read recent reports of this research in such magazines as *Scientific American* may well ask you about this information. At present, there is no evidence to support this contention, though research is continuing.

The Brain

The heaviest concentration of neurons in the human body is in the brain, and because most learning is assumed to take place in the brain, some study of the various brain functions is appropriate for students in the field of learning disabilities. Figure 2.2 presents a diagram of the various regions of the brain.

The brain is composed of three different regions—the brain stem, the **cerebellum,** and the **cerebrum.** Of course, each of these regions may be subdivided into many more sections or areas, and some of these areas are presented in Figure 2.3. However, understanding the complex functions of each minute part of the brain will not be necessary here. In order to understand some of the early theories relating to the field of learning disabilities, it is only necessary that you have some understanding of the major sections of the brain.

The brain stem is the lower part of the brain, as shown in Figure 2.2. This is the oldest part of the human brain, in evolutionary terms, and controls the life-sustaining functions of the body. Different portions of the brain stem control heartbeat and respiration. Often, in accident cases when other portions of the brain are "dead" in the sense that measurable electrical brain activity has ceased, this portion of the brain will continue to function, and

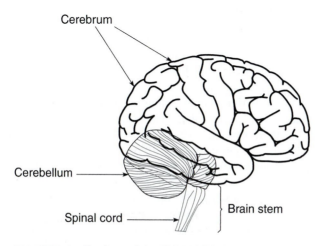

FIGURE 2.2   Regions of the Human Brain

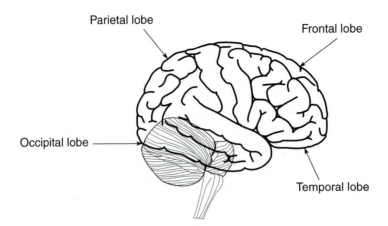

Parietal lobe

Frontal lobe

Occipital lobe

Temporal lobe

FIGURE 2.3   Hemispherical Lobes

that will serve to keep a person breathing and "alive." Sensory input and motor nerve output to the face area are also controlled here.

The cerebellum receives sensory input and controls most of the motor nervous system. The motor nervous system comprises the set of nerves that control bodily movement. Thus, balance, posture, and movements are controlled largely by this section of the brain.

The Cerebrum

The cerebrum is the largest part of the human brain. This part of the brain controls most of the higher-thought functions that we consider to be predominantly *human* thought functions. Although all mammals have some version of a cerebrum, this brain section is most developed in human beings.

The cerebrum is divided into two hemispheres, and that division of upper-brain activity has been the foundation for several theories of learning disabilities. The two hemispheres of the cerebrum are "cross-wired" in humans, in the sense that the left hemisphere is related to motor nerve control for the right side of the body, whereas the right hemisphere seemingly controls the left side of the body. In other words, a brain signal to move the right hand (such as in writing) is initiated in the left hemisphere of the cerebrum.

In addition to this cross-wiring of motor control, the two hemispheres seem to relate to different types of learning and brain activity. For example, in 90% of the adult population, language and linguistic forms of thought seem to originate in the left hemisphere of the brain (Robertson, 2000). The left hemisphere of the brain also seems to control other language systems such as reading numbers and logical thought. The right hemisphere of the cerebrum, for most adults, seems to control spatial orientation, time sequences, visual imagery, and creative expression in music. Of course, the functions of the hemispheres are reversed in certain individuals, and no one knows why some individuals develop differently. Interest Box 2.2 presents a more complete list of the types of functions that seem to be associated with the two hemispheres of the cerebrum for right-handed individuals.

You may hear the term *localized* used to mean that a particular type of learning activity is generally centered in one hemisphere or the other. Hence, language, for most of us, is localized in the left hemisphere, whereas spatial orientation seems to be localized in the right hemisphere.

The process of **localization** takes place during the first several years of life. In fact, children up until the age of 7 years or so tend to have hemispheres that act in a very similar fashion, and language becomes localized in one hemisphere or the other only after a certain age. If a child of, say, 4 years suffers a significant accident to the left hemisphere of the brain, the right hemisphere can, in some sense, carry the burden and learn to use language. However, if the same type of accident takes place in the adult brain (or in a child past 7 years), the individual is likely to suffer from a language deficit throughout life.

At least one early theory in the field of learning disabilities was based on this hemispheric specialization pattern. Orton (1937) noted that human beings were not born with this pattern of brain activity already established. Orton (1937) proposed that children suffering from learning disabilities had difficulty in reading because of some lag or incomplete development of normal cerebral dominance patterns. For example, if language functions

■ ■ ■ ■ ■ ▬▬▬▬▬▬▬▬▬▬▬▬▬▬▬▬▬▬▬▬▬▬▬▬▬▬▬▬▬▬▬▬▬▬▬▬

INTEREST BOX 2.2

FUNCTIONS ASSOCIATED WITH BRAIN HEMISPHERES

Left Hemisphere	*Right Hemisphere*
Expressive speech	Spatial orientation
Receptive language	Simple language comprehension
Language (general)	Nonverbal ideation
Complex motor functions	Picture and pattern sense
Vigilance	Performancelike functions
Paired associate learning	Spatial integration
Liaison to consciousness	Creative associative thinking
Ideation	Facial recognition
Conceptual similarities	Sound recognition
Temporal analysis	Nonverbal paired associate thought
Analysis of detail	Tactile perception
Arithmetic	Gestalt perception
Writing	Picture processing
Calculation	Intuitive problem solving
Finger naming	Psychic experiences
Right-left orientation	Humorous thoughts
Sequential processing	Simultaneous processing

Source: Information in the chart came from various sources but is summarized in *Dyslexia: Neuropsychological Theory, Research, and Clinical Differentiation* by G. W. Hynd and M. Cohen, 1983, New York: Grune & Stratton.

had not localized by the age of 10, the child with the slowly developing brain function would suffer from reading and language problems.

Also, the concept of *laterality* was based on the **hemispheric specialization** just described. This once influential idea was based on the concept that a student's preference for using one hand in writing (usually the right hand) developed as the hemispheres developed dominance in various areas of learning. If hemispheric dominance was slow or delayed, confusions in laterality were assumed to develop in which children had difficulty in determining which hand to write with or in following a line of print from one side of the page to the other. This *laterality confusion* was assumed to cause reading and written-language problems. However, these early ideas have largely been superseded by more recent evidence in neurophysiology.

Figure 2.3 presents a side view of one hemisphere of the cerebrum, and four separate areas are labeled. Each hemisphere of the brain includes these areas. In moving from the front of the brain to the rear, the **temporal lobe** controls hearing and auditory memory. The **frontal lobe** controls abstract thinking. The **parietal lobe** controls tactile sensations from the various body parts, and the **occipital lobe** deals with vision and visual perception. Each of these lobes in one hemisphere may communicate with the similar lobe in the other hemisphere through a bundle of nerve fibers in the center of the brain, known as the *corpus collosum*. Thus, although the two hemispheres are discrete in some ways, they do interact with each other in most learning tasks.

A basic understanding of these general cerebral areas can assist teachers in understanding some learning problems. For example, for a child with an injury to the lower rear portion of the skull, the occipital lobe may be negatively affected, which could result in visual-perceptual problems; at times, these can result in a learning disability. Further, brain-scanning studies have shown that the frontal lobe is highly involved in rehearsal of new knowledge as well as memory (Sousa, 2001). For example, when a child is considering a new fact or idea, he or she will often restate it and then try to think of other similar facts or ideas. This type of rehearsal involves a variety of brain areas, but the frontal lobe is highly involved, and this type of frontal lobe work will result in increased long-term memory for the fact or idea rehearsed in such a fashion. Clearly, a problem in the functioning of the frontal lobe can result in a wide variety of learning problems, including learning disabilities.

Research is progressing on cerebral brain functioning in all students, including those with learning disabilities, and a more complete picture of the interactions of the cerebral hemispheres has begun to emerge (Galaburda, 2005; Plante, Ramage, & Magloire, 2006; Robertson, 2000; Shaywitz & Shaywitz, 2006). Interest Box 2.3 presents a recent theory on reading disabilities that has developed as a result of emerging medical technologies and brain-scanning techniques.

ETIOLOGY OF LEARNING DISABILITIES

In the preceding discussion, we have briefly examined several medically based theories of *etiology,* or causation—theories that attempt to explain what causes a learning disability. The search for medically based causes has been a part of the history of learning disabilities since the earliest phases of study in the field, and any attempt to understand the current

INTEREST BOX 2.3
SUBTYPES OF LEARNING DISABILITIES

Rourke and his colleagues (Rourke, 2005; Rourke, Ahmad, Collins, Hayman-Abello, Hayman-Abello, & Warriner, 2002) have suggested that various brain-imaging techniques have progressed to the point from which learning disabilities may be identified by using these newly developed brain study techniques (Rourke, van der Vlugt, & Rourke, 2002). While historically an assumption was made that learning disabilities were based on some unspecified dysfunction in the brain, these researchers suggest that, using the modern brain study technologies, we can now document these brain dysfunctions (Rourke, 2005). These recently developed brain-scanning technologies are described later in this chapter.

Specifically, these researchers have proposed two subtypes of learning disabilities: nonverbal learning disabilities and basic phonological processing disabilities.

Nonverbal Learning Disabilities (NLD)

NLD are characterized by

1. Well-developed single-word reading/spelling processing
2. Efficient use of verbal information in social situations
3. Onset of disability symptoms after age 4
4. Excessive hyperactivity after age 4
5. Decreases in hyperactivity over the next decade of life
6. Possible withdrawal, anxiety, depression, social skill deficits in adolescence

Basic Phonological Processing Disabilities (BPPD)

BPPD are characterized by

1. Poorly developed single-word reading/spelling processing
2. More efficient use of nonverbal information than verbal information in social situations
3. Relatively normal social development and behavior

This general list of characteristics associated with each type of learning disability seems to result in notable differences in academic and behavioral performance. For example, the spelling errors of students with NLD are almost always phonetically accurate, whereas misspellings of students with BPPD are frequently phonetically inaccurate (Rourke, 2005). Based on these findings, differential educational intervention options may be called for.

It is interesting to note that, among the various disabilities (i.e., retardation, severe emotional disturbance, etc.), only learning disabilities has not been delineated/refined into subtypes. For example, students with severe emotional disturbance are managed differently in educational situations from those with mild behavioral disorders, and severe retardation results in different educational treatment than mild retardation. Clearly, this line of research on subtyping in learning disabilities holds much potential for expanding our understanding of learning disabilities, and teachers in the field should remain vigilant in reading the expanding research on subtypes of LD.

issues in the field of learning disabilities must begin with an attempt to understand the medically based assumptions upon which the field was founded. This section will present several potential medical causes of learning disabilities.

Genetic Influences

There is growing evidence that genetic influences may cause some learning disabilities (Galaburda, 2005; Wood & Grigorenko, 2001). Hallgren (1950), in an early investigation, studied 276 children and identified numerous reading and language problems among the relatives of the children. A genetic link was suggested as one possible cause for the reading problems of the children. Decker and DeFries (1980, 1981) conducted a series of studies of 125 children with reading disabilities and their families, and the results indicated that reading disabilities may be hereditary.

Other evidence for some genetic cause for learning disabilities comes from several *studies in identical twins.* Unlike fraternal twins—who come from two separate eggs and thus have different genetic information—identical twins come from the same egg. Studies of twins have shown that when reading problems exist, those problems are more likely to exist in both identical twins than in both fraternal twins, thus indicating a genetic cause for those reading problems (Wood & Grigorenko, 2001).

With the mapping of the human genome in 2000, investigations on genetic causes for learning disabilities have increased (Wadsworth, Olson, Pennington, & DeFries, 2000; Wood & Grigorenko, 2001). To date, portions of certain chromosomes have been implicated in the search for a genetic marker that would, under certain conditions, result in dyslexia. In particular, chromosome 15 has been implicated, but research has also focused on potential genetic markers associated with chromosomes 1, 2, 6, 13, and 14 (Raskind, 2001; Wood & Grigorenko, 2001).

Further, recent research suggests that genetic influences may account for over 50% of the cases of reading disabilities, and when only students with normal and above-normal IQs are considered, genetic influences may account for as much as 75% (Wadsworth et al., 2000). Although this research is medical in nature, teachers should be aware of the possibilities that may eventually result from this type of research, including specification of a primary genetic cause for many learning disabilities, assessment procedures based on genetic mapping, or even gene replacement therapy as a potential preventative measure for some learning disabilities (Wadsworth et al., 2000; Wood & Grigorenko, 2001).

Teratogenic Insult

Teratogenic insult increases the likelihood of malformations of the brain and central nervous system during pregnancy, and numerous teratogens have been identified. Several particularly damaging teratogens have been mentioned in the literature as potential prenatal causes of learning disabilities, though none has been exclusively associated with learning disabilities.

Alcohol.   The relationship between maternal use of alcohol and serious malformations of the fetus during pregnancy has become painfully clear. National media coverage of

fetal alcohol syndrome (FAS) has called public attention to the problem of mothers who ingest alcohol during pregnancy. The FAS problem appears to be associated with heavy use of alcohol, and children who demonstrate this syndrome typically have moderate to severe limitations in cognitive ability, along with numerous physical malformations. However, mild forms of this syndrome have been hypothesized and may result in a learning disability. It is unknown at present if children can be mildly affected by this syndrome, but the possibility exists that use of alcohol by pregnant women may result in learning problems that are later characterized as learning disabilities.

Smoking.   Numerous studies have demonstrated a link between maternal smoking during pregnancy and birth-related problems in infants. Some of the research has indicated a relationship between heavy smoking on the part of the mother and later reading problems and lower IQs among children.

Teratogenic Influences in Retrospect.   Several issues must be considered when discussing teratogenic influences on learning disabilities. First, all of this evidence is correlational in nature, and firm conclusions regarding maternal drug use as a potential cause of these problems will have to await further research. Second, numerous illegal drugs are in widespread use today. This section presented information on both alcohol and smoking as potential causes for learning problems because these two drugs have been more widely studied. However, other drugs may also result in learning disabilities. For example, the increased use of cocaine and a cocaine derivative—crack—has yet to receive widespread attention in the learning disabilities literature, though maternal use of crack is known to cause severe damage to the fetus that results in lowered intelligence, low birthweight, and addiction at birth.

The effects of both alcohol and smoking on unborn infants can be devastating. About the only bright spot in the literature is the fact that prenatal teratogenic insult is amenable to prevention. The dark side of the cloud is that once such an insult has been introduced into the environment of the fetus, the damage is done and no cure is possible.

Perinatal Causes

A number of events may negatively affect the child during the birth process, and some theorists have connected certain perinatal problems with learning disabilities. For example, premature birth seems to be related to later learning difficulties. Prolonged labor and the use of forceps to deliver the infant's head have been mentioned as potential problems that may lead to later learning disabilities. As is the case with the other causes discussed, the evidence for a link between perinatal difficulties and learning disabilities seems to be predominantly correlational in nature, and no direct causal links have yet been established.

Postnatal Influences

The list of potential postnatal causes for learning difficulty is nearly endless. For example, numerous types of head injury can result in certain learning disorders, as indicated by the soldiers with brain injuries studied by Goldstein and discussed in Chapter 1.

A number of chemicals present in our modern technological environment may produce certain types of learning disorders. Some research indicates that lead poisoning may create an increased danger of learning disabilities. For example, Needleman (1980) studied two groups of children. Children with high levels of lead in their teeth were compared with children who showed lower levels of lead. The children with higher levels of lead in their bodies scored lower than the other children on several important variables, including verbal performance, language processing, and attention.

Numerous other chemicals have been identified as potentially related to learning disabilities. However, many of the commonly mentioned chemicals (food additives, refined sugars, eggs, corn, and milk) have been linked to learning disabilities only tentatively, and the suggestions that these chemical agents cause learning disabilities is unsupported at present. _ Not true

Search for Medical Causes

As you read the last few sections of text, you may have noticed the various disclaimers that suggested the points under discussion had not been solidly demonstrated. The medical field has not continued to be the dominant partner in research on learning disabilities that it was during the first historical phase, and there are several reasons for the declining influence of medical approaches.

First, although numerous potential medical insults to the child's body or to the mother's body during pregnancy may cause learning problems, there is no evidence that a particular type of insult results in the particular problem—learning disabilities. In fact, every potential cause presented in this text may very well be a cause for just about any other type of disability.

Next, no single medical cause has been related to any particular type of learning disability. For example, medical science has demonstrated that an aberration of the 21st chromosome is the medical cause for trisomy 21, or Down syndrome. Also, heavy use of alcohol during pregnancy results in fetal alcohol syndrome, which is usually associated with some degree of mental retardation. However, with the possible exception of the emerging genetic evidence, there is no evidence of any single type of medical insult to the fetus or the child that routinely results in a learning disability. Consequently, the best one can do is become aware of the types of insults that cause learning problems and advocate against them. As a teacher, you may have the occasion to discuss drinking with the parent of a child who has learning problems, and such a discussion may result in more caution on the part of that parent relative to future children.

Another issue in the search for medical causes relates to the usefulness of the acquired knowledge in classroom situations. Even if a particular medical cause is found for a learning disability, teachers may not be able to make use of that knowledge. For example, knowing that a child suffered brain injury in an accident and that today's learning difficulties began at that time does not help a teacher decide what to do today to help that child learn.

Next, when medical treatments are used on children with learning disabilities—to control problem behaviors, for example—teachers are not generally in charge of the treatment. Medical causes for problems lead to medical solutions, and teachers are not trained to administer most medical treatments. As the discussion later in the chapter will demonstrate, teachers do play a vital role in drug treatment programs, but the main responsibility for such programs rests with the physician. Thus, the teacher is somewhat removed from decisions on use of this type of treatment.

At this point, it is obvious that medicine has not contributed greatly to the understanding of the etiology of learning disabilities. Because so many potential problems have been identified and no single problem or set of problems has been exclusively associated with learning disabilities, most theorists today no longer believe that medical concerns for etiology continue to be a major influence in the field. However, medical science has made significant contributions to the study of learning disabilities in areas other than etiology. Also, medical science will continue to affect the field as new and different diagnostic procedures are developed, and etiological concerns may be successfully addressed by medical science in the future.

MEDICAL DIAGNOSIS OF LEARNING DISABILITIES

In the area of assessment, medical science has made some progress. A nomenclature has been developed, and certain medically based assessment procedures have been used on an infrequent basis. Some of these assessment ideas involve use of expensive medical hardware, whereas other diagnostic procedures do not. This section presents the contributions of medical science in the area of assessment. First, the assessment nomenclature is presented; then the specific assessment procedures are discussed.

DSM-IV

Perhaps the primary medically based diagnostic system is that developed by the American Psychiatric Association. This system was developed in the context of general confusion regarding the types of attention and behavioral problems that children manifest in the academic environment.

Numerous terms have been used in recent years to identify attention problems that are abnormal and interfere with learning. These include *attention problems, attention-deficit disorders, attention-deficit hyperactivity disorders,* and *hyperactivity.* These terms reflect the changing terminology of the diagnostic criteria of the American Psychiatric Association, and as that organization gained increasing understanding of this constellation of related problems, the terminology changed fairly regularly. Further, there has been considerable confusion in the field regarding these terms because not all children with attention problems manifest both attention deficits and hyperactive types of behaviors.

McKinney, Montague, and Hocutt (1993) reviewed the extant literature on assessment of attention-deficit disorders and described three primary characteristics: inattention/distractibility, impulsivity and disinhibition, and hyperactivity. In addition to these primary characteristics, a number of studies (reviewed by McKinney and his co-workers, 1993) indicated that there are secondary characteristics, including conduct disorders, inappropriate social behaviors, and attention-seeking behaviors of all types. At present, little is understood about the relationship between these secondary characteristics and the primary characteristics. Clearly, much more information is needed on this type of disorder.

In 1994, the American Psychiatric Association revised the classification system for delineating various disorders in children. **DSM-IV** (*Diagnostic and Statistical Manual of Mental Disorders,* fourth edition, American Psychiatric Association, 1994) specifies several types of problems dealing with attention-related disorders in children. In 1993, the American Psychiatric Association published the most recent set of diagnostic criteria, and the terminology has now stabilized, based on that set of criteria. **ADHD** (attention-deficit hyperactivity disorder) is now considered the correct term for all disorders of this type. Interest Box 2.4 presents some of the associated behavioral indicators for the disorder, as reported by parents. Also, a revision of this classification system is in the planning stages and may address many of these issues. That revision will be called **DSM-V** (www.dsm5.org).

In order to be diagnosed under this classification system, children must manifest these characteristics at no later than 7 years of age. Also, the symptoms must be present in two or more settings (e.g., at school and at home). Next, the disturbance must cause clinically significant distress or impairment in social, academic, or occupational functioning (American Psychiatric Association, 1994).

Even with these newly revised criteria, a number of unanswered questions still remain. For example, the issue of **comorbidity** (i.e., how many children or youth manifest both ADHD and learning disabilities) is still unresolved. After a review of all available evidence, McKinney and his co-workers (1993) estimated that perhaps 10% of children with ADHD also demonstrate a learning disability, whereas between 15% and 80% of children

---

INTEREST BOX 2.4

BEHAVIORS INDICATIVE OF ADHD AS REPORTED BY PARENTS

INNATTENTIVE ADHD
- loses books and work materials
- easily distracted
- ignores instructions
- short attention span
- poor attention to details
- cannot finish homework in a timely manner

HYPERACTIVE-IMPULSIVE ADHD
- fidgety
- runs around the living room
- sits in unusual positions and moves constantly
- leaves his/her seat at the dinner table
- constantly talking
- impulsive and cannot wait for his/her turn

COMBINED ADHD
When children demonstrate the combined type of ADHD, any and all of the behavioral indicators reported above may be seen.

with learning disabilities also manifest ADHD. Perhaps this newly revised classification system will increase understanding of this medically based condition, which, in turn, should lead to clarification of the relationship between ADHD and learning disabilities.

Neurological Assessments

The medical field has not developed assessments that can identify a student with a learning disability, though several authors have suggested that certain brain-based cognitive tasks can assist in assessment. Fawcett, Nicolson, and Maclagan (2001), for example, presented evidence to suggest that a combination of phonological assessments and prescribed movements (threading beads, etc.) may eventually play a role in assessment of children with learning disabilities. However, school districts are far from using such medically based assessments currently.

More typical would be the use of an informal neurological examination, performed by a physician; occasionally, such reports will be included in the folders for students with learning disabilities. Hynd and Cohen (1983) presented a list of tasks that may be used in an informal assessment of neurological functioning, as shown in Interest Box 2.5.

The assessments listed in Interest Box 2.5 are fairly informal, and the physician can evaluate a number of central nervous system functions without using any diagnostic equipment. First, a medical history is taken, with particular attention given to the pregnancy and birth process as well as any unusual childhood diseases. These histories typically include various developmental milestones such as the age when the child first crawls, pulls himself or herself into an upright position, or walks. Any learning problems of immediate family members are noted.

Next, the physician will assess motor skills. The motor nerves control movement of the muscles and muscle groups. Strength is tested by having the subject push or pull against the physician's grasp. Eye-hand coordination is assessed, as is gross motor coordination. The physician may ask the subject to stand on one foot, walk heel to toe, hop, or skip and move the arms at the same time.

An evaluation of the deep-tendon reflexes is included. The knee and elbow reflexes are tested by a gentle blow (usually with a rubber or plastic hammer) to the tendons in the knee and elbow. Abnormal reflexes can indicate some type of damage to the central nervous system.

Next, the **cranial nerves** are examined. The cranial nerves control the movements of the facial muscles and sensory organs. Examination of cranial-nerve function consists of looking into the eye and observing various movements of the eyes, facial muscles, tongue, and mouth. A penlight is used to see if the patient can follow the light without turning his or her head, thus assessing motor control of the eye muscles. Also, pupilar reflexes are assessed by noting the degree of change in the pupil of the eye in response to bright light. The patient may be asked to identify certain smells and make chewing movements with his or her jaw to assess motor control in that area.

Through these informal techniques, physicians can note a number of potential irregularities in nerve and brain function. Difficulties with any particular aspect of these movements may also help the physician determine the location of the problem area within the central nervous system.

■ ■ ■ ■ ■ ▬▬▬▬▬▬▬▬▬▬▬▬▬▬▬▬▬▬▬▬▬▬▬▬▬▬▬▬

INTEREST BOX 2.5

COMMON PROCEDURES IN A NEUROLOGICAL EXAMINATION

1. Tests of cerebral functions
   Language usage
   Levels of consciousness
   Intellectual abilities
   Orientation
   Emotional status
2. Tests for cranial nerves
   General hearing, vision, and speech
   Motor movements of facial muscles
   Pupilar reflexes
3. Tests of cerebellar functions
   Finger-to-nose-to-finger

   Rapid alternating movements
   Heel-to-toe walking
   Standing—eyes open
   Standing—eyes closed
4. Motor functioning
   Muscle size
   Muscle tone
   Coordination
   Reflexes
5. Tests of sensory nerves
   Superficial tactile sense
   Superficial pain sense

Source: Information adapted from *Dyslexia: Neuropsychological Theory, Research, and Clinical Differentiation* by G. W. Hynd and M. Cohen, 1983, New York: Grune & Stratton.

Medical Technologies for Neurological Assessment

The EEG.   Because the brain and central nervous system are electrical systems, measurements of the flow of electricity during various learning tasks will provide some information about the areas of a subject's brain that are in use. The EEG, or electroencephalogram, is a device that produces a recording of the electrical activity of the brain. Electrical impulses are measured by taping electrodes on different parts of the scalp. The electrodes record the different electrical impulses and record that activity on a running record that can then be reviewed and interpreted (Sousa, 1995).

The CAT Scan.   A **CAT scan**—computerized axial tomography scan—utilizes a radiological technique to examine the structure of the brain. The x-ray beams are sent through the brain at different angles, and a computer puts the various pieces of information together to formulate a picture of the brain's structure, which can show areas of little brain activity.

The PET Scan.   The **PET scan**—positron emission tomography—involves the introduction of radioactive sugar isotopes into the brain through the bloodstream. The patient is required to perform certain functions, and the flow of blood is recorded by following the movement of the radioactive isotopes. The PET scan can picture different sections of the brain and give some indication of the metabolism. If a certain area of the brain is inactive, that type of problem may cause a learning disability (Sousa, 1999).

The MRI.   One nonradiological technique that has been developed is the **magnetic resonance imaging (MRI)** procedure. A magnetic field is created that results in certain measurable changes in brain tissue. The changes are then measured by radio frequencies and computerized enhancement in order to picture the various parts of the brain. Like the PET scan, this technique is used to demonstrate differences in the brain that may cause learning problems. However, this technique pictures brain structure and not brain activity.

The Functional MRI.   The functional MRI is an MRI that measures blood flow to and throughout the brain rather than brain shape or structure. Like the PET scan, a **functional MRI (fMRI)** can show which parts of the brain are active during a thinking task. Also, because it does not involve the introduction of any radiation into the brain (unlike the PET scans and CAT scans described above), this technique can be used on children with normal brains (Sousa, 1999). Because of the nonintrusive nature of this technique, the functional MRI holds the greatest potential for actually mapping brain activity during reading or math or science activities, and this is the brain-mapping technique most frequently used today to study children with learning disabilities (Joseph, Nobel, & Eden, 2001).

Use of New Techniques

Newly developed hardware has resulted in a profusion of research in medical science, and numerous studies have been performed on various groups of children with disabilities. In one recent study, Molfese and his co-workers (2006) used the EEG and demonstrated that various regions of the brain are differentially active in above-average readers when compared to lower-level readers. In a related study, Shaywitz and Shaywitz (2006) utilized the fMRI and have documented two specific brain areas that are associated with word analysis (i.e., sounding out words). Further, these two areas seem to be "underactivated" during the reading process among students with reading disabilities. Specifically, two areas in the rear of the brain—the occipito-temporal region and the parieto-temporal region—seem to be less stimulated during the reading process among students with reading disabilities than among other students. Further, Shaywitz and his co-workers (2003), in an experimental study, demonstrated that even among students with reading disabilities, effective instruction could reinvigorate these underactive brain areas. These researchers provided intensive instruction in a phonologically based reading instruction program—a program that emphasized letter sounds and phonics—for 50 minutes per day for a period of 8 months during one school year. Thus, this experimental group received a total of 105 hours of instruction. When compared with a control group after that time, the underactive areas of the brain were shown to be considerably more active, indicating that effective instruction involving intensive work on letter-sound relationships can alleviate reading problems among struggling readers. Further, these effects were still measurable one year after the experiment ended.

For our purposes, these results demonstrate several things. First, effective instruction on letter-sound relationships works for students with reading problems. Second, the brain-compatible research of today, unlike much of the early research on the human brain, often focuses directly on academic problems and on measuring specific academic outcomes. As this trend continues, teachers will need to remain current in their understanding of this research and the implications for the classroom. Obviously, should such a concrete understanding of neurological functioning develop, the field of learning disabilities would be profoundly affected. In a diagnostic sense, such a functional system of reading would allow the field to state categorically whether or not a particular child had a processing problem or a minimal brain dysfunction, as discussed in Chapter 1.

In addition to studies of language-based learning disabilities, certain theorists have indicated that nonverbal learning disabilities may be associated with specific malfunctions in the brain or CNS (Gross-Tsur, Shalev, Manor, & Amir, 1995; Sousa, 2001). For example, an abnormality in the right hemisphere of the brain may lead to nonverbal learning disabilities (i.e., learning disabilities that are not speech or language based, including visuospatial integration, memory problems, and attention problems). Gross-Tsur and her co-workers (1995) studied 20 children (averaging 9.5 years of age) with abnormalities in the right hemisphere who were identified as having learning disabilities and attention-deficit hyperactivity disorder in an attempt to use the newly developed assessment technologies to map out their brain-based learning problems. Students were included in the study if they were referred to a clinic for emotional and interpersonal problems, communication problems, poor visual/spatial skill, or either poor math achievement or behavioral indications of brain lesions. Contrary to expectation, of the 20 children in the study, only 4 children had abnormal indications of brain functioning.

Unrealized Promises

In spite of the optimism among certain theorists in the field, the promises of psychoneurologists seem a bit premature. The field has not widely embraced the use of the neurological assessment devices—either the assessment batteries or the medical technologies—and only a few assessment reports on learning disabilities in youngsters today included such information. Finally, as is the case with the medical search for the etiology of learning disabilities, psychoneurological assessment practices seem to hold great potential but have not yet begun to assist in the identification process for most children with learning disabilities (Bigler, Lajiness-O'Neill, & Howes, 1998). However, in some areas of the United States, assessment of this nature is increasing. It remains to be seen if the promise of medical science in the area of assessment will one day be realized.

MEDICAL TREATMENTS FOR LEARNING PROBLEMS

The major influence of medical science in the field of learning disabilities currently is in the area of treatments, specifically, in the use of medically prescribed drugs to combat hyperactivity that results in academic problems. Children who are hyperactive and demonstrate attention problems are less likely to learn. Medical science has devised a number of drug therapies to alleviate this problem, with notable success.

The use of various drug therapies on children with learning disabilities has grown in recent years. Rosenburg (1988) indicated that 60% of all special education teachers had some level of involvement with students who received medication; today 90% of these teachers have such involvement. Clearly, teachers should be aware of the supporting role that they will play in these interventions.

Types of Drug Interventions

Although most teachers of the learning disabled have come into contact with frequently used medications such as methylphenidate (Ritalin) or atomoxetine (Strettera), numerous other drugs are used to control children's behavior problems. Certain common drug-based interventions are intended to "make the child available for learning" by decreasing attention-deficit disorders and hyperactive behaviors that prohibit learning. Other medications are intended to combat aggressive behaviors in children or prohibit psychotic symptoms. Not all drug interventions are intended for the same purpose, but they are all generally intended to manipulate and control problem behaviors in some form.

Among the various medications used for students with learning disabilities and/or ADHD, there are several different types of medications. Stimulants are the most frequently used, including such common drugs as Ritalin and Concerta. However, some students do not respond to stimulant medication, and consequently, other medications have been developed. Interest Box 2.6 presents some of the commonly used medications for students with learning disabilities and/or ADHD. Further, a number of Websites provide parents and teachers with further information on these medications (www.pediatrics.about.com, www.strettera.com, www.adrugrecall.com, www.rxlist.com, www.chadd.org).

Note that each of these drug interventions has well-documented side effects. Although not all children demonstrate these side effects, these negative effects provide a rationale for using this type of intervention only as a last resort. Clearly, other behavioral control options should be considered prior to initiating a drug-based intervention to control a child's behavior.

Research on Efficacy

Approximately 2.5 million children between the ages of 4 and 17 take various ADHD medications, and in many of those cases, ADHD and learning disabilities are codiagnosed. While many parents have expressed concern related to utilization of these medications to curb attention problems, research indicates that many of those fears are unfounded. For example, approximately 80% of students with ADHD respond positively to stimulant treatment (CHADD, 2006; Iannelli, 2006), and in the majority of cases, both attention and academic achievement of students using these medications increase. Further, while documenting some side effects, research has shown that in the majority of cases, those side effects, if they appear at all, are not long lasting for the stimulant medications.

With those overall results noted, there have been recent reports of highly negative side effects in a very limited number of cases. The FDA recently received reports of 25 cases of sudden death and 54 cardiovascular incidents in patients taking Adderall for ADHD (CHADD, 2006). Other medications, Strettera is one example, have been linked to suicide ideation and/or suicide. Clearly, given the potential negative impact of these extreme side effects, research will be ongoing on these questions. However, it is clear that the stimulants that have been around a bit longer, and thus have been the subject of research over a longer time period (e.g., Ritalin or Dexedrine), are reasonably safe and have significant positive benefits for many students (Iannelli, 2006).

■ ■ ■ ■ ■

INTEREST BOX 2.6

MEDICATIONS COMMONLY USED TO TREAT STUDENTS WITH LEARNING DISABILITIES OR ADHD

STIMULANTS (used for attention-deficit disorder and/or hyperactivity)

Drugs: Ritalin and/or Concerta (methylphenidate), Dexedrine (destroamphetamine), Adderall (amphetamine combined with dextroamphetamine)

Possible side effects: appetite suppression, insomnia, dysphoric reaction, growth delay, headaches, stomachaches, jitteriness, and social withdrawal

Note: Among the stimulants, Adderall in particular has been linked with some extreme side effects, including possible links with heart attacks, high blood pressure, and/or sudden death. The FDA announced in February of 2006 that studies were under way on this medication and possible links to these extreme side effects.

ANTIDEPRESSANTS (used for depression, acute school refusal, and attention disorders)

Drugs: Tofranil (imipramine), Wellbutrein (bupropion hydrochloride), Aventyl (nortriptyline)

Possible side effects: dose-related dry mouth, blurred vision, constipation, sedation, cardiac toxicity, seizures

NEUROINHIBITORS (used for attention disorders and behavioral problems)

Drugs: Strattera (atomoxetine)

Possible side effects: excessive tiredness, insomnia, increase in heart rate and blood pressure, sexual side effects, painful urination, suicide ideation

NEUROLEPTICS (used for treating overt psychosis, unmanageable destructive behavior, severe aggression, and Tourette's syndrome)

Drugs: Haldol (haloperidol), Mellaril (thioridazine)

Possible side effects: sedation, dystonic reactions

Note: This information is provided only for general knowledge, and prior to taking any medication, a complete description and list of side effects should be considered by one's doctor.

Teacher's Role

Although drug interventions are prescribed by psychiatrists or other physicians, the classroom teacher has a crucial role in the intervention plan. This role involves five tasks, including documentation of unsuccessful nondrug interventions and indication that the behavior problem is not manageable by teacher-initiated instructional procedures, monitoring of the intervention and the effects of the intervention, and continued attempts at nondrug strategies.

First, as a teacher of children who are learning disabled, part of your responsibilities will be to indicate the extent of the behavior problem in measurable terms. Use of the behavioral strategies described in Chapter 10 will facilitate documentation of the behavior problem. In your report to the child-study team, you should state the number of behavioral disorders, the nature and severity of these disorders, and the frequency of them.

Next, you will report on several interventions you have tried that failed to alleviate the behavior problem. You should also have attempted several other intervention options for management of behavior. Various education/treatment options are discussed later in this text, including self-monitoring (a cognitively based intervention) and behavioral reinforcement strategies. These strategies should be tried prior to discussions of drug intervention. When you discuss such interventions with the physician and the assessment team, you will be much more prepared to make meaningful contributions if you present a summary of the other interventions you have attempted. Such presentation indicates you have used the professional interventions that are at your disposal.

After you have attempted several interventions, you may need to request assistance from the child-study team. The team will review your information and may request a medical evaluation. A drug intervention may then be one of the options considered. Such a request for assistance should be in written form—a letter to the child-study team chairperson, with copies to the principal and the director of special education. Some school districts recommend that teachers make their judgment known in a brief note to the child-study team chairperson and that the chairperson handle communication with others. Interest Box 2.7 presents a sample letter to a chairperson of a child-study team that indicates the type of information needed in such a recommendation.

After the drug program is initiated, you will have to monitor both the intervention and the effects of the intervention on the behavior and academic achievement of the student. You will be instructed concerning the administration of the drug, and you may need to monitor the time for administration. In most states, teachers are not allowed to administer the drugs, so your role will be to send the child to the school nurse for administration of the drug during the school day. You should investigate the local legal guidelines for drug interventions in your area.

In monitoring the effects of the intervention, only the teacher has the constant contact at school to provide useful information to the physician. Consequently, detailed records should be kept to provide information relative to positive effects of the intervention in the classroom. Chapter 10 provides information on collection of behavioral data that should be helpful in monitoring the effects of the drug intervention. Because of the importance of daily data collection in this type of situation, you may wish to take elective courses in behavior management or behavioral assessment to augment your new skills in this regard.

Finally, you must be prepared to continue behavioral and metacognitive interventions throughout the drug intervention. Such continued nondrug intervention attempts are conducted for two reasons. First, it is possible that, at some future point, an alternative intervention may show enough success that the drug dosage may be reduced. In some cases, the drug intervention may be eliminated altogether. Second, numerous studies indicate that behavioral interventions may enhance the effectiveness of drug interventions. The two seem to work nicely together to help control behavioral outbursts. Interventions of this nature are discussed in Chapters 10 and 11.

With this level of involvement in drug interventions, you will certainly wish to explore how drug interventions are handled by teachers of children who are learning disabled

INTEREST BOX 2.7

LETTER RECOMMENDING EVALUATION FOR DRUG INTERVENTION

William Johns
Resource Teacher
Barton Elementary School
Barton, MA 00572

Dr. Eoral Baxter
School Psychological Services
Barton School District
Barton, MA 00583

Dear Dr. Baxter:

Recently, I spoke with Mr. Coats, our fifth-grade teacher, about the behavior of Jamie Walker. In both my class and Mr. Coats's, Jamie is frequently out-of-seat and running around the room. His attention span is very short, and he does not finish a great deal of his work because of his low level of on-task time. Both Mr. Coats and I have had problems with Jamie's behavior in class, and we would like to request an evaluation by a physician in order to identify any potential medical causes of these behavior problems.

Jamie Walker has been in special education classes for children who are learning disabled for the last two years. He transferred to us from an out-of-district placement this fall. His behavior has repeatedly been discussed, and both Mr. Coats and I have instituted behavioral intervention programs to try to combat the frequent out-of-seat behaviors, as well as a noted tendency to leave classwork unfinished. Mr. Coats compiled a daily baseline count of out-of-seat behaviors and intervened through a behavioral contract. This had no notable effect. Further, I implemented a self-monitoring of behavior project in an attempt to increase the completion rate for in-class worksheets. This also showed no positive results.

We will be happy to share these baseline and intervention data with you. However, as you can see, we have implemented several interventions and have been unable to assist Jamie in maintaining sustained attention to his schoolwork. With your permission, I would like to contact the parents concerning this recommendation for an evaluation. If this seems appropriate to you, let me know, and I will schedule an appointment.

Thank you for your time on this matter. Please contact me if you require any additional information.

Yours,

William Johns

William Johns
Resource Teacher

in your local school districts. During your various laboratory field placements prior to student teaching, you can collect the policy statements from local districts concerning the use of teachers in monitoring drug-intervention programs.

Summary of Drug Interventions

The treatment area is the one area in which medical science has contributed greatly to the field of learning disabilities. Although research and early theories of learning disabilities were drawn from medicine, medical science has failed to realize the promises made in the areas of etiology and assessment. However, the treatments that have been provided are very frequently used throughout the field, and almost every practitioner has come into contact with this medical contribution.

Research has clearly demonstrated that drug interventions are effective in reducing behavior problems that hamper learning. Also, there is some recent evidence that these interventions may improve academic output. However, numerous issues are involved in the application of drug programs in the public schools, particularly when other interventions have not been attempted first. As a teacher of children with learning disabilities, you will almost certainly have to participate in some type of drug intervention for some students. Therefore, it is important to understand local school district policy on each of the five tasks that teachers must fulfill in order to participate in the supporting role for students whose education intervention includes these drug treatments.

SUMMARY

Medical science provided the historical foundations of the field. This chapter elaborates on the historical foundations detailed in Chapter 1 and shows the major contributions of medical science in the overall areas of etiology, assessment, and treatment. The search for medical causes of learning disabilities has not been particularly fruitful to date, though research in genetics is showing considerable progress. Likewise, the assessment recommendations suggested by the medical paradigm have not been widely implemented. There is some movement toward increased use of terms such as *ADHD* in school-based diagnosis.

However, in the area of treatments, medical science has provided several major classes of drugs that assist in the behavioral management of some children who are classified as having learning disabilities. Today, most teachers of children who are learning disabled are not affected to any great degree by the medical contributions in etiological or assessment concerns. Still, most practitioners will be exposed to children who are benefiting from medical treatments. For that reason, it is important to understand the teacher's role in the management of a drug treatment plan.

The following points will help you in summarizing this chapter:

- Medical science is the foundation of the study of learning disabilities, and many early theories in the field came from the medical profession.
- Studies of brain-based learning are progressing and show promise of identifying particular areas of the brain associated with particular learning problems.

■ Assessment strategies that are medically based have been developed, but few practitioners utilize these strategies today.

■ Medical treatments related to control of certain behavioral problems have been the major contribution thus far of medical science to the field of learning disabilities.

■ As a teacher of students with learning disabilities, you may encounter nomenclature from various disciplines, including genetics and medicine, and you need some familiarity with this nomenclature.

■ As a teacher, you may find that you are involved in the decision to implement a drug-based treatment plan. Therefore, you need a firm grasp of the role of the educator in implementation of these treatment approaches.

QUESTIONS AND ACTIVITIES

1. Describe the three major sections of the brain and the functions associated with each.

2. Describe the lobes of the cerebrum and the functions associated with each.

3. Identify the new technologies used in assessment of mental activities, and describe the basic principle behind each.

4. Contact a local school district, and identify the neurologists in your area who work with the schools in identification of neurological problems.

5. Describe the role of the teacher in drug-based intervention strategies.

6. Describe the subtypes of ADHD.

7. Obtain a local school district's written policy on drug interventions and review it. What is the teacher's role as stipulated in that policy?

REFERENCES

American Psychiatric Association (1994). *Diagnostic and statistical manual of mental disorders* (4th ed.). Washington, DC: Author.

Bigler, E. D., Laniness-O'Neill, R., & Howes, N. (1998). Technology in the assessment of learning disability. *Journal of Learning Disabilities, 31,* 67–82.

Booth, J. R., & Burman, D. D. (2001). Development and disorders of neurocognitive systems for oral language and reading. *Learning Disability Quarterly, 24,* 205–215.

CHADD (2006). *National AD/HD advocacy group urges that science drive further research and action on AD/HD medications.* National organization of Children and Adults with Attention Deficit Disorders. Retrieved from www.CHADD.org.

Commission on Excellence in Special Education (2001). *Revitalizing special education for children and their families.* Available from www.ed.gov/inits/commissionsboards/whspecialeducation.

Decker, S. N., & DeFries, J. C. (1980). Cognitive abilities in families of reading disabled children. *Journal of Learning Disabilities, 13,* 517–522.

Decker, S. N., & DeFries, J. C. (1981). Cognitive ability profiles in families of reading disabled children. *Developmental Medicine and Child Neurology, 23,* 217–227.

Fawcett, A. J., Nicolson, R. I., & Maclagan, F. (2001). Cerebellor tests differentiate between groups of poor readers with and without IQ discrepancy. *Journal of Learning Disabilities, 34,* 119–135.

Galaburda, A. M. (2005). Neurology of learning disabilities: What will the future bring? The answer comes from the successes of the recent past. *Learning Disability Quarterly, 28*(2), 107–110.

Gross-Tsur, V., Shalev, R. S., Manor, O., & Amir, N. (1995). Developmental right-hemisphere syndrome: Clinical spectrum of the nonverbal learning disability. *Journal of Learning Disabilities, 28,* 80–86.

Hallgren, B. (1950). Specific dyslexia: A clinical and genetic study. *Acta Psychiatrica Neurologica, 65,* 1–287.

Hynd, G. W., & Cohen, M. (1983). *Dyslexia: Neuropsychological theory, research, and clinical differentiation.* New York: Grune & Stratton.

Iannelli, V. (2006). *ADHD treatment guidelines.* Retrieved from www.pediatrics.com.

Joseph, J., Nobel, K., & Eden, G. (2001). The neurobiological basis of reading. *Journal of Learning Disabilities, 34,* 566–579.

Leonard, C. M. (2001). Imaging brain structure in children: Differentiating language disability and reading disability. *Learning Disability Quarterly, 24,* 158–176.

McKinney, J. D., Montague, M., & Hocutt, A. M. (1993). *A synthesis of research literature on the assessment and identification of attention deficit disorders.* Coral Gables, FL: Miami Center for Synthesis of Research on Attention Deficit Disorders.

Molfese, D. L., Key, A. F., Kelly, S., Cunningham, N., Terrell, S., Ferguson, M., Molfese, V. J., & Bonebright, T. (2006). Below-average, average, and above-average readers engage different and similar brain regions while reading. *Journal of Learning Disabilities, 39*(4), 352–363.

National Joint Committee on Learning Disabilities (NJCLD) (2005). Responsiveness to intervention and learning disabilities: A report prepared by the National Joint Committee on Learning Disabilities. *Learning Disability Quarterly 28*(4), 249–260.

Needleman, H. L. (1980). Human lead exposure: Difficulties and strategies in the assessment of neuropsychological impact. In R. L. Singhal & J. A. Thomas (Eds.), *Lead toxicity.* Baltimore: Urban & Schwarzenberg.

Orton, S. (1937). *Reading, writing, and speech problems in children.* New York: Norton.

Plante, E., Ramage, A. E., & Magloire, J. (2006). Processing narratives for verbatim and gist information by adults with language learning disabilities: A functional neuroimaging study. *Learning Disabilities Research and Practice, 21*(1), 61–76.

Raskind, W. H. (2001). Current understanding of the genetic basis of reading and spelling disability. *Learning Disability Quarterly, 24,* 141–158.

Richards, T. L. (2001). Functional magnetic resonance imaging and spectroscopic imaging of the brain: Application of fMRI and fMRS to reading disabilities and education. *Learning Disability Quarterly, 24,* 189–204.

Robertson, J. (2000). Neuropsychological intervention in dyslexia: Two studies on British pupils. *Journal of Learning Disabilities, 33,* 137–148.

Rosenburg, M. S. (1988). Review of *Children on medication: Vol. II. Epilepsy, emotional disturbance, and adolescent disorders. Behavior Disorders, 13,* 150–151.

Rourke, B. P. (2005). Neuropsychology of learning disabilities: Past and present. *Learning Disability Quarterly, 28*(2), 111–114.

Rourke, B. P., Ahmad, S. A., Collins, D. W., Hayman-Abello, B. A., Hayman-Abello, S. E., & Warriner, E. M. (2002). Child-clinical/pediatric neuropsychology: Some recent advances. *Annual Review of Psychology, 53,* 309–339.

Rourke, B. P., van der Vlugt, H., & Rourke, S. B. (2002). *Practice of child-clinical neuropsychology: An introduction.* Lisse, The Netherlands: Swets & Zeitlinger.

Shaywitz, B. A., Shaywitz, S., Blachman, B., Pugh, K., Fullbright, R., & Skudlarski, P. (2003). Development of left occipito-temporal systems for skilled reading following a phonologically-based intervention in children. Paper presented at the Organization for Human Brain Mapping, New York.

Shaywitz, S. E., & Shaywitz, B. A. (2006). Reading disability and the brain. In *Educating exceptional children: 2005/2006.* Dubuque, IA: McGraw-Hill.

Sousa, D. A. (1995). *How the brain learns: A classroom teacher's guide.* Reston, VA: National Association of Secondary School Principals.

Sousa, D. A. (1999). *How the brain learns* (video). Thousand Oaks, CA: Corwin Press.

Sousa, D. A. (2001). *How the special needs brain learns.* Thousand Oaks, CA: Corwin Press.

Wadsworth, S. J., Olson, R. K., Pennington, B. F., & DeFries, J. C. (2000). Differential genetic etiology of reading disability as a function of IQ. *Journal of Learning Disabilities, 33,* 192–199.

Wood, F. B., & Grigorenko, E. L. (2001). Emerging issues in the genetics of dyslexia: A methodological preview. *Journal of Learning Disabilities, 34,* 503–511.

CHAPTER THREE

COGNITION AND LANGUAGE CHARACTERISTICS OF STUDENTS WITH LEARNING DISABILITIES

CHAPTER OUTLINE

PRAGMATICS: LANGUAGE IN CONTEXT
  Code Switching
  Thought Units and Complexity
  Instructional Implications

Functional Communication
Research on Functional Communication
SUMMARY

WHEN YOU COMPLETE THIS CHAPTER, YOU SHOULD BE ABLE TO:

1. Describe the average IQ for the population of students with learning disabilities.
2. Define *learning aptitude* in terms of educational time.
3. Describe working memory.
4. Describe three separate aspects of attention and the anticipated characteristics of children who are learning disabled in each area.
5. Discuss for each area the learning-style characteristics of students with learning disabilities.
6. Describe the relationships between attention-deficit hyperactivity disorder and learning disabilities.
7. Describe the semantic and syntactic deficits that students with learning disabilities display.
8. Define *pragmatics* and discuss the types of capabilities that this concept represents.
9. Discuss the general evolution of studies of language in children who are learning disabled.
10. Describe the referential communicative skills of children with learning disabilities.

KEYWORDS

intelligence
gifted learning disabled
time-on-task
focus of attention
distractibility
selective attention
incidental recall
reticular activating system
comorbidity
short-term memory
long-term memory
working memory

encoding
storage
retrieval
explicit memory
semantic memory
episodic memory
implicit memory
memory strategy
learning style
alphabetic principle
phonemes
graphemes

phonemic manipulation
semantics
syntax
pragmatics
code switching
thought units
complexity
functional communication
narrative discourse
story schema
referential communication

INTRODUCTION

As you recall from the history reviewed earlier, the field of learning disabilities is predicated on the assumption that students with disabilities learn differently from other students. This assumption has led to numerous studies that demonstrate differences between students who have learning disabilities and students who do not, on a wide variety of cognitive learning characteristics (Commission on Excellence in Special Education, 2001). A great deal of the early research focused on identifying the characteristics that differentiated children who were clinically referred for learning disabilities from other children, and this early research formed the foundation for the more recent research conducted on children identified in public school settings as having learning disabilities.

Figure 3.1 indicates the presumed relationship between the various cognitive characteristics and the cognitive processes of a student with learning disabilities. For example, a student's intelligence is presumed to affect that student's learning, as are the student's language, memory, attention capabilities, and cognitive style or mode of learning. Each of these characteristics is discussed here.

INTELLIGENCE

Anticipated Levels of Intelligence

The definition of learning disabilities stipulates that these children have average or above-average **intelligence** (i.e., an average IQ of 100). However, early research studies indicated that the anticipated IQ levels for populations of students with learning disabilities were in the range of 90 to 93 (Gajar, 1979). This led to a challenge of the use of IQ in assessment of students with learning disabilities (Commission, 2001; Council for Exceptional Children, 2002). This lowered IQ figure probably reflects several things. First, intelligence, as

Standard I.Q Test

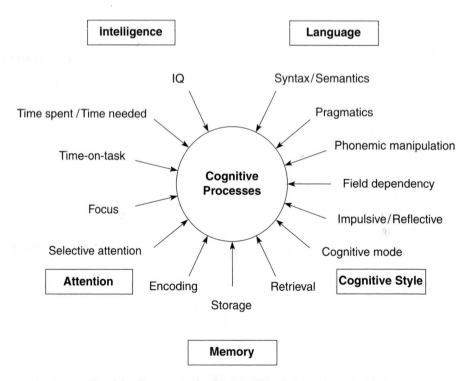

FIGURE 3.1   **Cognitive Processes of a Student Who Is Learning Disabled**

measured today in Western culture, is very dependent on verbal skill, and this dependence may deflate the average IQ levels reported for students with LD. Second, these figures are based on samples of students identified by the public schools as learning disabled, and there are numerous occasions when a child-study team will identify a child as disabled in order to receive services when the child does not meet the criteria established by the definition. Finally, these figures reflect the earlier years of serving students with disabilities and may not be accurate today.

There are some students with learning disabilities who display a level of intelligence in the gifted range. These students are known as **gifted learning disabled.** Some students with IQs above 130, or two standard deviations above the mean, also demonstrate an ability-achievement discrepancy. These students may be at or above grade level academically, but if there is a large discrepancy between their IQ and their achievement, they may be classified as learning disabled or gifted learning disabled. Research studies that examine the characteristics of this particular group of students are relatively rare. At present, no scholar can make data-based recommendations on appropriate educational programs for these students. Should they be handled just like any other child with a learning disability, or should they also receive enrichment activities and advanced placement in certain classes?

The Commission on Excellence in Special Education (2001) challenged the importance and use of IQ in the identification of students with learning disabilities, which resulted in an emphasis on response to intervention (RTI) in IDEA of 2004 (NJCLD, 2005). This new identification procedure places the future of this group of gifted students with learning disabilities in question. For example, even with a significant deficit between their IQ and achievement, one may assume that children with an IQ of 130 or more are likely to respond positively to an appropriately targeted intervention. Therefore, it could be possible that under the newly developed RTI eligibility procedures, this category of gifted learning disabled might actually cease to exist.

As a teacher in this field, you will probably be responsible for the education of gifted students with learning disabilities, at least for the next few years. You should remain abreast of the issues associated with gifted learning disabilities through reading appropriate journals in the field and other professional development activities. At this point, the existence of the category of the gifted learning disabled is an open question.

Meaning of Intelligence — *more than 100*

There is more than one definition of intelligence. The most prominent view has been that intelligence is a unified construct that, when measured on a standardized IQ test, represents a sum total of all the abilities of an individual. This is a relatively static view, in the sense that intelligence is viewed as residing exclusively within a child and that the whole of one's abilities can be summarized in a single IQ score. However, there are serious concerns about this definition (Mather & Roberts, 1994). Specifically, does an IQ figure represent an upper limit on the potential of a child to learn? What instructional information does an IQ score give to a teacher who is charged with the responsibility of teaching a particular student? These and other unanswered questions indicate the problems with the traditional view of intelligence. Still, this traditional view has dominated educational and psychological research, and every definition of learning disabilities that is based on a discrepancy between IQ and achievement presupposes that IQ is a unitary construct.

However, over the years various theorists have challenged that unified construct. As discussed in Chapter 1, Howard Gardner (1983) in his theory of multiple intelligences indicated that intelligence may be best represented by a series of relatively independent measures on various abilities and that a particular student may be quite strong in one area and somewhat weaker in another (Campbell, 1994; Campbell, Campbell, & Dee, 1996; Stanford, 2003). Although it is too early to determine what impact the multiple intelligences theory may have on the field, teachers of students with learning disabilities should be aware of the intelligences identified by Gardner and of the types of instructional activities that have been recommended based on this multiple intelligences theory.

As you recall, Gardner's suggestion was that human ability can best be understood in terms of eight rather independent types of abilities. These are the multiple intelligences he refers to:

interpersonal	the ability to relate well with others
intrapersonal	an ability to know/understand oneself
logico-mathematical	strengths in mathematical reasoning/logical thinking
naturalistic	strengths in categorization/naturalistic appreciation
bodily-kinesthetic	strong sense of one's body in space, efficient movement
linguistic	strengths in language—traditional measure of IQ
musical/rhythmic	abilities in rhythms/song/music
visual-spatial	strength in visual arts/visual interpretations

Based on this conceptualization of human intelligence as a set of relatively unrelated strengths/weaknesses, several researchers have suggested that instructional lessons be developed and formatted to address these various intelligences (Bender, 2002; 2005; Campbell, 1994; Sprenger, 2003; Tomlinson, 1999). For example, when planning a unit of instruction for a one- or two-week time period, teachers may wish to schedule a variety of activities that emphasize the strengths involved in more than one of the intelligences, thus giving students with learning disabilities—who presumably are strong in one or more intelligences but weak in others—the opportunity at some point during that lesson to demonstrate their particular strengths. Interest Box 3.1 presents a sample set of activities that may be appropriate for an inclusive fifth-grade class studying the solar system. Notice the types of activities that could be used to address the various intelligences.

In another alternative view of intelligence, John Carroll (1963) presented an alternative definition of aptitude. He defined aptitude as a function of time:

$$\text{APTITUDE} = f \text{ (time spent learning a task/time needed to learn)}$$

This definition of aptitude suggests that a teacher can increase a child's aptitude for a particular task by increasing the time spent in learning that task. By stating that aptitude was a function of time needed by a student to learn a particular task, in relation to time spent on learning, Carroll formulated a very optimistic view of aptitude. Although a teacher cannot control genetic makeup or cultural and environmental stimulation, the teacher does have control over learning time in the classroom. Thus, Carroll's historic paper forms the basis for studies of **time-on-task,** or the amount of time in which a student is engaged with

■ ■ ■ ■ ■ ▬▬▬▬▬▬▬▬▬▬▬▬▬▬▬▬▬▬▬▬▬▬▬▬▬▬▬▬▬

INTEREST BOX 3.1

**TEACHING TIPS: MULTIPLE INTELLIGENCE LESSON ACTIVITIES
FOR A UNIT ON THE SOLAR SYSTEM**

Over a 6- to 10-day unit of study on the solar system, you may undertake the following activities. On the first day, divide the class into teams, based on the relative strengths of each student in one intelligence. Then assign activities to the teams, based on their relative multiple intelligences strength. Some examples are listed below. On days 2, 3, and 4, give the teams time to work out their particular contributions, and on days 5, 6, 7, and 8, have teams present their work to the class. After a review on day 9, be ready for a unit quiz on day 10.

Here are activities that would be appropriate for various teams.

1. Interpersonal. Have students with interpersonal strengths develop a skit on how one body in the solar system may influence another (e.g., the gravity of the sun determining the flight of a comet). Have the skit presented to the class.
2. Intrapersonal. This intelligence may be hard to address in this unit. Emphasize this strength in the next unit of instruction with several activities.
3. Logico-mathematical. Use students with strengths in math to determine the relative decline of the sun's gravitational field on an inner versus an outer planet.
4. Naturalistic. Use students with this strength to describe the various types of objects within the solar system. Present these differences (e.g., the difference between a moon, an asteroid, and a comet) to the class.
5. Bodily-kinesthetic. Have these students develop an activity for the class using various class members to "walk" the orbits of planets, moons, and asteroids around the sun.
6. Linguistic. Have students with a strength in this area develop a descriptive poster about the definitions of objects in a solar system.
7. Musical/rhythmic. Have these students develop a song with lyrics that can assist the class members in remembering the objects in a solar system. Have them lead a lesson and teach the song to the class.
8. Visual-spatial. Have students with a strength in this area develop a graphic or chart depicting the solar system and write various facts about each object on the chart. Present this to the class, and keep it before the class for the entire unit.

the learning task. This historic formulation of aptitude as a function of time has received attention from theorists concerned with children who have learning disabilities (Kavale & Forness, 1986; Sousa, 2001) and created a new emphasis for research. In short, researchers began to study how children with LD used their time to attend to learning tasks.

ATTENTION

Like most concepts, attention is more complex than it seems. Many teachers frequently request that students "pay attention," yet very few teachers ever teach students what, exactly, that means. For example, is paying attention merely looking at the teacher? Does it consist of a quick response to the teacher? Is it looking out the window while listening intently to the teacher? Is it an active type of concentration on what the teacher is saying? As these questions demonstrate, there are numerous aspects to the concept of attention, and theorists have used different terms for these various aspects.

Time-on-Task

This aspect of attention is measured by a frequency count of, or a percentage of, time in which a student attends to a task. For example, the child who never seems to finish worksheets, even though he or she may be able to do the problems, may have a problem with time-on-task. Several other terms refer to the same general concept, including *engaged time* and *attention span.* Interest Box 3.2 presents an observational measurement system for assessing this measure of attention.

On-task time for students without disabilities ranges considerably, but many researchers indicate that these students are on-task around 60 to 85% of the time during instructional activities. In contrast, children with learning disabilities are on-task 30 to 60% of the time (Bender, 2002; McConnell, 1999).

Focus of Attention

The ability to focus one's attention on the most relevant stimuli is an essential component of learning. With so many stimuli in a typical classroom, if students cannot inhibit distracting stimuli, they will have difficulty in learning the task at hand. Teachers realize this need

■ ■ ■ ■ ■

INTEREST BOX 3.2
MEASUREMENT OF TIME-ON-TASK

In Bender's (1985) study, a fairly common observational procedure was used to assess time-on-task behavior. First, a record sheet with several columns was created. The columns indicated several categories of behavioral codes that capture all possible types of classroom behavior. On-task time is usually defined as eye contact with the task at hand. Although this definition includes some error—children can look at a task and be miles away mentally—the assumption is that the error works out to be roughly zero because children often stare blankly out the window while they listen to the teacher. In Bender's study, an observer coded the type of behavior occurring at the sound of a 10-second bell for the child with learning disabilities. Behavior for the matched child without such disabilities was coded at the sound of the next 10-second bell. Note that if a behavior occurs between bells, or when the observer is watching the other child, that behavior is ignored. Consequently, with this type of time-sampling procedure, frequency of only certain categories of behavior is tallied. Also, the behaviors should be coded on several different days in order to assure that daily fluctuations in behavior do not unduly bias the data. In the Bender study, three 20-minute observation periods on three separate days were used. At the end of the days, frequencies of behavior in each category were computed. The average frequencies for the group with learning disabilities was compared statistically with the average frequencies for the control group, and students with LD were less on-task than the comparison group.

to focus on the learning task and support students in this attempt by closing doors to busy hallways, pulling the shades when other students are on the playground, and, in some cases, providing relaxing music as a type of "white noise" background. Each of these common strategies indicates the importance teachers place on the **focus of attention.**

Unfortunately, the early research on the ability to focus attention among students with learning disabilities was inconsistent (Zentall, 1986). Most of this research has examined **distractibility** of such students, which is the opposite of the ability to focus attention. For example, many studies use teachers' ratings of the behavior of students with learning disabilities, and data collected in this fashion generally demonstrate that teachers rate students who have these disabilities as more distractible than students without disabilities (Bender & Wall, 1994).

However, several researchers have studied distractibility more directly, involving the use of laboratory learning tasks with intentional distractions built into the task or structured peripherally to the task. Rather than indicating that peripheral distracters impair the learning of children with disabilities, these laboratory tasks seem to suggest that such distracters facilitate learning (Zentall, 1986). Perhaps these distractions force the students to more actively focus their attention.

In addition, several teacher rating studies have indicated that students with learning disabilities do not demonstrate a higher level of reaction to distracting stimuli in the environment (Bender & Wall, 1994). This evidence clearly contradicts the earlier teacher ratings that indicated that teachers perceived those who were learning disabled to be more distractible than other students. Solid conclusions on the ability to focus attention among students with learning disabilities will have to await further research. Meanwhile, as a teacher, you may wish to continue to assist students to focus on the task by using some of the strategies mentioned here. Obviously, closing the classroom door is unlikely to impair a child's ability to focus on the task, and some research indicates that this type of strategy does facilitate higher levels of attention.

Selective Attention

Selective attention is the ability to identify the important aspects of a stimulus and disregard all of the other stimuli in the environment. Hagen (1967) developed a task to measure this aspect of attention; it focused on assessment of a student's ability to intentionally remember certain objects in relation to the number of objects remembered incidentally. Because of the importance of selective attention in the research on learning disabilities, one of the classic studies is reviewed here.

The early research by Hallahan, Gajar, Cohen, and Tarver (1978) on selective attention is a hallmark in research on this aspect of attention. These researchers used an adapted version of Hagen's (1967) task to measure central recall and incidental recall. Seven pictures of household items and line drawings of animals were paired on a poster, as presented in Figure 3.2.

Each stimulus card was presented for 12 seconds to children who were learning disabled and to others who were not. There were 18 different posters. Students were asked to attend only to the animals and to remember the order in which they were shown the animal pictures. The first 4 posters were used as practice trials and the last 14 as actual test items. The percentage of correct responses was used as the measure of central recall because the children were told, in effect, to center their attention on the animals. At the end of this task, the children were presented with seven paired boxes with the animals drawn in at the bottom and blank spaces at the top. Also, the students were given seven pictures of the household items to be matched to the animals and placed in the blanks. This was considered the measure of **incidental recall** because the children remembered these stimuli only incidentally. By subtracting the incidental recall score from the central recall score, the researchers obtained a measure of selective attention. Results showed that the students with learning disabilities were similar to the other group on incidental recall, but both central recall and selective attention scores for the group with learning disabilities were lower than for the other group. Hallahan and his co-workers stated that this selective attention deficit among children with learning disabilities supported Torgesen's conceptualization of these children as inactive learners.

More recent research on brain functioning has increased our understanding of how the brain selectively attends to various stimuli (Bender, 2002; Sprenger, 2003, 2002; Sousa, 2005, 2006; Wolfe & Nevills, 2004). This emerging brain research indicates that the selective attention process is fairly complex. In fact, at least three different neural networks are involved in selective attention (Sousa, 2006, p. 46). These include the following:

Alerting network—suppresses unimportant and/or background stimuli

Orienting network—prepares to process sensory input

Executive control—links the limbic system where memories first occur and directs neural processing in other areas of the brain

However, the ongoing research on how the brain functions has shown more than merely these three neural networks. For example, we now know much more concerning how the brain attends to stimuli from the various senses. For every sense other than the sense of smell, information is initially attended to and processed by the brain in the

FIGURE 3.2   Sample Item to Measure Selective Attention

same general fashion (Sprenger, 2003; Sousa, 2006). First, information enters through the senses, then goes through the brain stem and into a brain structure called the thalamus. This brain area sorts the information, sending visual information to the visual cortex, auditory information to the auditory cortex, and kinesthetic information to the cerebellum and the motor cortex. For information that seems to be a threat or seems to require immediate attention, a brain system called the reticular activating system releases chemical neurotransmitters that effectively focus attention immediately. Thus, this **reticular activating system** allows the brain to immediately attend to information that represents a threat to survival while also cataloging information that is not a threat for further brain processing (Sprenger, 2003).

Selective attention is a very important skill in classroom tasks. For example, when confronted with a blackboard full of information such as columns listing presidents, vice-presidents, and terms of office, a student is bombarded with information. The retrieval of the name of the vice-president in 1862 is a process of selective attention. The student must selectively seek the information required using a step-by-step process, ignoring all of the other information on the board. The student must ignore the column of presidents, find the column of dates, and scan down the dates until he or she finds the term of office that includes 1862, move to the vice-president list, and read the name. This is a highly selective process, which includes a degree of intentionality. This intentionality is also present when, as a student in a lecture hall, your mind wanders every few seconds from the lecture being presented. Perhaps the speaker says something that briefly triggers some unrelated thought about an earlier class or your students' behavior in class that day. As a mature learner, once you realize that your mind is wandering, you intentionally bring yourself back to the lecture hall and the topic at hand. The student who listens to the information the teacher is presenting instead of sounds in the hall is exercising the same selective attention capacity.

Attention-Deficit Hyperactivity Disorder

It would be impossible to discuss the attention problems of students with learning disabilities without addressing the **comorbidity** of learning disabilities and attention-deficit hyperactivity disorders (ADHD). As discussed in Chapter 2, attention-deficit hyperactivity disorders may coexist with a learning disability. Barkley (1990) indicated that as many as 26% of the students with ADHD may also manifest learning disabilities, and with the relationship between attention problems and learning disabilities relatively undefined, there will continue to be some confusion between ADHD and learning disabilities.

As McKinney, Montague, and Hocutt (1993) indicated, inattention is one defining characteristic of students with ADHD. However, other researchers have discussed the comorbidity (i.e., the coexistence) of learning disabilities and ADHD and have argued that these two groups of children may, in fact, be the same group (Bender & Wall, 1994). For example, during the 1970s and 1980s, a child was often considered learning disabled if a mainstream teacher indicated that the child had attention problems and if the child was a few grades behind in his or her reading skills. In those days, children with identified attention problems and reading deficiencies would have been placed in classes for students with learning disabilities. Stanford and Hynd (1994) directly compared three groups of students to address this comorbidity issue. The groups were made up of students with attention-deficit disorders with hyperactivity, students with attention-deficit disorders without hyperactivity, and students with learning disabilities. The behaviors of students with attention-deficit disorders without hyperactivity and the students with learning disabilities were shown to be very similar, according to the ratings of parents and teachers. However, there were some important differences in attention skills between these two groups. Certainly, more research will be forthcoming on this question of comorbidity of LD and ADHD, but you should anticipate numerous attention problems among your students with learning disabilities.

Summary of Research on Attention

The bulk of the evidence has demonstrated that students with learning disabilities are deficient in each aspect of attention behavior. These students are on-task less often than other children. In the majority of studies, children with disabilities are perceived as being more distractible. Finally, selective attention is lower among children who are learning disabled, and these children demonstrate a lag in the development of this important attention capability. Clearly, attention deficits among children with learning disabilities warrant further research attention, and further research is the only option that will clarify these important questions. As a teacher, you will want to follow the continuing research in each of these areas.

In addition to reading the ongoing research, there are several teaching tips that may facilitate attention skill, and thus learning, among the students in your charge who have learning disabilities. These are presented in Interest Box 3.3.

MEMORY AND CHILDREN WITH LEARNING DISABILITIES

Models of Memory

The importance of memory skills in academic learning cannot be overestimated (Liddell & Rasmussen, 2005). Research has linked memory deficits among children who are learning disabled with reading problems, language problems, difficulty in spelling, and other areas (Bender, 2002; Swanson, 1994). Finally, our own school experiences tell us that memory skills are used in many required tasks in the classroom.

Historically, memory has been differentiated into two levels: short-term memory and long-term memory (Swanson, 1994). **Short-term memory** represents storage of a limited amount of information (six to eight bits) for a limited amount of time (usually less than 15 seconds). **Long-term memory** has been defined as memory of a longer duration.

More recently, the term *working memory* has been used to describe a refinement and extension of short-term memory skills (Sprenger, 2002; Sousa, 2005, 2006; Swanson, 1994). **Working memory** represents the ability of a student to hold a small amount of information in short-term memory while working with that information and integrating it with other information. Swanson (1994) compared students with LD and students without on a number of short-term memory and working memory tasks and indicated that working memory was more influential in reading skill than short-term memory for both groups. In other words,

■ ■ ■ ■ ■ ▬▬▬▬▬▬▬▬▬▬▬▬▬▬▬▬▬

INTEREST BOX 3.3

TEACHING TIPS BASED ON ATTENTION RESEARCH

1. Offer numerous cues to attend to task during lecture and discussion. Cues such as "The next point . . . ," "Point number three . . . ," or "There are four specific examples of this I want you to have. First . . ." will cue students to attend to the points you make.
2. Visually monitor a child's eye contact with the assigned task at all times. You should always wander around the room when students are doing seatwork independently in order to scan visually and make certain that students stay on task.
3. Keep external distractions to a minimum. Draw shades if another class is on the playground outside your window. Consider using background music in your class to cover the routine classroom noise.
4. Question students on how they knew what aspect of a stimulus to attend to. Discuss the selective attention strategies in class.
5. Use special attention strategies. For example, use a colored marker to code the instructions on each worksheet for students who demonstrate attention problems.
6. Discuss the meaning of *paying attention* with your students. Show them the advantages of good attention skills in terms of finishing work more quickly and receiving more study time.
7. Teach children how to pay attention using self-monitoring (see Chapter 11).

short-term retention of isolated facts is less important than the skill of short-term retention in combination with the need to integrate that information with previous knowledge.

Memory has also been conceptualized as including three relatively distinct processes. **Encoding** refers to translating a sensory input into some representational form for storage. When a student picks one key word to help remember an important phrase, that is an encoding process. **Storage** refers to the durability of the memory, and **retrieval** refers to the process of recovering an encoded representation of a stimulus from memory (Torgesen, 1984).

Sousa (2006) presented a more recent model of memory processing that captures the multiple aspects of memory. This model represents our most recent understanding of how memory works in human beings and is presented in Figure 3.3. As indicated, information enters the brain from the environment through the senses (five arrows on left). This information immediately passes through the sensory register, represented as the side view of a venetian blind. If, based on past experience, the information seems important, the stimuli will pass through the sensory register. Alternatively, if the stimuli are deemed unimportant, they will be ignored and not stored in memory. Sousa (2006) postulated that all activities of the sensory register are unconscious, suggesting that many stimuli that are temporarily registered in the brain are eventually eliminated without any conscious thought.

If the stimuli pass through the sensory register, this will be noted for a brief period of time (usually 3 to 7 seconds) in short-term memory (Sousa, 2006). Short-term memory is represented by a clipboard and serves as merely a continuation of storage beyond the sensory register. In Sousa's model, short-term memory is an unconscious process.

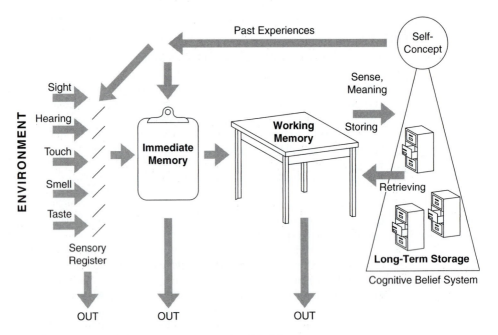

FIGURE 3.3   Sousa's Information-Processing Model

Source: From *How the Brain Learns,* 3rd ed., by D. A. Sousa, 2006, Thousand Oaks, CA: Corwin Press.
Reprinted by permission.

Working memory, in contrast, is a conscious process in which a person considers a stimulus (or new knowledge) in terms of attributing sense and meaning to it, based on previous knowledge (Sousa, 2006). For example, in the classroom in order for something to be learned (i.e., stored in long-term memory), the new knowledge must make sense to the student. This knowledge must be understandable in the terms and context the student has already mastered. Further, the new knowledge must have meaning. It must in some sense answer a question for the student or fill a gap in understanding that the student recognizes; the student must want to learn it. The worktable in the model represents the individual's conscious efforts to place the stimuli within the context of something that is already known.

In one sense, this working memory construct represents the constructivist perspective (see Chapter 1) in a nutshell, since all stimuli to be learned must be based on meaningful relationships that are constructed between the new knowledge and other knowledge that was learned previously (Sousa, 2006). If sense and meaning can be associated with the new knowledge, the likelihood of long-term memory storage is great. Otherwise, the new knowledge falls out of the system. Thus, the attachment of sense and meaning is the critical aspect of learning. In Sousa's model (2006), both encoding and retrieval would be functions of working memory. Instructional suggestions based on this emerging brain-based memory research deal predominantly with assisting a student to attach sense and meaning to new knowledge.

Note that long-term storage is represented in the model by filing cabinets (Sousa, 2006). This suggests a regulated system by which knowledge is associated with other relevant knowledge and is immediately available for retrieval. Also, long-term memory storage is part of the individual's cognitive system, self-concept, and past experiences and impacts future learning, as represented by the arrows from long-term storage to the sensory register and short-term memory.

Another conceptualization of memory involves memory of specific types of information, and these are referred to as explicit memory and implicit memory (Sprenger, 2003; Sousa, 2006). For example, **explicit memory** is memory of details, facts, and events (e.g., memory of one's name or locations of friends' homes). Explicit memory is the memory system teachers attempt to impact when helping students make connections between a known fact or principle and a new fact that has yet to be mastered. This memory system involves processing in the hippocampus and cerebrum (Sousa, 2006). Explicit memory may be further divided into two types. First, **semantic memory** involves general factual memory and memory connections (e.g., knowing where the state of Oregon is on the map or how to read a clock). Because semantic memory is tied to connections between facts, strategies such as mnemonic instruction function well to enhance semantic memory. Second, **episodic memory** involves memory that may be based on location and circumstance. For example, when asked to recall what you did at 1:00 P.M. yesterday, you first try to recall where you were and then what additional actions you engaged in (Sprenger, 2003).

Implicit memory describes memory for nonfactual information (e.g., how to hit a baseball) and is processed in various areas of the brain, depending upon the type of memory. That is, the implicit memory of how to hit a baseball may be processed by the motor cortex and cerebellum, whereas other types of implicit memory may be processed elsewhere. Researchers today further catagorize implicit memory into various areas, as noted below (Sousa, 2005).

Procedural memory—involves learning of motor skills (e.g., hitting a ball or driving a car)

Perceptual register memory—involves the structure and form of words and objects that may be prompted by prior experience; also involves our ability to complete fragments of words

Associative learning—involves memories that result from Pavlovian conditioning (e.g., when a conditioned stimulus and an unconditioned stimulus are paired together)

Nonassociative learning—involves the brain's tendency to briefly remember and then "screen out" information (e.g., noises of the city)

Research on Memory in Students with Learning Disabilities

Several researchers have summarized the relevant research and suggested that children with learning disabilities apparently have no distinctive difficulty with long-term memory (Cutting, Koth, Mahone, & Denckla, 2005; Swanson, 1994; Sousa, 2001). This is shown by a number of research studies that suggest that manipulation of motivation, selective attention, or coding ability for memory will improve the memory of children with learning disabilities to levels commensurate with children who do not have such disabilities (Swanson, 1994).

Rather, the memory problems among children with learning disabilities are twofold. They seem to be based on an inability in working memory to code information for memory storage and decreased motivation for such intentional mental efforts (O'Shaughnessy & Swanson, 1998). For example, several research studies have demonstrated that when supplied with a memory strategy, children who are learning disabled can perform memory tasks as well as children who are not (Swanson, 1999). This research suggests that memory-encoding strategies are differentially effective for students with learning disabilities. In other words, students without learning problems use some method of encoding the information without being told to, but students who are learning disabled apparently do not. Consequently, when a memory strategy is presented to both groups, the memory score of the group with disabilities increases, and the score of the control group remains constant. Clearly, one teaching recommendation for children with learning disabilities is the provision of strategies to assist them in performing tasks that involve the use of memory.

This body of research on memory is another factor in the development of the meta-cognitive perspective on learning disabilities, as discussed in Chapter 1. However, the metacognitive perspective is essentially an optimistic perspective because it suggests that provision of memory strategies enhances the child's memory.

Torgesen's (1984) work in the area of memory skills among children with learning disabilities is an excellent example of this optimistic view. In one of the early studies, Torgesen and colleagues (1979) demonstrated that rote memory differences between children who are learning disabled and those who are not could be eliminated if both groups were given a common **memory strategy.** Each group was comprised of 19 students. Two tasks were performed. In the first, 24 pictures of common objects were used. Every object belonged to one of six categories. After a practice trial, the children were shown the stimulus cards, asked to name each picture, and told to study the cards in any manner they chose for later recall. The study period lasted 3 minutes. The children with learning disabilities performed less adequately than the other children, thus demonstrating a memory deficit. However, the procedure was repeated again. This time, the students were told to sort the cards into groups that "go together in some way." A measure of immediate recall was then taken. Results demonstrated that those with learning disabilities recalled the same number of cards as the others when a memory strategy such as sorting the cards was provided. This study and others in the same series (Torgesen, 1984) have supported the metacognitive perspective on learning disabilities, as well as providing an optimistic prognosis for the learning disabled. These studies have provided a research basis for the use of memory strategies and other organizing strategies among students with learning disabilities. A provision of memory strategies seems to result in adequate memory performance of most children who are learning disabled.

Scruggs, Mastropieri, Sullivan, and Hesser (1993) demonstrated that a pegword or keyword type of strategy facilitated memory recall for factual information that students with learning disabilities obtained from expository text. A *keyword* or *pegword* is a word that sounds like the word or factual material to be mastered. For example, the word *agua* means "water" in Spanish. To master that word, a student may use the pegword *aqua* (which

agua = "water"

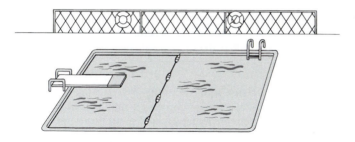

aqua = "blue water"

FIGURE 3.4   Mnemonic Keyword Method Representation of
agua = **"water"**

sounds like the word to be mastered) and imagine a picture of a blue-colored swimming pool, as depicted in Figure 3.4.

In a series of studies, Scruggs and associates have shown this to be an effective technique. The students who performed best on a recall test after reading a passage about dinosaurs was the group who received a pegword coupled with a picture to represent in some fashion the content of the factual information. This series of studies, like Torgesen's earlier work on memory, indicates that working memory of students with learning disabilities can be significantly enhanced by appropriate teaching techniques.

Instructional Considerations

With this model of memory in mind, there are a number of instructional considerations that will assist you in teaching. For example, emerging brain-based learning research has documented a primacy/recency effect in learning (Sousa, 2006). This effect suggests that in general children remember best the information that was taught first in a lesson (i.e., the primacy effect), next best what was taught last in a lesson (i.e., the most recent information or recency effect), and less well what was taught in the middle of a lesson. Equipped with this knowledge, the successful teacher will intentionally structure lessons to maximize the use of time to enhance memory. New information that is most critical will be taught first through discussion, visual display, and a variety of techniques. During "downtime" in the middle of the lesson, students should be encouraged to discuss the new information with each other—an approach that subtly encourages understanding. Finally, the new information should be taught directly a second time toward the end of the lesson to take advantage of the second learning opportunity (i.e., the recency effect). Brain-based research on memory offers a number of other instructional suggestions; several of these are presented in Interest Box 3.4.

INTEREST BOX 3.4
TEACHING TIPS BASED ON MEMORY RESEARCH

Brain-based learning research offers a number of specific guidelines concerning optimizing learning in the classroom (Sousa, 2006). Teachers should endeavor to build these techniques into their classroom.

I. Use Closure to Enhance Sense and Meaning
   A. Closure describes a working memory process a child uses to summarize what has been learned. Students should use closure frequently in their efforts to attach sense and meaning to the new learning.
   B. To initiate closure, the teacher gives directions that focus students on the new learning, such as "I'm going to give you about two minutes to think of the four facts about planets that we learned today; then we'll discuss them briefly." Note that this gives students specific instructions and also holds them accountable for their learning by mentioning a discussion at the end.
   C. Sousa (2005) noted that closure is different from review. In closure students do the work for themselves, whereas in review the teacher may lead the discussion.
   D. The teacher can use closure at various times in a single lesson. Closure may occur during the lesson when the teacher moves from one concept to the next. The teacher may say to the students, "Please reflect on the first three guidelines before we continue." Closure may also take place at the end of the lesson in order to connect all of the concepts into a meaningful whole.

II. Use the Primacy/Recency Effect
   A. The teacher should always endeavor to teach the new materials first (after getting the students' focus).
   B. The teacher should use the downtime portion of the lesson by structuring students' practice of the new concepts (Sousa, 2006).
   C. The teacher should again cover new material toward the end of the lesson. During that period each learner should attach sense and meaning to the new learning.
   D. Sousa (2005) suggests that the optimum lesson time is about 20 minutes. In that timeframe a student will experience a primacy effect for the first 10 to 12 minutes, downtime for the next 2 to 3 minutes, and a recency effect for the remaining 3 to 5 minutes. When teaching in a longer class period, the teacher may wish to divide a 40-minute period into two 20-minute periods.

III. Use Rehearsal to Enhance Retention
   A. Simple repetition works for short factual items (telephone numbers, dates, etc.).
   B. Cumulative repetition involves rehearsal of the first few lines (of a song or poem, etc.) and then expands to the next lines (Sousa, 2005). This is an effective technique for highly structured material.
   C. Elaborative rehearsal involves developing specific facts within the material to be learned. This may include paraphrasing, predicting, questioning, and summarizing (Sousa, 2005). Note the similarity between this type of rehearsal and the reciprocal teaching technique described in Chapter 11.
   D. Teachers should remind students of these specific strategies when appropriate and then provide time for students to reflect on a new concept.

LEARNING STYLE

Almost every educator recognizes that students learn in different ways, and over the last 20 years, the term **learning style** has been used to describe students' preferred ways of mastering content material (Sousa, 2006; Sprenger, 2003). Many in the field of learning disabilities believe that knowing the learning style preference of students with learning disabilities allows the teacher to better plan students' educational programs. However, there is considerable disagreement on what learning styles may exist, as well as over the importance of learning styles in the overall education of students with disabilities. Further, descriptions of learning style have involved a wide variety of ideas, including color preferences of students (i.e., the suggestion that certain colors may be more soothing and result in better retention; Sprenger, 2003), students' preference of the color of the lighting in the room, the use of relaxing music in the class, or the senses used by various children in the learning process. Moreover, a number of terms have been used in the past to refer to various learning styles, which are no longer utilized in the field. While a broad discussion of various other approaches to learning styles is not possible here, as a new teacher in the field you should be aware of these terms as well as the more recent approaches to learning styles. Some of the earlier terminology that was used to describe learning styles is presented in Interest Box 3.5, and you may hear co-workers utilize these terms in reference to students with learning disabilities.

In recent years, other conceptualizations of learning style have emerged that are more closely linked with research on brain processing. Perhaps the most useful learning-styles approach for students with learning disabilities is consideration of their preferred learning pathways, as described by Sprenger (2003). Sprenger presented a simple, yet direct, approach to learning style by delineating specific learning preferences based on various sensory systems. For example, some students seem to learn better when they utilize the visual memory preference. For those students, either print-oriented learning (i.e., reading for comprehension, which of course schools emphasize a great deal) or graph/chart-oriented learning (which schools are beginning to emphasize more—e.g., the use of graphic organizers) seems to work best to facilitate learning. Some research has suggested that students with learning disabilities may prefer graph/chart-based learning rather than print-only learning (Boon, Ayers, & Spencer, in press), and much of the recent research on the use of graphic organizers for students with learning disabilities supports this view of their learning style.

Another learning-style preference noted by Sprenger (2003) is the auditory/verbal memory preference. This involves both hearing and speaking about a topic when learning factual material and/or concepts. Students with this learning style seem to master material best when they are presented with the opportunity not only of hearing the material but also of talking about it with other students in a nonthreatening manner. The vocabulary of these students is typically quite varied, and they are also attuned to the pitch, tone, and rhythm of the spoken word (Sprenger, 2003). However, students with this learning style may be overly sensitive to various sounds, and thus common noises in the classroom may be quite distracting.

A third learning style identified by Sprenger (2003) is the kinesthetic/tactile memory preference. Students with this preferred mode of learning like to have their content

■ ■ ■ ■ ■

INTEREST BOX 3.5

HISTORIC CONCEPTUALIZATIONS OF LEARNING STYLE

1. **Field independence/field dependence**

   Definition: The ability to organize information based on dependence or independence from the perceptual field (or perceptual environment) of the stimuli

   Research: Some early research indicated that students with learning disabilities tended to be more field dependent, but few researchers have recently investigated this learning style among students with learning disabilities.

2. **Impulsive/reflective**

   Definition: The tendency to react instantly (or perhaps overreact) to stimuli in one's environment, with consideration of the results of one's reaction

   Research: Early research suggested that students with learning disabilities tended to be more impulsive than reflective and that this could account for ill-timed interactions at school. However, little research has been done recently on this variable.

3. **Cognitive mode**

   Definition: The tendency to encode information using a particular type of thinking (e.g., when you try to remember directions to a new location, do you mentally list all the turns, which would indicate auditory thinking, or do you mentally draw a map, indicating spatial thinking?)

   Research: Early research on this variable was somewhat simplistic and tried to place students with learning disabilities in one "cognitive mode" or another. However, unlike the previous learning styles, research is still ongoing in this area.

presented in terms of movement. Sprenger (2003, p. 38) refers to this as "whole body learning." Because some degree of hyperactivity has historically been associated with students with learning disabilities, many teachers believe that students with learning disabilities may learn best when taught concepts that can be represented by movement. For example, in teaching addition of positive and negative numbers, many teachers utilize a number line taped to the students' desks. For kinesthetic/tactile learners with learning disabilities, a large number line taped on the floor would work better, since it would allow the students to move along the number line and actually "act out" the addition of +3 and −4. Other students with this learning-style preference function best when they are allowed to represent their content in pictures or drawing.

   Given the increase in brain research, a number of researchers have delineated instructional suggestions based on learning-style preferences (Sprenger, 2003; Sousa, 2006), and these are presented in Interest Box 3.6. However, while there is considerable ongoing study of learning styles, teachers must be aware that the research on various learning styles is not as solid as might be wished. In fact, many suggest that consideration of learning-style preferences among students with learning disabilities is premature, based on the frequent changes in terms in this area. Clearly, more research is needed in this area on students with learning disabilities; ongoing research on brain functioning will help clarify this topic in the future.

STUDY OF LANGUAGE

One cognitive characteristic that requires extended review for prospective teachers of the learning disabled is the area of language (Sousa, 2006). Although not all children with learning disabilities demonstrate deficits in language, language delay and inappropriate use of language have been concerns in the field of learning disabilities historically, and many such students do have some problems in this area (Silliman & Scott, 2006).

As you may recall from Chapter 1, one of the early groups concerned with learning disabilities in children was a group of professionals interested in the development of language. This group, led by Kirk and Osgood, focused on language delay as a critical cause for academic problems in children with learning disabilities. This focus heightened

---

INTEREST BOX 3.6

TEACHING TIPS BASED ON LEARNING-STYLE RESEARCH

Although research on learning style is not conclusive, several theorists have suggested teaching strategies based on this research (Sousa, 2006; Sprenger, 2003). The following is an adapted synthesis of these suggestions:

1. In an attempt to respect the learning potential of both halves of the brain, all teachers should employ both visual and linguistic examples of problems in initial instruction, rather than rely merely on verbal explanations.
2. Accommodate the diagnosed learning styles of all learners in reading exercises. Schedule some short-duration assignments for those impulsive children who cannot persist in a long task.
3. Use a variety of social and instructional groupings for reading and other assignments, and base these to a degree on the preferences of the child.
4. Utilize holistic reading strategies that involve language-experience approaches and tactile-kinesthetic resources with "right-hemisphere-dominant" children.
5. Structure some instructional activities for each learning style in an effort to broaden and strengthen both weak and strong learning-style preferences.
6. Learn to ignore impulsive answers while encouraging the child to reflect on other possible solutions and select another answer.
7. Informally diagnose learning-style preferences repeatedly in an effort to remain cogizant of the instructional needs of the child.
8. Recognize that you will tend to teach according to your own learning style, so be sure to include techniques aimed at other learning styles also.
9. Use movement to represent content whenever possible.
10. Have students in pairs explain difficult concepts to each other.

the importance of language within the field, and some evidence has tended to support this emphasis. For example, Sousa (2001) pointed out that letter reversal problems may stem from the fact that some letters sound alike when a child's brain interprets the letters, even if the child is not saying the letters out loud. This may play a part in some reading disabilities. Others have suggested that various problems in interpretation of language may be the foundational basis for most learning disabilities (Abrahamsen & Sprouse, 1995; Mather & Roberts, 1994; Silliman & Scott, 2006; Ward-Lonergan, Liles, & Anderson, 1999). Clearly, language is one characteristic that has received and will continue to receive research attention.

Initially, several definitions of various terms used in the study of language may be in order. First, the smallest unit of sound that carries meaning is defined as a *phoneme* (Bender & Larkin, 2003; National Reading Panel, 2001). Note that phonemes do not refer to printed letters, but rather speech sounds that may or may not be associated with particular letters. For example, the word c / a / t has three phonemes in it, whereas the word c / o / m / e likewise has three phonemes. Further, the c in the word c / a / t will change the word from at to cat and therefore changes the meaning of the word. Likewise, the s used to form plurals in the English language may be considered a phoneme. When combined, all the languages of the world utilize approximately 90 phonemes, though only 44 phonemes are used in the English language (Sousa, 2001). Different researchers identify different numbers of phonemes in the English language; for example, the National Reading Panel (2001) stated that there are 41 phonemes.

Language Literacy and Reading Disabilities

The recent emphasis on phonemic and phonological awareness among students with learning disabilities has resulted in a variety of important research efforts, as well as a growing understanding of the importance of early literacy in developing reading skills (Bos, Mather, Silver-Pacuilla, & Nar, 2000; Kame'enui, Carnine, Dixon, Simmons, & Coyne, 2002; Silliman & Scott, 2006; Wolfe & Nevills, 2004). Early literacy may be thought of as the relationship between language and early reading skills, and research has demonstrated even more of a connection between the language to which a child is exposed and his or her later reading skill than was originally thought, particularly among young children with some degree of language delay (Silliman & Scott, 2006). First, we now understand much more concretely how the brain processes language and how that processing relates to reading (Sousa, 2006; Wolfe & Nevills, 2004). In fact, we now know that a student's reading ability utilizes the same brain areas as his or her spoken language (Shaywitz & Shaywitz, 2006). Further, if students do not develop competence in phonemic manipulation skills early during the process of learning spoken language, it is quite likely that they will demonstrate reading deficits, which are likely to result in a diagnosis of learning disability by grade 3 or 4. This developing knowledge has led to various assessment and instructional techniques to assist students in developing these phoneme manipulation skills, and research has demonstrated that students with learning disabilities benefit from such instruction (Kame'enui et al., 2002).

However, other insights have stemmed from this work also. First, we have learned how effective readers read. While context clues are important for most readers, almost all

readers recognize words primarily by decoding the letters in the words, based on the sound/
symbol (i.e., sound to letter) relationship (Chard & Osborn, 1999). Further, for students
who never learned to detect differences in phonemes, reading will be a nearly impossible
challenge. Next, we have learned the importance of the **alphabetic principle,** the principle
that states that there is a predictable relationship between **phonemes**—the sounds of spoken language—and **graphemes**—the letters and spellings used to represent those sounds.
In early literacy, generally prior to the beginning of formal reading training, most young
children develop a basic understanding of the alphabetic principle. For those who do not,
the initial training on letter recognition may be somewhat delayed, and this can result in a
learning disability. For this reason, the study of early language and language development
of young students has increased in importance during the last decade.

Phonemic Problems

Within the last decade, a great deal of research has demonstrated that students with learning
disabilities have difficulties in detecting and manipulating phonemes (Bender & Larkin,
2003; National Reading Panel, 2001). In some ways, this line of research may ultimately
prove to be the driving force behind research on learning disabilities, because researchers
have suggested that difficulties in phoneme awareness and phoneme manipulation skills
may be the foundational cause of almost all subsequent learning disabilities (Bender &
Larkin, 2003; Chard & Dickson, 1999; Kame'enui, Carnine, Dixon, Simmons, & Coyne,
2002; Lyon & Moats, 1997). Research has shown that many children with reading disabilities do demonstrate significant deficits in their ability to detect and manipulate phonemes
(National Reading Panel, 2001; Sousa, 2005). Clearly, if a child with a learning disability
cannot detect differences in speech sounds, and manipulate these differences in sounds, that
child will experience a significant deficit when trying to detect different sounds that are represented by different letters. Difficulty in such letter interpretation can result in significant
subsequent reading disabilities.

Researchers in learning disabilities have used the terms *phonemic awareness* or **phonemic manipulation** to represent this ability to detect and manipulate discrete speech
sounds, independent of manipulation of letters. Although different researchers identify
slightly different types of phonemic manipulation skills, Bender and Larkin (2003) specified 10 skills that serve as the basis for phonemic manipulation:

1. Detecting rhyming sounds
2. Recognizing the same initial sound in words
3. Isolating initial sounds
4. Categorizing onsets and rimes (An onset is the first sound in a word, and a rime is the
   rhyming sound that forms the end of the syllable.)
5. Isolating middle/ending sounds
6. Blending sounds into words
7. Segmenting or dividing sounds within words
8. Phoneme addition
9. Phoneme deletion
10. Phoneme substitution

Many research efforts have investigated phonemic problems as the primary basis for learning disabilities. The research on phonemic instruction has been summarized by Kame'enui and others (2002). There is a strong emphasis on the converging consensus that phoneme-based instruction is an essential skill in reading and a major problem for many students with learning disabilities.

Based on this growing consensus, researchers have offered various instructional strategies to strengthen phonemic skills (Bos, Mather, Silver-Pacuilla, & Narr, 2000; Chard & Dickson, 1999; Chard & Osborn, 1999; National Reading Panel, 2001). In order to provide some understanding of what phonemic instruction for students with learning disabilities entails, Interest Box 3.7 presents several samples of these learning activities.

Syntax and Semantics

Semantics refers to the knowledge and comprehension of words. Semantic skills may be measured by various receptive vocabulary tests. However, semantics is a broader concept than merely words in the sentence, as can be seen from the simple example in Figure 3.5. Compare the sentences below:

> I went home and died after the party.
> Her father died last week.

Obviously, the meaning of the word *died* changed to reflect the context. As this example illustrates, it is often difficult to entirely separate semantics from the next level of language—**syntax**. Syntax refers to the formal relationships between words in phrases or sentences. Examples of such relationships are the subject/verb relationship and the relationship between the verb and the direct object.

Wiig was one of the early researchers to study syntax and semantics (Wiig, Lapointe, & Semel, 1977). This research consistently demonstrated deficits in various semantic and syntactic abilities among children with learning disabilities. For example, these children demonstrate deficits in the ability to apply morphological rules (formation of plurals, verb tenses, and possessives are some examples). Also, comprehension and expression of syntactic structures have been identified as a deficit area among these children. These syntactic structures include relationships between words in sentences and phrases. Understanding who a pronoun applies to and what function is served by a direct object and an indirect object are examples of this syntactic skill. These deficits are apparent both in the child's understanding of the language of others and in his or her own production of spoken language. Finally, at least one of these studies demonstrated that oral language production did not automatically improve with age for students with learning disabilities as it does for other students (Wiig et al., 1977). This may suggest a critical period in which language intervention must take place if such intervention is to be effective.

Recent research has demonstrated that receptive language of particular types of information may be a problem for students with learning disabilities. Abrahamsen and Sprouse (1995) investigated the ability of students with learning disabilities to understand fables that were read to them and to select the correct moral for the fable. Based on the early research, which suggests that average students begin to understand figurative language (i.e.,

■ ■ ■ ■ ■ ■

INTEREST BOX 3.7

TEACHING TIPS: PHONEMIC MANIPULATION TEACHING ACTIVITIES

A Tactic for Detecting Rhyming Sounds.   Pair students up. When one says a word, his or her partner is required to say a rhyming word. Then the second student picks a word, and the first partner must say a rhyming word.

A Tactic for Recognizing the Same Initial Sound in Words.   Divide the class into teams, with each team including the children who sit in one row of desks. After you read a sentence, call on students on one team to give the initial sound in each word sequentially. For example, after reading the sentence, "The ball rolled under the large truck on the highway," the first student would be expected to give the initial sound in the word *The* or t / h / consonant blend. The child in the second seat would need to give the initial sound in the word *ball,* and so on. For each initial sound given correctly, the team earns one point. Next, give team 2 (or the students in the next row) another sentence. Depending on the grade level, you may wish to write the sentence on the board to help students with poor memory skills.

A Tactic for Isolating Initial Sounds.   Students should be required to isolate phonemic sounds, particularly at the beginning of syllables and words. For example, stress letter sounds in simple reading passages by asking questions about phoneme sounds:

"What is the first sound in b / a / l / l?"
"Can someone give me another word with the same first sound?"

A Tactic for Teaching Phoneme Substitution.   Identify two teams in the class, and have each number its members. Using a list of words, call out a word, and suggest a substitute for the initial consonant sound. Then have the first child on team 1 "Put the word together and say the whole word." The team gets two points if that student can put the word together correctly. If he or she cannot, the other team members can help. If the team gets the word correct, the team is awarded one point. Call out the next word and substitute a consonant sound for the first student on team 2; then return to team 1 for the next word.

metaphors, similes, idioms, and proverbs) in about the fourth or fifth grade, these researchers presented fables to two groups of students, 14 average learners and 14 students with learning disabilities. The students with learning disabilities were less capable of selecting the correct moral for the fable when four selections were presented, and they were also less capable of explaining their choices. Thus, ambiguity and subtle meanings seem to elude children with learning disabilities.

Perhaps a classroom example is in order. Many teachers issue multiple directions to students in the inclusive class, particularly when it is time to change subjects. However, the students in the class who are learning disabled may have some difficulty in understanding

FIGURE 3.5   Semantics in Context

the teacher's meaning. Imagine a teacher who says something like the following: "OK, that's it for spelling today, so you can put your books away. Get out your history homework to pass up. Get your history books and notebooks and put them on your desk."

Note that four separate commands are included in this brief set of instructions. The child must do something with spelling books, history homework, history books, and history notebooks. The child with learning disabilities may very well end up with the history homework sitting on the desk along with the history book and history notebook, when the teacher wanted the homework passed up to the front of the row. This child may also be inclined to misread the referent for the pronoun *them* in the last sentence, thinking that that pronoun also applied to the history homework. Misreading instructions such as this is a frequently mentioned problem whenever teachers discuss students with learning disabilities, and this problem is related to the inefficient use of language.

Most of the studies in this line of research were group comparisons that identified a group that had disabilities and a group that did not and then compared them on the variable of interest. Although such studies are useful in the early phase of development in a particular research area, they should lead to several other types of research. It is the responsibility of the researchers in any given area to show why a particular research area is important by demonstrating relationships between variables in the area and academic variables. Some indicators of semantics and syntax are related to school achievement, but research in these areas of language has failed to establish a case that these linguistic deficits represent a major cause of failure in school for children with learning disabilities (Feagans, 1983). Also, those variables that do relate to achievement tend to be variables that represent complex symbolic operations (understanding sentences, phrases, and morphological rules) as opposed to merely decoding words and speaking correctly. As a result, research emphasis shifted to studies of language beyond the study of isolated words and sentences in the 1980s and 1990s.

PRAGMATICS: LANGUAGE IN CONTEXT

Pragmatics, or the use of language in social contexts, is the final, most advanced level of spoken language. This aspect of language encompasses the social and cultural roles of the participants in the conversation. Theorists who study pragmatic language emphasize the ecologically based study of language in real communication situations, rather than scores on a test that may not indicate true communicative skill. Researchers in this area tend to measure the actual utterances a child uses when he or she communicates with other children and adults. Consequently, while studies of semantics and syntax tend to use test scores as variables, studies of pragmatics tend to be based on contrived situations in which students with disabilities have to communicate in some fashion.

Studies of language in the social context of children with learning disabilities were undertaken in the 1980s and 1990s (Feagans, 1983; Roth, Spekman, & Fye, 1995; Ward-Lonergan, Liles, & Anderson, 1999). Pragmatic language includes the ability to use language in spoken or written form, but there are several other skills included also. A definition of pragmatic language must include an element of social awareness, ability in conversational skills, awareness of nonverbal cues that may affect the conversation, as well as other intangibles not revealed in simple studies of word knowledge and syntax (Boucher, 1984, 1986; Feagans, 1983; Roth et al., 1995). Research in this area has consistently demonstrated that children with learning disabilities are deficient in their communicative abilities and in most other measures of pragmatic language (Bender & Golden, 1988; Boucher, 1984, 1986; Feagans, 1983).

Code Switching

One important aspect of pragmatic language is the ability to adjust one's language to the speaker in order to enhance communication. For example, a person generally uses a more simplistic language with a young child than with an older person. This language adaptation is referred to as **code switching.** Such adaptations may be made in a number of ways, including using more simple sentences or using fewer modifiers in each complete thought.

Early research suggested that children who are learning disabled do not switch codes as frequently as children who are not disabled (Boucher, 1984; Bryan, Donahue, & Pearl, 1981). In this research, asking questions, responding to inadequate messages, and persuasion were noted as difficult skills for children with learning disabilities to master (Boucher, 1986). Finally, these skills were cited as a possible reason for inadequate social skills among these children (Bryan et al., 1981). However, some research has challenged this evidence (Boucher, 1986). For example, Boucher conducted a series of studies that investigated these aspects of the pragmatic language of children who have learning disabilities. Several interesting measures of language were used, as presented in Interest Box 3.8.

INTEREST BOX 3.8
EXPERIMENTAL MEASURES OF LANGUAGE

Boucher (1984, 1986) used a number of interesting measures of language and communication skill. On occasion, a language specialist on a child-study team will present information based on this type of measure, so several of these are described here.

Sentence complexity is often coded by the type of sentence: simple sentence (one basic phrase), compound (two independent phrases joined by a conjunction), and complex (an independent phrase and a dependent phrase such as a prepositional phrase, which cannot stand alone as an independent sentence). The teacher who conducts instructional activities on sentence diagramming or dependent phrases is emphasizing sentence complexity, among other things.

T-units, or thought units, represent the shortest units into which a language sample can be cut without leaving any sentence fragments as residue. Note the following sentence: *The lady lived next door, and she was a loud singer.* This sentence consists of two thought units, five and six words, respectively, with a mean T-unit length of 5.5. Averages such as this suggest something about language maturity because it takes a certain mature understanding of language to convey meaning in brief, well-stated sentences.

Mean utterance length is a measure of language based on the average length of the utterance. New utterances are initiated if a child pauses for several seconds before continuing.

Real word count consists of the number of understandable words that a child can produce about any given subject. Nonsense words and words that cannot be understood are excluded.

Thought Units and Complexity

One problem in some of these studies was the limited size of the comparison groups. For example, five students who had learning disabilities were compared with five students who did not; with subject groups this small, one subject can easily bias the results for the entire group. However, Boucher (1986) indicated that smaller numbers of students in each group allowed for a more in-depth analysis of the statements made by each child. The results indicated that students with learning disabilities did use a less-sophisticated level of language than the control group. Specifically, students with learning disabilities used fewer complex sentences and fewer words in their completed thought (**thought units**) than did the students without such disabilities.

However, unlike the earlier studies, Boucher's (1984, 1986) studies indicated that students with learning disabilities do engage in code switching. In Boucher's studies, those students did use more simple sentences with peers and more complex sentences with adults. They also used longer thought units with adults than with peers.

Given the several discrepancies noted in the research, you will have to await further clarification on the exact nature of pragmatic language problems among students with learning disabilities. Also, you should attend to forthcoming research on these indicators of language skill and **complexity**. Research may show that pragmatic language problems lead to academic deficiencies in areas such as reading comprehension and subject-content classes such as history and science.

Instructional Implications

Ward-Lonergan and colleagues (1999) provided an example of research on pragmatic language that holds implications for teaching. These researchers used 49 adolescent males (29 had a learning disability) to study the effects of different teaching methods on each student's ability to retell the content from a social studies lecture. Two 5½-minute minilectures on social studies content were videotaped. In one lecture, the content was taught by comparison discourse (discussion in which comparisons formed the basis of the lecture). In the other lecture, causation was the organizing theme of the content. Each of these lectures was shown to the students, then each student was asked to retell verbally the content of the lectures. The student's retelling session was graded according to how many T-units were used. As anticipated, the 29 students with learning disabilities produced a significantly smaller number of T-units overall than did the students without disabilities. However, both the students with disabilities and those without managed to produce more T-units from content delivered in the comparison-based lecture than from content delivered in the causation-based lecture. This would suggest that in teaching students with learning disabilities, comparisons should be a primary basis for instruction, since relationships between content facts may be more clearly established in that context, whereas in a causation context such relationships may not be highlighted in the same fashion. This example illustrates how research on pragmatics in the context of the classroom can inform instructional efforts for students with learning disabilities.

Functional Communication

Several theorists have investigated the role of language or the functional intent of utterances (**functional communication**) used by students who experience learning disabilities in comparison with students who do not (Boucher, 1984, 1986). Boucher (1984), to give one example, categorized the statements by both groups of children according to the functional intent of the statements. These categories were recommended by Halliday (1975) and are presented in Interest Box 3.9.

Results of the comparison demonstrated that students with learning disabilities were different from the other students in the functional intent of their language. Specifically, the students with learning disabilities made more regulatory statements and more imaginative statements when interacting with peers than did the other students. Also, the students with learning disabilities made more informative statements and more unjustifiable or inappropriate statements when interacting with both peers and adults than did the other students.

Research on Functional Communication

Narrative discourse involves event-based stories in various forms, which are quite common in public school classes (Feagans, 1983). History lessons, reading-comprehension exercises, and various other school activities require an understanding of narrative and generally include an element of plot, understanding the relationship between the various discrete events, and placing the appropriate sentences in the correct sequence so that the story has meaning. The narrative involves the child's comprehension of the substance of the story either in spoken or written form.

■ ■ ■ ■ ■ ▬▬▬▬▬▬▬▬▬▬▬▬▬▬▬▬▬▬▬▬▬▬▬▬▬▬▬▬▬▬▬▬▬▬▬▬▬▬▬

INTEREST BOX 3.9
FUNCTIONAL LANGUAGE CODES

Halliday (1975) devised a system for coding the functional use of language by categorizing sentences according to their function. Basically, sentences were grouped according to the categories listed below. A sample sentence in each category is also provided (Boucher, 1984).

FUNCTIONAL CODE	SAMPLE SENTENCE
Instrumental	I want that pencil.
Regulatory	Please, do as I suggest.
Imaginative	Imagine a purple cow!
Interactional	We can agree with that.
Personal	Here I come.
Heuristic	Tell me why the sky is blue.
Informative	I may have something to tell you.
Ambiguous	(Includes sentences not easily coded.)

Research on children without learning disabilities has addressed the comprehension of story schema. **Story schema** has been defined as the subjective concept or the connection between the various events in the story. Certain students may not have an understanding of the hierarchical structure that forms the substance of the story. Teachers who have worked with readers who have disabilities have had the experience of teaching a child who did not seem to grasp the idea that the different events in a story were logically connected, either temporally or causally. Such unawareness demonstrates the lack of a story schema. Without such an awareness, or with an incomplete awareness, the reader will not actively search for connections between the events in the story.

Roth and colleagues (1995) investigated the connectedness of narrative stories produced by students with learning disabilities and students without disabilities. The students produced two narratives, one as a spontaneous story condition and one in response to a stimulus picture. These narratives were recorded and subsequently compared. Students with LD did not tie the various elements of their narratives together as specifically as students without LD. Students with learning disabilities also used fewer connection words to relate the thought units in the narratives to each other.

Other research with students who have learning disabilities has suggested that these children and adolescents do not understand the implications of story narratives when presented in either a written or oral mode (Feagans, 1983). The problem seems to be both the ability to recall critical information (see the discussion of memory in this chapter) and the ability to organize the events when required to do so (Feagans, 1983).

Feagans (1983) suggested that referential communication is a problem area for children with learning disabilities. **Referential communication** requires that a child communicate specific information to another and/or evaluate the adequacy of communication from another. Giving or receiving instructions is one example of referential communication. This referential communication skill, therefore, includes awareness of accurate and inadequate messages as well as choices based on such communication.

Some research has suggested that children with learning disabilities are deficient in recognizing and acting on communication when the content of the communication is less than adequate. For example, Spekman (1981) created dyads or paired groups of children, some of which included a child with learning disabilities and some of which did not. Each child in each dyad was to communicate information and act on information received from the partner in the dyad. This research design allowed for comparison on referential communication skills as well as listening competence in this type of communication. The children were told they could ask questions regarding incomplete communications. No differences were found in the ability to follow directions, to complete the task, or to ask appropriate questions, but the children with learning disabilities in the dyads gave less task-relevant information. Consequently, these dyads demonstrated less success in completion of the task than the dyads that included only normally functioning children.

One confounding variable that may have biased the results in the Spekman (1981) study was the ability of the students with learning disabilities to read the diverse nonverbal facial cues and expressions of the students in their dyads. This presents a dilemma because referential communication must involve a listener, and different listeners may produce different facial and nonverbal cues. Feagans and McKinney (see Feagans, 1983) solved this problem in a unique way. These researchers compared a group of children who were learning disabled to a group who were not on referential communication when the listener was a puppet. Obviously, the puppet presented the same facial cues to both groups, and a tape-recorded set of responses even allowed the puppet to give preset verbal responses while both groups of children were verbally communicating.

The task to be taught in the Feagans and McKinney study consisted of obtaining a piece of candy from a hiding place inside of a wooden box. The box was constructed so that several intertwining and movable sides had to be pulled in a particular order. This would allow the lid to open and make the candy available. First, each subject was taught how to open the box. Comprehension was assured by the child performing the task. Then the child was told to verbally teach this task to the puppet. This placed the child with learning disabilities in the role of teacher and required that the child give instructions to the puppet to open the box. The results demonstrated two things. First, the children with learning disabilities took longer to learn the task. Second, they were much less capable of communicating this knowledge to the puppet than were the other children.

The implications of this research for the classroom present a very real concern. If a child with learning disabilities does demonstrate a pragmatic language disability in referential communication skills, that student will be less capable of giving instructions to his or her classmates. This disability would affect that student's performance on all types of group projects that require verbal participation of each group member. Also, the child would have problems responding to instructions given by the teacher or other members of the group. Clearly, a disability in referential communication presents real problems in the typical elementary school classroom.

As a teacher, you will continue to see research in this area as well as studies that relate language deficiencies to various forms of failure in school subjects. However, the specific implications of these language-based deficits have not yet been presented in terms of rec-ommendations for teachers. The research does support several general recommendations for classroom tasks, and these are presented in Interest Box 3.10.

SUMMARY

For most of the cognitive characteristics discussed in this chapter, the evidence points to various deficits among school-identified populations of students with learning disabilities. For example, most populationwide studies indicate a lower level of intelligence among chil-dren who are learning disabled. However, this is questionable because so many measures of IQ depend almost entirely on linguistic ability. Gardner's concept of multiple intelligences may be a more fair and reasonable way to look at a student's capabilities overall. Research concerning on-task behavior and selective attention indicates that such children have defi-cits in each area. Also, deficits in working memory have been consistently demonstrated. This research has played a prominent role in the development of the metacognitive perspec-tive on learning disabilities.

The research on various cognitive-style indicators, although considerably less im-pressive than research on other cognitive characteristics, has also indicated that children with learning disabilities have deficits on various cognitive-style measures. These students tend to be more field dependent than students without disabilities. Also, children with learn-ing disabilities are more impulsive than other students, and this impulsivity has been related to low achievement. As a teacher, you need to become more aware of these characteristics of the learning disabled in order to structure educational activities for students with these characteristics.

This chapter has also demonstrated deficits among children with learning disabilities in phonemic manipulation, and in semantic, syntactic, and pragmatic language. Many of these children do not interpret or manipulate phonemes, and this deficit may prove to be the primary basis for many learning disabilities. Also, many students with learning disabilities do not really understand the grammatical rules that facilitate language usage; nor do they understand the relationships between words in sentences and phrases. However, there is some question as to whether these deficits actually cause or contribute to school failures in reading and other subject areas (Feagans, 1983). Research will continue on this issue.

Research on pragmatic language of children with learning disabilities has demonstrated deficits that could readily contribute to difficulties in social situations (Ward-Lonergan et al., 1999). Although recent research has indicated that such children do adapt their language to the situation and the age of the listener, they also use less complex sentences than other children. This indicates that they have a less sophisticated understanding of language than other children. The use of contrived tasks that result in consistent language samples has demonstrated these deficiencies in several of the more recent studies. Finally, researchers have begun to identify various language subtypes among children with learning disabilities in an effort to identify more specific instructional remedies for particular children.

As a teacher, you will have responsibility for the development of language in the students in your class who are learning disabled. Although most of the typical teacher's language instructional time is spent working on written language, the child's use of oral language must also receive attention because deficits in oral language may cause failures

■ ■ ■ ■ ■ ▬▬▬▬▬▬▬▬▬▬▬▬▬▬▬▬▬▬▬▬▬▬▬▬▬▬▬▬▬

INTEREST BOX 3.10

TEACHING TIPS BASED ON LANGUAGE RESEARCH

We are only beginning to understand the importance of language and language usage in academic subjects, and few researchers have made concrete teaching recommendations based on the new knowledge. However, the research will support some general guidelines for the classroom teacher (Feagans, 1983).

1. Be aware of the language demands of the task assigned. Attend to additional research and recommendations made by language specialists.
2. Look for unusual or ambiguous sentences in the stories that are assigned, and make a point to discuss these in class. Model both the correct and incorrect interpretation.
3. Insist on correct grammar, syntax, and word selection when speaking with students. While not embarrassing students who come from a nonstandard-English background, one function of all teachers is to prepare students to communicate effectively in the national language. Gently correct students, and expect them to follow your model.
4. Play videotapes of successful minority members of society, and discuss the correct use of English in the processes of interpersonal and career success.
5. Present additional lessons on grammar, syntax, and semantics to students with learning disabilities who need additional help, and always relate the paper-and-pencil work to the spoken language of the child.
6. Whenever necessary, seek the help of speech and language specialists, and follow their instructional advice.
7. Expand a child's utterances. If a child says, "That's a house," you both praise the child and expand the utterance by saying, "That's right. That is a house, with a brown roof." Expansion will assist children in developing more developed sentences.
8. In combination with praise for a child's speech production, you should also question the child to get him or her to continue speaking.
9. Read folktales and other literature aloud to your class, and discuss the idioms, metaphors, similes, and other expressive phrases that are used.
10. Provide sharing time in which students can talk about events that occurred over the weekend.
11. During all reading assignments, discuss the connectedness of the text by highlighting cause-and-effect relationships, and inviting students to predict the story outcome.

in school tasks such as reading comprehension, language arts exercises, and comprehension of subject matter. Your methods courses will prepare you with a number of options for instructional programming to improve language, which may include role-play, debate, argumentative language, and other exercises. Also, you will work closely with the speech teacher and language specialists for children with severe language problems.

The following points will help you study this chapter:

■ Students with learning disabilities typically have intelligence scores that fall in the low-average range (90 to 95).
■ Students with learning disabilities demonstrate problems in all three areas of attention: time-on-task, focus of attention, and selective attention.

- Students with learning disabilities typically demonstrate certain memory problems that involve working memory and encoding information for memory storage. Typically, these students do not demonstrate long-term memory problems.
- Students who are learning disabled tend to be more impulsive than students who are not.
- Students with learning disabilities tend to be more field dependent than other students.
- Students with learning disabilities demonstrate problems in phoneme manipulation, and these problems in language interpretation are believed to cause later reading disabilities.
- Students who are learning disabled use less complex sentences than students who are not.
- Students with learning disabilities apparently do switch codes as required by their understanding of the social situation, but their understanding of the situation may be incomplete.

QUESTIONS AND ACTIVITIES

1. From a member of your college educational psychology faculty, obtain a paper-and-pencil measure of cognitive mode, and have each member of the class take it. What does this reveal about your learning tendencies? Is it accurate for you?

2. Interview local psychologists, and find out what the average IQ is for local children with learning disabilities in the opinion of local child-study team members.

3. What is the relationship between the various measures of learning style and intelligence? Divide the class into research teams, and identify correlational studies to determine this relationship.

4. Identify any local workshops based on learning style, and elect a class representative to attend them and bring back information.

5. How are selective attention and memory strategies related? Can you present examples where local teachers use a memory strategy?

6. Select one of the papers in the area of distractibility research that demonstrates that students who have learning disabilities are not any more distractible than those who do not, and review

it for the class. Can you explain the differences in this area of research?

7. Interview a local speech pathologist, and ask him or her to identify the types of language problems that are common among children and adolescents with learning disabilities.

8. Identify recent articles in the study of phonemic manipulation among children who have learning disabilities, and track the references these theorists use that connect them to the language-based theorists of the 1940s and 1950s.

9. Collect an oral language sample from a local child, and analyze it in class, identifying the semantic, syntactic, and communication errors. Use the various codes described in the chapter.

10. Review the contradictory evidence on code-switching ability among children with learning disabilities. How can the subtype hypothesis account for these contradictions?

11. Review the report of the Commission on Excellence in Special Education (2001), and describe for the class the implications of this report for assessment of IQ.

REFERENCES

Abrahamsen, E. P., & Sprouse, P. T. (1995). Fable comprehension by children with learning disabilities. *Journal of Learning Disabilities, 28,* 302–308.

Barkley, R. A. (1990). *Attention deficit hyperactivity disorders: A handbook for diagnosis and treatment.* New York: Guilford.

Bender, W. N. (1985). Differences between learning disabled and non-learning disabled children in temperament and behavior. *Learning Disability Quarterly, 8,* 11–18.

Bender, W. N. (2002). *Differentiating instruction for students with learning disabilities.* Thousand Oaks, CA: Corwin.

Bender, W. N. (2005). *Differentiating math instruction: Strategies that work for K–8 classrooms.* Thousand Oaks, CA: Corwin Press.

Bender, W. N., & Golden, L. B. (1988). Adaptive behavior of learning disabled and non-learning disabled children. *Learning Disability Quarterly, 11,* 55–61.

Bender, W. N., & Larkin, M. (2003). *Reading strategies for students with learning disabilities.* Thousand Oaks, CA: Corwin Press.

Bender, W. N., & Wall, M. (1994). Social-emotional development of students with learning disabilities. *Learning Disability Quarterly, 17.*

Boon, R., Ayers, K., & Spencer, V. (in press). The effects of cognitive organizers to facilitate content-area learning for students with mild disabilities. A pilot study. *Journal of Instructional Practice.*

Bos, C. S., Mather, N., Silver-Pacuilla, H., & Narr, R. F. (2000). Learning to teach early literacy skills—collaboratively. *Teaching Exceptional Children, 32*(5), 38–45.

Boucher, C. R. (1984). Pragmatics: The verbal language of learning disabled and nondisabled boys. *Learning Disability Quarterly, 7,* 271–286.

Boucher, C. R. (1986). Pragmatics: The meaning of verbal language in learning disabled and nondisabled boys. *Learning Disability Quarterly, 9,* 285–295.

Bryan, T., Donahue, M., & Pearl, R. (1981). Learning disabled children's peer interactions during a small-group problem solving task. *Learning Disability Quarterly, 4,* 13–22.

Campbell, B. (1994). *The multiple intelligences handbook: Lesson plans and more.* Stanwood, WA: Campbell & Associates.

Campbell, L., Campbell, B., & Dee, D. (1996). *Teaching & learning through multiple intelligences.* Needham Heights, MA: Allyn and Bacon.

Chard, D. J., & Dickson, S. V. (1999). Phonological awareness: Instructional and assessment guidelines. *Intervention in School and Clinic, 34*(5), 261–270.

Chard, D. J., & Osborn, J. (1999). Word recognition instruction: Paving the road to successful reading. *Intervention in School and Clinic, 34*(5), 271–282.

Commission on Excellence in Special Education (2001). *Revitalizing special education for children and their families.* Available from www.ed.gov/inits/commissionsboards/whspecialeducation.

Council for Exceptional Children (2002). Commission report calls for special education reform. *Today, 9*(3), 6–15.

Cutting, L. E., Koth, C. W., Mahone, E. M. & Denckla, M. B. (2005). Evidence for unexpected weaknesses in learning in children with attention-deficit/hyperactivity disorder without reading disabilities. *Journal of Learning Disabilities, 36*(3), 259–269.

Feagans, L. (1983). Discourse processes in learning disabled children. In J. D. McKinney & L. Feagans (Eds.), *Current topics in learning disabilities, Vol. 1.* Norwood, NJ: Ablex.

Gajar, A. (1979). Educable mentally retarded, learning disabled, emotionally disturbed: Similarities and differences. *Exceptional Children, 45,* 470–472.

Gardner, H. (1983). *Frames of mind: The theory of multiple intelligences.* New York: Basic Books.

Hagen, J. W. (1967). The effect of distraction on selective attention. *Child Development, 38,* 685–694.

Hallahan, D. P., Gajar, A. H., Cohen, S. G., & Tarver, S. G. (1978). Selective attention and locus of control in learning disabled and normal children. *Journal of Learning Disabilities, 11,* 231–236.

Halliday, M. A. K. (1975). Learning how to mean. In E. Lenneberg (Ed.), *Foundation of language development: A multidisciplinary approach, Vol. 1.* New York: Academic Press.

Kame'enui, E. J., Carnine, D. W., Dixon, R. C., Simmons, D.C., & Coyne, M. D. (2002). *Effective teaching strategies that accommodate diverse learners* (2nd ed.). Upper Saddle River, NJ.: Merrill-Prentice Hall.

Kavale, K. A., & Forness, S. R. (1986). School learning, time and learning disabilities: The disassociated learner. *Journal of Learning Disabilities, 19,* 30–138.

Liddell, G. A., & Rasmussen, C. (2005). Memory profile of children with nonverbal learning disability. *Learning Disabilities Research and Practice, 20*(3), 137–141.

Lyon, G. R., & Moats, L. C. (1997). Critical conceptual and methodological considerations in reading intervention research. *Journal of Learning Disabilities, 30*(6), 578–588.

Mather, N., & Roberts, R. (1994). Learning disabilities: A field in danger of extinction? *Learning Disabilities Research and Practice, 9*(1), 49–58.

McConnell, M. E. (1999). Self-monitoring, cueing, recording, and managing: Teaching students to manage their own behavior. *Teaching Exceptional Children, 32*(2), 14–23.

McKinney, J. D., Montague, M., & Hocutt, A. M. (1993). *A synthesis of research literature on the assessment and identification of attention deficit disorders.* Coral Gables, FL: Miami Center for Synthesis of Research on Attention Deficit Disorders.

National Reading Panel (2001). Put reading first: The research building blocks for teaching children to read. Available from www.nationalreadingpanel. org/publications.

National Joint Committee on Learning Disabilities (NJCLD) (2005). Responsiveness to intervention and learning disabilities: A report prepared by the National Joint Committee on Learning Disabilities. *Learning Disability Quarterly 28*(4), 249–260.

O'Shaughnessy, T. E., & Swanson, H. L. (1998). Do immediate memory deficits in students with learning disabilities in reading reflect a developmental lag or deficit? A selective meta-analysis of the literature. *Learning Disability Quarterly, 21,* 123–148.

Roth, F. P., Spekman, N. J., & Fye, E. C. (1995). Reference cohesion in the oral narratives of students with learning disabilities and normally achieving students. *Learning Disability Quarterly, 18,* 25–40.

Scruggs, T. E., Mastropieri, M. A., Sullivan, G. S., & Hesser, L. S. (1993). Improving reasoning and recall: The differential effects of elaborative interrogation and mnemonic elaboration. *Learning Disability Quarterly, 16,* 233–240.

Shaywitz, S. E., & Shaywitz, B. A. (2006). Reading disability and the brain. *Educating Exceptional Children: 2005/2006.* Dubuque, IA: McGraw Hill.

Silliman, E. R., & Scott, C. M. (2006). Language impairment and reading disability: Connects and complexities. *Learning Disabilities Research and Practice, 21*(1), 1–7.

Sousa, D. A. (2006). *How the brain learns* (3rd ed.). Thousand Oaks, CA: Corwin.

Sousa, D. A. (2005). *How the brain learns to read.* Thousand Oaks, CA: Corwin.

Sousa, D. (2001). *How the special needs brain learns.* Thousand Oaks, CA: Corwin Press.

Spekman, N. (1981). Dyadic verbal communication abilities of learning disabled and normally achieving fourth and fifth grade boys. *Learning Disability Quarterly, 4,* 193–201.

Sprenger, M. (2003). *Differentiation through learning styles and memory.* Thousand Oaks, CA: Corwin.

Sprenger, M. (2002). *Becoming a "wiz" at brain-based teaching: How to make every year your best year.* Thousand Oaks, CA: Corwin.

Stanford, L. D., & Hynd, G. W. (1994). Congruence of behavioral symptomatology in children with ADD/H, ADD/WO, and learning disabilities. *Journal of Learning Disabilities, 27,* 243–253.

Stanford, P. (2003). Multiple intelligence for every classroom. *Intervention in School and Clinic, 39*(2), 80–85.

Swanson, H. L. (1994). Short-term memory and working memory: Do both contribute to our understanding of academic achievement in children and adults with learning disabilities? *Journal of Learning Disabilities, 27,* 34–50.

Swanson, H L. (1999). Cognition and learning disabilities. In W. N. Bender (Ed.), *Professional issues in learning disabilities* (pp. 415–460). Austin, TX: ProEd.

Tomlinson, C. (1999). *The differentiated classroom: Responding to the needs of all learners.* Alexandria, VA: Association for Supervision and Curriculum Development.

Torgesen, J. K. (1984). Memory processes in reading disabled children. *Journal of Learning Disabilities, 18,* 350–357.

Torgesen, J. K., Murphy, H., & Ivey, C. (1979). The effects of orienting task on memory performance of reading disabled children. *Journal of Learning Disabilities, 12,* 396–401.

Ward-Lonergan, J. M., Liles, B. Z., & Anderson, A. M. (1999). Verbal retelling abilities in adolescents with and without language-learning disabilities for social studies lectures. *Journal of Learning Disabilities, 32,* 213–223.

Wiig, E. H., Lapointe, C., & Semel, E. M. (1977). Relationships among language processing and production abilities of learning disabled adolescents. *Journal of Learning Disabilities, 9,* 292–299.

Wolfe, P., & Nevills, P. (2004). *Building the reading brain, preK–3.* Thousand Oaks, CA: Corwin.

Zentall, S. S. (1986). Effects of color stimulation on performance and activity of hyperactive and non-hyperactive children. *Journal of Educational Psychology, 78,* 159–165.

CHAPTER FOUR

PERSONALITY AND SOCIAL CHARACTERISTICS OF STUDENTS WITH LEARNING DISABILITIES

CHAPTER OUTLINE

WHEN YOU COMPLETE THIS CHAPTER, YOU SHOULD BE ABLE TO:

1. Define the major characteristics within the domain of personality development.

2. Present the major research findings in each personality area.

3. Differentiate between social acceptance and social skills.

4. Present the evidence for higher levels of loneliness, stress, depression, and suicide among students with learning disabilities.

5. Describe the growing concern for self-determination and self-advocacy of students with learning disabilities.

6. Discuss the results from research on the families of children with learning disabilities.

KEYWORDS

personality variables	temperament	social acceptance
self-concept	anxiety	social isolation
global self-concept	state anxiety	social rejection
locus of control	trait anxiety	sociometric rating
internal locus	suicide ideation	social competence
external locus	parasuicide	peer nomination
learned helplessness	self-advocacy	roster rating
attributions	self-determination	social skills

INTRODUCTION

Generally, the courses in educational psychology for teachers include a great deal of information on cognitive characteristics and only limited information on the personality and social development of children. Because the major emphasis in schooling has been academic growth, it seems reasonable to concentrate on the cognitive characteristics such as memory, intelligence, language, and attention, which may be related to growth in achievement. Research on students with learning disabilities has also followed this pattern, and only over the last 20 years has research appeared on the social and personality characteristics of these students (Bender, Rosenkrans, & Crane, 1999; Eisenman & Chamberlin, 2001; Elksnin & Elksnin, 2004; Handwerk & Marshall, 1998; Maag, Irvin, Reid, & Vasa, 1994; Sharma, 2004).

In spite of this pattern, there are several reasons for investigating these social and personality characteristics among students with learning disabilities. First, social and personality growth have been justifications for the need to educate children with disabilities. Many parents of these children realize that their child might never demonstrate normal academic growth, but the parents do want their children exposed to role models in the hope that this will foster growth in self-concept and social development. The rationale for inclusion of children with mild disabilities was based, in part, on the need for appropriate role models.

Second, many social and personality variables impact on academic achievement (Rothman & Cosden, 1995). For example, there is some evidence that an increase in self-concept may cause an increase in academic achievement (Rothman & Cosden, 1995). However, this direct causal relationship between self-concept and achievement is still the subject of some debate. Given these questions about the causal relationship, perhaps the best that can be said today is that certain personality variables among children and adolescents with learning disabilities may lead to suggestions for teaching methods, and various suggestions for teaching are presented throughout the chapter.

Third, certain personality variables may be related to the amount and quality of work that a special education teacher or a general education teacher expects from a student who is learning disabled. Teacher expectations can, in turn, be related to the quality of instruction provided for the students. This would suggest that personality variables may, in an indirect sense, lead to growth in academic achievement. Clearly, if personality variables determine the types of assignments given to students with disabilities, teachers must be trained to be aware of this potential prejudice in themselves and try to assure a fair opportunity for each student with a disability.

Next, there is some evidence that personality variables may begin to play a part in the identification of learning disabilities in children. For example, Handwerk and Marshall (1998) demonstrated that measures of behavioral functioning could distinguish between students with learning disabilities and students with emotional disturbance. With the difficulties in present identification procedures (discussed in Chapter 5), any variables that offer assistance in this regard deserve attention.

Finally, these personality and social competence variables will have an impact on the student with learning disabilities throughout his or her life (Elias, 2004; Elksnin & Elksnin, 2004). As these students mature and begin to function in the adult world, these variables play an increasingly important role in their job success and their relationships with others. The concept of self-determination, described below, is based in large measure on these personality variables. In fact, the ability of adults with learning disabilities to advocate for themselves in the workplace or in the everyday world of adults may be negatively impacted by less than optimal outcomes on these personality or social competence factors (Malian & Nevin, 2002). Thus, much of the recent research focus on self-advocacy or self-determination of students with learning disabilities stems from study of these personality and social competence issues.

Figure 4.1 depicts the personality and social-emotional variables that may affect both the academic performance and the overall well-being of the child with learning disabilities (Bender & Wall, 1994). The four general domains pictured are behavioral development, social development, emotional development, and cognitive development; and each of the variables that have been extensively studied in children and youth with learning disabilities is included. Although the variables are currently located under the domain in which their primary effect will be felt, it is quite possible to have any of these variables affect the student with learning disabilities in a variety of other domains as well. For example, a low self-concept presumably would lead to some degree of hampered social development, so that variable is located in the emotional development domain. However, low self-concept may also lead to lower academic achievement (Bender & Wall, 1994; Rothman & Cosden, 1995). This relationship is discussed in more detail later, but you should remember that

Behavioral Domain

ADHD
Conduct problems
Impulsivity
Adaptive behavior

Social Domain

Family interactions
Adult adjustments
Social competence
Social rejection

Cognitive Domain

Language usage
Cognitive skills
Academic skills

Emotional Domain

Risky behavior
Loneliness
Depression/suicide
Temperament
Anxiety
Self-concept

FIGURE 4.1   Major Domains of Development for Students with Learning Disabilities

any or all of the variables presented in this figure may very well affect—either positively or negatively—the successful development of the student with learning disabilities in any of these domains.

PERSONALITY, RISKY BEHAVIOR, AND SELF-DETERMINATION

Personality variables, also referred to as *emotional variables,* include such variables as self-concept, locus of control, temperament, anxiety, loneliness, depression, suicide ideation, and a willingness to engage in risky behaviors. Research concerning these characteristics among students with learning disabilities is presented here in a prioritized order. The variables are discussed in the order in which they have received research attention historically. Consequently, the results in the area of self-concept are much less tentative than the research on anxiety or loneliness, depression, and suicide because more studies have been done over a longer period of time concerning the self-concept of students with learning disabilities.

Self-Concept

Self-concept may be defined as the view one has of oneself, either overall or in relation to a particular situation or setting. It is sometimes important to distinguish between the first type of self-concept—**global self-concept**—and the second type of self-concept, which is restricted to one's self-perceptions in a particular setting. Most college students have a good overall self-concept, but if you think of a situation or even a particular class in which your abilities are not particularly apparent, you would have a lower self-concept in relation to that situation.

Students with learning disabilities have numerous situations in which they feel adequate for the demands of the situation, though many of these students feel less than adequate when confronted with academic tasks in school. For this reason, it is important to distinguish between global self-concept and school-specific self-concept.

Some of the self-concept measures that are commercially available make this distinction. For example, the Piers-Harris Children's Self-Concept Scale (Piers, 1984), one of the most frequently used self-concept measures, includes information on a total (global) score as well as on six different subscales. These include self-perceptions of behavior, intellectual status, anxiety, popularity, happiness, and personal attractiveness. The scale has a reading level of second to third grade and is normed for use through high school. Because the score on intellectual status is essentially a school-specific measure, this instrument makes a comparison between the global score and a school-specific score.

Assessment of self-concept can be conducted by the child-study team or by a teacher. Generally, it is a good idea to assess the self-concept of a randomly selected pupil of the same race and sex, from the same class, who is not disabled as an indicator of normal self-concept in that situation.

Research has been fairly consistent in demonstrating that younger students with learning disabilities have a lower global self-concept than other students (Bryan, Burstein, & Ergul, 2004; Gans, Kenny, & Ghany, 2004). However, studies regarding lower global self-concept among older students with learning disabilities are somewhat equivocal (Meltzer, Roditi, Houser, & Perlman, 1998). There is general consensus that older students with learning disabilities demonstrate lower self-concept on the particular school-specific tasks associated with their disability, such as reading, math, or language (Gans, Kenny & Ghany, 2004; Rothman & Cosden, 1995), rather than lower global self-concept. Research among adolescents with learning disabilities, in particular, has demonstrated lower school-specific self-concept scores. Bender & Wall (1994) suggested that there may be a developmental trend in which younger children with learning disabilities demonstrate a lower global self-concept, and older students, as they mature, may learn to think more highly of themselves in general while maintaining a lower self-concept relative to academic tasks. This type of developmental trend may explain the effects on self-concept for students with learning disabilities.

In an interesting variation on this research, Rothman and Cosden (1995) investigated the relationship between self-concept and the self-perception of learning disabilities among students identified as disabled. As children grow older, they may become more aware of what their disability is and of ways to cope with it. As an initial research question, Rothman and Cosden (1995) wanted to find out how one's understanding of one's own disability affected one's general self-concept. Fifty-six children with learning disabilities, from grades 3 to 6, were administered a battery of measures, including one that assessed the degree to which they believed their disability was modifiable and nonstigmatizing, rather than unchangeable and stigmatizing. Students with more positive perceptions of their learning disability did demonstrate both higher self-concept scores and higher academic achievement scores. Although this research doesn't directly address the issue of a developmental lag in development of a positive global self-concept, it does demonstrate that awareness of one's own disability can positively affect one's perception of oneself.

Locus of Control

Locus of control is an educational variable that has been identified more recently than self-concept. It may be defined as one's perception of control over one's environment. In some cases, this body of research is referred to as "attribution" research because it addresses a student's attribution of cause (Ring & Reetz, 2000). That perception may be **internal locus** (the belief that what one does oneself has a major impact on the environment) or **external locus** (the belief that one's fate is externally controlled by the environment). A simple example will demonstrate. If you studied each night for the next test in a course and still failed the test, you would develop a high external and low internal locus of control. You would find reasons for the failure in the external environment, such as ineffective teaching by the instructor or the lack of an accurate study guide. In short, continued failure in spite of continued attempts at school tasks leads to an external locus of control. Further, a high external locus of control, in turn, leads to a lack of motivation for study and for school in general. This has been referred to as **learned helplessness** since a high external locus of control generally results in individuals making very little effort (Palladino, Poli, Masi, & Marcheschi, 2000).

There are several methods of measurement that may be used to assess locus of control. First, numerous paper-and-pencil tasks ask the student to imagine himself or herself in a particular situation and then assess the locus of control. The following is a sample item from this type of measure:

> If you did really well on your next report card, it would probably be because:
> a. You had studied very hard.
> b. The teacher graded very leniently.
> c. You had prepared well and the teacher was lenient.

Answer "a" represents an internal locus of control. Answer "b" represents an external locus, and answer "c" represents a combined, internal/external, perspective. One problem with this type of measure is that such methods assume that students understand how to adopt the role described in the item. For example, in the sample question, the student has to be able to assume that he or she did well on the report card. This may be a difficult skill for some students with learning disabilities.

A second method is to assess students' **attributions** for success and failure directly. This entails giving them a task to do and asking them afterward how they did and why they succeeded or failed. The responses that the students give then have to be coded as either internal or external. This is a stronger method of measurement, and initial results that use this method with children and adolescents who are learning disabled suggest that these students are more externally oriented than students who are not.

Like self-concept, locus of control may be measured in a global fashion or in relation to school-specific variables. The research has suggested that students with learning disabilities have a higher external locus of control and demonstrate more learned helplessness than other students for school tasks (Bender & Wall, 1994; Palladino et al., 2000). This area of research is intriguing from the standpoint of the prospective teacher because it suggests an interaction effect. Specifically, among students with learning disabilities, those with a higher external locus of control for school tasks may respond more positively to higher levels of structure in the classroom. As one early example, Schunk (1985) observed 30 sixth-grade children with learning disabilities in a treatment study that involved instruction in subtraction using three strategies. The students were randomly assigned to one of the three groups. Group 1 set their own goals, group 2 had goals assigned for them, and group 3 had no stated goals for the instruction. Results indicated that achievement is directly related to goal setting. Group 1 performed better than the other groups, and group 2 performed better than the group with no goals. Clearly, teachers should encourage students to set realistic goals for each major task that is undertaken.

Temperament

Research has shown that certain personality characteristics may be relatively stable very early in the lives of young children. Specifically, characteristics such as task persistence or the level of reaction to various stimuli in the environment may be established as early as late infancy (Teglasi, Cohn, & Meshbesher, 2004). Measurement of these **temperament** variables is usually done by a teacher or parent rating of the most typical response of a child in relation to a particular setting. These ratings stress the question, How is a child likely to behave?

Keogh (2003) has provided the measurement device that has been most frequently used to assess temperament in children with learning disabilities and has assessed temperament variables among these students (Keogh, 1983). The early research generally shows some differences between students who are learning disabled and those who are not, and these differences typically favor the children without disabilities. The results to date suggest that children with learning disabilities are less task persistent and demonstrate less social flexibility than other children.

In a recent review, Teglasi, Cohn, and Meshbesher (2004) pointed out that there is little agreement on what dimensions exist under the broader term *temperament*. In fact, these researchers identified a variety of temperament constructs. These researchers identify five dimensions of temperament, which generally fall into two broad areas: reactivity and self-regulation. Reactivity may be defined as how one is predisposed to react to the environment and is typically discussed in five dimensions, as defined in Interest Box 4.1. Self-regulation involves one's ability to regulate or temper emotions and ranges from automatic self-regulation to highly effortful self-regulation. For example, individuals with high reactivity and little automatic self-regulation have to expend considerable effort to control their emotional reactions to events in the environment. Further, such intentional effort may take one's attention away from other tasks, such as those required in the academic environment, which is why many researchers consider temperament a critically important variable in understanding children and adolescents with learning disabilities (Bender & Wall, 1994; Teglasi, Cohn, and Meshbesher, 2004).

Research has shown that students with learning disabilities demonstrate certain differences in temperament from students without disabilities (Bender & Wall, 1994; Pullis, 1985). Further, researchers have begun to attend to the interaction between a student's temperament and the instruction he or she receives in the classroom (Pullis, 1985; Teglasi, Cohn, & Meshbesher, 2004). For example, Pullis (1985) has shown that a teacher's perceptions of a child's temperament result in different types of instructional assignments that can

■ ■ ■ ■ ■

INTEREST BOX 4.1
DIMENSIONS OF TEMPERAMENT

Activity Level—the tempo and vigor of motoric movement, and/or preferences for motor activity of greater or lesser intensity. High levels of activity have been associated with certain types of behavioral problems (Teglasi, Cohn, and Meshbesher, 2004).

Emotionality—the prevalence and intensity of emotional states (either positive or negative). Positive and negative emotional states are highly independent and are associated with different neural-biological systems. Moreover, research has shown that students with learning disabilities are more likely to experience negative emotions than others (Bryan, Burstein, & Ergul, 2004).

Attention Level—involves one's ability to, in an effortful manner, orient and attend to task; the opposite of this is referred to as distractibility. A related factor is inhibitory control—the ability to inhibit responses that may be inappropriate to the situation Traditionally, learning disabilities have been associated with high distractibility and poor inhibitory control (Bender & Wall, 1994).

Approach/Avoidance—involves the tendency to approach or avoid other persons and/or social situations.

Adaptability/Flexibility—involves the ability to adapt to often unanticipated changes in the environment. Some students with learning disabilities demonstrate less adaptability than their peers.

clearly affect the educational outcome. Understandably, teachers tended to assign different types of tasks to students who were different in task persistence. If a child can attend to a task for only approximately 10 minutes, a teacher should give that child a series of 10-minute tasks rather than a task that takes the entire period. This type of research (which identifies links between personality variables and teacher-selected instructional procedures) suggests that teachers need to be much more aware of the types of temperament and other relevant personality variables displayed by the children with learning disabilities in their class.

✳ Anxiety

Anxiety refers to behaviors that indicate a fear of situations or a more global, all-pervasive anxiousness. Fear of specific situations is called **state anxiety** because it is manifested only in specific situations. If a person demonstrates the more pervasive anxiety behaviors, this is called **trait anxiety** and is assumed to represent a more stable personality characteristic than the former (Lufi, Okasha, & Cohen, 2004; Margalit & Shulman, 1986). Obviously, there is some overlap with characteristics discussed earlier. For example, one subscore that may be obtained from the Piers-Harris Children's Self-Concept Scale (Piers, 1984) yields a score for self-perceptions of anxiety. Also, there is a parallel between school-specific self-concept, discussed previously, and state anxiety because both are related to specific situations.

Several research articles have suggested that students with learning disabilities are more anxious overall (trait anxiety) than other students (Margalit & Shulman, 1986; Margalit & Zak, 1984). For example, Margalit and Shulman (1986) studied the anxiety of 40 male preadolescents with learning disabilities (aged 12 to 14) who attended a special school. A comparison group of 40 male students of the same age was selected from a local public school. State anxiety and trait anxiety were measured for both groups. The scores indicated that youth who were disabled had higher levels of trait anxiety, whereas no difference on state anxiety existed between the two groups. Although this is a worthwhile study in an area in which we badly need information, there is one design problem in this research. Can you identify it?

Notice that the two groups of children compared were different for several reasons. First, one group had a learning disability, and the assumption behind the research is that the disability accounts for any differences between the groups in anxiety. However, the groups also differed in terms of where they attended school. Could this uncontrolled factor create a difference in trait anxiety? Are there particular schools that are located in dangerous areas of town in which any student would demonstrate more anxiety? The reader cannot assume that the measured differences in anxiety really result from learning disabilities. As a teacher and a professional, you must learn to look for examples of research problems in the studies you read in order to become more fluent in using the evidence in your field. Only through research can our profession ever develop an accurate picture of the anxieties of children with learning disabilities.

There is one further caution regarding this research, and that involves the number of studies in this area. Several studies are not enough to draw firm conclusions on this issue of state or trait anxiety. Unlike the studies on self-concept and locus of control presented earlier, these results must be viewed as tentative because only a few studies exist.

Although state anxiety can be related to a number of causes, one potentially important cause that is directly related to school is test anxiety (Lufi, Okasha, & Cohen, 2004). For example, if students with learning disabilities are highly test anxious, this could account for many of the academic problems they display. This area is just beginning to receive research attention, and no firm conclusions can be drawn concerning the degree to which students with learning disabilities are anxious about tests in the school environment. Swanson and Howell (1996) investigated test anxiety among a mixed group of students (i.e., some with learning disabilities, some with behavioral disorders, some with attention-deficit disorders, and some with various combinations of disability). Results indicated that lower test anxiety was related to effective study habits and effective, task-related self-instructions during task/test performance. Thus, effective self-instructions and effective study skills may help alleviate test anxiety to some degree, but much more research is needed.

In view of the preliminary nature of these results, no theorists have made specific recommendations regarding teaching strategies based on this personality variable. However, because of the increased research on the personality of students with disabilities and the nature of these early findings, this research area will be expanded in the future, and prospective teachers should be aware of this area. Also, the presentation of these results demonstrates how little we know about certain characteristics of children and adolescents with learning disabilities.

Loneliness, Depression, and Suicide

With the increasing awareness of differences between students with and without learning disabilities on variables such as self-concept, locus of control, and anxiety, a number of researchers have begun to study other indicators of mood states, including measures of loneliness, depression, and suicide (Bender et al., 1999; Palladino et al., 2000; Pavri & Monda-Amaya, 2000, 2001). Research on variables such as self-concept and locus of control is fairly plentiful, but there are only a few studies on loneliness, depression, and suicide among students with learning disabilities (Huntington & Bender, 1993). Nevertheless, these studies are important because of the crucial nature of these topics. Whereas deficits in self-concept indicate a problem that may or may not be severe, a student's attempt at suicide, in the context of loneliness or clinical depression, is automatically a crucial concern. As a practitioner, you may have to face clinical depression, chronic loneliness, and suicide or suicide attempts on the part of your students, and should you ever teach a student who attempts or succeeds at suicide, you will see the value of the research that addresses this critical problem.

Research has suggested that students with learning disabilities are more prone to loneliness, depression, and suicide than students without learning disabilities (Bender & Wall, 1994; Margalit & Levin-Alyagon, 1994; Palladino et al., 2000; Sabornie, 1994). However, the research conducted to date has not painted a clear picture in any of these research areas. For example, the bulk of the research on depression has generally demonstrated that students with learning disabilities are more likely to be depressed than nondisabled children (Newcomer, Barenbaum, & Pearson, 1995; Palladino et al., 2000; Wright-Stawderman, Lindsey, Navarette, & Flippo, 1996; Wright-Stawderman & Watson, 1992). However, other studies have failed to identify any differences in depression between these groups (Maag & Reid, 1994). The study by Newcomer and her co-workers illustrates one possible reason for these equivocal results. The study by Newcomer and colleagues (1995) was strong methodologically because a group of 85 students with learning disabilities was directly compared to a group of students without learning disabilities (unlike some research, which merely compares students with disabilities to the published data in the norm tables for students without disabilities). Also, multiple measures of depression were used by Newcomer and her colleagues; this added validity to the study overall. The measures of depression included both a self-rating, completed by the students with learning disabilities, and a teacher rating of depression for each subject. Although students with learning disabilities did not rate themselves as more depressed than the comparison group, the teachers did indicate higher depression among students with learning disabilities. This suggests that different measurement approaches on depression may yield different results—certainly a concern for researchers as well as teachers in the field.

Data on suicide or suicide attempts by children and youth with learning disabilities are particularly alarming (Bender et al., 1999; McBride & Siegel, 1997; Peck, 1985). In Peck's (1985) study, for example, the suicides reported by the Los Angeles Suicide Prevention Center were investigated for a 1-year period, resulting in a total of 14 suicides studied.

Half of those involved students with learning disabilities, even though students with learning disabilities account for less than 5% of the adolescent population. Other studies have indicated that **suicide ideation** (or thoughts of suicide) and **parasuicide** (actual suicide attempts that are unsuccessful) may likewise be more common among students with learning disabilities (Huntington & Bender, 1993). These results, although tentative, do suggest that some students with learning disabilities may need immediate counseling assistance.

Of course, much more research on these variables will appear in the literature during the next few years, and you should remain current in your understanding. However, if you have any suspicion that a student may be considering suicide or that a student appears unduly depressed over a period of days, you should mention that concern to the guidance counselor or school psychologist in your district. Depression and suicidal thoughts are not to be ignored. Interest Box 4.2 presents additional suggestions for the teacher who confronts this problem.

Risky Behaviors

As adolescents mature, they begin to seek their own identity, and in many cases, this quest is coupled with some degree of risk taking. Although some risky behavior is normal during adolescence, extreme risk taking (e.g., use of illegal drugs and unprotected sexual intercourse) can be quite dangerous, and research on adolescence has begun to investigate risky

---

■ ■ ■ ■ ■ ■

INTEREST BOX 4.2
TEACHING TIPS: WHEN A STUDENT MENTIONS SUICIDE

1. Take note of the several warning signs of suicidal thoughts. Students may make statements such as, "My family would be better off without me!" or "How many sleeping pills does it take to kill somebody?" Keep a written record (date, time, and what was said) for later use.
2. Elicit confirmation about any observed warning signals. Ask questions when the warning signs appear, such as, "Do you think about harming yourself often?" or "Have you ever tried to hurt yourself?" Also inquire to determine if the student has a definite plan for a suicide attempt. Such a plan would suggest the seriousness of the possibility of suicide. Also, remember: There is no evidence to suggest that asking this type of question can "prompt" students to actually commit suicide.
3. Be supportive of the concerns of the student, but also affirm a commitment to life.
4. Do not react with horror or panic. Do not try to shock the student by daring him or her to proceed, and do not downplay the seriousness of the student's concern. What may seem a solvable problem to you may not seem to be to the student.
5. If your questions seem to suggest that the student is serious, keep the student with you, or arrange for someone else to stay with the student. Do not leave the student alone.
6. Contact professional help. Report the incident to the school guidance counselor and the school psychologist, and request their immediate help. Most states and school districts require teachers to report students' threats of suicide.

behavior. Consequently, researchers have likewise begun to look at risky behaviors among adolescents with learning disabilities.

Substance abuse and/or risky sexual behaviors are not considered "personality" variables in the same sense as self-concept, anxiety, or depression, but there is an obvious relationship between the documented deficits in these personality traits among students with learning disabilities and their willingness to participate in these behaviors (Beitchman, Wilson, Douglas, Young, & Adlaf, 2001; Cosden, 2001). For this reason, researchers have investigated these risky behaviors among students with learning disabilities, and recent research has indicated that some students with learning disabilities indeed develop a set of high-risk behaviors—including smoking tobacco or marijuana, using cocaine and alcohol, or engaging in risky sexual behavior—prior to and during their adolescence (Beitchman et al., 2001; Blanchett, 2000; Lambert & Hartsough, 1998; Maag et al., 1994; Meltzer et al., 1998; Molina & Pelham, 2001). This research is still quite tentative and is ongoing, but because of the severely negative outcomes associated with such risky behaviors, these growing data must be investigated.

Maag and colleagues (1994) completed one of the initial studies on the relationship between self-concept and substance abuse among adolescents with learning disabilities. Two groups of adolescents, a nondisabled group and a group of 123 students with learning disabilities, were compared on their patterns of use of alcohol, tobacco, and marijuana. Students with learning disabilities, using several self-report measures, indicated that they used more tobacco and marijuana than students without disabilities; no difference was found in the use of alcohol between the two groups. Contrary to expectation, self-concept scores did not help predict which students used illegal drugs more frequently.

In a more recent study, Beitchman and co-workers (2001) studied 103 children, 59 of whom had demonstrated a learning disability by age 19. Records were searched to specify the point at which a learning disability had first been identified for these students. Those who had demonstrated a learning disability at both age 12 and at age 19 were more likely to develop a concurrent substance use problem at age 19 than were the nondisabled children in the study.

Although these initial results have caused concern, not all of the investigations of substance abuse among students with learning disabilities have shown a significant relationship between such abuse and a disability (Molina & Pelham, 2001; Weinberg, 2001). Also, these studies document the fact that a large number of students with learning disabilities do not engage in risky behaviors to any greater degree than do students without disabilities. Thus, much more research on this question is needed.

There is considerably less information available on risky sexual behavior among students with learning disabilities. Blanchett (2000), using a self-report questionnaire with a group of 88 young adults with learning disabilities, did document some risky sexual behavior among this group. These data indicated that 51% of adolescents with learning disabilities engaged in sexual behavior that would put them at risk for HIV during high school. Of those engaging in sexual behavior, the average age at which they began their sexual experiences was 15.9 years. Further, of those engaging in various forms of sex, 71% reported that some alcohol or drug use typically preceded the sex.

These data are inconclusive, and many of these studies are very recent, but this research does document the possibility that students with learning disabilities engage in risky behaviors more frequently than do other students. For this reason, these investigations are quite likely to continue. Also, if future research continues to indicate that students with learning disabilities display an increased tendency to engage in risky behaviors when compared with other students, one may anticipate that various preventative-treatment instructional curriculums may be developed for the classroom. As a concerned teacher, you should remain cognizant of this growing concern for the health and well-being of students with learning disabilities.

Self-Determination and Self-Advocacy

In view of the personality traits and risky behaviors described, it seems clear that some students with learning disabilities demonstrate personality issues that can have a negative impact on their overall lifelong outcomes. In particular, with these issues in mind, a number of researchers have become concerned with the ability of students with learning disabilities to envision a successful future for themselves and to advocate for themselves toward that future during school, during the postschool transition period, or later as these students move into adult life (Eisenman & Chamberlin, 2001; Malian & Nevin, 2002; Price, Wolensky, & Mulligan, 2002; Whitney-Thomas & Moloney, 2001). This ability is referred to as **self-advocacy,** or **self-determination.** Whitney-Thomas and Moloney (2001) used a series of in-depth, repeated interviews to encourage high school students with and without disabilities to describe their self-definition. Of course, one's definition of self (i.e., self-image) will in large measure determine what choices one will make at critical transition points in life. The weaker self-definition for students with disabilities documented in this study presents the field with some interesting challenges. Students with learning disabilities may have a weaker view of their own future, based on the difficulties that the disability has caused in their lives, and teachers may soon need to address this weaker self-definition.

Although definitions of self-determination vary greatly from one researcher to another (Malian & Nevin, 2002), it may best be conceptualized as the development of attitudes, abilities, and skills that empower students to specify—and ultimately to achieve—their own goals (Malian & Nevin, 2002; Price et al., 2002). Of course, this represents the ultimate development and the desired end result of a successful education, and the educator's responsibility is to assist every student with a learning disability to achieve this lofty goal. Price and colleagues (2002) presented a breakdown of this overall goal, as shown in Interest Box 4.3. A review of these individual components of self-determination will assist you in understanding the overall concept. As you read these components, note the relationship between the personality variables previously described and the individual components of self-determination.

Clearly, students with learning disabilities will be better served if they are taught to advocate for themselves, and the context of the educational meetings for developing IEPs seems to be one arena for such training. This is, perhaps, the first area in which the broader emphasis on self-determination is having an impact (Martin et al., 2006; Test, Fowler, Brewer, & Wood, 2005; Test et al., 2004; Wehmeyer, Field, Doren, Jones, & Mason, 2004). Research has shown than many students with learning disabilities can participate meaningfully in their IEP meetings, and other meetings concerning their education, such as transition planning meetings, disciplinary meetings, and so on (Carter, Lane, Pierson,

---

INTEREST BOX 4.3
COMPONENTS OF SELF-DETERMINATION

Behavioral Autonomy—progression from dependence to self-care and self-direction
- *Choice-making skills:* select from among alternatives based on preferences
- *Decision-making skills:* weigh adequacy of various solutions
- *Problem-solving skills:* respond in order to function effectively in one's environment
- *Goal-setting/attainment skills:* develop goals and perform necessary actions
- *Independence, risk-taking, and safety skills:* perform tasks without help

Self-Regulated Behavior—decide to plan, act, evaluate, and revise plans as needed
- *Goal-setting/attainment skills:* develop goals and perform necessary actions
- *Self-observation, evaluation, and reinforcement skills:* access, observe, and record what you discover
- *Self-instruction skills:* self-talk to provide prompts for problem solving
- *Self-advocacy skills:* speak up to defend oneself, a cause, or a person

Psychological Empowerment—internal locus of control, self-efficacy, outcome expectations
- *Internal locus of control:* belief that one has control over critical outcomes
- *Positive attributions of efficacy/outcome expectancy:* behavior leads to expectations

Self-Realization—accurate knowledge of individual strengths and needs, along with the ability to act in a manner that capitalizes on that knowledge
- *Self-awareness:* basic understanding of one's strengths, needs, and abilities
- *Self-evaluation:* ability to use/apply personal insights to real-world settings

---

& Glaeser, 2006; Martin et al., 2006). However, the level and quality of participation will be greatly enhanced when pre-IEP meeting training is provided for the student (Hammer, 2004). Further, teachers should not be satisfied merely to increase self-advocacy during IEP meetings, but rather should aim at increasing self-determination overall for their students. Interest Box 4.4 presents some general guidelines for increasing general self-determination for students with learning disabilities.

Summary of Personality, Risky Behavior, and Self-Determination

Although numerous other personality characteristics may eventually receive research attention, the preceding characteristics have received the most attention in the research on personality development among children and adolescents who are learning disabled. As is clear from these studies, these students experience more than an array of cognitive inabilities. Clearly, the continued failure in school-related tasks has taken a toll on most students with learning disabilities such that these students experience numerous personality problems that can lead to general unhappiness. However, we do not yet know how to interpret the long-term effects of many of these variables. For example, does a depressed self-concept result in a more seri-

■ ■ ■ ■ ■

INTEREST BOX 4.4
TEACHING TIPS TO INCREASE SELF-DETERMINATION

Several teaching recommendations may be based on the characteristics discussed in this chapter. The beginning teacher should consider implementation of these strategies in order to help strengthen the personality and ultimately the self-determination of children and youth with learning disabilities.

1. Separate the student's problem in learning from the student as a person. Offer corrective feedback for learning problems and praise for successes, but do not criticize the student personally.
2. Find something that the student knows and can demonstrate for the class. It may be a new dance, a hobby, an after-school job, or a brother's occupation, but include such presentations in your regular requirements when they are related to the class content. Provide an opportunity for students to be proud of themselves.
3. Offer highly structured tasks to students who require them. Externally oriented students will usually respond better to an organized task, so provide clear task instructions concerning how to read a chapter or a paragraph. For example, tell the student to review the questions at the end first, then the subheadings, and only then to read for the answers.
4. Reward (tokens or praise) all successful work that students do. Put corrected papers on the board, and request that the principal visit and comment on someone's paper when he or she is in class. Such "outside" praise can provide a real boost for many children with learning disabilities.
5. Encourage students to set goals for their learning. Do everything you can to encourage involvement and an internal locus of control.
6. Encourage attendance and active participation of the student in every IEP meeting. Discuss with the child in advance what the meeting will be like and the importance of his or her participation.
7. Discuss with each student his or her lifetime goals, and relate work in class to those goals.

ous clinical depression or in increased risky behaviors? Perhaps the growing literature on self-determination can shed light on the impact of these personality characteristics and risky behavior patterns among some students with learning disabilities.

SOCIAL DEVELOPMENT OF CHILDREN WITH LEARNING DISABILITIES

Over the years, research has documented that approximately 75% of students with learning disabilities manifest some type of social skills deficits (Kavale & Mostert, 2004). Further, one of the earliest rationales for including children with learning disabilities in general education classes was the assumption that placing these children in mainstream classes would foster social growth by providing nondisabled role models. This assumption has resulted in several areas of study, including social acceptance of students who are learning disabled, social skills, social competence, and social development in the family context.

Social Acceptance

The issue of **social acceptance** is concerned with the social relationships that students with learning disabilities are likely to have in inclusive classes. Such social relationships may reveal which boys or girls are not selected for softball teams at recess, for example. If a student is continually rejected for such activities, and if the rejections are unrelated to his or her ability in that particular area, such **social isolation** may lead to self-concept problems or general unhappiness (Sabornie, 1994; Vaughn & Haager, 1994).

A second drawback to low social acceptance is the fact that it may negatively affect academic performance. In many elementary classrooms, various educational activities are based on group work, group studying, and other academic tasks for which a certain minimum level of social acceptance is desirable. The same low socially accepted child with disabilities who is rarely chosen for the softball team may well be the last student in class chosen for a class debate.

Another reason for concern with low social acceptance of students with learning disabilities involves the negative long-term outcomes of lower social acceptance (Kavale & Mostert, 2004). Vaughn, La Greca, and Kuttler (1999) indicated that students with learning disabilities who suffered from lower social acceptance were more likely to drop out of school. In fact, students with learning disabilities who dropped out were less socially accepted than were students with disabilities who remained in school. For these reasons, every teacher who deals with students with learning disabilities must consider the issue of low social acceptance.

A distinction must be drawn between social isolation and **social rejection.** Although these may sound similar, there is, in fact, little relationship between the two terms. For example, many students suffer from low social acceptance or social isolation—perhaps the popular students merely fail to notice them or choose to play with other students—but that is different from actively rejecting students. Students who are actively rejected tend to be students who demonstrate clearly inappropriate social behaviors or noxious behaviors. Certain students may not bathe regularly, and their smell is offensive enough to result in active social rejection. Such social rejection is categorically different from social isolation.

There are several methods of measuring social acceptance. Self-ratings of social acceptance (of the type found on various self-concept measures) may be used. Teacher ratings that seek to identify the social stars and socially isolated students may also be used.

By far the most frequently used method is the use of *peer ratings* (sometimes referred to as a **sociometric rating**). This is the most accurate measure of social acceptance because this type of measure gives actual data on how frequently students accept pupils with disabilities in various classroom and extracurricular activities. A sociometric rating consists of a strategy used to encourage the peers of a child to rate the child's **social competence,** acceptance, or behavior. Basically, there are two strategies that may be used.

The first is called a **peer nomination** strategy (Vaughn et al., 1999). For example, students in mainstream or inclusive classes may each be asked to nominate three children with whom they would most like to play during recess (or with whom they would least like to play during recess). Tabulation of these results for the entire class would result in identi-fication of the "social stars" and the students who are socially rejected within the class. This is a fairly easy system to use and is the most common. However, this may not be helpful for the teacher or child-study team who wants information on a particular child because that child may be neither a star nor socially rejected.

The second type of sociometric strategy is designed to generate data on each member of a class. It is called a **roster rating** or peer rating, and every student in the class rates every other student in the class. For example, each student is given a roster that lists each class member with a Likert scale (a one- to five-point rating scale with one representing "never" and five representing "always") beside each name. The students are asked the question, How often would you like to play with this person? They then rate the social acceptance of every class member.

A number of studies have investigated the level of acceptance of students with learn-ing disabilities in inclusive classes, and most of the research has shown that children with-out learning disabilities do not readily accept students with learning disabilities (Bender et al., 1984; Sabornie & Kauffman, 1986), and this low social acceptance can result in feelings of loneliness among students with learning disabilities (Al-Yagon & Mikulincer, 2004; Sab-ornie & Kauffman, 1986; Vaughn & Haager, 1994; Wiener, 2004). Lower levels of social acceptance are particularly obvious in the research based on sociometric ratings. However, some research has indicated that there is not a one-to-one relationship between learning disability and lower social acceptance. There seems to be a group of students with learning disabilities who are as well accepted socially as the children without learning disabilities. For example, Ochoa and Palmer (1991) compared the sociometric status of 60 Hispanic students with learning disabilities with the status of children without learning disabilities. The researchers used both a nomination system and a roster-rating system to assure that some data were available on every child. Results indicated that Hispanic children who had learning disabilities were socially isolated more often than the children in the comparison group. However, not all such children were socially isolated. In that study, 30% of the chil-dren with learning disabilities received low social acceptance ratings, whereas 50% of the students with learning disabilities attained an average score on the sociometric ratings. This indicates that some students who are learning disabled experience the same levels of social acceptance as other groups of students who are not learning disabled.

Several reasons for the low social acceptance of students with learning disabilities have been suggested by research (Bender et al., 1984; Vaughn & Haager, 1994). For ex-ample, Bender and associates (1984) demonstrated that children with learning disabilities were not as well accepted in inclusive classes as average-achieving children. However, they were as well accepted as the children who went to a basic-skills reading program. This sug-gests that low social acceptance may be caused by low academic achievement or the stigma associated with a student leaving the class for any special education assistance, as opposed to social isolation that is a component of the disability itself.

Efforts to identify the possible causes of lower social acceptance and less-than-adequate social behavior of students with learning disabilities are continuing (Vaughn et al., 1999). For example, Kravetz, Faust, Lipshitz, and Shalhav (1999) compared 22 students with learning disabilities to 22 students without disabilities on a number of measures of interpersonal understanding. A clinical interview was conducted with each student, which consisted of having the student read a brief story involving a social problem and then say what the appropriate response would be for various characters in the story. The answers given by the children with and without learning disabilities were then rated on the degree of social understanding represented by each answer. Also, teachers completed a rating on each child's social behavior in the classroom. The results demonstrated that the social behavior of students with learning disabilities was considerably less appropriate than the behavior of their peers without disabilities. Also, the students with learning disabilities demonstrated less understanding of interpersonal situations. The important question of to what degree the social behavior of students with learning disabilities is dependent on their relative lack of interpersonal understanding was not answered by this study. However, even when the impact of interpersonal understanding was controlled for statistically within this study, students with learning disabilities still demonstrated a deficit in social behavior in the classroom. This suggests that a lack of understanding in social situations on the part of students with learning disabilities may not be the primary cause of the lower social acceptance associated with learning disabilities.

In another study, Vaughn, Elbaum, Schumm, and Hughes (1998) demonstrated that the social acceptance of students with learning disabilities may be affected by the type of instructional placement used. In this study, social relationships were examined for 185 elementary-aged students, 59 of whom had a learning disability. These students were educated in different schools. One school used a full-time inclusion placement in which a special education and a general education teacher co-taught in the classroom together for the entire day. In the other school, a collaborative instructional model was used in which the special education teacher was present in the classroom for only 1 to 2 hours per day. The students with learning disabilities in the collaborative instructional model demonstrated higher peer acceptance and generally fared better socially than children with learning disabilities in the full-day inclusion model.

Clearly, the research suggests several reasons for the lower social acceptance of students with learning disabilities, and this issue will need to be addressed in every classroom. Regardless of the ultimate cause or causes, it is clear that in order to receive the benefits of inclusive class placement, children who are learning disabled must be included in a meaningful fashion in class activities rather than merely sitting in the class without being an accepted member of it.

Social Skills and Behaviors

Researchers began to study the performance of children and adolescents with learning disabilities on specific social skills in the 1980s and 1990s (Most & Greenbank, 2000; Vaughn & Haager, 1994). This area of study may be differentiated from the earlier social acceptance research because the focus here was on the specific **social skills** and behaviors that these students lack. Research in this area was initiated by Tanis Bryan and colleagues, and specific behavior deficiencies among students with learning disabilities that result in less social acceptance have been identified. These generally include an inability to use language in social situations, an insensitivity to social cues, an inability to correctly perceive their own social status, and an inability to adapt to social situations (Bryan & Bryan, 1983).

Bryan's research on conversational competencies is interesting because it concerns crucial areas, and her research designs were both interesting and unique. She and her colleagues conducted a study in which they examined the conversational competence of children with learning disabilities (Bryan, Donahue, Pearl, & Sturm, 1981). The study included 20 children with disabilities (12 males and 8 females) in grades 2 and 4. A group of average achievers was randomly selected from several mainstream classes as a comparison group. Bryan set up a room with a TV camera to resemble a TV studio and discussed the role of TV talk show host with both groups of pupils. These children were then told to interview a guest as if they were the host of the show. These three-minute interviews were videotaped and analyzed for conversational content.

The strategies that the children with learning disabilities used for conducting the conversation were different from the strategies used by the comparison group. For example, the children with disabilities were less likely to produce the types of open-ended conversation that allow a conversation to continue. Consequently, the partners of the host who was learning disabled were less likely to produce elaborate responses. This lack of conversational competence may hamper the social relationships of children with learning disabilities.

Not only can conversational skills impede social development, but a child's ability to interpret the nonverbal cues of others in the conversation can lead to social problems (Dimitrovsky, Spector, & Levy-Shiff, 2000; Kravetz et al., 1999; Most & Greenbank, 2000). In one study, Most and Greenbank (2000) studied the ability of students with learning disabilities to interpret verbal and facial indicators of emotions in others. Sixty adolescents, 30 of whom had a learning disability and 30 of whom did not, were used. They were asked to interpret six different emotions expressed by an actor (happiness, anger, surprise, sadness, disgust, fear) and an emotionally neutral expression. The actor demonstrated these emotional cues in three ways: visual, auditory, and a combination of visual and auditory. The students with learning disabilities were less able to correctly perceive these emotional expressions in all three modes than were the students without learning disabilities. Also, the teachers evaluated the social skills of the students with learning disabilities as less adequate than their nondisabled peers.

Since the early research, a number of specific social skills have been identified in various sources in the special education literature. For example, various curriculum materials are available for instructing children and youth in a number of skills to enhance their social acceptability (Vaughn & La Greca, 1993). Many of these social skills programs utilize instructional scripts that facilitate the lesson. (Such scripts are described as a direct instructional technique in Chapter 10 of this text.) Other social skills training programs utilize role-play activities and puppets to illustrate situations and emphasize consideration of the feelings of others (Vaughn & La Greca, 1993).

While a number of social skills training programs have been developed, research on the efficacy of social skills instruction has been less than overwhelming (Kavale & Forness, 1996; Kavale & Mostert, 2004). Most of the research suggests very minor positive results from training in social skills, and while students with learning disabilities can learn many of the discrete social skills, such as those listed in Interest Box 4.5, the research does not demonstrate that learning discrete social skills results in either the use of those social skills in other settings (Bryan et al., 2004) or in higher levels of social acceptance overall.

■ ■ ■ ■ ■

INTEREST BOX 4.5

SOCIAL SKILLS IN THE COMMERCIALLY AVAILABLE MATERIALS

Starting conversation	Greeting skills
Controlling anger	Working in a group
Learning how to listen	Responding to others
Encouraging others to share ideas	Working cooperatively
Expressing oneself	Responding to aggression
Dating skills	Sex-role expectations
Being mad	Feeling left out
Feeling sad	Dealing with frustration

However, in spite of these questions, most teachers are implementing some type of social skills training program for students with learning disabilities who demonstrate these deficits. As a teacher in the field, you may be expected to implement such training using one of the available curricula, and you may wish to consult the research on this issue, as well as one or more of the reviews of these curricula (Kavale & Mostert, 2004; Vaughn et al., 1999).

Social Competence

The concept of social competence represents an interaction between personality development and social interaction. Research in both the personality and social development areas has indicated that these variables interact in a number of fairly complex ways (Malian & Nevin, 2002; Most & Greenbank, 2000; Rosenthal, 1992; Vaughn, McIntosh, & Spencer-Rowe, 1991). Rosenthal (1992) indicated that development of the psychological self is primarily dependent on successful interactions with others and that many of the personality deficits that are associated with learning disabilities (i.e., low self-concept, external locus of control, and experiences of learned helplessness) may be explained in terms of the relationship that students with learning disabilities have with significant others in their environment.

This interaction between personality characteristics and social development may be readily understood in terms of the information discussed previously on self-concept and loneliness. Presumably, if students with learning disabilities have a lower self-concept than other students, they may not tend to interact as frequently socially. This could lead to increased loneliness and a lack of opportunities to practice social skills such as conversation and greeting skills. This lack of practice, in turn, could contribute to further loneliness and a lower self-concept. Thus, this theory would suggest that students with learning disabilities would tend to have a weaker personality structure overall than students without disabilities.

There is some evidence for this type of interaction between the personality development of children and youth with learning disabilities and the social interactions of those individuals. For example, Pearl and Bryan (1992) investigated the ability of adolescents who have learning disabilities to resist peer pressure to engage in misconduct. Specifically, 74 students with learning disabilities and 85 students without learning disabilities were presented with pairs of statements that peers may utilize to encourage someone to engage in misconduct. The students with learning disabilities were much more likely to assume that persons who wished to elicit their support would use simple and direct requests rather than more subtle communications. These same students were also less likely to anticipate the use of requests that minimized the possibilities of getting caught in misconduct. Of course, this lack of ability to correctly "read" the intentions of the peers' statements may suggest that students with learning disabilities are more likely to be enticed by their peers to engage in misconduct. However, more research is necessary prior to firm conclusions on this question. At the very least, this evidence does suggest that students who have learning disabilities may be more apt to be led into inappropriate behaviors because of the overall weakness associated with these personality characteristics.

Perhaps Vaughn and co-workers have provided the best conceptualization for this interactive effect in their discussions of social competence (Vaughn & Haager, 1994; Vaughn & La Greca, 1993; Vaughn et al., 1991, 1999). Vaughn has argued that consideration of the variables discussed in this chapter individually may not be the most productive method for study. Specifically, she suggested the construct of social competence as an inclusive concept that includes both some of the personality variables and the social acceptance variables in order to understand the complex interrelationships between these measures. In this model of social competence, four components interact to create the overall social competence of an individual with learning disabilities. These include self-concept, positive relationships with others (as measured by social acceptance), the absence of maladaptive behaviors, and the component of effective social skills. Vaughn has also developed educational interventions for each of these different components, and these studies have shown some degree of success in increasing the social acceptance of students with learning disabilities (Vaughn & Haager, 1994; Vaughn et al., 1991).

This research on the comprehensive variable of social competence will affect you in a number of ways. First, as practitioners in the field begin to understand these complex phenomena better, more effective interventions will be developed. Teachers in the field will then experience increasing opportunities to utilize these instructional techniques. In most classes for children and youth with learning disabilities, at least a portion of the instructional time is allocated to instruction on social skills and social competence, and you should anticipate some instructional responsibilities in this area.

Families of Students with Learning Disabilities

The family lives of students with learning disabilities have received increasing research attention over the last two decades (Dyson, 1996; Falik, 1995; Johnson, 1993; Sharma, 2004; Voltz, 1994). Several factors have led to this growing interest. First, it has become increasingly apparent that a learning disability that is experienced by one member of a family can affect the entire family system, often in negative ways (Dyson, 1996; Falik, 1995; Knight, 1999). For example, Dyson (1996) demonstrated that having a child with a learning disability resulted in increased parental stress, which could negatively affect the parents' relationship to other children and even their relationship to each other.

Second, both educators and parents are noting that interventions are more effective if they begin early and involve the joint efforts of the teachers at school and the parents at home (Bjorck-Akesson & Granlund, 1995). Thus, researchers are attending much more to the dynamics of families that include students with learning disabilities (Falik, 1995) in an effort to foster earlier and more effective interventions.

Next, the efforts to study the postschool transition into adult life for students with learning disabilities have focused attention on the support that families provide during that transition phase (Morningstar, Turnbull, & Turnbull, 1995). Generally, family support is one crucial indicator of how well a student with a learning disability will make the adjustment from school to work, and this tends to focus attention directly on families of students with disabilities (Knight, 1999).

Finally, increasing efforts have been made recently to become more sensitive to the needs of minority students in special education, and this has evolved into a greater concern for involvement of minority parents in planning the school program for their children (Harry, Allen, & McLaughlin, 1995). All of these factors have tended to focus the efforts of researchers and teachers alike on the importance of the family in the lives of students with learning disabilities.

Research on Families.   Research on the family life of children who are learning disabled is less abundant than research on families with children who are severely disabled, and very little is known about the relationships between children with learning disabilities and their siblings. However, certain conclusions can be drawn concerning the attitudes of parents toward their children who are disabled. First, parents have lower academic expectations of these children than they have for nondisabled siblings (Bryan & Bryan, 1983). Also, parents tend to expect less desirable behaviors from children with disabilities than from their other children. Some evidence has suggested that the presence of children with disabilities in the family may restrict the social life of the parents (Martin, Brady, & Kotarba, 1992). Parents may experience lower levels of vitality in families that include children with disabilities. Waggoner and Wilgosh (1990), for example, conducted interviews with eight families that included children with learning disabilities, and those interviews documented these stresses on family life. Finally, some research suggests that parents tend to be somewhat more directive with students who are learning disabled than with students without disabilities (Bryan & Bryan, 1983).

Some researchers have suggested that certain types of family interactions may actually support and enhance the disabling aspects of this condition (Feagans, Merriwether, & Haldane, 1991; Green, 1990; Margalit & Almough, 1991). For example, many families with children who have learning disabilities, in comparison with other families, demonstrate a rather disjointed style of family communication, coupled with unclear behavioral expectations for the children and other family members (Green, 1990). Margalit and Almough (1991) indicated that Israeli families with children with learning disabilities were somewhat less supportive than families with children without disabilities. In short, certain types of families may operate in a manner that does not present a clear picture of appropriate social and interactive behaviors, and this would be a poor learning environment for any child, particularly one with a disability. This type of rather disjointed behavioral expectations may enhance or exacerbate the learning disability in some manner (Green, 1990; Knight, 1999).

Several researchers have investigated the relationship between the presence of an individual with learning disabilities in the family and the self-esteem of the brothers and sisters (Dyson, 1996). One might suppose that having a sibling with a learning disability may focus family attention and interactions around that child, to the exclusion of siblings.

Further, initial research indicated that sisters and brothers of students with learning disabilities demonstrated a lower self-concept. However, Dyson (1996) was not able to replicate that finding. Dyson (1996) investigated the self-concept of 19 siblings of individuals with learning disabilities and demonstrated no self-concept differences between those children and a comparison sample of students. Clearly, much more research will need to be done on how a learning disability in a family affects the siblings and the family system as a whole.

Family Involvement at School.   Ideally, families will cooperate with teachers, psychologists, and other educators to share information about a student's abilities in the home and nonschool social environments and jointly formulate an effective learning program for students with learning disabilities (Voltz, 1994). Parents know their children much better than teachers are likely to because parents typically spend much more time with them and see the children interact with others in a wider variety of environments than do teachers. Thus, parents have a great deal to contribute to the educational and social development of children, and this knowledge can be put to very good use in planning the individualized educational program for children with learning disabilities.

Unfortunately, this potential is realized much less frequently than most educators desire (Bjorck-Akesson & Granlund, 1995), and research has suggested that both school personnel and family members are responsible when the school-family relationship does not progress well. School responsibilities typically involve both systemic and professional barriers that tend to mitigate against parents becoming actively involved in planning with the special education teacher (Falik, 1995; Harry et al., 1995). Systemic barriers may be as simple as the fact that schoolteachers want to hold planning meetings after school hours, but most parents work until 5:00 P.M., and getting to school at 3:30 may be highly problematic for some parents, particularly single parents. Professional barriers may involve overuse of highly technical language, which parents may not understand, or the unintentional intimidation of the parent when confronted by a room full of professional teachers, psychologists, school administrators, and others.

In a recent naturalistic study, Harry and colleagues (1995) compiled data on participation of minority parents of 24 preschoolers with disabilities. A naturalistic study involves in-depth and systematic observations of family dynamics in the setting in which they occur. Rather than a preassigned list of measurement instruments and/or variables to study, the observations of the individuals in the natural environment result in establishing variables for study after the fact, and researchers are not limited by their preconceptions of what might be found. In this study, the researchers interviewed minority parents over a three-year period and observed interactions between those parents and schoolteachers at various meetings at the school. The researchers identified five deterrents to parental involvement of minority parents: late notices and inflexible scheduling of meetings, limited time for parental conferences, emphasis on documents rather than actual parental participation, use of jargon, and the structure of power (i.e., professionals' reading reports while parents listened established the experts and teachers as the knowledgeable participants and the parents as passive listeners). These researchers showed that, over time, these deterrents lead to decreasing advocacy by these minority parents for their children.

In addition to these school-based barriers to effective collaboration, the families of students with learning disabilities bear some responsibility for fostering effective collaboration with school personnel, and some families do not adequately meet this challenge to build effective communication mechanisms. In an effort to better understand what goes wrong in some families that include an individual with learning disabilities, Falik (1995) presented four prototypical patterns of negative family responses to a learning disability. According to Falik, some families may take an adversarial family stance and allow only limited involvement of the teacher or other professional in the family dynamics. Hence, these parents may be reluctant to consider instructional efforts that involve their time, such as a homework checkoff sheet for parents to review each night.

In a second scenario, one parent may become the outspoken advocate for the child with the school system, and sometimes even with the other parent. The advocacy-oriented parent may champion his or her child in ways that do not lead to effective communication with either school personnel or the other spouse. This can result in the other parent becoming somewhat resistant to any and all suggestions involving management of the learning disability. These families may become almost totally organized around the problems of one child—the child with the learning disability (Falik, 1995)—with one parent as the champion of the child and the other parent denying the existence of the learning disability.

In a third scenario, the family may willingly accept the learning difficulties, but become passively resistant to suggestions made by teachers (Falik, 1995). The parents' attitudes seem to convey that little is seriously wrong and, with the appropriate assistance, everything would be all right.

Finally, some families act out overt compliance with the expert's instructional treatment recommendations, but fail to carry through on any of the suggestions or requests for assistance (Falik, 1995). Of course, over time, this type of covert resistance will be transformed into more overt resistance, such as that demonstrated by the adversarial families previously described.

Strategies to Increase Family Involvement. With these potential negative scenarios in mind, every special education teacher should endeavor to break down the barriers that prohibit parents from becoming involved in the educational planning for their child. Numerous authors have suggested strategies for educators to use in facilitating increased parental involvement (Harry et al., 1995; Johnson, 1993; Knight, 1999; Voltz, 1994). Interest Box 4.6 presents a compilation of these strategies. As a concerned teacher, you should attempt any and all of them to assist in building a strong collaborative relationship with the parents of the students you teach.

One final concern is the issue of family advocacy for children with learning disabilities. Because of the involvement of many parents, a number of organizations have been formed to advocate for children with learning disabilities and their families (Hammill, 1993). Most of these organizations are relatively new, and some have a stronger focus on parental issues than others. Interest Box 4.7 presents some information on these organizations and an address or Website for each. You may wish to share this information with those parents who express an interest in this type of organization.

SUMMARY

This chapter has presented many different variables identified as relating to either academic or social outcomes of school for children with learning disabilities. Any variable that affects

■ ■ ■ ■ ■ ▬▬▬▬▬▬▬▬▬▬▬▬▬▬▬▬▬▬▬▬

INTEREST BOX 4.6

TEACHING TIPS FOR INCREASING PARENTAL COLLABORATION

1. Establish communication with parents as early as possible in the school year, preferably concerning a successful assignment their child completed or a high quiz score. This can be particularly important for minority parents (Voltz, 1994).

2. Write brief notes home to parents to compliment their child's work often. Set a goal for yourself of writing at least 10 brief notes per week to different parents, and attach them to the child's schoolwork.

3. Consider the parent's needs in establishing schedules for parent meetings. Plan one evening per grading period for such meetings for parents who can't get off work regularly to come to school after school hours (Harry et al., 1995). Call and personally invite parents to parent-teacher organization meetings, and let them know you look forward to talking with them.

4. Whenever possible, involve both parents. Avoid being caught working with only one parent, particularly in situations where the other parent may wish to deny the existence of the disability or the problems associated with it.

5. Always mention extended family members in your invitations to parents. In many families, particularly minority families, extended family members are crucial in the family dynamics (Harry et al., 1995).

6. Invite parents to "just drop in" to your class to watch their child when they can. An open door can lead to open communications.

7. Discuss class expectations for appropriate behavior with the parents, and inquire if those expectations differ from those at home. Be prepared to change your expectations if major differences exist, and be culturally sensitive to needs of minority students.

8. Try to ascertain, in a nonthreatening fashion, if the presence of a learning disability has affected the dynamics of the family (i.e., increased parental stress, sibling relationships, etc.). If difficulties exist, you may wish to recommend a local support group for the families (see Interest Box 4.7).

9. Be extremely reluctant to use sophisticated jargon in meetings with parents. Where highly technical language is necessary, always define it for parents, and request that other professionals also do so.

10. If difficulties arise in collaborative efforts with parents, ask another professional about appropriate strategies that may help remedy the situation.

these outcomes has a direct bearing on the reason for inclusion of these students because social growth was one of the original aims of the parents and educators who argued for increased inclusion.

Among the personality variables, self-concept is measured most frequently. Teachers may encounter measures of self-concept with some frequency in the reports and individual educational plans of their students with disabilities. Although locus of control, temperament, anxiety, loneliness, depression, and suicide have received increased research attention, these are rarely measured in today's identification procedures—except in the case of anxiety, which may be measured as one subscale of self-concept. However, research in these areas will

---

INTEREST BOX 4.7

ORGANIZATIONS AND WEBSITES FOR LEARNING DISABILITIES

- Learning Disabilities Association of America (LDA), 4156 Library Road, Pittsburgh, PA 15234.   www.ldanatl.org

This organization, formed in 1963, has around 50,000 members and concentrates mostly on parental concerns. This group has been a very effective advocacy group for children with learning disabilities (Hammill, 1993).

- Division for Learning Disabilities (DLD), 1920 Association Drive, Reston, VA 22091.   www.teachingld.org

This group was formed in 1982 and has approximately 13,000 members. It is made up predominantly of educators and researchers concerned with learning disabilities (Hammill, 1993).

- Council for Learning Disabilities (CLD), P.O. Box 40303, Overland Park, KS 66204.   www.cldinternational.org

This organization has about 4,000 members and attracts a large multidisciplinary membership of parents, psychologists, educators, and others (Hammill, 1993).

- International Dyslexia Association, 724 York Road, Baltimore, MD 21204. www.interdys.org

This is the oldest of the organizations that are specifically concerned with learning disabilities. Both a medical and an educational emphasis are maintained in this organization (Hammill, 1993).

- Children and Adults with Attention Deficit Disorders (CAADD), 499 NW 70th Ave., Suite 101, Plantation, FL 33317.   www.chadd.org

This organization advocates for students with ADHD and coexisting disorders. Since its founding in the late 1980s, membership has grown to over 20,000 persons worldwide.

- Research Websites

  LD Online: www.ldonline.org
  National Center for Learning Disabilities: www.ncld.org
  www.brainconnection.com

---

continue to increase, and you may find these measures in identification reports in the future. Also, you will find that these personality variables have a great bearing on the development of self-determination among children with learning disabilities.

Measures of social acceptance in inclusive classes are occasionally used today in the identification process. The information presented earlier will help you understand the types of information that may be provided. Also, certain ratings of behavior may yield information relative to peer status. However, these measures are not common in the identification process, and if you wish to have this information for a particular child, you may wish to administer a sociometric rating yourself in class.

Personality and social variables do explain a great deal about why some students learn and others apparently do not. Many teachers seek this information informally because it may have a bearing on how the teacher structures instructional groups or groups for activity periods. Information on personality and social variables may also suggest ways for you to approach the family of the child with learning disabilities in a request for home support of his or her educational goals. For these reasons, information on all of these variables among students who are learning disabled will be forthcoming.

The following points will help you study this chapter:

- Many students who have learning disabilities have a lower self-concept in academic situations than students who do not, and younger students with disabilities also have a lower global self-concept.
- Students with learning disabilities tend to be more external in their locus of control than students without learning disabilities.
- Some early research has suggested that students who are learning disabled may differ in overall temperament from other students. Also, these students demonstrate more anxiety and depression than other students.
- Students with learning disabilities will often need assistance in developing self-advocacy skills.
- Students with learning disabilities are not as frequently socially accepted as other students, though particular individuals may be.
- It is unclear, presently, why some students with learning disabilities are not accepted socially, though the suggested reasons range from lower achievement to inappropriate social behaviors.
- Parents of children with learning disabilities expect less of those children, in terms of both school achievement and behavior, than other parents expect of their children.

QUESTIONS AND ACTIVITIES

1. Form small groups in your class and look up some of the research by Sharon Vaughn in journals related to learning disabilities. Review in class her concept of social competence.
2. Through your curriculum center, obtain several measures of self-concept, and compare these to identify the types of scores and subscale scores that may be obtained from each. Discuss how a teacher may use these to obtain information about a child with learning disabilities.
3. Invite a local school psychologist to class to discuss measurement of personality and so-

cial variables. Find out how frequently he or she measures these variables for students with learning disabilities locally.
4. What are the reasons for the lack of information on siblings of children with disabilities? Can you find studies that present some information?
5. Describe the appropriate teacher response to a student's threat of suicide.
6. Identify the components of self-determination and discuss ways to develop these skills in your students.

REFERENCES

Al-Yagon, M., & Mikulincer, M. (2004). Patterns of close relationships and socio-emotional and academic adjustment among school-age children with learning disabilities. *Learning Disabilities Research and Practice, 19,* 12–20.

Beitchman, J. H., Wilson, B., Douglas, L., Young, A., & Adlaf, E. (2001). Substance use disorders in young adults with and without LD: Predictive and concurrent relationships. *Journal of Learning Disabilities, 34*(4), 317–332.

Bender, W. N., Bailey, D. B., Stuck, G. B., & Wyne, M. D. (1984). Relative peer status of learning disabled, educable mentally handicapped, low achieving, and normally achieving children. *Child Study Journal, 13,* 209–216.

Bender, W. N., Rosenkrans, C. B., & Crane, M. K. (1999). Stress, depression, and suicide among students with learning disabilities: Assessing the risk. *Learning Disability Quarterly, 22,* 143–156.

Bender, W. N., & Wall, M. E. (1994). Social-emotional development of students with learning disabilities. *Learning Disability Quarterly, 17,* 323–341.

Bjorck-Akesson, E., & Granlund, M. (1995). Family involvement in assessment and intervention: Perceptions of professionals and parents in Sweden. *Exceptional Children, 61,* 520–535.

Blanchett, W. J. (2000). Sexual risk behaviors of young adults with LD and the need for HIV/AIDS education. *Remedial and Special Education, 21*(6), 336–346.

Bryan, J. H., & Bryan, T. S. (1983). The social life of the learning disabled youngster. In J. D. McKinney & L. Feagans (Eds.), *Current topics in learning disabilities, Vol. 1.* Norwood, NJ: Ablex.

Bryan, T. S., Donahue, M., Pearl, R., & Sturm, C. (1981). Learning disabled children's conversational skill— The "TV talk show." *Learning Disability Quarterly, 4,* 250–259.

Bryan, T., Burstein, K., & Ergul, C. (2004). The social-emotional side of learning disabilities: A science-based presentation of the state of the art. *Learning Disability Quarterly, 27* (1), 45–52.

Carter, E. W., Lane, K. L., Pierson, M. R., & Glaeser, B. (2006). Self-determination skills and opportunities of transition-age youth with emotional disturbance and learning disabilities. *Exceptional Children, 72*(3), 333–346.

Cosden, M. (2001). Risk and resilience for substance abuse among adolescents and adults with LD. *Journal of Learning Disabilities, 34*(4), 352–358.

Dimitrovsky, L., Spector, H., & Levy-Shiff, R. (2000). Stimulus gender and emotional difficulty level:

Their effect on recognition of facial expressions of affect in children with and without LD. *Journal of Learning Disabilities, 33*(5), 410–416.

Dyson, L. L. (1996). The experiences of families of children with learning disabilities: Parental stress, family functioning, and sibling self-concept. *Journal of Learning Disabilities, 29,* 280–286.

Eisenman, L. T., & Chamberlin, M. (2001). Implementing self-determination activities. *Remedial and Special Education, 22*(3), 138–148.

Elias, M. J. (2004). The connection between social-emotional learning and learning disabilities: Implications for intervention. *Learning Disability Quarterly, 27*(1), 53–63.

Elksnin, L. K., & Elsknin, N. (2004). The social-emotional side of learning disabilities. *Learning Disability Quarterly, 27*(1), 3–8.

Falik, L. H. (1995). Family patterns of reaction to a child with a learning disability: A mediational perspective. *Journal of Learning Disabilities, 28,* 335–341.

Feagans, L. V., Merriwether, A. M., & Haldane, D. (1991). Goodness of fit in the home: Its relationship to school behavior and achievement in children with learning disabilities. *Journal of Learning Disabilities, 24,* 413–419.

Gans, A. M., Kenny, M. C., & Ghany, D. L. (2004). Comparing the self-concept of students with and without learning disabilities. *Journal of Learning Disabilities, 36*(3), 287–295.

Green, R. J. (1990). Family communication and children's learning disabilities: Evidence for Cole's theory of interactivity. *Journal of Learning Disabilities, 23,* 145–147.

Hammer, M. R. (2004). Using the self-advocacy strategy to increase student participation in IEP conferences. *Intervention in School and Clinic, 39,* 295–300.

Hammill, D. D. (1993). A brief look at the learning disabilities movement in the United States. *Journal of Learning Disabilities, 26,* 295–310.

Handwerk, M. L., & Marshall, R. M. (1998). Behavioral and emotional problems of students with learning disabilities, serious emotional disturbance, or both conditions. *Journal of Learning Disabilities, 31,* 327–338.

Harry, B., Allen, N., & McLaughlin, M. (1995). Communication versus compliance: African-American parents' involvement in special education. *Exceptional Children, 61,* 364–377.

Huntington, D. D., & Bender, W. N. (1993). Adolescents with learning disabilities at risk? Emotional well-being, depression, suicide. *Journal of Learning Disabilities, 26,* 159–166.

Johnson, H. L. (1993). Stressful family experiences and young children: How the classroom teacher can help. *Intervention in School and Clinic, 28*(3), 165–171.

Kavale, K. A., & Forness, S. R. (1996). Social skill deficits and learning disabilities: A meta-analysis. *Journal of Learning Disabilities, 29,* 226–237.

Kavale, K. A., & Mostert, M. P. (2004). Social skills interventions for individuals with learning disabilities. *Learning Disability Quarterly, 27*(1), 31–44.

Keogh, B. K. (2003). *Temperament in the classroom: Understanding individual differences.* Baltimore: Brookes.

Keogh, B. K. (1983). Individual differences in temperament: A contributor to the personal-social and educational competence of learning disabled children. In J. D. McKinney & L. Feagans (Eds.), *Current topics in learning disabilities, Vol. 1.* Norwood, NJ: Ablex.

Knight, D. (1999). Families of students with learning disabilities. In W. N. Bender (Ed.), *Professional issues in learning disabilities* (pp. 263–306). Austin, TX: ProEd.

Kravetz, S., Faust, M., Lipshitz, S., & Shalhav, S. (1999). LD, interpersonal understanding, and social behavior in the classroom. *Journal of Learning Disabilities, 32*(3), 248–255.

Lambert, N. M., & Hartsough, C. S. (1998). Prospective study of tobacco smoking and substance dependencies among samples of ADHD and non-ADHD participants. *Journal of Learning Disabilities, 31*(6), 533–544.

Lufi, D., Okasha, S., & Cohen, A. (2004). Test anxiety and its effect on the personality of students with learning disabilities. *Learning Disability Quarterly, 27* (3), 176–184.

Maag, J. W., Irvin, D. M., Reid, R., & Vasa, S. F. (1994). Prevalence and predictors of substance use: A comparison between adolescents with and without learning disabilities. *Journal of Learning Disabilities, 27,* 223–234.

Maag, J. W., & Reid, R. (1994). The phenomenology of depression among students with and without learning disabilities: More similar than different. *Learning Disabilities Research and Practice, 9*(2), 91–103.

Malian, I., & Nevin, A. (2002). A review of self-determination literature. *Remedial and Special Education, 23*(2), 68–75.

Margalit, M., & Almough, K. (1991). Classroom behavior and family climate in students with learning disabilities and hyperactive behavior. *Journal of Learning Disabilities, 24,* 406–412.

Margalit, M., & Levin-Alyagon, M. (1994). Learning disability subtyping, loneliness, and classroom adjustment. *Learning Disability Quarterly, 17,* 297–310.

Margalit, M., & Shulman, S. (1986). Autonomy perceptions and anxiety expressions of learning disabled adolescents. *Journal of Learning Disabilities, 19,* 291–293.

Margalit, M., & Zak, I. (1984). Anxiety and self-concept of learning disabled children. *Journal of Learning Disabilities, 17,* 537–539.

Martin, S. S., Brady, M. P., & Kotarba, J. A. (1992). Families with chronically ill young children: The unsinkable family. *Remedial and Special Education, 13*(2), 6–15.

Martin, J. E., Van Dycke, J. L., Christensen, W. R., Greene, B. A., Gardner, J. E., & Lovett, D. L. (2006). Increasing student participation in IEP meetings: Establishing the self-directed IEP as an evidence-based practice. *Exceptional Children, 72*(3), 299–316.

Martin, J. E., Van Dycke, J. L., Greene, B. A., Gardner, J. E., Christensen, W. R., Woods, L. L., & Lovett, D. L. (2006). Direct observation of teacher-directed IEP meetings: Establishing the need for student IEP meeting instruction. *Exceptional Children, 72*(2), 187–200.

McBride, H. E. A., & Siegel, L. S. (1997). Learning disabilities and adolescent suicide. *Journal of Learning Disabilities, 30*(6), 652–659.

Meltzer, L., Roditi, B., Houser, R. F., & Perlman, M. (1998). Perceptions of academic strategies and competence in students with learning disabilities. *Journal of Learning Disabilities, 31,* 437–451.

Molina, B. S. G., & Pelham, W. E. (2001). Substance use, substance abuse, and LD among adolescents with a childhood history of ADHD. *Journal of Learning Disabilities, 34*(4), 333–342.

Morningstar, M. E., Turnbull, A. P., & Turnbull, H. R. (1995). What do students with disabilities tell us about the importance of family involvement in the transition from school to adult life? *Exceptional Children, 62,* 249–260.

Most, T., & Greenbank, A. (2000). Auditory, visual, and auditory-visual perception of emotions by adolescents with and without learning disabilities and their relationship to social skills. *Learning Disabilities Research and Practice, 15*(1), 171–178.

Newcomer, P. L., Barenbaum, E., & Pearson, N. (1995). Depression and anxiety in children and adolescents with learning disabilities, conduct disorders, and no disabilities. *Journal of Emotional and Behavioral Disorders, 3*(1), 27–39.

Ochoa, S. H., & Palmer, D. J. (1991). A sociometric analysis of between-group differences and within-group status variability of Hispanic learning disabled and nonhandicapped pupils in academic and play contexts. *Learning Disability Quarterly, 14,* 208–218.

Palladino, P., Poli, P., Masi, G., & Marcheschi, M. (2000). The relation between metacognition and depressive symptoms in preadolescents with learning disabilities: Support of Borkowski's model. *Learning Disabilities Research and Practice, 15*(3), 142–148.

Pavri, S., & Monda-Amaya, L. M. (2000). Loneliness and students with learning disabilities in inclusive classrooms: Self-perceptions, coping strategies, and preferred interventions. *Learning Disabilities Research and Practice, 15*(1), 22–33.

Pavri, S., & Monda-Amaya, L. M. (2001). Social support in inclusive schools: Student and teacher perspectives. *Exceptional Children, 67*(3), 391–411.

Pearl, R., & Bryan, T. (1992). Students' expectations about peer pressure to engage in misconduct. *Journal of Learning Disabilities, 25,* 582–597.

Peck, M. L. (1985). Crisis intervention treatment with chronically and acutely suicidal adolescents. In M. Peck, N. Farbelow, & R. Litman (Eds.), *Youth suicide* (pp. 1–33). New York: Springer-Verlag.

Piers, E. V. (1984). *Piers-Harris Children's Self-Concept Scale, revised manual.* Los Angeles: Western Psychological Services.

Price, L. A., Wolensky, D., & Mulligan, R. (2002). Self-determination in action in the classroom. *Remedial and Special Education, 23*(2), 109–116.

Pullis, M. E. (1985). LD students' temperament characteristics and their impact on decisions by resource and mainstream teachers. *Learning Disability Quarterly, 8,* 109–121.

Ring, M. M., & Reetz, L. (2000). Modification effects on attributions of middle school students with learning disabilities. *Learning Disabilities Research and Practice, 15*(1), 34–42.

Rosenthal, I. (1992). Counseling the learning disabled late adolescent and adult: A self-psychology perspective. *Learning Disabilities Research and Practice, 7,* 217–225.

Rothman, H. W., & Cosden, M. (1995). The relationship between self-perception of a learning disability and achievement, self-concept, and social support. *Learning Disability Quarterly, 18,* 203–212.

Sabornie, E. J. (1994). Social-affective characteristics in early adolescents identified as learning disabled and nondisabled. *Learning Disability Quarterly, 17,* 268–279.

Sabornie, E. J., & Kauffman, J. M. (1986). Social acceptance of learning disabled adolescents. *Learning Disability Quarterly, 9,* 55–60.

Schunk, D. H. (1985). Participation in goal setting: Effects on self-efficacy and skills of learning dis-

abled children. *Journal of Special Education, 19,* 307–316.

Settle, S. A., & Milich, R. (1999). Social persistence following failure in boys and girls with LD. *Journal of Learning Disabilities, 32,* 201–212.

Sharma, G. (2004). A comparative study of the personality characteristics of primary-school students with learning disabilities and their non–learning disabled peers. *Learning Disability Quarterly, 27* (3), 127–140.

Swanson, S., & Howell, C. (1996). Test anxiety in adolescents with learning disabilities and behavioral disorders. *Exceptional Children, 62,* 389–397.

Teglasi, H., Cohn, A., & Meshbesher, N. (2004). Temperament and learning disability. *Learning Disability Quarterly, 27*(1), 9–20.

Test, D. W., Fowler, C. H., Brewer, D. M., & Wood, W. M. (2005). A content and methodological review of self-advocacy intervention studies. *Exceptional Children, 72*(1), 101–125.

Test, D. W., Mason, C., Hughes, C., Konrad, M., Neale, M., & Wood, W. M. (2004). Student involvement in individualized education program meetings. *Exceptional Children, 70*(4), 391–412.

Vaughn, S., Elbaum, B. E., Schumm, J. S., & Hughes, M. T. (1998). Social outcomes for students with and without learning disabilities in inclusive classrooms. *Journal of Learning Disabilities, 31,* 428–436.

Vaughn, S., & Haager, D. (1994). Social competence as a multifaceted construct: How do students with learning disabilities fare? *Learning Disability Quarterly, 17,* 253–267.

Vaughn, S., & La Greca, A. (1993). Social skills training: Why, who, what, how? In W. N. Bender (Ed.), *Learning disabilities: Best practices for professionals.* Boston: Andover Medical Publishers.

Vaughn, S., La Greca, A. M., & Kuttler, A. F. (1999). The why, who, and how of social skills. In W. N. Bender (Ed.), *Professional issues in learning disabilities* (pp. 187–218). Austin, TX: ProEd.

Vaughn, S., McIntosh, R., & Spencer-Rowe, J. (1991). Peer rejection is a stubborn thing: Increasing peer acceptance of rejected students with learning disabilities. *Learning Disabilities Research and Practice, 6,* 83–88.

Voltz, D. L. (1994). Developing collaborative parent-teacher relationships with culturally diverse parents. *Intervention in School and Clinic, 29*(5), 288–291.

Waggoner, K., & Wilgosh, L. (1990). Concerns of families of children with learning disabilities. *Journal of Learning Disabilities, 23,* 97–98.

Wehmeyer, M. L., Field, S., Doren, B., Jones, B., & Mason, C. (2004). Self-determination and student involvement in standards-based reform. *Exceptional Children, 70*(4), 413–425.

Weinberg, N. Z. (2001). Risk factors for adolescent substance abuse. *Journal of Learning Disabilities, 34*(4), 243–251.

Wiener, J. (2004). Do peer relationships foster behavioral adjustment in children with learning disabilities? *Learning Disability Quarterly, 27*(1), 21–30.

Whitney-Thomas, J., & Moloney, M. (2001). "Who I Am and What I Want": Adolescents' self-definition and struggles. *Exceptional Children, 67*(3), 375–390.

Wright-Stawderman, C., Lindsey, P., Navarette, L., & Flippo, J. R. (1996). Depression in students with disabilities: Recognition and intervention strategies. *Intervention in School and Clinic, 31*(5), 261–275.

Wright-Stawderman, C., & Watson, B. (1992). The prevalence of depressive symptoms in children with learning disabilities. *Journal of Learning Disabilities, 25,* 258–264.

CHAPTER FIVE

ASSESSMENT OF LEARNING DISABILITIES

CHAPTER OUTLINE

WHEN YOU COMPLETE THIS CHAPTER, YOU SHOULD BE ABLE TO:

1. Describe an assessment eligibility report that is based on ability-achievement discrepancies.
2. Describe an RTI assessment procedure.
3. Review a child-study team report to determine the type of perspective underlying the evaluation.
4. Identify the types of assessment information useful for eligibility decisions and instructional decisions.
5. Demonstrate a simple task analysis as an in-class assessment device.
6. List the types of daily work that should be used as informal assessments in child-study team meetings.
7. Describe the calculation of an ability-achievement discrepancy coupled with RTI as a basis for the eligibility decision.

KEYWORDS

intelligence testing	standard-score discrepancy	authentic assessment
eligibility	regression-based discrepancy	portfolio assessment
IEP	response to intervention (RTI)	dynamic assessment
curriculum-based assessment	educational consultant	strength-based assessment
criterion-referenced testing	norm-referenced tests	minimum competency tests
WISC-III	prereferral report	
subtest scatter	task analysis	
discrepancy	error analysis	

INTRODUCTION

The purpose of this chapter is to present the various assessment options currently in use with children who have learning disabilities, in the context of the information that has already been presented in the case-study reports, the history, and the perspectives on learning disabilities. Frequent references will be made to the case-study reports and the various perspectives on learning disabilities discussed in Chapter 1, and the individualized educational plans (IEPs) in the Appendix. Therefore, this chapter on assessment is intended to provide a gestalt experience in which your understanding of the field of learning disabilities comes together and you perceive the diverse perspectives and assessment procedures as a meaningful whole. Also, it may be useful to reexamine the information in the earlier chapters as you read.

BROAD PURPOSES OF ASSESSMENT

In special education, assessment is mandated for several reasons. First of all, assessment was historically seen as one method of protecting the interests of the child (Commission for Excellence in Special Education, 2001; NJCLD, 2005). For example, in earlier years in school systems that had classes for students with mental retardation, if a particular child became disruptive and did not complete the homework assignment, the teacher may have wanted to remove that child from the class. One convenient way to accomplish this was to ship the child out to a special education class, even though the child may not have been retarded. **Intelligence testing,** conducted on an individual basis, was intended to prevent this type of disservice to the child.

Second, there is a need in the schools to identify children who need help earlier (Fuchs & Fuchs, 2006). Many children occasionally fail a semester or grade, but not every child who fails is disabled (Commission, 2001). Failure can occur for a number of other reasons, ranging from disruptions at home to incomplete homework assignments. Clearly, the schools need some mechanism by which to screen children in order to decide which children demonstrate failure resulting from a learning disability. Therefore, a major reason for individualized assessment is the need to document the **eligibility** of a particular child for a particular type of special educational service provided by the school.

Another reason for assessment is the need to document the actual levels of performance on various classroom tasks in order to provide an individualized educational plan (**IEP**) (Commission, 2001). This need led to the recent emphasis on **curriculum-based assessment.** Much of the recent research in assessment has been directed toward assessment for instruction (Bryant, 1999; Jones, 2001), and almost all this research has demonstrated the effectiveness of periodic assessments conducted by the teacher on a weekly, biweekly, or daily basis (Fuchs & Fuchs, 2005; Jones, 2001). Theorists have argued that special education assessment, by virtue of being totally individualized, should compare a child's performance with a stated list of criteria or behavioral objectives that the child must master, rather than an arbitrary score derived from a norm group of children on a particular test (NJCLD, 2005). Consequently, concepts such as **criterion-referenced testing,** task analysis, curriculum-based assessment, and responsiveness to instruction have received increasing research emphasis. However, prior to discussion of these innovations, it is necessary to understand the use of psychometric assessment in identification of students with learning disabilities.

ASSESSMENT FOR ELIGIBILITY DECISIONS

As demonstrated in the discussion on definitions, and the recent passage of IDEA 2004, determining whether or not a child has a learning disability is a task about which there is little consensus at present (Commission, 2001; Gersten & Dimino, 2006; NJCLD, 2005). Consequently it is difficult to report on the best method to identify children or adolescents with learning disabilities. Since substantial change in how students' learning disabilities are documented can be expected in coming years, the most appropriate approach meanwhile

should include understanding both the new eligibility procedures as well as the more recently implemented eligibility procedures for documentation of a learning disability.

At present, new teachers in the field will probably be exposed to both more traditional
eligibility procedures for documenting a learning disability as well as the more recently
developed response-to-intervention procedures. In the sections below, the text will present
the more traditional eligibility assessment procedures first, as listed in Figure 5.1, and subsequently a discussion of response-to-intervention procedures.

FIGURE 5.1   Assessment for Eligibility

COMPONENTS OF LD DEFINITION	COMMON ASSESSMENTS
I. Psychological processing problem	
IQ assessment	WISC-III
(Subtest scatter/verbal)	Stanford-Binet
Performance deficit/subtest regrouping	Woodcock-Johnson Kaufman Assessment Battery for Children (K-ABC)
Visual-perception/visual-motor	Bender Gestalt Woodcock-Johnson WISC-III
Auditory perception/language	Test of Language Development Woodcock-Johnson WISC-III
II. Discrepancy	
Intraindividual differences	Woodcock-Johnson WISC-III
Ability-achievement discrepancy	WISC-III Woodcock-Johnson Peabody Individual Achievement Test–Revised (PIATr) Test of Written Language K-ABC
III. Exclusionary clause	
MR	IQ tests
Behavioral disorders	Class observations Teacher ratings of behavior Sociometric ratings
Mental disability	Physician's examination
Cultural/environmental/economic	Examination of school records History of speech improvements

Psychological Processes

The psychological processes component of the definition is intended to focus on the types of ability deficits that may prohibit learning. Consequently, many tests of auditory and visual perception or motor control can be subsumed under this component. The use of intelligence tests to demonstrate deficits or developmental imbalances in psychological processing also represents an attempt to effectively quantify the psychological process component of the definition.

Intelligence Assessment.   Currently, the Wechsler Intelligence Scale for Children, Third Edition (**WISC-III**), is the most commonly used assessment for measuring intelligence in children with learning disabilities. Other commonly used tests include the cognitive section of the Woodcock-Johnson Psychoeducational Battery, the Stanford-Binet Intelligence Scale, and the Kaufman Assessment Battery for Children.

The use of intelligence tests to document deficits in the basic psychological processes has been repeatedly attempted, and the roots of these efforts spring from the concept of "developmental imbalances." Developmental imbalance may best be understood as an uneven pattern of development, such that a student may function on grade level in math but significantly below grade level in reading. Thus, an imbalance will be shown when his or her academic scores in these areas are compared.

Most of the suggestions for documenting a developmental imbalance have used one of the standard IQ measures mentioned previously. For example, the subtests on the WISC-III (Wechsler, 1991) may be used to calculate a single score on general intelligence, but they may also be used to calculate two different scores: verbal intelligence and performance intelligence. Here the verbal IQ would represent language-based learning, and the performance IQ would represent visual interpretation, synthesis, and the ability to copy designs. If these two scores were widely discrepant, a developmental imbalance could, presumably, be identified and would account for a learning disability. While this distinction between verbal IQ and performance IQ will be discussed in the occasional assessment report, this concept is now considered discredited (Commission, 2001; Siegel, 1999).

Another conceptualization of this developmental imbalance idea involves analysis of **subtest scatter,** or how the scores on an IQ assessment are grouped (Watkins, 1996). If the range of the individual subtest scores is unusually high, this would tend to indicate an imbalance in normal cognitive development. However, numerous theorists have raised questions about the appropriateness of these types of calculations (Watkins, 1996), and like the development imbalances approach described previously, the subtest scatter concept has been discredited. However, many practitioners in the field still attempt to utilize this rationale in describing a learning disability, and you may find such a rationale in various assessment reports even today. Thus, you should be aware of this logic and the unproven theoretical rationale on which it is based.

Visual-Perceptal and Visual-Motor Tests.   The most common visual-perceptual and visual-motor tests used today are the Bender Visual Motor Gestalt Test and the Developmental Tests of Visual Motor Integration. Although most intelligence tests include some subtests that are basically visual in nature, IQ tests are not included in this general domain of tests because IQ tests also assess things other than visual perception and motor performance. Basically, the tests listed above involve only visual perception and motor responses to these perceptions. The test items generally involve copying various geometric designs in order to demonstrate an ability to adequately perceive and reproduce information, though there may also be figure-ground discrimination problems and reversals. Interest Box 5.1 presents two items from the Developmental Tests of Visual Motor Integration. These tests generally have very low reliabilities, and some authorities have recommended that use of this type of assessment be terminated (Council for Learning Disabilities, 1987). As a result, these tests are being used less and less often in assessment of children with disabilities.

Auditory and Language Processes Assessments.   Historically, the Illinois Test of Psycholinguistic Ability, the Peabody Picture Vocabulary Test, and the Wepman Auditory Discrimination Test were the most widely used instruments for assessment of auditory and language processes. However, early research demonstrated many of the same types of reliability problems with these instruments as were demonstrated with the visual-perceptual instruments (Council for Learning Disabilities, 1987). Also, the same debate that concerns visual-perceptual testing is applicable here: Many professionals today question the

■ ■ ■ ■ ■ ▬▬▬▬▬▬▬▬▬▬▬▬▬▬▬▬▬▬▬▬▬▬▬▬▬▬▬▬▬▬

INTEREST BOX 5.1
SAMPLE ITEMS FROM PERCEPTUAL-MOTOR TESTS

Many visual-perceptual tests assess a student's ability to visually perceive a geometric design and to copy that design. Both the Bender Visual Motor Gestalt Test and the Developmental Tests of Visual Motor Integration use this assessment procedure. The early assumption behind such tests was the belief that problems with letter and word reversals could be detected in this fashion. Note the tasks below and the similarity to commonly reversed visual stimuli. These items represent the types of tasks that are found on these visual-perceptual tests. Typically, the student would copy a number of these designs, and the examiner would grade the student on the quality of the copy (lines parallel, intersecting, angles correct, etc.).

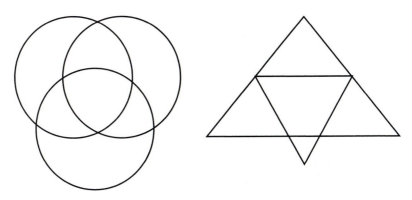

usefulness of these assessment instruments. However, many speech clinicians and learning disabilities teachers use various sections of these tests to assess language usage and supplement these assessments with classroom observations or recorded samples of children's language output.

A host of more recently developed instruments has been designed to assess language functioning. For example, the Tests of Language Development, which come in either a primary or intermediate version, are the most widely used assessments of language today. Likewise, the recent assessments by Wiig (the Let's Talk Inventory for Children or Adolescents) are well-designed assessments of language. These assessments are much more acceptable, from a technical assessment perspective, than the assessments that were utilized earlier.

Many intelligence tests have sections or subtests that provide information on verbal abilities and receptive or expressive language. Consequently, most professionals who need this type of information today utilize a verbal score from one of the frequently used tests of intelligence.

Process Testing Revisited.   Assessment of basic psychological processes or ability deficits grew from the early medical assumptions in the field. Both the perceptual-motor theorists and the language theorists produced assessments that were later shown to be less than technically adequate for educational purposes (Ysseldyke, 1983). More recently, the use of standardized IQ assessments as a basis to document these psychological processes (Commission, 2001) has become commonplace. However, in some areas, newer assessments that are more acceptable technically have been developed.

As professionals, each of you will have to take responsibility for decisions regarding assessment of psychological processes or ability deficits. For example, as a student, you should be aware of the debate concerning the use of these tests, and as a teacher (or future teacher), you should realize that many different perspectives concerning these tests are possible. Will you use these tests or sit as a member of a team that uses these tests to make educational decisions? What additional evidence is necessary in order to supplement the assessment findings in these areas? All these questions are unanswered at present. Perhaps the best strategy is to discuss these concerns with the director of special education in your district in order to find out the local and state perspectives regarding the use of these instruments. However, at this point, it must be stated that accurate, technically sound assessment of basic psychological processes is not possible psychometrically, given the low reliability and validity of most of these instruments (CLD, 1987).

Discrepancy Criteria

The belief that children with learning disabilities have a problem in school subjects prompted the **discrepancy** concept. In a very basic sense, would an educator wish to provide a specialized—and thus more expensive—program to a child who was capable of reaching his or her potential in the general education class without any modifications? The original discrepancy concept was merely an attempt to demonstrate that a child needed some type of extra assistance.

However, with the failure of assessments of psychological processes, the discrepancy component became the only defensible operationalized aspect of the definition. Consequently, many states now employ versions of this concept, and practitioners rely on this aspect of the definition more than on measures of psychological processes during the eligibility phase of assessment.

The ability-achievement discrepancy states that a child has a major deficit in some area of school achievement compared to his or her potential. This concept has had at least four major variations over the last 20 years, though only the most recent two aspects of this concept are directly relevant today (Commission, 2001). Interest Box 5.2 presents the historical development of the concept.

Standard-Score Discrepancies.   Many states and local districts employ a **standard-score discrepancy** procedure for identification of learning disabilities (Commission, 2001; NJCLD, 2005). In this procedure, scores from an intelligence test and an achievement test—usually a reading achievement test—that have the same mean and standard deviation are obtained. The achievement score is then subtracted from the intelligence test score, and if the discrepancy is great enough, a learning disability has been documented.

Because many tests will yield scores that have a mean of 100 and a standard deviation of 15, this procedure is relatively easy for teachers and child-study team members to use.

■ ■ ■ ■ ■ ■

INTEREST BOX 5.2
DISCREPANCY FORMULAS

There have been four major types of ability-achievement discrepancy calculations.

1. Some practitioners began to calculate a discrepancy between grade placement and achievement level by merely subtracting the latter from the former. This procedure suggested that a fifth-grader who was reading at a second-grade level must be disabled.
2. The "formula" calculations were the next to evolve. Because the procedure above did not take into account the child's level of intelligence, numerous theorists developed formulas that did. These formulas usually involved calculation of an expected achievement based on intelligence and grade placement, which was then compared to actual achievement to indicate a discrepancy.
3. Standard-score calculations were developed next. The formulas described above were generally based on mathematical manipulation of grade-equivalent scores (e.g., a 3.5 in reading). Calculations such as these are inappropriate mathematically because the standard deviations of the different grade-equivalent scores are different. Consequently, the concept of a standardized-score comparison was developed, where the practitioner would obtain an IQ score and an achievement score based on tests that have the same mean and standard deviation. These scores are mathematically comparable.
4. The regression-score table was developed from the standard-score procedure. As any statistics student knows, repeated tests resulting in scores that are either very high or very low tend to yield scores that regress toward (or fall back toward) the mean, and this can create error. Thus, some states use regression tables, which are basically standard-score comparisons that take this regression into account.

For example, school districts in the state of North Carolina regularly employ this method. Both the Wechsler Intelligence Scale for Children, Third Edition, and the cognitive battery of the Woodcock-Johnson, Revised, will yield IQ scores of this nature. The reading section of the Woodcock-Johnson, Revised, and the Peabody Individual Achievement Test, Revised, provide reading and math achievement scores that employ this metric.

However, the federal government failed to provide guidelines on how large the discrepancy between ability and achievement had to be before a student is considered disabled. State and local education agencies have chosen to define this discrepancy at various levels. For example, the state of North Carolina uses a 15-point (or a 1-standard-deviation) discrepancy while the state of Georgia has indicated that a discrepancy of 20 points is necessary in order to be eligible for placement in a class for the learning disabled. Certain theorists have recommended a 2-standard-deviation discrepancy prior to labeling a child as learning disabled. Clearly, a small discrepancy cannot be the sole indicator of a learning disability because, given the nature of standardized scores, as many as 17% of all public school students demonstrate a difference of 1 standard deviation between IQ and achievement. However, the smaller the discrepancy that is required, the more flexibility local decision makers have in assigning a child to a class for the learning disabled, and this desire for flexibility may be one reason the use of such procedures has continued. A sample discrepancy calculation is presented in Interest Box 5.3.

Regression-Based Discrepancy Tables.   A mathematical problem with the standard-score discrepancy procedure was soon identified. When a student is administered a series of tests and the scores are correlated, the scores of that student will tend to regress toward the mean, particularly if the scores are notably higher or lower than the mean. Consequently, the standard-score discrepancy procedure is likely to be much less accurate for a student whose IQ is particularly high or particularly low. As a result of this mathematical phenomenon, some states have produced tables of information that take this regression phenomenon into account even though based on the standard-score discrepancy concept. This is known as **regression-based discrepancy.** For example, Iowa uses regression tables of this nature. In states that use a regression table, the assessment personnel administer the intelligence and achievement tests and use the chart to identify the minimum discrepancy necessary to document a learning disability given that particular level of intelligence.

Exclusionary Clause

Although the discrepancy formulations discussed previously have received research attention, very little information is available on methods by which the exclusionary clause may be operationalized. For example, what types of data may be used to discriminate between a child with learning disabilities and some secondary behavioral problems and a child with behavior problems who also demonstrates achievement deficits? How are children who are culturally disadvantaged separated from children who are learning disabled, and how does a team of assessment professionals (which will include you, as a teacher) distinguish between a child who needs services in a class for the learning disabled, based on language deficits, and a child who needs a speech clinician's assistance? These are questions for which there are no easy answers.

■ ■ ■ ■ ■

INTEREST BOX 5.3

SAMPLE DISCREPANCY CALCULATION FOR ELIGIBILITY DETERMINATION

Alonzo Shanker is a 10-year-old student in Atlanta, Georgia, who was referred for evaluation with a possible learning disability. Georgia uses a 20-point discrepancy criterion for determination of eligibility for learning disability services, and such a discrepancy must be documented on at least two assessments. The psychologist used an IQ assessment and several reading assessments along with a clinical interview, teachers' ratings of behavior, and other assessments and documented the discrepancies as described below. Alonzo's scores were as follows.

- Stanford-Binet Intelligence Scale, 4th ed.

Verbal Reasoning	92
Abstract/Visual Reasoning	94
Quantitative Reasoning	90
Short-Term Memory	108
Test Composite Score	95

- Wechsler Individual Achievement Test

Basic Reading	76
Reading Comprehension	64
Total Reading	69

- Woodcock-Johnson Reading Comprehension Score   67

Discrepancies between the total composite IQ score (95) and the total reading scores (69 and 67, respectively) each indicated a discrepancy of more than 20 points (26 and 28 points, respectively). This is well over 1 standard deviation and surpasses the 20-point discrepancy criterion used in Georgia for documentation of a learning disability. Thus, a discrepancy has been documented for this student. Also, the evidence suggests that Alonzo demonstrated normal intelligence and very low reading scores in every area.

Of course, documentation of a discrepancy between IQ and achievement is only one facet of the identification process, and this procedure has been challenged (Council for Exceptional Children, 2002; Commission, 2001). Also, a difference of 20 points or more between IQ and other academic areas (e.g., writing, math, or spelling) can likewise be used to document a discrepancy for eligibility purposes.

This issue is further complicated by the nature of the exclusionary clause. The federal definition does not say that students with learning disabilities cannot also demonstrate other disabilities. Rather, the definition merely stipulates that those other conditions are believed to be secondary in nature and not the primary cause of the learning disability. Thus, a student with learning disabilities may also have secondary emotional or behavioral problems and/or come from an environmentally disadvantaged background.

Current practice and federal guidelines do give some indications concerning these distinctions. Because the last part of the definition indicates the conditions that are excluded as the primary cause of the learning disability, part of the assessment process for determining potential learning disabilities in children is identification of the characteristics that would indicate the presence and severity of these other conditions.

Distinction: Mental Retardation.   Children who are mentally retarded cannot technically be learning disabled, though there is every reason to believe that some children with retardation may demonstrate the characteristics of learning disabilities in terms of letter-reversal problems, language problems, perceptual problems, and behavioral problems such as hyperactivity. Still, if the IQ score and adaptive behavior of the child indicate that a placement in a class for children who are retarded is warranted, the child should not be considered learning disabled. The problem arises in situations where a child's IQ score is lower than normal (i.e., in the 74 to 85 range) but not low enough to warrant placement as retarded. Many such children are labeled learning disabled, in spite of the fact that their IQ is not in the normal range, which is usually assumed to be 85 or higher. Child-assessment teams may decide that such a label will result in services for the child that would be unavailable otherwise. Although such practice cannot be condoned, it can be readily understood by any professional who has ever been in the position of a team member who sees a child failing in the traditional general education class. Many scholars have called for more flexibility in placing this type of child in non–special education classes that have small numbers of students, more individualized instruction, and an emphasis on remediation. However, until additional services such as these are available, many students without any identifiable disabilities will continue to be placed in classes for children with learning disabilities.

Distinction: Emotional and Behavioral Disorders.   Unfortunately, the distinction between emotional problems and learning disabilities is vague. This is because emotional and behavioral disorders often have a negative effect on academic work, and depressed academic scores in an intelligent student may resemble a learning disability. Further, learning disabilities often have a negative emotional or behavioral effect and may therefore resemble an emotional or behavioral disorder. The guideline question or general rule of thumb in making this distinction is: Does the emotional problem cause the academic deficit, or does the academic deficit cause the emotional problem? In gathering evidence on this, several types of information may be sought. First, input from the teacher who referred the child concerning the child's behavior, peer relationships, and motivation in class may indicate that the child's problems are basically academic in nature. If the student seems emotionally healthy based on these indicators, the child is probably not emotionally disturbed or behaviorally disordered. Teachers are generally good observers of classroom behavior, and numerous ratings of behavior, which the general education teacher may be asked to complete, can provide this information.

   Next, the peers in the class can also provide information on the behavior and social skills of the student. Various informal roster-rating techniques may be used to elicit information on the social acceptance of the child. These devices require every child in the class to indicate the level of social acceptance of every other child in the class. When the results are tallied, the totals will indicate the level of acceptance of any child in the class. If both teacher ratings and sociometric information indicate major behavioral abnormalities or very low social acceptance, perhaps a placement as emotionally disturbed is more justified than placement as learning disabled. Under those conditions, the child-study team would want to gather more complete information, possibly including a therapeutic interview between the child and a trained counselor in order to determine the extent of the emotional disturbance.

It should be noted that teachers are not trained to conduct sociometric roster-rating procedures in most teacher education programs. Consequently, if such information is needed, child-study team members should be used to conduct this type of assessment. As in most cases involving assessment data, information from a sociometric assessment in the wrong hands can be detrimental.

Distinction: Medical Disability.   The definition of learning disabilities clearly excludes individuals who have visual, auditory, or motor deficiencies. Unlike the perceptual problems or basic psychological processes discussed previously, this phrase in the definition indicates problems that can be identified by visual, motor, or auditory screening and follow-up procedures. Although child-study assessment teams generally do not include a physician, assessments for medically based conditions can be obtained. In some cases, the school nurse, a speech clinician, or an audiologist may be able to provide initial screening in these areas. Medical causes for learning problems must not be overlooked in the initial procedures dealing with new referrals, though few referrals require more than brief hearing and visual-screening procedures.

Distinction: Cultural, Environmental, Economic Disadvantage.   One difficult distinction to be made is the discrimination between students with disabilities and students who have been raised in a depressed or language-poor environment. Although children who are poor and economically or environmentally disadvantaged may have a learning disability, the placement team must determine that the primary cause for the disability is not environmental disadvantage. Some practitioners have argued that this distinction need not be made at all because students who are culturally deprived need many of the same types of educational modifications as children with learning disabilities. Still, the current federal definition stipulates that this distinction be made, though no guidelines are currently available for making this distinction.

Distinction: Students Who Are Low Achieving.   Often, it is quite difficult to distinguish between students who have learning disabilities and students who are low achieving for other reasons (Commission, 2001; Fuchs & Fuchs, 2006). In fact, one reason for the recent emphasis on response to intervention is the fact that procedures used currently do not facilitate this distinction at all. While some individual research studies have suggested differences between students with learning disabilities and low-achieving students, school districts have not systematically attempted to make this distinction. Still, the intention of various legislative definitions of learning disabilities historically has been to exclude students who are low achieving from services unless they also manifested some documented disorder in the basic psychological processes described above.

Distinction: ADHD.   With the recent increase in students identified as demonstrating attention-deficit hyperactivity disorders, there is a growing concern related to how to distinguish students with learning disabilities from those with ADHD. The Commission on

Excellence in Special Education (2001) noted the similarities between ADHD and learning disabilities. Both groups do demonstrate problems in attention, and both may also demonstrate hyperactivity, impulsivity, and a lack of organizational skill. In fact, many students with ADHD have been considered "learning disabled" over the years, and determining the distinguishing characteristics of these groups has proven difficult. Further, Barkley (1990) indicated that as many as 40% of students with learning disabilities may also manifest attention-deficit disorders.

In a report on assessment and identification of students with attention-deficit disorders, Montague, McKinney, and Hocutt (1994) suggested that a number of procedures may be used for diagnosis, including teacher ratings, observational techniques, and interviews. Of course, these same techniques may also be employed when a learning disability is suspected, and use of the same techniques to identify these two groups merely confuses the discrimination process.

Given this difficulty in distinguishing these two groups, teachers should realize that the basis of the distinction is the documented discrepancy between ability and achievement. Although the size of the discrepancy required for an identification of learning disability changes from one state to another, if a large discrepancy is noted, the child will typically be identified as a student with a learning disability. Alternatively, if the child has attention problems, hyperactivity, and/or impulsivity, but does not demonstrate a large discrepancy between ability and achievement, the child will typically be identified as ADHD. Once identified as ADHD, the child may either receive special services in the regular education program or be placed in special education under the "other health impaired" category.

Response to Intervention

As discussed in previous chapters, federal law now allows the use of a child's **response to intervention (RTI)** as a documentation of his or her learning disability (Batsche et al., 2004; Marston, 2005; Scruggs & Mastropieri, 2002; Mastropieri & Scruggs, 2005). This is the most recent change in eligibility procedures, and in many ways, it is perhaps the most innovative (Fuchs & Fuchs, 2005, 2006; Gersten & Dimino, 2006). This approach resulted from the general dissatisfaction with previous approaches for documentation of a learning disability, in particular a dissatisfaction with the discrepancy criteria described in Chapter 1. In short, many policy makers believe that the discrepancy criteria results in overidentification of students with learning disabilities and thus increases the overall costs of special education (Fuchs & Fuchs, 2006). Other reasons for dissatisfaction with current eligibility procedures include inconsistency in definitions of learning disabilities from one state to another and the tendency of discrepancy procedures to identify as learning disabled students who have merely been exposed to poor teaching (Fuchs & Fuchs, 2006).

The RTI procedure involves actual implementation of several intervention procedures that under normal conditions would be expected to result in academic growth. In the absence of such academic growth, a learning disability is assumed to exist (Batsche et al., 2004; Fuchs & Fuchs, 2006). Conceptually, this is perhaps the most effective method for documenting the existence of a learning disability, and the RTI eligibility procedure now has many proponents (Fuchs & Fuchs, 2005, 2006; Gersten & Dimino, 2006; Marston, 2005; Scruggs & Mastropieri, 2002; Mastropieri & Scruggs, 2005), though others have raised concerns with this new procedure (NJCLD, 2005).

In the discussions available in the professional literature, a "tiered system" involving several interventions is typically recommended in order to "prove" a child has a learning disability (Batsche et al., 2004). For example, the National Joint Committee on Learning Disabilities described a three-tiered system of interventions (NJCLD, 2005). Perhaps an RTI example will best demonstrate this procedure; the description below is a synthesis of a variety of different research-based RTI models (Fuchs & Fuchs, 2005, 2006; Marston, 2005; Vaughn, Linan-Thompson, & Hickman, 2003; Vellutino et al., 1996).

Imagine a general education first-grade classroom including some 22 children. Under RTI procedures, the teacher would be expected to conduct some type of screening assessment in reading—perhaps a measure of word identification fluency—in the second or third month of the school year, in order to identify those children who may be struggling with reading. Early in grade 1, students may be expected to know perhaps 10 to 15 words (*a, the, he, she,* etc.), since some of these words may have been mastered in kindergarten and others would have been learned in the early fall of the first-grade year. After administering that assessment for every child, the teacher could then identify the lowest 25% of students in the class. These students would then be targeted for some type of scientifically validated instructional procedure in the general education classroom. Those students scoring above the lowest 25% would not be considered eligible for LD services. The intervention used for the lowest-scoring group of students would represent the first tier of the RTI process—that is, it would be the first attempt by the schools to remediate potential reading problems for these students.

Most researchers recommend that this first tier of intervention be viewed as the responsibility of the general education teacher (Fuchs & Fuchs, 2005; Gersten & Dimino, 2006). Federal legislation requires that the teacher use a reading curriculum supported by scientific research. Surprising as it may seem, many commercially available reading curricula are not supported by independent scientific research.

During the tier 1 intervention, the general education teacher would be expected to periodically monitor the child's progress on various reading variables. Fuchs and Fuchs (2005) suggest such progress monitoring be undertaken at least once per week over a period of 8 to 10 weeks. Children whose weekly scores showed growth in reading skill would not be considered for further services for the learning disabled. However, students who did not demonstrate appropriate growth would move into the second tier of intervention.

To continue the example of the classroom described above, Figure 5.2 presents a progress monitoring chart for the tier 1 intervention. The student, Hernandez, was monitored on his word identification weekly during an 8-week intervention. As the scores show, he did not master new words very well. The general education teacher selected a random set of 50 words from the most common 200 sight words (i.e., words commonly mastered in the early years) and had Hernandez read as many as he could in 1 minute. That teacher counted the words read correctly in 1 minute and then charted that score at least once each week. Fuchs and Fuchs (2005) suggest a learning rate of perhaps 5 words per week, for pre-primer and first-grade words. Based on this criteria, the data show that Hermandez was not learning quickly enough to demonstrate a positive response to his reading intervention. The data indicate that he was only mastering at most one or two new words each week. Thus, he would be considered for the second tier of intervention.

Early research on RTI suggests that around 33% of students referred for learning disabilities do not succeed in learning during the first tier of instruction in the general education classroom (Vellutino et al., 1996), suggesting that these students may demonstrate a

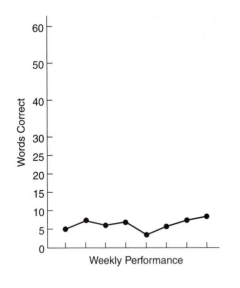

STUDENT NAME: _Hernandez_____

DATES: _9/24/06 – 11/14/06_____

FIGURE 5.2   Progress Monitoring/Tier 1 Intervention

learning disability. Based on these figures, perhaps two of the 22 children in this classroom would be judged unresponsive to the tier 1 instruction, and clearly Hernandez was one of those students.

Fuchs and Fuchs (2005) recommended that the second tier of intervention involve a more intensive reading instruction, involving small teacher-student ratios; they recommended instruction by either a teacher or paraprofessional and that there be no more than two or three students for this tier of the intervention. Instruction considered appropriate would include research-based direct instruction curricula in a variety of reading areas, such as phonics-based decoding skills, fluency, or reading comprehension. In the example, since Hernandez was not demonstrating mastery of words, his intervention would presumably be an intervention in word decoding and/or phonics. Most researchers recommend a more frequent performance-monitoring procedure in the tier 2 intervention phase than in tier 1 (Batsche et al., 2004; Marston, 2005). For example, Fuchs and Fuchs (2005) recommended progress monitoring weekly, while Vaughn, Linan-Thompson, and Hickman (2003) suggested monitoring progress twice a month. However, another possibility would be monitoring progress daily, and many computer-based educational curricula are currently set up to do this. The teacher can thereby develop a more comprehensive understanding of the child's progress, or lack thereof, in a much shorter timeframe.

Many researchers suggest that both general education teachers and special education teachers participate in the planning and intervention for students with reading difficulties in tier 2. Of course, this raises many questions concerning time and responsibilities of the teachers involved, and policy makers as well as researchers have yet to address such concerns. Different states will likely develop differing guidelines on who is responsible for tier 2 interventions, but most researchers suggest some involvement of special education personnel at this intervention level. A portion of federal funds for special education have been set aside for some degree of special education involvement at this point prior to the actual referral of the child for special education evaluation.

In progressing through these intervention tiers, students might be expected to successfully demonstrate academic growth with each increasingly intensive intervention. However, as you recall, the overall purpose of implementing RTI is to document students with specific learning disabilities. In this case, one might expect the opposite result—that is, fewer students succeeding in the instruction offered at each progressive tier. In fact, the extant research suggests that between 24 and 50% of students who were placed in tier 2 intensive instruction will not demonstrate appropriate academic progress, even though they are receiving intensive instruction (Vaughn et al., 2003; O'Connor, 2003). For students who do succeed in learning, progress monitoring reports will indicate their academic growth, and they will not be considered learning disabled. However, the 24 to 50% of students who do not succeed in tier 2 intervention will move to tier 3.

To return to our example, the tier 2 intervention for Hernandez involved placing him in an intensive phonemically based instructional program designed to teach him letter recognition, word decoding, and an increased vocabulary. Again, his progress in learning new words from the same word list was monitored, though in the tier 2 intervention, his word recognition was monitored daily for a period of four weeks. These data are shown in Figure 5.3. Even with the intensive intervention on phonics and word decoding skills, Hernandez still did not make adequate progress; therefore, he did not respond to instruction. Thus, he will move to tier 3 of the RTI process.

By the time Hernandez reaches the third tier of the RTI process, the eligibility team will be called together, and the child will be deemed eligible for services as a child with a learning disability. Clearly, for children who do not benefit from progressively intensive reading interventions, there is documented evidence of some type of learning problem. In this way, the RTI process promises to be a useful tool for documenting eligibility.

SAMPLE ELIGIBILITY REPORTS

The reports discussed next represent the most common type in the field today. These two reports present information that may be used to determine the eligibility of students for services in the class for students with learning disabilities. As you read through these reports, note the types of eligibility arguments that are presented to demonstrate that the child in question actually demonstrates a learning disability.

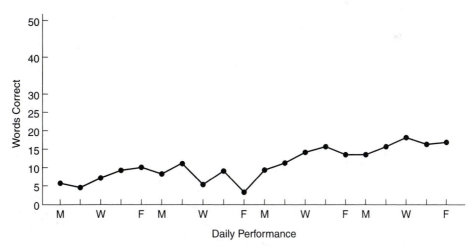

STUDENT NAME: _Hernandez_____

DATES: _11/15/06 – 12/18/06_____

FIGURE 5.3   Progress Monitoring/Tier 2 Intervention

Psychoeducational Team Assessment Report

In most cases involving diagnosis of a learning disability, a team of specialists is involved. This team may include a school psychologist, special education and general education teachers, school administrators, the child's parents, medical practitioners, and the student. The report in Interest Box 5.4 summarizes the types of information that the psychoeducational team might collect.

The psychoeducational team report includes a number of examples of the eligibility arguments based on the developmental-imbalances perspective. For example, the neurologist's report indicated that scores on a visual test were lower than would be expected for a child of this age. This led that professional to the conclusion that this child might have a learning disability. However, the psychologist used a different visual-motor assessment and concluded that there was no evidence of a visual-perceptual problem. The educational consultant's report was in agreement with the interpretation of the neurologist, in that there seemed to be evidence of a visual-perceptual problem and thus of a learning disability. Note that the summary for the entire team specifically highlighted the contradictory evidence on the presence or absence of a visual-perceptual problem. Finally, the educational consultants discussed the discrepancy between IQ and achievement in two areas.

Educational Consultant's Evaluation

Often, when a parent and a school district disagree concerning the diagnosis of learning disabilities, a private **educational consultant** will assess the child—or, in some cases, review assessment data—and render a decision concerning the child's eligibility for services. The report in Interest Box 5.5 represents the type of report an educational consultant might present.

As you can see from this report, the educational consultant has chosen to emphasize the developmental-imbalances perspective, by demonstrating a developmental imbalance between Adam's skill in hearing information compared to visual input. This is another example of the developmental imbalances eligibility argument that was discussed earlier in this chapter. Also, notice that the educational consultant documented a discrepancy between IQ and achievement as a major factor in the diagnosis of learning disability. Finally, you may wish to note the relative lack of educational suggestions presented in this report. Beyond the suggestions for placement and some work on writing skills, there is very little useful information in this report that could assist in planning educational activities for Adam.

Cultural Diversity and Eligibility Decisions

In spite of the best efforts of test manufacturers and educational personnel, research has shown that there is some degree of bias in many of the assessments used to document eligibility for services as learning disabled (Commission, 2001; Olivarez, Palmer, & Guillemard, 1992). This potential bias is particularly troubling when one considers that students with learning disabilities come from all cultures (Lerner & Chen, 1992). One growing concern with our eligibility assessment practices is the relatively limited cultural sensitivity of the assessment process (Hyun & Fowler, 1995; Leung, 1996). Many of the assessments

INTEREST BOX 5.4
PSYCHOEDUCATIONAL TEAM REPORT

NAME: Heather Demetri   **DATE OF BIRTH:** 4/24/98   **AGE:** 7-10

SCHOOL: Anderson Elementary   **GRADE:** 2   **DATE OF REPORT:** 3/6/06

TEAM MEMBERS: Dr. William Johnson, School Psychologist; Dr. Angela Brown, Educational Consultant; Dr. Tyler Gregson, Neurologist; Ms. Ann Duddley, Resource Teacher; Mr. John Franks, Second-Grade Teacher

REASONS FOR REFERRAL: Heather demonstrated difficulty in reading during her second-grade year in Mr. Franks's class. He contacted the parents and referred her to the child-study team.

NEUROLOGIST'S REPORT
Tests Administered.   Electroencephalogram, the Visual Motor Integration Test, and a clinical observation.

Test and Observation Results.   Heather was quite easy to work with. Rapport was established merely by explaining that I was going to ask her to do several fun things that she should consider as games. She was encouraged to do her best.

Heather's gait was quite normal, and observation of her gross motor movements indicated no problems in that area. Likewise, when she wrote her name and several other words on paper, she did not have any noticeable difficulty in fine motor control. An informal check (asking her to watch the end of a pencil) revealed no difficulty in following an object visually through space, even when she was asked to hold her head in a fixed position and just follow it with her eyes. Finally, Heather's brain wave scan indicated no abnormal patterns of electrical activity.

When asked to copy several designs on the blackboard, she consistently referred to the model that I had drawn, and, even under those conditions, she did not correct every mistake. Errors included lines that joined in the model but were not joined in her copies, incorrect angles, and an inability to draw concentric circles.

Similar to the informal observations reviewed above, Heather's score on the Visual Motor Integration Test indicated that she was functioning below her expected age range. She had difficulty copying the sets of figures on paper, thus indicating certain problems in perceptual-motor integration, which could affect her reading ability.

NEUROLOGIST'S SUMMARY
Close examination of the various tasks and test results suggests that Heather may be suffering from some type of minimal CNS dysfunction, and this may lead to the problems in school. The Visual Motor Integration Test certainly suggests that Heather's schoolwork may be impaired for paper-and-pencil tasks, and placement in a class for children with learning disabilities may be appropriate at this time.

PSYCHOLOGIST'S REPORT
Heather was friendly and verbal with the examiner, joining him at the test location. Rapport was quickly established. Heather did not seem bothered by the testing. She was cooperative and worked quickly on the items throughout the testing. These results probably represent her best efforts.

(continued)

INTEREST BOX 5.4 CONTINUED

Tests Administered. Wechsler Intelligence Scale for Children, Third Edition; Bender Visual Motor Gestalt Test; and clinical interview.

Test Results. On the WISC-III, Heather obtained a verbal IQ of 114, a performance IQ of 105, and a full-scale IQ of 111. This gives Heather a percentile rank of 75 and indicates that she is presently functioning within the high-average range of intelligence.

There is no significant difference between verbal and nonverbal scores, though there is some moderate intersubtest variability. Heather's scores in the verbal area range from superior (on a subtest measuring practical judgment) to below normal (on a subtest measuring abstract-concept formation). Her general information, arithmetic reasoning, and word knowledge are all in the average range.

Heather's scores on the performance area range from superior (on ability to recognize cause and effect in social situations) to low average (on grapho-motor speed). Nonverbal abstract thought and visual organization/manipulation are in the average range.

Heather's functioning on the Bender suggests that she is currently functioning at an age-appropriate level in the area of visual-motor coordination.

PSYCHOLOGIST'S SUMMARY

Heather is an intelligent young lady without any obvious learning disabilities. She is a friendly, outgoing child and should receive remediation in the regular class for any reading difficulties. Mr. Franks should be provided with support in terms of additional materials for use with Heather, and the team should reconsider this child if a problem persists over the next year.

EDUCATIONAL CONSULTANT'S REPORT

Test Results	Grade Equivalent	Standard Scores
Spache Diagnostic Reading Scales		
Word recognition	1.1	
Graded passages	1.2	
Motor Free Visual Perception Test		
Perceptual age	5–6	
Woodcock-Johnson Achievement Tests		
Reading cluster		71
Math cluster		87
Written language		80
Informal tasks involving written expression		

Interpretation. Heather's age-equivalent score of 5–6 on the Motor Free Visual Perception Test indicated below-average functioning in that area. Such weaknesses can, and often do, cause a delay in the acquisition of reading skills in the early grades.

Heather's standard score of 71 in reading suggested a reading level that was below average for her grade. Her performance was strongest in the word-attack subtest, which involved decoding nonsense words. Her weakest score was on the word-recognition subtest. Further analysis of reading skills on the Spache presented a comparable profile. Heather's performance on the word recognition was weaker than the score on the graded reading passages. Her oral reading was very slow and tended to be word-by-word reading without expression. However, she did seem to use context clues in the passages.

Heather earned a standard score of 80 on the written language cluster, which indicated below-average functioning in this area. The tests involve proofing and dictation and assess punctuation, spelling, and capitalization. She was lower than expected grade level in all of these areas. When asked to write several sentences about her favorite TV show, she produced four sentences, one of which had no verb. She did not capitalize the first word of one sentence, though she did capitalize the word *I* in one sentence. In several instances, her writing went over the line, even though she was using second-grade paper for this informal assessment. Her uppercase and lowercase letters were basically the same size, and, in one instance, she wrote well into the right margin. These types of problems may indicate a weakness in visual perception, as indicated on the perceptual test discussed previously. Also, this informal assessment supports the score on written language and indicates below-average achievement in this area.

Heather's standard score of 87 on the math cluster indicated a low-average functioning. There was little difference between her performance on paper-and-pencil calculations and applied problems. Heather was able to do beginning addition and subtraction problems without regrouping, but she misread several signs on the math problems. Heather counted and calculated using her fingers much of the time.

EDUCATIONAL CONSULTANT'S SUMMARY

Heather's visual-motor performance indicates a problem in that area that could cause a reading deficit. Her reading and writing standard scores are more than 2 standard deviations below her IQ score of 111, indicating a significant IQ/achievement discrepancy in these two areas. This documents a learning disability in reading and writing, and she will require a specialized educational placement in order to remediate these problems and to help her catch up to her grade-level peers. Ms. Duddley should work closely with Mr. Franks in an inclusion class setting to assist Heather in her academic progress.

RECOMMENDATIONS

Clearly, the test results are inconsistent, as are the recommendations of the psychologist and the educational consultant. At least one visual-perception test indicated a potential problem in that area, but Heather is clearly not mentally retarded. Further, there is no evidence from the teacher or in the clinical interview that these academic difficulties are a result of behavior or motivational problems. Finally, Heather's anticipated failure in the second grade this year provides evidence that some action should be taken. We, therefore, recommend that placement as a student with learning disabilities be initiated immediately, with a review of this placement at the end of the current school year. Further, the special education teacher and general education teacher will devise an inclusion class IEP in reading and language arts for completion during the next several months. Finally, the child-study team will assist in the decision concerning advancement or grade-level retention.

DATE: _____   SCHOOL: _____   SIGNATURES: _____

PSYCHOLOGIST: _____   PARENT: _____

ED. CONSULTANT: _____   TEACHER: _____

NEUROLOGIST: _____   PRINCIPAL: _____

SP. ED. TEACHER: _____

■ ■ ■ ■ ■

INTEREST BOX 5.5

EDUCATIONAL CONSULTANT'S REPORT

NAME: Adam Arter   **DATE OF BIRTH:** 5/12/96   **AGE:** 10–3   **GRADE LEVEL:** 4

EXAMINER: John C. Longerton, Ph.D.   **DATE OF EXAMINATION:** 8/5/06

History.   Adam has had continued problems in school, failing social science and science in the first half of the fourth grade this year. He was recommended for evaluation by his fourth-grade teacher, Ms. Juniper, who reports that Adam has difficulty completing class assignments and homework assignments in reading-dependent subjects. No problem was noted in math. Ms. Juniper placed Adam in the slowest reading group, but, even in that group, he is still having difficulty. Adam's mother reported that Adam spends from 1 to 2 hours studying each night, and she helps him frequently with his work. According to Adam's mother, Adam's most recent medical examination indicated no visual or auditory problem.

Tests Administered.   Tests administered included the Woodcock-Johnson cognitive ability cluster and the reading achievement cluster. Scores were also calculated for the perceptual speed cluster and the auditory memory cluster. Other tests administered included sections from the Brigance and the Piers-Harris Children's Self-Concept Scale. Also, a writing sample was obtained and analyzed.

	Standard Scores	*Grade Equiv.*	*Percentile*
Woodcock-Johnson			
Cognitive Ability Total	124	8.8	95
Perceptual Speed	93	3.7	32
Memory	108	6.4	71
Reading	91	3.9	28
Piers-Harris Self-Concept	48		41

In the Brigance Reading Comprehension Test, two brief reading sections were read at each grade level except for the second grade, where one section was read. There were five comprehension questions for each section.

Comprehension was 30% (or 3 of 10 questions correct), 70%, and 100%, for grades 4, 3, and 2, respectively.

These scores provide a relatively complete comparative picture of Adam's cognitive and emotional functioning. The standard-score column indicates scores that have a mean of 100 and a standard deviation of 15, except for the Piers-Harris standard score. This score has a mean of 50 and a standard deviation of 10. The percentile scores indicate the percentage of students who scored at or below Adam's score on each test. On all tests, the higher scores indicate more positive performance.

Cognitive Ability.   The present scores on cognitive ability indicate that Adam is functioning in the above-average range for his age. His scaled score of 124 is a good indication that Adam has above-average intelligence. However, closer examination of the perceptual speed score, which basically measures skill on a set of timed visual tasks, indicates a weakness in the ability to visually obtain information. When compared to Adam's skill in obtaining information through hearing, the scaled scores (93 and 108, respectively) indicate a 15-point difference, or a difference of 1 entire standard deviation between visual perception and auditory perception. Such discrepancies can be indicative of a learning disability, though many practitioners prefer to demonstrate a difference of 2 standard deviations before labeling a child as disabled.

Another indication of such impairment is the discrepancy between Adam's standardized intelligence score and his reading score. Such comparison addresses the issue of Adam's potential compared to his achievement. Comparisons between the cognitive-ability score and his reading score (124 and 91, respectively) clearly indicate that Adam is not realizing his potential. The difference between these scores is more than 2 standard deviations, and this difference is strong evidence of a learning disability.

Analysis of Academic Skill.   Adam's reading comprehension scores range from second grade to fourth grade. Overall, his instructional reading range appears to be around third-grade level. The Brigance and the Woodcock-Johnson reading scores both suggest that grade range. His ability to comprehend reading material is lower than his ability to recognize words and decode unfamiliar words on the subtests of the Woodcock-Johnson. Finally, Adam did have to move backward to the second-grade level before he did well on comprehension.

Adam's writing sample demonstrated a number of language arts problems, including consistent mistakes in spelling ("in till" for *until* on two occasions; "aspost" for *supposed*) and poor punctuation. His sentences were correct, but his paragraph structure was disorganized, and the paragraph was not indented. His writing was barely legible, and in many instances he wrote above the line. These skills are clearly not fourth-grade level.

Emotional and Behavioral Development.   The overall self-concept score was almost perfectly average. The teacher indicated that although Adam had trouble paying attention in class and was easily distracted, he had several friends with whom he usually played at recess. Also, Adam was not a severe behavior problem in class. Based on this information, there seemed to be no problems in the emotional or behavioral area.

RECOMMENDATIONS

Adam should be placed in the program for students with learning disabilities for 55 minutes each day in an attempt to identify and remediate his specific reading problems. His writing skills should also receive attention because he is weak in this area and these skills may be one reason for his failure on homework in the subject areas. The special education teacher should coordinate instruction in the language arts areas with Ms. Juniper's work schedule in the general education class and provide some tutoring on written work.

John C. Longerton, Ph.D.

John C. Longerton, Ph.D.
Educational Consultant

used to determine eligibility have norm samples that do not include appropriate representation of children in various minority groups (Leung, 1996). Also, in our increasingly diverse society, many minority groups that have been underrepresented in the population are now growing in size.

Several reports on the implementation of special education law indicated that there may be some bias in the frequently used eligibility assessment practices (Alexander, 1992; Commission, 2001). Specifically, these reports indicated that a higher percentage of minority children were referred to special education than one would anticipate, and concerns such as this have documented the need to increase our efforts to be sensitive to cultural differences that may account for differential test performance.

Although most authorities indicate the general validity of current IQ assessment procedures, there is still a need to validate a minority child's performance with other data (Leung, 1996). Rather than relying exclusively on test results, practitioners should collect other data, including interviews with parents about the child's functioning or direct observations of the child in school and perhaps at home. These data then can be used to cross-validate the assessment results and assure that a child is protected from subtle bias in eligibility decisions. Leung (1996) also encouraged teachers to consider their own assumptions relative to particular minority groups by asking themselves questions such as, "What assumptions do I make about the cultural group from which this child comes?" or "Will my attitude affect this child's performance?" Such self-examination should lead everyone in the field to more fair and equitable assessment and decision-making practices.

Most Western democracies value cultural diversity in their populations, and awareness of the strengths of cultural diversity is increasing. There have been recommendations for modifications of assessment practices for certain minority groups, but such modifications are far from normative in today's environment. Of course, when evidence of bias is found, educators have a moral obligation to make every effort to eliminate that bias in assessments. Some evidence has suggested that there may be a bias against male students in the identification process (Clarizio & Phillips, 1986; Leinhardt, Seewald, & Zigmond, 1982). Further, Olivarez and colleagues (1992) indicated that the commonly used assessment batteries for determination of eligibility tend to overestimate the achievement of African American and Hispanic students.

With this evidence of bias in hand, researchers and practitioners alike must make every effort to mitigate the effects of bias in the eligibility decision making. There are, as yet, only various sets of general guidelines for mitigating the negative consequences of bias. Chin and McCormick (1986) provided a set of guidelines, which are presented in Interest Box 5.6.

ASSESSMENT FOR INSTRUCTION

While child-study team members grapple with eligibility issues together, the teacher often faces the need for assessment information for instructional planning alone. Psychologists, social workers, school nurses, and educational-assessment consultants often perform some basic achievement testing, resulting in a score that compares a child with a group of children, but such information is not necessary or useful in planning individualized instruction

■ ■ ■ ■ ■

INTEREST BOX 5.6

TEACHING TIPS FOR TEACHING ETHNICALLY DIVERSE STUDENTS

1. Become informed about the different ethnic groups in your class, namely, their characteristics and learning styles.
2. Encourage students to share their cultures. Start by sharing your own cultural traditions.
3. Avoid textbooks and materials that present cultural stereotypes or that present cultural diversity negatively.
4. Learn about minority students' home and community interests, talents, skills, and potentials. Develop the instructional program to highlight these positive cultural aspects.
5. Find out how students in your class from racial or ethnic minority groups would like you to refer to their groups, and use those terms.
6. Integrate ethnic studies in the curriculum. Help students from minority groups gain a more positive self-image through those studies.
7. Make minority parents your partners in educating their children.
8. Treat all students equally; do not practice reverse discrimination with any group.
9. Be sure the assessment techniques you use are appropriate in terms of addressing cultural differences.
10. Avoid imitating the dialects or other speech patterns of minority students.

Source: Based on "Cultural Diversity and Exceptionality" by P. C. Chin and L. McCormick, 1986, in N. G. Haring and L. McCormick (Eds.), *Exceptional Children and Youth,* 4th ed., Columbus, OH: Merrill.

(Bryant, 1999). Based on current practice in most states, it is clear that you, as the teacher, will often know the child better than any other member of the assessment team—except, of course, the parents. Consequently, educational assessment for instruction is often the responsibility of the teacher. You need a great deal of preparation in such assessment, and most teacher education programs include at least one entire course devoted to individualized assessment of children with disabilities.

The information presented in Interest Box 5.7 is intended to briefly introduce the various approaches to individualized assessment for instruction. Note that a number of assessment examples are given as well as the dates when the assessments developed. The dates are rough estimates; once an assessment concept has been developed, commercially available instruments continue to be published over time. Still, the dates indicate the rough order in which these various assessment approaches have been developed and indicate that assessment practices are not static. No doubt the field will witness continuing change in assessment practices for students with learning disabilities.

Norm-Referenced Achievement Testing

Assessment for instructional purposes has been reformulated several times in recent history. Initially, norm-referenced academic achievement tests, administered on an individual basis, were used. **Norm-referenced tests** compare a student's performance to the performance of other students and often result in an age- or grade-equivalent score or a standardized score.

■ ■ ■ ■ ■

INTEREST BOX 5.7
ASSESSMENT FOR INSTRUCTION

TYPE OF ASSESSMENT	INSTRUMENTS	CONCEPT DEVELOPED
1. Norm-referenced testing	Kaufman Assessment Battery Test of Written Language Test of Language Development Peabody Individual Achievement Test–Revised (PIATr) Woodcock-Johnson	Early 1900s–1930
2. Informal observational reports		1960s
3. Criterion-referenced testing	Brigance Key Math—Revised Informal CRTs	1970s
4. In-class assessment	Task analysis Error analysis Analysis of daily classwork	1970s
5. Curriculum-based assessment	Precision teaching Informal CBAs	1980s
6. Alternative assessment	Authentic assessment Portfolio assessment Dynamic assessment	1990s

Historically, such tests were intended to separate individuals into instructional groups. However, these tests provided little information of instructional value because they had a limited number of questions at each discrete grade level. Consequently, although many of these tests may be used today in order to document eligibility in ability-achievement discrepancy procedures, few practitioners believe that these tests provide any realistic basis for instruction. Still, as a professional in the field, you will encounter tests of this nature as part of the assessment package for students who demonstrate learning problems.

Observational Reports

A number of informal observational reports are used to assess children and youth with learning disabilities. For example, when a student is first suspected of demonstrating a learning disability, the teacher may be asked to complete an informal observational assessment that is intended to document the specific types of problems the student has demonstrated in the general education class. This type of report is referred to as a **prereferral report** because the information is collected prior to the official referral for special education services.

However, informal observational checklists and observational reports may be used at any time, either before the referral or afterward. In many cases, a standardized, commercially produced behavioral checklist may be required, whereas in other cases, an informal observational record may be obtained.

Criterion-Referenced Testing

Because of the need for more complete information on a child's performance, tests were developed that compared a child's performance to a list of behavioral objectives in highly discrete skill areas rather than other children's performance. For example, a criterion-referenced test may assess only whole-number addition, with five items for each type of addition problem. Each of the objectives on such a test is keyed to a particular question or set of questions, and if the student missed a particular set of items, that discrete skill would be included in his or her IEP. Documentation of levels of performance in each relevant area on criterion-referenced tests results in complete information for instruction. The theoretical basis for such testing procedures is the behavioral perspective, presented in Chapter 1.

Curriculum-Based Assessment

One recent thrust in assessment is very similar to criterion-referenced assessment, but it is conducted much more frequently. Because the levels of student performance vary considerably over time, various theorists have recommended assessment based on the work a student does in class, which takes place on a daily or biweekly basis (Jones, 2001; King-Sears, Burgess, & Lawson, 1999; Phillips, Fuchs, & Fuchs, 1994). These frequent assessments help the teacher monitor student performance.

For example, one such procedure—precision teaching—requires that data on a child's completion rate for a particular type of problem be kept on a daily basis (Bender, 2002). Information such as this can be used to chart the student's achievement on a particular skill over time. By looking at the recent daily work, the teacher can quickly tell when a student has mastered a task. Also, the teacher can tell when the type of instructional activity is not increasing the child's comprehension and rate of successful problem completion. In short, teachers get a daily picture of student performance on which to base educational programming decisions (King-Sears et al., 1999).

Although curriculum-based assessment practices have demonstrated effectiveness, many teachers consider these procedures much too time-consuming for use in special education classes. Fortunately, however, these daily data collections can be utilized in a manner that does not take an undue amount of time (Jones, 2001). For example, a teacher may use only the last several minutes of each period to assess the timed performance of the students, and several students may be timed simultaneously. Also, students may be trained to chart their own behaviors over a period of several weeks in order to see their own progress.

Several scholars have recommended that eligibility decisions for children with learning disabilities be made on the basis of curriculum-based assessment (Bender, 2002; Commission, 2001; Fuchs & Fuchs, 2005), and the new RTI emphasis proposes exactly this utilization of curriculum-based measures. The curriculum-based assessment report presented in Interest Box 5.8 demonstrates how several daily curriculum-based measures

■ ■ ■ ■ ■ ▬▬

INTEREST BOX 5.8

CURRICULUM-BASED ASSESSMENT REPORT

RELEVANT INFORMATION

NAME: Thomas Whitehead

STUDENT AGE: 13 years, 8 months

GRADE PLACEMENT: Grade 5

RESULTS FROM STATE TESTING PROGRAM: California Achievement Test administered 4/16–4/18/06

READING GRADE LEVEL: 3.7   MATH GRADE LEVEL: 4.9

LANGUAGE ARTS GRADE LEVEL: 3.2

School History.   Thomas attended Woodbury Elementary from kindergarten through the fifth grade. He was retained in the second grade, and barely passed his work for the next two years. During the fifth grade, the mainstream teacher referred Thomas for services.

Curriculum-Based Assessment Information.   For the last several months, Thomas's resource and remedial reading classes have included curriculum-based assessment and learning-strategies procedures that result in daily assessments of curriculum objectives. He has received all of his reading and language arts instruction in the resource and remedial class placements. Charts of progress in each language arts area for the last grading period of the school year are presented in Figures 5.4 through 5.6. This information should be used to plan instruction for the resource and reading programs next year.

Teacher Interviews.   In interviews with the psychologist, both the remedial and resource teacher indicate that Thomas is still considerably behind his grade-level placement in reading and language arts. This is supported by the group test results above. The teachers recommend continued placement in each program for the year. Mr. Frederick, the resource teacher, has indicated that he works closely with Ms. Bornez, the general education teacher, on selection of particular learning strategies that may benefit Thomas. At this point, a test-taking strategy, a paragraph-comprehension strategy, and a chapter-in-text comprehension strategy have been mastered by Thomas in the resource class for use in the general education class. Also, Thomas has worked on identification of complete subjects and predicates in sentences. These instructional strategies should be continued, based on the strategy selection of Thomas and these teachers.

    Ms. Kokora, the remedial reading teacher, indicated that she works with Thomas on reading comprehension of third-grade basal reading stories and language arts skills. These skills include identification of parts of speech, identification of direct object and indirect object, and homonym selection. She has employed a curriculum-based assessment strategy in order to show Thomas his progress, and she reports that he is motivated by his attempts to reach the stated goals. She intends to continue these strategies.

    Ms. Bornez indicates that Thomas passed each subject last year in the general education class, but that his most difficult subjects were the reading-dependent subjects of history and science. A readability study of these texts showed that the texts were written at roughly the sixth- and eighth-grade levels, respectively. This is, unfortunately, not uncommon in many subject-area texts. However, when Ms. Bornez provided subject material in supplementary library books for Thomas on the third/fourth-grade level, he worked much harder and successfully completed the

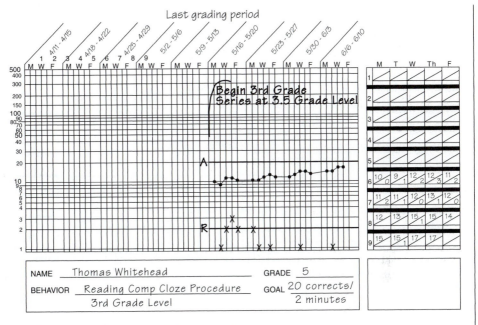

FIGURE 5.4   Performance on Cloze Procedure

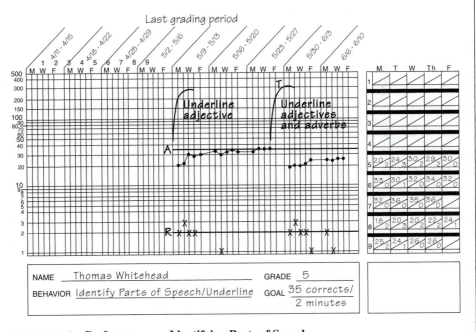

FIGURE 5.5   Performance on Identifying Parts of Speech

(continued)

INTEREST BOX 5.8   CONTINUED

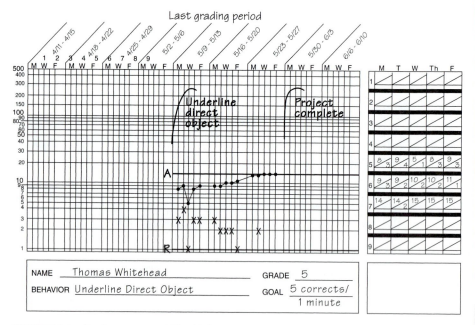

FIGURE 5.6   **Performance on Identifying Direct Objects**

work. Ms. Bornez indicated that she would continue to provide appropriate reading materials for these two subject areas. She further indicated that neither classroom behavior nor other subjects were problems.

RECOMMENDATIONS

Upon review of the charts and the teacher comments, the child-study team sees no indication that further assessment at this time would be beneficial. The team jointly accepts the recommendations of the teachers and recommends assignment of Thomas to one period per day in both the resource room and remedial reading program for the first half of the school year. The teachers will prepare a list of objectives and a curriculum-based assessment plan to be submitted for approval prior to the next meeting with the parent.

However, because strategy instruction may be completed by December, the team will review Thomas's progress in November and consider a reduction or elimination of the special educational placement in the resource room. This would place Thomas in the general education class for part of his reading/language arts instruction, and the team feels that he may be ready for such placement by December. Review scheduled for November 30, 2006.

SIGNATURES: _____

_____

_____

could be utilized for both instructional and eligibility determinations. Note the similarity between these precision teaching charts and the data described above for RTI procedures. Clearly, the RTI initiative is firmly rooted in the curriculum-based assessment research that has been conducted over the last two decades (Bender, 2002; Marston, 2005).

Interpretation of Curriculum-Based Assessment Charts.   Curriculum-based assessment charts portray the daily progress of Thomas's achievement over a period of weeks. This pattern of achievement is the most accurate method for measuring academic achievement. In the charts, you can see that Thomas made academic gains during the final weeks of school on each of the behavioral objectives from his IEP. For example, Figure 5.4 shows correct responses (dots) and errors (Xs) on a reading-comprehension cloze procedure (i.e., a "fill in the blank" procedure where the child must comprehend the content in order to fill in the blank) at the third-grade level. As the chart demonstrates, Thomas was moving toward his individual aim of 20 correct responses with no errors when school ended on June 10. Figure 5.5 demonstrates that, at the end of May, Thomas had met his aim of identification of adjectives and had begun a discrimination task concerning the identification of both adjectives and adverbs. Figure 5.6 demonstrates that Thomas was also moving toward his aim of identification of direct objects; that project was terminated when he met his aim in May.

These charts indicate the language arts areas that should be emphasized for Thomas next fall. Clearly, curriculum-based assessment exercises in reading comprehension at the 3.5 grade level should be initiated. Also, projects in identification of complete subjects and predicates, discrimination of adjectives and adverbs, and one or two other skills such as the identification of homonyms should be initiated.

In-Class Assessment Practices

In addition to monitoring types of assessment performed by teachers, several types of assessment practices are frequently used by teachers in order to plan instruction on a lesson-by-lesson basis. These include task analysis and error analysis. In-class assessments such as these, performed by the teacher who is with the child during his or her work each day, can be the most valuable type of assessment information for instructional planning.

Task analysis was developed by the behaviorists during the 1970s to allow a teacher to adequately describe a task to be completed by a child. This technique identifies particular steps or aspects of the skill to be mastered in order to diagnose precisely the child's level of understanding. A complete task analysis for a double-digit math problem is included in Interest Box 5.9.

Specification of the steps of the task at this discrete level will allow a teacher to introduce and explain the task to the child more completely during initial instruction. Also, task analysis such as this facilitates the second technique—error analysis—which is described below.

After the student has completed several problems, the teacher may find errors in the student's work. Analysis of these errors will allow the teacher to generate the rules or guidelines that the student used to complete the work. The teacher can then tell specifically what types of errors the child is likely to make, and specific instruction in these precise areas can be given. A complete **error analysis** is presented in Interest Box 5.10.

INTEREST BOX 5.9

TEACHING TIP: A SAMPLE TASK ANALYSIS

Task analysis is the delineation of specific aspects of a task in order to document the specific understandings and misunderstandings of the student with learning disabilities. The technique was originated in the behavioral school of thought. Below is a sample problem that identifies the specific tasks that must be performed by the student in order to complete a double-digit addition problem with regrouping.

Problem Requirements

$$\begin{array}{r} \overset{1}{2}\ 8 \\ +\ 3\ \ 5 \\ \hline 6\ 3 \end{array}$$

1. Add the digits in the 1's column (8 + 5).
2. Write down the first digit in the sum under the 1's column.
3. Write the second digit above the next column.
4. Add the three digits in the 10's column.
5. Write the answer under the 10's column.

Often, analysis of the specific aspects of a problem or educational task will assist the teacher in understanding the steps to explain to the child. For example, students who are encountering the problem above have probably already mastered two-digit addition without regrouping, and specification of the steps through task analysis clearly indicates the point at which this problem is different. The teacher then would begin instruction in step 3 above.

INTEREST BOX 5.10

SAMPLE ERROR ANALYSIS

The same problem that was task analyzed in Interest Box 5.9 is presented below, after the student attempted to complete it.

$$\begin{array}{r} 2\ 8 \\ +\ 3\ \ 5 \\ \hline 5\ 13 \end{array}$$

As is apparent in the student's attempt to complete the problem, the student with a disability correctly completed the first step, thus indicating a correct understanding of the starting point for the problem. However, the student's understanding breaks down here; he or she did not know where to write the two-digit answer. Therefore, this is the correct point at which to begin instruction.

Error analysis such as this can be performed in any subject area, on daily work, work samples from any other classes, and homework assignments, as well as test items. Obviously, the more of the child's work that can be analyzed, the more accurate the analysis of errors. Also, when an analysis of errors is completed, patterns of similar errors begin to emerge that indicate an incorrect understanding on the part of the child. This type of information is the most useful type of information to have when planning the day-to-day instruction of the child with learning disabilities. Effective teachers will prepare for assessment meetings with the child-study team by completing an error analysis in each relevant subject area, listing examples of the errors, and collecting daily work that displays these errors.

Innovative Assessment Practices

Over the last decade, there has been an effort within education to move toward assessments that have more bearing on how children actually perform various educational tasks (Bryant, 1999; Commission, 2001; Fuchs & Fuchs, 2006; Jones, 2001; King-Sears et al., 1999). These alternatives include authentic assessment (sometimes referred to as performance assessment), portfolio assessment, dynamic assessment, and strength-based assessment.

The term **authentic assessment** has been used to suggest that particular types of assessment practices are authentically related to a task that may be required of someone in the real world. In this concept of assessment, the individual must perform the task required in a real-world setting. Thus, the term *performance assessment* is sometimes used. The teaching example in Interest Box 5.11 illustrates authentic assessment practices.

If children can conduct the types of authentic tasks described—tasks that are required of adults in a real-world arena such as ecological studies—then the students may be said to understand the concepts. In short, they have been "assessed" in a much more authentic fashion than if given paper-and-pencil tests on the same topic in the school classroom. This type of assessment has many proponents among educators because this practice stresses the applicability of education to real-world problems.

For example, students of English or literature may create a school newspaper, doing various writing and editing jobs, as one example of authentic assessment. Alternatively, the students may jointly write an article each week for the local newspaper. As another example, high school students who take media production classes often can be involved in

■ ■ ■ ■ ■ ▬▬

INTEREST BOX 5.11
AN EXAMPLE OF AUTHENTIC ASSESSMENT

In a traditionally taught sixth-grade earth science class, the children may study concepts such as ecology, preservation of wetlands, the interdependence of life within a particular ecosystem, and so on. The class would then take a written test—with questions in multiple-choice or perhaps essay format—to demonstrate their knowledge. In contrast, using an authentic assessment model, the children would be assessed by actually applying their knowledge to real-world problems. For example, children may take a local field trip to a wetlands environment and perform a number of tasks demonstrating their understanding of the concepts that approximate tasks done in the real world by ecologists studying that ecosystem. Some of these assessments may include:

- Conduct tests on turbidity (i.e., clarity) of the water in streams feeding that environment
- Identify wildlife footprints for animals using the wetlands as a watering source
- Extract a water sample and, under a field microscope, count and identify the microbes in the water sample
- Compare the types and number of microbes to a record of microbes from the same wetlands conducted previously (if such a record exists)
- Conduct other experiments to determine the quality of the wetlands environment

running the school's television studio and producing the "Morning News"—the morning announcements for the school. These are just a few examples of authentic assessment; the only limit on what may comprise an authentic assessment or performance assessment is the teacher's imagination. Students generally find these assessments much more interesting and motivating than traditional instructional and assessment practices.

Portfolio assessment is one form of authentic assessment that, in addition to performance of real-world tasks, involves the student in the production of a file or portfolio that includes a number of projects designed and developed to demonstrate the student's skill in a particular area over time (Swicegood, 1994). This type of assessment originated in elementary education and has recently been applied in special education settings. Using portfolio assessment, teachers create a portfolio of student worksheets or homework, including numerous samples of the child's work—perhaps paragraphs written on topics selected by the student or math worksheets throughout a unit on multiplication. The teachers note the dates of completion for each assignment, and on the basis of the collected work samples, teachers identify strengths and weaknesses of the child.

In a sense, the portfolio or collection of student work becomes the basis for in-depth error analysis across the period during which the class papers, homework, or other work samples were collected. Using this portfolio, teachers and parents can gain a very accurate picture of where a particular child is and how that child is progressing toward the curriculum goals for the year (Swicegood, 1994). Also, many teachers find this form of ongoing assessment more manageable than the curriculum-based assessment charting plans described earlier in this chapter.

Portfolios vary considerably, and may include either a student's finished work on several projects in various areas or samples of the student's work in one particular area over time. For example, many teachers of writing include writing selections for a student from the beginning, the middle, and the end of the academic year. Thus, these written samples may be used to show a student's continuing progress in writing.

Dynamic assessment is, perhaps, the most interesting of these developing assessment concepts for the field of learning disabilities. In dynamic assessment, consideration is given not only to the student's performance on a particular task but also to the thought processes the student uses in performing the task (Bryant, 1999). For example, while completing a series of math problems that involve regrouping in the 10's place, the teacher may observe the student making an error and actually stop the student's work during one of the problems to inquire about why he or she wrote down a particular digit in the answer. Using this strategy, the teacher can begin to understand the dynamics of what the student was thinking while completing a problem (Bryant, 1999).

This assessment development is particularly intriguing when one considers the decidedly unorthodox thought processes that may be associated with a learning disability. If the teacher can, in a particular assessment, stop a child during a problem and discuss his or her solution immediately, the teacher may find out much more information on why a particular child often fails to complete that type of problem correctly.

Strength-based assessment is an assessment concept that emphasizes documentation of the strengths of students rather than merely cataloging their weaknesses (Epstein, 1999; Epstein, Rudolph, & Epstein, 2000). Michael Epstein developed this concept in an effort to specify an assessment alternative for students with disabilities. He indicated that, all too often, when students are identified as learning disabled, the teachers and professionals typically begin to describe them in terms of "deficits in" this or that subject area or "problems in" various academic or behavioral areas (Epstein & Sharma, 1998). Rather than focus on such negatives about a child, Epstein (1999) urged the field to develop ways to assess the strengths of the child in an effort to find educationally relevant ways to structure teaching activities on which the child can build.

Strength-based assessment may be defined as the assessment of competencies and characteristics that create a sense of personal accomplishment or contribute to satisfying personal relationships and promote one's personal and academic development (Epstein, 1999; Epstein et al., 2000). This concept of assessment based on strengths has appeal because it can help focus a child, and the eligibility committee itself, on the various factors that can assist the student in achieving his or her goals. Although this assessment focus has not been widely implemented as yet, one may well anticipate that the field will see increasing emphasis on strength-based assessment practices for all children with disabilities.

Other Issues in Assessment

Several other assessment issues often cause teachers some degree of confusion. First, if a teacher participates in an IEP meeting, he or she may wonder what types of assessment data to bring to the meeting. Clearly, the more complete and accurate the data that a teacher brings to the educational-planning conference, the more useful the information is. Information on both academic performance and any behavioral problems or social problems is very useful for such program planning. Interest Box 5.12 presents the general types of information that teachers should bring to such conferences. In addition to this general information, as RTI procedures are implemented in local school districts around the nation, teachers will be expected to bring data indicating their tier 1 and tier 2 intervention results. Charted data on a child's performance, such as those data presented in Figures 5.2 and 5.3 (pp. 152 and 153), would provide the best evidence of how well any particular child responded to instructional interventions (Bender, 2002; Gersten & Dimino, 2006). Thus, teachers should collect these data in advance of the meetings and have such data charts prepared for discussion at the meeting in order to determine the child's response to intervention.

The requirement in some instances to provide grades for report cards can be a challenge for teachers. For example, if a child's special education teacher has total responsibility for reading and language arts instruction, that teacher may be asked to grade the child in those subjects. Imagine a rather typical situation in which a fifth-grade child is completing third-grade-level reading and language arts assignments in a special education class with an "A" average. Should the child receive an "A" on these subjects on the report card? Will this confuse the parents and lead them to believe that their child is completing his or her work successfully? Is such a grading practice fair to other children?

Bender (1984) recommended that the child receive the best grade applicable in order to reinforce the effort and work that went into earning the "A." Also, a written statement should accompany the report card that reminds the parents that this grade indicates performance on work that is below grade level for that child. If you are faced with such a situation, you will also wish to ask your special education supervisor about local grading policies.

■ ■ ■ ■ ■

INTEREST BOX 5.12

**TEACHING TIPS: CHECKLIST OF ASSESSMENTS
FOR THE TEAM MEETING**

Effective preparation for a team meeting can earn you, the teacher, the respect of your professional colleagues on the team. Some teachers miss this opportunity to exchange knowledge of the child's functioning with other team members, but you should take advantage of the situation. Below is a list of assessments that you can complete before the meeting. Not all of these are appropriate or necessary in each instance, but you may wish to use this as a checksheet.

_____	A teacher rating of the child's behavior
_____	Criterion-referenced assessment in basic skill areas
_____	Error analysis in each relevant reading/language arts area
_____	Error analysis in each relevant math area
_____	A sight word and/or survival-skills word list
_____	Samples of work indicating patterns of various errors
_____	A log of critical behavioral problems over the last 2 weeks
_____	Copies of any notes to parents
_____	Sociometric information on social acceptance
_____	Copies of notes from the child's other teachers
_____	Precision-teaching charts in particular skill areas
_____	Instructional materials that the child is completing
_____	A student self-rating of self-concept
_____	Tier 1 and tier 2 response-to-intervention report/chart

Finally, one issue in assessment that has become an additional concern in the field of learning disabilities is the implementation of statewide assessment programs (Commission, 2001; CEC, 2002; Gronna, Jenkins, & Chin-Chance, 1998; Manset & Washburn, 2000; Thurlow, Ysseldyke, & Reid, 1997). In general education, there has been a movement to improve or reform education over recent decades, and this has resulted in increased use of group-administered, norm-referenced assessments that are mandated by the various states for particular grade levels.

Coupled with this move, an effort to set high standards for graduation from high school has resulted in the implementation of **minimum competency tests** in a number of states. In general, these are tests that document minimum competencies in literacy, math, and, in some cases, writing that are administered to all secondary students at a particular grade level. In many states using such minimum competency assessments, all students must pass prior to graduation from high school. Of course, this presents some concern for students with learning disabilities who, although passing all of their courses, may have particular difficulty on such standardized assessments.

As a result of the moves toward minimum competency testing, researchers have begun to investigate the impact of these statewide assessment initiatives on students with learning disabilities (Commission, 2001; Gronna et al., 1998; Manset & Washburn, 2000; Thurlow et al., 1997). As early as 1997, Thurlow and co-workers reported that 17 states had requirements for a minimum competency test or some other type of exit exam. More recently, that number has increased, and concerns have likewise increased. The Commission on Excellence in Special Education (2001) noted several problems in use of these assessments, which in many cases will not allow for modifications for students with learning disabilities. The commission notes:

> Despite the fact that IDEA requires participation of students with disabilities in statewide assessments, children with disabilities are often excluded from these assessments to establish the accountability and progress of schools. This is a major problem, as such assessments generally are designed without consideration of modifications or accommodations students with disabilities may need to complete the assessment. (Commission, 2001)

The commission responded to this problem by calling on test manufacturers to use universal design principles that would allow teachers to modify these assessments for students with learning disabilities without sacrificing accuracy or test integrity. Further, many researchers have expressed concern that these statewide testing programs, and the general move toward accountability for higher standards, may be driving the school curriculum to an inappropriate degree. This debate is ongoing, but many general education teachers feel that they must teach to the standards within the curriculum, as represented by these statewide assessments, even if those standards are clearly inappropriate for students with learning disabilities in the general education classes. As a professional in the field, you should remain cognizant of this ongoing debate within the field. You will probably find yourself administering one or more of these assessments as you begin/continue your teaching career.

SUMMARY

This chapter has presented information on assessment procedures for students with learning disabilities. Eligibility decisions were examined in terms of the various aspects of the federal definition of such disabilities. Although tests designed to measure basic psychological processes or ability deficits have not proven to be technically adequate, certain sections of intelligence tests provide some information on developmental imbalances that may indicate impaired psychological processes. The discrepancy criterion was shown to be the single most influential indicator of learning disability, though presence of an ability-achievement discrepancy is merely a necessary and not a sufficient indicator of such a disability. Also, the use of discrepancies may cease in the next few years as RTI procedures are phased in.

Assessment for instruction was shown to be the more recent emphasis in assessment for students with learning disabilities. Criterion-referenced assessment, curriculum-based assessment, various in-class assessments, and several examples of alternative assessments were presented. Assessment for instruction planning was shown to be the responsibility of you, as the teacher, though various child-study teams will, in many cases, assist with these tasks.

The following points should assist you in studying this chapter:

- Generally, psychological processes may be assessed using tests that are specific to that purpose or tests used to measure intelligence. The intelligence tests are more defensible in terms of technical standards than process tests.
- The discrepancy criterion is generally addressed by demonstrating a discrepancy between intelligence and achievement. Typically, this is done by using a standard-score discrepancy or a regression-based discrepancy table.
- The newly proposed RTI procedures will impact how professionals document a learning disability, and both special and general education teachers will play a role in RTI.
- The exclusionary clause in the definition of learning disabilities has not been adequately explained by scholars in the field, though this chapter presented some rough guidelines concerning how to differentiate between learning disabilities and other disabilities.
- Assessment for instruction may include norm-based assessments, observation reports, criterion-based assessments, curriculum-based assessments, in-class assessments, and alternative assessments. All of these are useful, but the last several are clearly the most appropriate assessments for instructional purposes.

QUESTIONS AND ACTIVITIES

1. What members of local child-study teams assist with assessment for instruction? Bring in a local team and several special education teachers for a round-table discussion of curriculum-based assessment.
2. What theoretical perspective provides the basis for curriculum-based assessment? For error analysis? For intelligence testing? For norm-based achievement testing?
3. Explain the RTI procedure using the charts in Figure 5.2 and 5.3. Are these similar to the charts later in the chapter? How?

4. Discuss the different purposes of assessment. How does assessment for documentation of eligibility relate to assessment for instruction?
5. Read the report of the Commission on Excellence in Special Education and discuss the recommendations on assessment with the class.
6. Present a debate between theorists who support curriculum-based assessment and those who support assessment of psychological processes.

REFERENCES

Alexander, L. (1992). To assure the free appropriate public education of all children with disabilities. *Fourteenth annual report to Congress on the implementation of the Individuals with Disabilities Act.* Washington, DC: U.S. Office of Special Education and Rehabilitative Services.

Barkley, R. A. (1990). *Attention deficit hyperactivity disorder: A handbook for diagnosis and treatment.* New York: Guilford.

Batsche, G., Elliott, J., Graden, J. L., Grimes, J., Kovaleski, J. F., Prasse, D., Reschly, D. J., Schrag, J., & Tilly, W. D. (2004). *Response to intervention:*

Policy considerations and implementation. Alexandria, VA: National Association of State Directors of Special Education.

Bender, W. N. (2002). *Differentiating instruction for students with learning disabilities.* Thousand Oaks, CA: Corwin.

Bender, W. N. (1984). Daily grading in mainstream classes. *The Directive Teacher, 6*(2), 4–5.

Bryant, B. R. (1999). The dynamics of assessment. In W. N. Bender (Ed.), *Professional issues in learning disabilities* (pp. 385–414). Austin, TX: ProEd.

Chin, P. C., & McCormick, L. (1986). Cultural diversity and exceptionality. In N. G. Haring and L. McCormick (Eds.), *Exceptional children and youth* (4th ed.) (p. 117). Columbus, OH: Merrill.

Clarizio, H. F., & Phillips, S. E. (1986). Sex bias in the diagnosis of learning disabled students. *Psychology in the Schools, 23,* 44–52.

Commission on Excellence in Special Education (2001). *Revitalizing special education for children and their families.* Available from www.ed.gov/inits/commissionsboards/whspecialeducation.

Council for Exceptional Children (CEC) (2002). Commission report calls for special education reform. *Today, 9*(3), 1–6.

Council for Learning Disabilities (CLD) (1987). The CLD position statement. *Journal of Learning Disabilities, 20,* 349–350.

Epstein, M. H. (1999). Development and validation of a scale to assess the emotional and behavioral strengths of children and adolescents. *Remedial and Special Education, 20,* 258–262.

Epstein, M. H., Rudolph, S., & Epstein, A. A. (2000). Using strength-based assessment in transition planning. *Teaching Exceptional Children, 32*(6), 50–55.

Epstein, M. H., & Sharma, J. M. (1998). *Behavioral and emotional rating scale: A strength-based approach to assessment.* Austin, TX: ProEd.

Fuchs, D., & Fuchs, L. S. (2006). Introduction to response to intervention: What, why, and how valid is it? *Reading Research Quarterly, 41*(1), 93–98.

Fuchs, D., & Fuchs, L. S. (2005). Responsiveness-to-intervention: A blueprint for practitioners, policymakers, and parents. *Teaching Exceptional Children, 38*(1), 57–61.

Gersten, R., & Dimino, J. A. (2006). RTI (response to intervention): Rethinking special education for students with reading difficulties (yet again). *Reading Research Quarterly, 41*(1), 99–108.

Gronna, S. S., Jenkins, A. A., & Chin-Chance, S. A. (1998). The performance of students with disabilities in a norm-referenced, statewide standardized testing program. *Journal of Learning Disabilities, 31,* 482–493.

Hyun, J. K., & Fowler, S. A. (1995). Respect, cultural sensitivity, and communication: Promoting participation by Asian families in the individualized family service plan. *Teaching Exceptional Children, 28*(1), 25–28.

Jones, C. J. (2001). CBAs that work: Assessment of students' math content-reading levels. *Teaching Exceptional Children, 34*(1), 24–29.

King-Sears, M. E., Burgess, M., & Lawson, T. L. (1999). Applying curriculum-based assessment in inclusive settings. *Teaching Exceptional Children, 32*(1), 30–39.

Leinhardt, G., Seewald, A. M., & Zigmond, N. (1982). Sex and race differences in learning disabilities classrooms. *Journal of Educational Psychology, 74,* 835–843.

Lerner, J., & Chen, A. (1992). Critical issues in learning disabilities: The cross-cultural nature of learning disabilities: A profile in perseverance. *Learning Disabilities Research and Practice, 7,* 147–149.

Leung, B. P. (1996). Quality assessment practices in a diverse society. *Teaching Exceptional Children, 28*(3), 42–45.

Manset, G., & Washburn, S. J. (2000). Equity through accountability? Mandating minimum competency exit examinations for secondary students with learning disabilities. *Learning Disabilities Research and Practice, 15,* 160–167.

Marston, D. (2005). Tiers of intervention in responsiveness to intervention: Prevention outcomes and learning disabilities identification patterns. *Journal of Learning Disabilities, 38*(6), 539–544.

Mastropieri, M. A., & Scruggs, T. W. (2005). Feasibility and consequences of response to intervention: Examination of the issues and scientific evidence as a model for the identification of individuals with learning disabilities, *Journal of Learning Disabilities, 38*(6), 525–531.

Montague, M., McKinney, J. D., & Hocutt, A. (1994). Assessing students for attention deficit disorder. *Intervention in School and Clinic, 29*(4), 212–218.

National Joint Committee on Learning Disabilities (NJCLD) (2005). Responsiveness to intervention and learning disabilities: A report prepared by the National Joint Committee on Learning Disabilities. *Learning Disability Quarterly 28*(4), 249–260.

O'Connor, R. (2003, December). *Tiers of intervention in kindergarten through third grade.* Paper presented at the national research center on learning disabilities responsiveness-to-intervention symposium, Kansas City, MO. (See the discussion of this paper in Marston, 2005.)

Olivarez, A., Palmer, D. J., & Guillemard, L. (1992). Predictive bias with referred and nonreferred black,

Hispanic, and white pupils. *Learning Disability Quarterly, 15,* 175–186.

Phillips, N. B., Fuchs, L. S., & Fuchs, D. (1994). Effects of classwide curriculum-based measurement and peer tutoring: A collaborative researcher-practitioner interview study. *Journal of Learning Disabilities, 27*(7), 420–434.

Scruggs, T. W., & Mastropieri, M. A. (2002). On babies and bathwater: Addressing the problems of identification of learning disabilities. *Learning Disability Quarterly, 25*(2), 155–168.

Siegel, L. S. (1999). Issues in the definition and diagnosis of learning disabilities: A perspective on *Guckenberger v. Boston University. Journal of Learning Disabilities, 32,* 304–319.

Swicegood, P. (1994). Portfolio-based assessment practices. *Intervention in School and Clinic, 30*(1), 7–16.

Thurlow, M. L, Ysseldyke, J. E., & Reid, C. L. (1997). High school graduation requirements for students with disabilities. *Journal of Learning Disabilities, 30,* 608–616.

Watkins, M. W. (1996). Diagnostic utility of the WISC-III developmental index as a predictor of learning disabilities. *Journal of Learning Disabilities, 29,* 305–312.

Wechsler, D. (1991). *Wechsler Intelligence Scale for Children* (3rd ed.). San Antonio, TX: Psychological Corporation.

Vaughn, S., Linan-Thompson, S., & Hickman, P. (2003). Response to treatment as a means of identifying students with reading/learning disabilities. *Exceptional Children, 69*(4), 391–409.

Vellutino, F. R., Scanlon, D. M., Sipay, E. R., Small, S., Chen, R., Pratt, A., & Denckla, M. B. (1996). Cognitive profiles of difficult to remediate and readily remediated poor readers: Early intervention as a vehicle for distinguishing between cognition and experiential deficits as basic cause of specific reading disability. *Journal of Educational Psychology, 88,* 601–638.

CHARACTERISTICS OF STUDENTS WITH LEARNING DISABILITIES

This section presents available information on the characteristics of students with learning disabilities. Information on reading, language, and mathematics characteristics is presented in Chapters 6 and 7 to provide background for the educational treatments discussed in the next section. Although many texts present information on the characteristics in these areas, this text presents information on how these characteristics are manifested in the public school. Chapter 8 indicates how these characteristics will affect the performance of the child with learning disabilities in elementary and secondary classrooms. Throughout this section, the emphasis is on the relationship between the characteristics typically associated with a learning disability and how these characteristics affect particular students in the classroom.

CHAPTER SIX

LEARNING CHARACTERISTICS IN READING AND LANGUAGE ARTS

CHAPTER OUTLINE

WHEN YOU COMPLETE THIS CHAPTER, YOU SHOULD BE ABLE TO:

1. Identify the major skills within the area of reading.

2. Discuss anticipated characteristics of students with learning disabilities in reading.

3. Describe the alphabetic principle and several instructional techniques to strengthen phoneme-based instruction.

4. Present research on the effects of pictures on the reading skills of students with learning disabilities.

5. Discuss the visually based and auditory/language-based treatments designed to improve reading comprehension of children who are learning disabled.

6. List several examples of oral reading errors that students with disabilities might make.

7. Describe the various areas of writing skills and delineate the problems that students with learning disabilities have in each area.

KEYWORDS

phonemes	reading fluency	visual imagery
dyslexia	testwiseness	semantic map
DIBELS	complex multiple choice	scaffolded instruction
phoneme-based instruction	cloze procedure	advance organizers
sight-word approaches	literal comprehension	story retelling
phonics approach	inferential comprehension	whole-language instruction

INTRODUCTION

Reading is the major problem area for most students who are learning disabled (Commission on Excellence in Special Education, 2001; Silliman & Scott, 2006). Perhaps as many as 90% of children with learning disabilities have problems in reading. The emerging evidence during the last decade seems to suggest that learning disabilities in reading begin much earlier than formal reading instruction in schools (Moats & Lyon, 1993; Padget, 1998). As discussed in Chapter 3, this evidence suggests that learning disabilities may begin in very young children as an inability to manipulate individual **phonemes** (Council for Exceptional Children, 2002; Kame'enui, Carnine, Dixon, Simmons, & Coyne, 2002; Sousa, 2005). An inability to recognize, distinguish, and reproduce phonemes would certainly provide one possible reason for difficulty in primary reading skills, and these difficulties would only be apparent academically, when children begin to learn the letter sounds in kindergarten and first grade. Presuming that these children then fall behind in their recognition of written letters and simple words, by the end of grade 1, they would display a significant learning disability.

With the passage of the No Child Left Behind federal legislation, the emphasis on reading instruction has increased dramatically, and has drastically affected instruction for students with learning disabilities. The act mandates, among other things, increased instructional emphasis on the early building blocks of reading, as well as statewide reading intervention plans for students at risk for reading failure. This includes many students with learning disabilities, some of whom may not have been identified. Further, these statewide plans must emphasize research-based reading instructional techniques, and this legal mandate has resulted in a growing emphasis on phonemic instruction (as described in Chapter 3), phonics, and comprehension strategies (Bos, Mather, Silver-Pacuilla, & Narr, 2000; Chard & Dickson, 1999; Kame'enui et al., 2002; National Reading Panel, 2000; Sousa, 2006). Clearly, the reading deficits demonstrated by many young children with learning disabilities, coupled with this new federal mandate, will result in increased emphasis on reading.

For older students with learning disabilities, deficits between their reading skill and their grade placement may range from a few months to five or six years, depending on the grade level of the individual student. Further, a reading deficit of several years may drastically affect the student's performance in numerous subject areas because the textbooks in those areas may be unreadable for the student who is learning disabled. For these reasons, reading problems are often the major concern in the education of these students. However, reading skills are not the only language arts problem area among students with learning disabilities. Research has documented a number of language arts problems that may be related to reading activities. These other areas include spelling, handwriting, note-taking, and writing composition. Deficits in any of these areas may severely limit a student's ability to perform in the public school classroom.

This chapter presents information on the reading and language arts characteristics of students with learning disabilities. The first section will focus on reading skills in order to demonstrate the comprehensive nature of reading as a foundation for discussion of many language arts problems. A review of research will present the information currently available on reading skills of students with disabilities. This will be followed by a discussion of the various reading-treatment approaches used currently in classes for those with learning disabilities. Finally, the characteristics of students with learning disabilities in each of the several language arts areas will be presented in order to demonstrate the types of language arts behaviors that you will encounter when you begin to teach these students.

READING DIFFICULTIES OF STUDENTS WITH LEARNING DISABILITIES

Over the years, research has consistently indicated that students with learning disabilities have numerous difficulties in reading (Commission, 2001; Padget, 1998). Various researchers have attempted to describe more specifically the types of reading problems demonstrated by students with learning disabilities (Kame'enui et al., 2002; MacInnis & Hemming, 1995; Mather & Roberts, 1994). For example, MacInnis and Hemming (1995) identified seven learning characteristics that are demonstrated by many students with learning disabilities; these are presented in Interest Box 6.1.

Whereas many students without disabilities may manifest one or two of these problems when they begin to acquire reading skills during the early school years, students

---

INTEREST BOX 6.1
READING PROBLEMS NOTED AMONG STUDENTS
WITH LEARNING DISABILITIES

Overdependency.   Students with learning disabilities seem to be overdependent upon others for direction in their learning. This is particularly devastating on reading assignments, which are typically individual assignments.

Difficulty Monitoring Performance.   Students with learning disabilities are not usually adept at monitoring their own understanding of reading material.

Failure to Modify Strategies.   Strategies needed for successful reading vary from one type of assignment to another. Reading a textbook requires different skills than reading a story, and students with learning disabilities fail to modify their reading strategies accordingly.

Memory Problems.   Students with learning disabilities demonstrate many memory problems and are less likely to retain their understanding from reading material.

Difficulty Mastering Letter Sounds and Vocabulary.   Students with learning disabilities have much more difficulty learning letter sounds, combinations of sounds, and vocabulary words.

Difficulty in Generalization.   These students fail to transfer concepts that have been learned in one context to another context.

Difficulty in Approaching a Task Positively.   Students with learning disabilities often display less than positive attitudes toward a challenging learning task, and this has been associated with repeated failure experiences throughout the early school years.

Source: Adapted from "Linking the Needs of Students with Learning Disabilities to a Whole Language Curriculum" by C. MacInnis and H. Hemming, *Journal of Learning Disabilities, 28,* 1995, 535–544.

---

with learning disabilities are likely to demonstrate many of these difficulties. Thus, the cumulative effect for many students with learning disabilities is overwhelming. They may have a difficult time in reading and many language arts skills, which are based on reading. Understanding these characteristics and the various instructional approaches should assist you in working with these students.

CONCEPTUALIZATION OF READING SKILLS

Reading is generally understood to mean extraction of meaning from words on the written page, and this overall definition serves well for the person who is not concerned with teaching reading. However, professionals in any field generally develop a professional language that is more exacting and specific than the terms used by the general public, and the field of reading has seen the development of such a language. For example, terms such as *phoneme awareness, decoding, structural analysis, inferential meaning,* and *literal comprehension* all represent a part of what the reading specialist refers to as *reading skill.* The terms defined below may be used to describe the reading problems of students with learning disabilities.

Although different theorists present different pictorial representations of reading, this text will use a schematic that includes four separate aspects of reading: decoding, word recognition, sentence comprehension, and comprehension of longer texts. Figure 6.1 presents the numerous terms in an organizational framework.

As you may note, the term **dyslexia,** which has been traditionally associated with learning disabilities research, is not in this hierarchy. There is considerable controversy over the definition of this term—and even whether the term should be used at all—among scholars in the field. Historically, the term has been widely used in the field.

Originally, *dyslexia* was defined as a specific malfunction in the brain or central nervous system that results in confusion in perception of letters or words. The assumption was that these confused perceptions resulted in continuing reading difficulties. The term was associated with the visual-perceptual perspective on learning disabilities, discussed in Chapter 1. Generally, dyslexic individuals do learn to read minimally, achieving a reading level around the second or third grade. Even this takes a great deal of effort, and no single teaching method has been shown to be more effective than any other for individuals who are dyslexic.

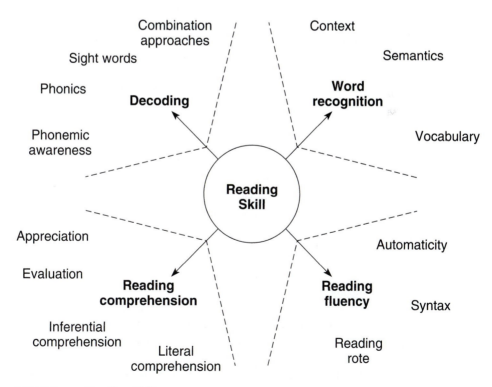

FIGURE 6.1   Reading Skills

However, although reading difficulties can be adequately measured, neither medical science nor educational psychology has been able to provide adequate diagnostic procedures to identify these brain-based, perceptual problems. Although this may soon change based on the application of the fMRI technology described in Chapter 2, a complete understanding of all brain processes involved in reading has not yet resulted (Sousa, 2005). Consequently, many researchers use the term *dyslexia* as if it meant any reading difficulty. At this point, other researchers and theorists in the field stopped using the term altogether because the definition was so imprecise. Research on this topic is continuing.

There is at least one other possible cause of dyslexia—the language or encoding capability of the individual with learning disabilities. Even if a child does correctly perceive the shape of the letters in a word, some type of language decoding is still necessary in order for the word to convey any meaning, and a deficiency in this language-based skill may be the cause of dyslexia (Shaywitz & Shaywitz, 2006). This represents a dramatic turnabout; whereas research in dyslexia was associated with the visual-perceptual perspective, this new position places the study of dyslexia firmly in the auditory/language perspective on learning disabilities. Although it is too early to evaluate this new position on research in the field, many researchers are excited by this shift and hope that some meaningful definition, measurement techniques, and educational treatments may soon be forthcoming from this shift in perspective on an old problem.

One final word: Many parents and teachers assume that all children with learning disabilities are dyslexics, but individuals who demonstrate these symptoms probably account for much less than 1% of the population in the public schools presently identified as learning disabled. Virtually none of the individuals who have learning disabilities with whom I have come into contact have been dyslexic, in the sense that they could learn to read well beyond second- or third-grade level when appropriate instruction was used. You should be aware that *dyslexic* and *learning disabled* are not synonymous, though many persons use these terms interchangeably.

Phonemic Awareness

A great deal of work has been done in the area of early reading skill, and as mentioned previously, much of this work has concentrated on phoneme manipulation skills (Bender & Larkin, 2003; Edelen-Smith, 1997; Haager, 2002; Kame'euni et al., 2002; NRP, 2000; Sousa, 2005). For example, Kame'euni and his colleagues (2002) investigated reading deficits among students with learning disabilities and have identified several fundamental principles in early reading, including the following:

1. Development of phonological awareness and manipulation, as described in Chapter 3
2. Understanding the alphabetic principle (i.e., that phoneme sounds are represented by letters, that the letter t results in a certain sound formed by placing the tongue behind the upper teeth and releasing a breath over the tongue as it is lowered—resulting in / t / sound
3. Automaticity with the alphabetic code or being able to quickly produce the sounds represented by letters

A student's mastery of these principles will result in effective reading skills, and failure to master these during the first couple of years of reading will typically result in a reading deficit. One can readily see in these principles the emphasis on phoneme manipulation and phonics. However, in addition to these general instructional principles, research has identified several "milestones" that may be considered stepping-stones for effective readers during kindergarten and grade 1 (Haager, 2002). Specifically, if a child achieves the following milestones or skills at the specified time in his or her reading lessons, then effective reading skills are quite likely to follow. Unfortunately, many children who are later identified as learning disabled do not reach these milestones as quickly as other students (Haager, 2002). The milestones are:

By 2 months into kindergarten	Recognize/manipulate onsets (initial sounds of words)
By the end of kindergarten	Successfully segment words into phonemes
By the middle of grade 1	Fluently manipulate phonemes in nonsense words
By the end of grade 1	Demonstrate oral reading fluency of 40 words per minute

In order to assess the level of students in relation to early literacy milestones of this nature, researchers at the University of Oregon developed the *Dynamic Indicators of Basic Early Literacy Skills* (Website: http://dibels.uoregon.edu/data/index.php). This measure is commonly known as **DIBELS.** DIBELS was developed as a quickly administered screening text to assess fluency in initial sounds, letter naming, phoneme segmentation, nonsense words, oral reading, retelling, and word use. The measures are designed as "one minute" assessments and are intended to be utilized frequently so as to monitor a student's progress in phonological awareness, alphabetic understanding, accuracy and fluency in reading connected text, vocabulary, and comprehension. The measures for each of these indicators of early literacy are reliable, and when used as recommended, the results can be used on a weekly or twice-a-week basis to document a student's early reading skills over time.

Today, many elementary teachers from kindergarten up through grade 3 are currently using DIBELS to assess students on skills such as recognition of initial consonant sounds, ability to name letters rapidly, and, ultimately, word recognition. For example, one goal would be recognition of eight initial phoneme sounds within two months of the beginning of kindergarten, whereas in January of the kindergarten year, students should be proficient at recognition of 25 initial sounds. For older children, one benchmark goal is for students to have established reading skills of 40 words per minute on oral reading fluency by the end of the first grade. Students who are reading at a rate of 19 words or fewer per minute at the end of the first grade are at risk for reading failure. DIBELS is a quickly administered screening assessment that many states have implemented on a statewide basis. For students suspected of having a learning disability in reading, early and periodic screening using DIBELS can provide an early opportunity for identification and remediation of early literacy phonemic problems.

As described in Chapter 3, the emphasis on phonemic awareness is relatively new in the field of learning disabilities. As you recall, phonemes are speech sounds that result in changes of meaning in a word, and many phonemes are represented by single letters. The mapping of speech sounds to letters is referred to as *phonics*. Although phonics instruction has been emphasized historically in reading instruction for students with learning disabilities, only recently have researchers become aware of the fact that, prior to teaching phonics, we must teach recognition of speech sounds without reference to the letters that represent them, at least for some children (Pullen & Justice, 2006). Interest Box 6.2 presents a set of additional activities that may be used to teach kindergarten and first-grade children phoneme manipulation skills, and you may wish to review the additional ideas for instruction presented in Chapter 3. Also, guidelines for phonemic instruction have been developed (Bender & Larkin, 2003; Edelen-Smith, 1997; NRP, 2000). When teaching a child who demonstrates significant disabilities in reading, teachers should consider **phoneme-based instruction** and use these general guidelines:

1. *Consider the hierarchy of phonemic skill.* The hierarchy of phonemic skills presented in Chapter 3 should provide the basis for instruction. The teacher should consider the individual child's reading problem in relation to the skills listed. Some children can detect different onsets but cannot blend sounds, whereas others can blend sounds but need assistance in segmentation of words. All of these skills are important for subsequent reading success for students with learning disabilities.

2. *Select only one or a few skills to teach.* Teachers should select only one or two skills from the hierarchy for the child to work on, bearing in mind that mastery of those skills will probably improve the child's work on the other skills as well. Activities for students with learning disabilities should be fun and should seem like "play" rather than drill (Edelen-Smith, 1997) because even very young children may have already established negative attitudes toward reading skills.

3. *Consider working on phonemic skills in isolation.* Whereas some students need specific work on phoneme detection, identification of initial onset sounds, and such, others may need work on phonemes in combination with phonics. The teacher must determine the appropriate level to emphasize, but teachers must recognize that many students with learning disabilities have failed to learn to read because educators have moved directly into phonics without adequate preparation on phonemic manipulation as a prerequisite.

4. *Use phoneme sounds.* When doing phoneme instruction, teachers may slip into using letter names rather than sounds for the instruction, and this should be avoided (Edelen-Smith, 1997). Rather, the teacher should use the sounds of the letters for the instruction, and it may help to represent those sounds by putting the letters between slash lines or brackets in the teacher's lesson plan (e.g., the teacher should say / h / a / t / rather than say "hat").

With these guidelines in mind, teachers working with students with learning disabilities should consider the child's skills in phoneme manipulation prior to initiating reading instruction. Of course, many critical questions are, as yet, unanswered in this research (NRP, 2000). For example, how old can a child with a learning disability be and still benefit from phonemic instruction?

■ ■ ■ ■ ■

INTEREST BOX 6.2

LESSON PLANS TO TEACH PHONEMIC MANIPULATION

I. THE GUESS-THE-WORD BLENDING GAME

Objective.   Students will be able to blend and identify a word that is stretched out into component sounds.

Materials Needed.   Picture cards of objects that students are likely to recognize (e.g., sun, bell, fan, flag, snake, tree, book, cup, clock, plane).

Activity.   Place a small number of picture cards before children. Tell them you are going to say a word using "snail talk"—a slow way of saying words (e.g., fffff lllll aaaaa ggggg). They have to look at the pictures and guess what the snail is saying. It is important to have each child guess the answer in his or her head so that everyone gets an opportunity to try it before hearing other answers. Alternate between having one child identify the word and having all children say the word aloud in chorus in order to keep them engaged.

II. A PHONEMIC SEGMENTATION INSTRUCTIONAL STRATEGY

Objective.   Students will be able to segment various parts of oral language.

Materials Needed.   List of brief phrases or poems children would know (e.g., "I scream. You scream. We all scream for ice cream").

Activities.   (a) Early instruction involves teaching the children to segment sentences into individual words. Have the children clap hands with each individual word. (b) As children advance, teach them to segment words into syllables. You may wish to start with children's names (Al-ex- an- der, Ra- chel). (c) When children have learned to remove the first phoneme from a word, teach them to segment short words into individual phonemes (s-u-n, s-t-o-p).

III. THE CHANGE-THE-LETTER GAME

*Objecti*ve.   Students will be able to detect the letter change and pronounce the word with the substitute letter.

Materials Needed.   List of word cards, each of which presents a simple noun with three letters and a picture of that object (consonant, vowel, consonant words, such as bat, cup, hat, and ham).

Activities.   Tell the students, "Mr. Sound will show you a word and then will change the first letter of the word. [Show a picture of a bat.] Say this word together." [The students say "bat."] Then tell the students, "Mr. Sound wants to change the first sound to an h. [Say the letter sound for h rather than the letter name.] If Mr. Sound changes that sound, what would be the matching picture?" Encourage each student to decide on the answer prior to calling on one of them for the answer.

Source: Adapted from "Phonological Awareness: Instructional and Assessment Guidelines" by D. J. Chard and S. V. Dickson, *Intervention in School and Clinic, 34,* 1999, 261–270.

Although most of the published information on phoneme instruction describes tactics for very young children—generally prekindergarten up through about grade 2 (Bos et al., 2000; Chard & Dickson, 1999; Kame'enui et al., 2002; NRP, 2000)—researchers have not adequately addressed the question of a third grader or even a sixth grader who is struggling in reading. Thus, the question of whether phoneme-based instruction should be offered in the higher grade levels remains unanswered. However, some preliminary research on this question is available. Bhat, Girffin, and Sindelar (2003) explored the efficacy of phonological awareness instruction among a group of middle school students with reading disabilities. Using an experimental, time-lag design, phonological instruction was offered first to 20 students with reading disabilities, while a second group of 20 students served as a control group for the first phase of the study. Afterward, phonological instruction was offered to the second group. Instruction in phonological awareness skills was provided on a one-to-one basis for each student, and this instruction included rhyming, identifying words with the same beginning or final sound, blending words, identifying syllables and phonemes, segmenting words, and phonemic deletion. Results indicated that provision of phonological instruction did result in increased word recognition skill.

A consensus that phoneme manipulation deficits may be the root cause of many learning disabilities has emerged (Kame'enui et al., 2002; Lyon & Moats, 1997; Moats & Lyon, 1993; Sousa, 2005), and various researchers have indicated that these deficits, even if present in a sixth- or eighth-grade child, must be addressed in order to facilitate progress in reading. This would suggest that phonemic instruction is very appropriate, even in the upper grades, for students who demonstrate deficits in this area. Of course, more research on this question will be forthcoming.

Several curriculums that address phonemic instruction have been developed for use with students with learning disabilities. For example, the Lindamood Phoneme Sequencing Program (Lindamood & Lindamood, 1998) presents a structured sequence of lessons to teach letter sounds, based on very small steps in letter-sound identification. Students are taught to discriminate likeness and differences between speech sounds, perceive the sameness or difference between the number and order of speech sounds, recognize minimal changes of speech sounds within syllables, and associate speech sounds with the alphabet. In this program, individual letter sounds are grouped together based on their sound. For example, the letters p and b are referred to as "lip poppers" by the teacher and students because the sounds of these letters involve a popping of the lips. In this pair, the letter p is considered the "unvoiced brother" and the letter b is considered the voiced sound; pronunciation of the letter b involves pronunciation of a voiced vowel sound, whereas pronunciation of a p does not. Other letters are grouped together by similarity of mouth and tongue movement. The letters m and n, for example, are referred to as "nose sounds." When students who have difficulty distinguishing sounds are taught these specifics of sound formation, they can better grasp the differences among phonemes.

Torgesen and Bryant (1994) developed the Phonological Awareness Training for Reading Program. In this program instruction in phonemes is divided into four sets of activities: warm-up, sound blending, sound segmenting, and reading/spelling. Rhyming activities focus the student's attention on letter sounds, and phonemic blending of sounds is emphasized next (Bender, 1999). This curriculum includes a wide variety of game boards, color-coded cards, letter-sound cards, picture cards, and audiotapes, all of which provide letter-sound examples. Research has demonstrated the efficacy of this program. Smith and

Simmons (1997) used a group of 31 first-grade students who were identified as at risk for reading failure, and three groups of children were formed. Ten children were exposed to the phonemic awareness curriculum for a period of six weeks. Ten others received exposure to the curriculum with enhanced review from the teacher, while the remaining children formed a control group and were taught via traditional instruction in the classroom. Children in the first two groups demonstrated enhanced phonemic awareness after the experimental period, compared to children who received traditional (i.e., nonphonemic-based) instruction. Based on this and other promising studies on phonemic awareness, teachers of children with learning disabilities should become familiar with one of the several programs designed to teach phonemic awareness and be prepared to implement that curriculum during their first year of teaching.

Finally, the Fast ForWord Reading Program developed by Scientific Learning Corporation (see the Website at *www.scientificlearning.com*) uses technology and synthesized speech to present phoneme problems to students with learning disabilities. The Fast ForWord Reading Program is built upon the latest research on how the human brain learns and focuses on phonemic-based instruction through several levels of reading. The Fast ForWord Reading Program involves a series of comprehensive computer-driven programs that cover reading skills from preschool through high school. In the early phoneme instructional programs, as a stimuli picture is presented on the screen, the student hears a series of phoneme sounds that represent the picture. One task involves the blending of these sounds to recognize the correct pronunciation of the word. Other tasks involve various other phonemic skills (e.g., detection of onsets and rhymes and phoneme substitution).

The computer program tracks the progress of the students and generates progress reports for the teacher. Subsequent programs present different skills in a variety of ways, most of which involve gamelike formats. The Fast ForWord Reading Program includes a series of instructional packages:

Basics	Intended for 4- to 7-year-olds who need to develop early reading skills such as phonemic awareness, letter naming, and letter sound skills.
Language	Used for students to develop the basic language skills that are the basis of reading, including working memory, reasoning, phoneme discrimination, and sound processing.
Language to Reading	Used for students to make the connection between oral and written language, including decoding, vocabulary, grammar, and beginning word recognition.
Reading	Concentrates on word recognition and fluency, advanced decoding, spelling, vocabulary, and passage comprehension.
Middle and High School	Emphasizes sustained focus and attention, listening comprehension, sequencing, and organization.

These programs have been piloted by Scientific Learning Corporation in a number of school districts, and the early research results are quite impressive, though few well-controlled studies are currently available in the journals. According to the pilot studies (that are briefly reviewed on the Website above), many students have demonstrated one- to three-year gains in reading and language in just two months of instruction. If these gains are eventually demonstrated for students with learning disabilities, this program will receive increased research attention.

Because many educators anticipate that effective instruction increasingly will be based to some degree on effective phonemic instruction software of this nature, reading programs such as this example may well represent the next approach to reading instruction. This would mean that the current generation of educators may well see schools retire the long practiced and venerated basal reading instructional approach for students with learning disabilities, as well as other students with reading deficits.

Sight-Word Approaches

Historically, reading was first taught using **sight-word approaches** for the first 6 decades of the last century. A sight-word approach involves students memorizing words by sight. The emphasis in this approach is on the meaning of the words, and whole words were often learned before the alphabet was introduced. Recognition of sight words is often aided by the configuration of the words (shape of the letters in the word, highlighted by boxes drawn around each letter). Also, sight words may be taught by using a tape recorder and letting the students hear the words.

Some research has indicated that basic lists of 200 to 300 sight words may account for up to 85% of the typical reading material in the first eight years of school. Consequently, it is very important for all children to master recognition of a set of basic sight words. However, early research on reading among children with learning disabilities indicated that, compared to other students, these students score consistently lower on word-recognition tests (Bender, 1985a). Clearly, the sight-word vocabulary of some of these students may be a limiting factor on their reading skill. Consequently, many teachers used sight-word lists as instructional tools for students who were learning disabled if the students did not respond favorably to other instructional approaches.

Phonics Instruction

Today, while selected lists of sight-words may still be utilized occasionally, teachers teach reading via a phonemic and phonics-based approach.

As described previously, the **phonics approach** involves the mapping of letters to speech sounds. These sounds represent a fairly complex sound/symbol coding system, and the student must master this system in order to "decode" an unknown word. Different vowel, consonant, and combination sounds are learned in isolation and then used as keys to pronounce unknown words. These sound/symbol relationships are often supplemented by the use of standard syllabication rules that indicate the number of distinct sounds in a word.

These complex sound/symbol relationships can represent major stumbling blocks for many students with learning disabilities. In certain cases, these students will decode part of the word, based on the easiest sound/symbol relationships, and merely guess at the remainder of the word. Other problems include a lack of understanding of multiple-sound consonants (g, c), vowels (a, e, i, o, u), or consonant blends (ch, pf).

Several researchers have suggested that an inability to decode words using phonological processing skills may be the most fundamental aspect of a learning disability (Moats

& Lyon, 1993; Padget, 1998). According to this argument, the inability to manipulate pho-nemes leads to difficulty in decoding words and many other reading problems.

Ackerman, Anhalt, and Dykman (1986) suggested that children with reading defi-ciencies may have sound/symbol problems that go beyond merely understanding the cod-ing nature of letters and sounds. Groups of children with reading disabilities and control children were compared on how well they could make an inference from two code-cueing words to a third target word. After ascertaining the appropriate reading instructional level for each child, researchers showed the students a target word and two cue words to assist in decoding the new target word. For example, the code words *shoe* and *got* were used to assist the child to decode the word *shot*. The children with disabilities did much worse than the control children, suggesting that problems with the use of coded clues as well as merely memory for those clues may cause problems in the use of phonics among these children.

Although study of phonics is usually restricted to the early years of school, Idol-Maestas (1981) indicated that instruction in a few basic phonics skills can yield impressive gains even in an adult's ability to read. The subject in that study was assisted in four skills: *r*-controlled vowels, short vowels, long vowels, and diphthongs. The 3-month instructional period resulted in instructional gains of over three years in total reading scores. Clearly, instruction in phonics may assist many students with learning disabilities in their reading progress.

WORD RECOGNITION AND COMPREHENSION

The ability to pronounce a word does not necessarily indicate an ability to understand a word's meaning. Thus, comprehension of words may involve more than recognition skills. Analysis of the context of the word (the use of the word in a sentence) may be used to emphasize word comprehension. Understanding the meaning of words is usually referred to as *semantics*.

Several authors have demonstrated low levels of vocabulary and a lack of under-standing of semantics among students with learning disabilities (NRP, 2000; Vogel, 1983). This may suggest that these students respond better to words when they are presented in context than in isolation because the context may help children with disabilities rec-ognize the word. However, research has indicated that merely using independent word strategies (i.e., dictionary and context clues) does not, in and of itself, assist students with learning disabilities in mastering new vocabulary (Bryant, Goodwin, Bryant, & Higgins, 2003). Clearly, teachers should employ additional strategies that are focused directly on learning new vocabulary terms. In this regard, researchers have investigated the efficacy of numerous strategies for enhancing vocabulary, including computer-assisted instruction, mnemonic instruction, direct instruction, and constant time delay (Bryant, Goodwin, Bry-ant, & Higgins, 2003; Jitendra, Edwards, Sacks, & Jocobson, 2004; Terrill, Scruggs, & Mastropieri, 2004). A brief synopsis of the various instructional techniques is presented in Interest Box 6.3. The research indicates support for each of the instructional strategies utilized; thus, teachers dealing with students with learning disabilities should implement one or more of these strategies.

Finally, analysis of the structure of the words is used to identify root words and suffixes or prefixes. Prefixes and suffixes frequently change the meaning of a word, and

INTEREST BOX 6.3

INSTRUCTIONAL STRATEGIES FOR TEACHING VOCABULARY TO STUDENTS WITH LEARNING DISABILITIES

TECHNIQUE	INSTRUCTIONAL PROCEDURE AND EFFICACY
Mnemonic Instruction	This instruction typically involves paired associate learning in which a new vocabulary term is paired with a known word (called a keyword), where the known word is similar in some fashion to the new term or represents a memorable action or event. Research is generally supportive of mnemonic instruction.
Direct Instruction	This method instruction involves specific instruction on words and word meanings, typically delivered in small-group fashion. Research on this technique is strongly supportive.
Constant Time Delay	This is an errorless learning procedure in which students are presented with words and/or word meanings and are expected to answer the problem if they know the answer. If they don't know the answer, the examiner will provide the answer in a period of three to five seconds, and the child is expected to repeat it, at which time the answer is counted correct (hence errorless learning). This method works well for vocabulary instruction.
Computerized Instruction	Typically, this approach involves individualized word sets of unknown words, with various instructional activities (e.g., multiple-choice exercises, matching) delivered via computer. Efficacy results are mixed on the effectiveness of this type of approach.

understanding this elaboration of word meaning is necessary in order to understand what is read. Structural analysis also includes an emphasis on other units of meaning, such as formation of plurals by adding s or es or the formation of possessives. Students with learning disabilities often demonstrate deficits in their ability to use these skills in determining word meaning.

READING FLUENCY

Reading fluency involves quick recognition of individual words, oral reading, and a student's understanding of whole phrases and sentences. Also, a student's ability to read quickly and with appropriate expression (i.e., appropriate use of punctuation) is critical. Students with learning disabilities have much more difficulty with fluent oral reading (Archer, Gleason, & Vachon, 2003; NRP, 2000). The types of errors students make in oral reading may include omission of words, mispronunciation, long hesitation while decoding words, and lack of comprehension.

Syntax is one aspect of reading fluency. Syntax refers to the relationships between words used in sentences. For example, in the sentence *John worked with Tom all summer, and he lived at the beach,* the pronoun *he* refers to John, and not Tom. Understanding the relationship of words in compound sentences is one aspect of syntax. Syntactic relationships such as the pronoun relationship, the direct object, and the indirect object of the sentence often confuse students with learning disabilities. In some cases, comprehension of entire sections of text or story lines depends on such syntactic structure. Also, sentence comprehension can become a problem during later school years because the sentences in textbooks tend to become more complex with numerous subordinated clauses. Clearly, one responsibility of the teacher of students with disabilities is to emphasize the comprehension of syntactic relationships.

However, reading fluency involves more than merely understanding syntax and sentences. As a student's early reading skills develop, that student spends less energy decoding individual letter sounds and words. Rather, entire words and even phrases are read together as a unit, with appropriate voice intonation and pauses for punctuation (Bender & Larkin, 2003; Chard, Vaughn, & Tyler, 2002). When students do not have to concentrate so much energy on recognition and decoding of the terms in the reading, they can invest more energy in reading fluently and in understanding the meaning of the passage. Thus, reading fluency serves as a bridge between decoding words and comprehension (Therrien & Kubina, 2006). Of course, students with learning disabilities often fail to make this transition to more sophisticated reading skills, and this presents consistent problems for these students during the later years of school. Thus, every teacher of students with learning disabilities should have some understanding of how to help students develop reading fluency.

Fortunately, much research has been done on appropriate strategies to increase reading fluency (Mastropieri, Leinart, & Scruggs, 1999; NRP, 2000). Fluency in reading develops as a result of monitored reading practice—that is, having students read text that is relatively easy for them and monitoring the errors. The National Reading Panel (2000) recognized the following levels of text difficulty:

Independent level	Relatively easy text for the reader, with no more than approximately 1 in 20 words difficult for the reader (95% success)
Instructional level	Challenging but manageable text for the reader, with no more than approximately 1 in 10 words difficult for the reader (90% success)
Frustration level	Difficult text for the reader, with more than 1 in 10 words difficult for the reader (less than 90% success)

The NRP (2000) suggested that students should be able to correctly read 95% of the words in a reading passage (i.e., making errors on only 1 in 20 words) in order for the passage to assist the student in developing reading fluency. Further, the various tactics that have been suggested as effective for developing reading fluency involve having someone monitor the oral reading of the student with the learning disability in one fashion or another (Chard et al., 2002; NRP, 2000). Several such tactics are presented in Interest Box 6.4.

There is one commonly used tactic that is no longer recommended as a fluency strategy. According to the National Reading Panel report (2000), individual oral reading—a tactic that has been used in the past—is now actively discouraged. In the past, teachers in

INTEREST BOX 6.4

TACTICS FOR DEVELOPING READING FLUENCY

Student–Adult Reading	A student reads one-on-one with an adult. The adult reads the text first, providing a model for the student, and the student then reads the text until the reading becomes fluent—perhaps three or four times through the passage.
Choral Reading	In choral (or unison) reading, students read along as a group.
Tape-Assisted Reading	In tape-assisted reading, students read along as they hear a fluent reader read the book on audiotape. On the first reading, the student should follow along with the words and point to each word as it is read. Next, the student should read along with the tape several times.
Partner Reading	In partner reading, paired students take turns reading aloud to each other, and more fluent readers may be paired with less fluent readers. Each partner may provide assistance to the other.

both special and general education classes would have students read aloud in class in order to monitor their reading fluency. While this is certainly a desirable goal, individual oral reading has caused considerable embarrassment for many students with reading problems. Consequently, the National Reading Panel discourages this technique and suggests substituting choral reading instead. While most teachers implement choral reading as "whole-class reading," choral reading may also be done in smaller groups (e.g., "Row 1, please read in unison the first paragraph"). By having four to six students read chorally, teachers will significantly reduce potential embarrassment and can still effectively monitor the reading of each individual child.

READING COMPREHENSION

Successful reading involves extraction of meaning from text. Comprehension of written material is a basic skill that heavily influences almost all aspects of educational achievement, and students with learning disabilities demonstrate deficits in this crucial skill. Research has demonstrated that reading levels of students with disabilities consistently fall considerably below those of their peers, even when intelligence scores are controlled (Bender, 1999; Bender & Larkin, 2003). Also, as the ability-achievement discrepancy discussion in Chapter 5 demonstrated, reading deficit has become a major factor in the identification process for learning disabilities in students. Clearly, comprehension is a major concern for teachers of children with learning disabilities.

Comprehension may involve relatively simple comprehension of the joint meaning of several sentences, more complex comprehension such as understanding paragraph structure and topic sentences in paragraphs, or understanding story structure (beginning, climax, etc.). A great deal of meaning may be gleaned from merely knowing the anticipated structure of the material that one is reading. Unfortunately, understanding the larger units of text structure is a weakness of many students with learning disabilities.

Measurement of Comprehension

Prior to looking at reading comprehension instruction, teachers must understand how comprehension is measured. As a teacher of the learning disabled, you will be frequently confronted with comprehension scores from various tests, and you must know the types of questions on the test in order to use the assessment data wisely. The most common measure of comprehension consists of answering questions about a text after the text is read. On this type of test, the student is required to read a brief paragraph or set of paragraphs and answer several multiple-choice questions. One problem with this type of test is that the student must correctly read the answers to the question in order to select the right one. If one answer has a word that is unknown, the student may choose incorrectly, not because of a lack of understanding of the test passage, but because of a lack of understanding of the possible answers.

Also, a lack of awareness of the structure of test questions (usually referred to as **testwiseness** skill) hampers many children with learning disabilities. For example, most multiple-choice tests have four answers consisting of one right answer, one answer that is partially correct but incorrect in a particular aspect, and two answers that are clearly wrong. Students who are testwise quickly identify the two incorrect distracter items and concentrate on careful reading of the remaining two items. A lack of knowledge of this testwiseness skill can lower a student's score, independent of his or her ability to read and comprehend the text. Scruggs, Bennion, and Lifson (1984) demonstrated that children who were learning disabled were less likely to demonstrate these testwiseness skills than other children.

Some tests currently use pictorial answers for the student. The student is asked to read a few sentences of a longer text and then select the correct picture from the possible choices. This eliminates the possibility of mistakes based on the words in the answer choices, but a lack of testwiseness skills may still have a negative impact on the student's score.

Another type of comprehension question is the **complex multiple-choice** question. The following is an example of a complex multiple-choice question:

Which of these gentlemen was president of the United States during the 19th century?

1. Abraham Lincoln
2. U. S. Grant
3. Robert E. Lee
4. Jefferson Davis

(a) 1 and 2 only
(b) 1 and 3 only
(c) 1 and 4 only
(d) 1, 2, and 3 only
(e) All of them

Questions of this type require a high level of concentration because of the answer format. A student must hold certain information in memory while he or she concentrates on additional information. This may be particularly difficult for children who have learning disabilities.

Finally, some recent assessments have begun to use a **cloze procedure,** in which the student must supply a missing word or phrase. The student reads a brief section of text and, based on that section, is expected to fill in a blank in the later portion of the same text. The assumption behind this procedure is that the student will understand the correct meaning of the section and supply the correct word or a synonym of that word.

As a teacher of children with learning disabilities, you may occasionally see a student who has received widely divergent scores on several reading tests. Parents may also be confused by widely different scores on reading for their child. As the professional, you must understand that different reading tests, because of the method of assessing comprehension, may measure different types of skills. You may be required to explain this to parents as early as your first year of teaching.

Levels of Comprehension

In addition to understanding the type of questions used to measure comprehension, you must understand the level of comprehension of written material. Generally, a hierarchical organization is depicted, with low-level comprehension items preceding higher-level, or more complicated, comprehension items. For example, low-level comprehension questions may require only **literal comprehension,** or direct recall of main points and details in the story. Other comprehension questions may be inferential in nature and require the student to draw conclusions from the text. Finally, evaluation of textual material is one of the higher levels of comprehension. Here, the student decides the worth of the text in relation to other similar texts.

Most tests of reading comprehension address literal and **inferential comprehension** adequately but address evaluation less adequately, because it is very difficult to prepare questions that assess the ability of a student to evaluate the quality of written material. Consequently, the higher levels of the comprehension hierarchy are often not included on reading comprehension tests.

Reading Comprehension Skills

Research results have demonstrated that children and adolescents with learning disabilities have difficulties comprehending what they read (MacInnis & Hemming, 1995). These students are less likely to recall the main idea and supporting details of a written text and are less likely to be able to draw appropriate conclusions from the text. Further, there may be several factors that interact to prohibit complete comprehension of multisentence texts among individuals with learning disabilities. Although each of the skills in the reading-skills hierarchy has been discussed as a separate, discrete skill, the reality is that these skills are overlapping and mutually supportive. Understanding the meaning of a sentence often gives some clue to decoding an unknown word in that sentence. Also, the ability to identify common types of phrases in sentences may help in oral reading fluency. The phrase *over the bridge* is more easily read than each word separately. In fact, good readers attend more to phrases than actual word-by-word reading.

In Chapter 3, the difficulties that children who are learning disabled have with pragmatic language (following the sequence of an extended narrative and being able to communicate that narrative) were discussed. Clearly, these difficulties in language usage may also complicate the understanding of information that is written. If one cannot understand a story when heard in spoken form, one may have more difficulty with the story in written form.

Also, comprehension of the written material is one clue to what the next words are. Likewise, letters are more accurately identified when they are found in words than in isolation. In short, scholars generally place reading comprehension at the top of the reading-skills hierarchy, but this skill permeates throughout the hierarchy, in a supportive fashion, in the development of all of the other reading skills. This is why the deficits that children with learning disabilities demonstrate in reading comprehension are of such concern to educators.

Although most of the research on comprehension has involved comprehension of basal readers in the elementary years, one special problem among the older population is comprehension of textbook material. As one may imagine, comprehension problems that adolescents with learning disabilities experienced during the early years of schooling have not disappeared, and comprehension of the text in history, science, or health class will present real problems for many of these students. Further, comprehension of text material is a different type of reading exercise when compared to comprehension of individual stories. For example, complete understanding of the material in text requires an understanding not only of the contents of the chapters, but of the organization of the several chapters into meaningful units (e.g., the relationship between chapters on vertebrates and invertebrates).

INSTRUCTIONAL STRATEGIES FOR IMPROVING COMPREHENSION

Research in the last two decades has yielded a number of very effective instructional approaches for improving reading comprehension (Bender, 1999; Das, Mishra, & Pool, 1995; Englert, Tarrant, Mariage, & Oxer, 1994; Kame'enui et al., 2002; Mariage, 1995; NRP, 2000; Padget, 1998; Schmidt, Rozendal, & Greenman, 2002). Some of these strategies involve the use of pictures or visual ability in activities that improve reading comprehension. Other techniques involve language usage in either prereading activities or postreading exercises to assist comprehension. One common theme in each of these strategies is an attempt to increase the active involvement or critical thinking on the part of the student. For this reason, most of these strategies may be conceptually related to the metacognitive perspective discussed in Chapter 1.

Visually Dependent Strategies

Visual Imagery.   Comprehension may be improved by the use of the imagination if students are systematically taught how to create a visual image of the material they are reading (Bender & Larkin, 2003; Ellis & Sabornie, 1988). In the **visual imagery** strategy, students must be instructed to close their eyes, think of the scene they read, identify the aspects of the scene that are necessary to understand the story, and create an image that includes these aspects. Exercises in imagery should be practiced each day for a period of time using low-reading-level paragraphs. Then the reading level of the paragraphs may be systematically increased over a period of days until an appropriate reading level is reached.

Semantic Map and Story Map.   Semantic-mapping and story-mapping exercises also represent visually based techniques for improving comprehension (Bender & Larkin, 2003; Boon, Ayres, & Spencer, in press; Mariage, 1995). In these exercises, students are presented with graphs, charts, or pictures and told to complete the exercise by reading the material and filling in the blanks in the chart. In more advanced instances, the students themselves may be required to aid in the development of the chart or **semantic map** as a part of the reading lesson. For example, in a semantic-mapping exercise in a small reading group, the class chooses a word that is central to the topic, and that word is placed in the center of the map. The class then brainstorms other words related to the keyword, and these are listed. The last list of words is examined in order to identify categories, and the categories are rearranged in order to group them around the central concept. The various meanings of the categories, terms, and concepts on the map are then discussed (Boulineau, Fore, Hagan-Burke, & Burke, 2004). A sample semantic map is presented in Figure 6.2.

   Both story-mapping and semantic-mapping techniques may be used in either group or individual instruction, and research has demonstrated the effectiveness of these techniques. Unlike the imagery strategy discussed earlier, these two strategies actually leave a written product, which may then be used for later study in order to master the content. Also, this technique (sometimes referred to as *participatory organizer* or *cognitive organizer*) is very useful for secondary students during both reading assignments and lecture assignments. The instructions for conducting a semantic map exercise are presented in Interest Box 6.5.

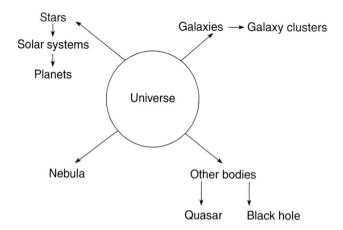

FIGURE 6.2   Semantic Map

■ ■ ■ ■ ■

INTEREST BOX 6.5

TEACHING TIPS: USING SEMANTIC MAPS

The interactive semantic-mapping procedure presented by Scanlon, Duran, Reyes, and Gallego (1992) is very useful to teachers who wish to employ this technique. The steps in the semantic-mapping process are described here.

1. Prepare a semantic map for your own reference.
   a. Conduct a content analysis. To begin, read the material, and identify the main concepts, with attention to superordinate concepts, coordinate concepts, and subordinate concepts.
   b. Depict superordinate concepts as central in the map, located on the center of a large sheet of paper.
   c. Using the headings in the text as guides, draw in coordinate concepts, depicting their relationship to the superordinate concept and to each other.
   d. Draw in the subordinate concepts.
   e. This map is for your reference, not to be shown to the students.
2. Have the students brainstorm the concept. Have them define their terms and explain what they mean.
3. Develop a clue list by skimming the text to glean important concepts. Students should be encouraged to use pictures and their former knowledge to identify the main concepts.
4. Develop the map with the group by focusing on what concepts are central (given the text content) and what topics are of lesser importance.
5. Have the students relate the concepts to each other and determine the concept that is deemed to be the focal point of the map. Encourage discussion between students.
6. Have the students refer to the text again and justify the relationships that are depicted on the map. Encourage the students to make modifications while they reread.
7. Review the map in its final form. Remind the students to utilize this map for their personal review and test preparation.

In a further elaboration of the semantic map concept, Hoover and Rabideau (1995) suggested using a semantic map to teach various types of study skills. For example, consider the testwiseness skills (including elimination of obviously wrong answers, etc.) described previously in this chapter. A semantic map that incorporates those testwiseness skills is presented in Figure 6.3. Notice how the task of taking multiple-choice tests is presented with test-taking skills, studying skills, and test-reviewing skills as the major organizers for the map. The specific subskills related to each area are presented as well. Use of semantic maps of this nature on a regular basis can greatly assist students with learning disabilities in learning to take multiple-choice tests, and other maps may help with other study skills.

Scaffolded Instruction.   One method of reading instruction that is related to the semantic map is the concept of **scaffolded instruction** (Das et al., 1995; Echevarria, 1995; Larkin, 2001; Mariage, 1995; Stone, 1998). Because students with learning disabilities often demonstrate a lack of organizational skills in reading, providing a systematic method to assist

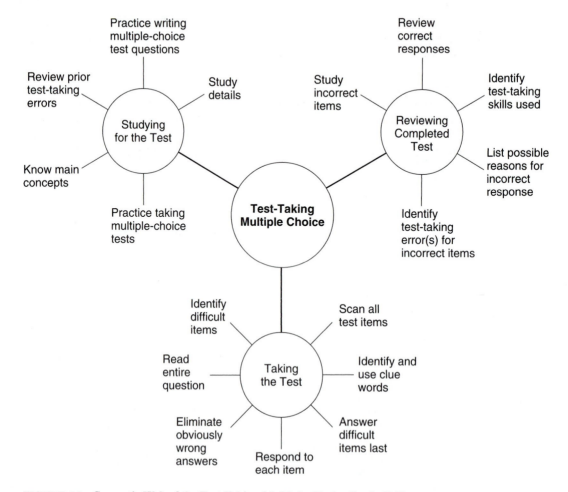

FIGURE 6.3   Semantic Web of the Test-Taking Multiple-Choice Study Skill

Source: From "Semantic Webs and Study Skills" by J. J. Hoover and D. K. Rabideau, 1995, *Intervention in School and Clinic, 30*(5), 292–296. Copyright 1995 by PRO-ED, Inc. Reprinted by permission.

them in gradually building their understanding and comprehension of a reading passage is often quite effective in improving their reading skills (Englert et al., 1994; Mariage, 1995).

As early as 1978, Vygotsky suggested that learning must be "scaffolded" or structured and supported by a person more competent in the particular skill under study (Echevarria, 1995). That mentor's role is to structure learning tasks that bridge the gap between the understandings a student currently has and the concept to be learned, using questions or learning tasks that approximate the final concept in a gradual shift from simple to more difficult concepts. Also, such scaffolds or learning supports might be represented in the form of suggested steps or guidelines. This would suggest that, rather than using a blank semantic map, students with learning disabilities may perform better with a map that indicates a series of organizational steps, which are scaffolded to support the student's growing comprehension.

Perhaps an example of this technique would illustrate the concept. Mariage (1995) presented a semantic map, based on a series of steps through which students may proceed to unpack the meaning in a reading passage on spiders, as presented in Figure 6.4. Using this procedure, students are encouraged to complete certain tasks prior to, during, and after reading. Those tasks include: (1) predicting what happens in a story, (2) organizing those predictions, (3) searching for main ideas, (4) summarizing the ideas, and (5) evaluating

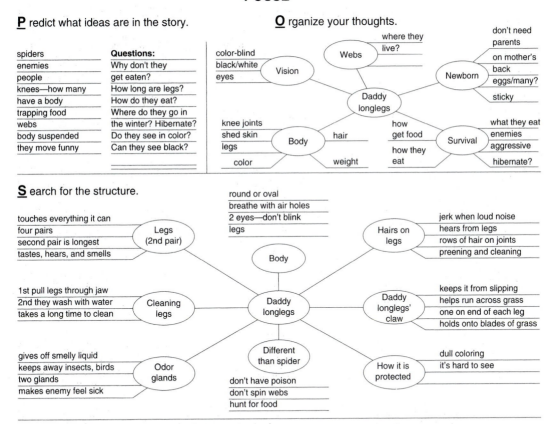

S ummarize. Summarize the main idea. Ask a "teacher" question about the main idea (check details).

E valuate. Compare. Clarify. Predict.

FIGURE 6.4   Partially Completed POSSE Strategy Sheet

Source: From "Why Students Learn: The Nature of Teacher Talk during Reading" by T. V. Mariage, 1995, *Learning Disability Quarterly, 18,* 214–234. Reprinted by permission.

the story. The acronym POSSE is used to provide a scaffold or a specified series of tasks for the student to perform. Adult supervision during the use of this acronym should result in improved performance. Figure 6.5 presents the types of questions students may use to complete the task.

Illustrations in Text.   Although the placement of illustrations in the basic reading texts improves the reading comprehension for nondisabled children, there is some evidence that pictures may hamper the reading comprehension of students who are learning disabled (Rose & Robinson, 1984). Some experts suggest that the presence of pictures may serve as a distracter. Also, as the metacognitive perspective on learning disabilities suggests (Chapter 1), children with learning disabilities may not cognitively engage themselves in the activity of seeking relationships between the pictures in the text and the written material. However, if a teacher highlights these relationships, the presence of pictures may enhance comprehension (Mastropieri & Peters, 1987). Still, this is speculative, and research is continuing on this issue of the usefulness of pictures in text for students who experience learning disabilities.

Language of POSSE

Reading Process	Comprehension Strategies	Self-Statements	Instructional Scaffolds
Before Reading	Predict • where did you get that idea? • ask questions Organize • categories • detail	• I predict . . . • I am remembering . . . • One question is . . . • One category might be . . . • A detail for that category is . . .	• POSSE strategy sheet • Self-statement cards • Teacher/student think aloud • Helper words • Reciprocal teaching • Mapping main ideas and details of passage
During Reading	Search • search for the main idea Summarize • main idea • ask questions about main idea	• While I am reading, I need to search for the main points the author is talking about • I think the main idea is . . . • A question about the main idea is . . .	
After Reading	Evaluate • compare new to known • clarify unclear words or referents • predict what author will talk about next	• I think we did (did not) predict this main idea • Are there any idea or word clarifications? • I predict the author will next talk about . . .	

FIGURE 6.5   LANGUAGE OF POSSE

Source: From "Why Students Learn: The Nature of Teacher Talk during Reading" by T. V. Mariage, 1995, *Learning Disability Quarterly, 18,* 214–234. Reprinted by permission.

Auditory/Language-Dependent Strategies

Some reading strategies involve the use of language, either before or after the text, in order to improve comprehension. The use of some type of warm-up activity preceding reading may generate interest and provide for some organizational understanding of the story prior to the actual reading. Alternatively, postreading activities requiring a student to retell a story also strengthen comprehension.

Advance-Organizer Techniques.   Research has shown that certain activities that cause the student to think about the story prior to reading may increase reading comprehension and oral reading performance (Bender, 2002; Mariage, 1995; Mason, Meadan, Hedin, & Corso, 2006). Discussion of the type of script, in terms of the plans and goals of the main characters in a story, leads to better retention of the main points of the story. These types of prereading activities are referred to as **advanced organizers.** Also, brief descriptions of a story with student input improve comprehension, such as, "This is a story about a bank robber who had some of his money stolen. How do you think he feels? What does he do when he catches the person who stole the money from him?" These questions would tend to improve the comprehension of students with learning disabilities.

Story Retelling and Self-Questioning.   In using a story-retelling technique (sometimes referred to as *paraphrasing* or *self-questioning* technique), the student is systematically taught to read passages and ask questions concerning the main idea and major supporting details. The student then retells the major events in the story prior to continuing with the comprehension questions. Research on this language-based strategy has shown that when students with learning disabilities are trained in **story retelling,** comprehension improves.

The TWA Strategy.   The TWA strategy for improving reading comprehension incorporates a variety of linguistically based cognitive techniques, including the advance organizer technique, but this strategy goes beyond prereading activity (Mason, Meadan, Hedin, & Corso, 2006). Students are encouraged to think and talk to themselves about various aspects of the reading content. First they are taught an acronym—TWA—that represents the steps to undertake before, during, and after reading a passage. The acronym represents the following steps.

> **T**   **Think before reading**—consider the author's purpose and what you already know about the topic.
>
> **W**   **While reading**—think about reading speed, linking new knowledge with things you already know, and, if necessary, rereading important parts.
>
> **A**   **After reading**—think about the main idea; verbally summarize information you have learned.

As these steps indicate, the first part of this tactic may be considered as an advance organizer, since it encourages the student to consider the text title and make some judgments about the author's purpose. Based on those predictions, the student can then check the accuracy of those predictions while reading. Further, research has shown that this technique works (Mason, Meadan, Hedin, & Corso, 2006). Specifically, the requirement for summarization of the reading content offers another opportunity to check predictions and reinforces enhanced comprehension of the entire passage (Hedin, Mason, & Sukhram, 2006).

Repeated Readings.   Offering the student the opportunity to repeat a reading has been shown to be a highly effective reading comprehension technique and to improve reading fluency among challenged readers (Knebel, Cartledge, & Kourea, 2006; National Reading Panel, 2000; Therrien & Kubina, 2006). In using this technique, students are exposed to the same reading passage for between three and seven readings in a short time period; many researchers have students read the same 5- to 10-paragraph text three or four times in the same day to enhance fluency and comprehension. Various types of instructional activities may be offered in conjunction with these repeated readings, such as instruction on content-specific vocabulary, paired readings, or discussion of the content of the passage. In a summary of research on repeated readings, the National Reading Panel (2000) indicated not only that this technique enhanced fluency and comprehension on the passage under study but also that repeated readings enhanced these skills for unpracticed passages to which the child had not been exposed. Thus, repeated readings is highly recommended as an instructional technique for students with learning disabilities (Therrien & Kubina, 2006).

Strategy Selection

Selecting the appropriate reading-comprehension strategy for use with a particular child is difficult. Further, there are no specific guidelines that can be offered for this decision. In a general sense, if a student tends to do better when material is presented visually, you may wish to try one of the visually based instructional strategies. However, research has not shown that aiming the instructional strategy toward a particular student's strength automatically increases comprehension. As the teacher, you will have to decide for each student on a trial-and-error basis which techniques seem to work best. Once you have found a technique that works for a particular student, present each reading assignment using that same instructional format.

Another option is the combination of several of the techniques discussed. For example, I used a combination of an advance-organizer technique and a story-retelling technique in a resource room for junior high students with learning disabilities. Students were told that, throughout the year, they were to use the "Five W" questions as an advance organizer. (This means they were to look for Who was in the story, What happens, When major events occur, Where the action is, and Why the story happened that way.) This was paired with the expectation that, after reading a story silently, the students would retell the story to the teacher, answering each of the questions. As this example illustrates, the various reading-comprehension techniques may be combined in numerous ways.

WRITING SKILLS

While the area of reading for students with learning disabilities has received much more attention than many other language arts areas, the area of writing has received increased attention over the last decade. In particular, the 1997 reauthorization of the Individuals with

Disabilities Act mandated the participation of students with learning disabilities in the general education curriculum, an emphasis that was reiterated with the reauthorization of IDEA in 2004 (Schumaker & Deshler, 2003). One outcome of these changes is the inclusion of students with learning disabilities in statewide assessment programs, and while nearly every state requires assessments in reading and math, 35 states also require assessment in writing (Council of Chief State School Officers, 1999). As a result, writing instruction has received increased emphasis, both in research literature as well as in classrooms for students with learning disabilities.

Many students who are learning disabled demonstrate problems in some area of writing—handwriting or written expression (Schumaker & Deshler, 2003). Unlike the difficulties associated with reading skills, the writing skills of these students have only recently been widely researched. We do know that many of these students demonstrate difficulties in printing and handwriting from their early years and that these difficulties are probably related to other problems, including language problems and cognitive planning ability. However, much work needs to be done concerning the types of difficulties in writing skills experienced by children with disabilities.

Handwriting

Students who are learning disabled often demonstrate problems in the earliest writing tasks, involving copying letters and words, as well as correct production of written letters during kindergarten and first grade. Interest Box 6.6 demonstrates some of these problems. Some theorists believe that these copying and writing problems may be symptomatic of deeper neurological or visual-processing abilities (see the visual-perceptual perspective in Chapter 1), whereas other scholars choose to ignore these potential causes and concentrate on the accurate letter-writing behavior (these scholars tend to come from the behavioral perspective). In addition to copying errors, other errors may include letter height, letter spacing within words, letter proximity to the line, and word spacing (Blandford & Lloyd, 1987).

Many of these handwriting problems are manageable with increased behavioral reinforcement for correct writing skill, suggesting that imperfect writing skills (in individuals without a physical disability) may be merely a matter of attention to the detail of correct letter formation and spacing. For students with severe problems, teachers should reward (on a word-by-word basis) every instance of correct handwriting.

Blandford and Lloyd (1987) presented an effective self-instructional procedure in which a card with seven self-checking questions was prepared and given to students with learning disabilities. The seven questions prompted students to think about the types of writing errors mentioned earlier, and each student was trained to use the card before submitting a written assignment. The handwriting improved markedly, and this improvement was sustained over a period of time, even after the card was no longer used. Clearly, this treatment approach should be attempted whenever a persistent handwriting problem becomes evident.

Spelling

Spelling is one language arts skill area that is essential when written products are required in classwork (Santoro, Coyne, & Simmons, 2006; Schumaker & Deshler, 2003). One early

INTEREST BOX 6.6

HANDWRITTEN SENTENCES OF CHILDREN
WITH LEARNING DISABILITIES

Note the height of the capital and lowercase letters in these sentences. Also, in several instances, the student wrote through the margin of the paper. Finally, when a student cannot follow the lines on the page, this may indicate a visual-perceptual problem.

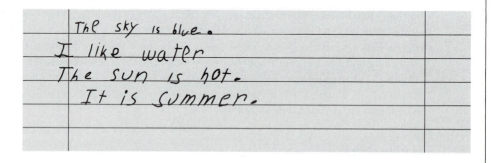

debate concerning spelling errors that such children made dealt with the cause of the errors. Because of the neurological and language problems among these students, several scholars argued that the spelling errors may be somewhat aberrant from the typical spelling errors found in the work of nondisabled children. If this were true, it may suggest that different types of spelling activities were necessary for children who have disabilities. However, research has shown that the spelling errors made by the learning disabled do not deviate from the types of errors made by younger children without learning disabilities (Gerber & Hall, 1987). Although students with learning disabilities typically do make more spelling errors than their age-mates, the same spelling strategies used to teach spelling to nondisabled children are likely to be effective in working with the spelling problems of the students with learning disabilities also. More recently, the importance of phonemic awareness as a basis for effective spelling among students with learning disabilities has been demonstrated (Berninger, Abbott, Rogan, Reed, Abbott, Brooks, Vaughan, & Graham, 1998; Chard & Dickson, 1999; Santoro, Coyne, & Simmons, 2006). Research has demonstrated that students need not only to understand letter sounds, but also to generate a mental representation of the sound-symbol relationship as well as to apply multiple spelling strategies (Berninger et al., 1998). Similar to the ongoing research on early reading (Moats & Lyon, 1993), the importance of phonemic awareness has become more obvious as a basis for spelling skills.

There are numerous spelling strategies available that have been shown to be effective with children who have learning disabilities (NRP, 2000; McNaughton & Hughes, 1999; Nulman & Gerber, 1984). For example, Nulman and Gerber (1984) demonstrated that a process of imitating a child's spelling errors, combined with a model of correct spelling, reduced a child's error rate. Other strategies may include modeling correct spelling with a brief time delay and strategy training that focuses on patterns of predictable letters within words.

Various authors have investigated error correction as an intervention to enhance spelling among children with learning disabilities (Kearney & Drabman, 1993; McNaughton, Hughes, & Ofiesh, 1997). For example, Kearney and Drabman (1993) demonstrated an inexpensive procedure for improving spelling performance. Students were tested daily on spelling words, and immediate feedback was given on the errors. On the first day, students took a conventional spelling test and were then instructed to write the error words five times, each time saying the letters as they wrote them. On the next day, students again took the spelling test and were required to write the error words 10 times, while saying each of the letters. Finally, on the next day, the students were required to take the test again and write the errors 15 times, each time saying the letters in the corrected words aloud. This procedure was shown to be very effective, and the authors suggested that the effectiveness of the procedure was related to the fact that this is a multisensory procedure. The students experienced both writing and saying the correct spellings on multiple occasions. Thus, this is an effective instructional procedure that requires no funds for purchase of curriculum or equipment.

One question that many teachers debate involves the use of spell-checking technology for students with learning disabilities. McNaughton, Hughes, and Ofiesh (1997) investigated the use of spell checkers coupled with an explicitly taught learning strategy designed to enhance a student's self-checking of spelling. Several students were included in a multiple baseline design, and spelling errors were tracked over time on their written products. The data showed that prior to any intervention, an average of 7.6% of the words in students' compositions included spelling errors, and even though students were using a spell checker at that point, students with learning disabilities only corrected 41% of those errors. However, after the intervention, which involved both the use of the spell checker and the strategy to emphasize self-checking of one's spelling, only 3% of the words in the students' compositions contained errors, and students were then correcting 75% of those words. The authors suggest that this is comparable to the self-correction rate of spelling errors among students without disabilities. Thus, while the use of spell checkers should be encouraged, teachers must do more than merely make these technologies available to students with learning disabilities; teachers must emphasize the importance of correction of spelling errors and should consider using learning strategies as one method to accomplish this.

Written Expression

The ability to express an opinion or argument in written form is a skill that is necessary during the later years of schooling. For example, essay questions on tests, homework assignments, and written work in class may require written expression beyond mere handwriting and sentence-structuring skills. Unfortunately, the difficulties that students with learning disabilities have in reading comprehension and spoken language probably interact to create difficulties in effective written-expression ability. The discussion of functional and narrative language in Chapter 3 indicated that these children had problems following information presented in narrative form and reproducing that narrative. Clearly, these difficulties in spoken language will affect the child's ability to express the same type of narrative in written form. The type of writing assignment also affects the written expression of children who are learning disabled. Interest Box 6.7 presents a sample of written expression of a student with learning disabilities.

Recently, researchers have begun to recommend strategies for improving the writing of students with learning disabilities. Some of these strategies depend on emerging computer technology and software (Montague & Fonseca, 1993; Williams, 2002). For example, Williams (2002) presented a case study on the use of developing speech-feedback technology to assist students with learning disabilities in writing. A student with poor writing skills used two computer-based software programs to enhance his writing. First, he used a word-prediction program that enabled him to write only a few letters of the desired word, and the computer provided the predicted word (based on the grammar, the letters previously typed in, etc.). This saved time and prevented many spelling errors on the part of the student. Next, after he had written a brief text, the student used a speech-feedback program that "read" the text selection; thus, the student had his work read out loud for revision purposes.

Montague and Fonseca (1993) used a program that assists the student with disabilities in focusing on the writing process and facilitates communication with the teacher concerning the student's writing. In that program, students are encouraged to develop plans for writing that include the overall organization and lists of major points. These points can then be sequenced into some logical order for written presentation. Also, revision of the written product is much less painful and time-consuming on the computer than in the traditional paper-and-pencil format. In addition, numerous computer programs are available that prompt a student during the writing process (Montague & Fonseca, 1993).

INTEREST BOX 6.7
WRITTEN EXPRESSION OF A STUDENT WITH LEARNING DISABILITIES

In this assignment, the student was instructed to write a paragraph about his favorite animal. Note that the student does recognize the general paragraph format, in that the first line is indented and he does not begin each sentence on a separate line. However, the intrinsic structure of a paragraph is not present. There is no readily identifiable topic sentence, nor do the sentences in the paragraph build upon each other to present supplemental information and more complex concepts. In a very real sense, this is merely a collection of sentences rather than a paragraph.

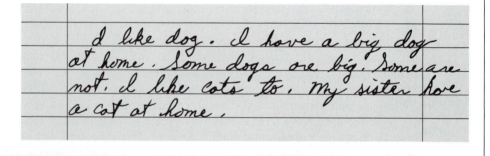

Troia, Graham, and Harris (1999) demonstrated the importance of thoughtful planning by students with learning disabilities when writing a story. Three fifth-grade students who were identified as learning disabled were taught to plan their writing selection by setting goals, brainstorming ideas, and sequencing their ideas. The multiple-baseline design demonstrated that after the students were trained in these planning strategies, their written stories got longer and the overall structure of the stories improved. Clearly, these three components of story planning should be taught to students with learning disabilities in all language arts classrooms.

Graves and Hauge (1993) suggested a self-monitoring checklist to assist students with disabilities in writing. The checklist, presented in Figure 6.6, presents a series of cues to the student that must be considered in planning a written composition and during the actual writing process. The student is instructed to use the card by specifying his or her decisions about each of the elements presented on the checklist in advance (Graves & Hauge, 1993). Also, after the writing process, this checklist could be used as a final check before turning in the assignment.

During the later years of school, writing assignments come in many forms and may include preparing research papers (Johnson & Bender, 1999). Because this type of writing assignment is relatively new for most students (i.e., this type of assignment usually begins in middle school or junior high school), students with learning disabilities are likely to need assistance with it. To meet this need, Korinek and Bulls (1996) developed a writing strategy called SCORE A, presented in Interest Box 6.8. Korinek and Bulls (1996) demonstrated the effectiveness of this strategy with five eighth-grade students with learning disabilities during a nine-week period. Four of the five students completed the assignment with a grade of "C" or higher. Thus, this strategy will assist students in the various steps in an extended research writing assignment, and these steps should be consistently applied over several such assignments until students have internalized this process.

Element	Check As I Plan:	Check As I Write:
Characters		
Setting		
Problem		
Plan		
Ending		

FIGURE 6.6   Self-Monitoring Checklist for Writing

Strategies such as these will assist students with disabilities in their writing endeavors. You should keep current with additional writing improvement strategies as they become available in the literature.

Note-Taking

One language arts skill that is essential in the upper grades is the ability to take notes when a teacher is speaking. To date, very little research on note-taking skills among students with learning disabilities is available. However, it may be assumed that because of the difficulties in language, written expression, and cognitive organization that these students demonstrate, note-taking is a very difficult task for them.

Research on note-taking among students with learning disabilities in recent years has indicated that the more cognitively involved students are with note-taking, the higher the recall of information (Igo, Bruning, McCrudden, & Kauffman, 2003). For example, students who must paraphrase information from a text when taking notes typically retain more information than do students who merely copy information, or (in the case of a Web-based textbook) cut and paste information to create their notes. Bender (2004) recommended that secondary teachers address this language arts skill by providing a participatory organizer for the students whenever a lecture takes place. The organizer may be either an outline form to be completed by the student during the lecture or a chart with appropriate spaces to be filled in. Semantic maps may provide an organizer to assist students in note-taking. Also, special education teachers should teach the important skills associated with listening to a lecture, identifying the main points, and arranging those points in some outline form to assist in note-taking.

In a recent study on note-taking among students with learning disabilities, Igo and his co-workers (2006) investigated use of computer technologies to assist in note-taking. Of course, computer-based note-taking, coupled with Web-based texts, offers the possibility of

■ ■ ■ ■ ■ ▬▬

INTEREST BOX 6.8
SCORE A: A STRATEGY FOR WRITING RESEARCH PAPERS

S   Select a subject
C   Create categories to be researched
O   Obtain sources on each topic or category
R   Read and take notes on each topic
E   Evenly organize the information

A   Apply the process writing steps
    a. Planning or prewriting
    b. Drafting
    c. Rewriting and revising

Source: Adapted from "SCORE A: A Student's Research Paper Writing Strategy" by L. Korinek and J. A. Bulls, *Teaching Exceptional Children, 28*(4), 1996, 60–63.

cutting and pasting content to formulate one's notes, as opposed to mentally constructing notes in non-Web-based learning, such as lectures and class discussions. Using seventh- and eighth-grade students with and without learning disabilities, Igo and his co-workers (2006) questioned the efficacy of cut-and-paste note-taking versus writing notes out and thus paraphrasing text. These researchers anticipated that writing notes out would result in increased comprehension, but instead, their results were mixed. Recall for written answers on texts was enhanced by writing out notes, whereas, contrary to expectation, recall on multiple-choice tests (which tend to be merely factual/literal recall) was enhanced by cut-and-paste note-taking. These results have implications for future research. First, more research will certainly be forthcoming on note-taking, since it is such a critical skill for secondary students with learning disabilities. Also, more research on electronic note-taking among students with learning disabilities will be undertaken in the near future. Teachers should utilize some computer-based note-taking for students with learning disabilities, while remaining current on this relatively new line of research.

WHOLE-LANGUAGE INSTRUCTION

During the 1990s, a number of theorists promoted an instructional approach referred to as **whole-language instruction** (Lerner, Cousin, & Richeck, 1992; MacInnis & Hemming, 1995). The traditional approach to language arts and reading instruction has seemed rather disjointed to some, and, as the organization of this chapter illustrates, reading and language arts skills have traditionally been broken down into numerous discrete areas for instructional purposes. However, the proponents of the whole-language instructional approach suggest that instruction that focuses on the discrete skills, rather than the holistic use of reading and writing as communication activities in a social context, fosters a rather sterile instructional climate where children cannot see the usefulness of the skills that they are forced to learn.

In the whole-language context, students are taught reading, language arts, spelling, writing, and other communication skills in the context of social relationships in the classroom (Bender, 1999). The focus for reading materials tends to be on real-world literature rather than artificially constructed reading curricula. Students practice discrete language arts skills only if their contextual writing samples indicate that they need extra work on those skills. Many teachers have chosen to restructure their reading and language arts instructional endeavors along these lines, and these teachers typically report that students seem to enjoy this type of curricular and instructional approach more than the traditional approach (Lerner et al., 1992).

However, a number of researchers suggest that whole-language instruction may not be an appropriate choice for students with learning disabilities (Lerner et al., 1992; Mather & Roberts, 1994; Moats, 1991; NRP, 2000). Contrary to the anecdotal claims of many teachers, Stahl and Miller (1989) demonstrated that this method was no more effective than traditional methods in terms of enhancing the reading achievement of students without disabilities. Further, Moats (1991) indicated that this method may not be effective for students who need work in phonological coding and sound blending, and many students with learning disabilities need that type of instruction. Thus, serious questions have been raised concerning the applicability of the whole-language instructional method for students with learning disabilities. Clearly, more research will be forthcoming on this question during the next several years, and until this question on efficacy is answered, teachers should use this method only in a limited fashion for students with learning disabilities.

SUMMARY

This chapter presented the reading and language arts deficiencies that students with learning disabilities demonstrate. Because of basic problems in phonemic awareness and spoken language, many of these children demonstrate reading difficulties. The reading-skills hierarchy, although presented as independent and discrete skills, is really a set of mutually interdependent skills. That is, problems in decoding may cause problems in comprehension, which may, in turn, eliminate the context clues necessary for decoding other words later in the text. Reading is a crucial area in almost every aspect of the school curriculum, including the secondary school content-area courses. For this reason, it is the responsibility of the teacher of the child with learning disabilities to select the strategies that allow that child to function successfully, given the reading demands of the curriculum.

These reading difficulties cause further problems in other language arts activities, including handwriting, spelling, written expression, and note-taking. In various classes and assignments, each of these language arts skills is necessary. Although much research and educational time typically go into reading, more research attention and more educational time in public school classes should be allocated to these reading-related language arts areas.

The following points should help you study this chapter:

- Almost all students with learning disabilities have difficulty in reading, and that difficulty affects their school performance in most subject areas.
- Reading may be conceptualized as four interdependent components: decoding, word recognition, reading fluency, and reading comprehension.
- Sight-word approaches involve memorization of various sight words without regard for particular letter sounds and should be used only after phonemic and phonics instruction have been implemented.
- Phonics instruction involves decoding the words based on letter sounds. This is the preferred method for teaching reading.
- Research has suggested that phonics instruction results in better reading skill overall than sight words for most students, though the sight-word approach may be the only successful approach for a particular child.
- Phonemic awareness instruction seems to hold great promise in alleviating the reading problems of many students with learning disabilities.
- Word analysis (study of root words, suffixes, and prefixes) results in improved word comprehension.
- Comprehension may be measured by a variety of methods, including multiple choice with written answers, multiple choice with picture answers, and cloze procedures.
- Comprehension should be viewed as a multilevel skill. The number of levels may vary, but most scholars would agree on at least a distinction between literal comprehension, inferential comprehension, evaluation, and appreciation.

- Different students with disabilities learn by different instructional approaches. As a result, the special education teacher should master both the visually dependent strategies and the auditory/language strategies for reading-comprehension instruction.
- Students who are learning disabled often demonstrate difficulty in other language arts areas such as handwriting, spelling, and written expression. Instruction in each of these areas is often the responsibility of the special education teacher.
- Whole-language instruction involves emphasis on language arts in social communication contexts, but questions have been raised about the effectiveness of whole-language instruction for students with learning disabilities.

QUESTIONS AND ACTIVITIES

1. Present to the class a critique of one of the research-treatment articles dealing with a reading-comprehension intervention study.

2. Obtain several copies of a basal reading text and a basal spelling text from the local public schools. Identify examples of phonics instruction from the texts. What examples of sight-word approaches can you find?

3. Review the research on phonemic instruction and report back to the class.

4. Review the research evidence on spelling errors of children with learning disabilities. What evidence supports/refutes the claim that these children make different types of errors?

5. Discuss in class the possible specific language-based causes for reading disabilities.

6. Obtain a writing sample from several students who are learning disabled, and compare it with the sample in text. What are the similarities?

7. Observe a secondary school class and casually identify the note-taking problems encountered by the students with learning disabilities in that class.

REFERENCES

Ackerman, P. T., Anhalt, J. M., & Dykman, R. A. (1986). Inferential word-decoding weakness in reading disabled children. *Learning Disability Quarterly, 9,* 315–323.

Archer, A. L., Gleason, M. M., & Vachon, V. L. (2003). Decoding and fluency: Foundation skills for struggling older readers. *Learning Disability Quarterly, 26*(2), 89–102.

Bender, W. N. (1985). Differential diagnosis based on task-related behavior of learning disabled and low-achieving adolescents. *Learning Disability Quarterly, 8,* 261–266.

Bender, W. N. (1999). Innovative approaches to reading. In W. N. Bender (Ed.), *Professional issues in learning disabilities* (pp. 83–106). Austin, TX: ProEd.

Bender, W. N. (2002). *Differentiating instruction for students with learning disabilities: Best teaching practices for general and special educators.* Thousand Oaks, CA: Corwin Press.

Bender, W. N. (2004). *Learning disabilities: Characteristics, identification, and teaching strategies* (5th ed.). Boston: Allyn and Bacon.

Bender, W. N., & Larkin, M. (2003). *Reading strategies for students with learning disabilities.* Thousand Oaks, CA: Corwin Press.

Berninger, V., Abbott, R., Rogan, L., Reed, E., Abbott, S., Brooks, A., Vaughan, K., & Graham, S. (1998). Teaching spelling to children with specific learning disabilities: The mind's ear and eye beat the computer or pencil. *Learning Disability Quarterly, 21,* 106–122.

Bhat, P., Girffin, C. C., & Sindelar, P. T. (2003). Phonological awareness instruction for middle school students with learning disabilities. *Learning Disability Quarterly, 26* (2), 73–88.

Blandford, B. J., & Lloyd, J. W. (1987). Effects of a self-instructional procedure on handwriting. *Journal of Learning Disabilities, 20,* 342–346.

Boon, R., Ayres, K., & Spencer, V. (in press). The effects of cognitive organizers to facilitate content-area learning for students with mild disabilities. A pilot study. *Journal of Instructional Practice.*

Bos, C. S., Mather, N., Silver-Pacuilla, H., & Narr, R. F. (2000). Learning to teach early literacy skills—collaboratively. *Teaching Exceptional Children, 32*(5), 38–45.

Boulineau, T., Fore, C., Hagan-Burke, S., & Burke, M. D. (2004). Use of story-mapping to increase the story-grammar text comprehension of elementary students with learning disabilities. *Learning Disability Quarterly, 27,* 1–17.

Bryant, D. P., Goodwin, M., Bryant, B. R., & Higgins, K. (2003). Vocabulary instruction for students with learning disabilities: A review of the research. *Learning Disability Quarterly, 26* (2), 117–128.

Chard, D. J., & Dickson, S. V. (1999). Phonological awareness: Instructional and assessment guidelines. *Intervention in School and Clinic, 34*(5), 261–270.

Chard, D. J., Vaughn, S., & Tyler, B. J. (2002). A synthesis of research on effective interventions for building reading fluency with elementary students with learning disabilities. *Journal of Learning Disabilities, 35*(5), 386–406.

Commission on Excellence in Special Education (2001). *Revitalizing special education for children and their families.* Available from www.ed.gov/inits/commissionsboards/whspecialeducation.

Council for Exceptional Children (CEC) (2002). Commission report calls for special education reform. *Today, 9*(3), 1–6.

Council of Chief State School Officers (1999). *State students assessment programs: A summary report.* Washington, DC: Author.

Das, J. P., Mishra, R. K., & Pool, J. E. (1995). An experiment on cognitive remediation of word-reading difficulty. *Journal of Learning Disabilities, 28,* 66–79.

Echevarria, J. (1995). Interactive reading instruction: A comparison of proximal and distal effects of instructional conversations. *Exceptional Children, 61,* 536–552.

Edelen-Smith, P. J. (1997). How now brown cow: Phoneme awareness activities for collaborative classrooms. *Intervention in School and Clinic, 33,* 103–111.

Ellis, E. S., & Sabornie, E. J. (1988). Teaching learning strategies to learning disabled students in post-secondary settings. In W. N. Bender, D. Benson, & D. Burns (Eds.), *College programs for the learning disabled.* New Brunswick, NJ: Rutgers University Press.

Englert, C. S., Tarrant, K. L., Mariage, T. V., & Oxer, T. (1994). Lesson talk as the work of reading groups: The effectiveness of two interventions. *Journal of Learning Disabilities, 27,* 165–185.

Gerber, M. M., & Hall, R. J. (1987). Information processing approaches to studying spelling deficiencies. *Journal of Learning Disabilities, 20,* 34–42.

Graves, A., & Hauge, R. (1993). Using cues and prompts to improve story writing. *Teaching Exceptional Children, 25*(4), 38–40.

Haager, D. (2002). *The road to successful reading outcomes for English language learners in urban schools.* Paper presented at the annual meeting of the Council for Learning Disabilities (October 11). Denver, CO.

Hawk, P. P., & McLeod, N. P. (1984). Graphic organizers: A cognitive teaching method that works. *The Directive Teacher, 6*(1), 6–7.

Hedin, L., Mason, L. H., & Sukhram, D. (2006, April 9–12). *The effect of TWA plus prompts for discourse on reading comprehension.* Paper presented at the annual meeting of the Council for Exceptional Children, Salt Lake City, UT.

Hoover, J. J., & Rabideau, D. K. (1995). Semantic webs and study skills. *Intervention in School and Clinic, 30,* 292–296.

Idol-Maestas, L. (1981). Increasing the oral reading performance of a learning disabled adult. *Learning Disability Quarterly, 4,* 294–301.

Igo, L. B., Bruning, R., McCrudden, M., & Kauffman, D. F. (2003). InfoGather: A tool for gathering and organizing information from the web. In R. Bruning, C. Horn, & L. PytliZilling (Eds.), *Web-based learning: What do we know? Where do we go?* Greenwich, CT: Information Age.

Igo, L. B., Riccomini, P. J., Bruning, R. H., & Pope, G. G. (2006). How should middle school students with LD approach online note taking? A mixed methods study. *Learning Disability Quarterly, 29* (2), 89–100.

Jitendra, A. K., Edwards, L. L., Sacks, G., & Jocobson, L. A. (2004). What research says about vocabulary instruction for students with learning disabilities. *Exceptional Children, 70* (3), 299–322.

Johnson, S. E., & Bender, W. N. (1999). Language arts instructional approaches. In W. N. Bender (Ed.), *Professional issues in learning disabilities* (pp. 107–139). Austin, TX: ProEd.

Kame'enui, E. J., Carnine, D. W., Dixon, R. C., Simmons, D.C., & Coyne, M. D. (2002). *Effective teaching strategies that accommodate diverse learners* (2nd ed.). Upper Saddle River, NJ: Merrill/Prentice Hall.

Kearney, C. A., & Drabman, R. S. (1993). The write-say method for improving spelling accuracy in children with learning disabilities. *Journal of Learning Disabilities, 26,* 52–56.

Knebel., S., Cartledge, G., & Kourea, L. (2006, April 9–12). *Repeated readings: An evidence-based strategy to improve urban learners' reading skills.* Paper presented at the annual meeting of the Council for Exceptional Children, Salt Lake City, UT.

Korinek, L., & Bulls, J. A. (1996). SCORE A: A student's research paper writing strategy. *Teaching Exceptional Children, 28*(4), 60–63.

Larkin, M. J. (2001). Providing support for student independence through scaffolded instruction. *Teaching Exceptional Children, 34*(1), 30–35.

Lerner, J. W., Cousin, P. T., & Richeck, M. (1992). Critical issues in learning disabilities: Whole language learning. *Learning Disabilities Research and Practice, 7,* 226–230.

Lindamood, P. C., & Lindamood, P. D. (1998). *Lindamood Phoneme Sequencing Program for Reading, Spelling, and Speech.* Austin, TX: ProEd.

Lyon, G. R., & Moats, L. C. (1997). Critical conceptual and methodological considerations in reading intervention research. *Journal of Learning Disabilities, 30*(6), 578–588.

MacInnis, C., & Hemming, H. (1995). Linking the needs of students with learning disabilities to a whole language curriculum. *Journal of Learning Disabilities, 28,* 535–544.

Mariage, T. V. (1995). Why students learn: The nature of teacher talk during reading. *Learning Disability Quarterly, 18,* 214–234.

Mason, L. H., Meadan, H., Hedin, L., & Corso, L. (2006). Self-regulated strategy development instruction for expository text comprehension. *Teaching Exceptional Children, 38* (4), 47–52.

Mastropieri, M. A., Leinart, A., & Scruggs, T. E. (1999). Strategies to increase reading fluency. *Intervention in School and Clinic, 34*(5), 278–292.

Mastropieri, M. A., & Peters, E. E. (1987). Increasing prose recall of learning disabled and reading disabled students via spatial organizers. *Journal of Educational Research, 80,* 272–276.

Mather, N., & Roberts, R. (1994). Learning disabilities: A field in danger of extinction. *Learning Disabilities Research and Practice, 9*(1), 49–58.

McNaughton, D. B., & Hughes, C. A. (1999). *InSPECT: A strategy for finding and correcting spelling errors: Instructor's manual.* Lawrence, KS: Edge Enterprises.

McNaughton, D. B., Hughes, C. A., & Ofiesh, N. (1997). Proofreading for students with learning disabilities: Integrating computer and strategy use. *Learning Disabilities Research and Practice, 12* (1), 16–28.

Moats, L. C. (1991). Conclusion. In A. M. Bain, L. L. Bailet, & L. C. Moats (Eds.), *Written language disorders: Theory into practice* (pp. 189–191). Austin, TX: ProEd.

Moats, L. C., & Lyon, G. R. (1993). Learning disabilities in the United States: Advocacy, science, and the future of the field. *Journal of Learning Disabilities, 26,* 282–294.

Montague, M., & Fonseca, F. (1993). Using computers to improve story writing. *Teaching Exceptional Children, 25*(4), 46–49.

National Reading Panel (NRP) (2000). *Teaching children to read: A report from the National Reading Panel.* Washington, DC: U.S. Government Printing Office.

Nulman, J. A. H., & Gerber, M. M. (1984). Improving spelling performance by imitating a child's errors. *Journal of Learning Disabilities, 17,* 328–333.

Padget, S. Y. (1998). Lessons from research on dyslexia: Implications for a classification system for learning disabilities. *Learning Disability Quarterly, 21,* 167–178.

Pullen, P. C., & Justice, L. M. (2006). Enhancing phonological awareness, print awareness, and oral language skills in preschool children. *Intervention in School and Clinic, 39* (2), 87–98.

Rose, T. L., & Robinson, H. H. (1984). Effects of illustrations on learning disabled students' reading performance. *Learning Disability Quarterly, 7,* 165–171.

Santoro, L. E., Coyne, M. D., & Simmons, D. C. (2006). The reading-spelling connection: Developing and evaluating a beginning spelling intervention for children at risk of reading disability. *Learning Disabilities Research and Practice, 21* (2), 122–133.

Scanlon, D. J., Duran, G. Z., Reyes, E. I., & Gallego, M. A. (1992). Interactive semantic mapping: An interactive approach to enhancing LD students' content area comprehension. *Learning Disability Research and Practice, 7,* 142–146.

Schmidt, R. J., Rozendal, M. S., & Greenman, G. G. (2002). Reading instruction in the inclusion classroom: Research based practices. *Remedial and Special Education, 23*(3), 130–140.

Schumaker, J. B., & Deshler, D. D. (2003). Can students with LD become competent writers? *Learning Disability Quarterly, 26* (2), 129–141.

Scruggs, T. E., Bennion, K., & Lifson, S. (1984). Learning disabled students' spontaneous use of test-taking skills on reading achievement tests. *Learning Disability Quarterly, 7,* 205–210.

Shaywitz, S. E., & Shaywitz, B. A. (2006). Reading disability and the brain. In *Educating Exceptional Children: 2005/2006.* Dubuque, IA: McGraw Hill.

Silliman, E. R., & Scott, C. M. (2006). Language impairment and reading disability: Connects and complexities. *Learning Disabilities Research and Practice, 21* (1), 1–7.

Smith, S., & Simmons, D.C. (1997, April). *Project phonological awareness: Efficiency and efficacy in phonological awareness instruction for prereaders at-risk of reading failure.* Paper presented at the annual meeting of the Council for Exceptional Children, Salt Lake City.

Sousa, D. A. (2005). *How the brain learns to read.* Thousand Oaks, CA: Corwin.

Stahl, S. A., & Miller, P. D. (1989). Whole language and language experience approaches for beginning reading: A quantitative research synthesis. *Review of Educational Research, 59,* 87–116.

Stone, C. A. (1998). The metaphor of scaffolding: Its utility for the field of learning disabilities. *Journal of Learning Disabilities, 31,* 344–364.

Terrill, M. C., Scruggs, T. E., & Mastropieri, M. A. (2004). SAT vocabulary instruction for high school students with learning disabilities. *Intervention in School and Clinic, 39* (5), 288–294.

Therrien, W. J., & Kubina, R. M. (2006). Developing reading fluency with repeated reading. *Intervention in School and Clinic, 41* (3), 131–137.

Torgesen, J. K., & Bryant, B. R. (1994). *Phonological awareness training for reading.* Austin, TX: ProEd.

Troia, G. A., Graham, S., & Harris, K. R. (1999). Teaching students with learning disabilities to mindfully plan when writing. *Exceptional Children, 65,* 235–252.

Vogel, S. A. (1983). A qualitative analysis of morphological ability in learning disabled and achieving children. *Journal of Learning Disabilities, 16,* 416–420.

Vygotsky, L. S. (1978). *Mind in society: The development of higher psychological processes* (M. Cole, V. John-Steiner, S. Scribner, & E. Souberman, Eds. & Trans.). Cambridge, MA: Harvard University Press.

Williams, S. C. (2002). How speech-feedback and word-prediction software can help students write. *Teaching Exceptional Children, 34*(3), 72–78.

CHAPTER SEVEN

LEARNING CHARACTERISTICS IN MATH

CHAPTER OUTLINE

WHEN YOU COMPLETE THIS CHAPTER, YOU SHOULD BE ABLE TO:

1. Describe the possible language and visual-perception-based causes of math deficits.
2. Describe the factors associated with automaticity in learning math facts.
3. Discuss the relationship between reading and capacity to complete word problems.
4. Discuss cognitive-strategy training in verbal math problem solving.
5. Identify one strategy for instruction for each area in math.
6. Identify the symptoms associated with nonverbal learning disabilities and how these impact achievement in math.

KEYWORDS

number sense	scope and sequence charts	linking
spatial ability	numeration	count-by
nonverbal learning disabilities	one-to-one relationship	multistep operations
numeral	sequencing	regrouping
counting-all	place value	complex operations
math standards	automaticity	cue words

INTRODUCTION

Most students with learning disabilities have disabilities that result in a negative impact on reading. However, there is no reason to believe that learning disabilities affect one curriculum area any more than another, and at present, there is much less information on the percentage of students identified as learning disabled who also have disabilities that impact negatively on math achievement (Gersten, Chard, Baker, & Lee, 2002). There is evidence to indicate that students with learning disabilities do have trouble in many areas of math (Babbitt & Miller, 1996; Bryant & Dix, 1999; Cawley, Parmar, Foley, Salmon, & Roy, 2001; Gersten et al., 2002; Grobecker, 1999; Maccini, McNaughton, & Ruhl, 1999; Miles & Forcht, 1995; Riccomini, 2005; Saunders, 2006). In all probability, some students have disabilities only in reading, some only in math, and some in both curriculum areas (Robinson, Menchetti, & Torgesen, 2002). Needless to say, these three different groups of students would have different instructional needs, as indicated in Figure 7.1.

Although there has been extensive research on the reading characteristics of children with learning disabilities, their learning characteristics in math have not been studied thoroughly (Gersten et al., 2002). For example, after an extensive literature search Maccini and colleagues (1999) found only six studies that looked at performance of students with learning disabilities in algebra. Gersten and his colleagues (2002) searched the literature and found only a very limited number of research studies on math interventions for students with learning disabilities. There are several possible reasons for this. First,

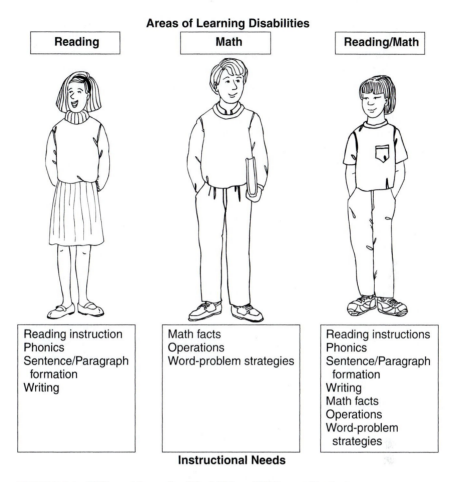

Areas of Learning Disabilities

Reading	Math	Reading/Math

Reading instruction
Phonics
Sentence/Paragraph
 formation
Writing

Math facts
Operations
Word-problem strategies

Reading instructions
Phonics
Sentence/Paragraph
 formation
Writing
Math facts
Operations
Word-problem
 strategies

Instructional Needs

FIGURE 7.1   **Different Learning Disabilities of Different Students**

although reading difficulties have been a major factor in the early history of the field, only recently have researchers begun to study math achievement. Early researchers tended to concentrate on reading because of the assumption that reading problems indicated a deeper underlying language problem. Today, we are aware of numerous possible relationships between language and math, but this is a relatively new research area in the field.

Next, not all studies have demonstrated achievement deficits in math between students with disabilities and other students (Cawley et al., 2001). Further, researchers and practitioners had not attended to the math achievement of children with learning disabilities until recently (Mastropieri, Scruggs, & Shiah, 1991).

Teachers and practitioners in the field may have received instructions to emphasize reading and language arts to the exclusion of math. Without openly articulating such a position, school administrators may have inadvertently assumed that deficits in reading affect other school subjects more than deficits in math.

Finally, the identification process, as it historically developed, may have inadvertently prejudiced the field of study. Although reading scores are frequently used in computation of an ability-achievement discrepancy, use of math scores to compute such a discrepancy is relatively rare, even though most states do allow such a procedure. This fact suggests the possibility that numerous students with a learning disability in math who do not demonstrate a problem in reading may not be identified at all. In fact, many children who are not presently identified as learning disabled may well need specialized instruction in math. This possibility suggests caution in interpretation of the studies that report no deficits in math achievement among these students because these populations—by use of the accepted selection and identification procedures—may have inadvertently eliminated many students who were disabled in math but not in reading.

At present, there is some evidence to support the existence of mathematics deficits among many students with learning disabilities, and as a teacher of these students, you may assume that one of your responsibilities will be to conduct instruction in mathematics. Further, with the implementation of the new RTI eligibility procedures, as described in previous chapters, the field may experience an increase in students with learning disabilities in math, since, presumably, this new procedure will allow for a student's response to a math intervention to be used in determining eligibility (Kroeger & Kouche, 2006). Of course, this will be determined over the next five years or so. Currently, we can identify certain relationships between the types of learning characteristics that these children demonstrate and the mathematics curriculum. Also, several recent educational treatment studies in mathematics will be discussed to demonstrate the type of instructional research currently under way.

COGNITIVE ABILITIES AND MATH SKILLS

Recent research on mathematics learning deficits among students with learning disabilities has suggested a number of possible relationships between cognitive deficits and problems in mathematics (Garrett, Mazzocco, & Baker, 2006; Kroeger & Kouche, 2006; Rourke, 1993, 2005; Robinson, Menchetti, & Torgesen, 2002), and in many conceptualizations, the concept of **number sense** seems to play a role. Number sense may be defined as a lack of understanding of the basic concepts that make our number system work, such as an understanding of:

- relative quantity (i.e., more than or less than, fewer or greater)
- one-to-one correspondence (i.e., one number represents a special number of items in a set of items)
- place value (i.e., not having a concept that numbers in various orders mean different things; 21 is different from 12)

Clearly, students with difficulties in understanding these concepts will have great difficulty in mastering even basic mathematics. In fact, some researchers have postulated the possibility that math learning disabilities may be based on difficulties in number sense (Bender, 2005; Gersten & Chard, 1999; Rourke, 2005). Further, some researchers have suggested that learning disabilities in math may be categorized into two different types of math disabilities, with difficulty in either "number sense" or "phonological difficulties in reading" being the distinguishing characteristic (Bender, 2005; Robinson, Menchetti, & Torgesen, 2002; Rourke, 2005).

For example, Robinson, Menchetti, and Torgesen (2002) postulated that some students experienced disabilities only in math and not in phonological manipulation, phonics, or reading. These researchers proposed that these types of math problems may be based on weak number sense overall. In contrast to these students with disabilities only in mathematics, other students with learning disabilities experience disabilities in both math and reading. Robinson et al. (2002) suggested that these students may have disabilities rooted in weak phonological processing, coupled with difficulties in understanding and manipulating numbers.

Finally, other researchers have investigated the relationship between mathematical ability and various cognitive processes directly. This information is summarized below.

Neurological Deficits

Several researchers have indicated that specific neurological deficits may play a role in learning disabilities in math (Geller & Smith, 2002; Rourke, 1993; Shalev & Gross-Tsur, 1993). For example, Rourke (1993) reviewed the available evidence and concluded that there were at least two different profiles of neuropsychological assets and deficits (typically represented by scores on particular subtests of an intelligence test) that may lead to learning disabilities in math. In a similar area, Shalev and Gross-Tsur (1993) analyzed the mathematical learning disabilities of a small group of children in Israel. They concluded that, for each child with a learning disability in math, a neurological disorder of some type could be specified. Results such as these suggest that studies of neurological abilities may reveal the factors that lead to learning disabilities that are particular to math.

In contrast, researchers who have developed educational treatments for learning disabilities in math have not specified particular types of cognitive deficits in their research designs. Mastropieri and colleagues (1991) reviewed the available literature in the field of learning disabilities and indicated that over 30 different studies had investigated specific educational intervention approaches for math problems among children and youth with learning disabilities. These researchers commented on the fact that in none of these studies did the researchers attend to the specific types of neurological problems demonstrated by the children in their study. One must conclude that, although a search for specific cognitive deficits is ongoing in the field, these data have to date had only a negligible effect on the educational treatment research on math deficits among children who are learning disabled.

Memory Deficits

As described in Chapter 3, memory deficits among students with learning disabilities are quite well documented, and many researchers and practitioners suggest that these memory problems play a role in math achievement deficits among students with learning disabilities (Geller & Smith, 2002; Jitendra, 2002). Geller and Smith (2002) suggested that problems in the perceptual register (see Sousa's model of memory in Chapter 3), as well as short-term memory, may negatively impact the math achievement of students with learning disabilities.

Wilson and Swanson (2001) investigated the relationships between working memory and mathematical computation skills and concluded that deficits in math result from specific deficits in the working memory system. Jitendra (2002), as another alternative, suggested using graphic representations of math problems to assist students with learning disabilities in their memory efforts. At present, a great deal of research is ongoing, and you should remain aware of the instructional options that may result from this research in the future.

Language Abilities

Language ability is probably an underlying factor in mathematics achievement, at least during the later years of elementary school math instruction, when word problems are used (Jordan, Levine, & Huttenlocher, 1996). However, language ability may also be required during the earlier years of school for the types of strategic planning required to do double-digit addition problems, as one example. Consider the metacognitive planning steps that are necessary to complete the following problem:

$$39$$
$$+26$$
———

To complete this addition problem, at least five steps must be planned and carried out. First, the digits 9 and 6 must be added, resulting in the answer of 15. The student must write in the 1's place the digit 5 under the 6 and hold the 10's-place digit (the 1). That digit must then be written above the 3. Finally, the three digits in the 10's column should be added. This type of metacognitive planning is a complicated exercise for some students with learning disabilities because the ability to conduct multistep problems obviously involves the child's language ability. Certainly, more complex problems with numerous steps are dependent on language ability and the ability to enumerate the correct steps to follow.

In a research effort, Jordan and colleagues (1996) demonstrated this relationship between language abilities and certain math problems. These researchers used 108 students in kindergarten and first grade, subdividing them according to their cognitive strengths and weaknesses. Based on individualized cognitive assessment, they formed four subgroups: nonimpaired students, students with delayed language, students with delayed spatial perception ability, and students with delays in both. After these groups were identified, they administered an extensive math assessment that included three types of math problems: math facts, verbal story problems, and nonverbal problems. Although the math-facts problems were presented to the children verbally ("How much is 3 + 4?"), that type of verbal problem is not as linguistically taxing as a story problem ("John has four toys and wants to share with his two friends. If each friend takes a toy, how many toys will John have left to play with?"). For the nonverbal problems, children watched the experimenter place a specified number of items on one side of a placemat and then cover the objects up. Next, the experimenter put several additional items on the other side of the mat and slid them under the cover to simulate addition. The student was then told to "Make yours like mine." The child was expected to put the correct number of items on his or her placemat.

The value of experimentation such as this is that it can suggest relationships between specific cognitive abilities and particular types of math problems. In this study, students with language delays performed less well than the nonimpaired group on verbal problems, but performed just as well as that group on nonverbal problems. The students with language delay performed as well as the nonimpaired students on the math-facts problems, even though these were presented verbally. This suggests that language delays may affect complete language tasks where manipulation of information is needed, but not straightforward verbal math facts. At the very least, this research demonstrates that language delay can negatively impact certain types of math problems while not impacting other areas.

One mechanism whereby language seems to directly affect math performance is the student's internal use of language to express various algorithms during problem solving (Van Luit & Naglieri, 1999). For example, many students with learning disabilities use very simple algorithms (i.e., rules for problem performance) in solving math problems. In solving the problem 3 × 6 some students may merely add 6 three times; thus their algorithm redefines the problem into 6 + 6 + 6. This algorithm represents the functional use of language to solve the problem during the initial stages of instruction. The expectation is that during later stages of learning the student will improve his or her memory skills and be able to access this knowledge without having to perform the multiple addition steps (Van Luit & Naglieri, 1999). Clearly, if a language delay inhibits the development and/or use of algorithms such as this, such a delay can severely impact math performance.

Spatial Abilities

Ackerman, Anhalt, and Dykman (1986) suggested that **spatial ability** may also be required in elementary school mathematics. Involvement of the ability to correctly perceive spatial relationships is certainly involved in the elementary curriculum in the pregeometric skills. As discussed in Chapter 1, one of the early groups of theorists—the visual-perception group—believed that children with learning disabilities were characterized by a lack of the ability to perceive spatial relationships correctly. This inability may have very real consequences in terms of mathematics achievement.

However, the study by Jordan and colleagues (1996) described previously did not demonstrate this proposed relationship between spatial abilities and nonverbal math disabilities. Students with spatial deficits, although somewhat delayed overall, performed as well as the nonimpaired children on each of the three types of math problems. Jordan and her co-authors suggested that students with spatial problems who were not language delayed may use their relative strength in language to offset their spatial delay in performing the math problem.

Nonverbal Learning Disabilities

The accumulation of information on the cognitive functioning of students with learning disabilities reported above, coupled with the increasing influence of recent research on how the brain and central nervous system learn (Rourke, 1993; Sousa, 2001, 2006), has resulted in an emerging interest in a specific type of learning disability—the nonverbal learning disability. Furthermore, specific disabilities in math seem to be expressly implicated in this type of learning disability. Rourke and his colleagues (Rourke, 1993; Rourke, Young, & Leenaars, 1989) have studied the cognitive profiles of students with learning disabilities and identified a specific, though relatively broad, pattern of symptoms associated with **nonverbal learning disabilities.**

As shown in previous chapters, most learning disabilities seem to consist of language-based problems, which seem to stem from an inability to understand, differentiate, and manipulate phonemes (Moats & Lyon, 1993). These learning disabilities thus may be more associated with the left brain hemisphere and the language production areas within the brain (Sousa, 2001, 2006). In contrast, nonverbal learning disabilities may stem from the brain functions typically associated with the right hemisphere, such as spatial orientation, mathematical understanding, and the ability to determine the relationships between objects in space. Students with nonverbal learning disabilities generally have a unique pattern of verbal strengths coupled with visual, perceptual, and/or organizational weaknesses (Robinson, Menchetti, & Torgesen, 2002; Silver, Pennett, Black, Fair, & Balise, 1999). Various researchers have further suggested that students with nonverbal learning disabilities are more likely to suffer from overt emotional problems stemming from a profound inability to interpret nonverbal social cues (Bender, Rosencrans, & Crane, 1999; Rourke et al., 1989). With this constellation of symptoms in mind, it seems apparent that students with nonverbal learning disabilities are likely to show more significant deficits in mathematics than in language or reading, though many students apparently suffer from both verbally based and nonverbal learning disabilities (Rourke, 1993). As more research becomes available on this specific type of disability, researchers and practitioners alike will develop an increasing understanding of appropriate treatments for these relatively unique children.

Beyond this information, very little is known and questions abound. For example, to what extent is mathematical skill related to auditory memory? If a child cannot remember the numbers he or she hears, does this affect achievement? As you may imagine, almost any cognitive ability may be related to mathematics skills, and much more information is needed concerning these relationships among students with learning disabilities.

TYPES OF MATH LEARNING DISABILITIES

With these cognitive deficits in mind, it is not surprising that research has identified a number of specific types of math learning disabilities (Bryant & Dix, 1999; Garnett, 1992; Mastropieri et al., 1991; Sousa, 2006). A list of the common types of disabilities that students with math learning disabilities demonstrate is presented in Interest Box 7.1.

Of course, with research on math learning disabilities progressing, lists of potential disabilities such as that shown in Interest Box 7.1 must be considered tentative. Undoubtedly, other math learning disabilities will be added to this list as research proceeds. Still, we do know some things about math learning disabilities. First, students vary considerably in how math learning disabilities are manifested. Some students will display all these problems, whereas other students with math learning disabilities will display only one or two of these problems. As Garnett (1992) indicated, some students develop conceptual understanding but demonstrate other problems such as erratic calculation procedures; yet others fail to grasp the basic number facts and number concepts.

Next, math disabilities can be quite pervasive. These various types of disabilities can create havoc in the math achievement of students with math learning disabilities. For example, if a student has a disability in grasping basic number sense concepts, this disability

■ ■ ■ ■ ■

INTEREST BOX 7.1
VARIOUS MATH LEARNING DISABILITIES

Conceptual understanding	Language of math
Written number symbol system	Basic number facts
Procedural steps of computation	Problem solving
Application of arithmetic skills	Lack of automaticity
Poor calculation strategies	Poor word-problem strategies
Counting sequences	Poor number sense

will be reflected in most of his or her math performance throughout school. It is possible for a student to have such a disability and no other problems at all, such that, without the disability, the mastery of complex word problems and even algebra and advanced algebra skills would be possible. However, the difficulty in number sense will certainly create difficulties in fractions, long division, and word problems. In fact, a math disability in mastery of basic number sense will be reflected throughout, and the student will probably not reach high levels of attainment in any math area.

Baroody and Kaufman (1993) described a young child with a math disability that involved the ability to copy or write numerals. (A **numeral** is a written digit or series of digits, whereas a *number* is a concept or an idea; whenever one speaks of numbers as written down, the correct terminology is *numeral.*) According to these researchers, numeral writing involves an accurate image of the numeral and a motor plan to write that numeral. These researchers recommended pairing a numeral with a letter with similar characteristics for teaching purposes. For example, a 2 would be paired with a capital Z, and a 5 would be paired with a capital S. The student would then learn the slight differences between the letters and the numerals.

Next, research has indicated that the strategies used by children with disabilities are not always hierarchical in nature (Garnett, 1992). Initially, researchers believed that children with learning disabilities learned an early set of strategies in math that were relatively immature. Counting on one's fingers would be an example. (This is referred to as a **counting-all** strategy. When adding 2 + 4, the student first "counts all" the numbers by saying "1, 2," and then "1, 2, 3, 4." The student will typically hold up one finger for each digit and then recount up to 6.) This strategy would then be shortened to a "counting on" the larger addend. In that strategy, the student would begin with the 4 and "count on" two more (Garnett, 1992).

During recent years, we have become aware that, rather than demonstrating a consistent replacement of immature strategies with more mature ones, most students demonstrate the use of multiple strategies at the same time, and children with disabilities may depend on very immature strategies much later in the elementary grades than other students. This can lead to fifth-grade students with learning disabilities attempting to complete double-digit addition with regrouping problems by using finger-counting strategies.

Although finger counting in middle- and upper-level grades would certainly be of concern, Jordan and her co-authors (1996) encouraged teachers to realize that this may be a compensatory strategy, used by a student to offset a language delay. Thus, teachers in lower grades should not try to "break the habit" of finger counting too early. Indeed, students with learning disabilities may depend upon this strategy over a longer period of time and at later grade levels than other students, and some use of finger counting should be encouraged for certain children.

Next, research has shown that math disabilities can be quite debilitating over the long term (Garnett, 1992). For example, many math disabilities persist into adulthood. It can be quite embarrassing for an adult with a math learning disability to have difficulty making change, balancing a checkbook, or completing any number of tasks that most adults do with relative ease. In fact, it is possible that a math disability can be more debilitating than a reading disability over the adult years.

Finally, research has recently suggested that overall, educators may not teach math as effectively as certain other subject areas, such as reading and language arts, and this could negatively impact students with learning disabilities even more than other students (Bender, 2005; Riccomini, 2005; Maccini, McNaughton, & Ruhl, 1999; Sanders, 2006). First, Bender (2005) has indicated that mathematics may be the singularly most "hated" topic in the public school curriculum, and this can build up an emotional barrier to successful achievement in math. Teachers will have to assist students in feeling comfortable in mathematics, in order to ensure student achievement.

Sanders (2006) recently studied the impact of mathematics instruction on two groups of high school students—those enrolled in algebra and those enrolled in technical math. Results demonstrated that students enrolled in algebra were much more likely to have mastered prerequisite skills in the lower and middle grades but that as many as 40% of students enrolled in high school technical math had not mastered even basic fractions. Clearly, this does not suggest that as a group teachers are doing an excellent job in teaching mathematics in elementary and middle school grades overall.

Riccomini (2005) took a different approach and investigated how well teachers were able to interpret error patterns in mathematics. As described in Chapter 5, an error analysis allows a teacher to draw conclusions about a child's understanding of particular problems in math, and thus the teacher will know where the child is making the error and how to teach that child more specifically. Riccomini's research indicated that teachers could correctly identify specific error patterns but would then not use this insight to focus their instruction specifically on the type of error the child made.

Of course, such research is not intended to paint a bleak picture of the instructional skills of all teachers in mathematics. Many are excellent teachers in mathematics, and successes of students with learning disabilities in many intensive high school and/or college math courses proves that. Still, we as a concerned group of professionals, should certainly pay more attention to mathematics instructional ideas and make certain that we do not shortchange our students in this critically important curriculum area.

MATH CURRICULUM STANDARDS

Because of the recent initiatives of the federal government and almost every state government, math curriculums have been delineated in terms of **math standards** or specific math objectives that should be met for each year of schooling (Maccini & Gagnon, 2002). This is one component of a national movement to hold schools and students accountable for certain standards within the curriculum and to tie school progress and/or graduation to those standards (Lanford & Cary, 2000). In fact, the individualized education plans for students with learning disabilities in many school districts around the nation must include curricular objectives from the state curriculum standards because students with learning disabilities must be provided with an opportunity to master the general education curriculum (Cawley et al., 2001; Matlock, Fielder, & Walsh, 2001). In spite of this relatively recent requirement, Maccini and Gagnon (2002) reported that many special education teachers were unaware of the new standards in math from the National Council of Teachers of Mathematics. Some understanding of the history of the "standards-based curriculum" in math education will help you understand the sequencing of math skills.

Many decades ago, school districts developed (often individually) lists of topics in math (and in other subjects) that were to be taught during particular grades. For example, based on these early plans, addition math facts were taught as early as kindergarten and grade 1; multiplication and division math facts were generally taught in grade 3. The earliest topical lists were referred to as **scope and sequence charts** because these lists of instructional objectives included not only the scope of instructional objectives in a subject area, but also the sequence of objectives and recommendations as to which year a particular objective would be taught. Thus, the scope and sequence charts represented a hierarchy of math skills, which was developmentally sequenced according to the cognitive level of the average child. Further, although math is our concern in this chapter, one should realize that scope and sequence charts were available for virtually every subject area (e.g., math, reading, language arts, history, and science).

With increasing political support for education over the last decade or so, many states have moved to state-approved curriculums (Cawley et al., 2001). Further, many professional organizations have likewise proposed certain standard requirements for instruction in various areas (Maccini & Gagnon, 2002). Of course, the scope and sequence charts from previous decades often became the basis for these standards-based curriculums in various areas, and math was no exception. Interest Box 7.2 presents a portion of a standards-based curriculum in math. Looking at math skills in terms of a developmental hierarchy, as represented by such a standards-based curriculum, will assist new teachers in understanding the basics of math instruction for students with learning disabilities.

Early Math Skills

Readiness Skills.   The earliest math skills in most standards-based curricula include pre-math objectives, which usually deal with such skills as sorting, understanding number sense, understanding sequencing, and identifying one-to-one relationships. For example, when a child first learns to count, he or she generally counts by using fingers. Such counting requires an understanding of each of these aspects of math skills. The child must know the words to say for each finger (**numeration**), the fact that when he or she holds up a new finger, another word is required (**one-to-one relationship**), and the correct order for the numeral names for each finger (**sequencing**). All mathematics achievement rests on such fundamental skills.

Very little information is available on the types of early math problems encountered among students with learning disabilities. In fact, Mastropieri and colleagues (1991) indicated that, of the 30 intervention studies available in the literature, none deals with

INTEREST BOX 7.2
MATH STANDARDS SAMPLE

KINDERGARTEN STANDARDS

Sorts objects by similarities

Arranges/orders objects according to size, shape, and color

Matches objects of sets one-to-one

Recognizes/names number of items in a set up to 5

Counts number of items in a set up to 10

Combines and separates sets of objects by a given characteristic

Selects numeral that names the number of elements of a set up to 10

Compares two objects according to size

Measures length by counting nonstandard units

Moves oneself or an object from one point to another using given directions

Sorts and identifies basic geometric shapes

Recognizes coins and bills as representing a system of exchange

Names coins up to 25 cents and bills up to 5 dollars

FIRST-GRADE STANDARDS

Determines amounts of money up to 50 cents and change to 25 cents

Applies units of measurement (time to half-hour, etc.)

Adds whole numbers—up to three one-digit numbers with no regrouping

Subtracts whole numbers—up to two digits with no regrouping

Recognizes different names for numbers—whole numbers up to 100 and fractions 1/2, 1/3, and 1/4

Relates numbers to models for numbers up to 60

Identifies the number of 10's and 1's in a given number

Recognizes sets that are equivalent

Recognizes ordinal numbers up to ninth

Identifies numerical relations—greater than, less than, equal to

Identifies standard geometric shapes and relations

Selects items belonging and not belonging to a given set

Identifies mathematical symbols (=, +, −, >, <)

Selects appropriate units to measure time

Selects appropriate operation—addition or subtraction—for a given problem

Organizes elements of sets according to characteristics

Determines sequencing of numbers, points on a number line, and shapes

Counts by 1's, 2's, 5's, and 10's

Interprets data on simple graphs

instructional practices for math readiness skills. This lack of information can be explained in two ways. First, the nature of the identification process could lead to this lack of data, particularly the calculation of the ability-achievement discrepancy. The identification process generally requires that a child demonstrate a deficit in reading, and because reading is an achievement area in school, it cannot be measured prior to school attendance. However, the early math skills generally develop in most children prior to public school entrance. In fact, the majority of the students identified as learning disabled are identified during the third- and fourth-grade years. This age of identification is the second reason for the lack of attention to math readiness skills. Math readiness skills are typically taught in preschool and kindergarten, and very few students are identified as learning disabled during those years. This has led many researchers to concentrate on math problems during the elementary school years rather than develop interventions for math readiness skills.

Assessment of Early Math Skills.   As a teacher, you must be prepared to examine potential deficits in number sense and early math skills for the students with learning disabilities in your class. Most of the students will have these skills, but you may find some children who do not. Obviously, remediation activities must be directed at the development of these skills prior to mastery of later objectives in the math skills charts, and such remediation is dependent on accurate assessment.

As an informal assessment, you may wish to sit down with the child and use a set of plastic counters, some paper, and a pencil. First, ask the child to count the counters, and allow the student to count through at least 21. This indicates an understanding of 1's and 10's. Ask the child to say the numbers that you do not say. Then count the counters by pointing to each one; every fifth counter or so, point to the counter and ask the child what number it is.

Ask the child questions concerning numeration such as, "What number comes after 68? What number comes next? And next?" Do this for several changes of 10's and 100's. You may also do this in written form by writing "68, 69, _____, 71, 72, _____, . . ." on a page and having the child fill in the blanks.

To assess the child's understanding of **place value,** draw 10 small boxes and 1 rectangular box that approximately equals the length of the 10 boxes together. Talk to the child about the fact that 10 small boxes equal 1 large one. Next, write 14 on the paper in large numerals, with the numerals slightly apart. Under the 4, draw 4 small boxes, and under the 1 draw a large rectangular box. Ask the child why the digit 1 is represented by a large box and how it could be represented by small boxes. Write 27 on the page, and ask the child to draw boxes for that numeral.

Other types of activities may also be used. For example, you may wish to draw a circle on the paper and place a number of counters in the circle in order to ask the student some questions about sets. The student may be instructed to create another set with one object included for each object in the original set. This allows some insight into the student's understanding of one-to-one correspondence.

As you can see, an observant teacher can assess early math skills with relative ease. These activities give you some insight into the early math skills of the child and may allow for better programming. For example, if a classroom teacher complains that a child cannot complete double-digit addition problems, that child's place-value skills must be investigated. As always with informal assessments, activities in this informal assessment should be completely described and the success rate noted. Such information will make your informal assessment useful to demonstrate progress later in the year. These assessment notes should be dated and placed in your files.

Math-Facts Skills and Automaticity

The math standards generally begin math-facts instruction in two operations—addition and subtraction—very early in the first-grade year. In some cases, math facts are studied in kindergarten. Beginning with this level of math skills, some research is available on math skills among children with learning disabilities, and that research has shown that many of these children have difficulty with mastery of basic math facts (Gersten & Chard, 1999). These problems, in turn, cause continued difficulty in mastering the later math curriculum. In fact, secondary students with disabilities tend to reach a plateau of mathematics performance at around the fifth- or sixth-grade achievement level (Bryant & Dix, 1999). This is partially caused by continuing difficulties in basic math facts.

Although most children who are learning disabled can correctly complete worksheets of basic math facts in addition and subtraction, these facts are generally not taught in a way that allows for use of the facts in more complex problems (Geller & Smith, 2002). For example, teachers during the early years often allow a child to compute addition facts using fingers or some other counter, and the child with learning disabilities may become quite proficient at this skill. However, such computations of simple math facts become cumbersome in problems that involve several computations. For example, hand calculation of math facts would be quite problematic in the double-digit addition and regrouping problem described earlier. Thus, one issue in early math deals with how quickly a child can recall specific math facts without having to use a counting method.

The concept of **automaticity** has been used to describe the speed with which children can recall math facts. First, children may need finger counting (or counters) to assist in early addition and subtraction facts. However, with repeated use and reinforcement for mastery of the facts by rote memory, most cognitive psychologists believe that the facts become automatic and that less cognitive processing is involved (Sousa, 2005). Apparently, around 50% of third-grade children who have no math disabilities have developed rapid automaticity. According to Hasselbring and colleagues (1987), this cognitive-processing capacity is a finite quality, and if less is used for the "math-facts" aspects of a problem, more of this capacity is available for other aspects of the problem's solution. In short, math facts should take some degree of mental energy during the early stages and become relatively automatic later. However, children with learning disabilities may develop automaticity much later than other children (Bender, 2005).

When a child learns math facts, or other rote memory material, the retention of that material is dependent on several factors, including frequency of use, complexity, and availability of practice in memory techniques. As discussed earlier, students who are learning disabled do not routinely devise effective methods of remembering material, even when they realize that they may be called on to remember the material later. Consequently, much of the research on memory skills among students with learning disabilities may have a bear-

■ ■ ■ ■ ■

INTEREST BOX 7.3
TEACHING TIPS: MEMORY STRATEGIES
FOR MULTIPLICATION FACTS

The memorization of multiplication facts or other math facts is usually considered essential for most students. Certainly this memorized set of facts facilitates higher math skills, including advanced multiplication, division, fractions, and decimal operations. The following strategies may prove helpful in memorizing these multiplication facts:

1. Have the student list the 3's times tables vertically and point out that, for the 3's tables, each successive times-table answer really represents the addition of another 3 to the former answer. The strategy, then, involves addition of a 3 to the answer in the previous math fact.
2. Use pencil marks as counters, and arrange these in sets to represent the problem. Point out that the number in each set is one multiplier and the number of sets is the other multiplier.
3. Have the student sing the answers to the difficult times tables, in the manner in which most people memorize the alphabet through song.
4. Develop drill and practice games for student use. Start these with the parents, and ask them to go through the times tables each night with the child.

ing on how these students are taught math facts. Interest Box 7.3 gives several examples of the types of memory strategies that may be used in mastery of math facts (Bender, 2005; Sousa, 2005).

A number of researchers have developed additional strategies for teaching basic math concepts and math facts (Bender, 2005; Hasselbring et al., 1987; Kroeger & Kouche, 2006; Sousa, 2006; Lembke & Foegen, 2006). Various adaptations of these strategies are possible, and in meeting the needs of students with learning disabilities in math you will need to be very creative. Several strategies to develop automaticity are presented in Interest Box 7.4.

Linking is a strategy by which one problem may be related to another problem for learning initial math facts (Garnett, 1992). For example, to assist a child in adding 5 + 6, the child should be taught to link that problem with a known problem (e.g., 5 + 5) and to count up from there. Garnett (1992) suggested that strategies such as this may assist the child in becoming more aware of math facts and may ease memorization.

One effective strategy for multiplication math facts is the **count-by** strategy described by McIntyre, Test, Cooke, and Beattie (1991). This strategy is similar to the counting-all strategy discussed for addition math facts, but the student is instructed to "count by" the multiplier a specific number of times. First, students must be taught to count by 3's, 4's, 5's, 6's, and so on. Then the problem 3 × 4 is translated to mean "count by 3 four times." This strategy has been used effectively with students with learning disabilities (McIntyre et al., 1991).

Garnett (1992) indicated that informal assessment should encompass both assessment of skills and attention to the specific strategies that children and youth utilize to complete the problems. For example, if the teacher can determine that a student is still dependent

INTEREST BOX 7.4

TEACHING TIPS: STRATEGIES FOR AUTOMATICITY IN MATH FACTS

1. Have the student practice flashcards with a peer tutor.
2. Have the student listen to math facts on a tape recorder.
3. Teach chunking strategies in which students learn facts as a group (i.e., 3 + 4 is the same as 2 + 5 since a 1 was taken from the first digit and added to the second).
4. Conduct a "math bee" on different levels for students who are slow to learn their math facts. Flashcards can be coded by difficulty level into several different groups.
5. Have a competition once a month for the "Facts Hall of Fame." The principal can direct the competition and give a reward to the winner each month.
6. Develop a tune and thus use music to make repetition useful.
7. Direct speed drills for the students to beat the clock, and reward the student for automaticity. A student should answer a math-facts problem in no more than 2 seconds for that answer to be considered automatic. Also, no obvious counting method (counting on fingers) may be used.
8. Give the students answer cards, and have the student respond to flashcards by holding up the correct answer card. Reward appropriately.

on a fairly simple addition strategy such as counting-all, rather than demonstrating automaticity for basic math facts, then additional instruction could be offered in one or more of the more complex strategies. Garnett (1992) indicated that, during informal assessment, teachers should ask what strategies children utilize to complete a problem. Also, careful observation can yield insight into the strategies that a child uses. Teachers should attempt to move students to increasingly more complex and mature strategies for all math facts and operations.

Place Value and Multistep Operations

Once math facts are learned to a reasonable level of automaticity, most math standards list place value and multistep operations as the next skill. **Multistep operations** involve execution of the same operation several times in order to complete the problem. For example, understanding **regrouping** in addition often requires that the student perform several addition exercises. This type of problem also requires some concept of place value. Students must understand that a digit in the 10's place really represents sets of digits from the 1's place. Instruction usually proceeds by having the student write the number to be "regrouped" above the appropriate column, prior to proceeding with the next step.

Note in this example the complex skills necessary. First, a student must understand the place-value concept. Next, a learning-strategy plan must be developed that indicates the sequence of steps to be followed in completing the addition. According to Pellegrino and Goldman (1987), students with learning disabilities may not possess the necessary memory and cognitive skills to complete this type of multistep problem. This type of problem does involve numerous operations and sequential steps, both of which require cognitive planning. In short, this is a fairly complex skill. Nevertheless, objectives that involve multistep operations such as this are found early during the elementary school years (grades 2 and 3, generally).

There is little information available on the abilities of students with learning disabilities in these areas. However, several researchers have suggested that students with learning disabilities in math will require many more concrete examples (Bender, 2005; Geller & Smith, 2002). For example, Bender (2005, pp. 47–67) recommended that the mathematics instructional approach known as CSA (concrete, semiconcrete, abstract) should be utilized much longer for students with disabilities. In this approach, math problems should be represented concretely (i.e., using counters, or objects that can be counted by hand) for lower-functioning students and/or students in lower grades. Semiconcrete teaching procedures (i.e., using tally marks rather than actual counters) should be employed for slightly more sophisticated learners. Students should move to abstract math problems only after proficiency in mathematical operations has been achieved. While almost all math curricula emphasize this type of CSA instruction in kindergarten through grade 2, Bender (2005) recommended that such instruction be continued in higher grade levels, including middle school, for students struggling in mathematics.

Geller and Smith (2002) recommended the use of a mental image to assist in multistep math problems. This concept, presented in Interest Box 7.5, is very similar to the visual-imagery strategy for reading comprehension discussed in Chapter 6.

It is interesting to note that math instruction in multistep problems is one of the few areas in which traditional instruction has paralleled the newly developed learning-strategies approaches. Elementary teachers four decades ago were listing the steps for problem completion on the board in the same terms that the learning-strategy literature today recommends. Clearly, as a teacher of students with learning disabilities, you will wish to use these strategies also. For example, many teachers produce a chart of the steps involved in a double-digit addition problem with regrouping in the 10's place and leave these steps on display all year. Each time a student completes a problem, he or she should be encouraged to state quietly the steps as they are completed.

Complex Operations

Math problems that involve **complex operations** are problems that include several different operations, as opposed to the same operation repeated several times. For example, a double-digit multiplication problem involves knowledge of multiplication math facts, understanding of regrouping, understanding of place value, and knowledge of addition. Because both addition and multiplication are involved, this type of problem is much more complex than the addition problem discussed earlier. Finally, the speed with which a student can complete these multiple operations may also be a concern.

We now know that students with learning disabilities demonstrate problems in complex computations (Bryant & Dix, 1999). With increasing complexity, the limitations of these students in memory and learning strategies become increasingly detrimental to performance. As the teacher, you should use the strategies developed in the elementary education literature and keep current with forthcoming research on various instructional techniques.

INTEREST BOX 7.5

TEACHING TIPS: USE OF MENTAL IMAGES IN MATH

Geller and Smith (2002) suggested that teachers use images to represent the solution to math problems. Although teachers in kindergarten and first grade often use concrete objects or pictures to represent math facts, use of these concrete stimuli should be continued into the higher elementary grades for children with learning disabilities.

Consider the math problem below. The problem may be represented by counters, as illustrated. In the second diagram, note how a set is identified around the counters to illustrate the concept of place value (i.e., 10 small ones traded for a big one).

$$
\begin{array}{r}
3\,6 \\
+\,4\,7 \\
\hline
\end{array}
$$

$$
\begin{array}{r}
{}^{1} \\
3\,6 \\
+\,4\,7 \\
\hline
8\,3
\end{array}
$$

Trade for ⟶

Word Problems

Within the last several years, numerous researchers have studied the performance of students with learning disabilities on word problems (Bryant & Dix, 1999; Desoete, Roeyers, & Buysse, 2001; Jitendra, DiPipi, & Perron-Jones, 2002; Xin, Jitendra, Deatline-Buchman, Hickman, & Post, 2002). Upon reflection, however, this is no great surprise. Studies of language use among these students have long been a staple of the research, and word problems involve use of language to solve mathematical problems.

The research evidence to date has demonstrated that students with learning disabilities are deficient in their word-problem-solving skill (Bryant & Dix, 1999; Miles & Forcht, 1995), and several studies have related this deficiency to reading deficiencies. The syntax, or the structure of sentences, in a word problem may be particularly difficult for some students with learning disabilities to understand, and if a student cannot read the problem correctly or understand the language of the problem, the student will not be able to complete the problem successfully.

Numerous instructional strategies have been recommended (Maccini et al., 1999; Xin et al., 2002; Jitendra, 2002; Jitendra et al., 2002), and most of these researchers recommend some type of cognitive training or learning-strategy intervention. For example, one method by which word problems may be made easier is identification of **cue words,** which generally indicate a particular operation ("John took six of the toys away" indicates subtraction because the words *took away* generally indicate that). Training to look for and identify these cue words may be an effective intervention for some children with learning disabilities. Bender (2005, p. 78) provided a list of cue words that typically indicate particular operations, as follows:

Addition	altogether, add, how many, put together, in all
Subtraction	take out, took away, left, gave away
Multiplication	problems that tell about one and ask for a total
Division	problems that tell about many and ask about one

Maccini and co-workers (1999) reviewed several studies on instructional techniques in algebra among students with learning disabilities. The various articles indicated that successful interventions include instruction on the specific knowledge associated with the problem as well as a general understanding of problem-solving approaches and self-regulation (i.e., self-checking) strategies. Numerous studies involved various visual cues (such as cue cards, which assist a student in identifying the correct steps) and the order of the steps in problem solution. Behrend (2003), as one example, suggested a method whereby students are taught to visualize the problem. He recommended a series of cognitively guided questions the teacher might use in order to help students picture the steps in a problem, as shown in Interest Box 7.6. Strategies such as this will assist students in visualizing the various steps in the problem and will also assist the teacher in understanding the student's cognitive interpretation of the problem. This type of strategy training should facilitate instruction in word problems.

While a variety of instructional approaches have been suggested for students with learning disabilities in the word-problem area (Babbitt & Miller, 1996; Miles & Forcht, 1995), there seems to be an increasing emphasis on the metacognitive or cognitive instructional perspective in the area of math, which is exemplified by the large number of learning-strategies approaches. Interest Box 7.7 includes a number of instructional recommendations common to many of these sources (Babbitt & Miller, 1996; Miles & Forcht, 1995).

Anchoring Math Instruction in Real-World Situations

Unlike reading, a skill that is used in a wide variety of school subjects, math instruction has traditionally been somewhat segregated from other subjects. Reading is necessary in social studies, science, and language arts, but math skills are not typically used in those other subject areas. Thus, math is relatively unsupported in other school subjects. Recently, several researchers and practitioners have recommended connecting math instruction for students with learning disabilities to real-world contexts that may include other school

INTEREST BOX 7.6

COGNITIVELY GUIDED VISUALIZATION DIALOGUE

PROBLEM

Jessica has 5 bags of candy. There are 4 pieces of candy in each bag. How many pieces of candy does Jessica have?

DIALOGUE

TEACHER: Remone, tell me about how you got your answer of 9?

REMONE: I wasn't sure, so I added 5 and 4.

TEACHER: Does that tell us how many pieces of candy there are? Do you want to try again?

REMONE: OK. I guess I have more than that.

TEACHER: There are 5 bags, and you need to think about how many are in each bag. Can you get that in your head?

REMONE: I got 4 pieces in each bag.

TEACHER: Yeah! That's right! Do you want to imagine 5 bags and pretend you can see into each bag. How many pieces in each bag?

REMONE: There are 4 pieces in each bag, so I've got a lot more. (The student may want to use counters or even draw a picture at this point.)

TEACHER: Why don't you draw circles and pretend they are bags and then put 4 pieces in each bag?

REMONE: I can do that in my head!

TEACHER: Great! When you see that, count all the pieces.

REMONE: There are 20 pieces. I've got a lot of candy!

TEACHER: Great! That's exactly right. You've got 20 pieces.

■ ■ ■ ■ ■

INTEREST BOX 7.7

TEACHING TIPS: TEACHING WORD PROBLEMS

1. Assist the student in "planning" how to complete the problem. Use an advance organizer that focuses on both the language within the problem and the necessary operations.
2. Demonstrate problem solutions repeatedly to the student. Prior to making a homework assignment, complete the first problem from that assignment in class, even if you have already completed initial instruction.
3. Have the child verbally state what he or she is doing, in order to "talk through the problem." Teach the student to give himself or herself verbal instructions out loud.
4. Teach the student to focus on cue words. Have the student circle the cue words in pencil in the problem.
5. Help the student to focus on important aspects of the problem. Concentrate first on what the student knows from the problem description and specifically what the student needs to know. After that, have the student write out a mathematical sentence to help solve the problem.
6. Whenever possible, use objects to demonstrate specific aspects of the problem. It may also help to visualize the problem mentally.
7. Emphasize the need to check every problem. Have the student consider if his or her answer really solves the problem.

subjects or even math applications from real-world scenarios presented via video (Bender, 2005; Bottge, Heinrichs, Chan, & Serlin, 2001; Cawley & Foley, 2002; Geller & Smith, 2002). According to the emerging brain-compatible instruction literature (Sousa, 2006), this technique is likely to enhance the memory of students with learning disabilities and increase achievement in math because they will more readily see the need for mastery of math skills and will practice those skills more frequently in a variety of contexts.

One emerging concept in the math curriculum involves basing instruction in the context of actual applications of the knowledge to be learned. This is referred to as *anchored instruction,* because knowledge is mastered more readily if it is anchored in a specific application context (Bottge et al., 2001; Xin, Glaser, & Rieth, 1996). Bottge and colleagues (2001) provided an example of anchored instruction by using 14 adolescents who were experiencing math difficulties (8 of whom were identified as learning disabled). In this study, use of video examples as an anchor for math word problems helped the students with learning disabilities in learning these problem-solving skills. The results indicated that the students in the remedial math class performed similarly to a comparison group of students without disabilities in a prealgebra class on the problem-solving skills taught using the video examples.

In another example of connecting math to real-world situations, Cawley and Foley (2002) suggested infusing the math curriculum with various aspects of the science curriculum, and provided various activity-based examples for primary, intermediate, and middle school students with mild disabilities. For students with learning disabilities in grades 3 to 5, these authors suggest developing word problems in elementary math that illustrate science concepts. Here is one such example.

The amount of work may be defined as force times distance, or

$$W = FD$$

If Tiamara used a force of 3 points to move a box 4 feet
across the floor, how much work did Tiamara do?

In this example, the science concept of force is explored while teaching word problems based on a simple algorithm used to determine work. Other types of problems that may be of particular assistance in the science curriculum might involve ratios or measurements. The creative teacher may also conceive of ways to involve math instruction in social sciences classes (e.g., the proportion of a population on a specific continent). By involving several content areas in math instruction, students with learning disabilities will demonstrate enhanced memory for the learning task in each subject area, and thus math will be "supported" in other subject areas.

CURRICULUM-BASED ASSESSMENT IN MATHEMATICS

Within the last decade, there has been an increasing reexamination of assessment practices in math for all students, including students with learning disabilities (Bryant, 1999; Grobecker, 1999). Within the area of math in particular, curriculum-based assessment has been advocated by a number of researchers (Fuchs & Fuchs, 1998; King-Sears, Burgess, & Lawson, 1999).

As described in Chapter 4, curriculum-based assessment involves repeated assessments—in many cases daily assessments—on the particular types of problems taught within the curriculum (King-Sears, Burgess, & Lawson, 1999). Ideally, there would be little distinction between instruction and assessment, since assessment would involve direct analysis of—and response to—the performance of the student on a particular set of skills. While a useful and practical assessment approach in many subject areas, curriculum-based assessment is especially effective in mathematics because of the straightforward nature of this curriculum area. For example, in this area, study of double-digit addition with regrouping always follows study of double-digit addition without regrouping. This level of structure in mathematics lends itself to curriculum-based assessment.

Curriculum-based assessment is firmly rooted in the behavioral perspective. There is often a negative reaction to the "reductionistic" aspects of behavioral thought—and by extension curriculum-based assessment. Specifically, proponents of the constructivist perspective (see Chapter 1) suggest that instruction and assessment of discrete math skills in the haphazard and relatively isolated fashion common in most classrooms diminishes learning, since math activities are not seen in relation to each other and a problem-solving approach is not typically applied—at least not to instruction of math facts and/or operations (Grobecker, 1999). Clearly, curriculum-based assessment practices may run afoul of the constructivists' perspective since the emphasis in curriculum-based instruction is on specific sequentially ordered facts and/or problems. In spite of this caution, as a practitioner you may expect to see increasing emphasis on curriculum-based assessment in mathematics for many students with learning disabilities for at least two reasons. First, curriculum-based assessment has earned the respect of practitioners as an effective instructional and assessment practice. Second, it has been structured into a wide variety of computer-based math instructional programs currently on the commercial market.

PROGNOSIS IN MATHEMATICS

The overall prognosis for mathematics achievement for students with learning disabilities as they finish school is not optimistic (Cawley et al., 2001). Although there are numerous exceptions, research has indicated that many of these children will function considerably below their peers (Cawley et al., 2001). Clearly, this indicates the overall need to attend to mathematics as a major skill area, and as a teacher, you will be required to address this area for many students with learning disabilities.

SUMMARY

This chapter has presented the evidence concerning math skills of students with learning disabilities. Although reading and language arts have been studied by researchers over a period of several decades, less information is presently available on the math skills of these students. These areas include early math skills, complex math operations, and the relationship between cognitive ability and mathematics achievement. However, in other areas—math facts, automaticity, and word problems—researchers are beginning to provide helpful instructional suggestions.

As a teacher of the learning disabled, you will be expected to instruct many students in many of the elementary math skills. Generally, the best recommendation is to utilize the suggestions from elementary math instruction courses and adapt those strategies for use in your classroom. Further, a general consensus favoring the use of learning-strategy instruction and anchored instruction has been noted, both in the area of math-facts instruction and in word-problem solving. More information on math instruction overall will certainly be forthcoming in the near future, and it is advisable to remain in touch with the literature on strategies for instruction in this important field.

The following points should help you in studying this chapter:

- Although much less is known about the learning characteristics of children with learning disabilities in math than in reading and language arts, we do know that most students with learning disabilities do not master the entire math curriculum.
- Math skills should be informally evaluated, based on the sequential context in which they are typically taught.
- Many children with learning disabilities have difficulty with memorization of math facts. This problem with *automaticity* may result from the memory problems discussed in earlier chapters.
- Word problems may present special difficulties for these students because the reading skills and reasoning skills necessary to complete the problem are lacking. Most of the current research on this issue suggests that students with learning problems should be taught various strategies to help them complete the correct sequence of steps for the problem.

QUESTIONS AND ACTIVITIES

1. Identify a general area in the math curriculum—early math skills or complex operations—and list a set of instructional strategies used in the elementary class for instruction in these areas. How may these strategies be adapted for use with children who have learning disabilities? What characteristics of these children form the basis for the recommendations for adaptations?

2. Obtain a set of completed math worksheets from a special education teacher in the local schools. Describe the types of math problems that are apparent.

3. Search the literature for information on correlates of math achievement. What types of skills on IQ tests seem to be related to math skills?

4. Compile an annotated list of strategies for instruction in word-problem solving. Start with the references for this chapter.

5. Discuss math instruction with a teacher of the learning disabled from the local schools. How much of his or her time is spent in math instruction? What are the approximate grade levels of the math instruction?

6. Obtain a copy of the math curricular standards from your state, review it, and share that with the class.

REFERENCES

Ackerman, P. T., Anhalt, J. M., & Dykman, R. A. (1986). Arithmetic automatization failure in children with attention and reading disorders: Associations and sequela. *Journal of Learning Disabilities, 19,* 222–232.

Babbitt, B. C., & Miller, S. P. (1996). Using hypermedia to improve the mathematics problem-solving skills of students with learning disabilities. *Journal of Learning Disabilities, 29,* 391–401.

Baroody, A. J., & Kaufman, L. (1993). The case of Lee: Assessing and remedying a numeral-writing difficulty. *Teaching Exceptional Children, 25*(2), 14–16.

Behrend, J. (2003). Learning-disabled students make sense of mathematics. *Teaching Exceptional Children, 9*(5), 269–274.

Bender, W. N. (2005). *Differentiating math instruction.* Thousand Oaks, CA: Corwin.

Bender, W. N., Rosencrans, C., & Crane, M. K. (1999). Stress, depression, and suicide among students with learning disabilities: Assessing the risk. *Learning Disability Quarterly, 22,* 143–156.

Bottge, B. A., Heinrichs, M., Chan, S., & Serlin, R. C. (2001). Anchoring adolescents' understanding of math concepts in rich problem-solving environments. *Remedial and Special Education, 22*(5), 299–314.

Bryant, B. R. (1999). The dynamics of assessment. In W. N. Bender (Ed.), *Professional issues in learning disabilities* (pp. 385–413). Austin, TX: ProEd.

Bryant, D. P., & Dix, J. (1999). Mathematics interventions for students with learning disabilities, In W. N. Bender (Ed.), *Professional issues in learning disabilities* (pp. 219–259). Austin, TX: ProEd.

Bullock, J. (1989). *This is Touch Math.* Colorado Springs: Innovative Learning Concepts.

Cawley, J. F., & Foley, T. E. (2002). Connecting math and science for all students. *Teaching Exceptional Children, 34*(4), 14–19.

Cawley, J., Parmar, R., Foley, T. E., Salmon, S., & Roy, S. (2001). Arithmetic performance of students: Implications for standards and programming. *Exceptional Children, 67*(3), 311–330.

Desoete, A., Roeyers, H., & Buysse, A. (2001). Metacognition and mathematical problem solving in grade 3. *Journal of Learning Disabilities, 34*(5), 435–449.

Fuchs, L. S., & Fuchs, D. (1998). General educators' instructional adaptation for students with learning disabilities. *Learning Disability Quarterly, 21,* 23–33.

Garnett, K. (1992). Developing fluency with basic number facts: Intervention for students with learning disabilities. *Learning Disability Research and Practice, 7,* 210–216.

Garrett, A. J., Mazzocco, M. M. M., & Baker, L. (2006). Development of the metacognitive skills of prediction and evaluation in children with or without math disability. *Learning Disabilities Research and Practice, 21*(2), 77–88.

Geller, C. H., & Smith, K. S. (2002). *Improving the teaching of math: From textbook concepts to real world applications.* Paper presented at the annual meeting of the Council for Learning Disabilities (October 11), Denver, CO.

Gersten, R., & Chard, D. (1999). Number sense: Rethinking arithmetic instruction for students with mathematical disabilities. *Journal of Special Education, 44,* 18–28.

Gersten, R., Chard, D., Baker, S., & Lee, D. S. (2002). *Instructional approaches for teaching mathematics to students with learning disabilities: Findings from a synthesis of experimental research.* Paper presented at the annual meeting of the Council for Learning Disabilities (October 11), Denver, CO.

Grobecker, B. (1999). Mathematics reform and learning disabilities. *Learning Disability Quarterly, 22,* 43–58.

Hasselbring, T. S., Goin, L. I., & Bransford, J. D. (1987). Developing automaticity. *Teaching Exceptional Children, 19*(3), 30–33.

Jitendra, A. (2002). Teaching students math problem-solving through graphic representations. *Teaching Exceptional Children, 34*(4), 34–39.

Jitendra, A., DiPipi, C. M., & Perron-Jones, N. (2002). An exploratory study of schema-based word-problem-solving instruction for middle school students with learning disabilities: An emphasis on conceptual and procedural understanding. *Journal of Special Education, 36*(1), 23–38.

Jordan, N. C., Levine, S. C., & Huttenlocher, J. (1996). Calculation abilities in young children with different patterns of cognitive functioning. *Journal of Learning Disabilities, 28,* 53–64.

King-Sears, M. E., Burgess, M., & Lawson, T. L. (1999). Applying curriculum-based assessment in inclusive settings. *Teaching Exceptional Children, 32*(1), 30–39.

Kroeger, S. D., & Kouche, B. (2006). Using peer-assisted learning strategies to increase response to intervention in inclusive math settings. *Teaching Exceptional Children, 38*(5), 6–13.

Lanford, A. D., & Cary, L. G. (2000). Graduate requirements for students with disabilities and practice considerations. *Remedial and Special Education, 21*(3), 152–161.

Lembke, E., & Foegen, A. (2006, April 9–12). *Monitoring your student's early math performance using curriculum based measurement.* Paper presented at the annual meeting of the Council for Exceptional Children, Salt Lake City, UT.

Maccini, P., & Gagnon, J. C. (2002). Perceptions and application of NCTM standards by special and general education teachers. *Exceptional Children, 68*(3), 325–344.

Maccini, P., McNaughton, D., & Ruhl, K. L. (1999). Algebra instruction for students with learning disabilities: Implications from a research review. *Learning Disability Quarterly, 22,* 113–126.

Mastropieri, M. A., Scruggs, T. E., & Shiah, S. (1991). Mathematics instruction for learning disabled students: A review of research. *Learning Disabilities Research and Practice, 6,* 89–98.

Matlock, L., Fielder, K., & Walsh, D. (2001). Building the foundation for standards-based instruction for all students. *Teaching Exceptional Children, 33*(5), 60–67.

McIntyre, S. B., Test, D. W., Cooke, N. L., & Beattie, J. (1991). Using count-bys to increase multiplication facts fluency. *Learning Disability Quarterly, 14,* 82–85.

Miles, D. D., & Forcht, J. P. (1995). Mathematics strategies for secondary students with learning disabilities or mathematics deficiencies: A cognitive approach. *Intervention in School and Clinic, 31,* 91–96.

Moats, L. C., & Lyon, G. R. (1993). Learning disabilities in the United States: Advocacy, science, and the future of the field. *Journal of Learning Disabilities, 26,* 282–294.

Pellegrino, J. W., & Goldman, S. R. (1987). Information processing and elementary mathematics. *Journal of Learning Disabilities, 20,* 23–32.

Riccomini, P. J. (2005). Identification and remediation of systematic error patterns in subtraction. *Learning Disability Quarterly, 28*(3), 233–242.

Robinson, C. S., Menchetti, B. M., & Torgesen, J. K. (2002). Toward a two-factor theory of one type of mathematics disabilities. *Learning Disabilities Research and Practice, 17*(2), 81–89.

Rourke, B. P. (2005). Neuropsychology of learning disabilities: Past and future. *Learning Disability Quarterly, 28*(2), 111–114.

Rourke, B. P. (1993). Arithmetic disabilities, specific and otherwise: A neuropsychological perspective. *Journal of Learning Disabilities, 26,* 214–226.

Rourke, B. P., Young, G. C., & Leenaars, A. A. (1989). A childhood learning disability that predisposes those afflicted to adolescent and adult depression and suicide risk. *Journal of Learning Disabilities, 22,* 169–175.

Saunders, S. (2006, April 9–12). *The algebra readiness of high school students in South Carolina: Implications for middle school math teachers.* Paper presented at the annual meeting of the Council for Exceptional Children, Salt Lake City, UT.

Shalev, R. S., & Gross-Tsur, V. (1993). Developmental dyscalculia and medical assessment. *Journal of Learning Disabilities, 26,* 134–137.

Silver, C. H., Pennett, H. D., Black, J. L., Fair, G. W., & Balise, R. R. (1999). Stability of arithmetic disability subtypes. *Journal of Learning Disabilities, 32,* 108–119.

Sousa, D. (2006). *How the brain learns* (3rd ed.). Thousand Oaks, CA: Corwin.

Sousa, D. (2001). *How the special needs brain learns.* Thousand Oaks, CA: Corwin Press.

Van Luit, J. E. H., & Naglieri, J. A. (1999). Effectiveness of the MASTER program for teaching special children multiplication and division. *Journal of Learning Disabilities, 32,* 98–107.

Wilson, K. M., & Swanson, H. L. (2001). Are mathematics disabilities due to a domain-general or a domain-specific working memory deficit? *Journal of Learning Disabilities, 34*(3), 237–248.

Xin, F., Glaser, C. W., & Rieth, H. (1996). Multimedia reading: Using anchored instruction and video technology in vocabulary lessons. *Teaching Exceptional Children, 29*(2), 45–49.

Xin, Y. P., Jitendra, A., Deatline-Buchman, A., Hickman, W., & Post, E. (2002). *Teach math word problem solving: Schema vs. traditional instruction.* Paper presented at the annual meeting of the Council for Learning Disabilities (October 11), Denver, CO.

CHAPTER EIGHT

STUDENTS WITH LEARNING DISABILITIES IN THE CLASSROOM

CHAPTER OUTLINE

WHEN YOU COMPLETE THIS CHAPTER, YOU SHOULD BE ABLE TO:

1. Discuss task orientation in inclusive classes at the elementary and secondary level.

2. Discuss the research on disruptive behavior of children and adolescents with disabilities during the elementary grades.

3. Present the research results on interactions between students with learning disabilities and teachers in elementary classes.

4. Define *adaptive behavior* and list the subcomponents of it.

5. Describe the types of instructional interaction that teachers and students with learning disabilities engage in during the school years.

6. List several instructional implications of adaptive behavioral research on children with learning disabilities in elementary classes.

7. List several instructional recommendations that may be made based on the research concerned with interaction between teachers and pupils with learning disabilities.

KEYWORDS

adaptive behavior	cumulative deficit	work-study model
task orientation	academic plateau	functional-skills model
disruptive behavior	motivation	learning-strategies model
hyperactivity	departmentalized curriculum	consultation model
teacher interactions	tutorial model	inclusive service delivery
instructional interactions	basic-skills remediation model	

INTRODUCTION

Much of the early research on students with learning disabilities involved only clinically identified populations. Students whose problems were severe enough to be referred to specialized educational or assessment clinics (usually on a university campus) tended to be more severely impaired than students identified by the public schools today. Also, much of the research reviewed earlier on characteristics of students with learning disabilities has involved studies of memory, attention, intelligence, or social skills on contrived laboratory tasks, more than ecological studies of these characteristics on typical school tasks in public school classrooms. This could raise questions concerning the accuracy or relevance of some of the research for public school classrooms. Only within the last three decades have children with learning disabilities been studied in classroom settings in elementary schools. As a teacher, you should have some understanding of the research that investigates the manifestations of learning disability characteristics in public school classes (Bender, 2002).

The purpose of this chapter is to present information on the typical behaviors and interaction patterns of students with learning disabilities at the elementary and secondary levels. Information presented here will focus on research conducted in inclusive classes. Some of the cognitive, language, and affective characteristics that were presented previously are discussed again here, but the focus here is on the manifestations of these characteristics in general education inclusive classes.

Regardless of the grade level where one is teaching, every teacher of students with learning disabilities needs some information concerning the educational characteristics of these students in secondary schools, as well as their interaction with the secondary school environment. Although achievement difficulties still abound in adolescent students with learning disabilities, many of these students also develop secondary emotional and social problems as a result of continued years of frustration and school failure. There is some evidence of increased risk for depression and suicide among adolescents with disabilities. No matter how successful an elementary program may be with a particular child, if that child reaches middle school or high school only to experience failure in school subjects, the total school experience for that student has not been successful and may lead to unfortunate results (Bryan, Burstein, & Ergul, 2004; Elksnin & Elksnin, 2004). This chapter will initially focus on students at the elementary level, followed by an emphasis on secondary students with disabilities.

ADAPTIVE BEHAVIOR OF CHILDREN WITH LEARNING DISABILITIES

read this

Adaptive behavior means one's ability to adapt to the environment. Although this term originated in the discussion of behavior of the mentally retarded, several theorists realized several years ago that the concept is appropriate for the learning disabled also (Bender, 1999; Bryan et al., 2004; Leigh, 1987; McKinney & Feagans, 1983; Weller & Strawser, 1981). McKinney and Feagans (1983) provided an early review of the numerous characteristics that comprise the concept of adaptive behavior, including task-oriented behaviors, disruptive behaviors, hyperactive behaviors, and interaction with teachers or peers. Weller and Strawser (1981) provided an early theoretical basis for studying adaptive behavior of children with disabilities and, in addition to these characteristics, included pragmatic language usage in the class. These characteristics have been described earlier, but some elaboration on how these problems are manifested in the elementary classroom is in order. The major issue is the ability of children with learning disabilities to adapt to the demands placed on them in the elementary classroom.

Various types of behaviors may result from inappropriate adaptive responses. For example, when a child does not know the correct answer to a question from the teacher, an inappropriate behavioral response—such as standing up and running across the room—may alleviate the need to respond to the question. The teacher would note this "hyperactive" behavior and presumably ask someone else the question. As this example illustrates, inappropriate behaviors may be adaptive in some sense from the perspective of the child, even if the teacher does not approve of them. In this case, the inappropriate behavior helped the child to avoid answering the question incorrectly.

A number of studies on children with learning disabilities have been conducted concerning specific aspects of adaptive behavior. These include studies on task orientation, disruptive behaviors, and hyperactivity (Elksnin & Elksnin, 2004; Teglasi, Cohn, & Meshbesher, 2004). (See Interest Box 8.1.)

■ ■ ■ ■ ■ ━━

INTEREST BOX 8.1
HISTORICAL FOCUS ON ADAPTIVE BEHAVIOR   *Skip*

With increasing research attention on the adaptive behavior of children with learning disabilities, assessment of adaptive behavior became a priority. The Weller-Strawser Adaptive Behavior Scale (Weller & Strawser, 1981) was published specifically to assess adaptive behavior of children and adolescents with learning disabilities. It is an important assessment instrument historically for several reasons. First, it was the first adaptive behavior scale designed specifically for use with populations of the learning disabled. Unlike adaptive behavioral scales designed for retarded or emotionally disturbed populations, which may not be appropriate for the learning disabled population (some include measures of teeth brushing, self-care, and other indicators that are not problem areas for this group), this scale was formulated specifically with children who have learning disabilities in mind.

Second, although other measures of task-oriented, hyperactive, and disruptive classroom behavior are available, this instrument includes a measure of pragmatic language in classroom situations. Given the nature of language problems among these children, this type of measure is essential.

The scale itself is a forced-choice teacher rating. In other words, two contradictory statements are made dealing with the same type of situation and specifying a particular trait or characteristic. The teacher must choose the option that best describes the child in question. In all, the teacher must make 34 different choices, which are then grouped into four general areas: ability to produce appropriate work in the classroom (roughly equivalent to task orientation), ability to use pragmatic language, ability to cope socially, and ability to engage in good relationships. Adequate reliability and validity for this instrument have been demonstrated in the manual, indicating that this measurement instrument meets generally accepted standards in the field.

Several comparison studies have indicated that children who experience learning problems are deficient in adaptive behavior (Bender & Golden, 1988; Leigh, 1987). In one study, Bender and Golden (1988) used the Weller-Strawser scale (Weller & Strawser, 1981). Adaptive behavior ratings of 54 children with learning disabilities and 54 children without such disabilities were compared. The children in the two groups were matched on race, sex, and class, which controlled for the possibility of idiosyncratic ratings by the teachers. The children with learning disabilities demonstrated less adaptive behavior in each of the four behavior categories. Specifically, they produced less classwork, used pragmatic communication less well, engaged in less constructive relationships, and demonstrated less ability to cope socially with the demands of the mainstream class.

Although the number of studies that look at adaptive behavior overall is small, a number of studies on children with learning disabilities have been conducted concerning specific aspects of adaptive behavior. These include studies on task orientation, disruptive behaviors, and hyperactivity. Many of these are reviewed in this chapter.

Task Orientation

Task orientation is an interaction between the several discrete aspects of attention discussed earlier. The research reviewed earlier demonstrated that students with learning disabilities are less on-task in elementary classes than other students (McKinney & Feagans, 1983; Teglasi, Cohn, & Meshbesher, 2004). Children without disabilities are on-task 60 to 85%

of the time; children with learning disabilities are on-task 30 to 60% of the time. In practical terms, this means that initially the children who are learning disabled will take perhaps twice as long to complete in-class assignments as the children who are not. When this time difference is compounded by increased distractibility and a lack of ability to selectively attend to the appropriate aspects of the task—even when the student is on-task—the deficit in overall task orientation is staggering.

From the perspective of the teacher, this creates scheduling problems in the inclusive class, as well as concern for the "downtime" of the other children who may have already finished a particular worksheet. Task orientation is also a problem in special classes for children with learning disabilities, where a group of five such children may finish the same reading assignment at five different times.

Many general education and special education teachers have devised methods of combating these task-orientation problems. Physical proximity to the child will usually result in increased on-task behavior. Creating an educational climate relatively free from overt distractions may decrease the distractibility of these students. Finally, instructional methods that focus on strategies for attacking particular educational tasks can improve the selective attention of children with learning disabilities.

Disruptive Behaviors

The prevalence of overtly **disruptive behavior** among students with learning disabilities was addressed early in the history of the field. Research in the 1980s and 1990s demonstrated that, overall, students with learning disabilities are no more disruptive than are other students in the classroom (Bender 2002, 1985; McKinney & Feagans, 1983; Slate & Saudargas, 1986). However, in spite of these results, teachers often report more disruption among students with learning disabilities than from others in the class (Bryan, Burstein, & Ergul, 2004). This inconsistency may be explained by the definition of the term *disruption* (i.e., studies defining disruption as "extreme behavioral problems" will document less disruption). Still, this inconsistent research result is important for teachers to note, because some general education teachers may believe that students with disabilities are more challenging to manage in the classroom; while this is true for some isolated students with learning disabilities, it is not generally true for students with learning disabilities.

Hyperactivity

Although teachers and professionals discuss **hyperactivity** as a major characteristic of children with learning disabilities, little research has demonstrated that this characteristic is present in students with disabilities more so than other students. However, one variable that impacts the level of hyperactivity of students with learning disabilities is the comorbidity of learning disabilities and attention-deficit hyperactivity disorder (ADHD). Comorbidity means that a child manifests the characteristics associated with more than one disability or disease. In the field of learning disabilities, the comorbidity with ADHD is always of concern, and this clearly impacts the task orientation of these students in the classroom (APA, 1993). Smith and Adams (2004) studied a large sample of children from the National Household Education Survey. In that data set, a large number of parents in different households were surveyed, and statistical data were compiled. Out of a total of 9,583 children, 3.7% (343 children) had comorbid ADHD and learning disabilities. Further, 3.6% manifested ADHD only, and 4.9% manifested only a learning disability. Clearly, with a relatively high comorbidity of learning disability and ADHD, teachers might well expect poorer task orientation among these students overall.

Teacher Interactions

Given the various adaptive behavior problems manifested by students with learning disabilities, one might well anticipate that teachers feel these students are more challenging to teach. Drame (2002) investigated teachers' perceptions of behavior and academic problems by studying 63 general education teachers. These teachers completed a variety of surveys to measure their attitudes toward academic skills and specific adaptive behavior problems as they related to teachers' tendencies to refer students with learning disabilities for special education placement. Results showed quite clearly that students were much more likely to be referred for services as learning disabled if, in addition to academic problems, they demonstrated inappropriate adaptive behaviors in the classroom.

Although no firm conclusions can be drawn from only one study, it is clear that adaptive behaviors such as task orientation, disruptive behavior, and hyperactivity problems of children with learning disabilities are a concern for teachers. Also, these studies suggest several implications for teachers in elementary classes. It seems clear that decisions concerning the types of instructional groups a teacher decides to use should be based in part on the adaptive behavioral skill of the children involved. Also, the average length of assignments may need to be modified, given the demonstrated problems in task orientation. Interest Box 8.2 presents suggestions for managing the adaptive behavior of children with learning disabilities in today's classrooms.

Research over the last decades has generally indicated that teachers interact with students with learning disabilities more frequently than with other students in the general education classroom (Alber, Heward, & Hippler, 1999; Bender, 2002; Bryan, Burstein, & Ergul, 2004). However, the quality of **teacher interactions** may be more important than the total number of interactions (Alber et al., 1999), and researchers over the last two decades have addressed the question of quality of teacher interaction.

The early research in the 1980s and 1990s suggested that teachers interacted more with students with learning disabilities because they had to manage behavioral problems more frequently (see Bender, 2002, p. 246, for a review). However, more recent research has shown that teachers in inclusive secondary classes interact with students with learning disabilities in a similar fashion as with students with no disabilities (Wallace, Anderson, Bartholomay, & Hupp, 2002). As a teacher, you should become more aware of the way you interact with students in an effort to focus more on instruction and on providing praise for students' work.

In a highly innovative study, Alber, Heward, and Hippler (1999) investigated an intervention that involved training students with learning disabilities to elicit more praise from their teachers in the general education classroom. Four students with learning disabilities and two general education teachers were the subjects in this study. Using a multiple

INTEREST BOX 8.2

TEACHING TIPS: MANAGING INAPPROPRIATE BEHAVIOR

1. Create a classroom atmosphere that encourages on-task behavior by rewarding the first few pupils in each instructional group who complete an assignment.
2. Monitor every child's behavior using eye contact with the child, physical proximity, and constant verbal cues to return to task. These cues and monitoring behavior should not be harsh or punitive in nature, but rather gentle reminders that the task is important and requires attention.
3. Organize instructional situations in which pupils get practice in persuasive argument or explanations of tasks to other students.
4. Use study carrels, white noise, and "quiet-study" periods to eliminate distractions that may cause off-task behavior.
5. Encourage role-playing among children with learning disabilities who have been in an argument, by attempting to get them to understand the other's feelings.
6. Offer instruction in groups in which each group member is given part of the necessary information to complete a project and must contribute to the product of the group. This should encourage cooperation between the persons in the group and improve social skills.
7. Structure classroom assignments to include more small-group instruction that is monitored by the teacher and less seatwork activity by individual children.

baseline design, each student was individually trained to recruit positive teacher attention by completing three behaviors in sequence: raising one's hand, waiting for the teacher's attention, and voicing a question about one's academic work (e.g., "How am I doing on these problems?"). The students were trained in these behaviors in the special education classroom and then applied these practices in the general education classroom, while independent observers noted both the student's recruiting behaviors as well as the general education teacher's response. The results indicated that once students were trained in appropriate recruiting, these students began to recruit more positive attention from the teachers using these appropriate behaviors. Further, the amount of praise provided by the general education teachers likewise increased. Finally, two of the four students with learning disabilities managed to maintain their appropriate recruiting behaviors during the maintenance period after the intervention was over, suggesting that this intervention procedure was self-sustaining for these students. The anecdotal evidence was even more exciting. The general education teachers began to perceive not only improved effort on the part of these students but also improvement in their academics (Alber et. al., 1999).

The good news about this innovative treatment is not only the efficacy of the intervention procedure but also the empowerment this procedure offers to students with learning disabilities. Specifically, with appropriate guidance, students with learning disabilities can be trained to improve their relationships with teachers in the general education classroom. In a sense, the special education teacher is likewise empowered. As a professional working with students with learning disabilities, you may find that students complain to you about their difficulty with a particular mainstream teacher. When this occurs, you should consider working with the student to implement this recruiting procedure in an effort to improve that relationship.

Clearly, interactions between inclusive class teachers and students with learning disabilities in the elementary grades are a critical concern, since such **instructional interactions** directly impact the early educational success of the child. Teachers should carefully monitor their instructional interactions with students with learning disabilities in order to ensure that students are appropriately challenged in the inclusive classroom and are not suffering undue embarrassment should they not understand the concepts discussed. Specifically, the types of questions teachers ask these students should mirror the types of instructional interactions with other students in the class. Interest Box 8.3 provides some guidelines for teachers to use in considering the types of questions to use for students with learning disabilities.

Skip —

COGNITIVE CHARACTERISTICS OF ADOLESCENTS WITH LEARNING DISABILITIES

Although the basic cognitive characteristics for students with disabilities were presented earlier, these characteristics are somewhat transformed by additional years of schooling.

INTEREST BOX 8.3

TEACHING TIPS: HOW TO QUESTION STUDENTS

Although there exists some uncertainty over which question formats are most appropriate, teachers may follow these suggestions:

1. It is probably wise to include both higher-level questions and lower-level questions in the instructional material as you would for other students.
2. Always present a ratio of higher-level questions and lower-level questions that seems most reasonable and appropriate for your students. You should closely observe the responses of your students to ascertain how they respond to each type of question and vary the percentage of questions accordingly.
3. Formulate numerous low-level comprehension questions based on direct recall of main ideas and details in reading material.
4. Formulate higher-level questions based on standard question formats. You may wish to remember that certain question formats typically result in questions that require some synthesis of different information from the study. For example, question phrases such as "Compare . . ." or "Defend the position that . . ." generally result in higher-level comprehension questions that require more than rote memory of story facts.
5. As a teacher, you must fight the tendency to make academic work too easy for children with learning disabilities by presenting only lower-level questions.
6. Always require the use of factual material in the acceptable answers to the higher-level questions.

This section is intended as a discussion of the transformation and interaction of the characteristics that have been previously discussed in order to present the types of behavior one might expect from adolescents with learning disabilities in public school classes.

Cumulative Deficit and Academic Plateau

The assumption behind public school is that the overall level of academic achievement increases throughout the school years. However, research has suggested that this may be an overly optimistic forecast for students with learning disabilities (Bender, 2002; Deshler, Schumaker, & Lenz, 1984). In fact, deficits in achievement seem to accumulate among these students. This cumulative-deficit problem is a potentially destructive reality for many secondary students with disabilities, as illustrated in Figure 8.1.

Basically, the concept of **cumulative deficit** suggests that as students with learning disabilities progress through school, they fall further and further behind. For example, as a child with a learning disability enters the early academic years, he or she may master only three-fourths of the reading content in the first grade. This child would be only one-

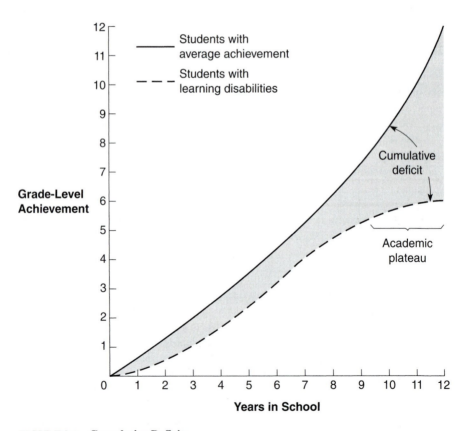

FIGURE 8.1   Cumulative Deficit

fourth of a year behind at the end of the first-grade year; and, given different levels of reading instruction, this is a manageable deficit for most first-grade teachers. However, if the same child again mastered only three-fourths of the reading content in the second grade, he or she would be half a year behind in reading at the end of the second year because the deficit is cumulative. This is still a manageable deficit in reading, but by the end of 12 years, the child would be reading at only the ninth-grade level, and even that figure seems to be overly optimistic. In fact, the mastery of only three-fourths of the first-grade curriculum makes it unlikely that the child will be able to master an equivalent amount of the second-grade content, and so the unmastered portion of the curriculum increases each year. The deficit is thus cumulative, and the prognosis for continued reading improvement throughout school among students with learning disabilities is not good.

Early research by Deshler and associates suggested that academic improvement may cease altogether for many of these students (Deshler, Schumaker, & Lenz, 1984; Deshler, Schumaker, Lenz, & Ellis, 1984). Adolescents who have learning disabilities seem to reach an academic plateau (with reading achievement scores around the fifth-grade level) during the tenth grade. Further, these students do not seem to progress at all thereafter.

This evidence certainly suggests that adolescents with learning disabilities will not be able to read materials in the subject areas that are written on grade level. Indeed, the students with these disabilities in the typical eleventh-grade class may be as much as six or seven years below grade level in reading. Although few teachers would hand a seventh-grade basal reader to a first-grade child, students with disabilities who have a deficit in reading are often placed in just this position in secondary classes.

To make matters worse, learning characteristics such as reading level often interact with instructional realities in the school. The readability of content-area textbooks may be so high that readability level further compounds the cumulative reading deficit. Although content-area texts generally present information at an appropriate conceptual level, many texts are written without the readability level in mind. It is not uncommon to find content texts in social studies, as one example, that are written several years above the grade level for which the text was intended (Putnam, 1992b). Imagine the following scenario: A student with learning disabilities is in a ninth-grade history class, the student's reading comprehension is fourth-grade level, and the text is written at a twelfth-grade level. Clearly, this student has virtually no opportunity to master this class unless major modifications are made in some fashion. Interest Box 8.4 lists several modifications that may enable this student to successfully complete that history class (Bender, 2002).

Adaptive Behaviors

Compared to children with learning disabilities, little information is available on the attention behaviors of adolescents with learning disabilities. Russ and colleagues (2001) recently demonstrated an inverse relationship between instructional group size and attention. Larger instructional groups were associated with lower levels of attention among students with disabilities. However, this study alone cannot be taken to suggest that merely reducing class size would increase attention for students with learning disabilities; nor does this result tell us if adolescents with learning disabilities attend to their work less than others in the secondary class.

INTEREST BOX 8.4

TEACHING TIPS: TEN TACTICS TO MODIFY READING ASSIGNMENTS

1. Obtain a high-interest, low-level reader on the same content that is covered in history class, and use this for several of the lower-level readers in the class.
2. Use partial outlines and charts (participatory organizers) that the student completes as he or she reads the assignment.
3. Assign the student a textbook in which another student has highlighted (with yellow markers) the topic sentences and important facts in each paragraph.
4. Indicate to the low-level readers the relationships between the text and the pictures in the text. Plan a class discussion around the pictures only.
5. Assign "tutors" to assist with reading and informal daily tests on the reading material.
6. Use alternative strategies (debate, role-play, discussion, and art-project strategies) rather than a unit test to allow the lower-level students to demonstrate comprehension.
7. Use specific learning strategies (summation after reading, paraphrasing the content, or elaboration) to assist the student in completing the task and to enhance comprehension.
8. Use individualized assignments and small-group assignments in order to increase understanding. Vary the modes of instruction.
9. Use cooperative instructional groupings in which the students take responsibility for each other's learning.
10. Use cubing to assist reading comprehension.

In one of the early studies, Bender (1985b) observed 18 high school students with learning disabilities in general education inclusive classes and compared their attention behavior to 18 other students. Teachers' ratings of behavior were also collected in order to capture as much information as possible concerning various aspects of adaptive behavior of adolescents who were learning disabled. The comparison group was a low-achieving group because adolescents with learning disabilities tend to be included in the lower-level secondary classes. Each student in the comparison was matched on race, sex, and class with a student in the learning disabled group. Finally, the student pairs were observed simultaneously by watching the student with disabilities for 10 seconds, the peer without disabilities for 10 seconds, and returning to the student with learning disabilities for the next 10 seconds. This captured instructional variations in the class.

The results of this multiple-measure study indicated that the students with learning disabilities were on-task less often than low-achieving students who were nondisabled. Also, the students with disabilities demonstrated more passive off-task behaviors than the low-achieving students. For example, when students with learning disabilities were off-task, they tended to demonstrate passive behaviors, such as staring off into space and playing with a pencil, rather than more disruptive behaviors. Neither the observed disruptions nor the teacher ratings of acting-out behavior indicated any difference in disruptive behavior between the two groups. When two different measurement methodologies (observation and teacher rating) indicate the same result, that result may be assumed to have more validity than a result from a study using only one measurement method. Consequently, this study indicated that adolescents who have learning disabilities are not more disruptive than low-achieving students in the secondary classes, though they are off-task more often than low-achieving students.

Research on the memory strategies among adolescents with learning disabilities suggests that the types of working-memory-strategy problems common among students in elementary grades who have disabilities may be common in secondary school as well (Hughes, 1996; Torgesen, 1984). Specifically, research suggests that teachers must incorporate memory-strategy instruction into their secondary-level classes.

SOCIAL AND EMOTIONAL CHARACTERISTICS IN SECONDARY CLASSROOMS

Secondary teachers generally indicate that, although academic problems are manageable, social and emotional problems such as poor self-concept, poor social skills and social relationships, lack of motivation, and poor attitudes toward school in general may be greater problems (Bender, 1999; Gans, Kenny, & Ghany, 2003; Tur-Kaspa, 2002). Bender (1994, 1999) suggested that personality, emotional, and social concerns may outweigh problems in academics among the adolescent populations who have learning disabilities. For example, consider the effect of the cumulative deficit in reading achievement described earlier. The typical male with learning disabilities in the early elementary grades may be only vaguely aware of the differences between his reading ability and the ability of other students in the class, but as his schooling progresses, he will become more aware of these differences. During the puberty period (grades 5 through 7, generally), he will become acutely aware of and embarrassed by his learning problems. At that time, it is often less embarrassing to answer the teacher rudely or make an inappropriate joke than to give an incorrect answer to a question in class. Consequently, disciplinary problems may result from attempts to hide or move the teacher's attention away from comprehension difficulties. For many students in the higher grades, attempts to cover an academic deficiency in such a fashion are quite common.

It should be pointed out that these social and personality problems seem to be demonstrated by some adolescents with learning disabilities and not by others (Bender & Wall, 1994; Lackaye, Margalit, Ziv, & Ziman, 2006). At present, there is no meaningful way to predict which children may demonstrate these problems in later years. Consequently, as a teacher who may work with adolescents who have learning disabilities, perhaps the best that you can do is to become aware of the possibility of some of these problems in some students.

Motivation and Emotional Well-Being

Teachers of secondary students with learning disabilities generally indicate that these students have certain problems in **motivation.** Although motivation for schoolwork is a common concern among all teachers, it is a particular problem for students who have repeatedly failed to successfully complete a particular learning task.

However, in the research on students with learning disabilities, there is no general measure of motivation of students. It seems surprising that, given the frequency with which the topic is discussed among teachers, no single questionnaire or rating yields information on this characteristic. Perhaps the concept of motivation can best be understood as an interaction between self-concept and locus-of-control orientation of adolescents with learning disabilities.

Self-Concept.   Research on the self-concept of adolescents with learning problems is very limited and often yields conflicting results. Several studies have indicated no difference between adolescents who have disabilities and those who do not, yet other studies have indicated some differences (Bender & Wall, 1994; Lackaye, Margalit, Ziv, & Ziman, 2006). As discussed earlier, self-concept may be defined in such a way as to include concept of oneself generally or concept in relation to specific school settings. The research tentatively suggests that adolescents with learning disabilities have an acceptable general self-concept (generally, they think they are OK people) but have a depressed self-concept in relation to academic settings. This can result in the student who may be a star pupil in math or vocational education courses, but who becomes completely unmotivated in reading-dependent courses such as history, science, or English in the secondary school curriculum.

Locus of Control.   *Locus of control* is defined as the perception of control over one's fate. Internally oriented persons believe that their own actions exert a major influence over their own fate, whereas externally oriented persons believe that factors outside of their own influence control their fate. Specifically, if adolescents with learning disabilities believe that their school fate (represented by grades) was not related to their efforts in studying, there would be little reason for these students to exert themselves. In the classroom, such a student may appear to be quite unmotivated, although in reality he or she would like to invest time in studying and class preparations. That student believes that such efforts are not related to the grades that are received.

Research on adolescents with learning disabilities has yielded conflicting results concerning the perception of locus of control of these students (Bender & Wall, 1994). However, the stronger studies that compared adolescents with and without disabilities indicate a difference in locus of control, with adolescents who have learning disabilities demonstrating a more external-locus-of-control orientation (Huntington & Bender, 1993).

Summary of Research.   Both self-concept and locus of control affect the effort that a student will invest in a learning task or homework assignment. Because of the lower self-concept and the tendency toward a perceived external locus of control among these students, teachers in secondary schools often are confronted with adolescents with disabilities who will not attempt homework, who do not put the time and energy into the seatwork in class (even when it is at an appropriate academic level), and who generally are poorly motivated to complete any school task. Teachers often feel a special need to reach out to these students in a personal way to encourage them to attempt the work. Unfortunately, even when personal rapport is developed between a teacher and an adolescent who has learning disabilities, the student may still refuse to make more than a cursory attempt at assignment completion. The potential interactions between the teacher's attempts to reach the student and the adolescent's external locus of control are varied and complex. These interactions may be further complicated if the student is severely depressed. Numerous problems can result even when the secondary teacher is sensitive to the student's emotional well-being.

A classroom example may be in order. Imagine a male with learning disabilities in the tenth grade in a vocational education class. Assume for the moment that the teacher is aware of the fact that this student helps his father in a lawnmower repair business and knows a great deal about two-cycle lawnmower engines. The teacher, in a concerned manner, attempts to create a brief success experience for the student by asking the student (in a nonembarrassing manner) to answer a question about two-cycle engines. The student refuses to answer or answers in a brief, incorrect mumble. The student knows the correct answer, and the teacher knows that the student knows the answer. The teacher asks again, and the student again refuses. The teacher, in disappointment and shock, turns to another student. Many teachers have been in this situation without completely understanding why a student who knows the answer will not answer the question.

Even when a student knows an answer, an external-locus-of-control orientation may prevent the student from answering. He may feel that if he answers, he has reinvested himself somehow in the very painful educational system that has consistently indicated that he is somehow a failure. In short, even when the answer is known and the teacher creates a positive situation, why try? The teacher also feels frustrated in the attempt to encourage successful participation in class. Thus, locus-of-control orientations can be very complicated motivational issues. Needless to say, many general education teachers who are otherwise very effective become discouraged and are unable to stimulate the adolescent with learning disabilities further. Should you eventually work with adolescents who have this disability, one challenge will be to continue to attempt to reach these students and encourage participation in class. Of course, this must be done in a nonthreatening manner.

To prevent the burnout experienced by some teachers, it is helpful to remember the pain that the adolescent with learning disabilities has experienced. The student is a social being and seeks approval socially from peers and teachers, and yet the student has been through years of school failure. Often, the student has been placed in impossible situations, where reading the assignment or completing the work is literally impossible. In a very real sense, an external orientation toward school failure may be viewed as a survival mechanism for the adolescent who is learning disabled. The entire school environment may have been telling that student that he or she is a failure for at least nine years, and an external locus of control allows the student the hope that such a message may be a mistake. Understanding the lack of motivation is relatively easy when one considers the responsibility of the school system in fostering such an uncaring attitude. Also, there are numerous reorganizations of the classroom environment that may be used to motivate such adolescents. These are reviewed briefly in Interest Box 8.5.

Depression and Suicide.   More recent research has, unfortunately, documented that the emotional difficulties of adolescents with learning disabilities are not confined to motivational problems. For example, a growing body of research has suggested that students with learning disabilities may be more at risk for depression and suicide than students without learning disabilities (Bender, 1999; Bender, Rosencrans, & Crane, 1999; Bender & Wall, 1994; Huntington & Bender, 1993; Maag & Behrens, 1989; McBride & Siegel, 1997). For example, Maag and Behrens (1989) investigated the prevalence and severity of depression of 465 secondary students. Multiple measures were used to assess depression, and the

■ ■ ■ ■ ■

INTEREST BOX 8.5

TEACHING TIPS: MOTIVATING THE ADOLESCENT WITH LD

Numerous authors have identified several motivational strategies that have been successfully used with secondary students who have learning disabilities. Although not all of these are possible for every secondary class, both mainstream and special education teachers should select the strategies that are appropriate for their classroom (Bender, 2002; Deshler et al., 1984).

1. Organize a token economy that rewards students for correct work when completed. Reinforcements may include privileges and extra time for student-selected activities.
2. Counseling has also been used in low-motivation situations. The counseling process should include information on the relevance of the material to be learned.
3. A contingency contract may be used with one student to encourage work completion. This is basically a written agreement between the teacher and the student that states the work to be completed and the student's self-chosen reward.
4. Verbal praise may also be used to encourage appropriate behavior. Either teacher or peer recognition may be used.
5. Cooperative group instruction may also be used to encourage meaningful participation. A student with learning disabilities will often complete work "for the team" that would not otherwise be completed.
6. Attribution training, which focuses directly on strengthening the student's internal locus of control, has also been shown to be effective. This focuses on internal motivation.
7. Self-monitoring procedures may also be effective in increasing a positive motivation, though research is still tentative.

results indicated that 20% of the male and 32% of the female junior high students with learning disabilities were severely depressed.

A number of researchers have indicated that this increased risk for depression may also lead to increased risk for suicide (Hayes & Sloat, 1988; Pfeffer, 1986). For example, Hayes and Sloat (1988) surveyed counselors in 129 Texas high schools to collect information on all suicide occurrences. Results indicated that over 14% of all suicide occurrences involved adolescents with learning disabilities, though that group accounts for only 4% of the secondary school population. These results were supported by Peck (1985), who indicated that, among all suicides reported to a Los Angeles suicide prevention center in one three-year period, 50% involved adolescents with learning disabilities. Clearly, teachers of students with learning disabilities may face adolescents with fairly severe depression or thoughts of suicide.

Social Life for Adolescents with Learning Disabilities

During adolescence, the social life of most individuals expands greatly to include significant others beyond the immediate family. For example, individuals usually begin to date formally during the junior high and senior high school years. The peer group becomes the norm-making group, and young persons are likely to spend as much or more of their waking hours with peers as with their family members. Consequently, the importance of social skills and social acceptance and the influence of the peer group increase during these school years.

As Chapter 4 demonstrated, the social acceptance of children who have learning disabilities is generally lower than for children without disabilities. However, during the adolescent years, social acceptance takes on an overwhelming degree of importance. For this reason, the teacher of the learning disabled must be aware of the available information concerning social acceptance of these adolescents.

Research has shown that the social acceptance of adolescents with learning disabilities is considerably below that of nondisabled students (Bender, 1987; Perlmutter, Crocker, Cordray, & Garstecki, 1983; Tur-Kaspa, 2002). However, the picture is not totally bleak. As Perlmutter and his co-workers (1983) indicated, there is a subgroup of students with learning disabilities who are very well regarded in the high school social climate. Also, among the other adolescents with learning problems, the research indicated that most of the students fell into a "neutral" range on the measurement scale rather than in the "active dislike" range. However, even with these qualifications, the picture for social acceptance of these adolescents is not as positive as one would like.

Researchers have speculated concerning the causes of this negative social behavior. Evidence suggests that adolescents with disabilities do demonstrate a certain lack of social sensitivity, which may play a part in the low social acceptance (Jackson, Enright, & Murdock, 1987). In fact, Leigh (1987) presented a comparison of children and adolescents with learning disabilities on ratings of communication and social skills, which seemed to suggest that ability in these areas decreased as children approached adolescence. Any or all of these factors could cause low levels of social acceptance among adolescents with learning disabilities.

SUMMARY OF EDUCATIONAL CHARACTERISTICS OF ADOLESCENTS WITH LEARNING DISABILITIES

As the preceding review demonstrates, the characteristics of many adolescents with learning disabilities are less than optimal for successful educational performance. Years of academic failure have often created an academic plateau of achievement around the fifth- to sixth-grade level. This prevents the student from meaningful involvement with many learning tasks in secondary schools. Also, this is compounded with attention, memory, and language problems that have not abated since the elementary school years. Finally, because of the inherent failure incorporated into the cumulative achievement deficit, the student may have developed low self-concept and perceived external locus of control that prohibit high levels of school motivation. Severe depression may develop, in some cases leading to thoughts of suicide. Also, the social skills and perceptions that are slow to develop increase the likelihood of being an outsider and not being socially accepted.

With this set of problems, the original cause of the particular learning disability (e.g., a lag in selective attention, a problem organizing material, a language delay) may seem almost trivial. Clearly, the secondary teacher of students with learning disabilities must deal with a great number of problems that the elementary teacher does not face. One additional problem, which is not related to the educational characteristics of the adolescent with disabilities, is the structure of schools and the expectations of the secondary school, compared to the elementary school. The next section presents several relevant aspects concerning the organization of secondary schools and secondary curriculum.

ADOLESCENTS WITH LEARNING DISABILITIES IN SECONDARY SCHOOL

Differences in School Organization

Departmentalized Curriculum.   There are numerous differences between the typical elementary classroom and the typical secondary classroom, and many of them impact on the educational opportunity of the adolescent with learning disabilities. First, the organization of the school day is different because in the typical secondary school the students change classes. This fact alone requires some degree of organization, particularly when a student must go to the locker during the break and get out the materials for the next several classes (books, homework assignments, projects, etc.). There may not be enough time during the next break to make a trip to the locker and return to a class across campus.

Pupil-Teacher Relationship.   The **departmentalized curriculum,** with a different teacher for each subject, means that the teachers know the adolescent with learning disabilities less well than did the general education elementary teachers. An elementary teacher typically has 25 to 30 students all day, but the secondary teacher may teach as many as 150 students a day (25 students in six different periods). For this reason, secondary teachers will generally be less well informed concerning the disabilities of any particular student.

Differential Teacher Preparation.   The training of the teachers at the elementary and secondary levels is quite different. Elementary teachers are taught to structure their classes around small-group, large-group, and individual-instructional formats. Also, a variety of instructional methods is used, including role-play, demonstrations, discussions, audiovisual materials, lectures, and field trips. Secondary teachers are much less varied in instructional technique and generally use only large-group instruction in a textbook/lecture format (Bender, 2002).

Teacher preparation differs because of certain historical reasons. Many of the early theories on child development suggested that the stages of human development stop around the age of 14. For example, both Freud and Piaget listed stages of development that ended at that age, and as public school curriculums were being formed during the early part of the 20th century, these theories were very influential. Teachers of children were presumed to need a healthy dose of child development courses and child psychology courses, whereas teachers for students above that age clearly needed more involvement in highly defined curriculum fields. In short, the assumption was that teachers of students above age 14 needed the same type of subject-area specialty that college instructors (teachers of adults) needed.

Practically speaking, most elementary teachers are taught to view each student as a growing, changing individual. Instructional groups are formed that facilitate individualized instruction or instruction with others at approximately the same developmental level. These teachers consider themselves teachers of children.

Secondary teachers consider themselves teachers of history, science, mathematics, and so on, instead of teachers of students. They have been trained to believe that instruction in the subject is their primary function, as opposed to instruction of students. These secondary teachers are trained to view their class as a unit rather than as a group of individuals with unique instructional needs. Further, the teacher preparation programs for secondary teachers generally include only a few child and adolescent development courses. As a result, these teachers are not usually taught how to individualize in their classes.

We now know that developmental stages proceed throughout life and that all teachers should differentiate their instruction to meet individual needs. Research has indicated that secondary teachers are not utilizing the types of instructional and test administration procedures that would facilitate learning for adolescents with disabilities (Klingner & Vaughn, 1999; Putnam, 1992a, 1992c). For example, Putnam demonstrated that adolescents with learning disabilities do not receive enough written feedback on test papers or on work assignments (Putnam, 1992c). The types of questions that secondary teachers utilize on classroom tests may further impair adolescents with learning disabilities (Putnam, 1992a).

In a recent synthesis of several research studies, Klingner and Vaughn (1999) identified a number of perceptions of adolescents with learning disabilities concerning the type of instruction they received in secondary school. This review suggests that the school environment as presently structured is not amenable to effective instruction for students with learning disabilities. Specifically, students with disabilities need modified grading practices, in-class assistance with homework, specific examples in classwork, frequent assistance with classwork and homework, and numerous other teaching modifications (Klingner & Vaughn, 1999). While a wide variety of modifications are available for students in secondary classes, research has consistently demonstrated that these modifications are not common (Baker & Zigmond, 1990; Klingner & Vaughn, 1999). Further, many of the accommodations made for students with learning disabilities have the effect of reducing the curriculum to memorization of a few meaningless and often unrelated facts rather than addressing basic concepts (Ellis & Wortham, 1999). In such a curriculum, learning is unlikely to take place, and classroom instruction is certainly less than stimulating.

Failure to provide accommodations, or providing inappropriate accommodations, to secondary students may lead to their increasing frustration with school, which can, in turn, cause students to drop out. Research has demonstrated that dropping out is a serious problem for students with learning disabilities (Levin, Zigmond, & Birch, 1985). Interest Box 8.6 presents several suggestions for helping secondary teachers prevent dropouts.

It would be hard to imagine a third-grade classroom in which the teacher does not form small groups for reading instruction, but many professionals in secondary schools have not been trained to apply this type of instructional model to the secondary class. Still, students with learning disabilities will benefit from a secondary teacher's knowledge of individualization practices. Different readings may be assigned, different tests given, and worksheets and participatory outlines for lectures may be used to provide help for secondary students with disabilities in the content-area classes. Group projects, debates, and art projects may also be used to demonstrate comprehension of subject material. All of these

INTEREST BOX 8.6

TEACHING TIPS: PREVENTING DROPOUTS

Some research suggests that as many as 50% of students with learning disabilities may drop out of school prior to graduation (Levin et al., 1985). However, this figure may be conservative because it is based on a specially designed program that was intended to reduce the dropout rate. In secondary schools where no specialized programs exist, the dropout rate may be higher.

Still, several factors may be identified that tend to encourage dropouts (Scanlon & Mellard, 2002). First, the secondary school, because of the departmentalized structure and regular class changes, is not organized in a fashion to encourage strong teacher/pupil relationships. Second, the phenomenon of cumulative deficit suggests that the academic level of adolescents with learning disabilities will not increase after a certain point. Several dropouts interviewed by Levin and his co-workers indicated that they had been encouraged to leave school for academic and behavioral reasons. Finally, as Johnson (1984) indicated, the major characteristics of the disability itself may change such that emotional and social concerns become at least as important as the attention or language problem that originally led to development of the learning disability. This leads to confusion among the professionals in terms of selection of appropriate programs for adolescents with disabilities.

Several general guidelines may assist you in combating the dropout problem:

1. Be sensitive to the emotional needs of the adolescents you serve. Self-concept and locus-of-control problems tend to be visible in many ways. Watch for the small signs—grades going down, sleepiness, a change in attitude, or other intangibles.
2. Discuss openly and honestly with each student any indications of changing motivation that you may notice. Adolescents must be treated as adults in these areas, even though they may not have complete understanding of the emotional or self-concept conflicts that they feel.
3. Discuss with each student his or her schoolwork from other classes in order to express your concern.
4. Indicate the advantages of finishing school relative to obtaining a good job, etc.
5. Find some way to make learning rewarding for each student, using the rewards that the student finds meaningful.
6. Find something in each student of which that student can be proud—something that the student does better than everyone else. Have the student showcase this skill.

strategies would facilitate inclusion of the secondary student who has learning disabilities (Bender, 2002).

At present, colleges and universities are only beginning to address these needs in the methods classes required of preservice secondary teachers. Consequently, as a special education teacher, you may be required to consult with secondary teachers in inclusive classes in order to help them begin to utilize these different methods of instruction more frequently.

Curriculum Emphasis Change.   Finally, the curriculum emphasis shifts between the early years of school and the secondary school years (Bender, 2002; De La Paz & MacArthur, 2003). Whereas the elementary grades are dedicated to instruction in basic skills such as reading, math, and language arts, the secondary curriculum includes a number of classes based on subject-area content. For example, few school districts have developed vocational education programs during the early years of school, though these are quite common in later school years. Also, because of the previously discussed training differences, the teachers in the subject areas generally do not consider basic-skill instruction as their responsibility. Secondary teachers view themselves as content specialists in history, health, science, and so on. As a result of this combination of factors and the low basic skill level of adolescents who are learning disabled, many of these students are left to wander through the secondary curriculum with little chance for success. This problem may also lead to the increasing number of these students who drop out of school prior to graduation.

Minimum Graduation Standards.   As one component of the standards-based curriculum movement, discussed in Chapter 7, many states have developed minimum standards tests that a student must pass before completing the secondary school curriculum and graduating from high school (Cawley, Parmar, Foley, Salmon, & Roy, 2001; Johnson, Kimball, Olson-Brown, & Anderson, 2001; Lanford & Cary, 2000; Manset & Washburn, 2000; Thurlow, Ysseldyke, & Reid, 1997). These assessments typically represent what is believed to be minimum basic competency for success in our society, and that is often specified as achievement roughly at the eighth-grade level. In some cases, these assessments are referred to as "exit tests" or "exit criteria." Other practitioners use the phrase "high-stakes" assessments, because failure on these tests may result in failure to graduate—a high-stakes result from the perspective of a student with a learning disability.

Further, for students with learning disabilities, who may be achieving in reading, math, and language arts at the fifth- or sixth-grade level (the typical post–high school achievement level for many such students), passing a high school standards test may be quite a challenge. As an alternative, many states offer students with disabilities an option of graduating with a nonstandard diploma (sometimes referred to as a certificate of attendance) that stipulates the child has attended a certain number of years of schooling (Lanford & Cary, 2000). Other states allow for a wide variety of accommodations in the graduation assessment for students with various disabilities. Although this may allow many students with learning disabilities to graduate from high school, this practice does raise concerns about the validity of the modified assessment (Johnson et al., 2001; Zurcher & Bryant, 2001). Regardless of how states address the issue of exit criteria assessments at the end of high school, this movement toward testing for high school graduation represents an additional demand on the adolescent with learning disabilities. As a teacher in the field, you should ascertain the graduation requirements for students with learning disabilities in your state and keep them in mind as you develop your individualized education programs for your students.

Educational Program Options
for Adolescents with Learning Disabilities   *read this*

Various scholars have identified the responses that secondary school personnel have made in order to accommodate the needs of the adolescent with learning disabilities (Deshler, Schumaker, Lenz, & Ellis, 1984; Johnson, 1984; Zigmond & Sansone, 1986). A synthesis of this research reveals several distinctly different program options that have been used over recent years for these adolescents. It is crucial that you, as a prospective teacher, understand these programs because such basic decisions as the curriculum that you will be using depend on the program option your school adopts.

First, many schools employ a content instruction model or **tutorial model** in which special education is used as a tutoring program for the content areas. In other words, the program for a particular adolescent with learning disabilities would include several inclusive classes in subject areas; and for one or two periods each day the student would receive instruction on content-area work (Johnson, 1984; Zigmond & Sansone, 1986). If your school system uses such a program, you will function as a tutor in the subject areas, even though you may not be certified to teach content areas such as history or science (McKenzie, 1991).

Numerous school systems have adopted a **basic-skills remediation model** in which the special education class period is used in reading, language arts, and math instruction, independent of the instruction in the inclusive classes. In this type of program, there is very little distinction between the learning disability teacher and the reading tutor.

A third type of program is the **work-study model,** which emphasizes job skills and job experiences as a part of the school day. Students may spend as much as half a day working at a job off the school campus (Zigmond & Sansone, 1986).

A **functional-skills model** of curriculum—which includes instruction in various survival skills such as completion of job applications, taxation forms, and the like—is another program option (Johnson, 1984). In many cases, this option may be combined with the other curricular emphases, including basic-skills remediation and work-study models.

With the increasing evidence that adolescents with learning disabilities may demonstrate a metacognitive deficit (see discussion of perspectives in Chapter 1), numerous secondary schools have adopted the **learning-strategies model.** This model was developed by Deshler and associates at the University of Kansas (Deshler et al., 1984) and includes a number of learning strategies designed to assist the adolescent with disabilities in coping with the demands of the standard high school curriculum (Bender, 2002).

Zigmond and Sansone (1986) discussed the **consultation model,** in which a learning consultant with specialized knowledge of learning disabilities works with the general education teachers in an effort to restructure the traditional high school curriculum. The consultant does not teach the adolescent with learning disabilities directly, but spends time working with the general education teachers in devising various instructional strategies to assist these adolescent learners.

Finally, with the increasing emphasis on providing a wide range of placement options, many school districts are providing an **inclusive service delivery** option. In inclusion programs, the special education teacher and general education teachers teach the students with and without disabilities together in the inclusive class. The inclusive service delivery model has been bolstered by an emerging instructional approach that is receiving increased national attention—the differentiated instruction approach (Bender, 2002; Tomlinson, 1999). This instructional procedure involves adapting the instructional strategies and tactics in the general education class to accommodate learners with more diverse learning needs. While differentiated instruction is not utilized exclusively for students with learning disabilities, such instruction can result in more successful learning endeavors for these students. This model is described in more detail in Chapter 9.

Selecting Educational Programming for Adolescents with Learning Disabilities

Given the types of learning problems associated with adolescents who are learning disabled and the structure of the school programs in secondary schools, you and the other professionals must find or create an educational program that is feasible for each student in your charge. The learning characteristics for each adolescent will vary, and as you can see, a number of program options exist for the adolescent with learning disabilities in secondary schools. Each of these includes certain assumptions, advantages, and disadvantages that may make the program more or less appropriate for a particular student. Interest Box 8.7 presents in brief some of the assumptions behind these several models, though for a more involved discussion of these issues, you should review the references at the end of this chapter.

In selecting a program, a teacher should confer with the entire child-study team, as well as the student and the parents, in order to provide the best type of program. Program options are frequently combined for particular students in order to provide the services that are needed. Also, the student and the parents should be included in the decision-making process, particularly concerning choices regarding vocational courses, work study, adapted curriculum, consultation, and other aspects of the program. Houck, Geller, and Engelhard (1988) reported that teachers of adolescents with learning disabilities include these students in educational planning meetings more than do middle school teachers. As students grow older, they should be involved more in selections of educational options. Such involvement is likely to encourage more participation and better behavior in the final years of public school.

SUMMARY

This chapter has presented research on manifestations of learning disabilities in elementary and secondary classrooms. It is clear that mere knowledge of cognitive, attention, language, and behavior characteristics of pupils with disabilities is not enough for the teacher who will teach these students. Knowledge of the specific manifestation of these characteristics in class must be provided so that you, as the teacher, may make informed judgments concerning behavior management and instruction.

First, the adaptive behavior patterns demonstrated by children and adolescents with learning disabilities are not consistent with success in inclusive classes. Task orientation of these pupils is very low because of the combined nature of the various problems in attention. Also, some pupils who are learning disabled may demonstrate hyperactive or disruptive behaviors in classes, resulting in additional problems with which the teacher must contend.

Next, interactions between general education teachers and pupils with learning disabilities have been shown to be less than optimal. These students are likely to hear many more statements concerning behavioral management than instruction. Also, the types of instructional questions asked of children with learning problems may be at inappropriate cognitive levels to assure maximum learning and school achievement. Clearly, you will have to decide regularly (if not daily) what types of instructional questions to ask because merely following the question formats of the teacher's manual does not abrogate your instructional responsibility to the individual student and is not as challenging for many

INTEREST BOX 8.7

ASSUMPTIONS BEHIND THE MODELS OF INSTRUCTION FOR ADOLESCENTS WITH LEARNING DISABILITIES

APPROACH	ADVANTAGES	DISADVANTAGES
Basic skills	Stresses basic reading and math skills that improve success. Emphasizes only skills necessary for success in school. Easily modeled on the elementary curriculum.	Turns special educator into a basic-skills tutor or reading tutor. Eliminates teaching of specialized methods that are replaced by remedial instruction.
Tutorial in subject areas	Complements the entire school curriculum rather than just basic skills. Subject-area teachers usually appreciate the help. Consistent with state-adopted curriculum standards.	Forces special teacher to teach subjects for which the teacher may not be certified. May overlook skills essential for life in order to cover the subject-area requirements.
Functional	Stresses essential skill areas used later in life. Students see relevance of this content.	Represents a view of potential that is pessimistic. Students may miss certain skills.
Work study	Students learn a job during school time. Research demonstrates importance of vocational preparation.	May represent a pessimistic view of the potential learner's ability to learn the usual curriculum. May eliminate the student from further educational possibilities.
Consultation	Can facilitate the use of newer and different instructional ideas because of consultant input.	Not supported by a strong research base. May lead to conflict between the general education teacher and consultant.
Inclusion	Maintains the student in the regular class.	The student may be lost in the class and not receive needed services.
Learning strategies	A research basis has been provided that demonstrates the effectiveness of this approach. Incorporates general education teachers into the instructional strategy. Provides ideas that generalize to other areas.	Very rarely used because of the limited dissemination of material. Requires input and participation from the general education teachers, who may choose not to give it.

teachers. Although there are no definitive rules concerning the types of questions that are most effective, you must make informed decisions now. This is part of the challenge, the responsibility, and the joy of being a professional educator.

An emphasis on students with learning disabilities and their interaction with secondary education programs is a recent research endeavor, and research is ongoing. Still, there are some conclusions available from this research. Adolescents with learning disabilities demonstrate deficits in achievement in many basic-skill areas, and these tend to increase over time. These deficits are compounded with the attention, language, and memory problems common to all students at any age who are learning disabled. However, the secondary school is generally less capable of meeting the needs of these students than are the elementary schools because of the structure of the school, the preparation of teachers, and the departmentalized curriculum. This combination of factors may contribute to the increasing dropout rate of adolescents with disabilities.

Researchers have specified several different educational programming models for use in the secondary schools. The models vary widely in the content of the recommended curriculum and the assumptions behind each model. As an educator concerned with students who are learning disabled, you will want to become familiar with the various models and the assumptions behind them. These instructional programming models may drastically affect the material you are expected to teach in your class.

The following points should help you in studying this chapter:

- The cognitive deficiencies presented earlier—lower intelligence, poor attention, language deficiencies, and memory problems—result in an inability of students with learning disabilities to adapt to the demands of the elementary school classroom.
- The attention problems of students who are learning disabled result in lower task orientation in elementary classrooms.
- Some students with learning disabilities may demonstrate hyperactive or disruptive behaviors, but most do not.
- Students who have learning disabilities interact with elementary teachers in ways that are less than optimal. These students receive many more commands to change behavior than instructional questions.
- The slower rate of achievement among students with learning disabilities tends to accumulate over the years so that they are much more deficient in reading skills compared to their classmates in high school than they were in the elementary grades.
- Students who are learning disabled tend to hit a plateau of achievement at around the fifth- or sixth-grade level and not progress much beyond that point, even in high school.
- Secondary students with learning disabilities have suffered through years of difficulty in schoolwork, and this often results in many motivation problems among these students. These students are at risk for severe depression and possibly suicide.
- The social life of many of these adolescents is less than satisfactory because they are not as socially accepted as their peers. However, there seems to be a group of students with learning disabilities who are socially accepted.
- The departmentalized curriculum in secondary schools makes organizational demands on students with disabilities that may result in emphasizing their disability.

- Various secondary instructional models are used with adolescents who are learning disabled, including tutorial instruction, basic-skills remediation, work study, functional-skills materials, and learning-strategies approaches.
- Differentiated instruction represents one new instructional model that should support students with learning disabilities in the general education classroom.

QUESTIONS AND ACTIVITIES

1. What reasons can you give for the dispute concerning the level of disruptive behavior among elementary school children with learning disabilities?

2. Interview a general education and a special education elementary teacher separately concerning adaptive behavior of pupils with learning problems. Compare and contrast their responses. Inquire concerning the strategies that these teachers use to manage behavior.

3. Study information on question formats and the relationship between question format and increased comprehension among elementary school children. What tentative conclusions may be drawn concerning appropriate question formats for children who have no disabilities?

4. Read the research presented here on teacher interaction patterns. Does this research support your own observations (from laboratory or clinical fieldwork experiences) concerning how teachers relate to pupils with learning disabilities in their classes?

5. Obtain a copy of Tomlinson's book *The Differentiated Classroom* (1999), and present a report on it to the class.

6. What program options are used in the local high schools in your area? Interview a teacher of the disabled about the types of instructional materials used and the possibility of work-study programs.

7. What is the relationship between teacher preparation and the level of individual instruction in elementary and secondary classes?

8. Discuss the development of attention behaviors. Is attention a phenomenon that develops over time? Read several of the articles referenced here, and present these to the class.

9. What does the research suggest about the effectiveness of the work-study model as an instructional option for adolescents with learning disabilities?

10. Discuss the limitations that the various instructional models place on adolescents who are learning disabled, in terms of further education and job placement opportunities.

11. List the several ways in which elementary students with disabilities and adolescents with the same condition differ in cognitive and social-emotional characteristics. What does this list suggest about possible outcomes of education?

REFERENCES

Alber, S. R., Heward, W. L., & Hippler, B. J. (1999). Teaching middle school students with learning disabilities to recruit positive teacher attention. *Exceptional Children, 65,* 253–270.

American Psychiatric Association (APA) (1993). *DSM-IV draft criteria.* Washington, DC: Author.

Baker, J. M., & Zigmond, N. (1990). Are regular education classes equipped to accommodate students with learning disabilities? *Exceptional Children, 56,* 516–526.

Barkley, R. A. (1990). *Attention deficit hyperactivity disorders: A handbook for diagnosis and treatment.* New York: Guilford.

Bender, W. N. (1985a). Differences between learning disabled and non-learning disabled children in temperament and behavior. *Learning Disability Quarterly, 8,* 11–18.

Bender, W. N. (1985b). Differential diagnosis based on task-related behavior of learning disabled and low-achieving adolescents. *Learning Disability Quarterly, 8,* 261–266.

Bender, W. N. (1999). Learning disabilities in the classroom. In W. N. Bender (Ed.), *Professional issues in learning disabilities* (pp. 3–26). Austin, TX: ProEd.

Bender, W. N. (2002). *Differentiating instruction for students with learning disabilities.* Thousand Oaks, CA: Corwin Press.

Bender, W. N., & Golden, L. G. (1988). Adaptive behavior of learning disabled and non-learning disabled children. *Learning Disability Quarterly, 11,* 55–61.

Bender, W. N., Rosencrans, C. B., & Crane, M. K. (1999). Stress, depression, and suicide among adolescents with learning disabilities: Assessing the risk. *Learning Disability Quarterly, 22,* 143–156.

Bender, W. N., & Wall, M. E. (1994). Social-emotional development of students with learning disabilities. *Learning Disability Quarterly, 17,* 323–341.

Bryan, T. (2005). Science-based advances in the social domain of learning disabilities. *Learning Disability Quarterly, 28* (2), 119–121.

Bryan, T., Burstein, K., & Ergul, C. (2004). The social-emotional side of learning disabilities: A science-based presentation of the state of the art. *Learning Disability Quarterly, 27* (1), 45–52.

Bulgren, J. A., & Carta, J. J. (1992). Examining the instructional contexts of students with learning disabilities. *Exceptional Children, 59,* 182–191.

Cawley, J., Parmar, R., Foley, T. E., Salmon, S., & Roy, S. (2001). Arithmetic performance of students: Implications for standards and programming. *Exceptional Children, 67*(3), 311–330.

De La Paz, S., & MacArthur, C. (2003). Knowing the how and why of history: Expectations for secondary students with and without learning disabilities. *Learning Disability Quarterly, 26* (2), 142–154.

Deshler, D. D., Schumaker, J. B., & Lenz, B. K. (1984). Academic and cognitive interventions for LD adolescents: Part I. *Journal of Learning Disabilities, 17,* 108–117.

Deshler, D. D., Schumaker, J. B., Lenz, B. K., & Ellis, E. (1984). Academic and cognitive interventions for

LD adolescents: Part II. *Journal of Learning Disabilities, 17,* 170–179.

Drame, E. R. (2002). Socio-cultural context effects on teachers' readiness to refer for learning disabilities. *Exceptional Children, 69*(1), 41–53.

Elias, M. J. (2004). The connection between social-emotional learning and learning disabilities: Implications for intervention. *Learning Disability Quarterly, 27* (1), 53–63.

Elksnin, L. K., & Elksnin, N. (2004). The social-emotional side of learning disabilities. *Learning Disability Quarterly, 27* (1), 3–8.

Ellis, E. S., & Wortham, J. F. (1999). "Watering up" content instruction. In W. N. Bender (Ed.), *Professional issues in learning disabilities* (pp. 141–186). Austin, TX: ProEd.

Gans, A. M., Kenny, M. C., & Ghany, D. L. (2003). Comparing the self-concept of students with and without learning disabilities. *Journal of Learning Disabilities, 36* (3), 287–295.

Gregory, G. H., & Chapman, C. (2001). *Differentiated instructional strategies: One size doesn't fit all.* Thousand Oaks, CA: Corwin Press.

Hayes, M. L., & Sloat, R. S. (1988). Preventing suicide in learning disabled children and adolescents. *Academic Therapy, 24,* 221–230.

Houck, C. K., Geller, C. H., & Engelhard, J. (1988). Learning disabilities teachers' perceptions of educational programs for adolescents with learning disabilities. *Journal of Learning Disabilities, 20,* 90–97.

Hughes, C. A. (1996). Memory and test-taking strategies. In D. D. Deshler, E. S. Ellis, & B. K. Lenz (Eds.), *Teaching adolescents with learning disabilities* (2nd ed.). Denver: Love.

Huntington, D. D., & Bender, W. N. (1993). Adolescents with learning disabilities at risk? Emotional well-being, depression, suicide. *Journal of Learning Disabilities, 26,* 159–166.

Ivarie, J., Hogue, D., & Brulle, A. R. (1984). An investigation of mainstream teacher time spent with students labeled learning disabled. *Exceptional Children, 51,* 142–149.

Jackson, S. C., Enright, R. D., & Murdock, J. Y. (1987). Social perception problems in learning disabled youth: Developmental lag versus perceptual deficit. *Journal of Learning Disabilities, 20,* 361–364.

Johnson, C. L. (1984). The learning disabled adolescent and young adult: An overview and critique of current practices. *Journal of Learning Disabilities, 17,* 386–391.

Johnson, E., Kimball, K., Olson-Brown, S., & Anderson, D. (2001). A statewide review of use of accommodations in large-scale, high-stakes assessments. *Exceptional Children, 67*(2), 251–264.

Klingner, J. K., & Vaughn, S. (1999). Students' perceptions of instruction in inclusion classrooms: Implications for students with learning disabilities. *Exceptional Children, 66* (1), 23–37.

Lackaye, T., Margalit, M., Ziv, O., & Ziman, T. (2006). Comparisons of self-efficacy, mood, effort, and hope between students with learning disabilities and their non-LD peers. *Learning Disabilities Research and Practice, 21* (2), 111–121.

Lanford, A. D., & Cary, L. G. (2000). Graduation requirements for students with disabilities: Legal and practice considerations. *Remedial and Special Education, 21*(3), 152–161.

Leigh, J. (1987). Adaptive behavior of children with learning disabilities. *Journal of Learning Disabilities, 20,* 557–562.

Levin, E. K., Zigmond, N., & Birch, J. W. (1985). A follow-up study of 52 learning disabled adolescents. *Journal of Learning Disabilities, 18,* 2–7.

Maag, J. W., & Behrens, J. T. (1989). Depression and cognitive self-statements of learning disabled and seriously emotionally disturbed adolescents. *Journal of Special Education, 23,* 17–27.

Manset, G., & Washburn, S. J. (2000). Equity through accountability? Mandating minimum competency exit examinations for secondary students with learning disabilities. *Learning Disabilities Research and Practice, 15*(3), 160–167.

McBride, H. E. A., & Siegel, L. S. (1997). Learning disabilities and adolescent suicide. *Journal of Learning Disabilities, 30*(6), 652–659.

McKenzie, R. G. (1991). Content area instruction delivered by secondary learning disabilities teachers: A national survey. *Learning Disabilities Quarterly, 14,* 115–122.

McKinney, J. D., & Feagans, L. (1983). Adaptive classroom behavior of learning disabled students. *Journal of Learning Disabilities, 16,* 360–367.

Peck, M. L. (1985). Crisis intervention treatment with chronically and acutely suicidal adolescents. In M. Peck, N. Farberow, & R. Litman (Eds.), *Youth suicide* (pp. 1–33). New York: Springer-Verlag.

Perlmutter, B. F., Crocker J., Cordray, D., & Garstecki, D. (1983). Sociometric status and related personality characteristics of mainstreamed learning disabled adolescents. *Learning Disability Quarterly, 6,* 20–30.

Pfeffer, C. R. (1986). *The suicidal child.* New York: Guilford.

Putnam, M. L. (1992a). Characteristics of questions on tests administered by mainstream secondary classroom teachers. *Learning Disabilities Research and Practice, 7,* 129–136.

Putnam, M. L. (1992b). Readability estimates of content area textbooks used by students mainstreamed into secondary classrooms. *Learning Disabilities, 3,* 53–59.

Putnam, M. L. (1992c). Written feedback provided by mainstream secondary classroom teachers. *Learning Disabilities, 3,* 35–41.

Russ, S., Chiang, B., Rylance, B. J., & Bongers, J. (2001). Caseload in special education: An integration of research findings. *Exceptional Children, 67*(2), 161–172.

Scanlon, D., & Mellard, D. F. (2002). Academic and participation profiles of school-age dropouts with and without disabilities. *Exceptional Children, 68*(2), 239–258.

Slate, J. R., & Saudargas, R. A. (1986). Differences in learning disabled and average students' classroom behaviors. *Learning Disability Quarterly, 9,* 61–67.

Smith, T. J., & Adams, G. (2004). The effect of comorbid AD/HD and learning disabilities on parent-reported behavioral and academic outcomes of children. *Learning Disability Quarterly, 27* (2), 101–112.

Teglasi, H., Cohn, A., & Meshbesher, N. (2004). Temperament and learning disability. *Learning Disability Quarterly, 27* (1), 9–20.

Thurlow, M. L., Ysseldyke, J. E., & Reid, C. L. (1997). High school graduation requirements for students with disabilities. *Journal of Learning Disabilities, 30*(6), 608–616.

Tomlinson, C. A. (1999). *The differentiated classroom: Responding to the needs of all learners.* Alexandria, VA: Association for Supervision and Curriculum Development.

Torgesen, J. K. (1984). Memory processes in reading disabled children. *Journal of Learning Disabilities, 18,* 350–357.

Tur-Kaspa, H. (2002). The socio-emotional adjustment of adolescents with LD in the kibbutz during high school and transition periods. *Journal of Learning Disabilities, 35*(1), 87–96.

Wallace, T., Anderson, A. R., Bartholomay, T., & Hupp, S. (2002). An ecobehavioral examination of high school classrooms that include students with disabilities. *Exceptional Children, 68*(3), 345–359.

Weller, C., & Strawser, S. (1981). *Weller-Strawser Scales of Adaptive Behavior for the Learning Disabled.* Novato, CA: Academic Therapy.

Zigmond, N., & Sansone, J. (1986). Designing a program for the learning disabled adolescent. *Remedial and Special Education, 7*(5), 13–17.

Zurcher, R., & Bryant, D. P. (2001). The validity and comparability of entrance examination scores after accommodations are made for students with LD. *Journal of Learning Disabilities, 34*(5), 462–471.

PLACEMENT, SERVICES, AND EDUCATIONAL TREATMENTS

This section presents information on the commonly used placement, services, and educational treatment approaches for children and adolescents with learning disabilities. Chapter 9 presents models of educational placements and service delivery. Behavioral treatments, discussed in Chapter 10, are the most influential type of educational treatment used today. Metacognitive treatments, presented in Chapter 11, are receiving the most attention by researchers in the field, and use of these strategies is increasing. Computer-assisted instruction is increasing in use as technology advances, and techniques and applications are covered in Chapter 12. In Chapter 13, characteristics and vocational and college opportunities for youth and adults with learning disabilities are presented. Finally, in Chapter 14, future issues in the field are explored.

CHAPTER NINE

EDUCATIONAL PLACEMENTS AND SERVICES

CHAPTER OUTLINE

WHEN YOU COMPLETE THIS CHAPTER, YOU SHOULD BE ABLE TO:

1. Describe the cascade of services and state the reasons for the importance of this model.

2. Identify the types of educational placements in which students with learning disabilities are typically found.

3. Describe the five types of resource rooms.

4. Identify the four curricular thrusts typically emphasized in special education for students who are learning disabled.

5. Describe the regular education initiative and its implications for the learning disabled.

6. Identify strategies that facilitate inclusion.

7. Describe Project RIDE.

8. Describe the implications of cross-categorical certification and placement practices for students with learning disabilities.

9. Discuss the efficacy of peer tutoring in elementary classes.

10. Describe several cooperative instructional plans for inclusive classes.

11. Describe the methods used in attribution training for the child with learning disabilities.

12. List the major biochemical agents that have been discussed as possible causes or cures for learning disabilities.

13. Describe differentiated instruction.

KEYWORDS

Deno's Cascade of Services
self-contained class
resource class
categorical resource rooms
inclusion movement
regular education initiative (REI)
ALEM
differentiated instruction
cubing

prereferral modification
Project RIDE
SWAT teams
cross-categorical placement
peer tutoring
cooperative instruction
jigsaw
jigsaw II
STAD

team-assisted individualization
group investigation
attribution training
scotopic sensitivity
Irlen lenses
megavitamins
trace elements

INTRODUCTION

One of the most difficult decisions that must be made, once a student is identified as learning disabled, concerns the type of educational placement to which he or she should be assigned. For example, should a child with learning disabilities be placed in a full-time special education class for the learning disabled, a resource room class, a general education class with certain modifications, or an inclusive classroom? Information on the various characteristics that the student displays is crucial in making these decisions, as is information on the different types of classes.

Deno (1970) formulated a model by which considerations concerning educational placement decisions may be made. Though this model was formulated a number of years ago, it is still very relevant to any discussion of educational placements because the model immediately preceded the passage of Public Law 94-142 and became the basis for many current educational-placement models. Also, the placement categories currently used by the federal government's Office of Special Education and Rehabilitation Services are adaptations of Deno's original categories (Danielson & Bellamy, 1989). Figure 9.1 presents a revision of **Deno's Cascade of Services.**

The model assumed that students would be relatively mobile and would be placed at different levels as their educational needs required. For example, early advocates of the model assumed that, if a child with learning disabilities in a general education class should need special help when he or she was learning cursive writing, a placement in the resource room would be arranged for one period each day for only a few weeks to assist with that problem. The length of placement was intended to vary with the type and severity of the educational problem, and a great deal of flexibility was envisioned.

Unfortunately, educational placements since the passage of PL 94-142 in the 1970s have not been nearly as flexible as this original assumption suggested (Kavale, 2000). Evidence has demonstrated that various states are implementing the laws and regulations regarding placement in very different ways (Danielson & Bellamy, 1989; Reschly & Hosp, 2004). For example, Danielson and Bellamy (1989) presented evidence suggesting that states vary widely in terms of where the special education students are placed. Some states use self-contained placements much more frequently than others, whereas other states emphasize inclusive placements. Finally, most researchers would agree that the ideal level of mobility envisioned in Deno's Cascade has not been realized. Many students who are placed in special education never leave the type of class into which they were originally placed, and this does not suggest the mobility within the placement system envisioned by Deno. Many practitioners hope that inclusive programs may provide increasing flexibility of placement (Kavale, 2000).

Because students with learning disabilities tend to demonstrate more mild problems than severe problems, the greatest number of children in the nation are served in the upper levels of the cascade. For example, it would be very difficult to find many students with learning disabilities in homebound instructional

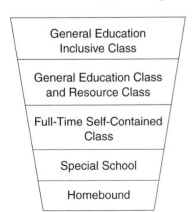

| General Education Inclusive Class |
| General Education Class and Resource Class |
| Full-Time Self-Contained Class |
| Special School |
| Homebound |

FIGURE 9.1   Cascade of Services

settings because their social skills, language skills, and academic skills are such that these students generally do quite well in a much less restrictive placement. This is not to suggest that no restrictive placements exist for students with learning disabilities. There are numerous private residential schools for these students throughout the country. However, the vast majority of students with learning disabilities may be found in public school placements at the higher levels within the model.

Over the last decade, there has been some modification to the overall service delivery scheme, generally referred to as the *inclusive schools* emphasis. In a broad sense, inclusive schools make every effort to include all students with disabilities at every severity level in the regular classes by providing the assistance required for the education of those children to the mainstream teachers (Kavale, 2000; National Association of State Boards of Education, 1992; Wallace, Anderson, Bartholomay, & Hupp, 2002; Zigmond, 2003). In many cases, special education teachers and general education teachers actually teach in the same classroom, in team teaching or co-teaching.

Perhaps the most useful way to develop an understanding of these models for placement is a historical approach. Initially, homebound and hospital programs were used with students who had any type of learning problem, but these models were never widely used with students with learning disabilities. Upon the initial recognition that learning disabilities were somehow different from mental retardation, the self-contained model for service delivery was very prominent—particularly during the years before federal legislation required educational services for students with disabilities. More recently, the resource room has been used more frequently. However, the inclusive model has received increasing attention during the last few years, and many school districts have shifted toward inclusive service delivery (Kavale, 2000; Reschly & Hosp, 2004). The next sections of the chapter will present each of these placement models in more detail.

SELF-CONTAINED CLASSES

The **self-contained class** is generally the most restrictive setting in which children with learning disabilities are found. In this type of placement, the student is removed from the general education class for all or most of the school day (Kavale, 2000). Typically, only a small percentage of all the children who are learning disabled in any given district will be found in this type of placement. Also, in many cases, children in self-contained classes are placed in other classes for a small part of the school day—perhaps one period in physical education, music, or art.

Teacher's Role

The responsibility of the teacher of the self-contained class for students with learning disabilities includes instruction in the entire curriculum. For example, the teacher will generally be expected to teach reading, language arts, mathematics, science, social science, health, physical education, and the fine arts. Other non-subject-area emphases may be added as well, including instruction in social skills, self-concept enhancement, or other areas. As you can readily see, this type of teaching load includes numerous instructional requirements.

In spite of these heavy teaching responsibilities, many teachers enjoy working in a self-contained setting. Also, many states enforce policies intended to lighten this burden somewhat. For example, many states set maximum student/staff ratios very low—8 students with learning disabilities per teacher or 12 students in classes that include a teacher and a paraprofessional (teacher's aide)—whereas a resource teacher may have a caseload of 20 to 25 students each day. Further, the teacher of the self-contained class generally does not have the responsibility for offering assistance to general education teachers to the same degree as does the resource teacher. Consequently, teachers in self-contained classes spend much less time interacting with other teachers than do resource or consultant special education teachers.

Students' Characteristics

The characteristics of the students with learning disabilities who are placed in self-contained rooms tend to set them apart somewhat from students with learning disabilities in resource or inclusive class placements. For example, students placed in self-contained classes generally receive all of their academic work in those classes. In other words, the child-study team decided that the academic deficits caused by the learning disability were so severe that the student could not succeed academically in inclusive classes. Consequently, the academic capabilities of students with learning disabilities in self-contained classes tend to be somewhat lower.

In one of the early studies on alternative placements for the learning disabled, Olson and Midgett (1984) compared the cognitive characteristics of students who were placed in self-contained classes and those placed in resource/inclusive placements. The two groups of students were compared on intelligence, learning aptitude, frequency of retention, chronological age, and achievement. The intelligence levels of the students in the self-contained classes were lower than for the students in the other placement.

Effectiveness of Self-Contained Placements

An article by Lloyd Dunn in 1968 was one of the most important articles in the history of special education (Kavale, 2000). Dunn briefly reviewed the effectiveness of special class placement for children with mental retardation and successfully argued that placement in regular education classes was as effective as self-contained placement in promoting academic and social growth. Because of the timing of this article, only eight years before the passage of PL 94-142, the Education for All Handicapped Children Act, this perspective had a profound impact on the acceptance of the concept of mainstreaming.

Later studies have confirmed that self-contained placement is more costly but not notably more effective than mainstream placements (Kavale, 2000). As recently as 2004, Zigmond reviewed research on various placements and concluded that there is little research for any type of placements. However, self-contained placements are still in use in some school districts in the nation. This is, no doubt, a consequence of the comparative administrative ease of using this type of placement. However, students with learning disabilities are not found in self-contained placements with the same frequency as children with other disabilities, particularly mental retardation.

Summary of Self-Contained Instruction

The self-contained class is one of the more restrictive educational placements used for students who are learning disabled. Students in these classes tend to be more severely impaired in some ways than others who are placed in resource or inclusive classes. Consequently, the teaching burden is lessened somewhat by most states in terms of the number of children in self-contained classes. However, instruction in these classes involves instructional responsibility for every subject in the school curriculum, plus the additional responsibilities imposed by the objectives on the individualized educational plans (IEPs).

You should remain aware of the research conclusions regarding the effectiveness of self-contained classes. At present, there is little empirical support for continued use of such placements for children identified as learning disabled (Kavale, 2000). Nationally, very few such students are found in self-contained classes because their characteristics usually allow for success in less restrictive placements.

RESOURCE ROOMS

Because of the frequency of resource room placements, there is a great deal of information available on this type of class. The **resource class** is a concept that has historical roots in both special education and remedial education for slow learners. Basically, the resource room was developed in response to the need for some limited specialized training by special educators for children with mild and moderate disabilities. In this placement, students are generally served in the general education class for most of the day, but may be "pulled out" of that class for one or two periods in the resource class; hence the use of the term *pull-out* program (Kavale, 2000).

This is one special education program option in which special educators and general education teachers must interact closely to provide an appropriate educational program. It is crucial that you, as a prospective special education teacher, understand the role and function of resource rooms.

Types of Resource Rooms

There are various types of resource rooms for students with disabilities. These are presented in Interest Box 9.1. As these definitions indicate, the concept of resource room programming is a multifaceted theoretical concept, and various states use different types of resource placement. For example, in some states, children identified as educable mentally retarded, learning disabled, and behaviorally disturbed will be placed in the same cross-categorical resource room program. In other states, these students may be in the same general education class, while being placed in separate **categorical resource rooms.**

Curricular Content in Resource Rooms

The question of which content should be taught in resource rooms has remained a hotly debated issue over the years. Some practitioners stress tutoring students with learning dis-

■ ■ ■ ■ ■ ▬▬▬▬▬▬▬▬▬

INTEREST BOX 9.1
DIFFERENT TYPES OF RESOURCE ROOMS

Categorical Resource Rooms.   These serve only students who have one particular disability. A resource room for students with learning disabilities could include only students identified as learning disabled; students identified as mentally retarded would go to another resource room.

Cross-Categorical Resource Rooms.   This type of placement serves several students with several disabilities functioning at about the same gross achievement levels. Students who are learning disabled, educable mentally retarded, and behaviorally disordered are often placed together in this type of resource room. This is the most common type of resource room.

Noncategorical Resource Rooms.   These serve as the resource room for all children with disabilities in states that do not recognize categorical distinctions.

Specific-Skills Resource Rooms.   This type of resource room aims its curricular content at one basic skill area (usually reading or math).

Itinerant Resource Programs.   These are programs where student visits to the resource room are not scheduled on a daily basis. Rural areas with very small schools in difficult-to-reach locations may provide one resource teacher for several schools, which he or she visits every other day.

abilities in subject matter content from the general education class (e.g., U.S history or language arts), while others stress only remediation in basic skills (e.g., reading or math). Others feel that students with disabilities should receive a functional life-skills curriculum, with an emphasis on things like making job applications, balancing checkbooks, and so on. The advantages and criticisms of each of these curricular approaches are presented in Interest Box 9.2.

Role of the Resource Teacher

In the 1980s and 1990s, the resource room became the most common placement for children with learning disabilities, with some states serving over 90% of their total population with disabilities in resource environments. Resource teachers provided a variety of services.

Basically, a resource room teacher is a person who is a resource for the entire educational community, including the child with disabilities, the parents and teachers of that child, administrators who are concerned and interact with that child, the psychologist and educational consultant who assess the child, and any others who may interact with the child in an educationally relevant fashion. This could also include, for example, a live-in grandparent who tutors the child twice a week.

Given such diversity of role responsibilities, various researchers have investigated the role of the resource teacher (Fore, Martin, & Bender, 2002). Evans (1981) collected information on percentages of time spent in nine basic activities that the resource teacher

■ ■ ■ ■ ■

INTEREST BOX 9.2

ADVANTAGES AND DISADVANTAGES OF VARIOUS CURRICULAR-CONTENT APPROACHES IN RESOURCE CLASSROOMS

TYPE OF APPROACH	ADVANTAGES	CRITICISMS
Basic-skills remediation	1. Stresses basic reading and math 2. Emphasizes only skills necessary for school and life success 3. Easily modeled on elementary curriculum	1. Turns the special educator into a basic-skills tutor 2. No difference between special class and reading/tutoring programs
Tutorial subject matter	1. Complements the regular education class curriculum rather than just basic-skills areas 2. General education teachers appreciate the help	1. Forces special educators to teach subjects in which they are uncertified 2. Attends to state graduation requirements more than child's needs
Functional skills	1. Stresses life-survival skills (checkbook skills, job forms, etc.) 2. Requires mastery of essential skills and provides the time to master them	1. Is a pessimistic view of the child's learning potential 2. Presents little opportunity for learning of many important topics
Learning strategies	1. Provides students who have learning disabilities with a set of cognitive strategies that can be used in all subjects 2. Research evidence indicates substantive support for this work	1. Time to teach the strategies must be taken from academic work 2. General education teacher may not follow up on strategy usage 3. Implementation usually requires attendance in a strategy workshop by the learning disabilities teacher

performed. Principals, classroom teachers, and resource teachers all gave information on the actual time spent in each activity by the resource person and the ideal amount of time that should be spent in each activity. Although Evans (1981) did not compare the different groups, she did compare the actual and desired percentage of time in each category. Results showed that there are several roles the resource teacher usually performs, and these do impact on the general education teacher and the education of the child with disabilities in the general education class.

The primary role of the resource teachers is one of instruction. Evans (1981) presented data to suggest that resource teachers spend 57% of their time in direct instruction of students. The resource teacher then has direct educational responsibility with various students coming to the resource room on a period-by-period basis.

The caseload of resource room teachers ranges from state to state. However, most states will allow from 20 to 25 students per resource room. Given that the students spend a majority of the school day in the general education class, this typically results in instruction for three to six students per period in the resource class. These numbers have been maintained at this relatively low level specifically to assure that individualized instruction is taking place. In spite of these low numbers, some resource room teachers still group students for resource instruction. Although this may be permissible for limited curricular emphases (e.g., social skills), such grouped instruction is clearly inappropriate if it comprises the majority of the resource time unless each student in the group has similar academic needs. The legal foundation of special education requires individualized instruction, and the teacher/pupil ratio in the resource room is kept low to allow for this requirement. Also, research has shown that students with learning disabilities learn better in smaller groups (Russ, Chiang, Rylance, & Bongers, 2001; Vaughn & Linan-Thompson, 2003).

Other roles for the resource teacher include assessment and diagnosis, eligibility team membership, prereferral services, consultation with general educators, and clerical work, such as IEP development, sending forms informing parents of their rights, and so on. In particular, the increase in paperwork has frustrated many resource teachers (Commission on Excellence in Special Education, 2001; Fore, Martin, & Bender, 2002). For this reason, the Commission on Excellence in Special Education sought to reduce unnecessary paperwork for special educators. As you may well guess, this attempt was not completely successful, and thus these noninstructional roles continue to expand over the years, with the result that many resource teachers feel that their instructional time is increasingly reduced.

Note that even with increased responsibilities in various areas, resource teachers are expected to provide some consultative support for general education teachers. Interest Box 9.3 provides a partial list of the types of services that may be provided to assist the general education teacher with various learning problems in the general education class.

Effectiveness of Resource Room Instruction

Research reviews have demonstrated that resource room instruction, coupled with general education instruction, is an effective educational placement option for students with mild and moderate disabilities (Kavale, 2000; Klingner & Vaughn, 1999). Research has tentatively suggested that resource room programming may be more successful with students who have learning disabilities and behavioral disorders than with mental retardation. However, the combination of general education and resource programming did result in increasing the academic achievement of all the groups. For this reason, we may well anticipate that resource placements for students with learning disabilities will continue to be one of the preferred placements.

■ ■ ■ ■ ■

INTEREST BOX 9.3

TEACHING TIPS: SERVICES PROVIDED BY THE RESOURCE TEACHER

The resource teacher is primarily responsible for teaching students in the resource class. How-ever, certain services may be offered to general education teachers if the provision of those services would enhance the likelihood of success for students with learning disabilities. These include the following types of activities:

1. Alternative testing situations in which tests from the mainstream class are taken in the resource room, where the teacher can help read the questions.
2. Assistance with homework or classwork assignments in the resource class.
3. Suggestions for materials and teaching approaches for use in the general education class.
4. Testing time to identify problem areas in the basic-skills curriculum, in order to enhance the general education teacher's planning.
5. Observations in the general education class, in order to identify problems that the child has.
6. Planning time so that the same content may be covered in the resource room and general education class at the same point during the year.
7. Crisis-intervention services to assist the general education teacher when a behavioral problem develops.
8. Other services as needed, when the resource teacher's time will allow them.

INCLUSION

Inclusive School Concept

In 1992, the National Association of State Boards of Education (NASBE) issued a report that called for placing all students with disabilities in general education classes, in the school nearest their home (given their grade-level considerations), and modifying those general education classes such that those students would receive an appropriate educa-tion. A heavy emphasis was placed on several aspects of education, including emphasis on (1) academics, (2) social-emotional development, and (3) personal and collective re-sponsibility and citizenship. The organization viewed this policy statement as supportive of education for all students with disabilities in the general education class, and this gave birth to the **inclusion movement** (Kavale, 2000).

Inside the Inclusive Classroom

Various school districts around the country have applied a variety of inclusive instructional models. One model involves co-teaching, wherein a special education teacher and a gen-eral education teacher both teach in the same classroom (Friend & Cook, 1992; Gately & Gately, 2001; Magiera & Zigmond, 2005). In this model, both co-teachers are responsible for the education of all of the students in the class.

As an example, imagine a third-grade classroom that is employing a co-teaching model. Two teachers would be present for a significant portion of the school day in the classroom. While the special education–certified teacher teaches a group of lower-level language arts students—some of whom are classified as learning disabled and some of whom are not—the elementary-certified teacher is teaching the remainder of the class in math in a small group that may, likewise, include some children with learning disabilities. Care is taken to ensure that neither teacher becomes merely the tutor or teacher's aide for the other teacher. Joint planning of all lessons is encouraged, and each teacher feels joint responsibility for all of the children in that class (Friend & Cook, 1992; Gately & Gately, 2001).

Because both the general education teacher and the special education teacher have skills that they bring to bear on the education of all of the children in the class, these teachers may feel more confident that they can deal with difficulties in the classroom. Typically, the general education teacher has a stronger background in the curriculum emphases, whereas the special education teacher may have stronger skills in modification of instructional materials to accommodate at-risk learners. Because of these diverse skills, the teachers frequently become a resource for each other as well as the students.

Several scholars have presented suggestions to facilitate inclusion, co-teaching, and/ or collaboration between general education and special education teachers (Bender, 2002; Friend & Cook, 1992; Gregory & Chapman, 2001; Tomlinson, 1999). These are presented in Interest Box 9.4.

Evolution of the Inclusive Class

The inclusive class concept originally evolved from two different arenas: politics and research. In the political realm, the regular education initiative (REI) was a political solution to continuing problems in financing the nation's growing special education programs (Kavale, 2000). In the research arena, the Adaptive Learning Environments Model was a research-based instructional model developed to assist in collaborative teaching between special educators and general education teachers.

In the 1980s, the federal government and many state governments became concerned with the definitional problems in the field of learning disabilities that result in everincreasing numbers of children being identified as learning disabled. Obviously, the more students who are identified, the more special education placements will cost. This administrative concern, coupled with the tentative evidence for the limited effectiveness of certain mainstream-with-resource placement models, led the federal government to an initiative that supports serving many students with mild disabilities (including learning disabilities) in the regular education class. Madeleine Will, assistant secretary for the Office of Special Education and Rehabilitative Services during the Reagan administration, formulated this policy at the federal level in 1988 (Kavale, 2000; Will, 1988).

This policy, the **regular education initiative (REI),** recommended the elimination of all pull-out programs, which remove special education students with mild disabilities from the general education classes (Kavale, 2000). The initiative also includes recommendations for providing consultative services to general education teachers in order to facilitate successful mainstream placements without resource room placements. The inclusion concept is based on REI.

INTEREST BOX 9.4

TEACHING TIPS: TEN TIPS FOR MAKING INCLUSION WORK

1. **Planning.** Teachers must work together in joint planning, not only of the lesson activities, but also in how they intend to conduct the activities.
2. **Time.** Planning time is crucial for joint teaching responsibilities. Teachers should work with their principal to ensure adequate planning, assessment, and instructional time.
3. **Communication.** Open discussions between the inclusion teachers are essential. Both teachers should be expected to bring issues and discomforts out into the open, in a professional manner, for discussion.
4. **Flexibility.** Both teachers in an inclusive classroom will be expected to modify the way they do things. Change becomes the constant in these classes.
5. **Preparation of Parents.** Teachers need to work with parents to assure them that their children will be receiving the specialized assistance that they require. If parents in a local area view inclusion as a withdrawal of commitment for special education children, the inclusion concept will not work in that local area.
6. **Joint Ownership.** Both teachers need to feel that the classroom is *their* classroom. If either teacher feels sole ownership of the class, the other teacher becomes a second-class citizen on educational decisions in that class.
7. **Disciplinary Policies.** Children with disabilities need more overall structure than some other children, and care should be taken to provide a solid disciplinary plan that both teachers will support and implement.
8. **Selection of Curricula.** Both teachers need to participate in the selection of curricula from within the identified curricular materials that are available. Each teacher needs to be intimately aware of the curricula and what the other teacher is doing.
9. **Timing.** Teachers should take care not to implement too many changes too fast. Rather, inclusion could be tried for one or two periods each day for the first year. Also, the individual needs of the children must determine which children are initially placed in inclusion settings.
10. **Varied Instruction.** Teachers should develop differentiated instructional options that challenge all students in the class.

As a research base, the proponents of inclusion focused on emerging research that supported providing numerous adaptations within the regular education class. This was the basis for recommending total inclusion of all students with disabilities in the general education classroom for the full day (Kavale, 2000). Wang and Birch originally (1984) developed the Adaptive Learning Environments Model (sometimes referred to as ALEM). The Adaptive Learning Environments Model (**ALEM**) is a proposed set of adaptations to be made in mainstream classes that are intended to facilitate successful academic growth without the need to pull students out of the mainstream class for resource placement (Wang & Birch, 1984). Components of the model include diagnosis and monitoring of students' academic progress, teaching of self-monitoring/self-management skills, and variable classroom structures such as team teaching, cooperative instructional groupings, and multiage groupings.

Although numerous studies have demonstrated the effectiveness of each of these educational strategies, the ALEM is the only model in which all of these innovations have been
evaluated together. The initial reports seemed to suggest that this model was effective in
increasing academic achievement, appropriate classroom behavior, and students' attitudes
toward school (Wang & Birch, 1984). However, Fuchs and Fuchs (1988) pointed out that all
of the supportive research has been done by the same theorists who developed the model.
Further, the model was evaluated in only one location—that in which it was developed.
The research results concerning the effectiveness of the model have also been challenged
(Kavale, 2000; Fuchs & Fuchs, 1988; Zigmond, 2003). Consequently, the effectiveness of
the ALEM approach is still open to question.

Research on Inclusive Classrooms

Recent research on inclusive classrooms has been somewhat equivocal—neither strongly
supporting inclusive practices nor totally condemning this type of placement (Austin, 2001;
Cawley, Hayden, Cade, & Baker-Kroczynski, 2002; Cook, Tankersley, Cook, & Landrum,
2000; Klingner, Vaughn, Schumm, Cohen, & Forgan, 1998; Salisbury & McGregor, 2002;
Zigmond, 2003). In considering the research basis for inclusion of students with learning
disabilities, one must be cognizant of a wide variety of research questions to consider. Issues involve how students, parents, and teachers feel about the inclusive classroom, preparation of general education teachers for inclusive teaching, and the overall efficacy of the
inclusive concept. Interest Box 9.5 presents a brief synopsis of this research on a variety
of questions.

With these results in mind, one may well ask why is the nation still moving toward
increased inclusive instruction? Although funding factors and concerns about availability of
teachers certainly play a role (i.e., one cannot place students in special education resource
rooms or self-contained classes without increasing the supply of teachers certified for those
teaching positions; Commission, 2001), perhaps the best understanding of this phenomenon
involves the historical commitment to educate every child in the least restrictive environment (Kavale, 2000). This has been a definitive commitment in special education since the
passage of the first federal special education legislation in 1974, and because of this historic
commitment, we may well expect this trend toward increased inclusion to continue for a
few more years, despite some of the efficacy evidence challenging inclusive instruction.

Academic Modifications in the Inclusive Class

Although the roles described for resource teachers may also be considered the primary
roles for the special education teacher in the inclusive class, one additional role of the
inclusive special educator involves assisting in modification of the curriculum materials in
the inclusive class (Bender, 2002). Some information is available on the types of curriculum
modifications that general education teachers can make in order to accommodate students
with learning disabilities that are included within the general education classes (Bender,
2002; Ellis & Wortham, 1999). Some suggestions for modifications of the curriculum are
presented in Interest Box 9.6 (p. 286), but every child will have different needs, and clearly

INTEREST BOX 9.5
SYNOPSIS OF RESEARCH ON INCLUSIVE CLASSES

1. *How do general education teachers feel about inclusion or co-teaching?* The majority of general education teachers are ambivalent about inclusion (Austin, 2001; Conderman & Morin, 2006; DeSimone & Parmar, 2006). For example, DeSimone and Parmar (2006) report that, while many teachers expressed support for inclusion, only 41% indicated that they believed students with learning disabilities could learn mathematics best in an inclusive classroom. Conderman and Morin (2006) indicated that many co-teachers with a special education certification felt "underutilized" in the inclusive secondary classes (e.g., used exclusively as paraprofessionals or tutors). The majority of teachers surveyed by Austin (2001) did not choose to co-teach, but they did find this teaching experience to be worthwhile after some exposure to the inclusive co-teaching model. However, in the view of students, the perceptions of general education teachers toward inclusion were quite negative; in one study, students indicated that general education teachers often made inappropriate substitute assignments rather than adapting the curriculum work to equalize the work demands (Pavik, McComas, & Laflamme, 2002).

2. *How do general education teachers feel about students with disabilities in the inclusive class?* Research has shown that general education teachers teaching in inclusive classes generally did not form strong positive attachments to students with disabilities as frequently as to students without disabilities (Cook et al., 2000). Further, the general education teachers expressed much more concern over the success of their instructional program for students with learning disabilities. These teachers generally do not believe that they are well prepared to undertake inclusive instruction (Kavale, 2000; DeSimone & Parmar, 2006). From the students' perspective, negative attitudes on the part of the teachers seemed to be the most deleterious of their school experiences (Pavik et al., 2002).

3. *Do general education teachers offer the types of differentiated instruction in the inclusive class that would facilitate effective learning for students with learning disabilities?* In general, the available research has suggested that many general education teachers do not have access to the types of instructional strategies that are likely to make the inclusive class an effective learning environment for students with learning disabilities (Austin, 2001). Also, research has shown that the instruction offered in most inclusive classrooms is not highly differentiated and that accommodations for students with learning disabilities are not routinely made. Thus, one would not anticipate effective learning for many students with learning disabilities in most inclusive classrooms (Baker & Zigmond, 1990, 1995; Council for Exceptional Children, 1993; Ellis & Worthan, 1999; Kavale, 2000; Learning Disabilities Association, 1993; Pavik et al., 2002).

4. *What type of placement do students with learning disabilities prefer?* A series of research articles has suggested that students with learning disabilities prefer receiving some type of general education and pull-out/resource program (Kavale, 2000; Klingner et al., 1998). In one study, guidance counselors rated students in inclusive classes as more depressed than students in self-contained classes (Howard & Tryon, 2002).

5. *What factors seem to facilitate successful inclusion?* Although several factors have been discussed as facilitative of inclusion, two have been widely discussed: administrative support and differentiated instructional practices. Administrators who are supportive of inclusion play a critical role in the success of inclusive programming in any school.

Administrators committed to addressing diversity in their students, who emphasize school improvement, and who exhibit innovativeness can clearly foster successful inclusion (Salisbury & McGregor, 2002). Also, general education teachers who demonstrate a commitment to differentiate the instructional strategies can foster successful inclusion (Baker & Zigmond, 1995; Bender, 2002). Finally, successful inclusion is likely in classes where all students—both with and without disabilities—demonstrate high levels of engagement and where teachers spend 75% or more of their time involved in instruction (Wallace et al., 2002).

6. *Does the evidence show that inclusive placements result in more learning?*   All of the previous questions are important, but the ultimate efficacy question is both simple and critical: Does inclusion work for students with learning disabilities? Unfortunately, at this point, the majority of studies seem to suggest that inclusive classes are no more effective than pull-out programs for students with learning disabilities (Kavale, 2000; Zigmond, 2003). Although some inclusive programs have been shown to be quite effective (Cawley et al., 2002; Rea, McLaughlin, & Walther-Thomas, 2002), these positive results, like the research reviewed previously on the ALEM program, tend to concern self-contained programs without extensive external research support. At this point, one

the needs of the student for particular modifications should be used as the primary guide for which modifications to undertake.

Differentiated Instruction for the Inclusive Class

As noted above, the inclusive class is the model strongly favored by federal legislation, and an emerging instructional innovation for inclusive classes has received increasing attention nationally—**differentiated instruction** (Bender, 2002; Gartin, Murdick, & Rhomberg, 2006; Gregory & Chapman, 2001; Stanford, 2003; Tomlinson, 1999). Carol Tomlinson (1999) first described the "differentiated classroom" as a general education classroom that involves a wide variety of instructional options, aimed at the increasingly diverse learning needs that typically characterize today's inclusive classes.

Consider the typical inclusive class. With 22 students in the class, a general education teacher may have 2 students with learning disabilities, 2 students with speech problems, 1 student with mental retardation, 2 students with behavioral disorders, 2 students with ADHD, and 3 gifted students. Thus, of 22 students, more than half would have some type of special instructional need. Of course, research has established that academic achievement of students with mild disabilities is inversely proportional to class size; in short, students with mild disabilities attain higher levels of achievement in smaller classes (Russ, Chiang, Rylance, & Bongers, 2001). However, in spite of this growing evidence, many students with learning disabilities are increasingly included in larger general education classrooms today. This example may seem a bit extreme, but all general education teachers in today's classrooms must learn to differentiate their instruction to meet the varied needs of highly diverse learners. Certainly, varying the question complexity, as discussed previously, could be one way to meet these diverse needs, and numerous authors have provided instructional ideas for students with learning disabilities in the differentiated classroom (Bender, 2005; Gartin, Murdick, & Rhomberg, 2006).

■ ■ ■ ■ ■

INTEREST BOX 9.6

TEACHING TIPS: MODIFYING THE CURRICULUM

Many general education teachers wish to assist the children with learning disabilities in their classes. It will help those teachers if you, the special education teacher, can provide them with some guidance concerning the types of modifications that may be made to enhance the likelihood of success. The following is a partial list of modifications that may assist in the mainstreaming of many children and youth with learning disabilities:

1. Provide advance organizers for stories.
2. Use audiovisual materials to illustrate points in lectures and readings.
3. Use assertive disciplinary procedures; provide clear consequences of good and bad behavior.
4. Pay attention to cognitive planning concerning task completion.
5. Monitor the on-task behavior of pupils at all times.
6. Use a variety of instructional groupings such as peer tutoring, team teaching, and cooperative instructional groups.
7. Give regular required assignments, and provide extensive feedback to illustrate strengths and weaknesses in the work.
8. Use different curriculum materials that cover the same content at lower reading levels.
9. Provide frequent use of unstructured time, computer reward time, or class privileges as rewards for good work and good behavior.
10. Use specialized instructional strategies such as precision teaching, self-monitoring, and so on geared to individual students' learning problems.
11. Use alternative test-taking approaches (oral administration, etc.).

Several authors have described a technique called **cubing** as one instructional option for differentiating the instructional demands for students with learning disabilities (Bender, 2002, 2005; Gregory & Chapman, 2001). Cubing is a technique that will assist students to consider a concept from six points of view. By envisioning the six sides of a cube as different levels of complexity, the students in the class may be assigned different "cube sides" and thus different levels of interaction with the concepts to be covered. In some cases, teachers actually make a six- or eight-inch cube and label the sides, and by tossing this out to various groups of students, assignments may be made that vary the level of complexity of the assignments. The sides may be labeled as follows:

Cube Side	Function	Use These Terms to Make the Assignment
Side 1	Describe it	recall, name, locate, list
Side 2	Compare it	contrast, example, explain, write
Side 3	Associate it	connect, make, design
Side 4	Analyze it	review, discuss, diagram
Side 5	Apply it	propose, suggest, prescribe
Side 6	Argue it	debate, formulate, support

By using cubing, students look at the same concept from six different perspectives, and the various levels of knowledge of different students may be addressed in this context. For example, some students consider initial descriptions of the concept, whereas others are involved in analysis of it or role-play activities in which students argue for or against a concept. Thus, this represents one way for teachers to address the differing intellectual needs of all students in the inclusive classroom and to offer differentiated instruction for students of varying abilities, including students with learning disabilities. In fact, using the cubing idea and/or many other, similar instructional techniques—such as varying the level of questions—the teacher will intentionally vary the demands and expectations of students. You may wish to review Bender (2002) for additional differentiated instruction ideas for students with learning disabilities. Concepts covered in this fashion are presented in a rich and multidimensional format and are considered by the students in a more complex fashion (Stanford, 2003).

Summary: Inclusive Classes

This type of service delivery model will probably be widely debated for the next few years. Although teachers seem initially pleased with this model, the research evidence is not supportive of this concept at present (Zigmond, 2003). Furthermore, numerous professional organizations have raised some valid concerns about the inclusion concept (Kavale, 2000). In spite of these concerns, there seems to be a broad general trend toward increasing availability of this service delivery model. You will want to review the journals in special education to identify new research findings on inclusion and to keep current on the ongoing debate.

ISSUES IN PLACEMENT

In addition to the debate on inclusion, a number of other concerns involve the appropriate placement of children with learning disabilities and other mild or moderate disabilities (Commission, 2001). These issues are generic and are not limited to learning disabilities. Discussion of them would be as appropriate in texts concerned with mental retardation and behavioral disorders as here. Nevertheless, as a prospective teacher, you should have some understanding of these complex placement issues because you will hear more about each of them.

Prereferral Modification

Because of the growing number of students being identified as learning disabled, there is increasing pressure to refer only those students who have more serious disabilities. Consequently, many school districts have instituted a system by which general education teachers must conduct (and document) the strategies they used in attempts to alleviate a problem before they refer a child to special education. Such **prereferral modification** strategies may be as simple as a single-subject design-reinforcement project to assist a student in increasing on-task behavior. Other projects may be more involved, such as institution of a team-teaching approach that allows a teacher time to work with the student on a one-to-one basis. The approaches presented here represent several different attempts to meet the need for more prereferral strategies.

Project RIDE.   **Project RIDE** stands for Responding to Individual Differences in Education (Beck & Weast, 1989). Several practitioners began to develop a team approach to solving problems that teachers were having with individual students in general education classes (Beck & Weast, 1989). Beck soon realized that teachers should be provided with information on effective instructional strategies for use in modification of general education classes. Further, Beck and associates collected data from groups of teachers in an effort to let the teachers identify the problems for which they needed solutions. A list of 40 common problems was generated. This included 20 academic problems (such as completing work on time, following oral directions, and organization of academic materials) and 20 social-behavioral problems (including talking out, stealing, and noncompliance). For each problem, a set of research-proven tactics was located in the literature, so that a teacher who had a problem with a student demonstrating out-of-seat behavior could use the tactics bank provided by Project RIDE to select a tactic that would be appropriate for his or her class. Between three and six different tactics were provided for each of the 40 problems, thus assuring each teacher of some selection. The selected tactic was then used to modify the general education class and eliminate the problem.

In the RIDE approach, teachers undergo training in describing behavior in measurable terms, team decision making, utilization of the RIDE tactics bank, and single-subject design interventions to implement the selected tactic. Extended in-service work is usually required for implementation of Project RIDE.

There is only one study on the effectiveness of Project RIDE (Beck & Weast, 1989). Project RIDE was implemented in six schools over a three-year period. Before implementing this prereferral system, 3.6% of the total school population was referred to special education, and this referral rate declined to 1.6% after Project RIDE was implemented. Further, the accuracy of referrals increased. Before Project RIDE was implemented, 54% of the referred students were declared ineligible for special education. This represents a great deal of wasted assessment time and money for students whose problems should have been handled in the general education class. However, after Project RIDE, only 20% of the referred students were considered ineligible. Clearly, teachers had become more adept at modifying their class to encourage success of the pupils who were at risk of referral.

Caution is in order here, for the same reasons as in the ALEM approach. Project RIDE has been implemented and evaluated only once, and that was done by the persons who developed it. However, this approach has the potential for assisting the general education teacher in identification of appropriate modification strategies.

Schoolwide Assistance Team.   Another type of prereferral intervention that several states have adopted is the implementation of schoolwide assistance **(SWAT) teams** (Chalfant, Van Dusen-Pysh, & Moutrie, 1979). This is a team of teachers (special education and general education) who listen together as a teacher describes a child in his or her class who may need additional assistance. The idea is to marshal the resources, ideas, and experience of the professionals based in the school to help alleviate the problem. The team discusses the problem and recommends a course of action or a modification for the mainstream teacher to use.

Different terms are used in different states for this procedure (*student/faculty support team, school resource team, school-based team,* etc.). Also, this procedure is incorporated into both ALEM and Project RIDE. As a beginning teacher, you will probably find that some type of schoolwide assistance team operates in your school district. You should begin to observe these meetings at the earliest possible time because you will probably be asked to participate in a team of this nature.

Response to Intervention as a Prereferral Intervention.   As described previously, an innovation in determining the existence of a learning disability involves documenting the failure to respond to a scientifically validated instructional intervention. Since this documentation takes place prior to classifying a student as learning disabled, the RTI process impacts, if not entirely supplants, the overall prereferral process. As described previously, the RTI would typically be implemented in two tiers, each of which involves documentation of how a student responds to an educational intervention. This process at some point may become the only required prereferral procedure, but it is too early to tell if this will be the case. As a new teacher in this field, you should continue your reading in the professional journals to follow this issue over the next several years.

Cross-Categorical Placement

A number of state school districts have begun to place children with several different types of disabilities in the same resource or self-contained class. In some instances, the states still identify the children by the traditional categories such as learning disabilities, mental retardation, and behavioral disorders and merely create a resource class that cuts across these definitional boundaries—hence, the term **cross-categorical placement.** Resource classes of this nature would include students with each of these conditions in them at the same period of the day.

Other states have decided that the learning characteristics of these three groups of children are so similar that separate labels for these conditions are not warranted. These states do not label students according to these categories, but rather use some type of generic label, such as *educationally handicapped,* and place the children together in the same class. Reschly and Hosp (2004) indicated that 20% of the states opted to allow for a cross-categorical identification of children with disabilities. Also, the Commission on Excellence in Special Education (2001) seemed to endorse this general merger of categories (Council for Exceptional Children, 2002).

A third option is the traditional categorical placement, in which children with learning disabilities go to the learning disabilities resource room, children who are educable mentally retarded attend an EMR resource room, and children with behavioral disorders attend a behavioral disorder resource room. This type of categorical placement is problematic from the perspective of principals in small schools or rural schools because there may not be enough students with each condition to warrant employment of three teachers with different training and certification.

Further, some early evidence suggests that different categorically based training of teachers does not result in improved educational performance by the students (Algozzine, Morsink, & Algozzine, 1988). For example, Algozzine and his co-workers (1988) investigated the potential differences in actual classroom instruction between teachers who were certified in the three categories. The evidence suggested no observable distinctions between the way they conducted their classes, even when different training was provided by these teachers. Based on this argument, there seems to be little rationale for categorical placement in resource rooms.

The issue of categorical/generic placement will continue to receive research attention. At present, most states still identify children with learning disabilities in a separate category from children with mental retardation and behavioral disorders. Also, professional groups such as the Council for Exceptional Children have taken positions that allow and encourage the use of this type of categorical placement. Nevertheless, this issue will affect you if you ever decide to move across state boundaries into a state with different placement and certification patterns. You should continue to keep abreast of this research debate.

SPECIALIZED INSTRUCTIONAL STRATEGIES

Within the context of these various instructional placements, students with learning disabilities do demonstrate some instructional needs that may not be present in other students. For example, students with learning disabilities, regardless of the instructional placement, will often demonstrate problems in attention, behavior, and social interaction that may require specialized instructional strategies that differ from the instructional practices used for other students. These may include peer tutoring, cooperative instruction, or attribution training. Other research seems to suggest the use of more esoteric instructional practices such as biofeedback and relaxation training. As a practitioner in the field, you will need some understanding of each of these instructional treatments.

However, in the field of learning disabilities, there have always been recommendations for instructional treatments that were not supported by research, and parents may well inquire about these. As a practitioner, you will need some understanding of these unsupported treatments as well because parents may read about them in the media and ask you questions about application of these treatments with their children. Regardless of the needs of the child, you will want to formulate the most effective instructional plan possible while avoiding instructional practices that are not supported by research. The next sections of this chapter will help you understand both the specialized strategies for use with students with learning disabilities and the several strategies that are not recommended at present.

Peer Tutoring

One intervention that has received increased research attention is the use of students to tutor each other (Burks, 2004; Mortweet, Utley, Walker, Dawson, Delquadri, Reedy, Greenwood, Hamilton, & Ledford, 1999; Saenz, Fuchs, & Fuchs, 2005). **Peer tutoring** may be conducted in either the general education or special education class. The original goals of tutoring involved improved academic work and improved social acceptance of children with disabilities. In some cases, the students are paired, with the expectation that on one day the first student will tutor the second and on the next day those roles will be reversed (Mortweet et al., 1999). Also, many special education teachers create opportunities for students without disabilities to be placed in the special education class for one period per day as a tutor. In my own teaching experience, I requested that two "study hall" students who wished to help teach be assigned to my room. In the literature, you will find many ways to acquire peer tutors from both inside and outside your own class.

Implementation of Peer Tutoring.   An implementation plan for peer tutoring must take several factors into account. First, obtaining the tutors is a major issue to be considered. If you intend to use tutors from your own class, the implementation is fairly easy. However, if you intend to obtain tutors from other classes in the school (or from a study hall class), this must be scheduled with the school administration and other teachers.

A second implementation issue concerns the level of training that tutors receive. The level of training is dependent on the types of tasks you want your tutors to accomplish. For example, if you wish your tutors only to grade objective papers and assist the students with self-checking quizzes, very little training is necessary, and the training may be accomplished by having the tutor observe the teacher do the tasks one day. The tutor will then be able to accomplish these tasks. However, if you want the tutor to assist in the implementation of a complex instructional method—a learning-strategies instructional lesson, for example—more extensive training will be necessary. This may involve a reading list concerning use of the strategies and strategy training overall, as well as a number of days of observation and guided practice while you offer critical input. Training of tutors becomes more involved as the complexity of the instructional task increases.

Several models for peer tutoring have been shown to be effective in the inclusive classroom (Burks, 2004; Mortweet et al., 1999; Sanez, Fuchs, & Fuchs, 2005). In the class-wide peer tutoring model, for example, each class member serves as a tutor for his peer-pal and then is tutored by the same peer-pal. Thus, this reciprocal tutoring results in increased integration for students with learning disabilities in the inclusive class. Also, research has repeatedly shown that this type of tutoring works to enhance learning by students with and without disabilities (Burks, 2004; Mortweet et al., 1999).

Summary of Peer Tutoring.   Peer tutoring is an instructional method that was intended to assist in the development of both academic and social skills among children with learning disabilities. Research has shown that both of these goals may be met in various tutoring situations, either in the inclusive class or in the special education class (Saenz, Fuchs, & Fuchs, 2005). The positive results of tutoring include increased academic achievement, improved levels of integration with nondisabled populations, improved self-concept, and improved academic and social skills among the tutors. Finally, unlike some of the more sophisticated interventions, tutoring may be implemented with relative ease. Generally, no special course work is required, and by reading a few of the research articles, you can get a feel for the methods by which tutoring may be implemented. You should consider using a tutoring system of some type in your class for students with learning disabilities.

Cooperative Instruction

Cooperative instruction was intended to facilitate the integration of special education populations into general education classes (Johnson, Johnson, Warring, & Maruyama, 1986). One reason for including special education students in general education classes, after Public Law 94-142 was passed, was to provide the children who had disabilities with nondisabled role models in order to facilitate the learning of social skills. However, special education practitioners soon noted that the students without disabilities tended not to include the students with learning disabilities and other disabilities in class and playground activities. This resulted in a lack of effective role models for the children with disabilities. Consequently, cooperative instructional activities were formulated, in part, to break down the barriers between those students who have disabilities and those who do not in general education class placements.

These types of instructional activities are routinely implemented in the general education class, and the special educator may serve a facilitating role by preparing the child with learning disabilities for such active participation. Also, you may have the occasion to assist a general education teacher, in an inclusive class, in the use of various cooperative instructional procedures.

Implementation of Cooperative Instruction. There are numerous cooperative instructional procedures, though perhaps the most widely used is the **jigsaw** (Aronson, Blaney, Stephan, Sikes, & Snapp, 1978). In this procedure, the class is divided into groups of three to five students. Each student is provided with certain information that the other students do not have, and the task for each student is to learn all of the information provided to every group member. The jigsaw groups may meet together for 45 minutes each day over a 5- to 10-day period. Also, on some days, students from different jigsaw groups who have been provided with the same information meet in "expert groups" and discuss the ways in which their portion of the information may best be made available to other group members. After a period of 10 to 15 days, each student takes a quiz on the material. Quizzes are graded individually on students' comprehension and recall.

One issue in implementation of cooperative instruction is the type of reinforcement (group or individual) you wish to give. In addition to the jigsaw method in which students receive individual grades, there are other cooperative instructional methods in which all of the students in a group receive the same group grade. Interest Box 9.7 presents several other methods of cooperative instruction, including **Jigsaw II, student team achievement division (STAD), team-assisted individualization,** and **group investigation.** Note the methods of group formation and reinforcement provided in each procedure.

Efficacy of Cooperative Instruction. Research results on cooperative instruction have been very positive (Bender, 2002; Johnson et al., 1986). For example, the academic achievement of students involved in cooperative instructional groups is generally higher than achievement for students in traditional instructional roles. Also, students with disabilities who have participated in cooperative instruction are generally more readily accepted socially than students who have not participated in such groups (Anderson, 1985; Johnson et al., 1986).

Summary of Cooperative Instruction Research. Cooperative instruction is an effective educational intervention for use with students in general education classes who are learning disabled. Positive research results in both academic achievement and social acceptance indicate the effectiveness of this technique. Although the procedure generally must be implemented in the general education class in order to have the desired social effects, the special education teacher who teaches in the resource room may also assist in this proce-

■ ■ ■ ■ ■ ■

INTEREST 9.7

TEACHING TIPS: USING COOPERATIVE INSTRUCTION

Jigsaw II.   This method differs from the original jigsaw (described in text) only in that both a pretest and posttest are given to each student, and these are compared to yield a gain score for each child. The average gain score for the group becomes each group member's score.

The Student Team Achievement Division (STAD).   In this method, five or six students are assigned to heterogeneous learning groups. First, a pretest on the new material is given to each student. Then worksheets are provided to team members. The teams work together and take another test individually. Each student's gains between the pretest and the posttest are averaged to provide a team score. High-scoring teams are rewarded.

Team-Assisted Individualization (TAI).   Heterogeneous groups of four to five students are formed. Based on a diagnostic assessment, each student is given specific unit materials. Each unit consists of an instruction sheet, worksheets, checklists, other activities, and a final test. Working in pairs, students check each other's worksheets, and a score of 80% or better means that a student can take the final test for that unit. Teams are reinforced together for exceeding preset standards and for completing units.

Group Investigation.   Students self-select into groups of two to five students and choose a topic from a potential list of topics for study. The group decides who should prepare what materials on subtopics in the group, and a final project, presentation, or report is prepared for presentation to the class.

dure by giving some study time in the resource class for use in mastery of the cooperative instruction materials. You should be prepared to recommend this instructional procedure to general education teachers who are having trouble with children in their classes who have learning disabilities.

Attribution Training

As discussed in earlier chapters, the metacognitive perspective on learning disabilities suggested that children with these disabilities were not emotionally and cognitively involved with the learning task. These students have a low internal locus of control, and this may hamper their academic endeavors (Bender, 2002). They are much more likely than nondisabled students to attribute their scholastic success to factors outside of their control, and this external locus of control leads to less involvement with academic tasks.

In order to combat this locus-of-control problem, several scholars have recommended that students with learning disabilities be subject to **attribution training** in which they learn to attribute success in schoolwork to such internally controlled factors as study time and effort (Shelton, Anastopoulos, & Linden, 1985; Tollefson, Tracy, Johnson, & Chapman, 1986). For the student with disabilities who is constantly making negative statements about his or her ability to complete schoolwork, an intervention of this type may be necessary.

Such training should result not only in increased internal perceptions of control, but also in improved efforts at completing schoolwork.

Implementation of Attribution Training.   Most of the research on implementation of attribution-training programs has utilized some form of a self-instructional set of statements that students employ (Shelton et al., 1985). For example, in the study by Shelton and colleagues, students were trained to practice saying positive things to themselves as they did their work. Examples of this could include "I really did a good job on that problem" or "This is a tough one, but hard work pays off." Initially, the students were trained to say these statements out loud, then to whisper them, and finally to say these positive things silently.

Were you to choose to implement a similar type of program with a student with learning disabilities, you would first keep a count of the number of negative statements made by that student for a period of 5 to 10 days to serve as baseline. Next, you would initiate an intervention phase. First, discuss with the student the positive effects of "thinking positively" about schoolwork. You would model for the student several different positive things to say, each of which encouraged internal attributions for success. The student should be told to do a task and say one of the positive things out loud. For the next problem, the student would whisper the positive statement, and finally for the third task, the student would say the positive thing silently. Intervention should continue for a number of days, and you should continue your count of the number of negative things that the student vocalizes each day. As the intervention takes effect and positive statements become habitual, the number of negative statements would decrease.

Efficacy of Attribution Training.   Research on the efficacy of attribution training has suggested that, at least for some students with learning disabilities, attribution training does result in increased internal locus of control (Shelton et al., 1985; Tollefson, Tracy, Johnson, Farmer, & Buenning, 1984). Also, several studies have suggested that attribution training resulted in improved task persistence. For example, the study conducted by Shelton and colleagues (1985) used 32 students—16 children who had learning disabilities and 16 who did not. All of the students were pretested on a locus-of-control measure and a self-concept measure. Afterward, both groups of students were randomly assigned to either an attribution-training group or a control group. The control group merely received the posttest on the two dependent measures and was not included in any training. Comparison of the experimental and control groups on the dependent measures indicated no pretraining differences in either self-concept or locus of control. The attribution-training group received six half-hour sessions per week for three weeks. During the training sessions, the students were instructed to read sentences aloud and to say "good things" to themselves as they read (e.g., "I tried hard and did a good job").

Results indicated that the attribution training did serve to improve the locus of control in students with disabilities. No improvement was noted on the self-concept measure. However, the reading persistence did increase as a result of the attribution training. Finally, a follow-up assessment indicated that the gains in internal attributions were maintained for the experimental group.

However, there are several cautions regarding the research on attribution training. Compared to certain other interventions discussed in this and previous chapters, there have not been as many studies on effectiveness of attribution training. Likewise, several questions remain unanswered. For example, should all children with learning disabilities be routinely trained in attribution training, or is this effective only for a particular subgroup of the population? Is there a certain age at which attribution training is more effective? These and other questions remain unanswered at present.

Summary of Attribution Training.   Attribution training can be effective in improving both a student's locus of control and task persistence. For certain students with learning disabilities, this type of treatment may have a notable impact on their overall efforts at school. Further, attribution training is relatively easy to implement, no special materials are required, and review of several research articles will give you an adequate picture of the techniques for application in your classroom. This is a technique with which each teacher should be familiar because you will often be responsible for a student or two who can profit from this technique.

Color Lenses

While many early theories concerning visual-perceptual deficits as potential causes of learning disabilities have not been supported by research (see Chapter 1), a more recent visually based theory has received initial research support. In 1983, Irlen postulated that some students with reading disorders might be overly sensitive to certain frequencies and wavelengths of the white light spectrum (O'Connor, Sofo, Kendall, & Olsen, 1990). Irlen (1983) identified a set of symptoms associated with these reading disorders and then noted that this oversensitivity, which Irlen termed **scotopic sensitivity,** could be corrected by wearing certain colored lenses **(Irlen lenses).** Thus, use of the colored lenses, or even colored transparencies to cover reading material, should result in improved reading and academic scores for those students.

Unlike the earlier theories on visual training, Irlen lenses have received some research support (O'Connor et al., 1990; Robinson & Miles, 1987; Whiting & Robinson, 1988). For example, O'Connor and his co-workers (1990) used the assessment developed by Irlen to assess scotopic sensitivity of 92 children with significant reading disabilities. Of that group, 67 children were classified as scotopically sensitive, and the remaining 25 were not. The children were then randomly assigned to various treatment groups, with some children receiving a transparency that the scotopic sensitivity measure indicated was the "right" color for that child, while other children received colored transparencies selected at random and/or clear transparencies. Children were instructed to use the transparencies to cover all of their reading material. Over the next few months, the children who received the colored transparencies improved their reading scores, and the researchers reported that most of the improvement occurred within one week of the beginning of the treatment. This type of research result is certainly encouraging. However, many more studies of the effects of this treatment are necessary before this treatment could be widely recommended for general use with children who have learning disabilities. If a parent or another teacher inquires about this treatment, you should present this synopsis of the research and then caution them against overly optimistic hopes.

Dietary and Biomedical Approaches

In addition to the recognized drug interventions discussed in Chapter 2, a number of alternative biochemical approaches have been recommended as treatments in the field of learning disabilities (Kavale & Forness, 1983; Silver, 1987; Thatcher & Lester, 1985). Some of these interventions recommend increasing certain types of chemicals in the body in order to combat various behavior and attention problems (Thatcher & Lester, 1985). Other treatments involve the limitation or elimination of certain elements from the diet of the child with learning disabilities (Silver, 1987).

At the outset, it is apparent that these treatments are not "educational" in the sense that the teacher does not control the diet of the child. For example, it does little good for a teacher to understand that a dietary deficiency is causing learning problems if the parents are not receptive to the possibility of changing a child's diet. However, teachers may eventually play a monitoring role, similar to the role described in prescribed drug interventions, should future research indicate that any of these dietary treatments holds promise for positive interventions for children with learning disabilities. At present, every teacher of these children should be aware of the most widely publicized dietary treatments.

A number of clinical reports have indicated that ingestion of refined sugars may be related to hyperactive behaviors (Silver, 1987; Thatcher & Lester, 1985). However, a number of research studies have been done in which the ingestion of sugar was increased in children in order to identify any increase in hyperactive behaviors and/or other behavior problems. These studies have not demonstrated any measurable behavior change related to ingestion of sugar, though there are a number of variables that could influence these results that were not controlled in the available research. For example, the type of breakfast eaten may hamper or enhance the effect of sugar ingestion. At present, there is little evidence that sugars impact behavior in most students with learning disabilities.

Use of **megavitamins** with patients exhibiting certain mental disorders has been common for a number of years (Silver, 1987). Several researchers have recommended specific treatment with vitamins. At present, there is no evidence to support the use of megavitamins in controlling the behavior problems among the learning disabled or any other group of children with disabilities (Silver, 1987).

Certain theorists have suggested that deficiencies in **trace elements** such as zinc, magnesium, chromium, and copper may be causally related to learning disorders (Fishbein & Meduski, 1987; Struempler, Larson, & Rimland, 1985). These elements are generally measured by a chemical analysis of the hair from the students with learning disabilities (Struempler et al., 1985). At present, there are no published data to support the theory that deficiencies in these elements cause learning disabilities or that treatments involving replacement of these elements result in increased learning potential or improved behavior (Silver, 1987).

SUMMARY

The most common types of educational placements for the learning disabled have been presented. The resource room has been the most frequently used placement, though inclusion placements have received the endorsement of the federal government. Inclusion placements also seem to be growing in popularity. Currently, it is not known how the professional debate on the efficacy of inclusion will turn out.

As you can see, the identification of children with learning disabilities who need special educational assistance is even more complex than the assessment issues in Chapter

5 may have indicated. Before a child is referred, numerous interventions should be undertaken to decide if the child can succeed in the general education class. Also, after a child is referred and determined to be eligible for services as a child with learning disabilities, various placement options should be considered before automatically selecting one. Further, the legal mandate in PL 94-142 must always be considered: Children with learning disabilities must be educated in the least restrictive educational environment that successfully meets their individual needs. A well-designed differentiated general education class will meet the needs of most students with learning disabilities.

As a teacher of the learning disabled, part of your role is advocacy for the rights of the children you serve. It is your responsibility to tactfully argue for the least restrictive placement for each child, in spite of initial opposition you may encounter on the part of the administrators or the general education teachers. You should try to provide assistance to these persons in order to facilitate both the success of the child with disabilities in the least restrictive placement and a positive attitude change on the part of general education teachers regarding inclusion of these children in more general education class activities.

The following points should assist you in studying this chapter:

- There is little evidence for effectiveness of self-contained placements for students who are learning disabled.
- Many students with disabilities receive services in resource rooms. The curricular content of these resource rooms varies and may include tutorial services, basic-skills instruction, survival curricula, or learning-strategies approaches.
- The role of the resource teacher is to become a resource for everyone involved in the school—pupils with disabilities, other teachers, administrators, and parents.
- Inclusion models of service delivery are growing in popularity, though recent research has challenged this model. This is the most frequently used model for students with LD.
- Modification of instruction prior to referral has been emphasized recently in order to maintain more children with mild disabilities in general education classes. Project RIDE and SWAT teams represent two approaches to prereferral modification.
- Cross-categorical placement involves placement of children with various disabilities—mild retardation, behavior disorders, and learning disabilities—in the same class. Some states have begun this type of service delivery placement.
- Cooperative instruction is an effective intervention to increase social acceptance of some children with learning disabilities in the general education classes.
- Peer tutoring generally results in improved academic performance and emotional well-being of both the tutors and the tutees.
- Attribution training generally employs a metacognitive model of instruction to effect positive change in a child's attributions for success.
- Various biochemical approaches have been discussed in the national press, including reduced sugar intake, increased trace-element intake, and ingestion of megavitamins. These treatments are not strongly supported by the majority of the available evidence.

QUESTIONS AND ACTIVITIES

1. Describe the relationship between ALEM and the regular education initiative. Consult the references listed in the chapter, and present a brief report to the class.

2. Describe the differences in the roles of self-contained teachers, resource teachers, and inclusion teachers.

3. What types of educational characteristics seem to suggest that children with learning disabilities require a different type of educational placement from those who are retarded or behaviorally disordered?

4. Consult local school districts in your area, and identify the types of certifications that most teachers have. Is there any type of cross-categorical certification in your state?

5. Describe Project RIDE, and discuss how this educational intervention may be used as a pre-referral intervention.

6. Observe the meeting of a school-based resource team in your local area, and present a report to the class on the actions taken.

7. Obtain information from a local school district on the number of children with learning disabilities served in each type of placement. What percentages were served in inclusive-only placements compared to resource and self-contained?

8. Interview teachers who have experience with co-teaching. Did they enjoy it? Why or why not?

9. What types of academic and social-emotional outcomes can you identify from the research literature for the tutors in a peer tutoring system?

10. Discuss the interaction between the types of tasks that tutors are required to perform and the level of tutor training necessary.

11. Form a study group to review the research on cooperative instruction. Then have the study group present a lesson to the class using a cooperative instructional strategy.

12. Review research on each of the different cooperative instructional strategies, and present an example of each method to the class.

13. Discuss the efficacy of attribution training on locus of control and persistence on school tasks.

14. Compare a differentiated lesson to a traditional direct instructional lesson.

REFERENCES

Algozzine, B., Morsink, C. V., & Algozzine, K. M. (1988). What's happening in self-contained special education classrooms? *Exceptional Children, 55,* 259–265.

Anderson, M. A. (1985). Cooperative groups tasks and their relationships to peer acceptance and cooperation. *Journal of Learning Disabilities, 18,* 83–86.

Aronson, R., Blaney, N., Stephan, C., Sikes, B., & Snapp, M. (1978). *The jigsaw classroom.* Beverly Hills, CA: Sage.

Austin, V. L. (2001). Teachers' beliefs about co-teaching. *Remedial and Special Education, 22*(4), 245–256.

Baker, J. M., & Zigmond, N. (1990). Are regular education classes equipped to accommodate students with learning disabilities? *Exceptional Children, 56,* 516–526.

Baker, J. M., & Zigmond, N. (1995). The meaning and practice of inclusion for students with learning disabilities: Themes and implications from the five cases. *Journal of Special Education, 29*(2), 163–180.

Beck, R., & Weast, J. D. (1989). Project RIDE: A staff development model for accommodating "at risk" students. Manuscript in preparation.

Bender, W. N. (2002). *Differentiating instruction for students with learning disabilities,* Thousand Oaks, CA: Corwin Press.

Bender, W. N. (2005). *Differentiating math instruction,* Thousand Oaks, CA: Corwin Press.

Burks, M. (2004). Effects of classwide peer tutoring on the number of words spelled correctly by students with LD. *Intervention in School and Clinic, 39*(5), 301–304.

Cawley, J., Hayden, S., Cade, E., & Baker-Kroczynski, S. (2002). Including students with disabilities into the general education science classroom. *Exceptional Children, 68*(4), 423–436.

Chalfant, J. C., Van Dusen-Pysh, M., & Moutrie, R. (1979). Teacher assistance teams: A model for within-building problem solving. *Learning Disability Quarterly, 2,* 85–96.

Commission on Excellence in Special Education (2001). *Revitalizing special education for children and their families.* Available from www.ed.gov/inits/commissionsboards/whspecialeducation.

Conderman, G., & Morin, J. (2006, April 9–12). *Secondary co-teaching: More than just the helper.* Paper presented at the annual meeting of the Council for Exceptional Children, Salt Lake City, UT.

Cook B. G., Tankersley, M., Cook, L., & Landrum, T. J. (2000). Teachers' attitudes toward their included students with disabilities. *Exceptional Children, 67*(1), 115–135.

Council for Exceptional Children (CEC) (1993). *Council for Exceptional Children policy on inclusive schools and community settings.* Reston, VA: Author.

Council for Exceptional Children (CEC) (2002). Commission report calls for special education reform. *Today, 9*(3), 6–15.

Danielson, L. C., & Bellamy, G. T. (1989). State variation in placement of children with handicaps in segregated environments. *Exceptional Children, 55,* 448–455.

Deno, E. (1970). Special education as developmental capital. *Exceptional Children, 37,* 229–237.

DeSimone, J. R., & Parmar, R. S. (2006). Middle school mathematics teachers' beliefs about inclusion of students with learning disabilities. *Learning Disabilities Research and Practice, 21*(2), 98–110.

Dunn, L. M. (1968). Special education for the mildly retarded: Is much of it justified? *Exceptional Children, 35,* 5–22.

Ellis, E. S., & Wortham, J. F. (1999). "Watering up" content instruction. In W. N. Bender (Ed.), *Professional issues in learning disabilities* (pp. 141–186). Austin, TX: ProEd.

Evans, S. (1981). Perceptions of classroom teachers, principals, and resource room teachers of the actual and desired roles of the resource teacher. *Journal of Learning Disabilities, 14,* 600–603.

Fishbein, D., & Meduski, J. (1987). Nutritional biochemistry and behavioral disabilities. *Journal of Learning Disabilities, 20,* 505–512.

Fore, C., Martin, C., & Bender, W. N. (2002). Teacher burnout in special education: The causes and the recommended solutions. *High School Journal, 86*(1), 36–44.

Friend, M., & Cook, L. (1992). The new mainstreaming. *Instructor* (March).

Fuchs, D., & Fuchs, L. S. (1988). Evaluation of the adaptive learning environments model. *Exceptional Children, 55,* 115–127.

Gartin, B. C., Murdick, N. L., & Rhomberg, M. A. (2006, April 9–12). *Differentiation of instruction in secondary classrooms.* Paper presented at the annual meeting of the Council for Exceptional Children, Salt Lake City, UT.

Gately, S. E., & Gately, F. J. (2001). Understanding coteaching components. *Teaching Exceptional Children, 33*(4), 40–47.

Gregory, G. H., & Chapman, C. (2001). *Differentiated instructional strategies: One size doesn't fit all.* Thousand Oaks, CA: Corwin Press.

Howard, K. A., & Tryon, G. S. (2002). Depressive symptoms and type of classroom placement for adolescents with LD. *Journal of Learning Disabilities, 35*(2), 185–190.

Irlen, H. (1983, August). *Successful treatment of learning disabilities.* Paper presented at the meeting of the 91st Annual Convention of the American Psychological Association, Anaheim, CA.

Jacobsen, B., Lowery, B., & DuCette, U. (1986). Attributions of learning disabled children. *Journal of Educational Psychology, 78,* 59–64.

Johnson, D. W., Johnson, R., Warring, D., & Maruyama, G. (1986). Different cooperative learning procedures and cross-handicap relationships. *Exceptional Children, 53,* 247–252.

Kavale, K. A. (2000). History, rhetoric, and reality. *Remedial and Special Education, 21*(5), 279–297.

Kavale, K. A., & Forness, S. R. (1983). Hyperactivity and the diet treatment: A meta-analysis of the Feingold hypothesis. *Journal of Learning Disabilities, 16,* 324–330.

Klingner, J. K., & Vaughn, S. (1999). Students' perceptions of instruction in inclusion classrooms: Implications for students with learning disabilities. *Exceptional Children, 66*(1), 23–37.

Klingner, J. K., Vaughn, S., Schumm, J. S., Cohen, P., & Forgan, J. W. (1998). Inclusion or pull-out? Which do students prefer? *Journal of Learning Disabilities, 31*(2), 148–159.

Learning Disabilities Association (LDA) (1993). Position paper on "Full Inclusion of All" students with learning disabilities in the regular education classroom. *LDA Newsbriefs, 28*(2), 1.

Magiera, K., & Zigmond. N. (2005). Co-teaching in middle school classrooms under routine conditions: Does the instructional experience differ for students with disabilities in co-taught and solo-taught classes? *Learning Disabilities Research and Practice, 20*(2), 79–85.

Mortweet. S. L., Utley, C. A., Walker, D., Dawson, H. L., Delquadri, J. C., Reedy, S. S., Greenwood, C. R.,

Hamilton, S., & Ledford, D. (1999). Classwide peer tutoring: Teaching students with mild mental retardation in inclusive classes. *Exceptional Children, 65*(4), 524–536.

National Association of State Boards of Education (NASBE) (1992). *Winners all: A call for inclusive schools.* Alexandria, VA: Author.

O'Connor, P. D., Sofo, F., Kendall, L., & Olsen, G. (1990). Reading disabilities and the effects of colored filters. *Journal of Learning Disabilities, 23,* 597–620.

Olson, J., & Midgett, J. (1984). Alternative placements: Does a difference exist in the LD populations? *Journal of Learning Disabilities, 17,* 101–106.

Pavik, J., McComas, J., & Laflamme, M. (2002). Barriers and facilitators to inclusive education. *Exceptional Children, 69*(1), 97–108.

Rea, P. J., McLaughlin, V. L., & Walther-Thomas, C. (2002). Outcomes for students with learning disabilities in inclusive and pullout programs. *Exceptional Children, 68*(2), 203–224.

Reschly, D. J., & Hosp, J. L. (2004). State SLD identification policies and practices. *Learning Disability Quarterly, 27*(4), 197–213.

Robinson, G. L., & Miles, J. (1987). The use of colored overlays to improve visual processing: A preliminary survey. *The Exceptional Child, 34,* 65–70.

Russ, S., Chiang, B., Rylance, B. J., & Bongers, J. (2001). Caseload in special education: An integration of research findings. *Exceptional Children, 67*(2), 161–172.

Saenz, L. M., Fuchs, L. S., & Fuchs, D. (2005). Peer-assisted learning strategies for English language learners with learning disabilities. *Exceptional Children, 71*(3), 231–247.

Salisbury, C. L., & McGregor, G. (2002). The administrative climate and context of inclusive elementary schools. *Exceptional Children, 68*(2), 259–281.

Shelton, T. L., Anastopoulos, A. D., & Linden, J. D. (1985). An attribution training program with learning disabled children. *Journal of Learning Disabilities, 18,* 261–265.

Silver, L. B. (1987). The "magic cure": A review of the current controversial approaches for treating learning disabilities. *Journal of Learning Disabilities, 20,* 498–512.

Stanford, P. (2003). Multiple intelligence for every classroom. *Intervention in School and Clinic, 39*(2), 80–85.

Struempler, R. E., Larson, G. E., & Rimland, B. (1985). Hair mineral analysis and disruptive behavior in clinically normal young men. *Journal of Learning Disabilities, 18,* 609–612.

Thatcher, R. W., & Lester, M. L. (1985). Nutrition, environmental toxins and computerized EEG: A minimax approach to learning disabilities. *Journal of Learning Disabilities, 18,* 287–297.

Tollefson, N., Tracy, D. B., Johnson, E. P., & Chapman, J. (1986). Teaching learning disabled students goal-implementation skills. *Psychology in the Schools, 23,* 194–204.

Tollefson, N., Tracy, D. B., Johnson, E. P., Farmer, A. W., & Buenning, M. (1984). Goal setting and personal responsibility training for LD adolescents. *Psychology in the Schools, 21,* 223–224.

Tomlinson, C. A. (1999). *The differentiated classroom: Responding to the needs of all learners.* Alexandria, VA: Association for Supervision and Curriculum Development.

Wallace, T., Anderson, A. R., Bartholomay, T., & Hupp, S. (2002). An ecobehavioral examination of high school classrooms that includes students with disabilities. *Exceptional Children, 68*(3), 345–359.

Wang, M. C., & Birch, J. W. (1984). Comparison of a full-time mainstreaming program and a resource room approach. *Exceptional Children, 51,* 33–40.

Whiting, P., & Robinson, G. R. (1988). Using Irlen colored lenses for reading: A clinical study. *Australian Educational and Developmental Psychologist, 5,* 7–10.

Will, M. (1988). Educating students with learning problems and the changing role of school psychologists. *School Psychology Review, 17,* 476–478.

Vaughn, S., & Linan-Thompson, S. (2003). What is special about special education for students with learning disabilities. *Journal of Special Education, 37*(3), 140–147.

Zigmond. N. (2003). Where should students with disabilities receive special education services? Is one place better than another? *Journal of Special Education, 37*(3), 193–199.

CHAPTER TEN

BEHAVIORAL TREATMENT INTERVENTIONS

CHAPTER OUTLINE

WHEN YOU COMPLETE THIS CHAPTER, YOU SHOULD BE ABLE TO:

1. Discuss the unifying factor among the diverse behavioral treatments for learning disabilities.
2. Present the rationale for using a token economy in the special educational classroom.
3. Describe a behavioral-contract intervention.
4. Describe a time-out intervention.
5. Define five types of time-out.
6. Describe an extinction intervention.
7. Describe an aversive contingency and give an example.
8. Describe a precision-teaching intervention project.
9. Describe a direct-instruction approach and identify its various components.

KEYWORDS

behavioral model of learning	time-out	phase change
behavioral contract	negative consequences	learning rate
ABAB intervention	extinction	direct instruction
positive behavioral supports	precision teaching	script
positive reinforcement	antecedent	Reading Mastery
baseline	consequence	
token economy	behavioral objective	

INTRODUCTION

The behavioral approaches to treatment of learning disabilities evolved during the third historical phase. As you may recall from Chapter 1, the third phase—the consolidation phase—began in 1963, when the various groups of theorists coalesced into one group concerned with learning disabilities. Within this coalition, a new interest in alternative educational treatments emerged. Because special education was in transition from specialized clinics and hospitals to public schools, educational treatments applicable in public school classes were sought, and behavioral approaches became dominant in educational psychology between 1965 and 1978.

Also at this time, the various visual-deficit hypotheses were losing influence in the field, and the behavioral perspective developed. This new perspective focused on remediation of academic skills and was dependent on behavioral philosophies. Consequently, many of the techniques seen today in classes for the learning disabled may be traced to roots in behavioral psychology.

Research indicates that many special education teachers use behavioral techniques with some frequency (Anguiano, 2001; Bender, 2002), and behavioral interventions do work to curb undesirable behavior (Burley & Waller, 2005; Graetz, Mastropieri, & Scruggs, 2006). For example, 90% of these teachers have reported using behavioral intervention strategies in their classes (Maheady, Duncan, & Sainato, 1982). The most significant of these techniques includes behavioral interventions such as behavioral contracting, token economies, positive reinforcement, time-out, and extinction procedures. Behavioral interventions have been criticized as both too rigid and too time-consuming (Bender, 2003). But the fact is that these techniques dominate special education classes today. These simple techniques can be easily applied even by first-year teachers (Anguiano, 2001) and work well for many students with learning disabilities (Bender, 2002). Also, several comprehensive instructional systems have been developed that are founded on behavioral psychology—precision teaching and direct instruction (Bender, 2002). As Figure 10.1 demonstrates, a wide variety of instructional ideas may be utilized to positively impact on a student's behavior. This figure includes only those ideas discussed in this chapter.

This chapter begins with a brief discussion of the behavioral foundations of these educational techniques. The first section is intended to bridge the gap between the theoretical discussions of behaviorism in which you participated during various educational psychology courses and the methods courses that will come later in your teacher preparation program. Then, each of the major behavioral techniques is discussed, and a classroom example is presented.

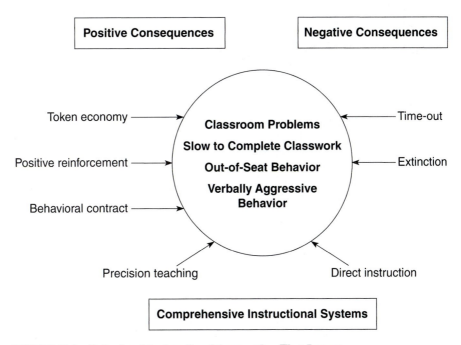

FIGURE 10.1   Behavioral Instructional Approaches That Impact Classroom Problems

COMMON GROUND AMONG BEHAVIORAL TREATMENTS

As you know, behavioral psychology concentrates on measurable behaviors, the antecedents that preceded those behaviors, and the consequences that follow. For behavioral psychologists, the accepted **behavioral model of learning** looks something like this:

Antecedent $\rightarrow$ Behavior $\rightarrow$ Consequence

Behavior was assumed to be controlled by the combination of antecedecnts and consequences that precede or follow the specific behavior. As a result, you—the teacher—can elicit and control the behavior of your students by (1) accurate measurement of those behaviors and (2) manipulation of the antecedents and consequences of those behaviors. In the broadest sense, then, *behavior modification techniques* may be thought of as a set of procedures designed to measure and manipulate behavioral change. This set of procedures empowers the teacher by focusing on the aspects of the learning environment that can be controlled by the teacher—the antecedents and consequences of behavior.

Behavioral psychologists have tended to concentrate more specifically on positive consequences of behaviors. *Positive reinforcement* is the application of a reward consequence that increases the target behavior, and strategies that utilize positive reinforcement in manipulation of behavior of students with learning disabilities are very frequent. Use of a token economy in special education classes represents one effective method for providing ongoing reinforcement. **Behavioral contracts,** which include a written agreement between a child and teacher specifying a change in behavior and a reward for the change, represent another example of positive consequences.

There has also been considerable use of negative consequences in educational treatments of children with learning disabilities (Bender, 2003; Carey & Bourbon, 2004). Procedures that deny reinforcement for behaviors generally decrease the likelihood of those behaviors in the future. These procedures include time-out, extinction, and the use of aversive contingencies.

Finally, one central aspect of behavioral psychology has been the insistence on accurate measurement of behavioral change. Consequently, most of the procedures reviewed in this section are based on an intervention design called **ABAB intervention** or single-subject design. Basically, the letter *A* stands for baseline phases where the target behavior is measured over a period of days without any intervention. The *B* stands for a period of intervention days, during which the intervention is applied. You may have read about single-subject educational interventions such as this in some of your earlier educational psychology courses. Several examples of these interventions are presented later in the chapter.

POSITIVE BEHAVIORAL SUPPORTS

Over the last decade, practitioners have utilized the term **positive behavioral supports** to delineate one or a series of behavioral interventions designed to promote positive behaviors among children with disabilities (Bender, 2003; Barbella & Lavong, 2006). Controlling the behavior of students with learning disabilities is no easier than controlling the behavior of any other student. Teachers should know how to manage students with learning challenges in the classroom, and positive behavioral supports, or interventions that support and extend positive behaviors on the part of students, should be used frequently by all teachers. These positive behavioral supports may be applied by one teacher for one child in a classroom or may be used in a schoolwide behavioral intervention plan designed to promote positive behavior. Interventions may range from simple interventions, such as use of a token economy, to more complex interventions, such as responsibility strategies or relaxation tactics (Bender, 2003).

In the late 1990s, the federal government mandated the preparation of behavioral improvement plans (or BIPS) for students who needed positive behavioral supports in the general education or special education classroom (Barbella & Lavong, 2006; Burley & Waller, 2005). These behavioral improvement plans are typically attached to the individualized education plan for students with learning disabilities. While not all students with learning disabilities require such support, many do (Bender, 2002; Kavale & Mostert, 2004). For example, Kavale and Mostert (2004) documented that 75% of students with learning disabilities display social skills deficits, with the result that many display inappropriate behavior in the classroom.

The following interventions represent the positive behavioral supports offered most frequently and include positive reinforcement, token economies, behavioral contracts, and responsibility strategies.

Positive Reinforcement

Positive reinforcement is the application of a desirable contingency in order to increase a behavior. Imagine the following situation. A student is fairly accurate in completion of his math problems but does not finish enough problems when a set of problems is assigned in class. You may wish to make reinforcement available on a daily basis, contingent on completion of all or most of the problems. You could easily initiate a simple positive-reinforcement project to increase the number of problems completed. A behavioral chart of such a project is presented in Figure 10.2.

This chart presents a standard ABAB design project. The chart has the number of days (or class periods or training sessions, whatever measure of time used) across the bottom and the scale for counting behaviors on the side. This format is standard in behavioral charting. Therefore, the dots on the first few vertical lines in the chart represent the behavioral count for the first few days of the project.

First, you would begin to chart the number of problems completed for five days. The numbers marked on each day indicate the number of problems completed correctly. This is the *A,* or **baseline,** phase, and it gives some measurable indication of the behavior prior to intervention.

Next, you would seek a reinforcer to which the student is likely to respond. If the student enjoys computer games, you may award one minute of computer game time for every five math problems completed correctly. As you can see, when this reinforcement was offered, the student began to finish many more math problems, as indicated on the chart for days 6 through 12.

A second *A,* or baseline, phase is included in sophisticated projects in order to assure that the behavior is responding to the intervention in the project and not some other change

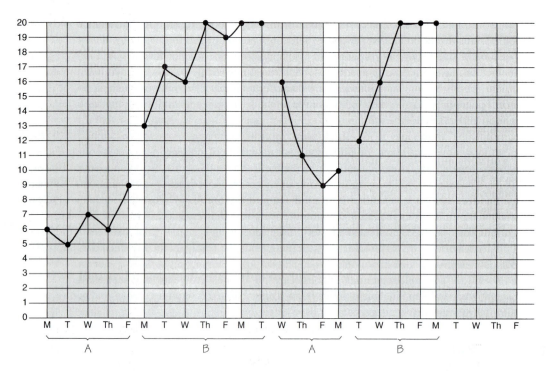

FIGURE 10.2   ABAB Intervention to Increase the Number of Completed Math Problems

in the environment that happened at the same time as the intervention. For example, if the student in this project had begun to receive a regular dosage of medication for an allergy at home on the same day as the intervention started, the drug could account for the positive change in behavior, and the teacher may be unaware of it. A second baseline phase is used to eliminate this possibility.

As you can see from the second baseline (days 13 through 16), the student began to drop off in the number of problems completed correctly. For that reason, the second intervention phase was initiated, and the number of problems completed began to go up.

A positive reinforcement project such as this is one of the easiest of the behavioral interventions to use because most classrooms include a number of privileges that students enjoy. All of these may be reinforcing for particular students.

Burley and Waller (2005) provided a recent example of a positive behavioral support plan involving the use of positive reinforcement to decrease disruptive behavior by a student with ADHD. Researchers recorded the number of class disruptions in one 55-minute class each day. After a baseline count of disruptive behaviors, the teachers met with the child to explain that he would receive reinforcement for each day in which he displayed no more than five disruptive behaviors, which represented a significant reduction in his overall disruptive behavior. Over a period of only 40 days, the disruptive behavior or this student was reduced considerably, indicating that even simple behavioral improvement plans can enhance behavior in a relatively short time.

Token Economy

A **token economy** is a system of payment for work completed and appropriate behavior in the classroom (Carbone, 2001). As a first step, the teacher and students must agree to a system of payment. Tokens (such as plastic counters, scratch and sniff labels, or play money) are obtained, and some system by which students and teacher agree on the amount of work required for certain payments is established. Finally, because the tokens have no intrinsic value, a set of rewards must be obtained for which the tokens may be traded at a later date. Some teachers operate a class store in which used or new retail items (usually five dollars or less per item) may be purchased. The teacher begins to reinforce students for appropriate behavior and correctly completed assignments, and students are offered the opportunity to trade for rewards once a week or so.

Here is an example. A token economy that involved play money was established in a resource class. The money used looked like real coinage in order to teach money recognition, counting, addition and subtraction, making change, check writing, and so on.

All of the students in the class were routinely reinforced for completion of accurate work. However, the class included a boy with learning disabilities who was frequently out of his seat inappropriately, was very fidgety, and disturbed others in the class. An ABAB intervention project was initiated to reduce out-of-seat behavior. The measurement chart for this project may be found in Figure 10.3.

First, out-of-seat behavior was defined specifically as any time the buttocks were not in contact with the seat of the desk. With that specific definition, measurement was less of a problem. For example, even when the student stood up in his chair, he was considered out of seat.

As you will note, the average of the first five days was 14 out-of-seat behaviors per class period. This is much too high, given that this student was only in the resource room for one 55-minute period per day. Clearly, out-of-seat behavior was interfering with his work.

During the intervention phase, the student was reinforced for remaining in his seat. For every four-minute period in which he did not leave his seat, he received 25 cents in the token economy. This was in addition to his regular payment for work completion. An egg timer was placed on his desk, and he was told to use the timer to remind him of each successful four-minute period. If he requested permission to leave his seat, such an instance was not counted as an inappropriate out-of-seat behavior. However, when he left his seat without permission, he was told to return to his seat and start the clock again. Results indicated that during the next eight days (the *B*, or intervention, phase), the student reduced his out-of-seat behavior to an average of one out-of-seat instance per period.

On days 14 through 17, a second baseline was initiated. The out-of-seat behaviors began to increase during that time, indicating that the initial decrease in out-of-seat behavior was a result of the token economy intervention. Because the intervention was shown to be effective, it was reinstituted, resulting in the last *B* phase in the project. As you can see, the

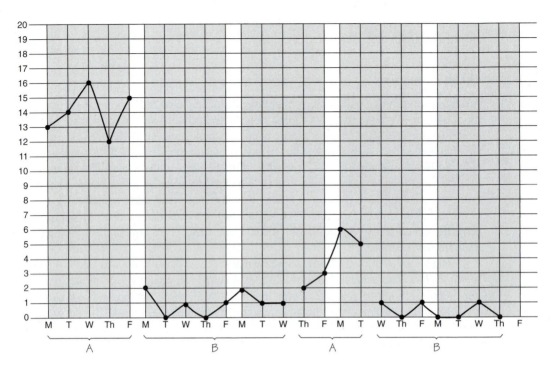

FIGURE 10.3   ABAB Intervention to Reduce Out-of-Seat Behavior

out-of-seat behaviors began to decrease again during this last phase. The student's out-of-seat behavior went down from an average of 14 instances per period to an average low of one per period during each treatment phase. Interventions of this nature work very well in controlling certain types of behavior (Bender, 2003).

As a teacher of the learning disabled, you may wish to establish some type of token economy in your classroom. This tactic, like most behavioral interventions, works in either the resource or the inclusive class. The token economy may be as simple as using plastic counters for tokens and exchanging these for class privileges such as choice of educational games during free time. Such a system would save the time of collecting goods for sale to the students in a store.

However, token economies that involve use of money can be used as instructional devices without taking undue instructional time, as discussed earlier. In one class, for example, students were highly motivated to correctly add their weekly monetary totals and check (through subtraction) the charge for their purchased rewards, even though the same students were not highly motivated to study addition and subtraction of decimal numbers in isolation. Counting, adding, and subtracting money were not considered part of the work, but rather part of the fun in the class. Students who were competent in these skills were given a checkbook in which they made deposits of weekly earnings and wrote checks for their purchases. These functional life skills were seen as privileges rather than merely as other educational activities to be completed. You may wish to review some of the research demonstrating the effectiveness of token economies and then decide which type of system would be appropriate in your class (Carbone, 2001; Salend, 1987).

Behavioral Contract

A behavioral contract is an agreement between a student and teacher that stipulates certain positive consequences that are contingent on demonstration of a particular behavior or a set of behaviors over a period of time. Generally, contracts stipulate tasks that the student will perform or behaviors that the student will demonstrate, the conditions or class activities during which the behavior will be measured, and the reward to be presented when the student has met the stated goal.

Even in classes where a token economy is in place, there is the occasional need for specific behavioral contracts between the teacher and certain students. Memory tasks provide a good example because these tasks can be very difficult for students with learning disabilities, and simple assignments such as memorization of multiplication tables present major hurdles. Interest Box 10.1 presents a sample form for a behavioral contract for Lorenzo.

Imagine the following situation. Lorenzo, a 12-year-old fifth-grade student with learning disabilities, had a problem in memorization of the times tables. This difficulty was hampering his other work in math also, and the math teacher approached you—the special education teacher—to request assistance. First, you would determine the extent of the problem by informal assessment of Lorenzo's ability to remember the lower times tables. Next, you would share the assessment with Lorenzo and his math teacher in an attempt to motivate Lorenzo to higher achievement. You should talk to Lorenzo about the importance of the times tables in his future work and in other everyday situations. You should ask him what types of reinforcers he would be willing to work hard for. Finally, you would challenge Lorenzo to a contract. Interest Box 10.1 presents the behavioral contract for this situation.

As you can see, the contract stipulates that Lorenzo will pass tests on the times tables that will be given daily and each week in order to assess his progress. When Lorenzo scores 90% on the test, he will be awarded a new football, which is being held in the class store exclusively for him.

Behavioral contracts are excellent ways to focus attention on particular learning problems. However, the rewards that students demand in contracts may be expensive, either in terms of money to purchase the reward or time allocated to class privileges. Also, other students in the class may demand the right of also working for a contractually stated reinforcer. This can be either an advantage or a disadvantage, depending on the number of students who request contracts and the teacher's time allocation to this procedure. Nevertheless, the contracts could be used on occasion by every teacher of the learning disabled for particularly difficult tasks.

Responsibility Strategy

Bender (2003) identified a positive behavioral support that involves offering a privilege or opportunity to a child. Many children misbehave simply because they do not realize that

■ ■ ■ ■ ■

INTEREST BOX 10.1

TEACHING TIPS: A BEHAVIORAL CONTRACT FOR LORENZO

This is a contract between _____Lorenzo_____ and _____Mr. Fisher_____. The contract

starts on ___11/1___ and ends on ___6/1___. We will renegotiate it on ___11/30___.

During ___math and resource period___, we agree to ___increase___

the specific behavior of ___correctly doing times tables___. This will be measured

by ___weekly & daily tests___. This project will continue until

the behavior is ___increased___ to ___90% correct___.

When the appropriate level of behavior is reached, _____Lorenzo_____ will

___win a new football___. The teacher will help by ___practice work each day___.

Student's signature _____

Teacher's signature _____

Date _____

they can gain positive attention by positive actions in the classroom. Thus, in order to encourage a child who misbehaves frequently to behave more positively, the teacher should seek out a privilege for the child. This should involve a task that the child is highly motivated to do and one that entails "bragging rights," or some degree of positive recognition in front of other students. Students will be motivated to do the selected task or privilege as his or her contribution to the class.

However, Bender (2003) does not use the typical behavioral approach, which suggests that a privilege should be contingent upon good behavior. While this tactic can work for many children, Bender suggests that the contribution or the responsibility that the child has should be highly visible to and highly valued by the class; thus, it will be required each day rather than merely as a reinforcement for positive behavior. The child should understand that his or privilege is important and that he or she can make that positive contribution to the class. The message the child hears should be, "Your contribution (i.e., doing this task for the class) is so important that we need you to do this even when you are having a bad behavior day." Research has shown that for many children with serious behavior problems, this responsibility strategy can work wonders (see Bender, 2003, for a review).

TECHNIQUES INVOLVING NEGATIVE CONSEQUENCES

Time-Out Procedures

Time-out procedures involve **negative consequences**—specifically, the removal of the possibility of reinforcement for a specified period of time—in order to decrease inappropriate behavior. This is one of the most frequently used procedures in classes for the learning disabled. In one survey, 45% of the teachers of students with learning disabilities indicated that they used some type of time-out procedure in their classroom (Maheady et al., 1982).

There are several different types of time-out procedures. These include activity time-out, teacher time-out, contingent time-out, ribbon time-out, exclusion time-out, and seclusion time-out. Definitions of these different procedures are presented in Interest Box 10.2. Each of the time-out procedures has been shown to be effective. However, you should realize that, because of the early forms of time-out applications, teachers generally mean either exclusion or seclusion time-out when they use the term. In the inclusion class, the exclusion time-out is generally the type utilized.

For example, in a resource class for learning disabilities, Thomas is demonstrating continued behavior problems. Basically, these problems begin by Thomas swearing

■ ■ ■ ■ ■ ▬▬▬▬▬▬▬▬▬▬▬▬▬▬▬▬▬▬▬▬▬▬▬▬▬▬▬▬▬▬▬▬▬▬▬▬▬▬

INTEREST BOX 10.2
TYPES OF TIME-OUT

Activity Time-Out.   This time-out requires that a given activity or material is removed from the child contingent on the display of misbehaviors. If the target behavior was swearing and the child was using a toy at the time, the toy should be removed for a given period of time.

Teacher Time-Out.   This procedure calls for the teacher to remove himself or herself from the child contingent upon the omission of some behavior. The teacher can turn away from the child for a given period of time.

Contingent Observation.   This is a procedure in which the child is removed from a group activity. The child is allowed to observe the group but is not allowed to participate in reinforcement.

Ribbon Time-Out.   This procedure entails the presentation of some item such as a ribbon or button that signals that a child is to receive continual reinforcement. The ribbon is removed contingent on misbehavior, and the child is not reinforced for a period of time.

Seclusion Time-Out.   This is a procedure in which the child is physically removed from the environment. This is usually reserved for severe aggressive behaviors and necessitates a special time-out room or seclusion area.

Exclusion Time-Out.   This is a procedure in which a child is sent to a different area of the same room—perhaps a time-out corner—and is thereby excluded from participation in the ongoing class activities.

at students as they walk past to retrieve assignments. Thomas is receiving reinforcements in the class by completion of the assigned work (through a token economy system). Also, Thomas is receiving a great deal of teacher and peer attention when he gets into trouble by swearing at students as they walk near him. After several weeks of this, you—the teacher— become quite frustrated at the necessity to call Thomas down so frequently.

In initiation of a time-out procedure, you will first wish to take some baseline data. Because Thomas is in your room for two periods before recess each day, you decide to count the number of instances of swearing at students on a daily basis. Figure 10.4 presents the graph of the daily count of swearing behavior.

As you can see, the first *A* phase (baseline data) suggested that Thomas was swearing at students an average of five times per day. At the end of the first baseline phase, you would present the data to Thomas and challenge him to discontinue that behavior. You inform him that, upon each instance of such behavior in the future, he will be sent to the time-out corner of the room. You would then locate the time-out corner away from other students and out of sight of them so that no reinforcement could be obtained from any source. During the intervention phase, you should send Thomas to the time-out corner upon each occurrence of swearing behavior and continue to chart the occurrences of that behavior.

Thomas's swearing behavior was changed as a result of the project presented above. As you can see, during the five-day baseline phase, Thomas averaged swearing five times each day. The intervention began on day 6 and continued through day 15. Each time Thomas swore, he was sent to the time-out corner of the room, where he could not see other students in the class. The class was instructed not to giggle or laugh when Thomas swore and to take

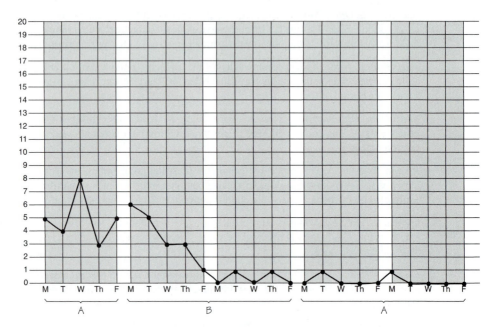

FIGURE 10.4   Single-Subject Intervention for Thomas's Swearing

no notice of his behavior while he was in the time-out corner. He had to remain in the time-out corner for three minutes after his final swear word. If he continued to swear in the time-out corner, he had to remain until he stopped and then wait an additional three minutes.

As the data demonstrate, Thomas's swearing began to decline when he was removed from the reinforcement of the class. During the last week of the intervention, he averaged less than one swearing behavior per day. In fact, he swore only twice during that entire week.

Baseline conditions were reinstituted during the third week, and the occurrences of swearing continued at very low levels. In this instance, Thomas had apparently broken the habit of swearing during the intervention phase. Because this project appeared to be successful, a second intervention was not instituted. At this point, class members have agreed not to reinforce Thomas for swearing, and that alone may cause further decreases in swearing. Consequently, no return to intervention conditions was necessary in this project.

Seclusion time-out is basically an intervention intended for a single student, but certain time-out procedures may be used with groups of children in the classroom. For example, the time-out ribbon procedure may be applied either to single individuals or to groups of children. Salend and Gordon (1987) evaluated the effectiveness of a group-oriented time-out ribbon procedure to decrease inappropriate talking of two groups of students. Five students with learning disabilities formed one group, and four students formed the other. These groups included every child in the special education class during the period. Talking was defined as any vocalization that occurred without teacher permission. The teacher and a trained observer recorded the number of inappropriate vocalizations for eight days. These data served as baseline data. An intervention phase was instituted for nine days. Both groups were then placed in a second baseline and a second intervention phase. During intervention phases, a time-out ribbon was presented to each by placing the ribbon on an easel under that group's name. For each two-minute period in which the group's ribbon was in place, the group received one token that could be used to buy tangible reinforcers. Each time a group member exhibited inappropriate vocalizations, the ribbon was removed, and the group lost the opportunity to earn tokens. Results indicated that the intervention phases reduced the inappropriate vocalizations for each group.

This study is interesting for several reasons. First, the study illustrates that time-out procedures that do not involve seclusion or exclusion are very effective. Second, time-out may be used as a group contingency rather than an individual contingency. Finally, a group contingency time-out such as this ribbon procedure is very easy to operate in an inclusive class. You may wish to consider such a procedure in your class.

Extinction Procedures

Extinction is the withholding of reinforcement for a previously reinforced behavior in order to decrease the frequency of the behavior. Of the techniques reviewed so far, extinction is, perhaps, the least well known. Maheady and colleagues (1982) reported that over 20% of the special education teachers surveyed had never heard of extinction. Nevertheless, the technique is very effective. Among the special education teachers who had tried extinction procedures, less than 10% reported failure (Maheady et al., 1982).

Imagine the following scenario: A girl with learning disabilities, Teressa, frequently asks for help when completing her spelling and language arts work. Although you, as the teacher, wish to help her as frequently as necessary, her requests for help from other class members are interfering with the other students' work. Also, when other class members help her, they may not take the time necessary to explain what they are doing in order to help Teressa learn the material. Consequently, some type of extinction procedure may be in order. Although the help she received from other class members was very reinforcing for Teressa, this reinforcement must be removed in order for her to stop the behavior of requesting help from the wrong persons.

In order to establish such a procedure, you would first take some baseline data for a period of approximately two weeks. The behavior chart in Figure 10.5 demonstrates that Teressa was requesting assistance an average of seven times per day in her 55-minute resource period.

After the baseline is established, you would begin the extinction procedure. As a first step, you would show the baseline data to Teressa and elicit her support in changing the behavior. Next, you may wish to talk to the class as a whole. Ask other class members to politely refuse to assist Teressa when Teressa happens to "forget herself" and ask them for assistance. Class members should be reminded to suggest that Teressa request the teacher's help should she need assistance.

As you can see from the data, the intervention was effective. After only two days, Teressa began to decrease her requests for help from the class. Note also that the teacher in this project chose not to include a second baseline or second treatment phase. This project is an AB design or baseline/treatment design. Although not as valid scientifically as the more extensive ABAB design discussed earlier, many teachers choose to use this type of procedure because the overall goal of the intervention has generally been accomplished by

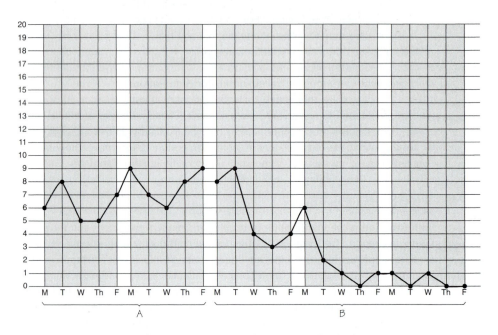

FIGURE 10.5   Reducing Teressa's Inappropriate Requests for Assistance

the end of the first intervention phase. As a practitioner in the classroom, you may terminate your intervention treatments at this point rather than include the last two phases for additional scientific exactness. However, most behavioral psychologists would insist that, at a minimum, the first baseline and intervention phases must be measured and charted in order to demonstrate any behavioral progress.

Video Monitoring Intervention

Video monitoring is a strategy that can be applied in several ways to impact the behavior of children with learning disabilities (Bender, 2003; Graetz, Mastropieri, & Scruggs, 2006). Video monitoring of inappropriate behaviors can serve as a mild punishment for students who display inappropriate classroom behavior. The approach involves the use of video monitoring of their inappropriate behavior (Bender, 2003). Many students with learning disabilities do not understand social situations as well as other students (Bryan, Burstein, & Ergul, 2004) and thus may not realize the effects of their behavior. Bender (2003) recommended videotaping students and capturing the response of other students to the target child's misbehavior. For many students with learning disabilities, it is mildly punishing to view such a video with the teacher and see other students' negative reactions to the inappropriate behavior; thus, the student might find that his or her attention-seeking wisecracks in the classroom are not considered funny by other students. This video intervention can provide a powerful reason for a child to decrease a particular type of attention-seeking behavior.

Of course, video monitoring may also be used to increase appropriate behavior. Graetz, Mastropieri, and Scruggs (2006) recently described the use of video monitoring to help a child compare his good behavior with less desirable behavior. These researchers made an "Oh, NO!" video that displayed inappropriate behavior and also a "Way to Go!" videotape that displayed desirable behaviors. They then used these videos in several "debriefing" sessions with the student, employing the videotape so the student could model his own positive behavior and then compare this model with his less desirable behavior. In this study, the student's disruptive behavior was reduced significantly.

Many school districts have guidelines as to how teachers may or may not use videotape with students. As a new teacher, you should ascertain what your local school board policy is regarding videotaping children in the classroom. Still, this strategy can greatly assist some students in improving their behavior, and it represents one research-proven tactic that you should include in your arsenal of behavior management strategies for students with learning disabilities.

Aversive Procedures

For some children with severe disabilities, aversive contingencies (very punishing contingencies) are used. For example, with severely retarded children or autistic children, various forms of aversive contingencies may be applied. If a child spits on his or her teacher, a drop of hot sauce may be placed on his or her tongue. Likewise, helmets or other headgear may be developed that squirt water in the face of children for self-destructive behaviors such as head banging (intentionally banging one's head against a hard wall) or dangerous and intentional self-injury. These aversives must be used only in extreme cases in which every other treatment option has been tried. Also, no single professional may be allowed to develop a behavioral plan based on these contingencies. Rather, a committee of professionals must agree that these extreme contingencies seem to be the only option for eliminating the self-destructive behavior.

The use of such aversives is quite rare (or indeed, unheard of) with children who are learning disabled, but any discussion of negative contingencies must mention these extreme examples because the national press has joined the debate concerning the ethics of these practices. Also, if you mention any behavioral treatment to parents or other teachers, some will respond quite negatively because of the extreme examples of these aversive treatments that have received national press. For that reason, you need to stay informed on the current use of these treatments, even though you will probably never use aversive contingencies with children identified as learning disabled.

SUMMARY OF BEHAVIORAL INTERVENTIONS

Each of the behavioral support interventions discussed has been shown to be effective in changing behavior of students with learning disabilities, students with many other disabilities, and students without disabilities. Also, many of these strategies are commonly used in special and/or inclusive classes for the learning disabled (Anguiano, 2001; Bender, 2003; Carbone, 2001). As you gain increasing experience in various special education settings, you will see various examples of token economies, contracts, time-out procedures, and perhaps extinction procedures. When you have such an opportunity, you should ask about the behavioral interventions and discuss different teachers' perceptions of the effectiveness of the intervention. Also, you may wish to evaluate the behavioral strategy yourself. If an intervention does not work for a particular child, try to determine why. Decide what additional interventions may be tried to alleviate the problem, and if you feel comfortable with your ideas, suggest a procedure to the teacher. In short, use your experiences with other special education teachers to gain insight into behavioral strategies in order to apply these strategies in your own classroom later.

Finally, you should realize that these several strategies represent only the most commonly used ones that have been derived from the behavioral psychologists. Many other strategies are available for classroom use (Anguiano, 2001; Carbone, 2001; Bender, 2003), and you will explore these additional strategies in later courses. As a teacher, you will wish to employ these strategies, and additional course work in behavioral interventions would be desirable.

SPECIALIZED BEHAVIORAL STRATEGIES

Because of the growing influence of behavioral psychology in education, a number of specialized educational treatments have been developed based at least partially on behavioral principles. Two of the more commonly discussed educational approaches are precision teaching and direct instruction. Both of these strategies are slightly more sophisticated than the behavioral strategies discussed earlier, and these strategies generally involve additional training experiences beyond the first methods course in the teacher education program. However, these strategies have been used successfully with children who have learning disabilities, and they represent promising educational interventions.

Precision Teaching

Lindsley (1990) used the precedents of behavioral psychology in order to formulate a method of evaluating instruction on a daily basis. Daily assessment allows for documentation of either success or failure of instructional techniques (Beck, Conrad, & Anderson, 1999; Bender, 2002; White, 1986). Because of daily assessment, precision teaching is a method that allows for specific educational improvements in a child's daily lessons in order to facilitate progress.

Precision teaching does not recommend a particular instructional method. The teacher is free to choose any preparational activity (**antecedent**) or any reinforcement (**consequence**) that will facilitate progress. Precision teaching provides a method of checking on the effectiveness of any method the teacher selects. This open-ended aspect of precision teaching makes this instruction/evaluation technique very adaptable for different classroom situations.

As reported in Chapter 5, many students with learning disabilities demonstrate poor task-oriented skills. This often results in students who do not finish their worksheets and assignments in an appropriate amount of time. Precision teaching can be a very effective method to use with such children because success is measured in terms of rate of work as well as mere accuracy.

For example, imagine that Alfred is a sixth-grade student with learning disabilities who is working on underlining simple subjects and predicates in your resource room. For the last several days, you have reviewed the guidelines for identification of subjects and predicates with Alfred and then given him a worksheet to complete. On each day, the worksheet has been only half completed, though you believe Alfred should be able to complete the entire worksheet. A precision teaching project is needed.

To begin the project, you would state the **behavioral objective** in terms of rate of work completion. An example of an objective in this format is:

> When presented with a set of simple sentences ranging in length from 7 to 12 words, Alfred will correctly underline the simple subject and simple predicate in 25 of those sentences in a three-minute time period.

With such an objective in hand, the initial stages of the project become relatively simple. On the first day, you review the guidelines for the task and give Alfred the worksheet as you had done previously. However, today you time his work and remove the worksheet after three minutes. Explain to him that you are timing him and want to see how quickly he completes his work. After you have checked the first three minutes of the work, you chart the number of correct and incorrect answers. You may then return the paper to him for the remainder of the period.

After several days of this, Alfred begins to get curious, and you may wish to share his charted results with him. You should encourage Alfred to assume ownership of the progress, as represented by the chart. If possible, get him to understand the importance of the task and the project. You may wish to offer reinforcement for reaching his stated goal. The data for the first four days are presented in the first section of the chart in Figure 10.6.

Alfred has demonstrated very little progress at the end of the first several days. This indicates that some change is necessary. Perhaps merely explaining the guidelines to Alfred is not enough. Perhaps several examples of how to identify subjects and predicates are necessary. The **phase change** line (the curved line on the top of the chart after the fourth day) indicates that the project was changed in some way on that day. The chart indicates that you added several examples and continued charting for several more days.

As you can see, Alfred's progress after he was presented with examples increased dramatically. After only seven more days, his correct **learning rate** was above his aim of 25 correct answers in three minutes. At that point, another phase of the project began. A different objective was specified, and Alfred began to identify complete subjects and complete predicates.

Many of the advantages of precision teaching are obvious in this example. First, by identifying the lack of improvement during the first four days of the project, you—the

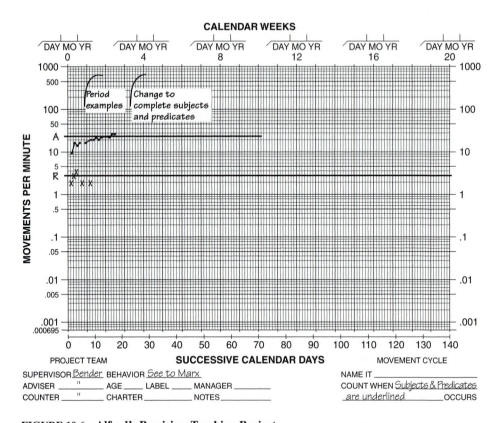

FIGURE 10.6   Alfred's Precision-Teaching Project

teacher—were able to change to an instructional method that was more effective for this student. If presenting examples had not worked, you would have seen that also, in several days, and would have changed instruction again until some method was found that resulted in measurable progress. This adaptability of instruction represents very responsive teaching when compared to traditional instructional methods. In some cases, teachers may have to wait until the unit test (administered in four weeks) before they find that merely reviewing the guidelines was not effective for Alfred. Precision teaching is highly responsive to the student.

Second, the charting of behaviors increases the likelihood for good communication between the teacher and the student. Both can see the stated goal, the progress toward that goal, and the distance to go before the goal is reached. This attention to measurement is characteristic of behavioral methods and very useful when communicating with students who have learning disabilities about their progress.

Third, there should be a direct relationship between the educational objectives on the individualized educational plan of a child with disabilities and the daily work that the child completes in the special education class. Precision-teaching projects represent one method by which such a direct relationship may be strengthened.

Finally, unlike certain other educational treatments for students with learning disabilities, precision teaching is relatively easy to initiate. Specialized curriculum materials, although sometimes helpful, are not essential because almost any worksheet that includes only one particular type of problem or educational task may be used during the project, and charting the rate of correct responses is a relatively simple task. Further, Beck and colleagues (1999) published a set of worksheets specifically for instruction in basic skills using a precision-teaching approach.

Research results on effectiveness of precision teaching have been very positive (see White, 1986, for review). Precision teaching has been used successfully in both elementary and high schools. Most of the research has used basic-skills curriculum areas such as language arts and math tasks. Finally, research has shown that precision teaching is useful for students with mild, moderate, and severe learning disabilities (White, 1986).

Direct Instruction

Direct instruction is a term that represents a teaching approach based on a set of effective instructional behaviors that the teacher should demonstrate in order to maximize the achievement levels of the students (Gersten & Baker, 1998). These teaching behaviors generally include specification of a behavioral objective; an initial direct-instruction phase in which the teacher models a problem and, through task analysis, identifies critical steps in the task solution; a teacher-guided explicit instruction phase; an independent practice phase with immediate feedback; and routine assessment with high levels of mastery required (Gersten & Baker, 1998).

Although the term *direct instruction* is used for a number of slightly different teaching approaches that specify some or all of these steps, the term most frequently refers to certain curriculum materials that have these behaviors incorporated into a scripted dialogue between the teacher and the student (Polloway, Epstein, Polloway, Patton, & Ball, 1986). These scripts are to be read when conducting the lesson, and they include alternative teacher dialogue in response to either correct or incorrect behaviors of the student. Interest Box 10.3 presents part of a **script.**

Research on direct-instruction programs with children who have learning disabilities has demonstrated the effectiveness of this approach (Gersten & Baker, 1998; Polloway et al., 1986). The research on direct instruction has demonstrated the effectiveness of this approach for basic-skills instruction in reading and language arts, as well as cognitive instructional

---

INTEREST BOX 10.3
A DIRECT-INSTRUCTION SCRIPT

> **TEACHER:**   Listen. Here's a rule. Just because someone important in one area says something is good or bad, you can't be sure it's true. (Repeat.)
>
> **TEACHER:**   When someone important in one area says something is good or bad in another area, can you be sure it's true?
>
> **STUDENTS:**   No.
>
> **TEACHER:**   No, just because someone important in one area says something is good or bad in another area, you can't be sure it's true.
>
> **TEACHER:**   OK, listen. George Bush says that Fords are the best family cars.
>
> **TEACHER:**   What do you know about George Bush?
>
> **STUDENTS:**   He's president.
>
> **TEACHER:**   In what area is George Bush important?
>
> **STUDENTS:**   Politics.
>
> **TEACHER:**   And what's this important person saying?
>
> **STUDENTS:**   That Fords are the best family cars.
>
> **TEACHER:**   So what is the other area that George Bush is talking about?
>
> **STUDENTS:**   Cars.
>
> **TEACHER:**   We're learning to judge what people say. Can you be sure what a politician says about Fords is true?
>
> **STUDENTS:**   No.
>
> **TEACHER:**   Why not?
>
> (Or prompt with, "What can you say when someone important says something is good or bad?")
>
> **STUDENTS:**   (Students should give the rule or respond with something like the following.) You can't be sure it's true, and politicians may not know very much about cars.
>
> **TEACHER:**   Listen, if I tell you that George Bush says that one good way to win an election is raising a lot of campaign money, can you be sure it's true?
>
> **STUDENTS:**   Yes.
>
> (Correction procedure: If a child answers "No," ask, "What do you know about the important person?")
>
> **TEACHER:**   Yes, you can be sure that's true. Why? (Accept the answer in varying forms.)

strategies involved in reading comprehension. Many of the early research studies focused on lower-achieving children and remedial skills. However, subsequent research demonstrated that direct instruction also works with higher-level cognitive skills such as critical reading and upper-level math problems (Darch & Kame'enui, 1987).

One may anticipate these research results because direct-instruction methods are founded on numerous behavioral principles that have been shown to be effective. These behavioral principles include specifying the target behavior in an objective, modeling the behavior, giving frequent feedback to the learner, recording accurate and frequent measurement of specific behavior, and achieving a high level of mastery.

A number of steps are necessary before you begin to apply direct-instruction techniques in your class, including obtaining appropriate curricular materials, familiarizing yourself with these, and selecting an appropriate group of students. For example, you may wish to identify a number of students who need reading-comprehension work at about the same level. These students would form a small reading group and would work in teacher-led instruction for 15 to 20 minutes each day. You would then obtain a set of materials (most curriculum centers in public schools have these materials) and conduct the lessons without straying from the prepared script. The routine assessments would be used to show progress, and many of the commercially available materials have progress charts used for monitoring the progress of each student individually. As this list of activities demonstrates, direct instruction can be a time-consuming instructional activity.

There are some teachers who feel that the scripted lessons that characterize direct-instruction curricula limit the teacher's role as instructional leader. You may wish to inquire about this aspect of direct instruction from teachers who are more experienced with these materials. Also, one of the best ways for you to learn the concept of direct instruction is to familiarize yourself with some of the commercially available materials. These include **Reading Mastery** (Englemann & Carnine, 1972) and *Corrective Reading Program* (Englemann, Becker, Hanner, & Johnson, 1980).

SUMMARY

The educational-treatment options presented in this chapter range from interventions for hyperactive behavior to educational interventions designed to improve academic achievement. As demonstrated by this range of interventions, behavioral-instructional principles are the major influence in instruction for the student with learning disabilities in public schools today. The effectiveness of reinforcement in token economies, behavioral contracts, time-out, and extinction has been amply demonstrated by both the research literature and the practical experience of most teachers. The fact that these interventions work accounts for the frequent use of the strategies (Bender, 2003; Maheady et al., 1982).

Perhaps less well known are the various specific instructional techniques that have been derived, in part, from behavioral principles. Precision teaching and direct instruction are both instructional methods that may involve extended course work. You will wish to take every opportunity to prepare yourself in these strategies for later use in your own classroom.

The following points should help you study this chapter:

- The behavioral model of learning is a very effective tool for conceptualizing an instructional process. Behavioral thought has been the dominant form of intervention for the learning disabled for the last 20 years.
- Many classrooms for students with learning disabilities currently employ various behavioral strategies such as token economies, behavioral contracts, extinction, and time-out. Each of these interventions has been supported by numerous research articles.
- Precision teaching is a behaviorally based strategy that requires specification of particular behaviors to be taught and specific measurement of the rate of change of those behaviors on a daily basis.
- Direct instruction is an instructional approach founded on behavioral principles. Teacher scripts are generally prepared, and the instruction consists of the teacher eliciting certain types of responses from the students and providing immediate feedback.

QUESTIONS AND ACTIVITIES

1. Check your college or university materials center, and find out if a corrective reading program is available. Report back to the class, and share the contents of the program.
2. Identify any teachers in your area who use a token economy. Describe their economy to the class.
3. Look through the research journals in special education, and find several examples of single-subject design experiments. Share these with the class.
4. What types of activities that were behavioral in nature were used when you were a student in elementary school?
5. Designate a group to investigate other behavioral-intervention strategies, and report back to the class on each.
6. Discuss the different types of tokens that may be used in a token economy and the advantages/disadvantages of each.
7. What types of activities have been shown to work well in a precision-teaching intervention? How about a direct-instruction intervention?
8. Prepare a chart for the class in which each of these behavioral strategies is paired with a description of the type of student and the type of educational task that would be most likely to facilitate success. What additional information do you need?

REFERENCES

Anguiano, P. (2001). A first year teacher's plan to reduce misbehavior in the classroom. *Teaching Exceptional Children, 33*(3), 52–55.

Barbella, R., & Lavong, A. (2006, April 9–12). *Tailor-made positive behavior support systems and data-driven decision-making: What suits you?* Paper presented at the annual meeting of the Council for Exceptional Children, Salt Lake City, UT.

Beck, R., Conrad, D., & Anderson, P. (1999). *Basic skill builders: Helping students become fluent in basic skills.* Longmont, CO: Sopris West.

Bender, W. N. (2003). *Relational discipline: Strategies for in-your-face kids.* Boston: Allyn & Bacon.

Bender, W. N. (2002). *Differentiating instruction for students with learning disabilities: Best practices for general and special educators.* Thousand Oaks, CA: Corwin Press.

Bryan, T., Burstein, K., & Ergul, C. (2004). The social-emotional side of learning disabilities: A science-based presentation of the state of the art. *Learning Disability Quarterly, 27*(1), 45–52.

Burley, R., & Waller, R. J. (2005). Effects of a collaborative behavior management plan on reducing disruptive behaviors of students with ADHD. *Teaching Exceptional Children Plus, 1*(4). Retrieved from http://escholarship.bc.edu/education/tecplus/vol1/iss4/2.

Carbone, E. (2001). Arranging the classroom with an eye (and ear) to students with ADHD. *Teaching Exceptional Children, 34*(2), 72–81.

Carey, T. A., & Bourbon, W. T. (2004). Countercontrol: A new look at some old problems. *Intervention in School and Clinic, 40*(1), 3–9.

Darch, C., & Kame'enui, E. J. (1987). Teaching LD students critical reading skills: A systematic replication. *Learning Disability Quarterly, 10,* 82–91.

Englemann, S., Becker, W. C., Hanner, S., & Johnson, G. (1980). *Corrective reading program.* Chicago: Science Research Associates.

Englemann, S., & Carnine, D. W. (1972). *DISTAR arithmetic III.* Chicago: Science Research Associates.

Gersten, R., & Baker, S. (1998). Real world use of scientific concepts: Integrating situated cognition with explicit instruction. *Exceptional Children, 65*(1), 23–36.

Graetz, J. E., Mastropieri, M. A., & Scruggs, T. E. (2006). Show time: Using video self-modeling to decrease inappropriate behavior. *Teaching Exceptional Children, 38*(5), 43–48.

Kavale, K. A., & Mostert, M. P. (2004). Social skills interventions for individuals with learning disabilities. *Learning Disability Quarterly, 27*(1), 31–44.

Lindsley, O. R. (1990). Precision teaching: By teachers for children. *Teaching Exceptional Children, 22*(3), 10–15.

Maheady, L., Duncan, D., & Sainato, D. (1982). A survey of use of behavior modification techniques by special education teachers. *Teacher Education and Special Education, 5*(4), 9–15.

Polloway, E. A., Epstein, M. H., Polloway, C. H., Patton, J. R., & Ball, D. W. (1986). Corrective reading program: An analysis of effectiveness with learning disabled and mentally retarded students. *Remedial and Special Education, 7*(4), 41–47.

Salend, S. J. (1987). Contingency management systems. *Academic Therapy, 22,* 245–253.

Salend, S. J., & Gordon, B. D. (1987). A group-oriented timeout ribbon procedure. *Behavioral Disorders, 12,* 131–136.

White, O. R. (1986). Precision teaching—Precision learning. *Exceptional Children, 52,* 522–534.

CHAPTER ELEVEN

METACOGNITIVE INSTRUCTIONAL APPROACHES FOR STUDENTS WITH LEARNING DISABILITIES

CHAPTER OUTLINE

WHEN YOU COMPLETE THIS CHAPTER, YOU SHOULD BE ABLE TO:

1. Describe the psychological foundations of metacognitive educational interventions.

2. Identify two types of learning strategies.

3. Draw and explain the metacognitive model of learning.

4. Describe a research treatment study that indicates the effectiveness of learning strategies for students with learning disabilities.

5. List and discuss the four stages of reciprocal teaching.

6. Describe a self-monitoring project designed to increase on-task behavior of a student who is learning disabled.

KEYWORDS

cognitive psychology	FISH	prediction
inner language	SCORER	question generation
self-monitoring	verbal rehearsal	summarizing
executive function	PLEASE	clarifying
learning strategies	FAST	scaffolded instruction
Donald Deshler	story map	self-correction
RIDER	story retelling	
SLANT	reciprocal teaching	

INTRODUCTION

The study of learning, generally referred to as **cognitive psychology,** may be traced to early leaders in educational psychology who studied cognitive development in children during the first decades of the past century. Educational leaders such as Jean Piaget, Jerome Bruner, Lev Vygotsky, Erik Erikson, and others developed numerous theories about how the intellectual abilities of children develop and grow (Fogarty, 1999). These early models of thought interacted with behavioral psychology in the 1960s and resulted in concentration on measurable indicators for learning.

Although behavioral psychology grew to be the dominant influence in the education of children with learning disabilities during the decade of the 1970s, cognitive psychology has been growing in influence since that time. By 1979, it was quite apparent that behavioral interventions were established as major educational treatments, and the effectiveness of those approaches had been demonstrated. According to behavioral psychologists, human learning follows the same laws as does learning in animals of lesser intelligence, and effective teaching consists of consistent implementation of behavioral interventions in order to influence learning.

However, psychologists who studied human learning, building on the early work of the psychologists previously mentioned, had never abandoned the idea that learning in human beings was somehow different from learning in primates and other mammals. By 1975, the evidence on behavior treatments used on children with disabilities had established that behavioral interventions worked, so cognitive psychologists could not ignore the behavioral model of learning. However, because of work done by cognitive psychologists with children without disabilities, the field of cognitive psychology could expand on the model of learning that the behaviorists proposed, resulting in a model of learning that has come to be known as *metacognition* or *cognitive behavior modification.* This metacognitive model has become increasingly important because numerous instructional strategies are being developed based on the model (Bender, 2002; Korinek & Bulls, 1996; Larkin, 2001; McIntosh, Vaughn, & Bennerson, 1995). In particular, Don Deshler and his colleagues have created numerous strategies based on metacognition (Deshler, 2006; Schumaker & Deshler, 2003).

METACOGNITIVE MODEL OF LEARNING

Learning has been described by behavioral psychologists as a function of antecedents and consequences, as discussed in Chapter 10. The model looks like this:

Antecedent   →   Behavior   →   Consequence

The cognitive psychologists could not disagree with the basic validity of this model because the evidence provided by behavioral psychologists for the model was overwhelming. However, the cognitive psychologists did stipulate a major refinement of this model. These theorists, particularly Michenbaum and his co-workers (Michenbaum, 1971; Michenbaum & Goodman, 1969), noted that in humans the role of inner language and self-instruction could be placed in the model as an intervening step between the antecedent and the behavioral response. As a result, the cognitive psychologists stipulated a model of learning that looks like this:

Antecedent   →   Inner Language   →   Behavior   →   Consequence

With this model in mind, cognitive psychologists have focused on providing instruction for this inner language component of the model. Most cognitively based instructional strategies focus on giving the students the correct set of inner language statements to be used as self-instruction while the student completes the task. Many of these cognitive instructional approaches provide models of the use of inner language and opportunities for practice in using the self-instruction.

As Figure 11.1 illustrates, human beings use inner language in most problem solving. Whereas the behavioral model works for all learning organisms, including human beings, the metacognitive model of learning utilizes the intervening variable that is available in learning among language-using human beings—**inner language**—which connects the environmental antecedents and the behavior. Consequently, these psychologists teach by manipulation of inner language while attending to the proven behavioral techniques.

FIGURE 11.1   Use of Inner Language by Problem-Solving Student

Later, the learning model that emphasized inner language became known as the *meta-cognitive model.* This term is roughly interpreted to mean thinking about thinking or the use of inner language to plan a thinking/learning activity.

Finally, the study of learning espoused by metacognitive psychologists has now expanded beyond mere inner language to include all self-planning of learning tasks (McConnel, 1999; Scanlon, 2002). When completing a task, there are two distinct types of cognitive activities occurring. One activity consists of the thinking processes that are directly related to the completion of the task. The other activity, generally referred to as *metacognition,* involves overall planning of the cognitive task, self-instructions to complete the task, and performance **self-monitoring,** or checking to see that each phase of the task is completed appropriately and in the appropriate order (Bender, 2002). Each of these tasks may involve the use of inner language or self-instruction as discussed previously. Some scholars use the term **executive function** to represent the process that involves thinking through a task and directing the performance of the task but not being directly involved in completing the individual cognitive steps of the task.

This model of metacognitive learning is one of the most important models of learning and instruction in the field of learning disabilities today. For example, textbooks have been written that emphasize only this model of learning for students with learning disabilities. Although this may be a bit restrictive, certainly future teachers of these students should be well versed in the instructional strategies that the metacognitive model promotes.

Research on the specific educational treatments has generated a large number of instructional ideas. Also, there are several different groups of scholars who have contributed notably to this body of research. The next sections of the text will present each of these diverse areas in an attempt to highlight the classroom implementation aspect of these cognitively based approaches.

Learning-Strategies Research

As discussed in Chapter 1, the metacognitive perspective has been the most influential perspective for research during the last several years. This perspective stressed the lack of involvement with the educational task in children with learning disabilities. In response to this perspective, various researchers began to develop a set of metacognitive strategies that enable the student to participate in the task in a more active fashion. Two types of metacognitive intervention strategies were developed—those that focused on an acronym representing the steps in the strategy and those that did not.

Learning strategies involving the use of acronyms to structure inner language were associated initially with **Donald Deshler** and his associates at the University of Kansas Learning Disabilities Institute (Boudah, Lenz, Bulgren, Schumaker, & Deshler, 2000; Deshler, 2006; Schumaker & Deshler, 2003). The strategies specified the steps for an adolescent student with learning disabilities to go through when completing specific tasks. These steps formed the basis of inner language for the student to use when completing the task. The acronym itself was to be memorized. Interest Box 11.1 presents the **RIDER** learning strategy. When applied in a consistent classwide or schoolwide fashion, this learning-strategies approach can greatly enhance learning (Lenz, 2006).

Since the earliest development of strategies, a number of these strategies have been developed for various types of tasks. Strategies have been developed for reading a paragraph, completing a multiple-choice test, reading a chapter in a subject-content area, studying captions under the pictures in a secondary text, and many other specific learning tasks.

SLANT is one example of a learning strategy intended for use on a specific learning task—note-taking (Ellis, 1991). SLANT is an acronym for the steps a student should go through in effective note-taking: *S*—Sit up; *L*—Lean forward; *A*—Activate your thinking; *N*—Name key information; and *T*—Track the talker. The student memorizes these steps and is given repeated practice in implementing each step. Time spent on this strategy will enhance a student's note-taking skills.

Test-taking skills represent one area in which students with learning disabilities often have problems. The **SCORER** strategy was developed to help students learn how to take multiple-choice tests. The acronym for this strategy is straightforward: *S*—Schedule your time; *C*—Clue word use; *O*—Omit difficult questions; *R*—Read carefully; *E*—Estimate your answers; *R*—Review your work. Research has indicated that this strategy can improve the test-taking skills of secondary students with learning disabilities.

A great deal of research has been conducted on learning strategies, including much recent research on word decoding, reading, and literacy (Archer et al., 2003; Deshler, 2006; Schumaker & Deshler, 2003; Whitaker et al., 2006). For example, Whitaker and her coworkers recently developed a strategy called **FISH** to assist students in decoding words at the elementary level. In this strategy, *F* indicates the student should "Find the rhyme,"

■ ■ ■ ■ ■ ▬▬▬▬▬▬▬▬▬▬▬

INTEREST BOX 11.1

TEACHING TIPS: RIDER: A LEARNING STRATEGY TO IMPROVE READING COMPREHENSION

A learning strategy consists of an acronym that indicates the actions a student is supposed to take while completing the educational task. A sample learning strategy is the RIDER strategy, which enables students to form visual images of material while they read in order to enhance recall and reading comprehension.

Read	Read the first sentence.
Image	Make an image of the material read.
Describe	Describe your image—(1) If you cannot describe it, explain why. (2) If you can make an image, compare it to the earlier image (from earlier sentences). (3) Describe the image to yourself.
Evaluate	Evaluate your image for completeness. Check to see that your image includes as much of the information as possible, and if it is complete, move on.
Repeat	Repeat the earlier steps for the next sentence.

which means they should identify the vowel, vowel sound, and the remaining sounds of the word. *I* suggests the student should "Identify the rhyme or word that ends with that sound." *S* means the child should "Say the rhyme," and *H* tells the child to "Hook the new onset (or beginning sound) to the rhyme." By applying this new learning strategy, using the same steps described above, the authors demonstrated in an action research project that students could not only learn to recognize rhymes directly taught and decode words involving those rhymes, but could also transfer this knowledge to rhymes that were not specifically taught using the FISH learning strategy. Thus, this learning strategy provided those children with a word-decoding strategy for simple word recognition.

As you can see, the array of tasks that can be addressed by strategy instruction is wide and includes many of the tasks that students with learning disabilities will have to perform to be successful in school (Lenz, 2006).

Strategy Instruction in the Classroom

Application of these learning strategies in classrooms for the learning disabled is a fairly complex affair. The University of Kansas group has recommended that a series of daily lessons be devoted to learning each of the strategies, as illustrated in Figure 11.2.

According to the suggested procedures, strategy instruction is to proceed in a relatively straightforward fashion. The teacher of students with learning disabilities should conduct the lessons with eventual application in each inclusive class. The recommended phases of strategy instruction are presented below.

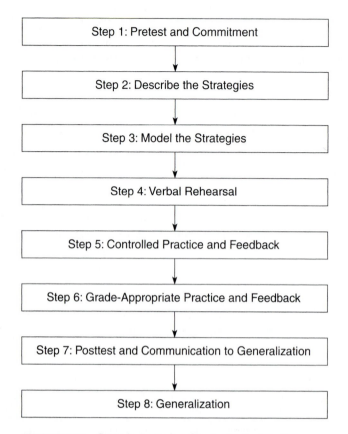

FIGURE 11.2   Steps in Learning-Strategies Instruction

        The first step takes place on the first day only and is devoted to the pretest and commitment phase. On the first day, each participating student is tested on the application of the strategy. Results are shared with the students, the importance of the strategy is emphasized, and students are requested to commit themselves to mastery of the strategy. The first instructional period (about 45 minutes) is devoted to this phase.

        The second step, on day 2, is devoted to providing a description of the new strategy for the students. The focus of the lesson is on the key elements of the strategy and application of the strategy. Students are encouraged to consider alternatives for strategy application.

        The third step, on day 3, is devoted to the modeling phase. The teacher speaks out loud as each step in the strategy is initiated, and generally several different tasks are completed. The teacher may also prompt the students and mention particularly difficult aspects of the strategy.

        The fourth step, on day 4 of strategy instruction, is **verbal rehearsal** of the strategy acronym. Students must identify the action to be taken in each step of the strategy and tell why each step is important to the strategy overall. This step takes one instructional period.

The fifth step of strategy instruction is practice in controlled materials. During strategy instruction, the difficulty of the material should not be allowed to impair mastery of the strategy. Consequently, the strategy is applied to materials that are below the student's mastery level. This often results in strategy instruction using materials that are several years below the student's current grade placement. A daily record of performance is kept, and the strategy is repeated over numerous instructional periods involving as many as 20 instructional days.

The next step is practice on grade-appropriate materials. This involves application of the strategy to materials with which the student is working in the special education class. This step usually takes 5 to 10 instructional periods, and a chart of progress is kept during this phase.

The last step is generalization. The student is trained to apply the strategy to materials from other classes. Instruction is provided on how to choose an appropriate task for the strategy that has just been mastered. Initially, during this phase, the special education teacher will check the assignments in order to assess strategy usage. Finally, during this phase, maintenance is emphasized by occasional postchecks of strategy application.

Research on Strategy Instruction

Research on learning strategies has demonstrated that this instructional method works very well with adolescents who have learning disabilities (Boudah et al., 2000; Deshler, 2006; Korinek & Bulls, 1996; Lenz, 2006; McIntosh et al., 1995). For example, Welch (1992) presented evidence that a strategy called **PLEASE** could be used to improve the paragraph writing of students with learning disabilities. The PLEASE strategy involves the following steps, as represented by the letters in the acronym: *P*—Pick a topic; *L*—List your ideas about the topic; *E*—Evaluate your list; *A*—Activate the paragraph with a topic sentence; *S*—Supply supporting sentences; and *E*—End with a concluding sentence and evaluate your work.

This strategy was used with two groups of sixth-grade students with learning disabilities. The study used a classic research treatment design in which one group of students was trained in the strategy and a comparison group was not so trained. The training for both groups took place several times each week over a 20-week period. After that training period, the paragraphs from these two groups were compared, along with an attitude measure to assess the students' perspectives about paragraph writing assignments. The results favored the group trained in the PLEASE strategy. Their paragraphs were much more developed than the paragraphs written by the other group. Also, the attitudes toward writing of the students in the experimental group improved significantly as a result of the metacognitive strategy treatment. This study indicates that there may be benefits resulting from metacognitive instruction beyond mere academic improvement on the specific task.

With additional research demonstrating the efficacy of learning-strategies instruction, a number of other researchers have contributed specific strategies for particular types of instructional problems that may be encountered by students with learning disabilities (Korinek & Bulls, 1996; Lenz, 2006; McIntosh et al., 1995; Scanlon, 2002). For example, Korinek and Bulls (1996) developed a strategy that may be used to assist students in preparing a research paper. The acronym used was SCORE A: *S*—Select a topic; *C*—Create categories for information about the topic; *O*—Obtain sources; *R*—Read and take notes; *E*—Evenly organize the information; and *A*—Apply the process writing steps.

Five students with learning disabilities in grade 8 were used to demonstrate the efficacy of the strategy. The students applied the strategy over a period of nine weeks, and subsequently, four of the five students received a grade of "C" or better on their papers.

McIntosh and colleagues (1995) developed a strategy to assist students with learning disabilities in social problem solving, based on the acronym **FAST**. When a student detects social hostility from someone, he or she should apply the following steps: *F*—Freeze and think about the problem; *A*—Alternatives to be generated to assist in solving the problem; *S*—Solution (i.e., determine which alternatives will work); and *T*—Try it. The FAST strategy was shown to assist students with learning disabilities in maintaining or increasing their social status.

A large number of additional studies have demonstrated the effectiveness of these techniques. This type of learning strategy is effective in most basic-skills areas, including reading, language arts, writing, spelling, and math. Also, strategies have been used with success to assist in reading comprehension of content-oriented classes such as science and history. Finally, the effectiveness of numerous strategies for specialized school tasks such as test-taking skills, paragraph writing, and comprehension of lecture information has been demonstrated.

OTHER METACOGNITIVE STRATEGIES

In addition to the research with strategies involving specific acronyms, a number of strategies have been developed that do not involve acronyms (Archer et al., 2003; Ashton, 1999; Dye, 2000; Hogan & Pressley, 1997). Various terms have been used to describe these activities, such as *graphic organizer, story frame,* **story map,** *semantic mapping, comprehension monitoring,* **story retelling,** and others.

None of these methods involves the use of specific acronyms that students must memorize, but each method does facilitate the students' use of inner language to accomplish the reading task because self-instructions must be given during the completion of the strategy. Archer, Gleason, and Vachon (2003) provided an example of this type of learning strategy. They devised a set of steps to assist older readers in a word-decoding strategy for multisyllabic words. The steps that older, struggling readers should follow to decode a word are:

1. Circle the word parts (prefix) at the beginning of the word.
2. Circle the word parts (suffix) at the end of the word.
3. Underline the letters representing vowel sounds in the rest of the word.
4. Say the parts of the word.
5. Say the parts fast.
6. Make it a real word (say it together).

When students with learning disabilities were taught this word-decoding strategy, their reading skills increased (Archer et al., 2003). Thus, this represents an example of strategy instruction that is not dependent upon use of an acronym.

INTEREST BOX 11.2

TEACHING TIPS: THE STORY-FRAME WORKSHEET

THE STORY-FRAME WORKSHEET

The problem in this story was _____

_____

It started when _____

_____

_____

After that, _____

_____

Then, _____

_____

The problem is solved when _____

_____

The story ends _____

_____

Another example of this is the story-frame strategy presented in Interest Box 11.2. In order to draw a meaningful picture of the material read, the student must actively describe the material to himself or herself. The student would first describe the problem to be resolved in the story, the initiation of the problem, the sequence of events, and the resolution of the problem. This use of inner language is one major factor in all cognitive strategies.

Research results on the efficacy of these strategies have been quite positive (Bowman & Davey, 1986; Johnson et al., 1986; Rose & Sherry, 1984). For example, the use of various strategies to preview reading material has been shown to be effective in improving reading comprehension. Instruction in monitoring comprehension during the reading tasks has been shown to improve comprehension. Requiring a student to retell a story after reading has been shown to be an effective method for improving recall of text information. Also, the use of pictures to organize information during and after reading is effective in improving recall of important information.

A review of the study by Rose and Sherry (1984) illustrates the use of a learning strategy that is not based on an acronym. Rose and Sherry (1984) studied the effects of two previewing procedures on oral reading performance. Five students with learning disabilities were used, and five separate AB interventions were reported. First, each student was observed during a two-minute reading session on each day of baseline. Observers counted the oral reading errors, including mispronunciations, omissions, substitutions, and unknown words. During the intervention phase, the students alternately used two previewing methods. Either they read the material silently to themselves as a preview technique, or they listened while the teacher read the material. The results indicated that both previewing methods were preferable to no previewing at all for four of the five students. However, the listening previewing method resulted in fewer errors than the silent-reading previewing technique for four of the five students.

The learning strategies that are not based on an acronym may be as simple as helping the child understand that previewing aids reading comprehension. Use of these simple strategies in your class will greatly facilitate your students' academic achievement.

RECIPROCAL TEACHING

Reciprocal teaching is an instructional method designed to promote metacognitive understanding of the material through a structured dialogue between the teacher and the students (Bender, 2002; Bruce & Chan, 1991; Palincsar & Brown, 1986, 1987). This method is a metacognitive method because the emphasis is placed on the correct dialogue in which a student must engage for successful task completion. Whereas the learning strategies presented earlier focused on the specific language a student should use during task completion, the reciprocal-teaching method focuses on the things the teacher can do to facilitate the students' use of metacognitive strategy planning. Interest Box 11.3 presents a sample dialogue from a classroom in which reciprocal teaching was employed (Palincsar & Brown, 1986).

Classroom Application of Reciprocal Teaching

When using a reciprocal-teaching approach, the teacher and the students take turns as the instructional leader. Whoever is the "teacher" assumes the role of leading a dialogue about a reading passage that the students read silently. The common goals of each member of the group are predicting, question generating, summarizing, and clarifying. Each of these goals is taught separately.

Prediction of what comes next in the text involves relevant background knowledge of the text. Also, predicting gives students a reason to read further—that is, to confirm or refute their predictions. Therefore, this strategy involves both comprehension of material being read and comprehension monitoring of material that has already been read.

Question generation gives the student the opportunity to identify the type of information that may make up test questions. Also, this activity may provide the occasion to discuss the method of study for various types of questions.

Summarizing information provides an opportunity to integrate information from different sections of the text. The most important ideas of the reading sections may be jointly identified and discussed.

Clarifying forces students to identify the major points of the reading selection and to identify concepts that may be difficult. Identification of difficult concepts is one aspect of reading comprehension that is particularly troublesome for students with learning dis-

■ ■ ■ ■ ■ ▬▬▬▬▬▬▬▬▬▬▬▬▬▬▬▬▬▬▬▬▬▬▬▬▬▬▬▬

INTEREST BOX 11.3
RECIPROCAL TEACHING DIALOGUE

STUDENT 1: What does an astronaut need when he goes into space?

STUDENT 2: A spacesuit.

STUDENT 3: It's called a pressure suit.

STUDENT 4: A helmet.

STUDENT 1: Those are all good answers.

TEACHER: Nice job! I have a question too. Why does the astronaut wear a pressure suit?

STUDENT 3: It keeps his blood from boiling.

STUDENT 4: It keeps his body temperature at a safe level.

TEACHER: Very good.

STUDENT 1: For my summary: This paragraph was about what astronauts need to take into space.

STUDENT 5: And why they need those things.

STUDENT 3: I think we need to clarify the blood boiling.

STUDENT 6: In zero pressure like space, liquids boil.

STUDENT 1: I have a prediction. In space there are many strange and wonderful stars and planets that astronauts see as they do their work. My prediction is that they'll describe some of these. What are some of the strange things you already know about that an astronaut may see?

STUDENT 6: A hurricane on Earth.

STUDENT 3: A double star.

STUDENT 5: Nebulae.

TEACHER: Good answers. Now, who will be our next teacher?

A teaching dialogue such as this is exciting for anyone who has ever attempted to involve students in discussions. Not only are numerous students participating, but the level of this small-group instructional dialogue indicates a great deal of metacognitive understanding on the part of the students. Each of the students was aware of the four basic metacognitive goals included in reciprocal teaching, and even if the students could not complete one of the goals, the students still were aware of the need to think about each step.

Reciprocal teaching is a cognitive instructional intervention that can be easily incorporated into almost any classroom. You may wish to read several of the articles in the references and consider using this method in your class.

abilities because these students will often read a selection and not realize that they did not understand part of the passage. Seeking clarification also allows the student to ask questions without embarrassment because the role of the students is to "question and clarify" the problem areas for other students.

Each of the four strategies is taught for a single instructional period, with the teacher conducting these lessons. Initially, each strategy is explained, and examples are given along with guided practice. By the fifth or sixth day, the teacher and students are using the strategies together to discuss reading material. At that point, the teacher continues to model the strategies, praises the students for using the strategies, and prompts the students to use additional strategies. By the end of a two-week period, the role of "teacher" is rotated, and the students become the facilitators.

Research Support for Reciprocal Teaching

Several studies have indicated that reciprocal teaching is useful in helping students understand written text (Bruce & Chan, 1991; Palincsar & Brown, 1985). These studies used various groups of students and concentrated on reading comprehension in the basic-skills areas. Also, some of the work has indicated that reciprocal teaching may be effective in reading comprehension of text material (Palincsar & Brown, 1986).

The early research indicated that reciprocal teaching was effective, but the application of this procedure was hampered by generalization problems. For example, although reciprocal teaching could be utilized in any class, it was typically taught in the special education classroom and not in the general education class. Bruce and Chan (1991) addressed this problem in a research study in which the procedure was taught in the special education class, and a generalization procedure was used in the general education class to encourage the students to use reciprocal teaching. The procedure involved memory cues to the students in the general education class to use the reciprocal-teaching strategies previously learned in the resource classroom. The results indicated that students would apply reciprocal-teaching procedures in various settings if such generalization was encouraged. This research does emphasize the need for special education teachers and general education educators to work together to assure that strategies learned in one setting are applied in various settings.

As a teacher of students with learning disabilities, you should plan to utilize this strategy with many of the students in your class. As indicated previously, this is not a technique that can be utilized for only one or two days. Rather, this strategy must be built into your classroom on a daily basis over a period of weeks. However, if such instruction is available to your students, you will find that they respond quite positively to reciprocal teaching. Like many of the metacognitive instructional strategies described in this chapter, this strategy has been shown to be effective, and these instructional procedures are gaining influence in the field.

SCAFFOLDED INSTRUCTION

The concept of *scaffolding* has been increasingly discussed as one metacognitive strategy that is effective for students with learning disabilities (Bender, 2002; Dye, 2000; Hogan & Pressley, 1997; Larkin, 2001). As you may recall from Chapter 1, the constuctivist view of learning suggests that learning is a process of mental construction whereby students build new knowledge in relation to previously learned material. In that construction process, a scaffold is an individualized, specialized instructional activity, tied to the child's current knowledge, that allows the child to bridge his or her current understanding and move toward new levels of comprehension of the material to be mastered.

Once a child's individual needs have been analyzed by the child and the teacher together, the scaffolds may be provided by the teacher or by curriculum material, a learning strategy, or an advance organizer (Bender, 2002; Dye, 2000)—any activity that can support the student as he or she approaches new concepts. This instructional technique can be quite effective as one method to differentiate instruction in inclusive classes because those classes would typically include students with widely varying abilities, and teachers need to consider the exact level of support needed by different students (Larkin, 2001; Scanlon, 2002).

Several authors have described the essential components of **scaffolded instruction** (Bender, 2002; Hogan & Pressley, 1997; Larkin, 2001). These individual components typically include the following:

- Preengagement, in which both curriculum demands and student needs are considered
- Establishment of a shared goal, after discussion with the child
- Active diagnosis of the current understanding and needs of the child
- Provision of assistance tailored directly to the child's needs
- Feedback to the child in his or her learning attempts
- Assistance in internalizing knowledge and generalization of newly learned skills

Many of these instructional components require that the teacher and student work closely together while the teacher actively diagnoses the child's current understanding of the problem at hand. Other components (e.g., provision of assistance tailored to the child's needs and provision of feedback) may be from a specifically selected learning task, a computer program, or specialized curriculum material. The key to scaffolding is not how a scaffold is provided, but rather the provision of just the right learning support at just the right moment and withdrawal of that scaffold as the child's learning grows. Over the next decade, one may expect to see many more research articles on learning scaffolds or metacognitive supports for learning for students with learning disabilities.

SELF-MONITORING

Self-monitoring strategies may be directed to improve either behavior or academic progress (Goddard & Heron, 1998; Scanlon, 2002; Snider, 1987). In this strategy, the student is trained to use inner language to periodically monitor his or her behavior or academic progress.

Here is one example of a self-monitoring strategy to improve attention. First, a cassette tape is prepared with a bell tone that rings at varying intervals (the intervals should average around 45 seconds in length). At the sound of each bell, the student asks the question, "Was I paying attention?" The student is trained to answer either yes or no on a recording sheet and immediately return to the worksheet.

The use of the silent question concerning one's behavior is the most critical aspect of this strategy, and dependence on such inner language indicates the relationship between this technique and other metacognitive intervention techniques.

Classroom Application of Self-Monitoring

Among the several strategies discussed in this chapter, self-monitoring to improve behavior is probably the most easily adapted to any classroom (Goddard & Heron, 1998). Only one or two days of instruction are necessary prior to implementation of this strategy, compared with 10 to 30 days for implementation of some of the other metacognitive interventions. Also, Hallahan, Lloyd, & Stoller (1982) have published a small booklet designed to give the novice teacher all the necessary information for implementation. An excerpt from that book is presented in Interest Box 11.4. It indicates the ease of implementation.

You should note the use of certain direct-instruction features in Interest Box 11.4. For example, both the teacher-scripted statements and the emphasis on modeling are based on the direct-instruction teaching practices described in Chapter 10. It is not uncommon to find that, once an effective idea has been proven—such as the direct-instruction teaching procedures described previously—that idea will then be incorporated into more recent innovations in instruction.

Research Support for Self-Monitoring

Self-monitoring to improve attention was developed and popularized by Daniel Hallahan and associates at the University of Virginia Learning Disabilities Institute (Bender, 2002), and numerous papers have demonstrated the effectiveness of this intervention (Goddard &

■ ■ ■ ■ ■

INTEREST BOX 11.4
TEACHING TIPS: SELF-MONITORING INSTRUCTIONS

"Johnny, you know how paying attention to your work has been a problem for you? You've heard teachers tell you, 'Pay attention,' 'Get to work,' 'What are you supposed to be doing?' and things like that. Well, today we're going to start something that will help you help yourself to pay attention better. First, we need to make sure that you know what paying attention means. This is what I mean by paying attention." (Teacher models immediate and sustained attention to task.) "And this is what I mean by not paying attention." (Teacher models inattentive behaviors such as glancing around and playing with objects.) "Now you tell me if I was paying attention." (Teacher models attentive and inattentive behaviors and requires the student to categorize them.) "OK, now let me show you what we're going to do. Every once in a while, you'll hear a little sound like this." (Teacher plays tone on tape.) "And when you hear that sound, quietly ask yourself, 'Was I paying attention?' If you answer 'yes,' put a check in this box. If you answer 'no,' put a check in this box. Then go right back to work. When you hear the sound again, ask the question, answer it, mark your answer, and go back to work. Now, let me show you how it works." (Teacher models entire procedure.) "Now, Johnny, I bet you can do this. Tell me what you're going to do every time you hear a tone. Let's try it. I'll start the tape and you work on these papers." (Teacher observes the student's implementation of the entire procedure, praises its correct use, and gradually withdraws his or her presence.)

Source: From *Improving Attention with Self-Monitoring* by D. P. Hallahan, J. W. Lloyd, and L. Stoller, 1982, Charlottesville: University of Virginia Institute for Learning Disabilities. Used by permission.

Heron, 1998; Hallahan & Sapona, 1983; Snider, 1987). This strategy has been shown to be effective across the grade levels (Bender, 2002).

For example, Prater, Joy, Chilman, Temple, and Miller (1991) used a self-monitoring strategy with one interesting variation. They incorporated a visual prompt—a poster that was designed to remind students of appropriate on-task behavior in a secondary classroom. The five students used the visual prompt poster and a self-recording sheet similar to the one described previously. The visual prompt poster included four reminders of appropriate on-task behavior: (1) eyes on the teacher or work; (2) sitting in seat, facing forward, feet on floor, or legs crossed; (3) using correct materials; and (4) working silently. Each of these statements was illustrated by a picture as an additional reminder to the students. Some of the students utilized the self-monitoring procedure in the special education class, whereas others used this procedure in the mainstream classes. When the bell tone was heard, each student was instructed to self-monitor his or her behavior using the visual prompt. Like the earlier studies with children with learning disabilities, this study indicated that the procedure worked quite well with adolescents. Also, one of the five subjects in this study was a 17-year-old African American female, and the results for that adolescent were as positive as for the four white males in the study. Inclusion of minority students strengthens this overall research design.

These studies have indicated the efficacy of self-monitoring as an intervention for children and adolescents with learning disabilities, including minority students. In addition, some results indicated that the frequency of problem completion increases, along with the increases in on-task time, as a result of self-monitoring (Snider, 1987), though this result is much more tentative. At the very least, self-monitoring will enhance the ability of many students with learning disabilities to stay on-task. Finally, there is some evidence that self-monitoring will work with students who have identified behavioral problems as well as students with learning disabilities (McLaughlin, Krauppmam, & Welch, 1985). Clearly, this is one metacognitive intervention that should be widely utilized by both general education and special education teachers to assist students who have attention-deficit problems.

With these results in mind, you should consider the types of tasks that you have a student complete while he or she is using a self-monitoring procedure. Self-monitoring of attention behavior should be used when a student is in the independent practice phase of learning or when that student is given a worksheet type of assignment to complete. The self-monitoring program should be used with students who have good understanding of the task and who demonstrate fairly high accuracy in problem completion. Students whose major problem is inability to stay on-task are good candidates for this intervention. Also, the intervention seems to work best on seatwork tasks that are done individually.

Some authors have recommended a slightly modified form of self-monitoring— **self-correction**—as an academic intervention for students with learning disabilities (Bender, 2002; Goddard & Heron, 1998; Hogan & Pressley, 1997; McConnel, 1999). For example, Goddard and Heron (1998) described a self-correction strategy by which a student with learning disabilities can learn to monitor and self-correct his or her spelling. They suggest several self-correction activities, including both letter-by-letter proofing and whole-word proofing.

In letter-by-letter proofing, a student is provided with a daily spell sheet that presents columns of words. The left-hand column, column 1, is a list of correctly spelled words that the student is to master, and the next four columns present either a correct spelling or a spelling variation of each of those words, as shown below:

Column 1	Column 2	Column 3	Column 4	Column 5
target	terget	target	targot	target
horse	hosrt	house	horse	harus

In this letter-by-letter proofing activity, the student would use a series of editing marks and correct each of the words in the last four columns. This type of self-correction exercise, provided on a daily basis, can assist students with learning disabilities in learning to spell the selected words. In the whole-word proofing, the same five-column format is used, but students write down the misspelled word correctly.

As a student's self-correction skills grow, this procedure results in the habitual self-monitoring of spelling performance on this and other written work. Of course, this self-correction, error-monitoring procedure is merely one instructional idea based on self-monitoring, and many other similar strategies have been developed. As you proceed in your education methods courses, you will encounter many self-monitoring techniques for students with learning disabilities.

SUMMARY

The various metacognitive interventions discussed in this chapter are based on the use of inner language to plan and organize strategies to facilitate the completion of schoolwork. For example, the learning-strategies acronyms developed at the University of Kansas facilitate the use of inner language for highly specific academic tasks in secondary school. These strategies have already received wide dissemination in classes for students with learning disabilities. The nonspecific strategies, such as text previewing, comprehension monitoring, scaffolding, and self-correction, are based on inner language for task planning. These strategies are also being used with increasing frequency.

Reciprocal teaching is an instructional method that focuses the child's metacognitive planning on specific types of tasks in order to improve reading comprehension. This strategy encourages the child to interact with the reading material in a well-planned manner.

Finally, self-monitoring of behavior is an example of the use of inner language to monitor appropriate behavior and academic performance in the classroom. The dependence on inner language is made clear by the questions that students are trained to ask themselves silently.

From a broader perspective, the relationship between each of these metacognitive strategies and the metacognitive perspective on learning disabilities is clear. The metacognitive perspective suggests that children with learning disabilities are uninvolved with the educational task and do not plan their educational tasks in any straightforward manner. As a result of this perspective, researchers began to focus on techniques that gave the student more responsibility for metacognitive planning of the solution for educational problems. Each of the metacognitive strategies presented in this chapter seeks to assure greater active involvement between the student who is learning disabled and the educational task. This focus has been the dominant theme in research on children with learning disabilities since around 1985, and there is every indication that these strategies will be more widely applied in classes for the learning disabled during the next decade.

The following points should help as you study this chapter:

- The metacognitive model of instruction is founded on the behavioral model of instruction and includes one additional element—inner language or self-instruction.
- Metacognition involves the student's overall planning of a learning task, self-instructions for that task, and self-monitoring of task performance.
- Learning strategies generally involve an acronym to be memorized, which represents the self-instructional steps in a learning task.
- Some learning strategies do not involve the use of acronyms, but rather the use of particular steps in comprehension. These include story mapping, retelling, and others.
- Reciprocal teaching is a metacognitively based instructional strategy for teacher-led small-group comprehension. It involves predicting, question generating, summarizing, and clarifying.
- Scaffolding involves the provision of an individually tailored support for the child's learning at a critical phase in the learning process.
- Self-monitoring of behavior is a metacognitive strategy designed to improve task orientation and academic performance.

QUESTIONS AND ACTIVITIES

1. Describe the common theoretical basis for the strategies presented in this chapter.
2. Compare and contrast the behavioral model of learning and the cognitive model of learning.
3. Search the information in your state, and identify workshops that focus on cognitive strategies. Can you associate any of these workshops with the University of Kansas learning strategies research?
4. Describe the scaffolding concept and develop a role-play activity to demonstrate this teaching idea.

5. Look in several basal reading texts from the local elementary school curriculum. Do you find the application of any of the strategies included in reciprocal teaching? What strategies?
6. Review some of the nonspecific strategies listed in this reference list. Report to the class on the effectiveness of these strategies.

REFERENCES

Archer, A. L., Gleason, M. M., & Vachon, V. L. (2003). Decoding and fluency: Foundation skills for struggling older readers. *Learning Disability Quarterly, 26*(2), 89–102.

Ashton, T. M. (1999). Spell CHECKing: Making writing meaningful in the classroom. *Teaching Exceptional Children, 32*(2), 24–27.

Bender, W. N. (2002). *Differentiating instruction for students with learning disabilities: Best practices for general and special educators.* Thousand Oaks, CA: Corwin Press.

Boudah, D. J., Lenz, B. K., Bulgren, J. A., Schumaker, J. B., & Deshler, D. D. (2000). Don't water down! Enhance content learning through the unit organizer routine. *Teaching Exceptional Children, 32*(3), 48–57.

Bowman, J. E., & Davey, B. (1986). Effects of presentation mode on the comprehension-monitoring behaviors of LD adolescents. *Learning Disability Quarterly, 9,* 250–256.

Bruce, M. E., & Chan, L. K. S. (1991). Reciprocal teaching and transenvironmental programming: A program to facilitate the reading comprehension of students with reading difficulties. *Remedial and Special Education, 12*(5), 44–54.

Deshler, D. (2006). An interview with Don Deshler: Perspectives on teaching students with learning disabilities (interview conducted by Steve Chamberlin). *Intervention in School and Clinic, 41*(5), 302–306.

Dye, G. A. (2000). Graphic organizers to the rescue! Helping students link and remember information. *Teaching Exceptional Children, 32*(3), 72–76.

Ellis, E. S. (1991). *SLANT: A starter strategy for class participation.* Lawrence, KS: Edge Enterprises.

Fogarty, R. (1999). Architects of the intellect. *Educational Leadership, 57*(3), 76–79.

Goddard, Y. L., & Heron, T. E. (1998). Pleaze, teacher, help me learn to spell better: Teach me self-correction. *Teaching Exceptional Children, 30*(6), 38–43.

Hallahan, D. P., Lloyd, J. W., & Stoller, L. (1982). *Improving attention with self-monitoring: A manual for teachers.* Charlottesville: University of Virginia Institute for Learning Disabilities.

Hallahan, D. P., & Sapona, R. (1983). Self-monitoring of attention with learning disabled children: Past research and current issues. *Journal of Learning Disabilities, 16,* 616–620.

Hogan, K., & Pressley, M. (1997). Scaffolding scientific competencies within classroom communities of inquiry. In K. Hogan & M. Pressley (Eds.), *Scaffolding student learning: Instructional approaches and issues* (pp. 74–107). Cambridge, MA: Brookline Books.

Johnson, D. D., Pittelman, S. D., & Heimlich, J. E. (1986). Semantic mapping. *The Reading Teacher, 39,* 778–783.

Korinek, L., & Bulls, J. A. (1996). SCORE A: A student research paper writing strategy. *Teaching Exceptional Children, 28*(4), 60–63.

Larkin, M. J. (2001). Providing support for student independence through scaffolded instruction. *Teaching Exceptional Children, 34*(1), 30–35.

Lenz, B. K. (2006). Creating school-wide conditions for high-quality learning strategy classroom instruction. *Intervention in School and Clinic, 41* (5), 261–266.

McConnel, M. E. (1999). Self-monitoring, cueing, recording, and managing: Teaching students to manage their own behavior. *Teaching Exceptional Children, 32*(2), 14–23.

McIntosh, R., Vaughn, S., & Bennerson, D. (1995). FAST social skills with a SLAM and a RAP. *Teaching Exceptional Children, 28*(1), 37–41.

McLaughlin, T. F., Krauppmam, V. F., & Welch, J. M. (1985). The effects of self-recording for on-task behavior of behaviorally disordered special education students. *Remedial and Special Education, 6,* 42–45.

Michenbaum, D. H. (1971). Examination of model characteristics in reducing avoidance behavior. *Journal of Personality and Social Psychology, 17,* 298–306.

Michenbaum, D. H., & Goodman, J. (1969). The developmental control of operant motor responding by verbal operants. *Journal of Experimental Child Psychology, 7,* 553–565.

Palincsar, A. S., & Brown, D. A. (1985). Reciprocal teaching: Activities to promote reading with your mind. In E. J. Cooper (Ed.), *Reading, thinking, and concept development: Interactive strategies for the class.* New York: The College Board.

Palincsar, A. S., & Brown, D. A. (1986). Interactive teaching to promote independent learning from text. *The Reading Teacher, 39,* 771–777.

Palincsar, A. S., & Brown, D. A. (1987). Enhancing instructional time through attention to metacognition. *Journal of Learning Disabilities, 20,* 66–75.

Prater, M. A., Joy, R., Chilman, B., Temple, J., & Miller, S. R. (1991). Self-monitoring of on-task behavior by adolescents with learning disabilities. *Learning Disability Quarterly, 14,* 164–178.

Rose, T. L., & Sherry, L. (1984). Relative effects of two previewing procedures on LD adolescents' oral reading performance. *Learning Disability Quarterly, 7,* 39–44.

Scanlon, D. (2002). PROVE-ing what you know: Using a learning strategy in an inclusive classroom. *Teaching Exceptional Children, 34*(4), 50–55.

Schumaker, J. B., & Deshler, D. D. (2003). Can students with LD become competent writers? *Learning Disabilities Quarterly, 28*(2), 129–141.

Snider, V. (1987). Use of self-monitoring of attention with LD students: Research and application. *Learning Disability Quarterly, 10,* 139–151.

Welch, M. (1992). The PLEASE strategy: A metacognitive learning strategy for improving the paragraph writing of students with mild learning disabilities. *Learning Disability Quarterly, 15,* 119–128.

Whitaker, S. D., Harvey, M., Hassell, L. J., Linder, T., & Tutterrow, D. (2006). The FISH strategy. *Teaching Exceptional Children, 38*(5), 14–18.

CHAPTER TWELVE

TECHNOLOGY FOR PERSONS WITH LEARNING DISABILITIES

CHAPTER OUTLINE

WHEN YOU COMPLETE THIS CHAPTER, YOU SHOULD BE ABLE TO:

1. Describe the various components of a multimedia stack.
2. Identify several instructional uses of the Internet.
3. List several research sites for student use on the Internet.
4. Discuss several software programs that have been developed specifically for students with learning disabilities.
5. Describe the various concerns in using multimedia and/or the Internet for instructional use.

KEYWORDS

assistive technologies	SALT	HyperCard
PDAs	CD-ROM	Inspiration software
multimedia	audio digitizer	cross-class projects
card	digital scanner	cyberpals
buttons	situated cognition	
stack	anchored instruction	

INTRODUCTION

With the advent of computers in the classroom in the 1980s and 1990s, many researchers began to explore the instructional technology applications for students with learning disabilities (Anderson-Inman, Knox-Quinn, & Horney, 1996; Blankenship, Ayres, & Langone, 2005; Boon, Fore, Burke, & Hagan-Burk, 2006; Castellani & Jeffs, 2001; Ferretti & Okolo, 1996; Hutinger & Clark, 2000; Stanford & Siders, 2001). A number of other researchers have described interventions that should assist adults with learning disabilities (Higgins & Raskind, 1995; Igo, Riccomini, Bruning, & Pope, 2006; MacArthur, 1998). Finally, another group of researchers has explored the policy implications associated with the newly developing applications of technology (Hauser & Malouf, 1996; Raskind, Herman, & Torgesen, 1995; Renard, 2000). Although it has become clear that computer applications should not be considered a magic pill that can cure disabilities, the applications of computer technology that assist persons with disabilities to compensate for their difficulties can be of great benefit to students with learning disabilities. For this reason, teachers who work with students with learning disabilities must explore these various computer applications and find ways to make these instructional applications work for students in their charge.

In 1993, a group of theorists met for a dialogue on technology for persons with learning disabilities (Raskind et al., 1995), and several applications have emerged from that meeting. First, the greatest thrust for technology applications for students with learning disabilities was identified as remediation in the traditionally addressed deficit areas of reading, writing, math, and memory, though the scholars in 1995 did acknowledge that the distinction between remediation and initial instruction in computer-based learning was somewhat blurry. Whereas initial instruction in a particular topic in traditional classrooms must always precede remedial work, use of the computer allows for initial instruction in a topic and remedial instruction simultaneously. Computer-assisted instruction blurs the traditional distinctions between various phases of learning.

Some discussion centered around the use of computer-based assessment as an identification procedure for students with learning disabilities (Raskind et al., 1995). In developing countries, where school psychologists are unavailable, a computerized identification procedure that would allow a teacher to assess and identify a student's learning disability could greatly facilitate services. However, others cautioned against assessment that was computer based and involved only a narrow view of the learning disability in the context of the classroom.

Information access was seen as another application of computer technologies that could greatly enhance the lives of persons with learning disabilities (Raskind et al., 1995). Online databases and CD-ROM information systems such as encyclopedias can assist in the quick access of needed information in forms that do not involve the necessity of reading. For example, in online databases and CD-ROM environments, information may be presented in video or audio format, charts, and graphs, rather than merely in text.

Finally, technology was viewed as having the capacity to foster talents of students with learning disabilities that may otherwise go unnoticed (Raskind et al., 1995). Persons who seem to think visually, rather than perform on paper-and pencil-tasks, may find their learning enhanced through the use of computer applications that involve the possibility of creativity in a variety of tasks.

These promises have largely come to fruition. By 1999, Walker had suggested that the computer had become more than merely another educational technology; the instructional applications currently available, coupled with the revolution in wireless and fiberoptic communications capability, as well as the Internet, have effectively raised the bar in society's conception of literacy. In short, today a person who is not computer fluent is effectively illiterate.

Clearly, students with learning disabilities should be offered every opportunity to benefit from these developing instructional options. In fact, since 1997, federal legislation has required special education teachers to consider **assistive technologies** applications for every child with an individualized education program (Lahm & Nickels, 1999), because technology today offers a wide array of instructional options for special education teachers. A partial list includes options for:

- Developing instructional techniques in reading, writing, and math (Castellani & Jeffs, 2001; Schetz & Dettmar, 2000; Symington & Stranger, 2000; Williams, 2002)
- Anchoring instruction in real-world contexts (Gersten & Baker, 1998)
- Setting up electronic pen pal programs around the globe (Stanford & Siders, 2001)
- Assisting students with transitions (Morgan, Ellerd, Gerity, & Blair, 2000; Trollinger & Slavkin, 1999)

- Connecting classes with other classes worldwide involved in the same study area (Hutinger & Clark, 2000)
- Developing individualized education programs and grading systems for special education classes

As this list demonstrates, special education and education in general will undergo a significant transformation as new computer technologies continue to develop. An exhaustive discussion of assistive technology applications is beyond the scope of this text, but a brief synopsis of several types of software in one subject area will contribute to understanding the importance of assistive technology for the student with learning disabilities.

While reviewing various assistive technology applications in the area of reading, Castellani and Jeffs (2001) identified a number of types of software that can greatly enhance reading instruction for many students with learning disabilities. For example, text-reading software allows the computer to read text and highlight text either word by word or letter by letter. It can also provide learning supplements such as definitions of terms, spell-checking, or large block word presentation. Visual concept organization software provides graphic organizers or semantic webbing templates for a student's work (Boon et al., 2006; Royer & Royer, 2004). Graphic-based software for writing can provide templates for story-boarding and framing the written work. Various writing templates provide specific types of documents, such as letters, résumés, outlines, and reports.

As an example of how several of these technologies can enhance the education for a student with a learning disability, Williams (2002) described the educational endeavors of a student with a learning disability. J. T. was spending an increased amount of time in the inclusive general education classroom, but often had difficulty in writing assignments because it took him so long to write words. Use of both a speech-feedback component (that enabled the computer to read what J. T. had just written) and word-prediction software (that allowed the computer to predict the word J. T. was typing in after only two or three letters and then supply the entire word) greatly enhanced J. T.'s written work, and he learned to write more quickly. These are merely a few of the applications of assistive technology currently available that can enhance the academic productivity of students with learning disabilities.

However, schools clearly have a long way to go in the functional utilization of this technology for instruction. While no business in today's world would fail to provide most of its employees with a computer and appropriate software and training, many students in public schools still have limited access to computers. Schools are working toward making a computer available for every student. In addition, using small notebook computers (mass produced and purchased on a low-cost state contract) and minimal software may be cheaper than purchasing textbooks for public school students. Clearly, teachers should anticipate changes in how we educate all students and, in particular, students with learning disabilities.

Because of the explosive growth of assistive technologies in education, many states are now requiring specific instruction for all teachers in assistive technology. For example, the state of Georgia requires that all teachers demonstrate technology competence by taking a three-semester-hour course in assistive technology for instruction. Further, the Council for Exceptional Children has assembled a panel of experts and generated a list of assistive technology competencies that every teacher of students with learning disabilities should master (Lahm & Nickels, 1999). The 51 technology-related competencies are grouped into eight areas:

1. Philosophical, historical, and legal foundations of assistive technology
2. Characteristics of learners as they impact technology
3. Assessment, diagnosis, and evaluation using technology
4. Instructional technology content and practice
5. Technology for planning and managing the learning environment
6. Technology for managing student behavior
7. Technology for communication and collaborative partnerships
8. Ethical practices in the application of assistive technology

With the increasing emphasis on assistive technology in the schools, teachers must ensure that all students—including those from ethnically diverse backgrounds or poorer students—have ready access to assistive technologies that will enhance their learning (Brown, Higgins, & Hartley, 2001). For students with learning disabilities such as J. T., assistive technology can make the difference between a successful school experience and an unsuccessful one. Denial, intentional or unintentional, of assistive technology to students with learning disabilities can negatively impact their educational endeavors, and teachers must struggle to keep up with this ever-changing landscape. Our students with learning disabilities deserve the very best instruction we can provide; in many cases this will often involve assistive technology of one type or another.

This chapter presents information on the recently developed technological applications of computers for persons with learning disabilities and suggests the directions these technologies may take in the future in your classroom. Certain applications have been widely discussed in the literature, while more recent developments have yet to be fully explored.

After a brief description of these applications, this chapter focuses on some of the recently developed computer-based instructional applications. Sections describing enhanced instruction through multimedia technology applications are presented, and Internet instructional options are explored.

TECHNOLOGY APPLICATIONS

Computer Applications

Many standard computer software applications can be used for students with learning disabilities (Lahm & Nickels, 1999; Raskind, 1993; Raskind & Higgins, 1998). For example, word-processing systems allow numerous students to review their written work for errors in sentence formation prior to printing the work. Currently on the commercial market, one may obtain proofreading programs that check for punctuation, grammar, and word usage, and these programs can greatly facilitate the writing skills of students with learning disabilities (Schetz & Dettmar, 2000; Strassman & D'Amore, 2002).

The spell-check system that is built into many word-processing systems may be especially beneficial to students with learning disabilities (Ashton, 1999; Raskind, 1993). This system, like the proofreading programs, allows the student to compose without the distraction of carefully reviewing for errors. The student composes his or her work and then activates the spell-checking aspect of the program. However, Raskind (1993) has cautioned against merely turning students loose with the spell-check package, because selection of the correct word from the list of word options provided by the spell-check can be a difficult task for many students with learning disabilities.

One skill that many older persons with learning disabilities seem to lack is the ability to organize their daily life. For example, numerous assistance programs for college students with learning disabilities incorporate some type of organizational training to assist those students in planning for work time on long-term assignments. Raskind (1993) indicated that computerized applications of data management—personal data assistants, commonly referred to as **PDAs**—may assist with that type of organizational problem. Likewise, many financial management computer programs may increase banking skills for a person with learning disabilities (Raskind & Higgins, 1998).

Secondary students with learning disabilities should be trained to use these systems in order to enhance their future performance in school. Teachers of students with learning disabilities should provide instruction on keyboarding skills and computer applications such as those in the student's individualized educational plan from the middle school years on up. Also, many teachers find that the novelty of computer usage provides extra motivation for many students with learning disabilities; these students will complete assignments on the computer (including editing and revision work) that they would not complete as a paper-and-pencil task.

Assistive Technologies

A number of researchers have identified an array of assistive technologies that may make life considerably easier for children and adults with learning disabilities (Blankenship, Ayres, & Langone, 2006; Morgan et al., 2000; Raskind, 1993; Raskind & Higgins, 1998; Symington & Stranger, 2000; Williams, 2002). These technologies may include print magnification systems for individuals with vision impairments, speech output devices, and enlarged computer keyboards. Although these assistive technologies were developed for students with other types of disabilities, there may be times when applications of these systems would benefit students with learning disabilities.

Several theorists have discussed the utilization of speech recognition systems to enhance (or in some cases facilitate) a student's written language (Raskind & Higgins, 1998; Williams, 2002). In sophisticated systems that are currently available, the computer is programmed to recognize the dictation of a particular person and to convert those spoken words to print. In these systems, the user dictates through a microphone, speaking clearly and slowly, and the words that the system understands appear on the screen. If the selected words are incorrect, the user can make changes and select the correct words from a menu on the screen. Some systems can translate 50 to 70 words per minute (Raskind & Higgins, 1998). For students with learning disabilities whose verbal skills exceed their writing skills, or merely for students who are intimidated by writing, such programs can provide a way to complete schoolwork by converting spoken language into written text. Further, these systems automatically learn the phonetic characteristics of a person's voice as he or she dictates text. This minimizes errors in future work.

Abbreviation expanders allow a student to develop an abbreviation for frequently used terms, and then the computer will expand the abbreviation (Raskind & Higgins, 1998). For example, a student writing a paper comparing invertebrate and vertebrate animals can simply type in "inv" or "ver" for invertebrate and vertebrate, respectively, and the computer expands that abbreviation to the full term. This can help students with learning disabilities speed up their work on writing assignments.

Speech synthesis and screen-reading capabilities are also now available. Speech synthesis devices generate speech. When coupled with a screen-reading device, these allow the computer to read text on the computer screen to the students with learning disabilities (Raskind & Higgins, 1998). This can be an effective tool in teaching students to read, as well as in supplementing their study skills. Further, programs that individually highlight words as they are read are now available, thus emphasizing visual tracking of the reading for students with learning disabilities.

A wide variety of other assistive technologies is available. Personal listening systems, as one example, can aid in the ability to attend to speakers and lecturers (Raskind & Higgins, 1998). The application of these types of assistive technologies to the field of learning disabilities has the potential for greatly expanding the arsenal of instructional approaches for these students. As a new teacher, you should constantly seek methods to employ computer-assisted instruction and assistive technologies in your class.

MULTIMEDIA-ENHANCED LEARNING

Multimedia applications for students with learning disabilities have exploded within the field (Glaser, Rieth, Kinzer, Colburn, & Peter, 1999; De La Paz & McArthur, 2003; MacArthur & Haynes, 1995; Wissick, 1996; Wissick & Gardner, 2000; Xin, Glaser, & Rieth, 1996). Applications of these instructional enhancements can create impressive academic gains and greatly enhance learning for students with learning disabilities. Consequently, every teacher should plan on building instructional programs around the application of these exciting computer-enhanced instructional innovations.

Multimedia and Learner Control

Multimedia involve the use of computer technologies to enhance text through making computer connections between the text material and additional clarification material. In multimedia, the text is presented along with the option of finding additional information about the text, such as identification of topic sentences, connections between prepositions and direct objects, or pronoun clarifications (MacArthur & Haynes, 1995). Multimedia give the user the power to jump from one topic to a related explanation or clarification in order to answer questions or explore further. This freedom of movement from one idea to another related idea represents a powerful instructional enhancement for students with learning disabilities.

To better illustrate this important attribute of multimedia-based instruction, consider an instructional unit in history. Thirty years ago, a teacher could use a chapter text or perhaps a filmstrip to teach certain topics in history. Both textbook chapters and filmstrips are *linear* media in that the information is presented in a linear, predetermined fashion; the film is viewed frame after frame, or the chapter is read one section at a time in the order predetermined by the book author (Bender & Bender, 1996). If while viewing a filmstrip on the Civil War a student is reminded of an associated topic by a particular frame, he or she must wait until the filmstrip is finished to pursue that associated topic through questions directed to the teacher or through looking up an answer in another medium. As this example illustrates, most traditional classroom lessons are still linear in orientation. This means that material is presented, one topic after another, in the order that is predetermined by the filmstrip content, the teacher, the text, or the presentation format. In each case, students must follow along, with very little room left for moment-by-moment inquiry.

Multimedia lessons are not linear. When a student using multimedia has a question or remembers an associated topic, he or she can immediately redirect the content and access the informational resources on the computer regarding the associated topic or question. This means that, at any time during the lesson, a student may view other information and return to the predefined lesson or continue on the self-selected branch of inquiry (Wissick & Gardner, 2000). One may view multimedia as trees with many branches. All the students start with the same root and trunk, but they may branch out to other information at any point, based on their curiosity and questions.

For students with reading-based learning disabilities, this can be a real advantage. Imagine, for example, that a student is reading a text and does not understand a passage involving use of a pronoun (i.e., the pronoun referent problem demonstrated by many students with learning disabilities). That student could suspend the text reading and select a review of pronoun referents for that section of the text. The computer would immediately highlight the pronoun and the correct referent in the text. The student could then return to his or her reading of the passage. This type of text enhancement is possible in the computer environment, but not in a traditional textbook reading assignment.

The method that many multimedia packages use for organization of information includes objects called stacks and cards. A **card** in this analogy would represent a single computer screen of information that would contain information in the form of graphics or text, as well as **buttons,** or sections on the screen where a student might "click" the mouse, which allows the user to view other cards. Cards may also include pronoun referents, identification of topic sentences within a paragraph, or changing screen displays that present charts and diagrams on the reading passage. Seeing information in a diagram form can help a student comprehend that information more than a reading presentation alone. A **stack** in this analogy may be thought of as a grouping of cards (best visualized as a stack of index cards). The use of buttons on the individual cards allows the student to control what information is presented, and the information may not be presented in a linear fashion. In a multimedia lesson, the student can choose, because of his or her interest, to skip from card number 6 directly to card number 86 and then move back to card number 8. The student has the choice of the order of presentation of information and thus has control over the information.

In a multimedia program, a stack may contain as many or as few cards as desired. Figure 12.1 is an example of a simple multimedia stack containing information on St. Augustine, Florida, which was first presented by Bender and Bender (1996). The first card gives the stu-

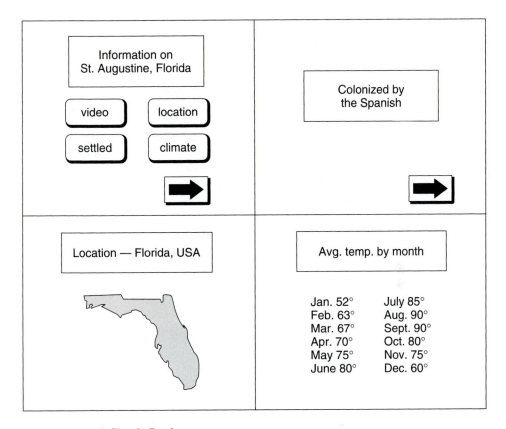

FIGURE 12.1   A Simple Stack

Source: From *Computer-Assisted Instruction for Students at Risk for ADHD, Mild Disabilities, or Academic Problems* by R. L. Bender and W. N. Bender, 1996, Needham Heights, MA: Allyn and Bacon. Reprinted by permission.

dent five options. By clicking the mouse on the button marked "video," the student will see a video of a carriage tour along the harbor of St. Augustine. Clicking on "settled," "location," or "climate" moves the student to the card (or screen) containing that information. By clicking on the arrow, the student can move through the stack in a linear fashion.

Multimedia Instruction for Students with Learning Disabilities

A number of multimedia software packages have been developed and used for students with learning disabilities (Ashton, 1999; Cawley & Foley, 2002; Inspiration Software, 2000; Symington & Stranger, 2000; Wissick & Gardner, 2000). MacArthur and Haynes (1995) described a multimedia text-enhancement system referred to as the Student's Assistant for Learning from Text (**SALT**). This program allows the teacher to develop enhanced versions of textbooks that provide a variety of reading comprehension supports. Once a text selection is entered into the SALT system, other enhancements, such as supplementary text, explanations, and compensatory support for decoding particular words in text, may be added. Main ideas within a passage may be presented in red type while the passage is presented in another color and a glossary of terms is presented. MacArthur and Haynes (1995) used this SALT system to instruct students with learning disabilities in grades 9 and 10 in a science textbook passage, and the results demonstrated that having these information options right at their fingertips can greatly enhance learning for students with learning disabilities.

Multimedia programs typically involve the combination of several different types of media (Ferretti & Okolo, 1996; Wissick, 1996). These may include audio playback systems for music and voice, text presentation systems, videotape presentations, brief movie clips, animation, and graphics. Using multimedia programs, a student would select a topic and be presented with a range of choices. These may include reading technical material, viewing a four-minute filmstrip or videotape, developing a diagram that illustrates concept organization, reviewing animated content, or listening to a human voice or audiotaped music. Each of these would be presented via the computer, under the moment-by-moment control of the student.

Multimedia Hardware for the Classroom

Obviously, to explore the world of multimedia software, students and teachers will need additional hardware beyond merely a computer and a printer. For multimedia presentations alone, the teacher has a number of different types of multimedia presentation formats to consider, including use of CD-ROMs and class projection systems.

CD-ROM discs allow for storing large amounts of data and text. CD-ROM discs look like CDs that play music, except CD-ROM discs are used to store not only sound, but also pictures, video, and text. CD-ROM drives come as standard equipment for most classroom computer systems today, but these drives may also be purchased as an add-on for your computer system. This type of disc is popular for storing reference material such as specialized encyclopedias, art libraries, and simulation programs. This material may then be referenced by students working on their own or teachers preparing a lesson.

For multimedia presentations in small groups, the computer monitor and speaker work fine because only one person or a small group is using the system, but some modifications may be needed if the system is to be used with the entire class. Class "scan converter" systems involve several different options. One is to invest in a computer in the classroom and a projection system that places the computer screen image on a large (perhaps 25- to 35-inches) television monitor. The second alternative is to utilize an LCD (liquid crystal display) panel. The LCD panel is plugged into the computer and placed on top of a high-light-intensity overhead projector. The result is that whatever is on the monitor is shown by the overhead projector on the projection screen at the front of the class. Both black-and-white and color versions of LCD panels are commercially available. Finally, various projection systems are now available that can project computer images directly onto a screen or television monitor.

The hardware described is necessary for presenting information that has already been developed in a multimedia format. However, many teachers and students create their own presentations in the multimedia environment, and this requires some additional hardware.

This may come with the purchase of a new multimedia-capable computer or may be added to existing computers within the classroom. For example, an **audio digitizer** allows students to create audio segments for computer presentations. Audio is an important part of the multimedia experience, including presentations of music, sound effects, and voice. Many multimedia applications include high-quality prerecorded sound. However, in some cases, users may have the option of recording their own sound, and use of an audio digitizer empowers the user to record audio. The digitizer converts sound to digital signals, which may then be stored in the electronic format. The user has the option of employing audio from tapes played into the microphone of the audio digitizer.

Visual images can be incorporated in multimedia in a variety of ways. Some multimedia software have graphics packages that allow the user to draw pictures, and some allow the use of pictures taken (or imported) from other sources, such as CD-ROMs or digital cameras. Users can also create their own computer images with a **digital scanner.** Scanners make computer-ready copies of flat visual images such as photographs and illustrations from books. A teacher or student, while creating a report, may scan maps, cartoons, and printed material for use in the report.

Instructional Applications of Multimedia

Several authors have described the instructional uses for preexisting multimedia packages (Okolo & Ferretti, 1996; Wilson, 1991; Wissick & Gardner, 2000). Several of these are presented below.

Multimedia in Teaching.   Teachers may use various commercially prepared multimedia presentations with students either individually or in groups. While presenting a lesson in astronomy, as one example, the teacher could use a software program to show movement of the planets, moons, and other objects. Perhaps the multimedia package would include videos taken by the moon rover vehicle. Programs such as these serve as a "high-interest" instructional tool for students with learning disabilities.

The preparation time involved in using preprepared multimedia for class presentations is minimal. Before the lesson, the teacher should locate the CD-ROM information to be shown to the class during the lesson. In most cases, the discs have a manual that includes a list of the information and bar codes that, when scanned, will show that information on your monitor. During the lesson, the teacher would only need to scan the proper bar code to display the information to the class. Note that the teacher can have the multimedia program go directly to the presentation material, without presenting other material. Again, the presentation of information is directly controlled and is nonlinear.

Prior to using multimedia instructional software programs, one should evaluate them in view of the learning characteristics associated with many students' learning disabilities (Bender & Bender, 1996). Instruction using multimedia is promising, but unless the motivational and interactive properties of the program are effective for your students, the full benefits of using the software will not be realized.

Keller and Keller (1994) developed an evaluation process that frames the issues to be considered in evaluation of software prior to use in the classroom. This process involves consideration of four interactivity components as well as four motivational aspects of the software. The four interactivity components are learner control, stimulus characteristics, learner responses, and consequences. Learner control involves the pacing, sequencing, and selecting of the instructional material by the student (for example, what selections a student may make within the program and when material is reviewed). Stimulus characteristics include the material presented and how it is presented. Learner responses include the emotional responses anticipated from the student, as well as the mechanical responses such as solving problems and note-taking. Consequences include the actions the program takes as a result of student responses.

Several motivational aspects must also be considered in order for a multimedia lesson to stimulate and sustain the motivation for a student with learning disabilities. First, the student's attention must be obtained. Second, the lesson must build relevance by connecting the lesson to the student's prior experiences. Third, the lesson should allow the student to build confidence that he or she will succeed in the lesson. Fourth, the student must receive some degree of satisfaction from the learning experience. These motivational aspects are, perhaps, even more important for students with learning disabilities because of the types of attention and motivational problems many of them demonstrate.

In addition to teaching presentations, multimedia offer significant opportunities for anchored instruction for students with learning disabilities. As you may recall from Chapter 7, anchored instruction involves specifying the relationship between the skills to be learned and real-world applications of those skills, such that the skills are anchored in real-world problems (Bottge, Heinrichs, Chan, & Serlin, 2001; Cawley & Foley, 2002; De La Paz & McArthur, 2003). **Situated cognition** is another term for this concept (Gersten & Baker, 1998). The multimedia environment offers teachers and students the opportunity to take virtual "field trips" and allows students to apply their knowledge in real-world scenes. Because many real-world application opportunities cannot be duplicated in the classroom, use of multimedia programs and computer technology allows teachers to focus on anchoring instruction in simulations or video reproductions of real-world learning situations. Thus, the cognitive exercises are situated in real-world contexts (Gersten & Baker, 1998; Xin et al., 1996).

For example, Glaser, Rieth, Colburn, and Peter (1999) combined a multimedia approach with **anchored instruction** to teach historical content related to the society in the United States during the periods immediately after World War I and World War II. Two "anchors" were selected to present sociological issues from those time periods. In this case, two videos were used: *To Kill a Mockingbird* and *Playing for Time*. Students were exposed to four phases in the anchored instruction. First, they watched the videos as anchors for the time periods under study. Next, they were expected to retell and segment the videos. Third, they discussed characterization of the main characters; and finally, they completed student research on the sociological factors for the time period. Class discussions were used in each phase of the discussion, and students were encouraged to "go beyond" the movie itself and discuss various issues, such as race or the role of women in the 1930s, and then make determinations as to the accuracy of the anchor. The results revealed an increase in students' questions about the time period under study as well as increasing complexity and quality of the students' understanding. As this research shows, rather than present history or other content in a rather static "written form," as done in the traditional history text, the multimedia environment offers the opportunity to present science, history, health, or other content with a rich tapestry of real-world "anchors" that make learning both more fun and a deeper cognitive experience.

Student Research.   A second use of multimedia involves student research (Trollinger & Slavkin, 1999; Wilson, 1991). Traditionally, when students were studying a topic or trying to find an answer to a question, they went to the library or used reference material in the classroom. In the library, they had access to books, encyclopedias, and films. Today students have access to information on many topics, including entire reference encyclopedias, in their classrooms in the form of CD-ROMs. With the interactive capabilities of multimedia, students can use such information on CD-ROMs as a specialized encyclopedia to learn about a topic. This allows students to seek out information and proceed at their own pace. This can greatly enhance learning for students with learning disabilities.

Again, note that, in addition to putting information at their fingertips, multimedia hardware presents it in a nonlinear fashion. For example, while a student is reading the answer to one question, he or she may think of a second question. Rather than stopping and finding a book with information on the second question, the student can immediately research the second question without getting up. When the student is finished with the second question, he or she can return to the first topic or continue with other topics.

However, this freedom of movement can have some drawbacks if it is unmonitored. Imagine a student with extreme hyperactivity clicking from one interesting visual image to another every 10 seconds (Wissick & Gardner, 2000). Would we assume that learning was taking place in that context? Clearly, for students with the types of attention difficulties and organizational problems demonstrated by many students with learning disabilities, the choices presented by these immediate-access features of multimedia may be either a blessing or a curse. The innovative multimedia programs will help many students immediately access information on topics of interest, but teachers should monitor the students' selections to assure that they remain on-task and not merely bounce quickly between the options and opportunities that most multimedia programs present. In other words, students with organizational problems can "get lost" among the numerous options presented by multimedia, and teachers must actively guard against such use because little learning will take place under those conditions (O'Neil, 1996).

Authoring System for Students.   Although instructional presentations involving multimedia can greatly enhance instruction, perhaps their most exciting use is the creative design of multimedia presentations by either teachers or students. Many researchers recommend teaching students with learning disabilities to create multimedia presentations (Ferretti & Okolo, 1996; Wissick, 1996; Wissick & Gardner, 2000). In this application, the students will be required to use an authoring system such as HyperCard, published by the Claris Corporation, to put together a report on a specific topic. This creative activity could also be assigned as a cooperative group project. Various other authoring systems are available that allow students to create multimedia reports (as opposed to merely writing a book or research report).

Authoring systems may best be understood as computer programs that help organize the information in a way that allows easy access by the users (Lewis, 1993). Authoring systems allow the student or teacher to put together text and graphics as well as allowing the user to skip through the content to find the needed information.

Yarrow (1994) recommends a set of instructional procedures that may be used to teach students with learning disabilities to create multimedia presentations using **Hyper-Card.** This procedure will take approximately six weeks. Initially, students are paired, and each pair selects a topic from one of the classes with which to create an interactive tutorial. The students are encouraged to use text, pictures, graphics, sound, and animation in their presentations. The first part of the assignment is for each group to create an outline of its "stack." The students are limited to creation of a relatively small, predetermined number of choices for cards within the stack, and questions on the cards are limited to six in either a multiple-choice or true/false format. This provides structure and prevents students from getting lost in the creative process. Most students follow the format of presenting information in a creative way and then asking a question. This format provides the user with an interactive strategy that includes immediate reinforcement.

Computer-Assisted Instruction for Students with Learning Disabilities

A number of authors have explored the use of computer-assisted instruction to aid comprehension of challenging subject matter by the generation of concept maps or organized study guides (Blankenship, Ayres, & Langone, 2005; Boon, Fore, Burke, & Hagan-Burk 2006; Mastropieri, Scruggs, Abdulrahman, & Gardizi, 2002; Okolo & Ferretti, 1996; Royer & Royer, 2004; Strum & Rankin-Erickson, 2004). For example, Mastropieri, Scruggs, Abdulrahman, and Gardizi (2002) used a software program called Inspiration (2000) that facilitates the creation of spatial organizers to assist students in mastering content. In this study, four teachers were trained to utilize the **Inspiration Software** in secondary world history classes. Tenth-grade students with and without learning disabilities were exposed to either traditional instruction or instruction using the Inspiration software. When using the software, students were instructed in the content of the class and were provided spatial organizers that contained the general outline with blank boxes for the content they were to learn. During the teachers' presentation of the content, the students were to complete the organizers, and later, students went to the computer lab to use the Inspiration software to develop both completed organizers and outline notes of the content. Results indicated that students learned 32% more content information when they utilized the Inspiration software than they did in the more traditional instruction. Further, most of the students indicated a strong preference to "study" using the software program; many asked if they could obtain copies of the software for home use or use in other subjects. This strong student preference for using the Inspiration software has been documented in other studies as well (Boon, Fore, Burke, & Hagan-Burk, 2006). Thus, these data clearly indicate the power and appeal of computerized instruction for today's students.

A number of instructional software programs have been developed specifically for students with learning disabilities and/or reading disorders (Anderson-Inman et al., 1996; Torgesen & Barker, 1995; Wissick & Gardner, 2000). A single chapter such as this cannot review all of these programs, but several examples may assist you in understanding the potential for multimedia instruction for students with learning disabilities.

Anderson-Inman and colleagues (1996) described a series of computer-based instructional strategies that were designed to assist middle school and secondary students with learning disabilities in study strategies. Strategies were developed to assist in several study skills necessary in the secondary classroom, including real-time note-taking, studying a textbook, and synthesizing content material; and this research indicated that students with learning disabilities could master these strategies. For many secondary students with learning disabilities, these study skills are essential for successful completion of high school and/or higher education.

Because reading deficits seem to be prevalent among many students with learning disabilities, a number of programs have been developed that assist students with learning disabilities in this area. In the area of reading, computer-assisted instruction has been shown to be effective in almost every reading skill area from vocabulary instruction to reading comprehension for older students (Bryant, Goodwin, Bryant, & Higgins, 2003; Mastropieri, Scruggs, Abdulrahman, & Gardizi, 2002). Beck and Roth (1984) developed a program that focused on reading skill. The Hint and Hunt program involves decoding medial vowels and vowel combinations. Part of it deals with initial instruction on vowel sounds; a second part involves a game in which students decode words the computer pronounces using digitized speech. Jones, Torgesen, and Sexton (1987) demonstrated that students with learning disabilities both mastered and generalized decoding skills for vowel sounds using this program.

Efficacy of Multimedia Instruction

Many students with learning disabilities can greatly benefit from multimedia because the pacing, attention, and motivational factors are under their individual control. Also, programs that deal specifically with the types of learning problems demonstrated by students with learning disabilities have been developed and will continue to be developed.

Further, the research on the efficacy of multimedia instruction for students with learning disabilities has shown that multimedia instruction does work quite effectively (Blankenship, Ayres, & Langone, 2005; Boon, Fore, Burke, & Hagen-Burk, 2006; Boyle, Rosenberg, Connelly, Washburn, Brinckerhoff, & Banerjee, 2003; MacArthur, 1998; Torgesen & Barker, 1995; Wissick & Gardner, 2000). For example, Mastering Fractions, one of the Core Concepts programs, has been used in numerous studies to ascertain the efficacy of this type of instructional program (Miller & Cooke, 1989). Research has shown that this multimedia program is effective in teaching large and diverse classes, including students with learning disabilities (Castellani & Jeffs, 2001; Hofmeister, 1989; Hofmeister, Engelmann, & Carnine, 1986; Miller & Cooke, 1989; Petersen, Hofmeister, & Lubke, 1988; Williams, 2002; Wissick & Gardner, 2000). These studies conclude that almost all of the students who had disabilities or were at risk for academic problems performed similarly to the regular education students in their academic performance on content covered via multimedia instruction.

This research also demonstrated several special benefits for students with academic problems. Miller and Cooke (1989) reported positive comments about the program from numerous students. Most of the students involved made comments like "I liked it a lot" and "It was easier." Other comments by students included statements such as "It [laser disc instruction] didn't treat me different," "I felt like I could keep up," and "I liked it [having a combined class]."

In summary, using high-quality multimedia instruction can facilitate learning for students with learning disabilities and other students at risk for learning problems (Anderson-Inman et al., 1996; Blankenship, Ayres, & Langone, 2005; Boon et al., 2006; MacArthur, 1998; Raskind & Higgins, 1995). Numerous other advantages were reported in these studies, including students seem more motivated, lessons may be replayed for individual students, and the teacher is free to circulate and thus can immediately correct the student's errors.

INSTRUCTIONAL APPLICATIONS OF THE INTERNET

The development of the Internet and the search engines that allow relatively easy navigation of the Internet present unparalleled instructional opportunities for all students, including those with learning disabilities (Guptill, 2000; Hutinger & Clark, 2000; O'Neil, 1996; O'Neill, Wagner, & Gomez, 1996; Renard, 2000; Scardamalia & Bereiter, 1996; Stanford & Siders, 2001). Although use of the World Wide Web for instructional purposes is still evolving, at least four types of applications for students without disabilities have been initiated to date. These range from simple communication procedures to sophisticated **cross-class projects.** Because these have developed so recently, there is virtually no evidence about their efficacy for students with learning disabilities. However, there is every reason to assume that numerous advantages will be realized from careful application of these practices for students with learning disabilities, and research will certainly be forthcoming in each of these areas.

Cyberpals Projects

Electronic mail (more commonly called e-mail) involves the use of computer technology to deliver messages through interconnected computers (Hutinger & Clark, 2000). These messages can be delivered worldwide instantly and are certainly much cheaper than any form of traditional communication. Consequently, for the first time in history, teachers can anticipate helping students develop relationships across almost any distance with a relatively quick timeframe (usually daily, limited by time zones rather than the Web itself). This places the old concept of pen pals on a relatively cheap, worldwide scale, that of cyberspace. Thus, students can develop communication-based friendships with their **cyberpals,** who may be in a class down the hall or in a classroom in Great Britain, Australia, or New Zealand.

For students with learning disabilities, there are a number of advantages to structuring such communication. First, many students, as their cyberpal friendships develop, will want to develop their own communication skills; thus, writing instruction can be greatly enhanced (Trollinger & Slavkin, 1999). The savvy teacher can also use this simple vehicle to develop skills in spelling and even suggest that cyberpals develop a study project together. In fact, many communication skills can be developed using a cyberpals approach, and many e-mail users have noted that an easy intimacy can develop with cyberpals. This can encourage students to continue to use the Internet for communication with their cyberpals long after projects are completed or even after the school year ends. Thus, even for students who are unduly shy about communication with other students, the Internet may hold the potential for breaking down certain barriers.

For the teacher who wishes to develop long-distance cyberpal relationships for his or her students, there is a concern regarding how to find other teachers and students to communicate with in order to develop these relationships. Fortunately, the Internet provides a number of Website locations that list schools and classes with people who may wish to participate in this type of relationship. Interest Box 12.1 presents a number of other opportunities for searching out schools or teachers that may likewise be interested.

Publishing Students' Work

A second possible use of the Internet is to display students' work on a worldwide basis. Many teachers display the work of students with learning disabilities on a classroom bulletin board, and this can have extremely positive effects on the students' motivation. The Internet provides an opportunity to display students' work to a worldwide audience, and the motivational effects can be even more profound for many students.

In order to display students' (or for that matter, teachers') work, a school may wish to develop a Website address that may then be accessed by others who are connected to the World Wide Web (Monahan & Tomko, 1996). Many schools have developed Websites

■ ■ ■ ■ ■ ▬▬▬▬▬▬▬▬▬▬▬

INTEREST BOX 12.1
TEACHING TIPS: WEB-BASED PROJECTS

Teachers who are interested in joining others around the United States and the world to collaborate on a project can find resources on the net. These are sites that help beginning teachers get started and also list schools that can be contacted.

TEChPLACEs.   TEChPLACEs is a site designed by teachers and a university design team to emphasize connecting early education special needs students to students in other environments. The site involves four components: (1) "All About Us," a location to post class-produced Web pages about the students' own class; (2) "Our Community," a location to post information about each class community; (3) resource links to screened Websites related to teachers, families, and educational products; and (4) an e-mail option (Hutinger & Clark, 2000). For more information, visit the Website: *www.techplaces.wiu.edu.*

Classroom Connect.   Classroom Connect is a K–12 educators' guide/magazine on using the Internet and commercial online services. In each issue, you can find tons of resources to help you understand the Internet, find keypals for your students, and find resources, lesson plans, and other things to help the beginning teacher. The format is easy to read and understand and is one of the most up-to-date magazines for teachers to use. There is a section, referred to as "Connected Teacher," that allows teachers to locate cyberpals for students in their classes. Also, under the "Teacher Search" section, you may identify other teachers and classes that are interested in cross-class projects. This is one Website that every teacher should utilize. For more information, visit the Website: *www.classroom.net.*

that allow the world to have access to information about the school, ongoing projects, or other things the school wishes to publish. Several of these schools may also be found at the Websites listed in Interest Box 12.1.

One of the interesting types of student and/or teacher publications available on the Web is the virtual museum. Students can collect pictures, video segments, text stories, or personal examples on a particular topic and construct a site on their school's home page to display those in a museum format. McKenzie (1996) described a series of virtual museums on the Web that were created by students as a learning project and later became a source of information for others. In one example, a group of elementary students and teachers created a site called Ellis Island and included information about immigration. Many of the students, who were first-generation Americans, contributed family stories about how their families arrived in this country, including pictures and information on their voyages from Laos, Cambodia, Greece, and Russia. A second example McKenzie (1996) described is the Fairhaven Turn of the Century Museum, which concentrates on local history of that area.

Research Applications

Website Research.   Perhaps the primary use of the World Wide Web is for research (Hutinger & Clark, 2000). For example, when a student has to write a book report or paper on a particular topic, in addition to use of the library, he or she may log on to the World Wide Web and use a search program to find information on the topic of interest. Of course, the search programs (sometimes referred to as *search engines*) have been recently developed and are certainly not as exact as the more traditional indexing systems used in the library. However, because of the size of the Internet, students are virtually guaranteed to find from this source information that will not be available in the school library. Interest Box 12.2 lists a number of interesting Internet locations that your students may find useful for research.

However, this recently developed technology has led to a relatively new problem: plagiarism that is almost undetectable (Renard, 2000). As students explore the rich resources available on the Internet, they will discover a number of Internet locations that provide excellent resource information, as well as other locations that are established with the sole goal of facilitating cheating. Renard (2000) lists "Evil house of cheat," "Homework world," and "Cheater.com" as examples. While the teacher will wish to see selective use and synthesis of information from a variety of sources coupled with analytic thought in students' work, students may be tempted to merely cut and paste information together for their reports. Renard (2000) suggests a variety of ways to make assignments cheat resistant, including becoming aware of how and why students plagiarize, avoiding using the same topics every year, requiring higher-level thinking skills and creative responses, and teaching students to document sources from the Internet.

Online Mentoring.   In addition to information such as texts, pictures, and preshot videos, the Internet also offers an instructional interaction possibility that could only be dreamed of several years ago. O'Neill and colleagues (1996) described the option of online mentoring. This is a very sophisticated use of the Internet that involves connecting students interested in a particular topic with scientists who are doing work on that topic in an online mentoring situation. For example, students interested in earth science were connected with scientists

■ ■ ■ ■ ■ ■

INTEREST BOX 12.2
PLACES OF INTEREST ON THE WORLD WIDE WEB

ACCUWEATHER.COM
www.accuweather.com
Students enjoy seeing the actual weather they can expect on any given day. The information on this site can easily be used to supplement science lessons in earth science, biology, climatology, and so on.

AMERITECH
www.ameritech.com:1080/ community/education/
Check out "Ameritech Schoolhouse," a guide to Internet resources for teachers, students, and parents in *Internet InfoCenter* (located on the home page).

CENTERS FOR DISEASE CONTROL
www.cdc.gov
Get the latest information available.

DISCOVERY.COM
www.discovery.com
This site is a rich resource for teachers. At this location, under Discovery School, teachers will find more than 2,000 Web links that present some information on almost every topic, ranging from free lesson plans in a wide variety of areas to videos/ books on every topic imaginable, including professional development for teachers. The Web location, Science Fair Central, at this address presents a variety of online science experiments for teachers to pull up. For students, the site presents the World Book Encyclopedia online as well as help with homework in all areas. Also, information on upcoming television shows from the Discovery Channel will be featured. The "Mydiscovery" section allows students to join in for free e-mail, but the e-mail comes with certain advertisements and e-mail notices on upcoming shows and other information. Teachers should carefully consider any board-of-education policies concerning this type of advertising prior to using this e-mail service for students.

FED WORLD
www.fedworld.gov
This is the hub for contacting more than 135 government bulletin boards and information.

INTERNIC
www.internic.net
This is a good source for Internet basics. Follow the path: Information Services/InterNIC InfoGuide/Internet Resources/Education K–12/ Gopher Menu.

LIBRARY OF CONGRESS
www.loc.gov
The Library of Congress location allows students to search the Library of Congress for information on virtually any topic. The location is user friendly, since guides to using the site are provided. Information may be obtained on Congress at Work, Using the Library, and Copyrights. The section "American Memory" allows students to download video segments, sound, and other notes of historical interest. Many students use these brief audio/video segments to

(continued)

INTEREST BOX 12.2   CONTINUED

create multimedia reports. Imagine the impact of actually seeing a brief segment of the famous "I Have a Dream" speech by Dr. Martin Luther King, Jr., in a report on the Civil Rights Movement of the 1960s.

LIGHTSPAN.COM
www.gsn.org
Promote distance learning by helping K–12 teachers and their students design and participate in collaborative projects that foster networking on the Internet. This location also offers teachers the opportunity to earn extra income for tutoring.

NATIONAL SCIENCE TEACHERS ASSOCIATION
www.nsta.org
You can preview NSTA periodicals and learn about organization-sponsored science projects. You can also access the NSTA FTP server or learn about online and off-line resources.

NETWATCH!
www.pulver.com
Track new Internet audio and video products like CU-SeeMe, NetPhone, RealAudio, and other utilities that facilitate real-time voice communication and broadcasting.

WORLD HEALTH ORGANIZATION
www.who.int
Get information from the WHO.

U.S. DEPARTMENT OF EDUCATION
www.ed.gov
Get up-to-date information from the U.S. Department of Education (ERIC site).

In using these Websites for your students, teachers should remember that Web addresses do change and sites often go down while a particular location reconstructs the Website. Consequently teachers should preview the Web locations that they plan to use immediately prior to the class in which they plan on accessing them. While most of the Web addresses in this list are accessed hundreds of thousands of times each day, teachers should not count on the popularity of a particular Website as an indicator of either quality or availability. However, a little diligent digging on the part of the teacher can often turn up gems for students to use in their research work.

studying earthquakes and avalanches. While the students conducted their research in preparation for a project in that area, they were able to ask questions directly of scientists.

Obviously, this will take some time from the mentors (O'Neill et al., 1996). Mentors would be expected to respond frequently to students' inquiries, make suggestions for further reading, and guide students in formulating meaningful questions. Also, finding appropriate mentors will take a considerable amount of the teacher's time. Interest Box 12.3 lists a number of other suggestions and considerations in the development of an online mentoring program for your students.

■ ■ ■ ■ ■

INTEREST BOX 12.3

TEACHING TIPS: DEVELOPING ONLINE MENTORING

1. Identifying effective telementors can be time-consuming. Seek mentors at local colleges, universities, on the Internet itself, and from local civic groups.
2. Develop a page of information about your mentoring program needs and the time commitments required of mentors. Keep time commitments minimal (i.e., three or four e-mail exchanges a week).
3. Seek to develop sustained interactions between the students and the mentors. Use mentors for projects that will cover a number of weeks.
4. Monitor the mentors' work and offer "coaching" suggestions. Many of those individuals may not have served as mentors before, and they will usually appreciate the input.
5. Critically evaluate the student's work as a work in progress, prior to final submission.
6. Incentives are necessary for both the mentor and the student. Should a mentor request that the student complete a specific task, consider using the student in that fashion (given time constraints, etc.).
7. Involve the mentors directly in evaluating students' projects. Seek their input for final quarterly grades. This encourages them to feel part of the process and may elicit cooperation during the next term.

Cross-Class Projects

Teachers using the Internet as a research vehicle for their students with learning disabilities will quickly realize that numerous more sophisticated options arise (Strassman & D'Amore, 2002). The ease of communication that often develops between students can be an appropriate basis for academic projects done between students in different classes, different schools, or different countries. For example, whereas the Eastern Band of the Cherokee never left their native homelands in North Carolina and Tennessee, the Western Band of the Cherokee were forcibly removed to Oklahoma during the last century. Imagine the powerful nature of a history project jointly developed between children in these locations. As another example, students in an oceanfront fishing community may wish to communicate with students on the Chesapeake Bay, in St. Louis, or in other riverfront communities. Development of projects on the economies of riverfront communities compared to oceanfront communities could be an excellent cross-class project for students or groups of students.

Strassman and D'Amore (2002) provided an excellent example of how students interacting via computer (in this particular case, using a local area network, or LAN, rather than the Internet) provided an excellent vehicle for learning to write. Students used an electronic read-around program combined with online synchronous chats to discuss various tasks. These combined assistive technologies allowed students to "think collectively" while using writing skills during the online discussion of the assigned task. As Strassman and D'Amore (2002) indicate, writing progresses through a series of predictable stages (e.g., brainstorming, prewriting notes, outlining, initial draft, editing, etc.). Much of this work can be done as group work online when students are provided options to discuss their assignments. Also, the very use of the keyboard in online chats builds both typing and writing skills. Finally, students are often more motivated to discuss these aspects of their assignment in an online environment than during traditional in-class discussions.

Cautions about Internet-Based Instruction

There are several cautions regarding instruction of this nature for students with learning disabilities, as well as for other students (Dwyer, 1996; O'Neil, 1996; Renard, 2000; Wissick & Gardner, 2000). Teachers must make certain that serious learning is taking place. Because the Internet is so attractive and interesting to some students, they can easily get lost in the intricate selections that are provided (a problem that may also be a concern when using multimedia instruction). Clearly, moving from site to site every 30 seconds does not allow any understanding or synthesis of knowledge to develop (O'Neil, 1996; Wissick & Gardner, 2000).

To combat this problem, teachers will have to carefully monitor the activities of students on the Internet in order to assure that learning is taking place. This concern is particularly important for students with learning disabilities, who may have organizational problems that are accentuated by the nearly infinite selections available on the Internet. Teachers may wish to provide a "lab sheet" or set of instructions about which Websites a student should look at when completing the first few projects on the Internet. Also, cross-class projects will require fairly extensive guidance from the teachers involved.

A more widely recognized concern involves the fact that the Internet is largely unregulated, and thus there are available numerous topics (e.g., pornography, overt violence) that are inappropriate for children. To deal with this issue, which some have referred to as a "security" issue, there are generally two possibilities. First, several software companies have developed products that limit student access to topics teachers and parents would probably deem inappropriate.

A second option involves the student's responsibility to identify on the Internet locales that teachers or parents may deem inappropriate and avoid them. Some teachers have signed agreements with both students and parents that commit the students to avoid inappropriate sites, to exit them should they find them accidentally, and to notify the teacher and/or parent that such a site was entered and then exited because of inappropriate material. As a preventive measure, you should discuss your planned use of the Internet for instruction with your principal and consider any school district policies that may apply prior to using this tool.

SUMMARY

This chapter has presented information on the increasingly complex and sophisticated computer-based instructional programs for students with learning disabilities, including multimedia and instructional use of the Internet. Some research is available on the efficacy of computer-assisted instruction for students with learning disabilities, and that research demonstrates that computer-assisted instruction can be quite effective. In fact, some theorists suggest that technological applications can profoundly enhance learning for students with learning disabilities.

However, research on use of multimedia instruction has only recently become available. Also, numerous theorists in the broad field of education are urging caution in believing the promises of technology (O'Neil, 1996). Only time will tell if many of these promises are realized.

The following points should assist you in studying this chapter:

- Multimedia involve programs that include options for use of different media, including synthesized speech, video, audio, graphics, and animation, along with text.
- Multimedia involve the possibility of developing in the computer textual material that has the option for built-in explanations, clarifications, and/or additional supplemental material.
- Multimedia programs have been found to be effective in assisting students with learning disabilities learn in a number of content areas.
- Use of the Internet as an instructional tool is just developing, but it promises to offer a wide array of educational opportunities.
- Cautions about the use of the Internet for instructional purposes should be addressed in discussion with your principal and in consideration of any districtwide policies that may apply.

QUESTIONS AND ACTIVITIES

1. Describe a software program that was designed for use with students with learning disabilities. What options does that software offer that are unavailable in the traditional classroom?
2. Obtain any multimedia instructional program in reading and review it for the class.
3. Plan and develop a multimedia program designed to introduce parents to the concept of learning disabilities. What types of topics would be appropriate, and what video segments can you find (check the Internet) that should be included?

4. Bring in a teacher from the local schools, and interview him or her about use of both multimedia and the Internet for students with learning disabilities.
5. Form a group of students, and review the article by Wissick and Gardner (2000). Hold a debate about the applications of multimedia in classes for students with learning disabilities.
6. Look up the Inspiration software online. Consider how you can use this with your class.

REFERENCES

Anderson-Inman, L., Knox-Quinn, C., & Horney, M. A. (1996). Computer based study strategies for students with learning disabilities: Individual differences associated with adoption level. *Journal of Learning Disabilities, 29,* 461–485.

Ashton, T. M. (1999). Spell CHECKing: Making writing meaningful in the classroom. *Teaching Exceptional Children, 32*(2), 24–27.

Beck, I. L., & Roth, S. F. (1984). *Hint and Hunt teachers' manual.* Allen, TX: Developmental Learning Materials.

Bender, R. L., & Bender, W. N. (1996). *Computer assisted instruction for students at risk for ADHD, mild disabilities, or academic problems.* Boston: Allyn and Bacon.

Blankenship, T., Ayres, K., & Langone, J. (2005). Effects of computer-based cognitive mapping on reading comprehension for students with emotional behavior disorders. *Journal of Special Education Technology, 20,* 15–23.

Boon, R. T., Fore, C., Burke, M. D., & Hagan-Burk, S. (2006, April 9–12). *Students' attitudes and perceptions toward technology: What do the users have to say.* Paper presented at the annual meeting of the Council for Exceptional Children, Salt Lake City, UT.

Bottge, B. A., Heinrichs, M., Chan, S., & Serlin, R. C. (2001). Anchoring adolescents' understanding of math concepts in rich problem-solving environments. *Remedial and Special Education, 22*(5), 299–314.

Boyle, E. A., Rosenberg, M. S., Connelly, V. J., Washburn, S. G., Brinckerhoff, L. C., & Banerjee, M. (2003). Effects of audio texts on the acquisition of secondary-level content by students with mild disabilities. *Learning Disability Quarterly, 26* (4), 203–214.

Brown, M. R., Higgins, K., & Hartley, K. (2001). Teachers and technology equity. *Teaching Exceptional Children, 33*(4), 32–39.

Bryant, D. P., Goodwin, M., Bryant, B. R., & Higgins, K. (2003). Vocabulary instruction for students with learning disabilities: A review of the research. *Learning Disability Quarterly, 26* (2), 117–129.

Castellani, J., & Jeffs, T. (2001). Emerging reading and writing strategies using technology. *Teaching Exceptional Children, 33*(5), 60–67.

Cawley, J. F., & Foley, T. E. (2002). Connecting math and science for all students. *Teaching Exceptional Children, 34*(4), 14–19.

De La Paz, S., & MacArthur, C. (2003). Knowing the how and why of history: Expectations for secondary students with and without learning disabilities. *Learning Disability Quarterly, 26* (2), 142–154.

Dwyer, D. (1996). A response to Douglas Nobel: We're in this together. *Educational Leadership, 54*(5), 24–26.

Ferretti, R. P., & Okolo, C. M. (1996). Authenticity in learning: Multimedia design projects in the social studies for students with disabilities. *Journal of Learning Disabilities, 29,* 450–459.

Gersten, R., & Baker, S. (1998). Real world use of scientific concepts: Integrating situated cognition with explicit instruction. *Exceptional Children, 65*(1), 23–35.

Glaser, C., Rieth, H., Kinzer, C., Colburn, L., & Peter, J. (1999). A description of the impact of multimedia anchored instruction on classroom interactions. *Journal of Special Education Technology, 14,* 27–43.

Guptill, A. M. (2000). Using the Internet to improve student performance. *Teaching Exceptional Children, 32*(4), 16–21.

Hauser, J., & Malouf, D. B. (1996). A federal perspective on special education technology. *Journal of Learning Disabilities, 29,* 504–511.

Higgins, E. L., & Raskind, M. H. (1995). Compensatory effectiveness of speech recognition on the written composition performance of postsecondary students with learning disabilities. *Learning Disability Quarterly, 18,* 159–176.

Hofmeister, A., Engelmann, S., & Carnine, D. (1986). *The development and validation of an instructional videodisc program.* Washington, DC: Systems Impact.

Hutinger, P. L., & Clark, L. (2000). TEChPLACEs: An Internet community for young children, their teachers, and their families. *Teaching Exceptional Children, 32*(4), 58–63.

Igo, L. B., Riccomini, P. J., Bruning, R. H., & Pope, G. G. (2006). How should middle-school students with LD approach online note taking? A mixed methods study. *Learning Disability Quarterly, 29* (2), 89–100.

Inspiration Software, Inc. (2000). *Inspiration 6.0 computer software.* Portland, OR: Author.

Jones, K., Torgesen, J. K., & Sexton, M. A. (1987). Using computer-guided practice to increase decoding fluency in learning disabled children: A study using the Hint & Hunt I program. *Journal of Learning Disabilities, 20,* 122–128.

Keller, B. H., & Keller, J. M. (1994). Meaningful and motivating interactivity in multimedia instruction: Design and evaluation guidelines. Presented at 11th International Conference on Technologies in Education, London, March 27.

Lahm, E. A., & Nickels, B. L. (1999). What do you know? Assistive technology competencies for special educators. *Teaching Exceptional Children, 32*(1), 56–64.

Lewis, R. B. (1993). *Special education technology: Classroom applications.* Pacific Grove, CA: Brooks/Cole.

MacArthur, C. A. (1998). Word processing with speech synthesis and word prediction: Effects on the dialogue journal writing of students with learning disabilities. *Learning Disabilities Quarterly, 21,* 151–166.

MacArthur, C. A., & Haynes, J. B. (1995). Student assistant for learning from text (SALT): A hypermedia reading aid. *Journal of Learning Disabilities, 28,* 150–159.

Mastropieri, M. A., Scruggs, T. E., Abdulrahman, N., & Gardizi, W. (2002). *Computer-assisted instruction in spatial organization strategies to facilitate high school content-area learning.* Fairfax, VA: Graduate School of Education, George Mason University.

Mastropieri, M. A., Scruggs, T. E., Spencer, V., & Fontana, J. (2003). Promoting success in high school world history: Peer tutoring versus guided notes. *Learning Disabilities Research and Practice, 18,* 52–65.

McKenzie, J. (1996). Making WEB meaning. *Educational Technology, 27*(7), 30–32.

Miller, S. C., & Cooke, N. L. (1989). Mainstreaming students with learning disabilities for videodisc math instruction. *Teaching Exceptional Children, 21*(3), 57–60.

Monahan, B., & Tomko, S. (1996). How schools can create their own Web pages. *Educational Leadership, 54*(5), 37–38.

Morgan, R. L, Ellerd, D. A., Gerity, B. P., & Blair, R. J. (2000). That's the job I want! How technology helps young people in transition. *Teaching Exceptional Children, 32*(4), 44–47.

Okolo, C. M., & Ferretti, R. P. (1996). The impact of multimedia design projects on the knowledge, attitudes, and collaboration of students in inclusive classrooms. *Journal of Computing in Childhood Education, 7,* 223–251.

O'Neil, J. N. (1996). On surfing—and steering—the net: Conversations with Crawford Kilian and Clifford Stoll. *Educational Leadership, 54*(5), 12–17.

O'Neill, K. D., Wagner, R., & Gomez, L. M. (1996). Online mentors: Experimenting in science class. *Educational Leadership, 54*(5), 39–43.

Petersen, L., Hofmeister, A., & Lubke, M. (1988). A videodisc approach to instructional productivity. *Educational Technology, 28*(2), 16–22.

Raskind, M. (1993). Assistive technology and adults with learning disabilities: A blueprint for exploration and advancement. *Learning Disability Quarterly, 16,* 185–198.

Raskind, M. H., Herman, K. L., & Torgesen, J. K. (1995). Technology for persons with learning disabilities: Report on an international symposium. *Learning Disability Quarterly, 18,* 175–184.

Raskind, M. H., & Higgins, E. L. (1995). Effects of speech synthesis on the proofreading efficiency of postsecondary students with learning disabilities. *Learning Disability Quarterly, 18,* 141–158.

Raskind, M. H., & Higgins, E. L. (1998). Assistive technology for postsecondary students with learning disabilities: An overview. *Journal of Learning Disabilities, 31*(1), 27–40.

Renard, L. (2000). Cut and paste 101: Plagiarism and the net. *Educational Leadership, 57*(4), 38–43.

Royer, R., & Royer, J. (2004). Comparing hand drawn and computer generated concept mapping. *Computers in Mathematics and Science Teaching, 23*(1), 67–81.

Scardamalia, M., & Bereiter, C. (1996). Engaging students in a knowledge society. *Educational Leadership, 54*(5), 6–11.

Schetz, K. F., & Dettmar, E. (2000). Collaborating with technology for at-risk readers. *Teaching Exceptional Children, 32*(4), 22–27.

Stanford, P., & Siders, J. A. (2001). E-pal writing! *Teaching Exceptional Children, 34*(2), 21–25.

Strassman, B. K., & D'Amore, M. (2002). The Write technology. *Teaching Exceptional Children, 34*(6), 28–31.

Strum, J., & Rankin-Erickson, J. (2004). Effects of hand-drawn and computer-generated concept mapping on the expository writing of middle school students with learning disabilities. *Learning Disabilities Research and Practice, 17* (2), 124–139.

Symington, L., & Stranger, C. (2000). Math = success: New inclusionary software programs add up to a brighter future. *Teaching Exceptional Children, 32*(4), 28–33.

Torgesen, J. K., & Barker, T. A. (1995). Computers as aids in the prevention and remediation of reading disabilities. *Learning Disability Quarterly, 18,* 76–88.

Trollinger, G., & Slavkin, R. (1999). Purposeful e-mail as stage 3 technology. *Teaching Exceptional Children, 32*(1), 10–16.

Walker, D. (1999). Technology and literacy: Raising the bar. *Educational Leadership, 57*(2), 18–21.

Williams, S. C. (2002). How speech feedback and word prediction software can help students write. *Teaching Exceptional Children, 34*(3), 72–78.

Wilson, K. (1991). Bank Street College of Education. *Proceedings of the Multimedia Technology Seminar, Washington, DC,* pp. 51–57.

Wissick, C. A. (1996). Multimedia: Enhancing instruction for students with learning disabilities. *Journal of Learning Disabilities, 29,* 494–503.

Wissick, C. A., & Gardner, J. E. (2000). Multimedia or not to multimedia? That is the question for students with learning disabilities. *Teaching Exceptional Children, 32*(4), 34–43.

Xin, F., Glaser, C. W., & Rieth, H. (1996). Multimedia reading: Using anchored instruction and video technology in vocabulary lessons. *Teaching Exceptional Children, 29*(2), 45–49.

Yarrow, J. (1994). Across the curriculum with HyperCard. *Technological Horizons in Education Journal, 21*(8), 88–89.

CHAPTER THIRTEEN

ADULTS WITH LEARNING DISABILITIES

CHAPTER OUTLINE

WHEN YOU COMPLETE THIS CHAPTER, YOU SHOULD BE ABLE TO:

1. Describe the cognitive, social, and vocational outcomes of education for individuals with learning disabilities.

2. Identify the types of educational experiences that seem to be related to vocational success after school.

3. Review the variety of vocational programs available today for those identified as learning disabled.

4. Discuss the types of modifications in the typical college curriculum that students with learning disabilities generally require.

5. Present a rationale for further societal assistance for adults who are learning disabled.

6. Discuss the rationale for understanding the prognosis for students with learning disabilities in the post–high school transition period.

7. Describe a self-advocacy training program for young adults with learning disabilities.

KEYWORDS

transition
emotional-social outcomes
retrospective study
longitudinal study
academic/cognitive outcomes
vocational outcomes
interpersonal skills

job-related academic skills
vocational skills
vocational high schools
community-based vocational
   training
Section 504
ADA

college students with learning
   disabilities
student support services
administrative flexibility
faculty support
self-advocacy

INTRODUCTION

During the decades of the 1980s and 1990s, scholars and practitioners in the field of learning disabilities became more cognizant of the needs of youth and adults after the public school years (Benz, Lindstrom, & Yovanoff, 2000; Blalock & Patton, 1996; Brinckerhoff, 1996; Bullis et al., 2002; Commission on Excellence in Special Education, 2001; Evers, 1996). The early research on disabilities was principally focused on research dealing with elementary school children, but more research began to appear that attended to the problems of adolescents with learning disabilities during their high school years. This was followed by an increase in the number of studies dealing with adults with such disabilities after they completed school (Lehmann, Davies, & Laurin, 2000; Madaus et al., 2006; Levine & Nourse, 1998). Particularly within the last 15 years, research has been conducted on postschool success of students with learning disabilities.

This chapter will present information in several areas that should help you in understanding the types of opportunities the student with learning disabilities has after school. It is important that you are aware of this for several reasons. First, you may find that your teaching position involves instruction for secondary students with learning disabilities, in which case you will need to be aware of the types of postschool options those students have. You may need that information in informal counseling sessions with the students you teach. Next, parents will frequently ask for long-term prognosis information. You should be prepared to answer their questions concerning the anticipated outcomes for their children and youth with learning disabilities. For example, it helps many parents just to realize that some students with learning disabilities do continue their education, while others find meaningful employment with future opportunities for advancement. This information should be made available to parents as their needs require. Finally, awareness of the postschool outcomes for students with learning disabilities may provide you with some guidance concerning how to structure your educational program as you write the individualized educational plans. Specific transition planning information must be included on the IEP after the student reaches the age of 16 (Dunn, 1996; Katsiyannis, DeFur, & Conderman, 1998). Knowing the types of courses that adults with disabilities report as meaningful may give you some indication of the curriculum areas that should be emphasized. Each of these reasons provides some rationale for studying postschool outcomes of students identified as learning disabled.

The first section of this chapter will discuss the general characteristics of young adults with learning disabilities. This information will supplement the characteristics information concerning high school students with disabilities presented earlier. Next, the vocational outcomes of these students will be presented, based on a number of research studies that have included postschool follow-up on adults with learning disabilities. Finally, a section on college programs for the learning disabled is presented.

CHARACTERISTICS OF YOUTH AND ADULTS WITH LEARNING DISABILITIES

The **transition** period between public school and postschool activities is difficult for the most capable of students, and this difficulty only increases when the adolescent has some type of disability. For example, the academic deficits that plague students with learning disabilities may prevent participation in either a four-year college program or a two-year vocational school program after graduation. This automatically limits the student's options to some type of employment, but the same academic deficits may limit the student in that arena also. Consequently, understanding the fear and frustrations that many of these young people display during the period immediately before finishing secondary school is very important. Also, a firm grasp on the characteristics that young people with disabilities display is one important aspect of understanding their postschool transition opportunities. As Figure 13.1 illustrates, there are numerous potential directions for these young people to take upon completion of high school, and most of these individuals will be very appreciative of your assistance in this transition.

Dunn (1996) presented a status report on the postschool transition of students with learning disabilities that identified numerous myths about these students. For example, although students with learning disabilities do experience more successful outcomes than students with certain other disabilities (e.g., severe retardation; see Heal & Rusch, 1995),

FIGURE 13.1   Adolescent with Learning Disabilities: Difficult Choices

students with learning disabilities are nevertheless less adept at successful postschool transition than their nondisabled peers. For example, only approximately 16% of students with learning disabilities attend a two-year or four-year college after high school (Wagner, Blackorby, Cameto, Hebbeler, & Newman, 1993)—a percentage significantly lower than the general population of high school graduates. Further, Sitlington (1996) indicated that many students with learning disabilities have significant difficulties in adjustment to adult life, even in such relatively mundane activities as maintaining a home, community involvement, and personal relationships. However, there is some positive news to report. Over the last decade, the number of students with learning disabilities that attended higher education has increased steadily, and that number has more than tripled over the last three decades (Madaus et al., 2006). Still, there exists a less-than-optimistic picture for successful transition for many students with learning disabilities (Dunn, 1996; Sitlington, 1996). Because of this growing concern, additional research has been conducted in this area, and as a teacher, you will want to understand the issues involved in research with adults with learning disabilities, as well as the research results.

Horn, O'Donnell, and Vitulano (1983) discussed the importance of careful selection of outcome measures when postschool transition is discussed. Specifically, the end of the 12 years of public schooling provides an appropriate time to summarize the effects, or outcomes, of the schooling effort. Measures of basic-skills achievement are certainly one group of variables to look at regarding how students with learning disabilities do after school, but these may not be the most important variables. For example, other outcome measures may include the frequency of employment, job satisfaction, or other vocationally oriented measures. Further, personal/social success measures may also be considered more important outcome measures than reading level. These **emotional-social outcomes** would include self-concept, locus of control, satisfaction with one's social life, and other variables dealing with emotional and social concerns. The research in each of these areas is presented based on studies of the post–high school population of students with learning disabilities.

There is one major problem with much of the research dealing with youth and adult populations with learning disabilities that should be noted. Most of the early research was retrospective in nature, whereas longitudinal research is generally considered to be stronger research. An explanation of these two types of research is in order in this chapter because research on adults who are learning disabled is based largely on this retrospective research design.

When a behavioral scientist wishes to study the manifestation of learning disabilities over time, there are several ways to do it. First, the scientist may start with a group of persons after they finish school, obtain the data that the school collected in earlier years, and statistically relate those data to today's outcomes. This is a **retrospective study,** because the study was planned and conducted retrospectively by using data that were collected earlier. The problem with this type of study concerns the types of data gathered by the school. Because of the retrospective nature of the study, the scientist was not around when the early data were collected, and consequently he or she has to use the data that were considered important at the time. This is a particular problem in a field such as learning disabilities because the various historical perspectives on the subject have tended to emphasize different variables. For example, very few secondary schools collected any data on classroom behavior of students with learning disabilities during the 1980s because it was only during that decade that scholars began to realize the importance of that variable. Consequently, retrospective studies done today could not adequately address questions concerning long-term effects of classroom behavior of these students.

A more effective method for studying the phenomenon over time is the **longitudinal study.** In this type of study, the behavioral scientist designs the study from the first years and collects any data he or she wishes to use. The scientist then follows the group of individuals with learning disabilities over the next several years in order to identify causal relationships between the variables that were measured and the postschool outcomes. Because of the expense (in both money and research time) of longitudinal research, most of the research on transition between school and adult life has been retrospective in nature. Without doubt, longitudinal studies of youth and adults with disabilities are presently under way and will become available in the literature in the future. However, at present, our understanding of this transition period in the lives of these students is still tentative at best, because much of what we know is based on the weaker retrospective designs.

Academic and Cognitive Outcomes

Research has indicated that many of the cognitive and academic characteristics associated with problems in school linger after the 12th grade is over (Benz et al., 2000; Evers, 1996; Gregory, Shanahan, & Walberg, 1986; Lindstrom & Benz, 2002; Lock & Layton, 2001; Reiff & DeFur, 1992; White, 1992). Gregory and colleagues (1986) conducted a retrospective study and compared various outcome measures for seniors in high school with and without learning disabilities. Gregory and his co-workers used a data set designed to predict **academic/cognitive outcomes** for all high school seniors in the secondary schools in the United States. Over 26,000 students completed a survey with information about themselves, and 439 of these students identified themselves as having learning disabilities. This group was compared to the nondisabled group on various academic variables, and the results demonstrated that the academic deficits of students with disabilities in reading, math, and language arts are very apparent as late as the last year in school. As discussed in previous chapters, the reading level of adolescents with learning disabilities seems to peak at around the fifth- or sixth-grade level and improves very little thereafter. Also, these indicators of academic achievement suggest that the ability-achievement discrepancy is still fairly large for most youth with learning disabilities. Further, deficits in reading comprehension, written work, and verbal language problems continue to plague adults with learning disabilities after the postschool transition period. These levels of achievement performance present problems in either further schooling or entrance into the workforce.

Emotional and Social Outcomes

Sitlington and Frank (1993) studied postschool transition of students with disabilities and included numerous social and emotional postschool adjustment variables. In an early follow-up of a group of students with disabilities, Sitlington and Frank (1990) used a retrospective design in an interview format to investigate living arrangements for students with learning disabilities one year after high school graduation. The data demonstrated that only 27% of these students were living independently, whereas the remaining students were living with parents and/or relatives. However, when the researchers interviewed the same group two years later (a longitudinal study), the data revealed that 49% of the group was living independently.

These studies are important for several reasons. First, this study series demonstrates how a longitudinal research design can paint a more complete picture than a retrospective study. Second, it demonstrates the importance of using outcome variables that reach beyond merely academic achievement and/or employment status. In point of fact, the quality of one's life, as well as the personal satisfaction one gleans from one's life, is often more associated with numerous social and emotional factors than with employment status. Thus, the studies that focused on a broad array of social and emotional factors over the years are important.

Whereas discussion of academic outcomes may be dealt with rather briefly, discussion of emotional and social outcomes is more involved because of the number of variables that may be measured. Initially, variables such as self-concept and locus of control were studied, but more recently the discussion branched out to cover some of the less frequently measured characteristics.

In many ways, the recently developed data on emotional and social outcomes for young adults with learning disabilities are not encouraging (Beitchman, Wilson, Douglas, Young, & Adlaf, 2001; Benz et al., 2000; Dickinson & Verbeek, 2002; Mull, Sitlington, & Alper, 2001; Price & Gerber, 2001; Witte, Philips, & Kakela, 1998). Research has shown that, in almost every area, students with learning disabilities, in general, demonstrate more social-emotional problematic outcomes than those without disabilities. For example, students with learning disabilities demonstrate lower self-concept and higher external locus of control than those without disabilities (Gregory et al., 1986). Further, some studies document higher levels of substance abuse problems among students with learning disabilities (Beitchman et al., 2001), though other studies do not (Molina & Pelham, 2001). Research has shown that college students with learning disabilities live with parents more often than other young adults and have fewer social contacts than students without learning disabilities (Mithaug, Horiuchi, & Fanning, 1985).

Another question involves legal problems among students with learning disabilities. Some research has suggested that as many as 4% of adolescents with learning disabilities have some involvement with legal services (Bender, Rosenkrans, & Crane, 1999; Gregory et al., 1986). In fact, there are 134,000 youth incarcerated in public and private juvenile correctional facilities, and between 25 and 50% of these youth have a disability (Bullis et al., 2002; Quinn et al., 2005). While most of these incarcerated students manifested an emotional or behavioral problem, some 38% of the incarcerated youth with a disability demonstrated a learning disability (Quinn et al., 2005). Clearly, there is a substantial segment of students with learning disabilities who have some problems with the law.

Variables in the social-emotional domain include depression and suicide, and the available evidence suggests that students with learning disabilities may be at higher risk for both depression and suicide (Bender et al., 1999). Rourke's research (summarized in Rourke, Young, & Leenaars, 1989) has indicated that the central nervous system problems that caused the learning disabilities during the school years may also be responsible for an increased risk of depression and suicide among adult populations with learning disabilities. Although no researcher would suggest that the present understanding of the neurological basis of emotional states of mind is complete, recent technologies (discussed previously) have allowed for conjectural hypotheses that indicate that CNS problems may very well lead to these negative emotional outcomes.

The bulk of information available—self-concept, locus of control, delinquency, depression, suicide data, and social activity variables—does not present a positive social prognosis for young people with learning disabilities in the immediate postschool period (Dunn, 1996; White, 1992). However, these results are based on averaged scores for groups with and without disabilities, and there will always be some youth with disabilities who adjust quite readily during the transition period. Also, there is some possibility that this bleak picture improves after several years, as young people begin to find employment and/or higher education endeavors around which they can build a social life (Sitlington & Frank, 1993). Finally, research has pointed out that these outcomes, though negative overall, are much more positive than the social-emotional outcomes for students with other, more severe disabilities (Shalock, Wolzen, Ross, Elliot, Werbel, & Peterson, 1986). As research progresses, we may find a more positive picture than the present data indicate, and you should continue to read the most current research on these questions.

Post-High School Vocational Outcomes

Research has documented that students with learning disabilities often enter the workplace after high school, but that they frequently do so in minimum wage jobs and tend to remain in those jobs longer prior to moving up, if indeed they move up at all (Benz et al., 2000; Johnson, Stodden, Emanuel, Luecking, & Mack, 2002). Further recent research has documented wage differences between young adults with learning disabilities and nondisabled individuals (Dickinson & Verbeek, 2002) that suggest lower than desirable employment outcomes for these students. Also, other research has suggested some gender inequity that further hampers the early career development of young women with learning disabilities (Lindstrom & Benz, 2002). Finally, in spite of federal mandates to develop reasonable workplace accommodations for individuals with disabilities based on the Americans with Disabilities Act of 1990, research has shown that employers do not have much information about either the requirements for accommodations or the specific accommodations that may be required for employees with learning disabilities. In fact, most of the employers interviewed for this study seemed to believe that making the work environment physically accessible (wheelchair ramps, etc.) was the only workplace accommodation requirement (Price & Gerber, 2001). Clearly, based on these data, the initial vocational outcomes for students with learning disabilities are not as positive as one may hope, and one of the initial problems is our conception of what we mean by positive **vocational outcomes.**

The types of vocational outcome variables measured in the studies vary widely. Most research studies report merely an overall percentage of students with learning disabilities and/or other disabilities who are presently employed at some point after high school. However, this figure may be misleading. Many individuals change jobs frequently during the turbulent postsecondary years, and a simple indication of percentage of individuals employed at any one time may be misrepresentative—that is, some individuals who would normally be employed may be between jobs. A better type of outcome measure is the percentage of time employed since leaving school. This type of outcome measure captures information concerning the overall employment status of the students for each of the years since graduation and is used in studies today.

Another outcome measure that has been investigated is the relationship between the students' instructional program and postschool outcomes (Evers, 1996). For example, does increasing vocational education classes result in better postschool adjustment? Do differential special education placements for students with learning disabilities result in different outcomes? Is resource or self-contained placement more likely to result in positive outcomes? The retrospective data available to date do not adequately address these questions because students with more severe impairments tended to be found in self-contained placements, and those students performed more poorly on postschool adjustment measures. However, retrospective research cannot determine if the poor outcome is caused by the type of program or the severity of the learning disability. Longitudinal research on this type of vocational outcome variable will be necessary in order to determine the differential effectiveness of the type of educational program.

Researchers have addressed several other educational program questions, and some data are available at this point (Blalock & Patton, 1996; Dunn, 1996; Evers, 1996; Heal & Rusch, 1995; Lindstrom & Benz, 2002). For example, Evers (1996) reported on a number of studies that investigated the relationship between the type of academic program received by students with learning disabilities and their subsequent postschool employment success. The available studies indicated that students with learning disabilities who receive some experience in vocational education and/or paid outside work experience during high school are more successful in obtaining and keeping a job. Although not all studies support this conclusion (e.g., Heal & Rusch, 1995), increased vocational preparation would seem to be in order for students with learning disabilities.

Whereas vocational educational experiences do positively affect the graduate's post-school employment success, research has indicated that academic classes may not be related to postschool success for students with learning disabilities (Heal & Rusch, 1995). For example, Gregory and colleagues (1986) indicated that academic outcomes may have little relationship to vocational outcomes, given the types of jobs that these young people obtain. Although some youth who have learning disabilities have reading levels that make the traditional white-collar jobs (law, journalism, teaching, etc.) possible, the vast majority of these young people take jobs that involve less work with written language and/or mathematics. Also, the data presented from the Colorado survey (Mithaug et al., 1985) indicated that a majority of youth with disabilities took jobs that paid the minimum wage. In that type of job, there would be less need for reading and math activities.

Recommendations by Youth with Learning Disabilities for Educational Program Change

Several of the follow-up studies involving young people with learning disabilities provided an opportunity for those former students to indicate the types of educational experiences that they found helpful (Lehmann et al., 2000; Mithaug et al., 1985; Shalock et al., 1986). For example, the students with mild disabilities in the Colorado study (Mithaug et al., 1985) indicated that both special education and vocational education courses were helpful in postschool vocational and personal success. Over half (55%) of the students thought that special education was helpful, and 57% thought that vocational education was helpful. Only 39% thought that regular education courses were helpful. These data may be interpreted to indicate that more time in the secondary school curriculum should be spent on vocational and special education areas, even if time in other areas of the curriculum is reduced.

Learning Disability Characteristics during the Transition Period

In summary, vocational outcomes present the brightest picture of postschool success among the several types of outcomes measured (Evers, 1996). Further, many would argue that this type of outcome is preferable because academic success may not be related to the types of jobs that young people with learning disabilities generally take, and social-emotional problems may be overcome during the next several years as the youths mature. However, it is not pleasant to find that the enormous amount of educational time spent on basic-skill instruction for these students is not effective in helping them catch up to nondisabled youth by the end of their school years. Also, the perception by these young people that regular education is not particularly helpful is troubling. Finally, the emotional and social development of youth with learning disabilities remains a concern because of the negative picture presented by the research and the potential connection between learning disabilities and juvenile delinquency (Sitlington, 1996) and depression/suicide (Bender et al., 1999).

VOCATIONAL OPPORTUNITIES

As scholars in the field became concerned with the needs of the adults identified with learning disabilities, it became apparent that vocational opportunities play a crucial role in successful lifetime outcomes for many of these adults. For this reason, vocational education is one of the more important aspects of education for the secondary student with learning disabilities who does not plan on furthering his or her education after high school (Benz et al., 2000; Evers, 1996; Katsiyannis et al., 1998). For example, Shalock and his co-workers (1986) used a number of subject characteristics, school curriculum variables, and community variables to explain the vocational success of 108 children with disabilities (including 62 youths who had learning disabilities). The number of vocational courses taken by the students was a major indicator of successful job performance after school. Finally, as noted earlier, when young people with learning disabilities are interviewed after their school years, they indicate that vocational education is an important aspect of their education (Lehmann et al., 2000).

Data from a number of follow-up studies of graduates of secondary programs with learning disabilities indicated that between 55 and 70% of those graduates are employed (Mithaug et al., 1985). This is similar to the employment rate for nondisabled youth (Reiff & DeFur, 1992). However, the problems noted for research studies reviewed earlier also apply to these studies. First, these large-scale follow-up studies are retrospective in nature, and retrospective research is generally not as strong methodologically as longitudinal research. Second, these data may not accurately represent the number of young people with learning disabilities who are employed because the percentages in some studies may include all disabling conditions. Shalock and his co-workers (1986) presented some data on employment, computed for different disabilities, that indicated that 72% of youth identified as learning disabled are employed after high school. However, Shalock's data represent the follow-up of a specialized type of vocational program in high school, and that program may have increased the number of these students who were employed. Based on all of these figures, the best estimate on the percentage of such youth with learning disabilities employed after high school seems to range between 60 and 70%.

Finally, there is some evidence that students with learning disabilities who come from a rural area may have a better prognosis in terms of postschool employment than students with learning disabilities in urban areas. In one study by Karpinski, Neubert, and Graham (1992), over 70% of the students with learning disabilities who finished school in a rural area were employed, whereas over 60% of the students with learning disabilities who dropped out of school were likewise employed. These percentages compare quite favorably to the percentages of individuals employed in urban areas. This may reflect the manner in which students obtain employment during the immediate postschool years. Connections with family and friends in the community are the source for most job offers to students with disabilities (Heal & Rusch, 1995), and those community connections may be somewhat stronger in less fluid, more traditional rural communities.

Vocational Opportunities for Adults with Learning Disabilities

During the postschool transition years, many young people who are learning disabled find jobs. However, locating and obtaining a job is not an easy or automatic task. For example, Minskoff, Sautter, Hoffman, and Hawks (1987) surveyed 326 employers from six states concerning attitudes about hiring the disabled. Most employers were positive about hiring the disabled in general, but a more negative reaction was noted relative to hiring persons identified as learning disabled. The results indicated that this negative reaction was related to prejudice against such persons and a lack of experience in supervising this type of worker.

In addition to difficulty in finding jobs, many of the employment opportunities that are available may be less than optimal. For example, results from a study of graduates of special education programs in Colorado indicated that 43% of students with mild disabilities earned approximately the minimum wage and 33% had never received a salary increase. This again seems to indicate that individuals who are mildly disabled tend to obtain jobs that offer very little advancement and poor future earnings potential.

Because of the importance of finding appropriate jobs during the postschool transition period, many practitioners and researchers are developing tools to assist students with disabilities in finding jobs. Morgan, Morgan, Despain, and Vasquez (2005) described a Website that is specifically designed to assist youth with disabilities in finding the types of jobs they may wish to explore. In fact, many computer-based programs are currently available that use either pictures of work activities and/or full-motion video to present jobs to students. The Your Employment Selections (YES) program (Morgan, Ellerd, Gerity, and Blair, 2000) presents a video that allows students to review job activities and then select a short list of 5 to 10 jobs they prefer. In this computer-based program, information on over 120 different jobs is included.

Apparently, students with learning disabilities can, with effort, attain jobs after graduation, but these tend to be low-level jobs. More research is needed concerning the length of time for which these young people stay in entry-level positions; and, again, you should remain current in your reading of this continuing research. This employment picture indicates a concrete need to attend to vocational education for many of these youths. It is difficult to overestimate the importance of vocational programming in the lives of many persons who have learning disabilities (Evers, 1996).

Content of Vocational Programs

Concerns for appropriate content of vocational programs have increased as scholars within the field have noted the importance of vocational programs in postschool transition (Benz et al., 2000; Johnson et al., 2002). Okolo and Sitlington (1986) addressed this issue of curricular content by identifying three basic reasons for employment problems of young people with learning disabilities: **interpersonal skills, job-related academic skills,** and specific **vocational skills.**

As earlier chapters have demonstrated, these students demonstrate a deficit in interpersonal skills. It should come as no surprise, therefore, that these deficits cause problems with the entry-level jobs that youth with disabilities take. In an early study, Brown (1976) surveyed 5,213 employers throughout the state of Texas in order to identify the reasons for rejecting job applicants after the initial interview. Of the 10 most common reasons, 9 related to interpersonal skills of the applicants. When one considers the hiring process, these data are not surprising. If an employer considers hiring a person, that person may be assumed to have the prerequisite academic skills for the job. Consequently, if problems develop later on, interpersonal skills are the major remaining cause. Several researchers have recommended that youth with learning disabilities be provided with specific training in interpersonal skills in order to prevent this problem.

Job-related academic skills represent another important content area for vocational education. Clearly, reading is an important academic skill, though job-related reading is different from the read-to-learn tasks in school curriculums. Job-related reading tends to have higher concentrations of charts, graphs, lists of directions, and written instructions than school curriculum materials. These types of activities are characteristic of reading in vocational courses, which may explain why students with learning disabilities valued those courses more than general curriculum courses.

Finally, job-related vocational skills are an essential component of any successful vocational curriculum. For example, skill in using the actual tools that are used on the job is one major reason for success or failure of students with disabilities in their postschool employment. Clearly, expertise with highly specific vocational skills will affect the success of youth with learning disabilities who enter the workforce.

Vocational Programs for Youth with Learning Disabilities

When considering the vocational program during the last years of schooling of youth with learning disabilities, one startling fact becomes apparent: Students who have learning disabilities do not participate in vocational education as frequently or as intensively as they should (Evers, 1996). For example, only about 2% of the students enrolled in vocational programs are disabled, though 10% of the school populations have a disability. Perhaps one reason for this lack of participation in vocational programs is a lack of coordination between the special education teachers and the vocational teachers. Special educators tend to emphasize basic-skills remediation and tutoring in academic subjects, whereas vocational educators tend to emphasize exclusively vocational skills and not interpersonal skills or job-related responsibilities. Clearly, more coordination between these two groups is desirable in order to more adequately prepare youth with learning disabilities for vocational opportunities after school.

In order to encourage more effective vocational outcomes, several models of vocational education have been developed. These range from classroom-based study about various vocations to community-based vocational placements and work-study programs.

Classroom-Based Vocational Studies. Numerous components of vocational programs may be offered on an in-house basis in the public school classroom. For example, Gaylord-Ross, Siegel, Park, and Wilson (1988) discussed the importance of the functional-life-skills curriculum model in vocational preparation. This functional curriculum model was discussed previously as one possible curricular thrust of secondary educational programming in resource rooms. Life skills such as filling out job applications, tax forms, and other such activities complement vocational education at the secondary level.

More recently, Cronin (1996) suggested that this emphasis on life skills needs to be somewhat broader. She presented a review of the literature on interventions designed to enhance life skills for students with learning disabilities and suggested including various emphases that go well beyond filling out job applications, tax forms, or banking paperwork. Interest Box 13.1 presents a list of skills that should be emphasized as a part of the comprehensive life-skills program for students with learning disabilities.

Various career-awareness and career-exploration activities may also be delivered in vocational classrooms during the school years. Some scholars recommend that these types

■ ■ ■ ■ ■ ▬▬▬▬▬▬▬▬▬▬▬▬▬▬▬▬▬▬▬▬▬▬▬▬▬▬▬▬▬▬▬▬▬▬▬▬▬▬▬

INTEREST BOX 13.1

SKILLS WITHIN THE COMPREHENSIVE LIFE-SKILLS CURRICULUM

Career education	curriculum designed to teach individuals the skills that enable the individual to have a career (i.e., the skills used in particular jobs, such as auto mechanic, etc.)
Daily living skills	personal care skills and/or skills that facilitate successful interactions with others (appropriate dress and grooming, appropriate interaction skills)
Functional academics	practical applied skills, taught in the context of daily, real-world activities (completing tax forms, checkbooks, etc.)
Survival skills	everyday coping skills needed in adulthood, which are necessary to function in the everyday environment (using bank machines, sophisticated telephone systems, etc.)

of vocational activities be initiated during the elementary or middle school years (Gaylord-Ross et al., 1988). Career counseling may also begin at this time.

Vocational High Schools.   Although most secondary schools have some vocational classes, many secondary schools specialize in making a wide array of vocational classes available to the students. Classes at **vocational high schools** would include many types of occupational training that would be unavailable in the traditional, academically based secondary class. Courses in small-engine repair, auto mechanics, dental hygiene, secretarial work, woodworking, horticulture, carpentry, and agriculture may be available, with several levels of each course offered. Research has shown that training in vocational classes such as these results in better employment outcomes for students with mild disabilities (Evers, 1996). Also, these students indicate that the vocational aspect of their high school training was one of the most important (Lehmann et al., 2000).

Community-Based Vocational Training.   Classroom-based vocational education and vocational classes are important components of vocational programming, but **community-based vocational training** is crucial for successful transition outcomes. In community-based vocational training, the students are trained at worksites in the community in order to learn to function successfully on the job itself. The San Francisco Unified School District has one such program that places students with mild disabilities at two locations in the city. Seniors in high school complete training for jobs involving typing, filing, and message delivery, as well as effective work habits. On four afternoons each week, the students work in a local business for three to four hours (Gaylord-Ross et al., 1988). Employers agree to hire those students who complete the training and meet their standards. Various work-study programs such as this have had very positive impacts on the transition employment outlook for adolescents with learning disabilities during the postschool transition period.

Postsecondary Vocational Training.   Research has suggested that between 8 and 16% of all individuals with mild disabilities attend vocational schools after completion of high school (Wagner et al., 1993). The types of classes typically offered by vocational schools are specialized classes that prepare a student exclusively in job-related skills. This training is similar to the vocational classes offered in secondary schools, though the classes tend to be more rigorous.

Summary of Vocational Transition Options

Research has shown that the majority of youth with learning disabilities enter the workforce upon completion of high school. Both retrospective studies and surveys of these students have indicated that vocational programming is one of the most meaningful types of educational experience for these students. Clearly, vocational education works for many of these adolescents and youth.

However, only a small percentage of students who participated in vocational courses at the secondary level are disabled. Further, only a small percentage of students with learning disabilities continue into vocational schools in the postsecondary school period. Consequently, there is a great deal of concern that students with learning disabilities are not receiving the type of vocational education that is needed. This may be related to the difference between the special education system and the vocational education system, which allows teachers in each area to continue their own business with very little integrated programming for adolescents with disabilities. As a teacher of students with learning disabilities, should you find yourself employed in a middle or secondary school, you will want to work on improving the collaboration between special educators and vocational educators in order to increase the positive outcomes for such adolescents as they enter the postschool years. Also, you will frequently plan the postschool transition activities for students with learning disabilities in conjunction with these students and their parents, in order to make all options for success possible.

COLLEGE OPPORTUNITIES FOR YOUTH WITH LEARNING DISABILITIES

College for Students with Learning Disabilities

Federal law, beginning with **Section 504** of the Rehabilitation Act of 1977 and continuing with the **Americans with Disabilities Act (ADA)** of 1990, requires institutions of higher education to provide reasonable accommodations that will help students with disabilities attain a college degree (Mull et al., 2001). Because of this legislation, there has been a fairly significant increase in the number of students with learning disabilities who attend college (Greenbaum, Graham, & Scales, 1995; Levine & Nourse, 1998; Madaus et al., 2006; Murray, Goldstein, & Nourse, 2000; Sparks & Ganschow, 1999). However, some 60% of students with learning disabilities receive no postsecondary education at all. The research indicates that 16% of students with learning disabilities attended a two- or four-year college within five years after high school graduation; 16% attended vocational schools. Further, this percentage drops somewhat after the first year of higher education (Levine & Nourse, 1988). Still, these figures, taken together, do indicate that a number of students with learning disabilities will attend college programs of one type or another (Madaus et al., 2006; Wagner et al., 1993).

College-Bound Adults with Learning Disabilities

The students with learning disabilities who go to college are not notably different in many ways from those who only complete high school. For example, their reading and academic scores tend to be low, and this inevitably results in difficulty in reading the texts required by college courses (Cohen, 1988). The problems that many teachers note concerning organization of assignments and scheduling are still very much in evidence among **college students with learning disabilities** (Madaus et al., 2006). Also, college students with learning disabilities report high levels of stress associated with schooling (Cohn, 1998). Bacon and Carpender (1989) compared college students with and without learning disabilities and noted some differences in the techniques by which college students with disabilities recall a story. Further, there is some evidence that students with disabilities demonstrate slightly more variability between IQ subtests than nondisabled college students (Salvia, Gajar, Gajria, & Salvia, 1988).

Lehmann, Davies, and Laurin (2000) invited 35 college students with disabilities to identify some barriers to their success in college. Four general types of barriers were reported from this focus group: (1) attitudinal barriers (the students noted a general lack of acceptance as well as a lack of understanding on the part of their peers and their professors); (2) a lack of student support services offered by their college; (3) the need for financial resources that can be extended into a longer than traditional timeframe; and (4) the need for self-advocacy skills to be able, at a minimum, to describe their disability to others. These data, which come directly from the persons we wish to provide services for, are most compelling; colleges and universities simply must provide more of the types of services that college-age adults with learning disabilities need.

There is one difference between youth with disabilities who are successful in college and those who are not. Students with learning disabilities who succeed in college tend to use strategies that compensate for their learning disabilities in some fashion (Cohen, 1988; Trainin & Swanson, 2005). Cohen (1988) interviewed 25 students who were identified with learning disabilities prior to entering a university program. Information on the cognitive and academic levels of these students was also obtained. Results indicated that the students had each found some combination of methods that compensated for their learning disabilities. For example, some students kept a daily/ weekly assignment schedule; others completed all homework assignments, read assignments aloud, and highlighted textbooks or purchased textbooks that were previously highlighted. Some strategies were identified that were specific to particular classes. In math classes, the students with learning disabilities tended to rely on more help from instructors and friends in the class, but in reading-based curriculum areas, the students tended to use strategies such as highlighting, which they could do by themselves. Also, the students tended not to use strategies that are frequently recommended. For example, few students had requested extra time to read essay exams, and only 3 of the 25 students had ever tried audiotaped textbooks. Only 9 of the 25 had ever tape recorded a lecture.

In a similar, though more detailed study, Trainin and Swanson (2005) examined the way successful college students with learning disabilities compensated for their reading deficits. In this study, 20 college students with learning disabilities who were scoring average or above average on their college grades were compared to 20 students without disabilities. While achievement levels for the groups were comparable, the data indicated that successful college students with learning disabilities did demonstrate lower scores on a number of academic skills, such as word reading, processing speed, semantic processing, and short-term memory. However, this study went beyond an academic comparison to investigate how these groups used a variety of "compensation strategies"—strategies that would tend to help students with learning disabilities compensate for these academic deficits. The compensation skills included the use of metacognitive learning strategies and seeking help. The results demonstrated that in each of these categories, successful college students with learning disabilities used the compensation strategies more than did the comparison group of students without disabilities.

Services Offered by Colleges

Given the academic deficits of young people with learning disabilities in college, one may expect that the college curriculum is simply too difficult for these students. In fact, a number of modifications may be made that allow access to the basic knowledge in the college curriculum without compromising the overall integrity of the curriculum. Many colleges and universities have begun to offer these modifications to students with learning disabilities in order to meet the requirements of Section 504 of the Rehabilitation Act of 1973, and the Americans with Disabilities Act of 1990. Although not specifically aimed at learning disabilities, these acts mandated that services be provided for all individuals with disabilities in order to encourage economic independence for students with disabilities.

Although federal legislation thus mandates reasonable accommodations for students with learning disabilities in college classes, this promise has not been fully realized to date at many institutions of higher education. For example, some research on instruction in college classes has suggested that college faculty frequently fail to provide instructional accommodations to students with learning disabilities (Bourke, Strenhorn, & Silver, 2000). Scott and Gregg (2000) suggested that college faculty may need additional in-service training in order to understand what accommodations may be necessary for students with learning disabilities. In fact, data from the study by Scott and Gregg (2000) documented that non-tenure-track faculty (i.e., generally younger, lower-ranking faculty members) reported that it was easier to provide accommodations for students with learning disabilities than did tenure-track (or more senior) college faculty members. This may suggest that college faculty who received their degrees more recently had more experience in teaching students with learning disabilities in college classes than their more senior college faculty counterparts.

Rose (1991) presented a synopsis of a technical assistance project that was designed to assist community college personnel to deal effectively with students with learning disabilities in their classes. Several specific needs were addressed, each of which illustrates a serious concern for students with learning disabilities. Five modules were developed, including modules on assessment, learning strategies, counseling, academic skills, and service networking. The modules on assessment and academic skills improvement are included because students with learning disabilities need both specialized assessment and academic assistance. The emphasis on learning-strategy instruction is included because the same metacognitive strategies that work for high-school-aged adolescents with learning disabilities will work for these students when they attend college. The counseling module was designed to prepare rehabilitation counselors and academic advisers to assist students with learning disabilities. Finally, the module on service networking was intended to assist college faculty to coordinate services for students with learning disabilities. Each of these five major concerns should be addressed when a student with learning disabilities is considering a college program.

Today, as a result of both Section 504 and the Americans with Disabilities Act, most colleges and universities offer some type of support for students with disabilities, in general, and learning disabilities, in particular; these are typically referred to as student support services. In most cases, such services involve study assistance and perhaps specialized assessment options. Other types of student support services may include administrative support and perhaps even support for college faculty who may be teaching students with learning disabilities for the first time. This hierarchy of services is discussed below.

Student Support Services.   Many types of support services may be offered directly to the students with disabilities (Janiga & Costenbader, 2002). For example, some students require tutors for particular courses, and some colleges may have guidelines for provision of tutoring without cost for students with learning disabilities. Other college students with learning disabilities need someone to assist them in time-management skills. Someone from the staff of the college learning disabilities program should be prepared to meet with a student on a regular basis throughout the first year of the program in order to assist in developing appropriate work skills and time-management/assignment-management skills. In fact, some youth with disabilities who have not fully developed the coping strategies discussed earlier will probably enter college each year, and effective programs for these students should make some provision whereby each of these coping skills may be taught.

Many colleges offer courses for minority or economically disadvantaged groups, which may assist certain students with learning disabilities. For example, Rutgers University teaches a noncredit course on study skills called *Learning to Learn*. This course focuses on the types of cognitive-based learning strategies used for adolescents with learning disabilities in high schools.

Many college students with learning disabilities indicate that the most important aspect of the college support program is emotional and social support. Effective college programs for such students tend to include some mechanism—such as weekly problem-solving meetings—that encourages the students to get together for mutual discussion of problems and mutual support (Dalke & Schmitt, 1987). Many programs provide a facilitator or discussion leader for this activity.

Provision of **student support services** for college students with learning disabilities may take the form of a summer institute for college-bound students. Dalke and Schmitt (1987) described such a five-week summer program at the University of Wisconsin–Whitewater in which students with learning disabilities participate prior to their first year of college. Assessment, instruction in learning strategies, academic reinforcement, campus awareness, and emotional-social support are provided. This type of support indicates a strong commitment to these college students.

With these support services in mind, there are two overall considerations in selecting a college program: comprehensiveness and individualization. The prospective student should consider the comprehensiveness of services offered. A service plan that includes some type of summer orientation and training program, tutoring in various classes, assessment as needed, emotional support, and accommodations in program planning should meet the needs of most students. However, even when comprehensive services are provided, an individually tailored program is critical. Students should not settle for a program that attempts to fit all students with learning disabilities into one standard program. Rather, case managers should meet with the student with learning disabilities to individually plan appropriate services.

Assessment Services.   Many colleges and universities offer assessment and remedial recommendation services for students with learning disabilities (Lehmann et al., 2000). Some colleges and universities use assessment to confirm the diagnosis, though identification of learning disabilities at the college level is hotly debated by some scholars in the field (Siegel, 1999). For example, should students who have not been previously identified with learning disabilities seek such a diagnosis in order to reduce class assignments, reduce required hours, or earn the right for alternative test-taking arrangements? Some studies of cognitive and academic abilities of youth with learning disabilities indicate little substantial difference between college students with and without such disabilities (Salvia et al., 1988; Trainin & Swanson, 2005), making it questionable whether cognitive assessment is of benefit in identifying learning disabilities during the college years.

Although the utility of cognitive assessment is debatable, assessment of academic strengths and weaknesses is certainly helpful in determining the types of courses to be taken and the timing of those courses. For example, if a student has a disability that affects math, he or she may wish to take the required math courses only during those semesters when the student is taking other courses in areas that are not problematic. Taking two physical education classes and one general history class along with the difficult math class may be a good idea.

Many colleges and universities offer assessment services on a fee basis, where students must pay the bill. In some cases, college faculty members who specialize in studies of learning disabilities will conduct these assessments, whereas other campuses have paid staff members to perform them. Also, some colleges will allow participation in their program for college students with learning disabilities based on assessments conducted during the late high school years. Certainly, unless assessment directly benefits the student, there is little reason to justify the expense of excessive testing, and students should inquire concerning this assessment prior to choosing a college learning disabilities program.

Administrative Support.   Many colleges offer certain types of **administrative flexibility** in order to promote success of college students with learning disabilities. Some schools allow students to take less than the required minimum number of hours each semester without sacrificing full-time student status. This is particularly important for students who have financial aid or dormitory space that is allocated based on status as a full-time student.

Also, if students with learning disabilities should wish to compete in athletic events, some easing of grade restrictions may be necessary.

Some colleges may have graduation requirements that prohibit students with disabilities from completing the program. In some instances, flexibility on the part of the college dean of curriculum is required (Shaw, 1999; Siegel, 1999). For example, if such a student has met all of the requirements for graduation except a foreign language requirement, the dean of the college may have to approve the student's graduation without the specified foreign language course. In other instances, state college and university systems institute statewide requirements. For example, in Georgia, a graduation examination is required by the board of regents of the university system. As a general policy, several colleges and universities make certain modifications in this requirement for students with learning disabilities.

This type of administrative flexibility is an important consideration in selection of a college program. When considering participation in a college program, the student with learning disabilities can usually get some indication of the level of administrative flexibility by inquiring about the types of modifications that have been made in the past by college and university administrators.

The outcome of one court case emphasizes the need for flexibility on the part of college administrators in accommodating students with learning disabilities (Shaw, 1999; Siegel, 1999). Students with learning disabilities successfully sued Boston University when the university changed its policy of allowing course substitutions for the foreign language requirement (Wolinsky & Whelan, 1999). Six students were awarded damages when the court ruled that requesting a course substitution for the foreign language requirement was a reasonable modification (Wolinsky & Whelan, 1999). Thus, based on this court decision, one may expect increasing flexibility on the part of various university administrators in providing certain accommodations for students with learning disabilities.

Support for College Faculty.   One of the toughest issues facing proponents of programs for college students with learning disabilities is the cultivation of empathy on the part of the college faculty. College faculty should be offered support for modifying their classes in order to accommodate these students (Scott & Gregg, 2000). However, the literature concerning college programs for such students does not include a great emphasis on this aspect of services, and this is disappointing.

Some research has become available on how college faculty respond to students with learning disabilities. Houck, Asselin, Troutman, and Arrington (1992) conducted some research on the types of modifications that college faculty were making for students with learning disabilities. Two groups were surveyed and compared: college faculty and students with learning disabilities. Generally, there was a high level of agreement that college faculty would attempt to work with students who have learning disabilities in order to help them succeed. However, there were several areas of disagreement. Students felt that professors were less likely to make course accommodations such as note-takers, taped lectures, and alternate or extra-credit exams than professors indicated they were. Also, professors were more likely to agree that having a learning disability limited one's choice of major.

Accommodations for college classes are not difficult. For example, college faculty who lecture frequently could easily incorporate participatory organizers and outline suggestions into the lecture classes. Study guides for upcoming tests also help many students with learning disabilities to focus their study time. College faculty should be encouraged to provide these types of accommodations, and they should be provided with administrative support for these modifications because these class accommodations will take time.

Clearly, this **faculty support** is more difficult for a college to undertake than the services mentioned previously because it involves attitude change on the part of the college faculty. However, many colleges are conducting workshops for faculty members in order to make them more cognizant of the needs of youth with learning disabilities.

Legal Requirements

Brinckerhoff, Shaw, and McGuire (1992) reviewed several court cases that suggest that college faculty are required to provide the types of accommodations discussed previously. Specifically, Tufts University Medical School was required to provide an alternative test format for a student with learning disabilities, and the University of California settled a case out of court when a student requested additional time on a math exam. Likewise, the University of Alabama was required to provide auxiliary aides and services (transportation and hearing assistance) to part-time students who needed such services. Clearly, these legal precedents do indicate that college students can expect reasonable accommodations to assist them in coping with the college curriculum, even if they are part-time students who are not enrolled in a degree program.

Selection of Colleges for Students with Learning Disabilities

There is little hard information on exact selection criteria that should be used when students with learning disabilities choose a college or university. Shaywitz and Shaw (1988) provided some guidelines for use by college personnel in admission decisions regarding these students. Also, McGuire and Shaw (1987) recommended consideration of three types of factors: the characteristics of the student, the general characteristics of the institution under consideration, and the specific characteristics of the learning disabilities support program at that institution. The general types of services previously discussed will provide some guide to the types of services available. However, selection of a college or university program is always a very personal decision, and the importance of making the correct decision cannot be overemphasized. Consequently, a college-bound student with learning disabilities, in conjunction with his or her parents, secondary teachers, and guidance counselors, should carefully weigh each of these factors.

Self-Determination and Self-Advocacy

As information on adults with learning disabilities has accumulated, numerous researchers have begun to speak of self-determination as a major goal of intervention programs (Brinckerhoff, 1994; Field, 1996; Kling, 2001; Rojewski, 1996). Unlike educational choices made for, with, and by children with learning disabilities (i.e., which courses to take in middle school, etc.), choices made by adults are much more likely to affect the individual for a lifetime. Choices may be as fundamental as choosing to go to college, go to technical school, or work after high school. Clearly, self-determination must play an increasing role in the life of the individual with learning disabilities as that person matures into adulthood.

Field (1996) points out that federal law mandates that students with learning disabilities be involved in development of their transition plans (i.e., those components of the IEP relating to transition). Among the various definitions of self-determination in the literature, Field (1996) indicated that most include some emphasis on freedom to make informed choices and control one's own fate and life circumstances.

Brinckerhoff (1994) suggested that self-advocacy skills should also be included in this developing emphasis. As one example, adults with learning disabilities will eventually confront situations in which they have no teacher, no advocate, no peer coach, no parent, and perhaps no close friends present. This would suggest that adults with learning disabilities will need to advocate successfully for themselves. Thus, students with learning disabilities should be taught specifically about their disability, their rights under the various federal laws, and how to advocate for themselves when entering the job market and/or entering a higher education program. Interest Box 13.2 presents some examples of the types of knowledge that may be included in self-advocacy training.

With this growing emphasis on self-determination and **self-advocacy** in mind, a number of theorists have indicated a need for self-advocacy training among students with learning disabilities prior to completing high school (Kling, 2001; Lock & Layton, 2001). First, college students with disabilities themselves have indicated that they feel a need for self-advocacy (Lehmann et al., 2000), and this may be one reason that students with learning disabilities who enter college often do not successfully complete either a two-year or a four-year college program. Next, recent training research has shown some wage discrimination against individuals with learning disabilities (Dickinson & Verbeek, 2002), and self-advocacy training would be one way to combat such inadvertent discrimination. Further, research has documented that coordinators of support services for students with learning disabilities in college believe that self-advocacy skills need much more emphasis in high school in order to prepare these students for college (Janiga & Costenbader, 2002). Finally, in one study, although 90% of the young adults with learning disabilities thought that their disability affected their job performance in some way, only 30% disclosed their disability to their employer (Madaus, Foley, McGuire, & Ruban, 2002), in spite of their legal right to receive reasonable accommodations on the job based on the Americans with Disabilities Act. These factors together clearly demonstrate a need for self-advocacy training.

Kling (2001) recommended self-advocacy training for all students with learning disabilities, based on a simple learning strategy mnemonic: ASSERT.

A	Awareness of the disability—student's self-identity and reflection
S	State the disability—students state the nature of the disability
S	Strengths and limitations—students state their individual strengths/weaknesses
E	Evaluate problems and solutions—students consider solutions to various problems
R	Role-play—students role-play the potential solutions to gain practice
T	Try it—students try the selected strategy in the real world

■ ■ ■ ■ ■ ▬▬▬▬

INTEREST BOX 13.2

**TEACHING TIPS: SELF-ADVOCACY SKILLS FOR ADULTS
WITH LEARNING DISABILITIES**

- Knowledge of what a learning disability is and what it involves
- Knowledge of legal rights under IDEA of 2004, Section 504, and the Americans with Disabilities Act
- Understanding of the available support services at the agency, the work environment, or the school
- Determination of reasonable accommodations that may make success more likely
- Understanding independence versus dependence versus isolation
- Practice in self-advocacy through role-play and coaching through a self-advocacy situation

Kling (2001) suggested that use of this mnemonic could assist students with learning disabilities across the age span in developing self-awareness and self-advocacy. Clearly, this is one way for teachers of secondary students with learning disabilities to prepare them for the task of self-advocacy as young adults. As research has shown, students with learning disabilities need these self-advocacy skills in order to successfully enter the world of postsecondary education (Dickinson & Verbeek, 2002; Janiga & Costenbader, 2002; Kling, 2001).

Transition Planning for Young Adults with Learning Disabilities

With the array of postschool options for students with learning disabilities ranging from continued vocational or college education to entering the workplace, planning for this postschool transition has been increasingly emphasized for these students (Benz et al., 2000; Lehmann et al., 2000; Lindstrom & Benz, 2002; Madaus et al., 2006; Steer & Cavaiuolo, 2002). In the 1990 revision of the Individuals with Disabilities Education Act, legislation was passed that required schools to address transition service needs on the IEP (Katsiyannis et al., 1998). This plan is often referred to as an individual transition plan or ITP. Several studies have indicated that the degree to which students are goal directed in their transition process is related to positive transition outcomes (Benz et al., 2000; Steer & Cavaiuolo, 2002), and these data merely increase the emphasis on effective planning for postschool transition.

Based on this legislation, schools have implemented a variety of options for postschool transition planning. First, almost all programs for secondary students with learning disabilities implement a school-to-work transition planning team (Reiff & DeFur, 1992) with this planning goal in mind. Typically, such a team consists of the student and his or her parents, general education and special education teachers, guidance counselors, and vocational placement persons. Planning begins with the desires and goals of the student and specifies annual goals to reach the overall goal, including those for the postschool years. Figure 13.2 presents a rough planning guide that may be used for this purpose.

FIGURE 13.2 Transition Services Planning Guide

Based on _____(student's name)_____ interests, aptitudes, and needs, the following desired postsecondary transition outcomes have been identified to date:

Desired Postsecondary Education Outcome(s)	Desired Postsecondary Employment Outcome(s)	Desired Postsecondary Community Living Outcome(s)
Adult Education _____	Full-Time Competitive Employment _____	Living Alone, with Friends or Partner _____
Vocational Training _____	Part-Time Competitive Employment _____	Living with Family _____
Community College _____	Full-Time Supported Employment _____	Transportation Independently _____
College or University _____	Part-Time Supported Employment _____	Transportation Support _____
Tech Prep _____	Apprenticeship _____	Independent Living Support _____
Other _____	Sheltered Workshop _____	Community Participation _____
	Other _____	Other _____
Specialized transition services or planning needed in this area? Yes ___ No ___	Specialized transition services or planning needed in this area? Yes ___ No ___	Specialized transition services or planning needed in this area? Yes ___ No ___

Statement of Needed Transition Services:

Based on _____(student's name)_____ interests, needs, and desired postsecondary outcomes identified, this IEP team has determined that _____ is in need of specialized transition services and/or support in the following areas:

Desired Long-Range Outcome: _____

_____

_____

Annual Goal: _____

_____

_____

Annual Objective(s): _____

_____

_____

Activities/Resources: _____

_____

Time Line(s): _____   Review Date: _____

Person(s)/Agencies Responsible: _____

Source: From "Transition for Youths with Learning Disabilities: A Focus on Developing Independence" by H. B. Reiff and S. DeFur, *Learning Disability Quarterly,* 1992, *15,* 237–249. Copyright © 1992 Council for Learning Disabilities. Reprinted by permission.

Next, teachers may wish to consider some type of informal assessment to assist with transition planning (Clark, 1996). Things such as interest inventories completed by the young adult with learning disabilities may be helpful, as well as ratings of job performance by several employers and/or co-workers.

Unfortunately, after a decade of implementation, research has suggested that schools have not yet fully implemented effective transition planning processes (Johnson et al., 2002). In the opinion of some researchers, some school districts have not yet reached minimal compliance with the law, while others find that their transition planning endeavors are regarded as secondary in the school culture. Clearly, the growing emphasis on transition will continue, and as a teacher of students with learning disabilities, if you should take a secondary teaching position, you will need to actively advocate for effective transition services in your school and school district in order to meet the needs of the students in your charge.

SUMMARY

The available evidence demonstrates that learning disabilities persist into adulthood. Both academic deficits and less-than-positive emotional-social characteristics persist, at least for the first five or six years after high school graduation. Based on these variables, it seems clear that learning disabilities are a lifelong phenomenon and that public school efforts to "cure" them have not been successful. The best that public school interventions can achieve is to develop appropriate compensatory strategies that help the adult with learning disabilities to cope successfully with his or her environment.

However, the employment opportunities that await these adults are less than satisfactory. There is prejudice against employment of such individuals, and some research suggests that many of them may end up in entry-level jobs at minimum wage. Still, a sizable majority of adults with learning disabilities join the workforce, which provides an opportunity for them to lead relatively independent lives.

Most adults with learning disabilities pursue either employment or higher education after high school. Percentage estimates vary concerning how many of these students go in either direction, though some research indicates that between 60 and 70% are employed. This indicates a need to develop strong vocational educational programs for the student with disabilities throughout the later years of public school and beyond.

Another group of adults with learning disabilities pursues higher education, and approximately 16% pursue vocational education at a postsecondary level. Colleges and universities are recognizing this need and are structuring programs to assist such students in college, though this restructuring is a long-term process. Although no clear guidelines are available concerning what an effective college program should include, teachers of secondary students with learning disabilities who may be applying for postsecondary education should investigate the various programs offered by colleges and universities in the local area.

The following points should assist you in studying this chapter:

- The transition period between the end of high school and meaningful integration into society after several years has received increasing study recently.

- The outcomes for students with learning disabilities are not as positive as most professionals would like. Outcomes in several areas are not at all positive, including academic and cognitive outcomes as well as social-emotional outcomes. Vocational outcomes are somewhat more positive.
- Many young people with learning disabilities take minimum-wage types of jobs after high school, and these workers tend to stay at minimum wage longer than their nondisabled co-workers.
- Youth with learning disabilities indicate that both special education and vocational education courses in high school were important in helping them after graduation. However, those students generally indicate that the remainder of their high school education was not helpful.
- Between 30 and 45% of the students with learning disabilities who finished high school attended some type of postschool educational program. Some of these young people continue their education in community colleges or vocational schools, whereas others attend four-year colleges.
- The services offered by colleges and universities for students with learning disabilities include assessment, student support services such as tutoring and counseling, administrative support, and support for college faculty in course modification. The best programs include all of these services.

QUESTIONS AND ACTIVITIES

1. Describe a retrospective study, and identify alternative research designs that provide more complete information.

2. Discuss the prognosis for adults with learning disabilities during the postschool transition years.

3. Obtain information concerning the programs offered for students with learning disabilities at your college or university. Prepare a fact sheet on the services offered, and place these services in the hierarchy of services discussed in this chapter.

4. Write to three postsecondary vocational schools in your area, and request information concerning the number of students who are identified as learning disabled. Does this number represent an accurate picture?

5. Discuss the types of outcome variables that should be included in follow-up studies of young people with learning disabilities. Which do you think are the most important?

6. What rationale can be provided for exempting students who are learning disabled from the foreign language requirements at the college level?

7. Compare the information in earlier chapters on characteristics of adolescents with learning disabilities and the information on youth presented here. What information is still needed on these groups?

8. Describe the hierarchy of services that college programs for students with learning disabilities may provide.

9. Describe the college faculty perceptions of students with learning disabilities.

10. Obtain several ITPs from friends, family, or the local schools, and review these for the class.

11. Describe the types of compensation strategies used by successful college students with learning disabilities.

REFERENCES

Bacon, E. H., & Carpender, D. (1989). Learning disabled and nondisabled college students' use of structure in recall of stories and text. *Learning Disability Quarterly, 12,* 108–118.

Beitchman, J. H., Wilson, B., Douglas, L., Young, A., & Adlaf, E. (2001). Substance use disorders in young adults with and without LD. *Journal of Learning Disabilities, 34*(4), 317–332.

Bender, W. N., Rosenkrans, C. B., & Crane, M. K. (1999). Stress, depression, and suicide among students with learning disabilities: Assessing the risk. *Learning Disability Quarterly, 22*(2), 143–156.

Benz, M. R., Lindstrom, L., & Yovanoff, P. (2000). Improving graduation and employment outcomes of students with disabilities: Predictive factors and student perspectives. *Exceptional Children, 66*(4), 509–529.

Blalock, G., & Patton, J. R. (1996). Transition and students with learning disabilities: Creating sound futures. *Journal of Learning Disabilities, 29*(1), 7–16.

Bourke, A. B., Strenhorn, K. C., & Silver, P. (2000). Faculty members' provision of instructional accommodations to students with LD. *Journal of Learning Disabilities, 33*(1), 26–32.

Brinckerhoff, L. C. (1994). Developing effective self-advocacy skills in college bound students with learning disabilities. *Intervention in School and Clinic, 29,* 229–237.

Brinckerhoff, L. C. (1996). Making the transition to higher education: Opportunities for student empowerment. *Journal of Learning Disabilities, 29,* 118–136.

Brinckerhoff, L. C., Shaw, S. F., & McGuire, J. M. (1992). Promoting access, accommodations, and independence for college students with learning disabilities. *Journal of Learning Disabilities, 25,* 417–429.

Brown, K. W. (1976). What employers look for in job applicants. *Business Education Forum, 30,* 7.

Bullis, M., Yavanoff, P., Mueller, G., & Havel, E. (2002). Life on the "outs"—Examination of the facility-to-community transition of incarcerated youth. *Exceptional Children, 69*(1), 7–22.

Clark, G. M. (1996). Transition planning assessment for secondary-level students with learning disabilities. *Journal of Learning Disabilities, 29,* 79–92.

Cohen, S. E. (1988). Coping strategies of university students with learning disabilities. *Journal of Learning Disabilities, 21,* 161–164.

Cohn, P. (1998). Why does my stomach hurt? How individuals with learning disabilities can use cognitive strategies to reduce anxiety and stress at the college level. *Journal of Learning Disabilities, 31,* 514–516.

Commission on Excellence in Special Education (2001). *Revitalizing special education for children and their families.* Available from www.ed.gov/inits/commissionsboards/whspecialeducation.

Cronin, M. E. (1996). Life skills curricula for students with learning disabilities: A review of the literature. *Journal of Learning Disabilities, 29,* 53–68.

Dalke, C., & Schmitt, S. (1987). Meeting the transition needs of college bound students with learning disabilities. *Journal of Learning Disabilities, 20,* 176–180.

Dickinson, D. L., & Verbeek, R. L. (2002). Wage differentials between college graduates with and without learning disabilities. *Journal of Learning Disabilities, 35*(2), 175–184.

Dunn, C. (1996). A status report on transition planning for individuals with learning disabilities. *Journal of Learning Disabilities, 29*(1), 17–30.

Evers, R. B. (1996). The positive force of vocational education: Transition outcomes for youth with learning disabilities. *Journal of Learning Disabilities, 29,* 69–78.

Field, S. (1996). Self-determination instructional strategies for youth with learning disabilities. *Journal of Learning Disabilities, 29,* 40–52.

Gaylord-Ross, R., Siegel, S., Park, H. S., & Wilson, W. (1988). Secondary vocational training. In R. Gaylord-Ross (Ed.), *Vocational education for persons with handicaps.* Mountain View, CA: Mayfield.

Greenbaum, B., Graham, S., & Scales, W. (1995). Adults with learning disabilities: Educational and social experiences during college. *Exceptional Children, 61,* 460–471.

Gregory, J. F., Shanahan, T., & Walberg, G. (1986). A profile of learning disabled twelfth-graders in regular classes. *Learning Disability Quarterly, 9,* 33–42.

Heal, L. W., & Rusch, F. R. (1995). Predicting employment for students who leave special education high school programs. *Exceptional Children, 61,* 472–487.

Horn, W. F., O'Donnell, J. P., & Vitulano, L. A. (1983). Long-term follow-up studies of learning disabled persons. *Journal of Learning Disabilities, 9,* 542–554.

Houck, C. K., Asselin, S. B., Troutman, G. C., & Arrington, J. M. (1992). Students with learning disabilities in the university environment: A study of faculty and student perceptions. *Journal of Learning Disabilities, 25,* 678–684.

Janiga, S. J., & Costenbader, V. (2002). The transition from high school to postsecondary education for students with learning disabilities: A survey of college service coordinators. *Journal of Learning Disabilities, 35*(5), 462–468.

Johnson, D. R., Stodden, R. A., Emanuel, E. J., Luecking, R., & Mack, M. (2002). Current challenges facing secondary education and transition services: What research tells us. *Exceptional Children, 68*(4), 519–531.

Karpinski, M. J., Neubert, D. A., & Graham, S. (1992). A follow-along study of postsecondary outcomes for graduates and dropouts with mild disabilities in a rural setting. *Journal of Learning Disabilities, 25,* 376–385.

Katsiyannis, A., DeFur, S., & Conderman, G. (1998). Transition services—Systems change for youth with disabilities? A review of state practices. *Journal of Special Education, 32*(1), 55–61.

Kling, B. (2001). Assert yourself: Helping students of all ages develop self-advocacy skills. *Teaching Exceptional Children, 32*(3), 66–70.

Lehmann, J. P., Davies, T. G., & Laurin, K. M. (2000). Listening to student voices about postsecondary education. *Teaching Exceptional Children, 32*(5), 60–65.

Levine, P., & Nourse, S. W. (1998). What follow-up studies say about postschool life for young men and women with learning disabilities: A critical look at the literature. *Journal of Learning Disabilities, 31*(3), 212–233.

Lindstrom, L., & Benz, M. R. (2002). Phases of career development: Case studies of young women with learning disabilities. *Exceptional Children, 68*(1), 67–83.

Lock, R. H., & Layton, C. A. (2001). Succeeding in postsecondary ed. through self-advocacy. *Teaching Exceptional Children, 34*(2), 66–71.

Madaus, J. W., Foley, T. E., McGuire, J. M., & Ruban, L. M. (2002). Employment self-disclosure of postsecondary graduates with learning disabilities: Rates and rationales. *Journal of Learning Disabilities, 35*(4), 364–369.

Madaus, J. W., Ruban, L. M., Foley, T. E., & McGuire, J. M. (2006). Attributes contributing to the employment satisfaction of university graduates with learning disabilities. *Learning Disability Quarterly, 26*(3), 159–170.

McGuire, J. J., & Shaw, S. F. (1987). A decision-making process for the college bound student: Matching learning, institution, and support program. *Learning Disability Quarterly, 10,* 106–111.

Minskoff, E. H., Sautter, S. W., Hoffman, F. J., & Hawks, R. (1987). Employer attitudes toward hiring the learning disabled. *Journal of Learning Disabilities, 20,* 53–57.

Mithaug, D. E., Horiuchi, C. N., & Fanning, P. N. (1985). A report on the Colorado statewide follow-up survey of special education students. *Exceptional Children, 51,* 397–404.

Molina, B. S. G., & Pelham, W. E. (2001). Substance use, substance abuse, and LD among adolescents with a childhood history of ADHD. *Journal of Learning Disabilities, 34*(4), 342–351.

Morgan, R. L., Ellerd, D. A., Gerity, B. P., & Blair, R. J. (2000). That's the job I want! How technology helps youth in transition. *Teaching Exceptional Children, 32*(4), 44–49.

Morgan, R. L., Morgan, R. B., Despain, D., & Vasquez, E. (2005). I can search for jobs on the Internet! A website that helps youth in transition identify preferred employment. *Teaching Exceptional Children, 38*(6), 6–11.

Mull, C., Sitlington, P. L., & Alper, S. (2001). Postsecondary education for students with learning disabilities: A synthesis of the literature. *Exceptional Children, 68*(1), 97–118.

Murray, C., Goldstein, D. E., & Nourse, S. E. (2000). The postsecondary school attendance and completion rates of high school graduates with learning disabilities. *Learning Disabilities Research and Practice, 15*(2), 119–127.

Nisbet, J. (1988). Professional roles and practices in the provision of vocational education for students with disabilities. In R. Gaylord-Ross (Ed.), *Vocational education for persons with handicaps.* Mountain View, CA: Mayfield.

Okolo, C. M., & Sitlington, P. (1986). The role of special education in LD adolescents' transition from school to work. *Learning Disability Quarterly, 9,* 141–155.

Price, L. A., & Gerber, P. J. (2001). At second glance: Employers and employees with learning disabilities in the Americans with Disabilities Act era. *Journal of Learning Disabilities, 34*(3), 202–211.

Quinn, M. M., Rutherford, R. B., Osher, D. M., & Poirier, J. M. (2005). Youth with disabilities in juvenile corrections: A national survey. *Exceptional Children, 71*(3), 339–345.

Reiff, H. B., & DeFur, S. (1992). Transition for youths with learning disabilities: A focus on developing independence. *Learning Disability Quarterly, 15,* 237–249.

Rojewski, J. W. (1996). Educational and occupational aspirations of high school seniors with learning disabilities. *Exceptional Children, 62,* 463–476.

Rose, E. (1991). Project TAPE: A model of technical assistance for service providers of college students with learning disabilities. *Learning Disabilities Research and Practice, 6,* 25–33.

Rourke, B. P., Young, G. C., & Leenaars, A. A. (1989). A childhood learning disability that predisposes those afflicted to adolescent and adult depression and suicide risk. *Journal of Learning Disabilities, 22,* 169–175.

Salvia, J., Gajar, A., Gajria, M., & Salvia, S. (1988). A comparison of WAIS-R profiles on nondisabled college freshmen and college students with learning disabilities. *Journal of Learning Disabilities, 21,* 632–636.

Scott, S. S., & Gregg, N. (2000). Meeting the evolving education needs of faculty in providing access for college students with LD. *Journal of Learning Disabilities, 33*(2), 158–167.

Shalock, R. L., Wolzen, B., Ross, I., Elliot, B., Werbel, G., & Peterson, K. (1986). Post-secondary community placement of handicapped students: A five-year follow-up. *Learning Disability Quarterly, 9,* 295–303.

Shaw, R. A. (1999). The case for course substitutions as a reasonable accommodation for students with foreign language learning difficulties. *Journal of Learning Disabilities, 32,* 320–328.

Shaywitz, S. E., & Shaw, R. (1988). The admissions process: An approach to selecting learning disabled students at the most selective colleges. *Learning Disabilities Focus, 3,* 81–86.

Siegel, L. S. (1999). Issues in the definition and diagnosis of learning disabilities: A perspective on *Guckemberger v. Boston University. Journal of Learning Disabilities, 32,* 304–319.

Sitlington, P. L. (1996). Transition to living: The neglected component of transition programming for individuals with learning disabilities. *Journal of Learning Disabilities, 29*(1), 31–39.

Sitlington, P. L., & Frank, A. (1990). Are adolescents with learning disabilities successfully crossing the bridge into adult life? *Learning Disability Quarterly, 13,* 97–111.

Sitlington, P. L., & Frank, A. (1993). *Iowa statewide follow-up study: Adult adjustment of individuals with learning disabilities three vs. one year out of school.* Des Moines: Iowa Department of Education.

Sparks, R. L., & Ganschow, L. (1999). The Boston University lawsuit: Introduction to the special series. *Journal of Learning Disabilities, 32*(4), 284–285.

Steer, D. E., & Cavaiuolo, D. (2002). Connecting outcomes, goals, and objectives in transition planning. *Teaching Exceptional Children, 34*(6), 54–59.

Trainin, G., & Swanson, H. L. (2005). Cognition, metacognition, and achievement of college students with learning disabilities. *Learning Disability Quarterly, 28*(4), 261–272.

Wagner, M., Blackorby, J., Cameto, R., Hebbeler, K., & Newman, L. (1993). *The transition experiences of young people with disabilities: A summary of findings from the National Longitudinal Transition Study of Special Education Students.* Menlo Park, CA: SRI International.

White, W. J. (1992). The postschool adjustment of persons with learning disabilities: Current status and future projections. *Journal of Learning Disabilities, 25,* 448–456.

Witte, R. H., Philips, L., & Kakela, M. (1998). Job satisfaction of college graduates with learning disabilities. *Journal of Learning Disabilities, 31*(3), 259–265.

Wolinsky, S., & Whelan, A. (1999). Federal law and the accommodation of students with LD: The lawyers' look at the BU decision. *Journal of Learning Disabilities, 32,* 286–291.

CHAPTER FOURTEEN

ISSUES IN THE FUTURE OF LEARNING DISABILITIES

CHAPTER OUTLINE

WHEN YOU COMPLETE THIS CHAPTER, YOU SHOULD BE ABLE TO:

1. Describe the relationship between changes in the definition of learning disabilities and growing emphasis on subtype research.

2. Describe the current and anticipated impact of the research on brain-compatible learning in the field of learning disabilities.

3. Discuss the rationale for development of competencies required for teachers of the learning disabled.

4. Define *burnout* and indicate some of its potential causes.

5. Describe PIP and the rationale for its utilization.

6. Describe the Commission for Excellence in Special Education and the No Child Left Behind legislation and the impact of these factors on preschool education for children with learning disabilities.

KEYWORDS

No Child Left Behind (NCLB) Act	co-occurring disorders	professional improvement plan
high-stakes testing	subtyping research	(PIP)
AYP	nonverbal LD	in-service
highly qualified	burnout	journals

INTRODUCTION

In preparing a chapter on the future of learning disabilities, any author must realize that he or she is in the business of making predictions—perhaps educated guesses—based on current trends. Although this is always problematic, in today's environment, it is even more so. As described in Chapter 1 and numerous subsequent chapters, the Commission on Excellence in Special Education (2001) issued a report on special education that resulted in major changes in the field of learning disabilities when recommendations were codified into IDEA for 2004. Thus, things in this field may change rather drastically, which makes a chapter such as this one particularly difficult to write.

Of course, in one sense, such uncertainty is quite common in the history of learning disabilities. Not only have the issues raised by the commission (e.g., definition, assessment, instructional interventions) long been discussed in this field, but the future of learning disabilities has always been a hotly debated topic as well (Hammill, 1993). Given this historic debate, any of the major issues discussed in this book may drastically change the nature of services provided for children with learning disabilities during the next several years. Issues involving definition, placement of these students in inclusive classes, and the response to intervention as an eligibility tool to identify students with learning disabilities are critically important and will reshape the field considerably. However, these issues have been discussed previously and will not be presented again here. Rather, this chapter presents other issues that are being discussed today in virtually every teachers' lounge in virtually every school. These include issues such as the implications of recent federal legislation, preparation of highly qualified teachers, high stakes testing and meeting state educational standards, and brain friendly instruction, as well as other issues specific to learning disabilities such as co-occuring disorders and subtyping research. These are presented to illustrate the types of scholarly debate that you will hear during the next several years.

You should think about these issues and be prepared to take a position on each issue and defend it with research. The ability to defend one's judgments on tough issues in the field is one mark of a professional teacher. At the end of the chapter, a summary statement concerning future directions will be offered as a challenge to you as a new professional in the field.

NO CHILD LEFT BEHIND: NEW ISSUES IN EDUCATION

In January of 2002, President Bush signed a landmark piece of legislation into law, referred to as the **No Child Left Behind (NCLB) Act.** This legislation was intended to ensure that every child complete the first several years of school with the required reading skills to successfully negotiate the increasingly complex curriculum from grades 4 through 12 (Simpson, LaCava, & Graner, 2004; Yell, Katsiyannas, & Shiner, 2006). The legislation requires states to implement a statewide plan for reading instruction, based on research-proven reading instructional principles, to ensure that no child is left behind in reading prior to grade 3.

With the passage of No Child Left Behind, a variety of issues have arisen that impact educators, generally, and special educators, in particular. These include, at a minimum, the issue of high-stakes assessment, meeting adequate yearly progress (often called AYP; Yell et al., 2006) toward achieving statewide educational goals, and the issue of the qualifications of teachers themselves—namely, the "highly qualified" teacher. These issues have been hotly debated among educators and likely will continue to be critical issues for teachers in the years to come.

High-Stakes Testing

While various state assessments have always been part of the education scene, only as recently as 1997 did federal legislation mandate that students with disabilities were to be included in statewide assessment programs (Kohl, McLaughlin, & Nagel, 2006). Such a mandate resulted from the worthy goal of ensuring that students with disabilities can participate in the benefits derived from studying the general education curriculum; thus, this mandate was a part of the broader national move toward inclusion.

More recently, the No Child Left Behind legislation has mandated that states develop a series of high educational standards and institute appropriate required assessments to document that students are meeting these standards (Elliott & Marquart, 2004; Fletcher et al., 2006; Ysseldyke et al., 2004). In essence, the federal legislation requires states to administer assessments periodically and to ensure that all students—and, in particular, various subgroups of students within the schools, such as racial minorities or students with disabilities—are achieving success toward learning the standards in the school curriculum. This was the origin of the title for this legislation—no child should be left behind in reading during the early grades.

Whereas NCLB only dealt with assessment in the elementary grades (Yell et al., 2006), this emphasis on assessment has revitalized the entire "assessment for accountability" issue. In many states, passage from grade to grade, or even graduation from high school, may be associated with successful completion of the required assessments in various grade levels. Thus, some of these assessments have high stakes (i.e., serious effects and implications) for various learners, including students with disabilities. Of course, accommodations for various disabilities are allowed under the guidelines; for example, many practitioners allow extra time as one accommodation for students with learning disabilities (Elliott & Marquart, 2004; Kohl et al., 2006).

Still, there is considerable debate—not to mention some degree of anger—among special educators relative to the implementation of the various high-stakes assessments, as well as other provisions of the No Child Left Behind legislation. One recent press release by the Council for Exceptional Children proclaimed, "No Child Left Behind Makes No Sense for Students with Disabilities" (CEC, 2003). In the national press, **high-stakes testing** has both been praised as resulting in improved education for students with disabilities as well as cursed for resulting in higher dropout rates (Ysseldyke et al., 2004). Further, while more research is certainly needed, the extant research indicates that such testing is having both positive and negative effects on students with disabilities. Interest Box 14.1 presents some of the research conclusions—both positive and negative—relative to implementation of high-stakes testing.

While the NCLB legislation did not initiate the move toward high-stakes testing, the use of assessments has certainly received increased emphasis because of NCLB. As an educator, you will hear many debates about both NCLB and high-stakes assessment during your teaching career, and you may find that your school struggles with various provisions of that legislation for many years to come.

Adequate Yearly Progress

The NCLB legislation also mandated the establishment of yearly goals for schools and school districts, and these goals are generally stated in terms of the average achievement levels for students and subgroups of students within the schools (Yell et al., 2006). Of course, the establishment of rigorous goals is intended to emphasize and enhance learning for all students, and this is certainly a worthy goal. Further, goals were established in such a fashion that the benchmarks or criteria for having meet the standards increase each year through the year 2014. Thus, schools might be expected to have 75% of third graders achieving the goal of reading at grade level by the year 2004, while the goal for 2005 might be for 80% of all students to be reading on grade level. Of course, the school would

■ ■ ■ ■ ■ ▬▬▬▬▬▬▬▬▬▬▬▬▬▬▬▬▬▬▬▬▬▬▬▬▬▬▬▬▬

INTEREST BOX 14.1

**POSSIBLE POSITIVE AND NEGATIVE EFFECTS
OF HIGH-STAKES ASSESSMENT**

**POSSIBLE POSITIVE EFFECTS OF HIGH-STAKES
TESTING MENTIONED IN THE LITERATURE**

1. Improved performance of students with disabilities on statewide assessments. This may suggest increased study efforts on the part of the students.
2. Increased participation rates of students with disabilities. While many states historically excluded students with disabilities from local or statewide testing programs, the NCLB legislation has decreased such exclusion and increased participation on these assessments.
3. Increased expectations for students with disabilities due to the setting of higher curriculum standards.
4. Increased alignment between IEP goals and objectives and standards on the state curriculum. Thus, special education students have benefited from increased exposure to the general education curriculum content.
5. More students with special needs are placed in general education classes.
6. Increased graduation rates among students with disabilities, according to some research reports.

**POSSIBLE NEGATIVE EFFECTS OF HIGH-STAKES
TESTING MENTIONED IN THE LITERATURE**

1. Increase in students referred and identified for special education services.
2. Increased dropouts resulting from high-stakes testing required for high school graduation.
3. Narrowing of curricular emphasis to include only content assessed on the tests.
4. Less teacher flexibility to emphasize local content that may not be emphasized on the statewide assessment (i.e., teachers may be less likely to teach about the science of the cleanup of Lake Erie for schools located on the lake, or to teach Civil War history for schools located near Civil War battlefields).
5. Possible detrimental effects on motivation of students with special needs, or other learners who are challenged by the curriculum.
6. Increased test anxiety or school anxiety among students with learning disabilities.

These are some of the possible positive and negative effects of high-stakes testing mentioned in the literature (Elliott & Marquart, 2004; Fletcher et al., 2006; Ysseldyke et al., 2004). More research is needed before these effects can be documented with certainty.

▬▬▬▬▬▬▬▬▬▬▬▬▬▬▬▬▬▬▬▬▬▬▬▬▬▬▬▬▬▬▬▬▬▬▬▬▬

have various specialized breakdowns of these goals, relating to various educationally challenged groups of students. For example, the school might also have goals related to minority children, non-English-speaking children, or children in special education (e.g., 80% of all minority children reading on grade level by 2005, etc.).

Of course, every school faculty member wishes to meet their school goals, and this can be a hotly debated local issue. Newspapers around the country have begun to report whether individual schools have met their standards or not. Thus, school faculty are very concerned with meeting adequate yearly progress toward their goals.

However, there have been a number of concerns stated with **adequate yearly progress (AYP),** as it is currently implemented. First, many schools in socioeconomically challenged areas are struggling to meet their AYP, and faculty at those schools protest that the specific challenges in teaching students from socioeconomically challenged families are not recognized in setting AYP goals. Further, because many distinct groups have been "broken out" for individual aggregation of scores, many highly successful schools have likewise not met AYP toward their goals. For example, in a high socioeconomic area in which schools include few children from impoverished homes or few non-English-speaking children, it is still possible for such schools to fail to meet AYP if their students with disabilities—as one subgroup of the school population—do not do well on the tests. The faculty in such a highly successful school might well feel aggrieved if their school was identified in the local press as having "not met AYP" because of only one subcategory of students—those with disabilities.

Clearly, meeting AYP will be a concern for many educators, since every educator wants to be a part of a successful school. Successful schools will not want to be stigmatized when students with disabilities do not meet their subgroup goals. Such scenarios can result in friction in the working relationship between special and general educators. Clearly, these issues are complex and generate strong feelings on all sides. You, as a new teacher in learning disabilities, should seek to understand the general perception of other educators in your area, as well as the national debate on meeting AYP. It is a certainty that this issue will continue to generate strong feelings and discussion over the next few years.

Highly Qualified Teachers

Another result of the NCLB legislation is that students are now assured of having teachers that are "highly qualified" to teach in their subject area (King-Sears, 2005). Being **highly qualified** typically means having a degree in the subject area you teach, and NCLB limits the definition of that term exclusively to content-area subjects (King-Sears, 2005). While this would seem to be simple enough for educators who teach specific subject areas in departmentalized schools (e.g., a secondary history teacher should have both a teaching certificate and extensive educational course work specific to history), this becomes more problematic when applied to special educators. Traditionally, special educators have provided expertise in instructional pedagogy rather than in particular content areas, and thus, the definition of "highly qualified" holds serious implications for many special educators (King-Sears, 2005). In point of fact, many special educators, in both resource and/or inclusive class placements, find themselves teaching virtually every subject in the school curriculum. According to the new standard of "highly qualified," teachers who have been teaching content area for decades are no longer considered highly qualified. In some cases, teachers have been told to go back to school to take content courses in reading, math, history, or science to get highly qualified! Of course, it is unrealistic to expect this group of special educators to complete a full undergraduate major in each subject area. Perhaps nothing has so impacted the education of special education teachers as this "highly qualified" provision within the No Child Left Behind legislation, and various states are developing

different ways for teachers in special education to earn additional course credits or participate in various workshops to become "highly qualified" in subjects they teach.

As a practitioner in the field, you should discuss this issue of "highly qualified" with
your undergraduate or graduate adviser and find out how districts in your state are implementing this provision. Likewise, you should ask questions about the "highly qualified"
requirements when applying for jobs in various school districts. There is some flexibility
on the part of some educational administrators in some districts but not in others, and this
may well influence where you choose to teach.

CO-OCCURRING DISORDERS

The issue of **co-occurring disorders** is becoming a concern for many professionals in the
field (Bender & Wall, 1994; Fletcher, Shaywitz, & Shaywitz, 1994; Lyon, 2000; Smith &
Adams, 2006). Specifically, the increasing numbers of students with attention-deficit hyperactivity disorders have caused concern because services for these students may tend to
draw funding away from services for students with learning disabilities. At present, these
two disabilities are considered to coexist or co-occur in many individuals, and researchers
have not yet teased out the distinctions between these two groups. Smith and Adams (2006)
indicate that these comorbid disorders tended to result in increased behavior problems,
which may suggest that these conditions are separate conditions. In fact, Fletcher and colleagues (1994) suggested that researchers should consider these two groups together in their
research designs until some clarification is forthcoming.

Bender and Wall (1994) suggested that the issue of co-occurring ADHD and learning
disabilities has resulted from changes in the definition of learning disabilities over the last
several decades. Historically, students who were demonstrating attention and organizational problems were considered to have a learning disability. However, during the last three
decades, a more rigid definition, based on the discrepancy between IQ and achievement
(as described in Chapter 1), has been implemented in almost every state. This has been a
grassroots change that took place without any federal mandate. However, implementation
of this discrepancy aspect of the definition did have the effect of eliminating some students
with attention, hyperactive, and/or impulsive problems from the classes for students with
learning disabilities if those students did not manifest the required discrepancy between
IQ and achievement. Obviously, one might have predicted that, with those students now
receiving no educational services, parents would become angry and form advocacy groups
to speak out for increased services. Consequently, ADHD—a heretofore obscure condition
that was identified in psychiatric and not in education literature—has taken on a whole new
form, and the numbers of children with ADHD have increased dramatically. Thus, the issue
of co-occurring disorders between learning disabilities and ADHD may in fact be a definitional issue (Lyon, 2000). We may see a point in the future where these two disabilities
are viewed as different manifestations of the same disability. In point of fact, Stanford and
Hynd (1994) have identified a number of similarities between students with ADHD, inattentive type, and students with learning disabilities. Clearly, future research will be needed
to tease out the merits of the distinction between these two groups.

SUBTYPING RESEARCH

With continued increases in both the numbers and the types of children who are considered learning disabled, there will be some need to identify the various subgroups of children who make up the learning disabilities population. At present, learning disabilities is one of the few recognized conditions that do not have empirically identified subgroups. For example, in mental retardation, the distinction between mild mental retardation and moderate mental retardation is widely recognized and easy to document. Likewise, in the area of behavioral disorders, the distinction between children with conduct disorders and those with personality disorders is fairly easy to document. Only the area of learning disabilities has had no historically documented subgroups that could be empirically distinguished from each other.

Efforts to identify empirically based subtypes among students with learning disabilities—referred to as **subtyping research**—has been under way for some 20 years (Catts, Hogan, and Fey, 2003; Cornoldi et al., 2003; Kavale & Forness, 1987; McKinney, 1984; McKinney & Speece, 1986; Silver et al., 1999), and most of the research indicates that various subgroups do exist within the population that is currently identified as "learning disabled." In most subtyping research, data on a number of students are gathered, and, through complex mathematical procedures, groups of students who share similar characteristics are identified (McKinney, 1984). A number of early subtype studies found that children with learning disabilities could be clustered into meaningful groups. For example, there is a subgroup of children who demonstrate problems on visual-learning tasks, a group with problems on auditory-learning tasks, and a group who seem to have a problem with both types of tasks (McKinney, 1984). Identification of these groups is consistent with the original concerns of scholars in the field and could have been anticipated, but this subtype research represents the first time that these differences were documented empirically.

Perhaps the subtyping research that holds the most promise is the work of Rourke and his colleagues. As presented in Chapter 2, Rourke (Rourke, 2005; Rourke et al., 2002; Rourke, van der Vlugt, & Rourke, 2002) suggests that a minimum of two subgroups of students with learning disabilities exist. The majority of the population of students with learning disabilities seem to suffer from basic phonological processing disabilities, which are characterized by poorly developed single-word reading and spelling processing, and relatively normal social development and behavior. In contrast, **nonverbal learning disabilities** seem to be characterized by well-developed single-word reading/spelling processing; excessive hyperactivity; and various emotional problems, possibly including withdrawal, anxiety, depression, and social skill deficits. While this particular line of subtype research is ongoing, it has become clear that these two basic subtypes do exist and do seem to have different learning strengths and weaknesses. Specifically, Cornoldi and his colleagues (2003) indicated that nonverbal learning disabilities tended to be associated with inadequate mental processing in the right hemisphere of the brain, whereas phonological processing is typically a left hemisphere function.

The hope of many theorists in the field has long been that through subtyping research, we may be able to identify subgroups of children with learning disabilities who profit from particular types of instruction (Catts et al., 2003; Cornoldi et al., 2003; McKinney, 1984; Rourke, 2005). Clearly, if different educational interventions are shown to be effective with different subgroups of students, the implications for all educators would be profound. Certainly, more research will be forthcoming in the area of subtyping research.

SERVICES FOR ADULTS WITH LEARNING DISABILITIES

As indicated in Chapter 13, practitioners have increased the emphasis on services intended to ease the transition between the school years and the early adult years (Benz, Lindstrom, & Yovanoff, 2000; Blalock & Patton, 1996; Brinckerhoff, 1996; Evers, 1996; Janiga & Costenbader, 2002; Kohler & Field, 2003). Although this topic was covered in Chapter 13, there are several important issues that should be highlighted in the context of the future directions of the field.

First, the emphasis on adults with learning disabilities parallels a broader focus on postschool transition into the world of work for all students (Johnson, Stodden, Emanuel, Luecking, & Mack, 2002). Citizens of the United States are inquiring, through their representatives, about the quality of the "product" of the school years—an informed, financially independent citizen who can get and hold a good job and make a contribution to society. Thus, this aspect of the lifelong focus on individuals with learning disabilities is one part of a more comprehensive concern with the quality of schooling overall, as well as the effectiveness of schools in preparing independent citizens.

Given this context, the emphasis on transition services for individuals with learning disabilities will continue to grow over the next decade (Kohler & Field, 2003). You may also anticipate that increasing funds, from both federal and state sources, will be directed toward this growing emphasis. This could result in an increase in the teaching positions that focus exclusively on transition issues, and you may find that you are offered jobs in which your teaching responsibilities would be focused exclusively on transition.

Coupled with this emphasis on transition, there has been an increasing emphasis on the use of technology to focus on the adaptive needs of adults with learning disabilities in the workplace (Raskind, Herman, & Torgesen, 1995). Chapter 12 illustrated many newly developing applications for students with learning disabilities, and many of those innovations can assist adults in the workplace. For example, spell-checking programs and computer-based writing/typing have helped many individuals with learning disabilities acquire certain office jobs that, prior to the advent of these technologies, would have been inappropriate for them. Thus, the growing interest in technology has added to the emphasis on services for adults in the postschool transition period. You may assume that additional applications of technology that will open up further job markets for adults with learning disabilities will be forthcoming.

IMPLICATIONS OF BRAIN-COMPATIBLE RESEARCH

As discussed in Chapter 1, the last decade of the 1900s witnessed an explosive growth in our understanding of how the human brain and central nervous system work (Bender, 2002; Bender & Larkin, 2003; D-Arcangelo, 1999; Jensen, 1995; Sousa, 2001, 2005; Sylwester, 1995), and these data hold implications for our understanding of every aspect of cognitive functioning. Several recent books have related the brain-compatible research directly to learning disabilities (Bender, 2002; Sousa, 2001), and one may anticipate a profound effect on this field based on the developing notions of brain-compatible instruction during the next decade. The emerging insights about the neural pathways involved in human learning promise to affect several theoretical approaches described previously, including multiple intelligences theory, constructivism, and brain-compatible learning strategies (Gardner, 1993; Perkins, 1999; Sousa, 2005; see descriptions of these in Chapter 1).

Specifically, the medical technique referred to as functional magnetic resonance imaging (or functional MRI) allows researchers to actually view the learning process in the human brain while the living human subject performs different types of cognitive tasks. Early studies documented that different areas of the brain were associated with language, math, music appreciation, and reading. In particular, reading was found to be a highly complex process that seemed to be related to a number of different areas within the human brain (D-Arcangelo, 1999; Rourke, 2005).

Other researchers have studied a wide variety of cognitive functioning (Rourke, 2005; Sarouphim, 1999; Swanson, 1999). For example, a number of researchers have begun to identify the specific types of memory problems manifested by students with learning disabilities (O'Shaughnessy & Swanson, 1998; Swanson, 1999). Rather than the ill-conceived notions about short-term memory problems that proliferated in the 1970s, specific working memory deficits across the age span have now been documented, emphasizing the need for more rigorous training in memory strategies for students with learning disabilities. Gardner (1993) and others (Sarouphim, 1999) have begun to question the dated construct of intelligence as merely one unified factor, opting instead for a multifactored approach. This concept will entirely redefine the fundamental aspect of the definition of learning disability, since the discrepancy component of the LD definition is dependent on a measure of general intelligence.

Based on these emerging insights on human learning, specific suggestions for assessment and instruction have been developed for the elementary and secondary classroom (Bender, 2002; Jensen, 1995; Sarouphim, 1999; Sousa, 2001; 2005), and these instructional practices will certainly affect the education of children and youth with learning disabilities. As the influence of behaviorist thought continues to wane and studies of metacognitive strategies and brain-compatible instructional techniques increase, this area of brain-compatible instruction may impact all fields of education as profoundly as any theory in the history of the field. Certainly, the realms of cognitive strategies instruction, multiple intelligences, and constructivism will be influenced by this emerging knowledge. As a beginning professional in this field, you should watch for research articles in this area and perhaps even consider participating in one of the numerous workshops on brain-compatible learning and instruction.

TEACHING IN THE FIELD OF LEARNING DISABILITIES

As this discussion of issues in the field of learning disabilities shows, teachers in the field face a number of challenges typically not confronted by other teachers. Perhaps for this reason, there has always been a teacher shortage in the field of special education. Thus, finding, preparing, and retaining qualified teachers are critical to the field, not to mention critical to the education of students with learning disabilities. The discussion presented below focuses on several issues within the field of teacher preparation for working with children with learning disabilities.

A National Teacher Shortage

There has historically always been a shortage of teachers in special education (McLeskey, Tyler, & Saunders, 2002), and this shortage continues. However, there is some evidence that the shortage may be getting worse over the last decade (Billingsley, Carlson, & Klein, 2004), and given the additional requirements imposed by the "highly qualified" provisions of NCLB, one might suppose that this shortage will continue to grow. Further, there is some debate about how the field should deal with this teacher shortage problem.

Specifically, evidence suggests that many teachers certified to teach students with learning disabilities enter the field and then choose to leave in only a few years (Billingsley et al., 2004). Therefore, the teacher shortage problem will probably not be solved by merely recruiting more teachers into special education; in point of fact, recruitment efforts alone will not alleviate the shortage, since teachers who do enter the field leave special education teaching for other teaching positions or leave the classroom entirely. Rather than emphasize recruitment, many have recommended study of why teachers leave and the implementation of programs to support teachers who are new to the field, in the hope that such support programs will retain teachers in special education.

Billingsley and her co-workers (2004) undertook a survey study to investigate the types of working conditions and support provided to special education teachers in the initial years of their careers. Over 5,000 teachers responded to the survey. Most respondents reported receiving informal support from another teacher, and those indicated that such support was more valuable than other formal forms of support. Further, approximately 60% of the teachers responding to the survey indicated that they participated in some type of formal teacher mentoring, whereby the beginning teacher was formally partnered with a veteran mentor teacher. Finally, the overall climate of the school was highly related to the teacher's desire to remain in the teaching field. Clearly, these forms of support represent one option for retaining teachers in the field; as a teacher new to the field, you should investigate options for mentoring at any school district where you apply for a job. Many times, having the support of a mentor teacher can make or break the first-year teaching experience, and you should strive for a teaching position that offers such support.

Teacher Burnout

Special education teaching is a high-stress field, and teacher burnout is a problem because it helps to create part of the national shortage of teachers (Commission, 2001). **Burnout** represents a generalized and pervasive feeling of dissatisfaction with teaching and may lead to inadequate teaching if teachers remain in the classroom after they begin to burn out. Teachers who are less than satisfied with their roles as teachers of students with learning disabilities may be less responsive to the needs of those students. Consequently, poor instructional experiences for the students may result. For these reasons, professionals have begun to study burnout in order to combat it.

Some tentative conclusions may be stated about burnout (Billingsley et al., 2004; Fore, Martin, & Bender, 2002; Zabel & Zabel, 1983). First, it is more likely to occur in younger, less experienced teachers than in older teachers. This is to be expected because younger teachers will generally be less efficient at meeting the varied demands in the work situation than more experienced teachers. Further, burnout seems to be related to the types of training that teachers receive (Zabel & Zabel, 1983). In other words, teachers who are better trained tend to burn out less often than teachers who are not well prepared.

At present, there is no overall indicator of the level of burnout among teachers of students with learning disabilities compared to teachers of other children with disabilities, nor is there any single indicator of the overall percentage of teachers who are burned out. Perhaps the best one can do is speculate on some tentative causes of burnout. The first of these causes is supported by the evidence, whereas the last two are purely speculative. First, as noted, burnout seems to be related to inadequate training prior to entering the classroom. Clearly, this is under the teacher's control, and victims of burnout may wish to take additional course work or in-service experiences prior to reentering the classroom. Also, providing the beginning learning disabilities teacher with a mentor teacher who is more experienced in working with these students may help.

It is possible that burnout is related to some service delivery factors (Billingsley et al., 2004; Fore, Martin, & Bender, 2002). For example, teachers who work with highly violent children or children with very severe academic problems may be subjected to more stress than teachers whose students demonstrate less severe problems. Placements in special classes as well as mainstream classes may need to be rearranged in order to lessen the load of particular teachers who seem to have the most problematic children.

Finally, burnout may also be related to the use of ineffective educational treatments in the field. Many of the treatments used historically to remediate the problems of children with learning disabilities have not been effective. If teachers continue to use these treatments and see their ineffective nature, those teachers may begin to feel somewhat inadequate, and burnout could result. Clearly, use of more effective instructional strategies should provide a more satisfying work environment for teachers of students who are learning disabled.

Several suggestions that may prevent burnout in the careers of beginning teachers are presented in Interest Box 14.2. As a new teacher in the field, you may wish to complete as many of these activities as you can during your first years of teaching.

PROFESSIONAL IMPROVEMENT

Improvement of one's skills and abilities with each succeeding year in the profession must be one goal of every teacher of students with learning disabilities. To illustrate this type of professionalism, consider some medical and legal examples. Would you wish to go to a doctor who last participated in medical training over 25 years ago, without any additional training? What would be the level of care provided by that physician? Likewise, would you wish to retain an attorney who had not remained current in his or her awareness of recent

■ ■ ■ ■ ■ ▬▬▬▬▬

INTEREST BOX 14.2

**TEACHING TIPS: RECOMMENDED ACTIVITIES
TO PREVENT BURNOUT**

1. Remain current in your professional skills. Read about and practice new instructional techniques on a planned and regular basis. If you consider yourself a professional, and take actions consistent with that view, you are probably less likely to burn out.
2. Attend professional conferences. At the very least, it helps to know that other teachers of the learning disabled face the same types of problems that you do. Also, you may find an idea or two you wish to try.
3. Consider a change in your job within the field. Move to another learning disabilities class in your district, and work with younger or older students. Perhaps moving to another school would help.
4. Take additional course work in related fields such as counseling, behavior management, behavioral disorders, or early childhood education.
5. Consider supervising a student teacher.
6. Teach, on an adjunct basis, a college-level class for preservice teachers.
7. Design and conduct some research with faculty from a local college or university that is intended to rectify a problem you face in your class.
8. Discuss your burnout feelings with other teachers, and elicit ideas they use to avoid burnout.
9. Contact students whom you taught in the past, and find out what types of instruction they felt was most helpful.
10. Take responsibility for your own burnout feelings, and work in some fashion to alleviate those feelings.

▬▬▬▬▬▬▬▬▬▬

case law? More pointedly, do you wish to send your children to a teacher who had his or her most recent training over 25 years ago?

As these examples demonstrate, all teachers should make a yearly effort to remain current in their professional field. This responsibility is part of the definition of *professionalism.* Many states require periodic courses for recertification, and this is certainly a step in the right direction. However, teachers in such states should not assume that such course work every third or fifth year is enough. Rather, teachers who take their professional responsibilities seriously will want to go further.

One method is the creation of a written agreement between a teacher and his or her supervisor or principal that specifies a set of professional activities in which the teacher will engage during the coming year. Some states and school districts have taken the positive step of requiring such documentation of professional improvement from each teacher.

The **professional improvement plan (PIP)** is a document that represents an agreement between a teacher and a school district and generally specifies the activities in which a teacher will engage during the following year in order to professionally improve his or her teaching performance. Activities such as reading research articles, participation in presentations or **in-service** classes, implementation of new teaching techniques, completion of additional course work from universities, creation of annotated bibliographies, implementation of computer-assisted instruction programs, conducting research, observations of other classes, serving as mentor teacher to new teachers, and many other activities are appropriate for the PIP. Almost any activity that encourages either more effective instruction or more awareness of recent research in the field would be appropriate.

Such professional improvement planning may be more necessary in the field of learning disabilities than in other areas. The field has existed for only 40 years, and this is a brief history compared to other areas such as research on mental retardation. Consequently, the learning disabilities field has had a notable number of "false starts" in terms of research. As discussed in Chapter 9, several of the educational treatments that were recommended by pioneers in the field only 20 years ago are presently viewed as unproven and have been discarded. Also, as Chapter 1 demonstrated, the definitions of the term learning disability continue to change on a regular basis. Chapter 5 indicated that assessment perspectives have changed drastically during the last several years. Each of these changes indicates that teachers in this field, even more than other teachers, must continue to remain involved with research in order to remain up to date.

What does it mean to be involved with research? This question can be answered with three mandates: read research, apply research, and conduct research.

Reading Research

Teachers of pupils with learning disabilities should read several articles monthly from the major **journals** in the field. Although articles from teacher magazines may provide information on a new idea for your class, the only manner in which a teacher can remain current with research is to subscribe to and regularly read one of the major journals in the field. The *Journal of Learning Disabilities* and the *Learning Disability Quarterly* are major journals that are highly regarded. Other journals that have articles relating to learning disabilities include *Exceptional Children, Psychology in the Schools, Journal of Special Education,* and *Teaching Exceptional Children.* Also, subscriptions for some of these journals are included in membership of certain organizations. For example, by joining the Council for Learning Disabilities, one interest group in the field, you will receive *Learning Disability Quarterly.*

It is difficult to imagine a physician who does not subscribe to at least one medical journal or an attorney who does not order at least one law journal, yet it is quite common for teachers who have finished their training to stop referring to the major journals in the field. Do not allow yourself to accept such a low professional standard. Make a point of reading at least one journal each month in order to remain current in your profession.

In order to document these efforts for your PIP, you may need to prepare an annotated bibliography of the articles or a brief synopsis of each article. Requirements for reviewing 20 to 30 articles during the next year are not uncommon, and that reading requirement is consistent with the workload of a beginning teacher.

Applying Research

Effective teachers try out the new ideas they read about in the journals. Teachers study and apply self-monitoring, precision teaching, cooperative instruction, peer tutoring, token economies, behavioral contracting, mnemonic instruction, and learning-strategies instruction merely because they read about a strategy in a journal. This type of initiative seems to characterize the most effective teachers of students with learning disabilities. These teachers are always willing to attempt a new idea in order to improve their teaching for the students in their classes. In an effort to facilitate this type of endeavor, this text has noted the strategies that may be applied based on reading several articles, as well as those strategies that may require additional course work or in-service study.

The challenge for you is clear: It is your task to read and apply new ideas in your classroom on a periodic basis. This represents the responsiveness to research that has characterized our field throughout its short history. Perhaps a good goal would be to apply at least one new teaching technique in every five or six months of teaching. In that fashion, you will at least experiment with approximately 10 new techniques during your first five years in the classroom. You may then choose to retain the ones that work and forgo use of the ones that do not seem applicable in your situation.

Currency in instructional technique is particularly difficult in some fields. For example, because of the advance of technological applications for teaching, one could spend 24 hours daily reading research about applications of newly developed software for students with disabilities. Clearly, this is one area in which beginning teachers will have to concentrate in order to remain aware of the vast array of research and to apply some of those research-proven software packages in their classes. However, as your efficacy as a teacher increases, you will become both more comfortable in your job and more widely respected. You should therefore make an effort to study the new technologies and apply that research in your classroom.

Documentation of the use of these new strategies in your classroom may be necessary for the PIP, and such documentation may be handled in several ways. First, you may produce some type of written report of these strategies complete with information that documents their effectiveness. Another option is to invite the principal or supervisor to observe you while you engage in the new strategy or instructional method. That supervisor could then write a brief report of the activity for your PIP documentation.

Conducting Research

Most of the research that is published in the journals is conducted by university and college faculty, whereas some is conducted by public school administrators and supervisors. Only rarely does one see an article in which a classroom teacher conducts research. Nevertheless, teachers should frequently conduct research—though in order to fully understand this injunction, the definition of research may need to be expanded. For example, if a teacher conducts a learning-strategy project or a single-subject design intervention in order to alleviate a classroom problem, that may be considered research in some sense. A problem was noted and measured, a hypothesis stated, and research conducted to validate the hypothesis. The results would then be shared with parents, school psychologists, and other teachers in order to communicate about the problem and its elimination. All teachers of students with learning disabilities should find ample opportunities to participate in this type of research intervention in their classes. The usefulness of research such as this is not dependent on publication. When you share successful single-subject intervention research with parents and other professionals, you gain respect in their eyes, and that is one worthy goal of such research. Conducting intervention research of this nature and sharing the results will contribute to a positive professional reputation for you.

In many instances, teachers have conducted projects in which the quality and general instructiveness of the finished product warranted publication in the journals. When a teacher demonstrates the effectiveness of a new idea or merely modifies an old idea, he or she should be encouraged to publish that research. Generally, such teachers find it helpful to work with someone who has publication experience in their efforts to publish research results. This desire to share effective strategies is one mark of a professional teacher.

A final option you should explore is participation in ongoing research in your school district. For example, many school districts encourage college and university faculty to conduct research in the public school classes for students with learning disabilities because this serves to keep public school faculties more current in research. This usually involves some degree of time commitment to the research, and you will need to weigh that time commitment against the positive gains for the school district. In many instances, researchers will return to the district after the research is concluded and share the results with the faculty involved. Also, there may be individual publication possibilities for you in particular research projects. Finally, when possible, all teachers of students with learning disabilities should encourage and participate in research if our knowledge of these students and methods of instruction is to continue to grow.

Documentation of research participation is fairly straightforward. First, if you participate in an ongoing research project at your school, this may be stipulated in the original PIP agreement at the beginning of the school year. Next, if you find that a particular intervention is necessary during the year, you may amend your PIP in order to include that intervention project when it is completed.

Some PIPs for supervisory personnel in a school district require publication of articles in major journals. Such a requirement is ambitious at best, and may be quite excessive for teachers, but the field of learning disabilities and the broader field of special education in general could only be improved if public school personnel took a more active hand in providing substantive literature in the field. If you publish a paper in one of the journals or teacher magazines, you should amend your PIP during that year to include that accomplishment.

Participation in Ongoing Professional Development

Many PIPs specify that teachers will participate in various workshops, in-service meetings, and university classes. For example, if you have noted a problem in handling disciplinary matters in your learning disabilities class, you may wish to take a university course on classroom behavioral management. Likewise, if you have several students who may profit from a metacognitive approach, you may wish to participate in a short-term workshop on learning strategies. Documentation of these activities would be provided merely by attendance records.

Many teachers who choose not to publish results of their work do share their innovative ideas by presenting various workshops and in-service sessions at state, regional, or national meetings. For example, the national meeting of the Council for Exceptional

Children has numerous presentation forums in which teachers share their innovative ideas. Documentation of attendance and presentations at meetings such as these should certainly be included in your PIP.

Serving on Professional Committees

In the field of learning disabilities, a great deal of work remains to be done. At times, state or local education agencies will form working committees to deal with issues regarding applications of the definition of learning disabilities, identification issues, certification standards, and many other tasks. Likewise, many of the organizations concerned with learning disabilities (e.g., Council for Learning Disabilities, Council for Exceptional Children) have committees that debate professional issues within the field. Service on such working committees is another professional activity that can improve your professional skills. For the PIP, documentation of work on these types of committees can usually be handled by a letter from the committee chairperson.

Summary of Professional Improvement

The educational opportunities for students with learning disabilities will continue to improve only if the professional preparedness of the teachers of these students continues to improve. Therefore, it is the responsibility of each teacher to set goals, at least on a yearly basis, and conduct activities that may improve his or her abilities and skills in instruction of these students.

Although some states and school districts require PIPs from each professional, there is no reason why teachers in other districts should not use a PIP to stipulate their own goals for professional improvement. Even in districts where PIPs are not required, many principals would be very pleased to see individual teachers who set and attain on a yearly basis goals that are consistent with professional improvement. Such goal setting can indicate your desire to be the most effective professional you can be. As a beginning teacher, after your first few months of teaching, you may wish to consider devising a PIP and sharing it with your supervisor and principal. They would then be able to give you guidance and feedback concerning your intended improvement areas, and such participation would indicate to them your willingness to learn.

AN UNCERTAIN FUTURE AND A CHALLENGE

In some fields of study, an author can say with some degree of certainty what the future is likely to include. As the continued discussions of issues over the last chapters have indicated, such is certainly not possible in the field of learning disabilities. Any of the major issues that have been presented in the last several chapters may affect the field drastically. Clearly, the field of learning disabilities is dynamic and growing, with much work yet to be done. Your active involvement in the professional meetings and major debates in the field will result in a sense of excitement concerning future directions of the field in general.

Inherent in this transitional turmoil is a challenge to every teacher who chooses to work with students with learning disabilities. It is the responsibility of every practitioner to engage in the professional debates and other professional responsibilities that further the growth of the field. As a beginning teacher, you should challenge yourself to continue the improvement of services for students who have learning disabilities. You should actively engage in debate on service delivery issues such as services to preschool children or adults with learning disabilities. You should participate in the debates regarding the types of educational placements that most facilitate academic and social growth among these children. You should develop a PIP for each year you teach and continually strive to improve your professional abilities and skills. If you can engage in these activities, you should then assume that the field will provide opportunities for your advancement, either in the classroom or in some administrative capacity.

Finally, you should challenge yourself to enjoy working with students with learning disabilities. When all is said and done, the best teachers—while highly skilled and having set high personal standards—tend to be the teachers who really like the students. Find ways to make your teaching pleasurable for yourself and for the students in your class. In that fashion, you will find that you can have the type of positive intellectual and emotional impact in the lives of students that you, and they, desire. This is an exciting field in which to make a difference in the lives of children who need a helping hand, and you may find that you love the profession of teaching students with learning disabilities. There are scores of these children whom you will teach in the future who await your teaching expertise. The challenge is clear: They deserve the best teacher you can be.

The following points will help you study this chapter:

- The only certainty in the future of the learning disabilities field is professional debate on a number of issues, especially those generated by NCLB.
- The learning disabled population is expanding because of difficulty in identification—based on difficulty in the definition of *learning disabilities*—and the continual addition of different groups of children with various problems to this population.
- Teacher burnout has become a problem in the field of learning disabilities. This may be related to inadequate preparation of teachers initially and continued use of ineffective treatments. However, it is the individual teacher's responsibility to combat burnout through professional involvement and continual self-challenge.
- The professional improvement plan should be completed each year in order to maintain professional involvement in the field.
- The increasing number of students identified as ADHD has resulted in increasing concern relative to co-occurring disorders. The field of learning disabilities will have to sort out these issues in the next decade.
- Concerns for transition to adult life will receive a great deal more attention in the next 10 years.
- The most effective teachers are the teachers who enjoy working with pupils who have learning disabilities. These teachers continually read research, apply research in their classrooms, and conduct research.
- The applications of computer-assisted instruction and assistive technologies may soon revolutionize the field.

QUESTIONS AND ACTIVITIES

1. Stage a debate on the relative merits and problems of providing services for preschool students with learning disabilities.
2. Review the No Child Left Behind legislation, and present a report to the class.
3. Identify several articles in the research journals that were written by teachers. Do you find a different perspective in those articles?
4. Form small groups, and prepare several PIPs as if you were teaching in a local school district.

What activities could you include that were not named in this chapter? Share these with the class.
5. Interview several local school principals about burnout among teachers. What types of activities can those professionals recommend that may inhibit burnout?
6. Identify several assistive technologies, and present these to the class.

REFERENCES

Bender, W. N., & Larkin, M. J. (2003). *Reading strategies for elementary students with learning difficulties.* Thousand Oaks, CA: Corwin.

Bender, W. N. (2002). *Differentiating instruction for students with learning disabilities: Best practices for general and special educators.* Thousand Oaks, CA: Corwin Press.

Bender, W. N., & Wall, M. E. (1994). Social-emotional development of students with learning disabilities. *Learning Disability Quarterly, 17,* 323–341.

Benz, M. R., Lindstrom, L., & Yovanoff, P. (2000). Improving graduation and employment outcomes of students with disabilities: Predictive factors and student perspectives. *Exceptional Children, 66*(4), 509–529.

Billingsley, B., Carlson, E., & Klein, S. (2004). The working conditions and induction support of early career special educators. *Exceptional Children, 70*(3), 333–347.

Blalock, G., & Patton, J. R. (1996). Transition and students with learning disabilities: Creating sound futures. *Journal of Learning Disabilities, 29*(1), 7–16.

Brinckerhoff, L. C. (1996). Making the transition to higher education: Opportunities for student empowerment. *Journal of Learning Disabilities, 29,* 118–136.

Catts, H. W., Hogan, T. P., & Fey, M. E. (2003). Subgrouping poor readers on the basis of individual differences in reading-related abilities. *Journal of Learning Disabilities, 36*(2), 151–164.

Commission on Excellence in Special Education (2001). *Revitalizing special education for children and their families.* Available from www.ed.gov/inits/commissionsboards/whspecialeducation.

Cornoldi, C., Venneri, A., Marconato, F., Molin, A., & Montinari, C. (2003). A rapid screening measure for the identification of visuospatial learning disability in schools. *Journal of Learning Disabilities, 36*(4), 299–306.

Council for Exceptional Children (CEC) (2003, October 29). *No Child Left Behind Act makes "no sense" for students with disabilities, say special education teachers.* Reston, VA: Author.

D-Arcangelo, M. (1999). Learning about learning to read: A conversation with Sally Shaywitz. *Educational Leadership, 57*(2), 26–31.

Elliott, S. N., & Marquart, A. M. (2004). Extended time as a testing accommodation: Its effects and perceived consequences. *Exceptional Children, 70*(3), 349–367.

Evers, R. B. (1996). The positive force of vocational education: Transition outcomes for youth with learning disabilities. *Journal of Learning Disabilities, 29,* 69–78.

Fletcher, J. M., Francis, D. J., Boudousquie, A., Copeland, K., Young, V., Kalinowski, S., & Vaughn, S. (2006). Effects of accommodations on high-stakes testing for students with reading disabilities. *Exceptional Children, 72*(2), 136–152.

Fletcher, J. M., Shaywitz, B. A., & Shaywitz, S. E. (1994). Attention as a process and as a disorder. In G. R. Lyon (Ed.), *Frames of reference for the assessment of learning disabilities: New views on measurement issues.* Baltimore: Paul H. Brooks.

Fore, C., Martin, C., & Bender, W. N. (2002). Teacher burnout in special education: The causes and the recommended solutions. *The High School Journal, 86*(1), 36–44.

Gardner, H. (1993). *Multiple intelligences: The theory in practice.* New York: Basic Books.

Hammill, D. D. (1993). A timely definition of learning disabilities. *Family and Community Health, 16*(3), 1–8.

Janiga, S. J., & Costenbader, V. (2002). The transition from high school to postsecondary education for students with learning disabilities: A survey of college service coordinators. *Journal of Learning Disabilities, 35*(5), 462–468.

Jensen, E. (1995). *The learning brain.* Del Mar, CA: Turning Point.

Johnson, D. R., Stodden, R. A., Emanuel, E. J., Luecking, R., & Mack, M. (2002). Current challenges facing secondary education and transition services: What research tells us. *Exceptional Children, 68*(4), 519–531.

Kavale, K. A., & Forness, S. R. (1987). The far side of heterogeneity: A critical analysis of empirical subtyping research in learning disabilities. *Journal of Learning Disabilities, 20,* 374–382.

King-Sears, M. E. (2005). Are you highly qualified? The plight of effective special educators for students with learning disabilities. *Learning Disability Quarterly, 28*(3), 187–189.

Kohl, F. L., McLaughlin, M. J., & Nagel, K. (2006). Alternate achievement standards and assessments: A descriptive investigation of 16 states. *Exceptional Children, 73*(1), 107–123.

Kohler, P. D., & Field, S. (2003). Transition-focused education: Foundation for the future. *Journal of Special Education, 37*(3), 174–183.

Lyon, G. R. (2000). Learning disabilities. In *Annual Editions: 00/01: Educating exceptional children.* Guilford, CT: McGraw-Hill.

McKinney, J. D. (1984). The search for subtypes of specific learning disability. *Journal of Learning Disabilities, 17,* 43–50.

McKinney, J. D., & Speece, D. L. (1986). Academic consequences and longitudinal stability of behavioral subtypes of learning disabled children. *Journal of Educational Psychology, 78,* 365–372.

McLeskey, J., Tyler, N., & Saunders, S. (2002). *The supply and demand of special education teachers: A review of research regarding the nature of the chronic shortage of special education teachers.* Gainsville: Center on Personnel Studies in Special Education, University of Florida.

O'Shaughnessy, T. E., & Swanson, H. L. (1998). Do immediate memory deficits in students with learning disabilities in reading reflect a developmental lag or deficit? A selective meta-analysis of the literature. *Learning Disability Quarterly, 21*(2), 123–150.

Perkins, D. (1999). The many faces of constructivism. *Educational Leadership, 57*(3), 6–11.

Raskind, M. H., Herman, K. L., & Torgesen, J. K. (1995). Technology for persons with learning disabilities: Report on an international symposium. *Learning Disability Quarterly, 18,* 175–184.

Rourke, B. P. (2005). Neuropsychology of learning disabilities: Past and present. *Learning Disability Quarterly, 28*(2), 11–114.

Rourke, B. P., Ahmad, S. A., Collins, D. W., Hayman-Abello, B. A., Hauman-Abello, S. E., & Warriner, E. M. (2002). Child-clinical/pediatric neuropsychology: Some recent advances. *Annual Review of Psychology, 53,* 309–339.

Rourke, B. P., van der Vlugt, H., & Rourke, S. B. (2002). *Practice of child-clinical neuropsychology: An introduction.* Lisse, The Netherlands: Swets & Zeitlinger.

Sarouphim, K. M. (1999). Discovering multiple intelligences through a performance-based assessment: Consistency with independent ratings. *Exceptional Children, 65,* 151–161.

Silver, C. H., Pennett, H. D., Black, J. L., Fair, G. W., & Balise, R. R. (1999). Stability of arithmetic disability subtypes. *Journal of Learning Disabilities, 32,* 108–119.

Simpson, R. L., LaCava, P. G., & Graner, P. S. (2004). The No Child Left Behind Act: Challenges and implications for educators. *Intervention in School and Clinic, 40*(2), 67–75.

Smith, T. J., & Adams, G. (2006). The effect of comorbid AD/HD and learning disabilities on parent-reported behavioral and academic outcomes of children. *Learning Disability Quarterly, 29*(2), 101–112.

Sousa, D. A. (2005). *How the brain learns to read.* Thousand Oaks, CA: Corwin.

Sousa, D. A. (2001). *How the special needs brain learns.* Thousand Oaks, CA: Corwin.

Stanford, L. D., & Hynd, G. W. (1994). Congruence of behavioral symptomatology in children with ADD/H, ADD/WO, and learning disabilities. *Journal of Learning Disabilities, 27*(4), 243–253.

Swanson, H. L. (1999). Cognition and learning disabilities. In W. N. Bender (Ed.), *Professional issues in learning disabilities* (pp. 415–460). Austin, TX: ProEd.

Sylwester, R. (1995). *A celebration of neurons: An educator's guide to the human brain.* Alexandria, VA: Association for Supervision and Curriculum Development.

Yell, M. L., Katsiyannas, A., & Shiner, J. G. (2006). The No Child Left Behind Act, adequate yearly progress, and students with disabilities. *Teaching Exceptional Children, 38*(4), 32–39.

Ysseldyke, J., Nelson, J. R., Christenson, S., Johnson, D. R., Dennison, A., Triezenberg, H., Sharpe, M., & Haws, M. (2004). What we know and need to know about the consequences of high-stakes testing for students with disabilities. *Exceptional Children, 71*(1), 75–94.

Zabel, M. K., & Zabel, R. H. (1983). Burnout among special education teachers. *Teacher Education and Special Education, 6,* 255–259.

OBJECTIVES FOR THE IEPs OF STUDENTS WITH LEARNING DISABILITIES

This appendix presents pages from the individualized educational plans (IEPs) for several students discussed in Chapter 5. These pages represent the sections of the students' IEPs that list specific goals and behavioral objectives. As you read these IEP pages, note the relationship between the weaknesses cited in the assessment reports and the specific objectives marked on the IEP. You may wish to refer to these IEP sections throughout your reading of the first several chapters of the text.

IEP OBJECTIVES FOR ADAM ARTER

In formulating individualized educational plans for students with learning disabilities, some school districts use forms that list the typical types of objectives in various academic and behavioral areas. The first IEP presented in this appendix (see Figure A.1) conforms to this type of format. In formulating the IEP, the committee would review the educational-assessment data that were provided and check on this form each objective that should be included in Adam's educational program for the next year. Also, formats such as this generally include several blank spaces so that a committee may write in an objective that is specific to a particular child with disabilities.

Note the concentration on objectives that deal with reading comprehension (Figure A.2), paragraph-writing skills (Figure A.3), and on-task behavior (Figure A.4). These were the skills that were identified as weaknesses in the evaluation of Adam's academic competence. Consequently, these objectives should provide the focus of the instructional and remediational efforts for Adam during the next school year. The teacher who works with Adam in the learning disabilities class during the next year would concentrate his or her efforts on these identified weaknesses. The criteria dates by each objective indicate the level of mastery of the objective and when that level of mastery is to be assessed. The dates vary throughout the year, indicating that some work is completed early in the year, whereas other topics take the entire year.

The method of evaluation is often stated in terms of the curriculum materials used in the classroom—the contractions test from the language arts text and the use of context clues from the basal reading book. Because many curriculum materials include various assessments, it is usually advisable to use assessments that are directly related to the materials the child has studied. These assessments should be noted on the IEP.

Note also the several objectives that relate to on-task behavior. Inclusion of these objectives resulted from the teachers' comments on Adam's tendency to be highly distractible. Many children with learning disabilities show signs of distractibility, so it is not at all uncommon to find objectives such as these on the IEP. As you read through the metacognitive and behavioral treatments described in the text, the interventions recommended for Adam's distractibility will come into sharper focus.

Finally, because Adam demonstrated no weaknesses in math or other areas, the IEP pages that include these objectives were omitted from Adam's IEP. Of course, if future assessment or grades in mainstream classes should indicate a weakness in other areas, additional pages could be appended to the existing IEP in order to provide a detailed educational program for Adam throughout the year.

Date Initiated ___9__ / __1__

Student Name ___Arter, Adam___

Student # ___8638___

Page ___1___ of ___4___

Teacher ___Ms. Juniper___

School ___Westwood___

OBJECTIVES	CRITERIA FROM	TO	OBJECTIVE METHOD OF EVALUATION	DATE REVIEWED	MASTERY YES	NO
To improve reading recognition the student will:						
___ Identify letters.						
___ Identify beginning consonant sounds.						
___ Identify medial consonant sounds.						
___ Identify ending consonant sounds.						
___ Correctly identify short vowel sounds.						
___ Correctly identify long vowel sounds.						
___ Correctly identify consonant digraphs.						
___ Correctly identify vowel blends.						
___ Correctly identify diphthongs.						
___ Correctly decode CVC phonetic patterns.						
___ Correctly decode CVVC phonetic patterns.						
___ Correctly decode CVCE phonetic patterns.						
___ Correctly decode r-controlled words.						
___ Correctly decode compound words.						
___ Correctly decode prefixes.						
___ Correctly decode suffixes.						
___ Correctly decode root words.						
___ Correctly decode word endings (ing, ed, er, est).						
___ Read basic sight vocabulary.						
___ Read abbreviations appropriate to grade level.						
X Read contractions appropriate to grade level.	4/1 100%	5/12	Contraction test from language book			
X Read comfortably.	9/1 90%	12/15	Pre/Posttest from basal reading series			
___ Use context clues to decode appropriate new words.						
___ Complete incomplete sentences orally and in writing.						
___ Give antonyms, synonyms, and homonyms for words.						
___ Be able to read and relate a sequence of events.						
(Write in Other Appropriate Objectives for Reading Recognition)						

Parent Signature _____

FIGURE A.1   Short-Term Objectives: Reading Recognition

Date Initiated 9 / 1

Student Name Arter, Adam

Student # 8638

Page 2 of 4

Teacher Ms. Juniper

School Westwood

OBJECTIVES	CRITERIA FROM	CRITERIA TO	OBJECTIVE METHOD OF EVALUATION	DATE REVIEWED	MASTERY YES	MASTERY NO
To improve reading comprehension at the grade level, the student will:						
___ Define the vocabulary.						
X Read and answer questions verbally or in writing regarding the sequence of the story.	9/1 90%	5/15	Weekly basal reading exercises			
X Read selections and answer questions regarding facts and details.	" 90%	"	Sequences			
X Read and answer questions verbally or in writing regarding the main idea.	" 90%	"	Main Idea Supporting detail			
X Read and answer questions verbally or in writing regarding inferences or drawing conclusions.	" 90%	"	Drawing conclusions Bornell Lift Specific Skill Services			
___ Read and answer questions verbally or in writing regarding the skills of separating facts and opinion.						
___ Read and answer questions verbally or in writing regarding the skills of separating reality and fantasy.						
X Read and answer questions verbally or in writing regarding cause-and-effect relationships.	" 80%	"	Monthly teacher-made tests			
X Read and answer questions verbally or in writing regarding predicting outcomes.	" 80%	"	Monthly teacher-made tests			
___ Read and answer questions verbally or in writing regarding the interpretation of comparison and contrast relationships.						
___ Interpret charts, graphs, and tables.						
___ Follow written directions.						
___ Use context clues appropriately.						
(Write in Other Appropriate Objectives for Reading Comprehension)						

Parent Signature _____

FIGURE A.2 Short-Term Objectives: Reading Comprehension

Date Initiated ___9___ / ___1___

Student Name ___Arter, Adam___

Student # ___8638___

Page ___3___ of ___4___

Teacher ___Ms. Juniper___

School ___Westwood___

OBJECTIVES	CRITERIA FROM	CRITERIA TO	OBJECTIVE METHOD OF EVALUATION	DATE REVIEWED	MASTERY YES	NO
To improve written expression the student will:						
___ Compose grammatically correct sentences.						
___ Use appropriate vocabulary.						
___ Write correct answers to comprehension questions given a reading passage on the student's reading level.						
___ Punctuate correctly (periods at the end of sentences, abbreviations, initials, question mark after a question, commas between the date and the year, commas between a city and a state, an exclamation point, quotation marks, apostrophes).						
___ Capitalize correctly (beginning of sentences, names of people, books, cities, states, countries or special days).						
___ Use a dictionary to determine correct spelling, parts of speech and correct word usage in a sentence.						
___ Identify parts of speech (nouns, pronouns, verbs, adjectives, adverbs, conjunctions, prepositions, and interjections).						
___ Use an index.						
x Use an encyclopedia accurately.	9/1	5/15		Every 2 weeks		
___ Organize objects, information and ideas into logical groupings and orders.						
x Compose paragraphs using correct grammar, spelling, punctuation and word usage.	"	"		Every week		
x Compose essays using correct grammar, spelling, capitalization, punctuation and word usage.	"	"		Every unit (History)		
___ Compose a report using correct grammar, spelling, capitalization, punctuation, word usage and report style.						
(Write in Other Appropriate Objectives in Written Expression)						

Parent Signature _____

FIGURE A.3   Short-Term Objectives: Written Expression

Date Initiated ___9___ / ___1___

Student Name ___Arter, Adam___

Student # ___8638___

Page ___4___ of ___4___

Teacher ___Ms. Juniper___

School ___Westwood___

OBJECTIVES	CRITERIA FROM	TO	OBJECTIVE METHOD OF EVALUATION	DATE REVIEWED	MASTERY YES	NO
The student will:						
x Utilize time effectively. Improve on-task behaviors.	9/1	10/30 on-task 80%	Time sampling observation while student uses a self-monitoring system of on-task self-management			
_ Recognize and acknowledge feelings in self and others.						
_ Appropriately express feelings.						
_ Participate in required activities without teacher intervention. Decrease number of required teacher interventions.						
_ Arrive at class on time.						
x Begin promptly. Decrease time required to begin work.	9/1 90%	12/15	Event record compiled by teacher/reinforcement for beginning work			
x Remain on-task until work is complete.	9/1 90%	5/15	Chart assignments completed each week			
_ Attempt to solve a problem with an academic task before asking for assistance.						
_ Organize and complete assignments within a given amount of time.						
_ Find acceptable ways of using unstructured time when tasks are completed. Reduce unacceptable behaviors during unstructured time.						
_ Accept responsibility for classroom materials and personal belongings.						
_ Accept differing personalities and changing situations by maintaining appropriate behaviors. Reduce inappropriate behaviors in these situations.						

(Write in Other Appropriate Objectives for Behavior)

Parent Signature _____

FIGURE A.4 Short-Term Objectives: Behavior

IEP OBJECTIVES FOR HEATHER DEMETRI

The objectives for Heather Demetri follow the format previously discussed. The committee, after consideration of the assessment information, merely checked the appropriate objectives from the list of objectives in the various subject areas.

You may wish to note the relationship between the objectives on these IEP objective pages (Figure A.5; Figure A.6; Figure A.7) and the information provided in the assessment report. The objectives that have been included here follow the strengths and weaknesses indicated in various parts of the committee's assessment report for Heather. Note that several objectives (telling time and money concepts) have been included without any assessment evidence indicating the need for them. This occurs frequently when a classroom teacher indicates to the committee the need for remedial work in a particular area.

The terminal dates with each objective indicate that Mr. Franks, Heather's teacher, is using several different types of assessments. For some objectives, he will use teacher observations at specified time periods, whereas for other objectives, he intends to use weekly or daily assessments. When assessment is that frequent, a chart of progress similar to the curriculum-based assessment charts discussed in Chapter 5 may be made.

Name **DEMETRI**   **Heather**   Birthdate **4** / **24** / **98**
      Last   First   Middle

Implementer **Ms. Lee**

ANNUAL GOALS:

✓ 28. To improve basic reading skills to the ____**3.0**____ level   ✓ 29. To improve reading comprehension skills to the ____**2.5**____ level

GOAL #	SHORT-TERM OBJECTIVES	CRITERIA FOR MASTERY	METHOD OF EVALUATION	DATE REVIEWED	MASTERY YES	In Prog.
28.	✓ a) Given basic sight vocabulary words in isolation and in context, the student will read the words orally.	DOLCH LIST 100%	Criterion Referenced Tests	11/30		
	___ b) Given unknown words, the student will utilize word attack skills to decode: 1. ___ vowels 4. ___ digraphs 7. ___ other _____ 2. ___ consonants 5. ___ diphthongs 3. ___ blends 6. ___ multisyllable words		Teacher Observation Teacher Recordings Work Samples			
	✓ c) Given passage(s) to read, the student will demonstrate the ability to utilize word attack and sight word competencies when reading: 1. ✓ words 2. ✓ content materials	90% 90%	Teacher Observation and Recording	3/1		
	✓ d) Given passage(s) to read orally, the student will demonstrate expression and fluency.	90%	Teacher Observation	3/1		
28.						
29.	___ a) Given passage(s) to read at his/her current instructional reading level, the student will answer comprehension questions of the following type:		Teacher Observation and Criterion Referenced Testing			
29.						

Sub-table within Goal 29 a):

	read orally	read silently	answering orally	answering in writing
1. factual	a.	b.	c.	d.
2. inferential	a.	b.	c.	d.
3. vocabulary	a.	b.	c.	d.

FIGURE A.5   Short-Term Objectives: Basic Reading

Name __DEMETRI__ __Heather__ _____ Birthdate __4__ / __24__ / __98__
     Last   First   Middle

Implementer __Ms. Lee__ _____ Date to Begin __9__ / __1__ Date to Review __6__ / __1__

ANNUAL GOALS:

✔ 30. To improve math calculation skills to the __3.0__ level   ✔ 29. To improve math reasoning skills to the __3.0__ level

GOAL #	SHORT-TERM OBJECTIVES	CRITERIA FOR MASTERY	METHOD OF EVALUATION	DATE REVIEWED	MASTERY YES	In Prog.
30.	✔ a) Given math problems in basic whole number operations, the student will compute the answers using: 1. ___ ☐ digit(s) w/out regrouping [+] [−] [×] 2. ✔ ☒ digit(s) with regrouping [×] [×] 3. ___ ☐ digit divisor & ☐ digit dividend w/out remainder [÷] 4. ___ ☐ digit divisor & ☐ digit dividend with remainder	90%	Criterion Referenced Tests	11/1		
	___ b) Given basic math facts, the student will demonstrate recall 1. ___ + 2. ___ − 3. ✔ × 4. ___ ÷	100%	Criterion Referenced Tests	daily CBA		
	___ c) The student will compute problems in the following areas: 1. ___ fractions 2. ___ decimals 3. ___ percents 4. ___ measurement 5. ___ Other _____		Criterion Referenced Tests			
30.						
31.	___ a) The student will demonstrate competencies in the following area(s): 1. ✔ time 2. ✔ money 3. ___ measurement 4. ___ word problems		Criterion Referenced Tests			
31.	① Telling time on clock face to the minute	90%	CRTs	monthly		
	② Counting correct change from a $1.00 purchase	90%	CRTs	monthly		

FIGURE A.6   Short-Term Objectives: Math Calculation

Name   **DEMETRI**   **Heather**   Birthdate   **4** / **24** / **98**

        Last   First   Middle

Implementer   **Ms. Lee**   Date to Begin   **9** / **1**   Date to Review   **6** / **1**

ANNUAL GOALS:

✓ 32. To improve written expression skills in ✓ sentences,   ___ 34. To improve oral expression skills in the ___ classroom,

      ✓ paragraphs, ___short stories.   ___community, with ___ peers, with adults.

___ 33. To improve listening comprehension skills to the _____ level.

GOAL #	SHORT-TERM OBJECTIVES (referenced to long term goals)	CRITERIA FOR MASTERY	METHOD OF EVALUATION	DATE REVIEWED	MASTERY YES	In Prog.
32.	✓ a) Given a picture or topic and asked to write a sentence, paragraph, story, or report the student will use: 1. ✓ complete sentence(s) 6. ✓ capitalization 2. ___ age appropriate vocabulary 7. ✓ punctuation 3. ___ imaginative ideas 8. ___ grammar and word usage 4. ✓ correct spelling 9. ___ topic sentence 5. ___ logical sequence	20 sentences 80% correct	Work Samples	each week		
	✓ b) Given spelling words that the student can read, he/she will spell the words correctly when using: 1. ___ lists and sentence tests 2. ___ application of learned words in written assignments	80%	Criterion Referenced Tests weekly spelling words (20)	each week		
	✓ c) The student will demonstrate legible handwriting using: 1. ✓ manuscript 2. ___ cursive 3. ___ correct formation of letters 4. ___ correct size relationships 5. ___ correct placement of letters 6. ___ correct spacing between words 7. ___ accurate copying from paper or book 8. ___ accurate copying from board 9. ___ using age appropriate speed	90%	Work Samples	each day		
33.	___ a) Given oral direction(s), the student will follow _____ direction(s). ___ b) After hearing a passage or story, the student will be able to answer questions of the following type(s): 1. ___ factual 2. ___ inferential 3. ___ sequence		Teacher Observation Teacher Observation			
34.	___ a) The student will express himself/herself orally: 1. ___ one-one interaction 5. ___ logical sequence of thoughts 2. ___ small groups 6. ___ appropriate vocabulary 3. ___ large groups 7. ___ appropriate articulation 4. ___ complete sentences 8. ___ appropriate volume		Teacher Observation			

FIGURE A.7   **Short-Term Objectives: Written Expression**

GLOSSARY

ABAB intervention   a type of research treatment study in which the "A" phases represent a baseline count of behavior and the "B" phases represent the application of a treatment to change the behavior. The design is a reversal design because after the first treatment, the design is reversed, and another baseline or "A" phase is initiated.

academic/cognitive outcomes   a term used in the literature on postschool transition to discuss the academic and cognitive results of education. Academic and cognitive outcomes for students with learning disabilities are not positive.

academic plateau   the tendency for students with learning disabilities to reach a plateau in academic achievement during high school. Many such adolescents reach approximately a fifth-grade level in achievement and cease to progress.

ACLD   Association for Children with Learning Disabilities; one of the first organizations of professionals and parents concerned with educational issues for this population.

adaptive behavior   refers to behavior that is adaptive to the public school classroom environment. Most students with learning disabilities demonstrate poor adaptive behavior skills.

ADHD   attention-deficit hyperactivity disorder; a term for a type of learning disability that is characterized by attention problems.

administrative flexibility   a term used to indicate that the college administration is supportive of programs to assist students with learning disabilities in college programs.

advance organizers   a strategy or organizing idea presented in advance of a learning task in order to facilitate successful completion of that task. Review of an outline prior to reading a section of history text is one example of an advance organizer.

ALEM   Adapted Learning Environments Model; one method for providing prereferral assistance to students who are at risk of becoming disabled. This model also provides services to students in mainstream classes who have already been identified as disabled.

alphabetic principle   the concept that discrete sounds in our language are represented by discrete written shapes (i.e., letters) and that knowing which sounds letters represent can assist in learning to read.

Americans with Disabilities Act (ADA)   legislation that states the civil rights of individuals with disabilities, such as the freedom to work and the right to expect reasonable accommodations in the workplace.

anchored instruction   instruction that is "anchored" in real-world situations (e.g., an interactive computer video that assists students with disabilities in mastering tasks such as shopping).

antecedent   an event that precedes and has some measurable effect on a behavior.

anxiety   a fear or pervasive uneasiness that may result in unsuccessful performance in particular settings.

assistive technologies   devices or systems that enhance communication skills, such as print magnification systems, speech output devices, enlarged computer keyboards, etc.

attribution training   instruction designed to change a student's locus of control through changing the student's attribution for successful experiences.

attributions   the cause-effect relationships identified by students when asked why they performed a certain way (i.e., some students attribute their academic scores internally, responding, "I really studied hard," or "I just can't seem to learn"; whereas others attribute their academic progress to external (nonself) factors, responding, "That was a hard test. Why did the teacher make it so difficult?").

audio digitizer   a piece of hardware that allows a user to import sound onto a computer disc, and thus, into a computer system.

authentic assessment   an assessment practice that is authentically related to a real-world task.

automaticity   ability to recall automatically certain rote-memory facts such as math facts. Automaticity is demonstrated by the ability to recall math facts within 2 seconds of the visual or auditory presentation of the fact.

axon   the long section of a neuron through which the nerve impulse travels.

AYP   adequate yearly progress; the requirement that all schools will make adequate yearly progress toward their educational goals, as defined under NCLB legislation.

baseline   the initial phase of data collection in a behavioral intervention project. This phase measures the strength or frequency of a behavior prior to intervention in order to have a measure of behavior to compare with data collected during later intervention phases.

basic-skills remediation model represents one curriculum thrust that is frequently used with students who have learning disabilities. This model emphasizes instruction in the basic skills of reading, writing, and mathematics.

behavioral contract a written contract between a teacher and a student that specifies a required task, conditions of task performance, criteria used to evaluate the task, and the reward for task completion.

behavioral model of learning a model of learning that specifies that the conditions that control learning are the antecedents that precede the task and the contingencies or consequences that follow the behavior. The full model expressed in temporal form is Antecedents Behavior Consequences.

behavioral objective specifies a learning task to be completed by the student and includes three components: the specific behavior to be completed, the conditions under which the behavior will be completed, and the criteria used to judge completion.

biofeedback a system whereby information of physical indicators of stress is provided to the subject in an effort to reduce stress. This technique is currently being used to combat hyperactivity in students with learning disabilities.

BPPD basic phonological processing disabilities; namely, learning disabilities characterized by poorly developed single-word reading/spelling processing, more efficient use of nonverbal information than verbal information in social situations, and relatively normal social development and behavior; approximately 80% of students with a learning disability demonstrate BPPD.

burnout the tendency for some teachers to grow tired of the stresses associated with teaching the learning disabled.

buttons marked sections on a computer screen that, when pressed or "clicked" with a mouse, cause certain functions to take place, such as the immediate movement to another computer screen.

cards a metaphor for a single computer screen and the information presented on that screen.

CAT scan computerized axial tomography scan is a radiological technique used to examine the structure of the brain. X-rays are sent through the brain at different angles, and the images are computerized to form a picture of the brain's structure from any angle.

categorical resource rooms resource rooms that serve children with only one type or category of disability.

CD-ROM a laser-based technology that provides one mechanism by which computerized information or computer programs may be stored.

cerebellum the part of the human brain that receives sensory input and controls most of the motor nervous system.

cerebrum the largest part of the human brain, which controls higher thought and language functions.

clarifying a reciprocal teaching strategy in which students are prompted to identify the major points of a reading selection as well as any concepts that may be difficult; the latter is particularly significant for students with learning disabilities, who often find this aspect of reading comprehension difficult.

classroom transition phase the period in the field of learning disabilities when researchers began to identify educational methods for use with students with learning disabilities in typical classroom settings rather than clinical settings.

clinical phase the phase in the history of the field of learning disabilities in which research information was based exclusively on children who demonstrated problems severe enough to be treated by specialized educational clinics or institutions.

cloze procedure a procedure for assessment of reading comprehension that requires the student to "close" a sentence by filling in the blank or providing a meaningful word for the blank, which results in a sentence that makes sense.

CNS the central nervous system, which is made up of the brain and the spinal column. It is the first of the nervous systems to develop in the fetus.

code switching the ability to change or adapt one's language according to the cognitive level of the audience. Code switching usually involves the use of simpler words and simpler sentences.

cognitive-processing perspectives a set of perspectives that dominated the LD field during the 1960s and 1970s, which postulated that some mental processing function (such as perception, memory, etc.) was the basis for all learning disabilities.

cognitive psychology the study of learning processes such as memory, associative learning, and intelligence.

college students with learning disabilities represents a new concern for the field. Some reports indicate that a number of students with learning disabilities can complete college.

community-based vocational training educational training of students with disabilities that is based on activities taking place in the community.

comorbidity the coexistence of two (or more) different disabilities in the same child.

complex multiple-choice multiple-choice questions that have sublevels of choices within the main level of answers.

complex operations operations in math that require the student to complete several different types of operations in one problem.

complexity refers to the use of more sophisticated forms of sentence construction in communication and to the depth of one's understanding of language.

consequence the event that follows a behavior and controls the likelihood of future occurrences of the behavior.

consultation model the learning disabilities specialist provides consultation to the mainstream teacher on educational strategies for the child.

co-occurring disorders the manifestation of several types of mental disorders at once, such as the co-morbidity of ADHD and LD in the same student.

cooperative instruction the use of instructional techniques that require students to cooperate with each other in order to complete a project successfully.

count-by a strategy for learning multiplication facts.

counting-all a strategy for learning addition facts.

cranial nerves nervous that control movement-official muscles and sensory organs.

criterion-referenced testing refers to detailed assessments of academic achievement that have specific behavioral objectives keyed to each question or set of questions. Consequently, if a student has problems completing one of the items, the teacher knows exactly which objective should be the major focus of instruction.

critical mathematics interview a diagnostic procedure designed by Crawley to determine a student's proficiency in basic math skills.

cross-categorical placement placement in resource rooms that serve children with a number of different disabling conditions—thus, the population cuts across the categories of disabilities.

cross-class projects a type of interactive school learning project in which students in different classes, different schools, and/or different countries cooperate to complete the work.

Cruickshank, William had a profound influence on the early history of the field by developing the hypothesis that an environment in which the stimuli are controlled will result in improved learning.

cubing an instructional procedure whereby the sides of a cube require differing levels of cognitive interaction with an assignment (i.e., one side may involve describing a construct, another side may require the student to compare/contrast the construct with another construct, and another side may require a student to analyze the construct more deeply).

cue words words in a math word problem that give some general hint concerning the operations necessary for successful problem solution.

cumulative deficit refers to the tendency for a deficit between achievement and grade placement to accumulate over the years of school such that secondary students with learning disabilities demonstrate much larger deficits than students in the lower grades with the same disabilities.

curriculum-based assessment ongoing (daily or bi-weekly) assessment of student performance on specific curriculum tasks to demonstrate progress in achievement.

cyberpals the use of the Internet to create electronic mail between students using the older concept of pen pals.

dendrites the connective tissues within a neuron that connect one neuron to another.

Deno's Cascade of Services a service delivery idea developed by Deno that suggests a variety of flexible service placement options for children with disabilities.

departmentalized curriculum an approach in which subject areas in secondary schools are taught by different departments or groups of teachers, resulting in the need to change classes and teachers for each subject.

Deshler, Donald credited with the development of numerous learning strategies at the University of Kansas Learning Disabilities Research Institute.

developmental imbalances one of several ability-deficit perspectives. This idea was based on the suggestion that a learning disability may be caused by uneven growth in particular mental abilities. For example, auditory memory may lag behind auditory discrimination, and that imbalance may cause a learning disability.

DIBELS Dynamic Indicators of Basic Early Literacy Skills, an assessment used to assess fluency in reading initial sounds, letter naming, phoneme segmentation, nonsense words, oral reading, retelling, and word usage.

differentiated instruction the suggestion that teachers should vary their instructional practices (i.e., differentiate) according to the various learning styles and/or multiple intelligences of their students.

digital scanner a piece of computer hardware that can "scan" written documents and immediately store the content on computer discs.

direct instruction a teacher-led instructional procedure that provides students with specific instructions on a task, modeling, teacher-led practice, independent practice, and frequent feedback on their performance.

DISCOVER Discovering Intellectual Strengths and Capabilities through Observation while allowing for Varied Ethnic Responses; a performance-based assessment instrument for multiple intelligences.

discrepancy the concept that children and youths with learning disabilities have abnormal patterns of development across domains, resulting in significant differences between measures of different types of abilities and skills.

discrepancy criteria one aspect of the definition of learning disabilities that suggests that students with learning disabilities must demonstrate a substantial difference between their anticipated achievement, as indicated by intellectual ability, and their actual achievement—hence the ability-achievement discrepancy.

disruptive behavior behavior that disrupts the instruction of other students in the classroom.

distractibility a tendency to be drawn off-task by stimuli in the learning environment.

Doman/Delacato two researchers who developed patterning or neurological organization—a treatment for learning disabilities that has never been shown to be effective.

DSM-IV the *Diagnostic and Statistical Manual of Mental Disorders* (4th ed.); a classification system published by the American Psychiatric Association for identifying various kinds of disorders in children.

DSM-V an update of DSM-IV, which is due for release in 2007.

dynamic assessment an assessment practice that is related to the task as well as to the thought processes involved in performing the task.

dyslexia a term that indicates an inability to read. Generally, the term is most frequently utilized by theorists who assume that an inability to read is associated with brain-based abnormalities.

educational consultant a person who may consult with parents on educational matters related to the child in question; included in the consultation may be an assessment or interviews with the child.

eligibility the determination of whether a child has a disability and is thus eligible for special services.

emotional-social outcomes a term used in the literature on postschool transition to discuss the emotional and social results of education for people who are disabled.

encoding the process by which a short-term memory may be coded for storage and later recall.

episodic memory memory that may be based on location and circumstance; (e.g., when asked to recall what you did yesterday, you first try to recall where you were and then to recall additional actions, or "episodes," you engaged in).

error analysis the process whereby a student's errors on academic work may be analyzed in order to identify the level of the student's understanding of the problem for further instruction.

etiological criteria criteria in early definitions of learning disabilities that indicated that a disability must be associated with a particular medically based cause.

exclusionary criteria the aspect of the definition of learning disabilities that suggests that a learning disability cannot be a result of any known handicapping condition.

executive function a term used by cognitive psychologists to describe a person's thinking about his or her thinking and learning process (metacognition).

expansion/retrenchment phase the most recent phase in the history of learning disabilities, in that the number of children identified as learning disabled has expanded.

explicit memory represents memory of details, facts, and events.

external locus one aspect of a student's locus of control that suggests that the student perceives control of his or her fate as resting with external factors in the environment rather than his or her own efforts.

extinction a behavioral procedure whereby behaviors may be decreased through intentional ignoring.

faculty support a term that indicates the level of support that college faculty receive from the college administration for including students with learning disabilities in college classes.

FAST a learning strategy acronym for development of effective social behaviors.

Fernald, Grace developed an educational technique used to instruct children in word recognition that included various activities enabling a child to see, hear, write, and sense the motion of writing a word all at the same time. Visual, auditory, kinesthetic, and tactile (VAKT) sensations were all utilized.

fetal alcohol syndrome a birth defect associated with maternal intake of alcohol during pregnancy.

FISH a learning strategy acronym designed to assist elementary students in decoding words.

focus of attention generally described as an ability to grossly focus one's attention on a particular stimulus.

frontal lobe a section of the cerebrum that controls abstract thinking.

Frostig, Marianne had a profound influence on the field by asserting that learning disabilities were the result of perceptual problems based on dysfunctions in the brain and central nervous system.

functional communication a child's ability to communicate in his or her environment, including conversational skills.

functional MRI (fMRI) a version of magnetic resonance imaging that measures blood flow and can show the activity of the brain during a thinking task.

functional-skills model   one model of instruction for students with learning disabilities that stresses functional life skills rather than academic subjects.

gifted learning disabled   a term used to indicate that a person is both intellectually gifted and learning disabled.

global self-concept   one form of self-concept that is not specific to particular situations or changes in setting.

group investigation   one form of cooperative instruction.

Halstead, W. C.   prepared one of the early neurological test batteries that is occasionally used with children with learning disabilities.

hemispheric specialization   the differences in brain hemispheric function that develop in a young child prior to the age of 7 or 8, typically resulting in a left-hemispheric specialization for language function, as one example.

highly qualified   a provision in the No Child Left Behind legislation requiring that all teachers be trained in the subject area they are teaching.

high-stakes testing   assessments required prior to grade passage or graduation.

hyperactivity   a higher level of activity or an increased or unusual tendency to frequent movement—either in-seat fidgeting or movement around the class.

HyperCard   an authoring program to allow students and teachers to create hypermedia programs.

IEP   individualized educational plan; an instructional program based on multidisciplinary assessment and designed to meet the individual needs of students with disabilities.

implicit memory   describes memory for nonfactual information (e.g., how to hit a baseball).

inactive learner perspective   the most recent perspective on children with learning disabilities. It suggests that these children are inactive in the learning process—they do not cognitively plan the educational task and are not motivated to participate actively in it.

incidental recall   the level of recall of extraneous information in the visual or auditory field, or the ability to recall information that was not the primary focus of the memory exercise.

inclusion movement   a philosophy that advocates placement of students with disabilities and special education teachers in regular classrooms and that incorporates cooperative learning and team-teaching models.

inclusive service delivery   a program option offered by some secondary schools in which special education teachers and regular classroom teachers teach adolescent students with and without disabilities in mainstream classes.

inferential comprehension   a level of comprehension that requires students to go beyond rote recall of main ideas and details and to draw conclusions from written text.

inner language   the self-dialogue that forms the basis of most cognitive thought. The use of strategies that teach children with learning disabilities to give themselves silent task instructions through inner language has become widespread in the field.

in-service   training that teachers undertake after they are employed in a teaching position. In-service is typically required for continuing certification.

Inspiration Software   software designed to assist students in developing a graphic organizer in order to master content in a variety of educational areas.

instructional interactions   interactions between a teacher and a student based on instructional statements. These may be contrasted with teacher/student interactions that result from behavioral management statements.

intelligence   the capacity of adaptation to one's environment, which, in humans, is usually highly dependent on one's facility with language.

intelligence testing   tests that are designed to measure intelligence.

internal locus   one possible perception of locus of control that refers to the sense that control over one's fate results from the actions that one takes—thus, the locus of control is internal.

interpersonal skills   a set of skills that enable one employee to get along well with his or her co-workers.

Irlen lenses   colored lenses provided for students whose reading disorders are attributed to an oversensitivity to certain frequencies and wavelengths of white light.

ITP   individual transition plan, which is sometimes part of the IEP. The ITP addresses the post–high school needs of young people with disabilities as they move from school into the work world; vocational programming is critical in helping make this transition to adulthood.

jigsaw   a cooperative-instructional strategy in which various group members are given only part of the information necessary for problem solution and the students are required to pool all of their information to complete the task.

jigsaw II   a cooperative-instructional strategy similar to jigsaw, except that both a pretest and posttest are given to each student, and these are compared to yield a gain score for each child. The average gain score for the group becomes each child's score.

job-related academic skills   skills that are directly related to employment, including skills such as using a specialized tool, performing a specific task, etc.

journals   scientific periodicals in which every scholarly article is read and critiqued by other researchers in the field prior to publication.

Kirk, Samuel   coined the term *learning disabilities* and was one of the most important figures in the early history of the field. He also co-authored the ITPA, a test that was used to document the existence of a learning disability for many years.

language deficit   a measurable deficit in language ability. For example, many students with learning disabilities demonstrate a deficit in the ability to understand semantics and syntax.

language theorists   one of the most influential groups of scholars in the early history of the field of learning disabilities. This group included Kirk, Myklebust, and other notable scholars.

laser disc   a recently developed method of communicating with the computer and of storing information.

LDA   The Learning Disabilities Association, which was originally formed as the ACLD or Association for Children with Learning Disabilities; a parental and professional advocacy group.

learned helplessness   a learned lack of motivation related to a high external locus of control.

learning rate   the number of problems completed correctly in relation to the amount of time needed to complete those problems. Learning rate is usually displayed as a chart of corrects in a specified time across a number of days.

learning strategies   a cognitively based instructional method that is intended to structure the child's inner speech in order to result in successful task completion. Many learning strategies are associated with a particular acronym that students memorize in order to remember the steps in the strategy.

learning-strategies approach model   one instructional thrust used with students who are learning disabled, based on instruction in various metacognitive learning strategies for application in mainstream classes.

learning style   a child's preferred way of learning (i.e., some children prefer seeing information, some learn best by hearing information, and some learn best when information can be physically represented, for example, by walking through a simple addition problem on a number line on the floor).

linking   a strategy for learning initial math facts by which an unlearned problem may be related to a problem for which the solution is already known.

literal comprehension   literal understanding of written material. Literal comprehension is usually thought to include recall of main idea, recall of supporting facts and details, and general understanding of the story plot.

localization   the tendency for specific higher brain functions to become associated with one brain hemisphere or the other.

locus of control   the perception of control over one's fate—usually discussed in terms of internal control (where one's own actions determine one's fate) or external control (where environmental conditions determine one's fate).

longitudinal study   a method of research that traces development of individuals over a period of years and in which the investigator designs the study and is involved in the data collection from the first stages.

long-term memory   the ability to recall information over long periods. Generally, the length of memory referred to as long term in research ranges widely from 1 or 2 minutes to a number of years.

Luria, Alexander   a Soviet neuropsychologist who developed a set of assessments to diagnose brain-based learning problems—the Luria-Nebraska.

magnetic resonance imaging (MRI)   a nonradiological technique in which a magnetic field is created that results in certain measurable changes in brain tissue; used to demonstrate differences in brain activity that may cause learning problems.

math standards   standards that comprise the mathematics curriculum; most state math standards are based on the standards generated by the National Council of Teachers of Mathematics.

megavitamins   use of massive doses of vitamins as a treatment for learning disabilities. To date, no widely recognized research has supported this practice.

memory strategy   a mental exercise designed to assist students in encoding information for long-term memory storage.

metacognition   a student's ability to think about, preplan, and monitor performance on an educational task.

minimum competency tests   assessment designed to document minimum capability to survive in society.

motivation   the desire to participate meaningfully in education in an effort to learn. Generally, motivation is discussed in terms of locus of control, self-concept, and task persistence.

multimedia   an enhanced computer presentation and/or authoring system, which allows for importing and presentation of more than merely text. This may include sound, voice, music, pictures, etc.

multiple intelligences   an instructional approach developed by Howard Gardner, based on the theory that humans demonstrate eight relatively discrete types of intelligence and that instructional tactics directed to these various "intelligences" will enhance learning.

multistep operations   operations in math that require the student to complete the same operation several times in order to complete the problem. Double-digit addition is one example.

narrative discourse refers to a type of language that tells a story. Elements such as sequencing and cognitive reasoning are important elements in narrative discourse.

negative consequences consequences of behavior that tend to decrease the future likelihood of a behavior.

neurological perspective one of the ability-deficit perspectives that results in the perception that brain-based deficits that can be measured are the major cause of a learning disability.

neuron one brain cell composed of axons and dendrites.

neurotransmitters a host of chemicals that transmit messages across the synaptic gap between dendrites in order to excite other neurons in the brain and nervous system.

NLD a nonverbal learning disability; a type of learning disability characterized by well-developed single-word reading/spelling processing, efficient use of verbal information in social situations, excessive hyperactivity after four years, and possible behavioral problems, such as withdrawal, anxiety, depression, social skill deficits in adolescence; approximately 20% of students with a learning disability demonstrate NLD.

No Child Left Behind (NCLB) federal legislation mandating many school reforms, including documentation of meeting adequate yearly progress toward rigorous educational standards and the provision that all children be taught by a teacher who is highly qualified in the subject area.

nonverbal learning disabilities learning disabilities that are associated more with nonlinguistic mental functions (i.e., visual reversals or social/emotional deficits) rather than language-based skill.

norm-referenced tests a class of assessments that compare a student's performance to the performance of a norm group. These tests generally result in a grade equivalent or standardized score rather than a set of objectives for future instruction and are therefore considered the opposite of criterion-referenced tests.

number sense the ability to understand number concepts at an early stage; includes concepts such as more than, less than, and that a two-digit number is larger than a one-digit number.

numeral a digit that has been written down.

numeration the ability to count or understand a series of numbers and the logical, sequential connection between them.

occipital lobe the portion of each hemisphere of the cerebrum that deals with vision and visual perception; located in the rear of the head, behind the parietal lobe.

one-to-one relationship one of the basic mathematical relationships, based on the awareness that an object in one set may be paired with an object in another set.

Orton, Samuel one of the early theorists in the field of learning disabilities who developed the concept that learning problems were associated with problems in the development of hemispheric dominance for language.

parasuicide actual suicide attempts that are unsuccessful.

parietal lobe the portion of each hemisphere of the cerebrum that controls tactile sensations from various parts of the body; located in the top rear of the head, between the frontal and occipital lobes.

patterning the positioning of bodily appendages in a manner that approximates reflexive positions of infancy in order to repattern the neural connections and facilitate learning. This method, developed by Doman and Delacato, has yet to receive research validation.

peer nomination a strategy of rating social competence that depends on the ratings of peers.

peer tutoring a structured instructional system in which peers instruct each other in academic skills.

perceptual-motor theorists a group of early theorists who described learning disabilities in terms of perceptual-motor abnormalities. This group included Cruickshank and Kephart.

personal data assistant technological devices used to assist many individuals in recalling information, such as daily schedules, telephone numbers, homework assignments, etc.

personality variables a number of variables that have an impact on educational achievement. These typically include self-concept, locus of control, anxiety, and temperament, among others.

PET scan positron emission tomography; involves the use of radioactive isotopes injected into the brain through the bloodstream while the flow of isotopes is recorded to investigate brain function.

phase change a term used in precision teaching to indicate a change in a student's instructional program.

phoneme-based instruction instruction that begins with phonemic manipulation and continues into phonics (or the relationship between discrete sounds and letters).

phonemes individual letter sounds and/or the smallest individual sound that carries meaning.

phonemic manipulation a child's ability to detect and manipulate discrete sounds; students must be able to detect, through hearing, the difference between the initial consonant sounds of b and d (as in *bed* and *dead*) prior to receiving instruction in which letters represent those sounds.

phonics approach   instruction in reading that is dependent on knowledge of letter sounds used to determine word pronunciation.

place value   the value change represented by digits in the 1's place, 10's place, 100's place, etc.

PLEASE   a learning strategy used to improve paragraph-writing skills (Pick a topic, List ideas, Evaluate the list, Activate the paragraph, Supply supporting sentences, and End with a concluding sentence).

portfolio assessment   a portfolio of student worksheets consisting of samples of the same type of work.

positive behavioral support   behavioral interventions (e.g., positive reinforcement, behavioral contract, etc.) that may be provided to assist a student in the classroom.

positive reinforcement   the provision of a desirable consequence contingent on a specified behavior that tends to increase the likelihood of future occurrences of that behavior.

pragmatics   the use of language in social situations or for purposes of pragmatic communication. Pragmatics is usually defined to include subtle, nonverbal cues in interpretation of language as well as understanding of the language itself.

precision teaching   an instructional monitoring approach developed by Lindsley that is based on daily curriculum-based assessment procedures and that features use of a standard measurement chart and frequent measures of learning rate.

prediction   one of four steps in reciprocal teaching that requires students to predict the outcome of a story or text.

prereferral modification   an intervention that is attempted prior to referral for special education services. Generally, these interventions are attempted while the child is still being served in mainstream classes in order to continue the child's successful progress in the mainstream and make special education assessment and placement unnecessary.

prereferral report   a report based on information collected prior to the official referral for special education services; documents the specific types of problems the student has demonstrated in the mainstream class.

professional improvement plan (PIP)   a detailed plan listing professional activities that will be undertaken to improve oneself as a professional teacher.

Project RIDE   a procedure whereby teachers may locate ideas for dealing with problem children. Project RIDE is very useful in providing novel ideas for prereferral services.

psychological processing criteria   the hypothesized "brain-based" abilities that were assumed to be underlying learning and learning problems.

question generation   one of four steps in reciprocal teaching that requires students to ask questions of material before they read.

reading fluency   one's ability to read quickly and without interruption; typically measured as "words read correctly per minute."

Reading Mastery   a set of curriculum materials that feature direct instructional techniques for instruction in math and reading.

reciprocal teaching   a metacognitive instructional method that requires students to complete four steps during a lesson, including predicting, questioning, and summarizing.

referential communication   one's ability to use references such as common pronouns, and to understand to whom those pronouns apply, or one's ability to give directions, or to receive verbal instructions.

regression-based discrepancy   calculation of an ability-achievement discrepancy based on standard score comparisons that take into account the mathematical phenomenon of regression to the mean.

regrouping   the restructuring of the digits in a math problem to increase or decrease the numeric value in the 10's, 100's, or 1,000's column. The terms historically used were *carrying* and *borrowing*.

regular education initiative (REI)   an initiative of the federal government that supports education of many students with mild handicaps, including learning disabilities, in the mainstream class.

Reitan-Indiana   a neurological test battery for children between the ages of 5 and 8 years.

relaxation training   instruction in certain mental imagery techniques that result in increased relaxation and decreased problem behaviors.

resource class   a class that is intended to be a resource for everyone concerned with the education of children with disabilities. Typically, the resource teacher teaches the child with learning disabilities directly for a brief period each day and serves as a resource teacher for the mainstream teachers who work with the child for the majority of the school day.

response to intervention   involves documenting how a student responds to an educational intervention; likely will become one method by which a learning disability may be identified and documented.

reticular activating system   a system of neural connections that allows the brain to immediately focus attention on information that represents a threat to survival while also cataloging information that is not a threat for further brain processing.

retrenchment phase the last historical period in the field of learning disabilities, during which the field defended itself from becoming lost in several overriding movements, including inclusion and accountability for definitional distinctions between LD and other special education groups.

retrieval the ability to retrieve information once that information has been stored in long-term memory.

retrospective study a method of research that uses previously existing data from past records.

RIDER a learning strategy for comprehension of individual sentences that uses the following steps: Read, Image, Describe, Evaluate, and Repeat.

Ritalin a frequently prescribed medication used to reduce hyperactivity.

roster rating a measurement device consisting of a list of students in the class used by each student to rate his or her class members on social acceptance or some similar sociometric measure.

SALT Student's Assistant for Learning from Text—a hypermedia program that allows a teacher to create enhanced text.

scaffolded instruction the building of understanding based on identification of a child's previous level of understanding and provision of supports for additional understanding from that point on.

scope and sequence charts lists of topics in content areas that are designed to identify the scope of the subject for a particular grade level and the sequence for instruction in those topics.

SCORER a strategy developed to help students with learning disabilities take multiple-choice tests; the acronym stands for Schedule your time; Clue word use; Omit difficult questions; Read carefully; Estimate your answers; Review your work.

scotopic sensitivity a term used to denote an oversensitivity to certain frequencies and wavelengths of white light.

script a written lesson used in direct instructional programs that specifies the dialogue that teachers and students should engage in to promote learning.

Section 504 a section of the Rehabilitation Act of 1973 that requires schools and other institutions to make reasonable accommodations for individuals with disabilities; many students without noted disabilities still have a "504 Educational Plan," which notes the accommodations those students require for success in the general education curriculum.

selective attention a child's ability to selectively attend to the stimuli that is being directly taught.

self-advocacy the ability and willingness to appropriately, and in a professional manner, advocate for one's own self-interest; many students with disabilities receive training in self-advocacy.

self-concept the perception that one has of oneself.

self-contained class a class that remains with one teacher for the entire day.

self-correction an instructional procedure whereby students are taught and required to self-correct their work as they reflect on their errors and how to avoid future errors on that type of work.

self-determination synonymous with self-advocacy; an ability and willingness to appropriately, and in a professional manner, advocate for one's own self-interest; many students with disabilities receive training in self-determination.

self-monitoring a metacognitive instructional technique that requires children to repeatedly ask themselves whether they were paying attention in order to increase their level of attention.

semantic map a picture or diagram that depicts a major term and associated terms. Often, a semantic map will be used to explore the meaning of a story or the various definitions of a term.

semantic memory involves general factual memory and memory connections (e.g., knowing where the state of Oregon is on the map, or how to read a clock).

semantics understanding the meaning of words, and correct use of words.

sequencing the act of identifying the sequence of events in a story.

short-term memory the ability to hold a stimulus in brief memory capacity—usually measured in less than 10 seconds.

sight-word approach one historical approach to reading in which students were trained to recognize whole words in context without regard to individual letter sounds.

situated cognition synonymous with anchored instruction; instruction that is "anchored" in real-world situations (e.g., an interactive computer video that assists students with disabilities in mastering tasks such as shopping).

SLANT a learning strategy for note-taking skills that incorporates the following activities: Sit up, Lean forward, Activate your thinking, Name key information, and Track the talker.

social acceptance the level of overall peer acceptance experienced by students with learning disabilities. The opposite of high social acceptance is general indifference, not active rejection of these students.

social competence overall social ability; the interaction in an individual between self-concept, positive relationships with others, the absence of maladaptive behaviors, and effective social skills.

social isolation the level of active peer rejection or dislike; experienced by only a few students with learning disabilities.

social rejection   the active social rejection of students, usually based on some noxious behavior or extremely unpleasant social intercourse style.

social skills   skills that facilitate social interactions such as listening, conversation, and interpretation of social cues and nonverbal cues.

sociometric rating   a measurement technique used to generate a rating of a child's popularity.

spatial ability   one of several cognitive abilities associated with mathematical ability. Spatial ability involves understanding visual or auditory perceptions of distance and objects in relationship to one another in space.

stack   a series of computer screens that presents information in a hierarchical fashion.

STAD   student team-assisted divisions; one form of cooperative instructional techniques.

standard-score discrepancy   the calculation of an ability-achievement discrepancy based on intelligence tests and achievement tests that have a common metric or common calculation for obtaining the standard scores (usually the same mean and standard deviation).

state anxiety   anxiety that is experienced as a result of exposure to a particular environment.

storage   refers to the ability to store information in short- or long-term memory.

story map   a graphic outline of a story that identifies the overall problem or plot, the sequence of major events, and the conclusions.

story retelling   a reading-comprehension instructional technique that involves retelling the main points of a text after the text is read.

story schema   refers to the underlying cognitive understanding of the story parts or the idea that the introduction, plot, characters, climax, and story ending are related to each other in a particular fashion.

strength-based assessment   concept emphasizing documentation of students' strengths rather than their weaknesses.

student support services   refers to teams of educators who offer assistance when teachers have problems with a child before he or she is classified as a special education child. Typically, student support services are viewed as attempts to support a child in the mainstream class and make special education placement unnecessary.

subtest recategorization   refers to the practice of regrouping certain subtests on intelligence assessments in a fashion that was not recommended by the test manufacturers in order to demonstrate a developmental imbalance in a child with learning disabilities.

subtest scatter   one variation of the developmental imbalance idea that suggests that identification of

learning disabilities may be based on measuring the variation between the subtest scores on a standardized intelligence test.

subtyping research   a series of studies in the literature on learning disabilities that represents attempts to identify various subgroups within the larger heterogeneous population of learning disabled.

suicide ideation   contemplation of suicide; thoughts of suicide.

summarizing   one of four steps in an instructional method called reciprocal teaching, which requires the child to summarize information after reading and discussing it.

SWAT teams   schoolwide assistance teams; one type of student support team designed to assist with problems in mainstream classes before students are referred for special education placement.

syntax   the use of words together in phrases or sentences or understanding of words in relation to each other.

task analysis   a behavioral procedure whereby each small step in a task is listed and analyzed in order to understand precisely where a student's understanding of the process breaks down.

Task Force I   proposed an early definition of the term *learning disabilities.*

task orientation   the percentage of time that a student is making eye contact with the assigned task.

teacher interactions   the relationships between teachers and students of all types; significant factors include teacher expectations, teacher/student communication, and frequency and quality of interaction.

team-assisted individualization   one form of cooperative instructional teaching that requires that students in teams assist each other in learning new material.

temperament   one of several personality variables studied among children with learning disabilities. This variable refers to one's overall personality approach to events in life, including such elements as task persistence, the level of reaction to events, and social capabilities.

temporal lobe   the portion of each hemisphere of the cerebrum that controls hearing and auditory memory; located in the front of the head, below the frontal lobe.

teratogenic insult   involves exposure to various chemicals during pregnancy, such as alcohol or tobacco, possibly resulting in birth defects.

testwiseness   the knowledge and use of certain test-taking skills, including awareness of logic whereby certain answer options may be eliminated.

thought units   a measure of language usage that breaks spoken language into complete thoughts for purposes of measurement.

time-on-task the percentage of time in which a student is on-task or attempting to complete an educational task. Time-on-task is usually measured by observing a student's eye contact with the educational task.

time-out the withdrawal of reinforcement, contingent on a misbehavior, resulting in a decrease in that behavior.

token economy a positive-reinforcement system utilizing tokens for appropriate behavior that can be redeemed at a later time for reinforcement.

Touch Math a touchpoint system of math calculation whereby each numeral is accompanied by dots placed on the numeral. The number of dots corresponds both to the number and to the major visual characteristics of the numeral symbol.

trace elements elements that may cause learning problems, even when found only in small quantities inside the body.

trait anxiety anxiety that is a global trait of a certain person's personality rather than a response to a situation.

transition refers to the movement from one educational setting to another or to the change from educational endeavors to post–high school activities such as work and community participation.

tutorial model a model of instruction used for students with learning disabilities in which the special education teacher tutors the students in academic subjects.

verbal rehearsal a memory technique in which verbally repeating a word or fact is used to assist in later recall.

visual imagery teaching a child to imagine a picture or image of the events in a story in order to increase comprehension and recall of the story.

visual-perceptual/motor theorists theorists asserting that impaired visual perception and delayed motor development are possible causes of learning problems.

vocational high schools high schools that specialize in providing a wide array of vocational courses.

vocational outcomes the postschool vocational possibilities of a student with learning disabilities. These outcomes should indicate the success of vocational programs, resulting from vocational education during the school years.

vocational skills the set of skills directly related to a job that makes the job possible. Use of a tape measure, hammer, and paint gun would be vocational skills for a carpenter. These may be contrasted with work-related skills, such as punctuality and effective peer relationships, that are related to success on the job but do not directly involve skills required for a particular job.

whole-language instruction an approach to the teaching of language skills that incorporates instruction in reading, language arts, spelling, writing, and other communication skills together in the context of social interactions in the classroom.

WISC-III the Wechsler Intelligence Scales for Children, third edition; one of the most frequently used intelligence assessments.

working memory a conscious process whereby sense and meaning are attributed to a new stimulus based on previous knowledge.

work-study model one model of vocational instruction that results in a student studying school subjects for part of the school day and working on a local job site for the remainder of the day.

NAME INDEX

SUBJECT INDEX